ABOUT LANGUAGE

A Reader for Writers

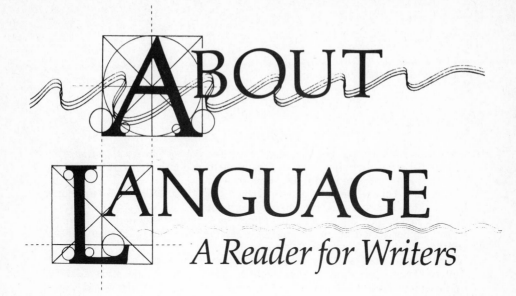

ABOUT LANGUAGE
A Reader for Writers

Second Edition

WILLIAM H. ROBERTS
University of Lowell

GREGOIRE TURGEON

HOUGHTON MIFFLIN COMPANY   BOSTON

Dallas   Geneva, Illinois   Palo Alto   Princeton, New Jersey

For Matt, Amy, and Becky

For my father, the best teacher

Acknowledgments

Charles Barber. "The Origin of Language" from *The Story of Speech and Language* by Charles Barber. Copyright © 1964 by Charles Barber. Reprinted by permission of Harper & Row and Pan Books Ltd., London.

Bell Telephone Laboratories. "A Lustful Twig." Copyright © 1976 Bell Telephone Laboratories, Incorporated; reprinted by permission.

Beryl Lieff Benderly. "The Multilingual Mind" by Beryl Lieff Benderly. Copyright © 1981 by Beryl Lieff Benderly. All rights reserved. Reprinted by arrangement with the Virginia Barber Literary Agency, Inc.

Stephen Vincent Benét. "American Names" from *Ballads and Poems* by Stephen Vincent Benét. Copyright 1931 by Stephen Vincent Benét and renewed 1959 by Rosemary Carr Benét. Reprinted by permission of Henry Holt and Company, Inc.

Hannah Benoit. "French Resistance," reprinted by permission of the author from *The Boston Globe*, March 12, 1984.

W. F. Bolton. Excerpt from *A Living Language: The History and Structure of English*, by W. F. Bolton. Copyright © 1982 by Random House, Inc. Reprinted by permission of Random House, Inc.

Daniel J. Boorstin. "The Rhetoric of Democracy," copyright © 1973, by Daniel J. Boorstin, author of *The Americans* and *The Discoverers*, available in Vintage Paperback (Random House).

(*Acknowledgments continue on page 529.*)

Printed in the U.S.A.

Library of Congress Catalog Card Number: 88-81360

ISBN: 0-395-43232-4

ABCDEFGHIJ-B-9543210-89

Contents

(Annotated format; a brief table of contents begins on page xvii.)

historians describes the social history of advertising, its qualities today, and its far-reaching implications.

With a memorable voice, the author details some of the specific language tricks that skillful but dishonest advertisers use in their efforts to persuade us to buy their products.

Natural carries weight with today's consumers, but the word often serves as part of "the 'natural' ploy" of advertisers eager for sales.

A well-known lexicographer sketches the history of emotional appeals in advertising for personal care products, which we perhaps now need because advertisers have told us we need them.

Many of the chapter's assertions about advertising language are illustrated in six representative ads for technological products, corporations, and organizations.

This important essay reveals the most common techniques used to bend language so that it perpetrates deceptions for political (and other) purposes.

Two inaugural addresses exemplify how two stylists use language to establish the tone of their administrations and to articulate their political philosophies.

Chapter 10

Many writers view word processing with skepticism, puzzlement, and even fear, but as Zinsser explains in this chapter from *Writing with a Word Processor*, most reservations about the new writing technology are unfounded.

For this author, a professor of humanities, society's apparent veneration of computer languages (as opposed to human languages) signals a fundamental problem with the way we now treat each other.

Computer jargon, now solidly embedded in our language, is mere "techno-babble" for this critic of the computer's contributions to everyday English.

While Americans have embraced the computer's contributions to the English lexicon, the French have exhibited linguistic chauvinism when faced with computer terminology, a reaction that Benoit considers both typical and self-defeating.

The author, an anthropologist, describes recent findings about how the brain handles language, findings that remind us that the brain and the computer are not analogous.

Contents

(Brief format; an annotated table of contents begins on page v.)

Chapter 10

Language and Technology   490

Preface

This second edition of *About Language: A Reader for Writers* is meant to help students become more conscious of language and more able to use it responsibly. The choice of reading selections was guided by our belief that an introduction to the complex, subtle, and manipulative nature of language will help students understand the ways in which language shapes our world and thought—and that such an awareness will help students to write with more skill and confidence.

Organization and Coverage

About Language is an anthology of sixty-one classic and contemporary reading selections, organized around ten language issues:

- Chapter 1, "The Process of Writing," looks at prewriting, writing, and revising through the eyes of such writers as Peter Elbow, Donald Murray, William Zinsser, and Donald Hall. The chapter also includes an unusually sensitive essay by Pico Iyer, "In Praise of the Humble Comma," published in 1988 in *Time*.
- Chapter 2, "Names and Naming," examines the names we give to people and places—from surnames to women's names to nicknames to place names—and discusses what these names in turn reveal about us.
- Chapter 3, "Dictionaries," looks at the origin of dictionaries, the process of compiling dictionaries, and the sometimes surprising influence of dictionaries (Malcolm X, "Get Hold of a Dictionary"). The chapter also includes an article on the role of the lexicographer, written expressly for this edition of *About Language,* by Anne Soukhanov, executive editor of the American Heritage dictionaries.
- Chapter 4, "Language Development," has essays on the origin of language (Charles Barber, Lewis Thomas), the history of the English language (Paul Roberts), and the growth of American English (H. L. Mencken). A recently published, entertaining article by Susan Trausch looks at how rapidly language can change.
- Chapter 5, "Slang, Taboo, and Euphemism," explores the origins, contexts, and implications of these aspects of language. John Updike's short story "A&P" is included to show how slang contrasted with more formal language can represent the transition from adolescence to adulthood.
- Chapter 6, "Language, Identity, and Discrimination," examines how language can include and exclude people from groups and also set one group apart from others. Several points of view are presented in essays

on black speech, bilingualism, and sexism and racism in language. A 1987 article by Alfie Kohn explores recent sociolinguistic research on the difference between male and female speech patterns.

- Chapter 7, "Jargon," analyzes both the uses and abuses of "in-language," especially in such fields as medicine, journalism, education, and law. "Legal Trees," a poem first published in 1988 in the *Atlantic*, parodies in legal language Joyce Kilmer's poem "Trees."
- Chapter 8, "Language and Advertising" reveals the subtle, persuasive, manipulative use of language in advertising. In addition to essays—from Daniel Boorstin's "The Rhetoric of Democracy" to Carl Wrighter's "Weasel Words: God's Little Helpers"—the chapter reproduces six advertisements for students to analyze.
- Chapter 9, "The Political Voice," includes George Orwell's classic "Politics and the English Language," two presidential speeches, and other essays that explore the ways in which politicians use language to lead, inspire—and deceive. Paul Chilton's "Nukespeak: Nuclear Language, Culture, and Propaganda" explores a frightening new language.
- Chapter 10, "Language and Technology," explores issues from writing with a word processor to the effect of computers on everyday language. The last essay in the text, "The Multilingual Mind" by Beryl Lieff Benderly, explores some recent surprising discoveries about the way the brain handles language.

Apparatus

All reading selections are followed by questions on content, questions on structure and style, and assignments for writing and projects. The Instructor's Manual for *About Language* suggests answers to the questions following each selection. The Manual also offers ways of approaching particular selections or specific aspects of selections.

Each of the ten chapters concludes with additional assignments and research projects. Students are invited to write longer papers and to take on more complex projects or activities.

New to the Second Edition

- Twenty-two new reading selections, many first published since 1985
- New material on many aspects of language, including bilingualism, jargon, euphemisms, "nuclear language," advertising, speech patterns, compiling dictionaries, and nicknames
- New sequence of chapters to help students build on previous knowledge (for example, advertising is now placed before politics so that

students can explore persuasive language in familiar and then less familiar contexts)

- Expanded material in "Additional Assignments and Research Topics" (for example, assignments on "Sniglets" and oxymorons in Chapter 2, which engage students in language activities that encourage creative thinking)
- Expanded Chapter 1, with substantially more material on revision
- New—and more—advertisements for students to analyze

Acknowledgments

We extend thanks to our colleagues and students at the University of Lowell and to our wives, Patsy and Sue, for yet more patience and insight.

We also wish to thank the following individuals for their constructive comments and suggestions on the developing manuscript: Donna Alden, New Mexico State University; Judith Anderson, Clark State Community College, OH; Dennis Bingham, The Ohio State University; Nemia M. Chai, Columbus College, GA; Thomas L. Erskine, Salisbury State College, MD; Nola Garrett, Edinboro University, PA; Barbara Jameson, University of New Mexico; Terrance B. Kearns, University of Central Arkansas; Michael J. McDowell, Portland Community College, OR; Harold Nelson, Minot State University, ND; Al Past, Bee County College, TX; Gerald D. Poulin, Roane State Community College, TN; and Mary Jo Stirling, Santa Monica College, CA.

W.H.R. & G.T.

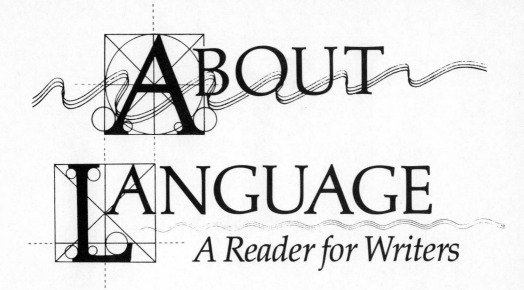

ABOUT LANGUAGE
A Reader for Writers

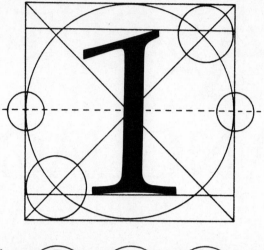

The Process of Writing

Your roommate is a good writer, but no matter how hard you try, you don't seem to have a talent for writing. While his essays show "convincing content . . . efficient structure . . . good use of evidence," your own essays are returned with comments such as "focus unclear . . . confusing structure . . . lacks fresh ideas."

Perhaps your sister writes well, too. Three days before her assignment is due, she can sit down and write, write, write. Words stream from her pen—so many words that, she claims, the hardest part of an assignment is "cutting out what's not good." Meanwhile, for you writing is agony. Writing means confronting an intimidating empty page. Writing means laboring through every sentence, feeling certain that "cutting out what's not good" means cutting out most, if not all, of it.

You can tell yourself that good writers are born, not made—or that being a poor writer isn't your fault. The truth about writing, though, is this: Good writing is not born; it's made. Good writing is the result of a process. "Making" good writing is every writer's true job, and in this chapter, professional writers and teachers offer advice on various aspects of the writing process.

The chapter begins with two selections that address the common question about writing, "How do I get ideas?" Peter Elbow's "Freewriting" and Jack Rawlins's "Five Principles for Getting Good Ideas" both explain ways to set the writing process in motion. The writing of a "typical" student essay is the subject of "How to Say Nothing in Five Hundred Words," by Paul Roberts. The strategies he advocates can help you produce well-crafted essays that are not merely competent but interesting.

The next three selections address revision, the aspect of writing that most students (and others) understand least. Donald M. Murray takes a fresh approach in "Internal Revision: A Process of Discovery." For Murray, writing itself *is* rewriting. Marvin H. Swift provides an extended, specific illustration of revision in "Clear Writing Means Clear Thinking Means . . . ," and William Zinsser analyzes the problem of "cluttered writing" and offers a solution in "Simplicity."

The chapter concludes with two selections that discuss, with remarkable feeling, two other important aspects of writing. Pico Iyer's "In Praise of the Humble

Comma" reveals how punctuation captures both the human voice and the spirit of an entire culture. Donald Hall's "An Ethic of Clarity" then adds further dimension to the term "good writing." For Hall, good prose is clear prose that honestly expresses the writer's character.

One idea runs through all the selections in this chapter. Good writing is not magic. It's the product of careful thought and work. Through a process, and through sensitivity to language and meaning at every step of that process, we *make* good writing.

Freewriting

Peter Elbow

Student writers know the truth in the German proverb "Every beginning is hard." Getting ideas, the first step in the writing process, can be agonizing, but in this selection from his book *Writing without Teachers,* Peter Elbow describes the technique of freewriting and how it can make beginning easier. Elbow's analysis shows that, when writing, we usually try to combine two separate tasks: producing and editing. Elbow's advice: Don't try to do two jobs at once.

1   The most effective way I know to improve your writing is to do freewriting exercises regularly. At least three times a week. They are sometimes called "automatic writing," "babbling," or "jabbering" exercises. The idea is simply to write for ten minutes (later on, perhaps fifteen or twenty). Don't stop for anything. Go quickly without rushing. Never stop to look back, to cross something out, to wonder how to spell something, to wonder what word or thought to use, or to think about what you are doing. If you can't think of a word or a spelling, just use a squiggle or else write, "I can't think of it." Just put down something. The easiest thing is just to put down whatever is in your mind. If you get stuck it's fine to write "I can't think what to say, I can't think what to say" as many times as you want; or repeat the last word you wrote over and over again; or anything else. The only requirement is that you *never* stop.

2   What happens to a freewriting exercise is important. It must be a piece of writing which, even if someone reads it, doesn't send any ripples back to you. It is like writing something and putting it in a bottle in the sea. The teacherless class helps your writing by providing maximum feedback. Freewritings help you by providing no feedback at all. When I assign one, I invite the writer to let me read it, but also tell him to keep it if he prefers. I read it quickly and make no comments at all and I do not speak with him about it. The main thing is that a freewriting must never be evaluated in any way; in fact there must be no discussion or comment at all.

3   Here is an example of a fairly coherent exercise (sometimes they are very coherent, which is fine):

> I think I'll write what's on my mind, but the only thing on my mind right now is what to write for ten minutes. I've never done this before and I'm not prepared in any way—the sky is cloudy today, how's that? now I'm afraid I won't be able to think of what to write when I get to the end of the sentence—well, here I am at

5

the end of the sentence—here I am again, again, again, again, at least I'm still writing—Now I ask is there some reason to be happy that I'm still writing—ah yes! Here comes the question again—What am I getting out of this? What point is there in it? It's almost obscene to always ask it but I seem to question everything that way and I was gonna say something else pertaining to that but I got so busy writing down the first part that I forgot what I was leading into. This is kind of fun oh don't stop writing—cars and trucks speeding by somewhere out the window, pens clittering across people's papers. The sky is still cloudy—is it symbolic that I should be mentioning it? Huh? I dunno. Maybe I should try colors, blue, red, dirty words—wait a minute—no can't do that, orange, yellow, arm tired, green pink violet magenta lavender red brown black green—now that I can't think of any more colors—just about done—relief? maybe.

4   Freewriting may seem crazy but actually it makes simple sense. Think of the difference between speaking and writing. Writing has the advantage of permitting more editing. But that's its downfall too. Almost everybody interposes a massive and complicated series of editings between the time words start to be born into consciousness and when they finally come off the end of the pencil or typewriter onto the page. This is partly because schooling makes us obsessed with the "mistakes" we make in writing. Many people are constantly thinking about spelling and grammar as they try to write. I am always thinking about the awkwardness, wordiness, and general mushiness of my natural verbal product as I try to write down words.

5   But it's not just "mistakes" or "bad writing" we edit as we write. We also edit unacceptable thoughts and feelings, as we do in speaking. In writing there is more time to do it so the editing is heavier: when speaking, there's someone right there waiting for a reply and he'll get bored or think we're crazy if we don't come out with *something*. Most of the time in speaking, we settle for the catch-as-catch-can way in which the words tumble out. In writing, however, there's a chance to try to get them right. But the opportunity to get them right is a terrible burden: you can work for two hours trying to get a paragraph "right" and discover it's not right at all. And then give up.

6   Editing, *in itself,* is not the problem. Editing is usually necessary if we want to end up with something satisfactory. The problem is that editing goes on *at the same time* as producing. The editor is, as it were, constantly looking over the shoulder of the producer and constantly fiddling with what he's doing while he's in the middle of trying to do it. No wonder the producer gets nervous, jumpy, inhibited, and finally can't be coherent. It's an unnecessary burden to try to think of words and also worry at the same time whether they're the right words.

7   The main thing about freewriting is that it is *nonediting*. It is an exercise in bringing together the process of producing words and putting them down on the page. Practiced regularly, it undoes the ingrained habit of editing at the same time you are trying to produce. It will make writing less blocked because words will come more easily. You will use up more paper, but chew up fewer pencils.

8   Next time you write, notice how often you stop yourself from writing down something you were going to write down. Or else cross it out after it's written. "Naturally," you say, "it wasn't any good." But think for a moment about the occasions when you spoke well. Seldom was it because you first got the beginning just right. Usually it was a matter of a halting or even garbled beginning, but you kept going and your speech finally became coherent and even powerful. There is a lesson here for writing: trying to get the beginning just right is a formula for failure—and probably a secret tactic to make yourself give up writing. Make some words, whatever they are, and then grab hold of that line and reel in as hard as you can. Afterwards you can throw away lousy beginnings and make new ones. This is the quickest way to get into good writing.

9   The habit of compulsive, premature editing doesn't just make writing hard. It also makes writing dead. Your voice is damped out by all the interruptions, changes, and hesitations between the consciousness and the page. In your natural way of producing words there is a sound, a texture, a rhythm—a voice—which is the main source of power in your writing. I don't know how it works, but this voice is the force that will make a reader listen to you, the energy that drives the meanings through his thick skull. Maybe you don't *like* your voice; maybe people have made fun of it. But it's the only voice you've got. It's your only source of power. You better get back into it, no matter what you think of it. If you keep writing in it, it may change into something you like better. But if you abandon it, you'll likely never have a voice and never be heard.

Questions on Content

1. What is the only absolute requirement for freewriting?

2. What effect does freewriting have on the editing process?

3. Many writers feel that the opening is the most difficult part of the writing process. According to Elbow, how does freewriting make beginning easier?

4. What important distinction does Elbow make between speaking and writing? How is the difference both an advantage and a disadvantage for the writer?

5. What does Elbow mean by "compulsive, premature editing" (paragraph 9)? How does freewriting help establish a sound relationship between producing and editing?

Questions on Structure and Style

6. We have all been frustrated by unclear directions, yet we probably don't realize that giving clear directions for even simple tasks is not easy—until we try giving directions to someone else. Go over Elbow's directions for freewriting in paragraph 1. Are they clear enough to follow without confusion? Why or why not?

7. How would you describe Elbow's tone in this essay? Who is Elbow's intended audience, and is the tone appropriate for that audience?

8. Why does Elbow include the example of freewriting in paragraph 3? Does this example affect your willingness to try freewriting?

9. What effect does Elbow achieve with these concrete figures:
   A. "It is like writing something and putting it in a bottle in the sea" (paragraph 2).
   B. ". . . and then grab hold of that line and reel in as hard as you can" (paragraph 8).

10. Why does Elbow use the pronoun *we* so frequently in paragraph 5?

Assignments

1. Try following Elbow's advice and freewriting for ten minutes. On the basis of this experiment, decide whether frequent freewriting would help you, and discuss how it would or would not.

2. Elbow emphasizes that the writing process has two stages: producing and editing. Write a brief essay describing your own writing process. Be sure to include the relationship between producing and editing as it affects your writing. Based on your response to Elbow's essay, do you see any adjustments you could make in your own approach to writing? What prewriting must you do before you begin to write this essay?

Five Principles
for Getting Good Ideas

Jack Rawlins

When you start to write, merely "getting ideas" is usually not enough. Good writers get *good* ideas. In this selection from his book *The Writer's Way*, writing teacher Jack Rawlins points out how this happens. Rawlins addresses the much larger issues of thinking and responding. Good ideas come to us when we think—critically and creatively—*and* we respond. In order to be successful at these tasks, we must be actively engaged with the world.

1   Brains that get good ideas follow five principles:

Don't begin with a topic.

Think all the time.

To get something out, put something in.

Go from little, concrete things to big, abstract things.

Connect.

We'll talk about each in turn.

Don't Begin with a Topic

2   Essays rarely begin with subject matter alone. Why would a person say out of the blue, "I think I'll write about linoleum, or the national debt"? Nor are the kernels of essays always "good ideas"—they often aren't *ideas* at all, in the sense of whole assertions. Thinking begins in lots of ways:

- **With a question:** "Is there any real difference between the Republicans and the Democrats anymore?" "Why is Ralph so mad at me?"
- **With a problem:** "I'm always behind in my work." "Violent crimes against women are on the increase."
- **With a purpose:** "I want to tell people about what's really going on in this class." "I want to let people know about alternatives to traditional medicine."
- **With a thesis:** "There are cheaper, healthier alternatives to regular grocery stores." "Old people are the victims of silent injustice in our culture."

- **With a feeling:** anger, frustration, surprise.
- **With a sensation or image:** a smell, a glimpse of a bird in flight, an eye-catching TV ad.

What shall we call that thing an essay begins with—the seed, the spark, the inspiration, the sense of "gotcha"? I'll call it a *prompt*.

Think All the Time

3   If you have a sense of humor, you know that the surest way to prevent yourself from being funny is to have someone (even yourself) demand that you be funny *now*. Comedians have always bemoaned the fact that people introduce them to friends by saying, "This is Milton. He's a riot. Be funny, Milton." Thinking's the same way. Being put on the spot is the surest way of preventing the creative juices from flowing.

4   So don't expect to discover a good prompt by sitting down for a scheduled half-hour of profundity. Minds that think well think all the time. One prolific student wrote that she goes through the world "looking for *writable* things" and is thought weird by her friends because she scribbles notes to herself at parties.

5   Thinking all the time sounds like work, but it isn't. Your mind works all the time whether you want it to or not, the same way your body moves all the time. Any yogi will tell you that it takes years of practice to learn to turn the mind *off*, even for a minute or two. And it's physiologically impossible for your brain to get tired, which is why you can study or write all day, go to bed, and find your mind still racing while your body cries for rest. So I'm really not asking your brain to do anything new; I'm just asking you to *listen* to it.

To Get Something Out, Put Something In

6   One popular, poisonous image for thinking is the light bulb flashing on over someone's head—the notion that ideas spring from within us, caused by nothing. To become good thinkers, we have to replace that image with another; think of ideas as billiard balls set in motion when something collides with them. Ideas are *reactions*—we have them in response to other things.

7   A thinker thinks as life passes through him and does what I call "talking back to the world." Many of us separate our input and output modes; we are either putting information into our brains or asking our brains to produce thoughts, but we don't do both at the same time. I call such people data sponges. But the best time to try to get things out is when things are going in. Let them bounce off you and strike sparks. People do this

naturally until they've been taught to be passive; try reading a book to a three-year-old, and listen to her react to everything she hears and sees, or take her to a movie and watch her struggle not to talk back to the screen.

8   Are you a data sponge? To find out, answer the following questions.

Do you find yourself mentally talking back to the newspaper when you read it?

Do you write in the margins of books you read?

Are at least 25 percent of the notes you take during course reading or lectures your own thoughts, questions, doubts, and reactions?

As you meet up with life's outrages, do you find yourself complaining to imaginary audiences?

After a movie, do you feel like you're going to burst until you find someone to talk about it?

When you listen to a speaker or a teacher, do you find yourself itching to get to the question-and-answer period?

If you said yes to these questions, you're not a sponge. If you said no, you're going to have to practice your reacting skills.

Go from Little, Concrete Things to Big, Abstract Things

9   This principle is a logical consequence of the one before. Since ideas come best in reaction to life's incoming billiard balls, the best thinking follows a predictable course: from little, concrete bits of experience to large, abstract implications. You see an ad on TV and start thinking about it, and it leads you to speculations on American consumerism, media manipulation, and the marketing of women's bodies. You overhear a snippet of conversation between a parent and child at the grocery store and start thinking about it, and it leads you to speculations on American child-rearing practices, the powerlessness of children, parental brainwashing, and antiyouth bigotry.

10   Here's what going from little particulars to big issues is like. I was sitting doing nothing one day when my eyes fell on a box of Girl Scout cookies. The box had on it a picture of a girl and the slogan, "I'm not like anyone else." I reacted. I thought, "Gosh, that sounds lonely." And I valued the reaction enough to notice it and think about it. It led me to a big issue: How does Americans' love of individuality affect their ability to be members of a culture? And I formulated a thesis: Americans love their individuality so much that they'll cut themselves off from everything and everyone to get it. Being unlike everyone else is a curse, because it means you're separated from other human beings by your differentness. I was raised a proud individualist, and I've only recently realized that the reward for being unique is loneliness.

11   I went from little things to big issues when I drew essays out of Sally's life.* When she mentioned that she couldn't drink too heavily in high school because it would affect her shot-putting, I instantly saw the abstract issue illustrated by her experience: People who have things they love dare not practice self-destructive behavior, because they'll destroy what they love in the process. So alcoholism or drug abuse is neither a crime nor a disease nor a moral failure in the individual; it's a symptom of a social failure, the failure of our society to offer the alcoholic or drug addict a life too precious to risk destroying.

12   Beginning writers want to start with large abstractions, in the mistaken belief that the bigger the topic is, the more there is to say about it. It doesn't work out that way. Usually the first sentence of the essay tells whether the writer knows this or not. Essays on friendship that begin "Friendship is one of the most important things in life" are doomed, because the writer doesn't know it. Essays that begin "Mary was my best friend in high school" will thrive, because the writer does know it.

Connect

13   Those who think well make connections between things. An essay begins when two previously unrelated bits in the brain meet and discover a connection. Usually a new stimulus hitches up with an old bit stored long ago in the memory; the incoming billiard ball hits an old one that's just lying there, and they fly off together.

14   It's hard to learn the connecting skill if you don't have it already. Here's what it feels like inside. One day I was sitting in an English Department faculty meeting, and we were discussing an administrative change. A colleague said, "We couldn't do that until we were sure our people would be protected." I thought momentarily, "I wonder how he knows who 'his people' are?" Months later I was vacationing in a small mountain town and picked up the local newspaper. On the front page was an article about the firing of a group of non-union construction workers. The boss had asked the union for workers, but none were available, so he trained out-of-work mill workers. Later the union rep showed up, announced that union workers were now available, and insisted that the others be fired. Something clicked, and I had an essay. My colleague's attitude and the union rep's were the same: I'll watch out for "my people," and everyone else can watch out for himself. I wanted to talk about why people think that way and how they learn to rise above it.

15   How did I make that connection? Incredible as it sounds, and unbeknownst to me, I must have been checking everything that came into my brain against the faculty-meeting remark for a possible connection. Or

* Sally is a student and subject of an interview presented earlier in Rawlins's discussion.

perhaps I had opened a file in my mind labeled "people who think in terms of those who belong and those who don't" and dumped anything related in there as it came along.

16   I just read a great essay by Arthur Miller connecting the current prayer-in-school political debate with his memories of saying the Pledge of Allegiance in elementary school. What brought the two things together? Miller must have checked prayer in schools against everything in his memory relating to state-mandated loyalty and come up with recollections of third grade. That sounds exhausting, but we all know that when something clicks in memory, we haven't "worked" at all—in fact, the way to bring the connection that's on the tip of the tongue to the surface is to forget about it and let the subconscious do its work unwatched.

17   *The more unlike two things are and the less obvious the connection between them is, the fresher and more stimulating the connection is when you make it.* Finding a connection between mountain climbers and sky-divers is merely okay; finding a connection between inflation rates and the incidence of breast cancer will make the world open its eyes. This is the Head Principle. Mr. Head was an aviation engineer who got interested in downhill skiing. Apparently no one had ever connected aircraft technology and skiing before; Mr. Head took a few runs down the hill and realized that he could make a better ski if he simply made it according to the principles and with the materials used in making airplane wings. He invented the Head ski, the first metal ski, and made millions of dollars. He then did the same thing in tennis, by inventing the Prince racket. Apparently aircraft engineers didn't play tennis either.

18   The Head Principle says you can't predict what will connect with what. So you can't tell yourself what information to seek. You can only take in experience and information voraciously and stir it all up together. If I had been formally researching stupid faculty remarks, I'd never have thought to read up on northern Californian construction workers. If you're writing about Charles Dickens and you read only about Charles Dickens, you're just guaranteeing you won't make any connections except those other Dickens scholars have already made. Instead, go read *Psychology Today*, read Nixon's memoirs, see a movie, watch a documentary on insect societies, or visit a mortuary. As you talk back to all of it, keep asking yourself, "What is this like? When have I thought things like this before? When was the last time I reacted like this?" When I read about the construction workers, I reacted, and I remembered that I'd had a conversation with myself like that one before sometime. Perhaps that's the key to connecting.

19   It's easy to block ideas from coming by practicing the exact opposite of our idea-getting principles. Just set aside a time for idea-getting, cut yourself off from the outside world by locking yourself in a stimulus-free study room, and muse on a cosmic abstraction. If you're doing any of that, your idea-getting regimen needs overhauling.

1. How does Rawlins define the term *prompt* (para-graph 2)? Rawlins contrasts a prompt with another writing element. Which one?

2. Why is being a "data sponge" (paragraphs 7–8) not helpful for a writer? What tasks would a data sponge most likely perform well?

3. Paragraphs 9 through 12 discuss the need to distin-guish between the concrete and the abstract, and the need to begin writing with the concrete. Exam-ine paragraphs 9 through 12, and underline all of Rawlins's "abstract things." How much of the four paragraphs consists of abstract things? Exam-ine other paragraphs, perhaps 6 through 8 or 17 through 19. Overall, how would you estimate the ratio of abstract to concrete things in this selection? What can we conclude from this ratio?

4. Rawlins defines what he calls the Head Principle (paragraphs 17–18) and explains its importance for writers. Aside from writers, who would find the Head Principle useful?

5. Why do you think Rawlins spends so much time discussing his own experiences? Why is this tactic valuable and not merely self-indulgent as he offers advice to students?

6. Rawlins begins by referring to "brains that get good ideas" (paragraph 1). What effect does he create by using the word *brains* rather than *people* or *writers*?

7. Rawlins sometimes employs words that are not scholarly, such as *gotcha* (paragraph 2), *hitches up* (paragraph 13), and *stupid* (paragraph 18). What im-pression do we have of Rawlins because he uses words like these? How do these words contribute to Rawlins's style? How would you describe this style?

8. The author obviously knows the importance of transitions. Circle the transitions in paragraphs 5 and 14.

9. The structure of this reading selection is simple and efficient. Where does Rawlins state his thesis? Why is paragraph 19 a good conclusion?

Assignments

1. Rawlins states that "thinking begins in lots of ways" (paragraph 2). He then lists some of the most common ways. Try to recall a good idea you once had—perhaps it involved asking a special person for a date or explaining an awkward situation to a friend. If you have trouble recalling a single good idea, remember that you need to define the vague word *good*. In your case, *good* may mean useful, profitable, entertaining, or something else. Once you've identified the idea, write a paragraph (or an essay) in which you trace the evolution of the idea. How did it begin? Who played a role? Was your age, location, job, or some other factor a crucial one? Overall, how far removed is the idea from the "place" where it began?

2. Rawlins writes that "the Head Principle says you can't predict what will connect with what" (paragraph 18). Pick one of the following topic pairs, and in an essay, explain how the two can actually "connect."

    a subway and false teeth

    rabbits and mountain climbing

    your roommate and your last job

    teachers and fresh vegetables

    Such an exercise is obviously not what Rawlins intends, but the results (which are often entertaining) illustrate how easily connections can be made when we are receptive to the idea of making them. (A classroom activity can involve devising topic pairs to be used by the entire class.)

How to Say Nothing in Five Hundred Words

Paul Roberts

Most students want their writing to be lively and interesting, and methods for achieving these goals are the subject of this informative, amusing selection. Paul Roberts wrote several books on linguistics, but he also spent many years teaching, in the process reading countless five-hundred-word essays by students. In this selection he details, with wry humor, his pained reaction to the "typical" student essay, and he explains credible ways in which students can make their prose both clear and refreshingly noticeable.

1   It's Friday afternoon, and you have almost survived another week of classes. You are just looking forward dreamily to the weekend when the English instructor says: "For Monday you will turn in a five-hundred-word composition on college football."

2   Well, that puts a good hole in the weekend. You don't have any strong views on college football one way or the other. You get rather excited during the season and go to all the home games and find it rather more fun than not. On the other hand, the class has been reading Robert Hutchins in the anthology and perhaps Shaw's "Eighty-Yard Run," and from the class discussion you have got the idea that the instructor thinks college football is for the birds. You are no fool. You can figure out what side to take.

3   After dinner you get out the portable typewriter that you got for high school graduation. You might as well get it over with and enjoy Saturday and Sunday. Five hundred words is about two double-spaced pages with normal margins. You put in a sheet of paper, think up a title, and you're off:

WHY COLLEGE FOOTBALL SHOULD BE ABOLISHED

College football should be abolished because it's bad for the school and also bad for the players. The players are so busy practicing that they don't have any time for their studies.

This, you feel, is a mighty good start. The only trouble is that it's only thirty-two words. You still have four hundred and sixty-eight to go, and you've pretty well exhausted the subject. It comes to you that you do your best thinking in the morning, so you put away the typewriter and go to the movies. But the next morning you have to do your washing and some math problems, and in the afternoon you go to the game. The English instructor turns up too, and you wonder if you've taken the right side after all. Saturday night you have a date, and Sunday morning you have to go to church. (You can't let English assignments interfere with your religion.) What with one thing and another, it's ten o'clock Sunday night before you get out the typewriter again. You make a pot of coffee and start to fill out your views on college football. Put a little meat on the bones.

WHY COLLEGE FOOTBALL SHOULD BE ABOLISHED

4   In my opinion, it seems to me that college football should be abolished. The reason why I think this to be true is because I feel that football is bad for the colleges in nearly every respect. As Robert Hutchins says in his article in our anthology in which he discusses college football, it would be better if the colleges had race horses and had races with one another, because then the horses would not have to attend classes. I firmly agree with Mr. Hutchins on this point, and I am sure that many other students would agree too.

5   One reason why it seems to me that college football is bad is that it has become too commercial. In the olden times when people played football just for the fun of it, maybe college football was all right, but they do not play football just for the fun of it now as they used to in the old days. Nowadays college football is what you might call a big business. Maybe this is not true at all schools, and I don't think it is especially true here at State, but certainly this is the case at most colleges and universities in America nowadays, as Mr. Hutchins points out in his very interesting article. Actually the coaches and alumni go around to the high schools and offer the high school stars large salaries to come to their colleges and play football for them. There was one case where a high school star was offered a convertible if he would play football for a certain college.

6   Another reason for abolishing college football is that it is bad for the players. They do not have time to get a college education, because they are so busy playing football. A football player has to practice every afternoon from three to six and then he is so tired that he can't concentrate on his studies. He just feels like dropping off to sleep after dinner, and then the next day he goes to his classes without having studied and maybe he fails the test.

(Good ripe stuff so far, but you're still a hundred and fifty-one words from home. One more push.)

7   Also I think college football is bad for the colleges and the universities because not very many students get to participate in

it. Out of a college of ten thousand students only seventy-five or a hundred play football, if that many. Football is what you might call a spectator sport. That means that most people go to watch it but do not play it themselves.

(Four hundred and fifteen. Well, you still have the conclusion, and when you retype it, you can make the margins a little wider.)

8   These are the reasons why I agree with Mr. Hutchins that college football should be abolished in American colleges and universities.

9   On Monday you turn it in, moderately hopeful, and on Friday it comes back marked "weak in content" and sporting a big "D."

10   This essay is exaggerated a little, not much. The English instructor will recognize it as reasonably typical of what an assignment on college football will bring in. He knows that nearly half of the class will contrive in five hundred words to say that college football is too commercial and bad for the players. Most of the other half will inform him that college football builds character and prepares one for life and brings prestige to the school. As he reads paper after paper all saying the same thing in almost the same words, all bloodless, five hundred words dripping out of nothing, he wonders how he allowed himself to get trapped into teaching English when he might have had a happy and interesting life as an electrician or a confidence man.

11   Well, you may ask, what can you do about it? The subject is one on which you have few convictions and little information. Can you be expected to make a dull subject interesting? As a matter of fact, this is precisely what you are expected to do. This is the writer's essential task. All subjects, except sex, are dull until somebody makes them interesting. The writer's job is to find the argument, the approach, the angle, the wording that will take the reader with him. This is seldom easy, and it is particularly hard in subjects that have been much discussed: College Football, Fraternities, Popular Music, Is Chivalry Dead?, and the like. You will feel that there is nothing you can do with such subjects except repeat the old bromides. But there are some things you can do which will make your papers, if not throbbingly alive, at least less insufferably tedious than they might otherwise be.

Avoid the Obvious Content

12   Say the assignment is college football. Say that you've decided to be against it. Begin by putting down the arguments that come to your mind: it

is too commercial, it takes the students' minds off their studies, it is hard on the players, it makes the university a kind of circus instead of an intellectual center, for most schools it is financially ruinous. Can you think of any more arguments, just off hand? All right. Now when you write your paper, *make sure that you don't use any of the material on this list.* If these are the points that leap to your mind, they will leap to everyone else's too, and whether you get a "C" or a "D" may depend on whether the instructor reads your paper early when he is fresh and tolerant or late, when the sentence "In my opinion, college football has become too commercial," inexorably repeated, has brought him to the brink of lunacy.

13   Be against college football for some reason or reasons of your own. If they are keen and perceptive ones, that's splendid. But even if they are trivial or foolish or indefensible, you are still ahead so long as they are not everybody else's reasons too. Be against it because the colleges don't spend enough money on it to make it worthwhile, because it is bad for the characters of the spectators, because the players are forced to attend classes, because the football stars hog all the beautiful women, because it competes with baseball and is therefore un-American and possibly Communist-inspired. There are lots of more or less unused reasons for being against college football.

14   Sometimes it is a good idea to sum up and dispose of the trite and conventional points before going on to your own. This has the advantage of indicating to the reader that you are going to be neither trite nor conventional. Something like this:

15   We are often told that college football should be abolished because it has become too commercial or because it is bad for the players. These arguments are no doubt very cogent, but they don't really go to the heart of the matter.

Then you go to the heart of the matter.

Take the Less Usual Side

16   One rather simple way of getting into your paper is to take the side of the argument that most of the citizens will want to avoid. If the assignment is an essay on dogs, you can, if you choose, explain that dogs are faithful and lovable companions, intelligent, useful as guardians of the house and protectors of children, indispensable in police work—in short, when all is said and done, man's best friends. Or you can suggest that those big brown eyes conceal, more often than not, a vacuity of mind and an inconstancy of purpose; that the dogs you have known most intimately have been mangy, ill-tempered brutes, incapable of instruction; and that only your nobility of

mind and fear of arrest prevent you from kicking the flea-ridden animals when you pass them on the street.

17   Naturally personal convictions will sometimes dictate your approach. If the assigned subject is "Is Methodism Rewarding to the Individual?" and you are a pious Methodist, you have really no choice. But few assigned subjects, if any, will fall in this category. Most of them will lie in broad areas of discussion with much to be said on both sides. They are intellectual exercises, and it is legitimate to argue now one way and now another, as debaters do in similar circumstances. Always take the side that looks to you hardest, least defensible. It will almost always turn out to be easier to write interestingly on that side.

18   This general advice applies where you have a choice of subjects. If you are to choose among "The Value of Fraternities" and "My Favorite High School Teacher" and "What I Think About Beetles," by all means plump for the beetles. By the time the instructor gets to your paper, he will be up to his ears in tedious tales about a French teacher at Bloombury High and assertions about how fraternities build character and prepare one for life. Your views on beetles, whatever they are, are bound to be a refreshing change.

19   Don't worry too much about figuring out what the instructor thinks about the subject so that you can cuddle up with him. Chances are his views are no stronger than yours. If he does have convictions and you oppose him, his problem is to keep from grading you higher than you deserve in order to show he is not biased. This doesn't mean that you should always cantankerously dissent from what the instructor says; that gets tiresome too. And if the subject assigned is "My Pet Peeve," do not begin, "My pet peeve is the English instructor who assigns papers on 'my pet peeve.' " This was still funny during the War of 1812, but it has sort of lost its edge since then. It is in general good manners to avoid personalities.

Slip Out of Abstraction

20   If you will study the essay on college football [near the beginning of this essay], you will perceive that one reason for its appalling dullness is that it never gets down to particulars. It is just a series of not very glittering generalities: "football is bad for the colleges," "it has become too commercial," "football is a big business," "it is bad for the players," and so on. Such round phrases thudding against the reader's brain are unlikely to convince him, though they may well render him unconscious.

21   If you want the reader to believe that college football is bad for the players, you have to do more than say so. You have to display the evil. Take your roommate, Alfred Simkins, the second-string center. Picture

poor old Alfy coming home from football practice every evening, bruised and aching, agonizingly tired, scarcely able to shovel the mashed potatoes into his mouth. Let us see him staggering up to the room, getting out his econ textbook, peering desperately at it with his good eye, falling asleep and failing the test in the morning. Let us share his unbearable tension as Saturday draws near. Will he fail, be demoted, lose his monthly allowance, be forced to return to the coal mines? And if he succeeds, what will be his reward? Perhaps a slight ripple of applause when the third-string center replaces him, a moment of elation in the locker room if the team wins, of despair if it loses. What will he look back on when he graduates from college? Toil and torn ligaments. And what will be his future? He is not good enough for pro football, and he is too obscure and weak in econ to succeed in stocks and bonds. College football is tearing the heart from Alfy Simkins and, when it finishes with him, will callously toss aside the shattered hulk.

22   This is no doubt a weak enough argument for the abolition of college football, but it is a sight better than saying, in three of four variations, that college football (in your opinion) is bad for the players.

23   Look at the work of any professional writer and notice how constantly he is moving from the generality, the abstract statement, to the concrete example, the facts and figures, the illustrations. If he is writing on juvenile delinquency, he does not just tell you that juveniles are (it seems to him) delinquent and that (in his opinion) something should be done about it. He shows you juveniles being delinquent, tearing up movie theatres in Buffalo, stabbing high school principals in Dallas, smoking marijuana in Palo Alto. And more than likely he is moving toward some specific remedy, not just a general wringing of the hands.

24   It is no doubt possible to be *too* concrete, too illustrative or anecdotal, but few inexperienced writers err this way. For most the soundest advice is to be seeking always for the picture, to be always turning general remarks into seeable examples. Don't say, "Sororities teach girls the social graces." Say, "Sorority life teaches a girl how to carry on a conversation while pouring tea, without sloshing the tea into the saucer." Don't say, "I like certain kinds of popular music very much." Say, "Whenever I hear Gerber Sprinklittle play 'Mississippi Man' on the trombone, my socks creep up my ankles."

Get Rid of Obvious Padding

25   The student toiling away at his weekly English theme is too often tormented by a figure: five hundred words. How, he asks himself, is he to achieve this staggering total? Obviously by never using one word when he can somehow work in ten.

26   He is therefore seldom content with a plain statement like "Fast driving is dangerous." This has only four words in it. He takes thought, and the sentence becomes:

> In my opinion, fast driving is dangerous.

Better, but he can do better still:

> In my opinion, fast driving would seem to be rather dangerous.

If he is really adept, it may come out:

> In my humble opinion, though I do not claim to be an expert on this complicated subject, fast driving, in most circumstances, would seem to be rather dangerous in many respects, or at least so it would seem to me.

Thus four words have been turned into forty, and not an iota of content has been added.

27   Now this is a way to go about reaching five hundred words, and if you are content with a "D" grade, it is as good a way as any. But if you aim higher, you must work differently. Instead of stuffing your sentences with straw, you must try steadily to get rid of the padding, to make your sentences lean and tough. If you are really working at it, your first draft will greatly exceed the required total, and then you will work it down, thus:

28   It is thought in some quarters that fraternities do not contribute as much as might be expected to campus life.

Some people think that fraternities contribute little to campus life.

29   The average doctor who practices in small towns or in the country must toil night and day to heal the sick.

Most country doctors work long hours.

30   When I was a little girl, I suffered from shyness and embarrassment in the presence of others.

I was a shy little girl.

31   It is absolutely necessary for the person employed as a marine fireman to give the matter of steam pressure his undivided attention at all times.

The fireman has to keep his eye on the steam gauge.

32   You may ask how you can arrive at five hundred words at this rate. Simple. You dig up more real content. Instead of taking a couple of obvious points off the surface of the topic and then circling warily around them for six paragraphs, you work in and explore, figure out the details. You illustrate. You say that fast driving is dangerous, and then you prove it. How long does it take to stop a car at forty and at eighty? How far can you see at night? What happens when a tire blows? What happens in a head-on collision at fifty miles an hour? Pretty soon your paper will be full of broken glass and blood and headless torsos, and reaching five hundred words will not really be a problem.

Call a Fool a Fool

33   Some of the padding in freshman themes is to be blamed not on anxiety about the word minimum but on excessive timidity. The student writes, "In my opinion, the principal of my high school acted in ways that I believe every unbiased person would have to call foolish." This isn't exactly what he means. What he means is, "My high school principal was a fool." If he was a fool, call him a fool. Hedging the thing about with "in-my-opinion's" and "it-seems-to-me's" and "as-I-see-it's" and "at-least-from-my-point-of-view's" gains you nothing. Delete these phrases whenever they creep into your paper.

34   The student's tendency to hedge stems from a modesty that in other circumstances would be commendable. He is, he realizes, young and inexperienced, and he half suspects that he is dopey and fuzzy-minded beyond the average. Probably only too true. But it doesn't help to announce your incompetence six times in every paragraph. Decide what you want to say and say it as vigorously as possible, without apology and in plain words.

35   Linguistic diffidence can take various forms. One is what we call *euphemism*. This is the tendency to call a spade "a certain garden implement" or women's underwear "unmentionables." It is stronger in some eras than others and in some people than others but it always operates more or less in subjects that are touchy or taboo: death, sex, madness, and so on. Thus we shrink from saying "He died last night" but say instead "passed away," "left us," "joined his Maker," "went to his reward." Or we try to take off the tension with a lighter cliché: "kicked the bucket," "cashed in his chips," "handed in his dinner pail." We have found all sorts of ways to avoid saying *mad:* "mentally ill," "touched," "not quite right upstairs," "feebleminded," "innocent," "simple," "off his trolley," "not in his right mind." Even such a now plain word as *insane* began as a euphemism with the meaning "not healthy."

36   Modern science, particularly psychology, contributes many polysyllables in which we can wrap our thoughts and blunt their force. To many

writers there is no such thing as a bad schoolboy. Schoolboys are malad-
justed or unoriented or misunderstood or in the need of guidance or lacking in continued success toward satisfactory integration of the personality
as a social unit, but they are never bad. Psychology no doubt makes us
better men and women, more sympathetic and tolerant, but it doesn't
make writing any easier. Had Shakespeare been confronted with psychology, "To be or not to be" might have come out, "To continue as a social
unit or not to do so. That is the personality problem. Whether 'tis a better
sign of integration at the conscious level to display a psychic tolerance
toward the maladjustments and repressions induced by one's lack of orientation in one's environment or—" But Hamlet would never have finished
the soliloquy.

37   Writing in the modern world, you cannot altogether avoid modern jargon. Nor, in an effort to get away from euphemism, should you salt your
paper with four-letter words. But you can do much if you will mount guard
against those roundabout phrases, those echoing polysyllables that tend to
slip into your writing to rob it of its crispness and force.

Beware of Pat Expressions

38   Other things being equal, avoid phrases like "other things being equal."
Those sentences that come to you whole, or in two or three doughy lumps,
are sure to be bad sentences. They are no creation of yours but pieces of
common thought floating in the community soup.

39   Pat expressions are hard, often impossible, to avoid, because they come
too easily to be noticed and seem too necessary to be dispensed with. No
writer avoids them altogether, but good writers avoid them more often
than poor writers.

40   By "pat expressions" we mean such tags as "to all practical intents and
purposes," "the pure and simple truth," "from where I sit," "the time of
his life," "to the ends of the earth," "in the twinkling of an eye," "as sure
as you're born," "over my dead body," "under cover of darkness," "took
the easy way out," "when all is said and done," "told him time and time
again," "parted the best of friends," "stand up and be counted," "gave
him the best years of her life," "worked her fingers to the bone." Like
other clichés, these expressions were once forceful. Now we should use
them only when we can't possibly think of anything else.

41   Some pat expressions stand like a wall between the writer and thought.
Such a one is "the American way of life." Many student writers feel that
when they have said that something accords with the American way of life
or does not they have exhausted the subject. Actually, they have stopped
at the highest level of abstraction. The American way of life is the complicated set of bonds between a hundred and eighty million ways. All of us

know this when we think about it, but the tag phrase too often keeps us from thinking about it.

42   So with many another phrase dear to the politician: "this great land of ours," "the man in the street," "our national heritage." These may prove our patriotism or give a clue to our political beliefs, but otherwise they add nothing to the paper except words.

Colorful Words

43   The writer builds with words, and no builder uses a raw material more slippery and elusive and treacherous. A writer's work is a constant struggle to get the right word in the right place, to find that particular word that will convey his meaning exactly, that will persuade the reader or soothe him or startle or amuse him. He never succeeds altogether—sometimes he feels that he scarcely succeeds at all—but such successes as he has are what make the thing worth doing.

44   There is no book of rules for this game. One progresses through everlasting experiment on the basis of ever-widening experience. There are few useful generalizations that one can make about words as words, but there are perhaps a few.

45   Some words are what we call "colorful." By this we mean that they are calculated to produce a picture or induce an emotion. They are dressy instead of plain, specific instead of general, loud instead of soft. Thus, in place of "Her heart beat," we may write, "Her heart *pounded, throbbed, fluttered, danced.*" Instead of "He sat in his chair," we may say, "He *lounged, sprawled, coiled.*" Instead of "It was hot," we may say, "It was *blistering, sultry, muggy, suffocating, steamy, wilting.*"

46   However, it should not be supposed that the fancy word is always better. Often it is as well to write "Her heart beat" or "It was hot" if that is all it did or all it was. Ages differ in how they like their prose. The nineteenth century liked it rich and smoky. The twentieth has usually preferred it lean and cool. The twentieth century writer, like all writers, is forever seeking the exact word, but he is wary of sounding feverish. He tends to pitch it low, to understate it, to throw it away. He knows that if he gets too colorful, the audience is likely to giggle.

47   See how this strikes you: "As the rich, golden glow of the sunset died away along the eternal western hills, Angela's limpid blue eyes looked softly and trustingly into Montague's flashing brown ones, and her heart pounded like a drum in time with the joyous song surging in her soul." Some people like that sort of thing, but most modern readers would say, "Good grief," and turn on the television.

Colored Words

48   Some words we would call not so much colorful as colored—that is, loaded with associations, good or bad. All words—except perhaps structure words—have associations of some sort. We have said that the meaning of a word is the sum of the contexts in which it occurs. When we hear a word, we hear with it an echo of all the situations in which we have heard it before.

49   In some words, these echoes are obvious and discussable. The word *mother*, for example, has, for most people, agreeable associations. When you hear *mother* you probably think of home, safety, love, food, and various other pleasant things. If one writes, "She was like a mother to me," he gets an effect which he would not get in "She was like an aunt to me." The advertiser makes use of the associations of *mother* by working it in when he talks about his product. The politician works it in when he talks about himself.

50   So also with such words as *home, liberty, fireside, contentment, patriot, tenderness, sacrifice, childlike, manly, bluff, limpid*. All of these words are loaded with associations that would be rather hard to indicate in a straightforward definition. There is more than a literal difference between "They sat around the fireside" and "They sat around the stove." They might have been equally warm and happy around the stove, but *fireside* suggests leisure, grace, quiet tradition, congenial company, and *stove* does not.

51   Conversely, some words have bad associations. *Mother* suggests pleasant things, but *mother-in-law* does not. Many mothers-in-law are heroically lovable and some mothers drink gin all day and beat their children insensible, but these facts of life are beside the point. The point is that *mother* sounds good and *mother-in-law* does not.

52   Or consider the word *intellectual*. This would seem to be a complimentary term, but in point of fact it is not, for it has picked up associations of impracticality and ineffectuality and general dopiness. So also such words as *liberal, reactionary, Communist, socialist, capitalist, radical, schoolteacher, truck driver, undertaker, operator, salesman, huckster, speculator*. These convey meaning on the literal level, but beyond that—sometimes, in some places—they convey contempt on the part of the speaker.

53   The question of whether to use loaded words or not depends on what is being written. The scientist, the scholar, try to avoid them; for the poet, the advertising writer, the public speaker, they are standard equipment. But every writer should take care that they do not substitute for thought. If you write, "Anyone who thinks that is nothing but a Socialist (or Communist or capitalist)" you have said nothing except that you don't like people who think that, and such remarks are effective only with the most naive

readers. It is always a bad mistake to think your readers more naive than they really are.

Colorless Words

54   But probably most student writers come to grief not with words that are colorful or those that are colored but with those that have no color at all. A pet example is *nice,* a word we would find it hard to dispense with in casual conversation but which is no longer capable of adding much to a description. Colorless words are those of such general meaning that in a particular sentence they mean nothing. Slang adjectives like *cool* ("That's real cool") tend to explode all over the language. They are applied to everything, lose their original force, and quickly die.

55   Beware also of nouns of very general meaning, like *circumstances, cases, instances, aspects, factors, relationships, attitudes, eventualities,* etc. In most circumstances you will find that those cases of writing which contain too many instances of words like these will in this and other aspects have factors leading to unsatisfactory relationships with the reader resulting in unfavorable attitudes on his part and perhaps other eventualities, like a grade of "D." Notice also what *etc.* means. It means "I'd like to make this list longer, but I can't think of any more examples."

Questions on Content

1. According to Roberts, how can a writer make a dull subject interesting?

2. Roberts suggests that writers should select topics and put down all the arguments that come to mind. He then says that writers should make a point of not using any of these arguments. What is *his* point?

3. According to Roberts, writers should always choose the side of a topic that looks hardest and least defensible. Why?

4. What is the difference between colorful and colored words?

5. What are euphemisms, and what do they ordinarily do to student writing?

**Questions
on Structure
and Style**

6. How would you describe Roberts's tone in this essay? The tone seems to change in paragraph 10. Why?

7. Roberts is addressing student writers. What type of relationship does he establish with that audience?

8. Roberts uses informal diction, especially in the first part of this essay. Such phrases as "a good hole in the weekend," "for the birds," and "sporting a big 'D' " are examples. What effect does this diction achieve?

9. Is there a thesis in this essay? If so, where?

10. What do you think is Roberts's purpose in this essay? How does Roberts use organization to achieve this purpose?

Assignments

1. Choose a potentially "dead" topic like "my pet peeve," "fraternities," "popular music," or "household pets." Make a list of original approaches you could take that would make the topic alive and vibrant.

2. Write the essay you thought about in assignment 1.

3. Choose a sample of your writing and evaluate it, using the standards that Roberts establishes in his essay.

Internal Revision:
A Process of Discovery

Donald M. Murray

While a professor at the University of New Hampshire, Donald M. Murray published many articles addressed to teachers of writing. In the following selection, Murray advises teachers to remember that revision is not merely proofreading or manuscript preparation. Instead, revision is the discovery of meaning itself and is "almost always . . . the most exciting, satisfying, and significant part of the writing process."

1   Writing is rewriting. Most writers accept rewriting as a condition of their craft; it comes with the territory. It is not, however, seen as a burden but as an opportunity by many writers. Neil Simon points out, "Rewriting is when playwriting really gets to be fun. . . . In baseball you only get three swings and you're out. In rewriting, you get almost as many swings as you want and you know, sooner or later, you'll hit the ball."

2   Rewriting is the difference between the dilettante and the artist, the amateur and the professional, the unpublished and the published. William Gass testifies, "I work not by writing but rewriting." Dylan Thomas states, "Almost any poem is fifty to a hundred revisions—and that's after it's well along." Archibald MacLeish talks of "the endless discipline of writing and rewriting and rerewriting." Novelist Theodore Weesner tells his students at the University of New Hampshire his course title is not "Fiction Writing" but "Fiction Rewriting."

3   And yet rewriting is one of the writing skills least researched, least examined, least understood, and—usually—least taught. The vast majority of students, even those who take writing courses, get away with first-draft copy. They are never introduced to the opportunities of serious revision.

4   A search of the literature reveals relatively few articles or books on the rewriting process. I have a commonplace book which has grown from one thin journal to 24 3-inch-thick notebooks with more than 8,000 entries divided into prewriting, writing, and rewriting. Yet even with my interest in the process of rewriting—some of my colleagues would say my obsession—only four of those notebooks are labeled rewriting.

5   I suspect the term rewriting has, even for many writers, an aura of failure about it. Rewriting is too often taught as punishment, not as an opportunity for discovery or even as an inevitable part of the writing

process. Most texts, in fact, confuse rewriting with editing, proofreading, or manuscript preparation. Yet rewriting almost always is the most exciting, satisfying, and significant part of the writing process.

The Writing Process

6   The most accurate definition of writing, I believe, is that it is the process of using language to discover meaning in experience and to communicate it. I believe this process can be described, understood, and therefore learned. Prewriting, writing, and rewriting have been generally accepted as the three principal divisions of the writing process during the past decade. I would like to propose new terms for consideration, terms which may emphasize the essential process of discovery through writing: *prevision, vision,* and *revision.*

7   Of course, writing will, at times, seem to skip over one part of the writing process and linger on another, and the stages of the process also overlap. The writing process is too experimental and exploratory to be contained in a rigid definition; writers move back and forth through all stages of the writing process as they search for meaning and then attempt to clarify it. It is also true that most writers do not define, describe, or possibly even understand the writing process. There's no reason for them to know what they are doing if they do it well, any more than we need to know grammatical terms if we speak and write clearly. I am convinced, however, that most writers most of the time pass through the following distinct stages.

8   *Prevision.*   This term encompasses everything that precedes the first draft—receptive experience, such as awareness (conscious and unconscious), observation, remembering; and exploratory experience, such as research, reading, interviewing, and note-taking. Writers practice the prevision skills of selecting, connecting, and evaluating significant bits of information provided by receptive and exploratory experience. Prevision includes, in my opinion, the underestimated skills of title and lead writing, which help the student identify a subject, limit it, develop a point of view towards it, and begin to find the voice to explore the subject.

9   *Vision.*   In the second stage of the writing process, the first draft—what I call a discovery draft—is completed. This stage takes the shortest time for the writer—in many cases it is written at one sitting—but it is the fulcrum of the writing process. Before this first draft, which Peter Drucker calls "the zero draft," everything seems possible. By completing this vision of what may be said, the writer stakes out a territory to explore.

10   *Revision.*   This is what the writer does after a draft is completed to understand and communicate what has begun to appear on the page. The writer reads to see what has been suggested, then confirms, alters, or develops it, usually through many drafts. Eventually a meaning is developed which can be communicated to a reader.

The Importance of Discovery

11   My main concern in this chapter is revision. But to be able to understand what I consider the most important task in the revision process, we have to appreciate the fact that writers much of the time don't know what they are going to write or even possibly what they have written. Writers use language as a tool of exploration to see beyond what they know. Most texts and most of our research literature have not accepted this concept or dealt with its implications.

12   Elie Wiesel says, "I write in order to understand as much as to be understood." The poet Tony Connor gives a recipe for writing a poem: "Invent a jungle and then explore it." William Stafford states, "You don't know what's going to happen. Nobody does." I have included at the end of this chapter forty-seven other quotations from my commonplace book which testify to the essential ignorance writers feel many times about what they are writing.

13   In teaching writing I often feel that the most significant step is made when a student enters into the writing process and experiences the discovery of meaning through writing. Yet this process of discovery has not been generally explored or understood for a number of reasons. First of all, it has not been experienced by nonwriters or admitted when it is experienced by writers in the less imaginative forms of writing. One professor of philosophy, after reading a text of mine, confessed he had been ashamed of the way he wrote, that he didn't know what to say or how to say it when he sat down to write. He had to write and write and write to find out what he had to say. He was embarrassed and didn't want his colleagues to know how dumb he was. When he read my book he found his activities were legitimate. I suspect such unjustified shame is more prevalent than we like to admit. Another professor told me recently that he makes assignments he could not complete by his own deadline. He explained, "My students are smarter than I am. I have to rewrite and rewrite many drafts." Yet he neither "confesses" this to his students nor allows them the opportunity to perform the writing task essential for them to achieve publication.

14   Most professors who are aware of the process of rewriting to discover meaning are uncomfortable thinking about it, to say nothing of discussing it in class. Discovery seems the province of the "creative writer," the writer

who deals in poetry, fiction, or drama. Such activities are not quite respectable in the academic community, where we too often have a sex manual attitude: it's okay to read about it as long as you don't do it. But I am an academic schizophrenic, a "creative" writer and a "noncreative" writer. As the chairperson of a rather large department, I spend a good deal of my time writing memos to deans and vice provosts. (That's really creative writing.) I also moonlight occasionally as a corporate ghostwriter. I publish texts, novels, poems, and "papers." And in all of these roles I find the process of discovery through language taking place. I do not agree with the educational segregation of functional and imaginative writing, creative and noncreative writing. I know the process of discovery takes place when I write fiction and nonfiction, poetry and memos. To produce letters, reports, novels, essays, reviews, poems, and academic papers that say something, you have to allow language to lead you to meaning.

15   In drafting this paper I found myself writing, as I attempted to define the writing process, that the writer, after the first draft, is "not dealing with the vision but a fact." The word vision surprised me. It appeared on the page without premeditation. In reading it over I cut the sentence but decided the word was a better term than *writing* to describe the second stage of the writing process and, working from that point, saw the virtue of using the term *revision* for rewriting and then tried on the term *prevision* for size and found it fit, although I can't find it in my dictionary. I'm not sure that this is a discovery of enormous value, but it was fun; and I think this accident of language, this business of using words I didn't know I was going to use, has helped me understand the writing process a little bit better.

16   I suspect most of us have experienced many similar discoveries, but we feel it a failure: if we had a bit more IQ, we would have known the right word. I find few English teachers are comfortable with the concept of uncalculated discovery. They simply do not believe the testimony of writers when they say they write what they don't know, and this may indeed be an uncomfortable concept if you spend your classroom hours analyzing literature and telling your students exactly why the writer did what he or she did, as if literature resulted from the following of a detailed blueprint. Writing, fortunately for writers, is much more exciting than that. The writer does plan but keeps adapting those plans to what is discovered on the page.

17   The writer, however, who lives in the academic community—and today most of us do—is surrounded by people who seem to know precisely what happens in a piece of literature. The other night my colleague, the poet Charles Simic, said his favorite poems were the ones he didn't understand, an unsettling confession in a department of English. It is hard to admit that you don't know what you're doing when you write. It seems a bit

undignified, perhaps even cause for the removal of tenure. Surely my governor would think I ought to know what I'm doing when I sit down to write—I'm a full professor, for goodness sake—and yet I don't. And hope I never will.

18   Listening to a lecture the other day, I found myself doodling with language. (The better the lecture the more likely a piece of writing will start to happen on my notebook page.) From where I sat in the lecture hall, I could see an office door, and I watched a person in that office get up and shut the door against the lecture. It was an ordinary act, yet, for no reason I can recall, I found myself writing this on the page:

> I had an office at a university, an inside office, without window or air. The classrooms up and down the corridor would fill up with words until they spilled over and reached the edge of my half-opened door, a confident, almost arrogant mumble I could no longer bother to try to understand. Was I to be like the makers of those words, was I already like the students in my own Freshman sections? Perhaps the only good thing about this position was that Mother was dumbly proud and Father puzzled and angry, "Is this where they put you, an educated man? The union would kill me."
>   If I hadn't killed a man, my life would have seemed trite. . . .

19   I have followed this short story for only a couple of pages in the past few days. I am ashamed to reveal the lines above—I don't know if they will lead me to a story—but I'm having fun and think I should share this experience, for it is revealing of the writing process. I did not intend to write a short story. I am working on a novel, a book of poems, and articles such as this one. Short fiction is not on the menu. I did not intend to write an academic short story. I do not like the genre. I do not particularly like the character who is appearing on my page, but I am interested in being within his head. I have not yet killed a man, to my knowledge, and I have never been a teaching assistant, although I have known many.

20   I want to repeat that there was absolutely no intent in what I was doing. The fact that the character had killed a person came as a total surprise to me. It seems too melodramatic, and I don't like this confessional voice, and I do not like the tense, and I have trouble dictating these words from my notebook to my wife, because they keep changing and leading me forward. I do not know if the killing was accidental or premeditated. I don't know the victim. I don't know the method. I don't know if it was imaginary. I do know the phrase "killed a man" appeared on the page. It may have come there because of what the father said; or, since in the next paragraph I discovered that the young man feels this one act gives him a certain distance from life, a sort of scenic overlook from which to view life, perhaps

that idea came from the word "position" in the first paragraph. In my lower middle-class background, even a teaching assistant had a position, not a job. A little more of this kind of thing, however, and the story will never be written.

21   Writers must remain, to some degree, not only ignorant of what they are going to do but what they are doing. Mary Peterson just wrote me about her novel, "I need to write it before I can think about it, write it too fast for thought." Writers have to protect their ignorance, and it is not easy to remain ignorant, particularly in an English department. That may be one reason we have deemphasized the experience of discovery in writing.

22   Discovery, however, can be a frightening process. The terror of the empty page is real, because you simply do not know what you are going to say before you say it or if indeed you will have anything to say. I observe this process most dramatically at those times when I dictate early drafts of nonfiction to my wife, who types it on the typewriter. We have done this for years, and yet rather regularly she asks me to repeat what I have said or tell her what I am going to say so that she can punctuate. I don't think, after many books and many years, that she really believes me when I claim I can't remember what I've just said or that I don't know what I'm going to say next.

23   This process is even more frightening when you engage in the forms of writing that take you inside yourself. "There's not any more dangerous occupation in the world," says James Dickey of poetry. "The mortality rate is very, very high. Paul Valéry once said, 'one should never go into the self except armed to the teeth.' That's true. The kind of poets we're talking about—Berryman, Crane, Dylan Thomas—have created something against which they have no immunity and which they can not control."

24   Finally, many expert readers who teach English, and therefore writing, are ignorant of the process of discovery because it is not, and should not be, apparent in a finished work. After a building is finished, the flimsy scaffolding is taken away. Our profession's normal obsession with product rather than process leads us towards dangerous misconceptions about the writing process. I believe increasingly that the process of discovery, of using language to find out what you are going to say, is a key part of the writing process. In light of this I would like to reexamine the revision process.

The Two Principal Forms of Revision

25   The more I explore the revision process as a researcher and the more I experience it as a writer, the more convinced I am that there are two principal and quite separate editorial acts involved in revision.

26   *Internal revision.*   Under this term, I include everything writers do to discover and develop what they have to say, beginning with the reading of a completed first draft. They read to discover where their content, form, language, and voice have led them. They use language, structure, and information to find out what they have to say or hope to say. The audience is one person: the writer.

27   *External revision.*   This is what writers do to communicate what they have found they have written to another audience. It is editing and proofreading and much more. Writers now pay attention to the conventions of form and language, mechanics, and style. They eye their audience and may choose to appeal to it. They read as an outsider, and it is significant that such terms as *polish* are used by professionals: they dramatize the fact that the writer at this stage in the process may, appropriately, be concerned with exterior appearance.

28   Most writers spend more time, *much* more time, on internal revision than external revision. Yet most texts emphasize the least part of the process, the mechanical changes involved in the etiquette of writing, the superficial aspects of preparing a manuscript to be read, and pass over the process of internal revision. It's worth noting that it is unlikely intelligent choices in the editing process can be made unless writers thoroughly understand what they have said through internal revision.

29   Although I believe external revision has not been explored adequately or imaginatively, it has been explored. I shall concentrate on attempting to describe internal revision. . . .

30   After the writer has completed the first draft, the writer moves toward the center of the writing process. E. M. Forster says, "The act of writing inspires me," and Valéry talks of "the inspiration of the writing desk." The writer may be closer to the scientist than to the critic at this point. Each piece of writing is an experiment. Robert Penn Warren says, "All writing that is any good *is* experimental: that is, it's a way of seeing what is possible."

31   Some pieces of writing come easily, without a great deal of internal revision. The experience is rare for most writers, however, and it usually comes after a lifetime of discipline, or sometimes after a long night of work, as it did when Robert Frost wrote "Stopping by Woods on a Snowy Evening." The important thing to understand is that the work that reads the most easily is often the product of what appears to be drudgery. Theodore Roethke wisely points out that "you will come to know how, by working slowly, to be spontaneous."

32   I have a relatively short 7-part poem of which there are 185 or more versions written over the past 2 years. I am no Roethke, but I have found it important to share with my students in my seminar on the teaching of

writing a bit of the work which will never appear in public. I think they are impressed with how badly I write, with how many false starts and illiterate accidents it took for me to move forward towards some understanding of the climate in a tenement in which I lived as an only child, surrounded by a paralyzed grandmother and two rather childlike parents. The important thing for my students to see is that each word changed, each line crossed out, each space left on the page is an attempt to understand, to remember what I did not know I remembered.

33   During the process of internal revision, writers are not concerned with correctness in any exterior sense. They read what they have written so that they can deal with the questions of subject, of adequate information, of structure, of form, of language. They move from a revision of the entire piece down to the page, the paragraph, the sentence, the line, the phrase, the word. And then, because each word may give off an explosion of meaning, they move out from the word to the phrase, the line, the sentence, the paragraph, the page, the piece. Writers move in close and then move out to visualize the entire piece. Again and again and again. As Donald Hall says, "The attitude to cultivate from the start is that revision is a way of life."

Discovery and Internal Revision

34   The concept of internal revision is new to me. This essay has given me the impetus to explore this area of the writing process. The further I explore the more tentative my conclusions. This chapter is, indeed, as I believe it was meant to be, a call for research, not a report of research. There are many things I do not understand as I experience and examine the process of internal revision. But in addition to my normal researches, I am part of a faculty which includes seven publishing writers, as well as many publishing scholars and critics. We share our work in process, and I have the advantage of seeing them discover what they have to say. I also see the work of graduate students in our writing program, many of whom are already publishing. And I watch the writing of students who are undergraduates at the university, in high school, in middle school, and in elementary school. And I think I can perceive four important aspects of discovery in the process of internal revision.

35   The first involves *content*. I think we forget that writers in all forms, even poetry, especially poetry, write with information. As English professors and linguistic researchers, we may concentrate on stylistic differences, forgetting that the writer engaged in the process of internal revision is looking through the word—or beyond the word or behind the word—for the information the word will symbolize. Sitting at a desk, pausing, staring out the window, the writer does not see some great thesaurus in the sky; the writer sees a character walking or hears a character speaking, sees a

pattern of statistics which may lead toward a conclusion. Writers can't write nothing; they must have an abundance of information. During the process of internal revision, they gather new information or return to their inventory of information and draw on it. They discover what they have to say by relating pieces of specific information to other bits of information and use words to symbolize and connect that information.

36   This naturally leads to the discoveries related to *form and structure*. We all know Archibald MacLeish said that a poem should not mean but be, but what we do not always understand is that the being may be the meaning. Form is meaning, or a kind of meaning. The story that has a beginning, a middle, and an end implies that life has a beginning, a middle, and an end; exposition implies that things can be explained; argument implies the possibility of rational persuasion. As writers bring order to chaos, the order brings the writers toward meaning.

37   Third, *language* itself leads writers to meaning. During the process of internal revision (what some writers might call eternal revision), they reject words, choose new words, bring words together, switch their order around to discover what they are saying. "I work with language," says Bernard Malamud, "I love the flowers of afterthought."

38   Finally, I believe there is a fourth area, quite separate from content, form, or language, which is harder to define but may be as important as the other sources of discovery. That is what we call *voice*. I think voice, the way in which writers hear what they have to say, hear their point of view towards the subject, their authority, their distance from the subject, is an extremely significant form of internal revision.

39   We should realize that there may be fewer discoveries in form and voice as a writer repeats a subject or continues work in a genre which he or she has explored earlier and become proficient with. This lack of discovery— this excessive professionalism or slickness, the absence of discovery—is the greatest fear of mature, successful writers. They may know too much too early in the writing process.

Questions on Content

1. In paragraph 6, Murray cites the three standard names for the divisions of the writing process: prewriting, writing, and rewriting. Why does he then rename these divisions?

2. Murray says of revision: "Eventually a meaning is developed which can be communicated to a reader" (paragraph 10). Why is the word *eventually* so important to understanding the process of rewriting?

3. Murray claims that "most professors who are aware of the process of rewriting to discover meaning are uncomfortable thinking about it, to say nothing of discussing it in class" (paragraph 14). According to Murray, why is this true? What can we infer about professors who demonstrate such a reluctance?

4. Why does Murray include the "story about a story" that he presents in paragraphs 18 through 20? How do you feel about Murray after reading this account?

5. What are the differences between internal and external revision as Murray defines each? Why is internal revision more important?

6. Murray refers to, and quotes from, many well-known professional writers (see paragraphs 30 through 33 for several examples). What do such quotations add to Murray's presentation? Why are they *not* simply efforts by Murray to show off?

**Questions
on Structure
and Style**

7. Paragraphs 1 through 5 serve as an introduction. Why do they work well at leading readers into Murray's presentation? Why does Murray *not* begin with his description of the writing process (paragraphs 6–10)?

8. Why is Murray's use of a phrase like "doodling with language" (paragraph 18) characteristic of his writing style? How would you describe that style?

Assignments

1. Murray points out that "writers use language as a tool of exploration to see beyond what they know" (paragraph 11). In other words, writers understand that through writing, they find out what they think. Sometimes speaking can have the same result. Think of a time when you discovered something about yourself *because* you spoke, perhaps when you rebuked or congratulated someone. What did you learn? That you had more courage than you believed? Less courage? Less patience? Stronger

feelings? In a paragraph or an essay, explain how using language allowed you to discover something about yourself.

2. Murray states that in writing a first draft, "the writer stakes out a territory to explore" (paragraph 9). How does this idea compare with your own understanding of what a first draft should be? Do you too consider a first draft simply a beginning? In a short essay, explain your reaction to Murray's statement.

Clear Writing Means Clear Thinking Means . . .

Marvin H. Swift

▬▬▬▬▬▬▬

Marvin H. Swift taught for years in the business world and knows the problems of business writing. In this article (which appeared in the *Harvard Business Review*), he discusses writing a memo, clearly a business-related task; but his advice for managers can help anyone who writes. Swift shows how revision can sharpen thinking, and he also shows how courage has its own role in the writing process.

▬▬▬▬▬▬▬

1 If you are a manager, you constantly face the problem of putting words on paper. If you are like most managers, this is not the sort of problem you enjoy. It is hard to do, and time consuming; and the task is doubly difficult when, as is usually the case, your words must be designed to change the behavior of others in the organization.

2 But the chore is there and must be done. How? Let's take a specific case.

3 Let's suppose that everyone at X Corporation, from the janitor on up to the chairman of the board, is using the office copiers for personal matters; income tax forms, church programs, children's term papers, and God knows what else are being duplicated by the gross. This minor piracy costs the company a pretty penny, both directly and in employee time, and the general manager—let's call him Sam Edwards—decides the time has come to lower the boom.

4 Sam lets fly by dictating the following memo to his secretary:

To: All Employees
From: Samuel Edwards, General Manager
Subject: Abuse of Copiers

It has recently been brought to my attention that many of the people who are employed by this company have taken advantage of their positions by availing themselves of the copiers. More specifically, these machines are being used for other than company business.

Obviously, such practice is contrary to company policy and must cease and desist immediately. I wish therefore to inform all concerned--those who have abused policy or will be abusing it--that their behavior cannot and will not be tolerated. Accordingly, anyone in the future who is unable to control himself will have his employment terminated.

If there are any questions about company policy, please feel free to contact this office.

Now the memo is on his desk for his signature. He looks it over; and the more he looks, the worse it reads. In fact, it's lousy. So he revises it three times, until it finally is in the form that follows:

To: All Employees
From: Samuel Edwards, General Manager
Subject: Use of Copiers

We are revamping our policy on the use of copiers for personal matters. In the past we have not encouraged personnel to use them for such purposes because of the costs involved. But we also recognize, perhaps belatedly, that we can solve the problem if each of us pays for what he takes.

We are therefore putting these copiers on a pay-as-you-go basis. The details are simple enough . . .

Samuel Edwards

This time Sam thinks the memo looks good, and it *is* good. Not only is the writing much improved, but the problem should now be solved. He therefore signs the memo, turns it over to his secretary for distribution, and goes back to other things.

From Verbiage to Intent

5   I can only speculate on what occurs in a writer's mind as he moves from a poor draft to a good revision, but it is clear that Sam went through several specific steps, mentally as well as physically, before he had created his end product:

- He eliminated wordiness.
- He modulated the tone of the memo.
- He revised the policy it stated.

Let's retrace his thinking through each of these processes.

Eliminating Wordiness

6   Sam's basic message is that employees are not to use the copiers for their own affairs at company expense. As he looks over his first draft, however, it seems so long that this simple message has become diffused. With the idea of trimming the memo down, he takes another look at his first paragraph.

> It has recently been brought to my attention that many of the people who are employed by this company have taken advantage of their positions by availing themselves of the copiers. More specifically, these machines are being used for other than company business.

He edits it like this:

> Item: "recently"
> Comment to himself: *Of course; else why write about the problem? So delete the word.*
>
> Item: "It has been brought to my attention"
> Comment: *Naturally. Delete it.*
>
> Item: "the people who are employed by this company"
> Comment: *Assumed. Why not just "employees"?*
>
> Item: "by availing themselves" and "for other than company business"
> Comment: *Since the second sentence repeats the first, why not coalesce?*

And he comes up with this:

> Employees have been using the copiers for
> personal matters.

He proceeds to the second paragraph. More confident of himself, he moves in broader swoops, so that the deletion process looks like this:

> Obviously, such practice is contrary to company
> policy and ~~must cease and desist immediately. I~~
> ~~wish therefore to inform all concerned--those who~~
> ~~have abused policy or will be abusing it--that~~
> ~~their behavior cannot and will not be tolerated.~~
> ~~Accordingly, anyone in the future who is unable~~
> ~~to control himself will have his employment~~
> ~~terminated.~~ will result in dismissal.

The final paragraph, apart from "company policy" and "feel free," looks all right, so the total memo now reads as follows:

> To: All Employees
> From: Samuel Edwards, General Manager
> Subject: Abuse of Copiers
>
> Employees have been using the copiers for
> personal matters. Obviously, such practice is
> contrary to company policy and will result in
> dismissal.
>
> If there are any questions, please contact this
> office.

Sam now examines his efforts by putting these questions to himself:

> Question: Is the memo free of deadwood?
> *Answer: Very much so. In fact, it's good, tight prose.*
>
> Question: Is the policy stated?
> *Answer: Yes—sharp and clear.*

Question: Will the memo achieve its intended purpose?
Answer: Yes. But it sounds foolish.

Question: Why?
Answer: The wording is too harsh; I'm not going to fire anybody over this.

Question: How should I tone the thing down?

To answer this last question, Sam takes another look at the memo.

Correcting the Tone

7   What strikes his eye as he looks it over? Perhaps these three words:

- Abuse . . .
- Obviously . . .
- . . . dismissal . . .

The first one is easy enough to correct: he substitutes "use" for "abuse." But "obviously" poses a problem and calls for reflection. If the policy is obvious, why are the copiers being used? Is it that people are outrightly dishonest? Probably not. But that implies the policy isn't obvious; and whose fault is this? Who neglected to clarify policy? And why "dismissal" for something never publicized?

8   These questions impel him to revise the memo once again:

To: All Employees
From: Samuel Edwards, General Manager
Subject: Use of Copiers

Copiers are not to be used for personal matters. If there are any questions, please contact this office.

Revising the Policy Itself

9   The memo now seems courteous enough—at least it is not discourteous—but it is just a blank, perhaps overly simple, statement of policy. Has he really thought through the policy itself?

10   Reflecting on this, Sam realizes that some people will continue to use the copiers for personal business anyhow. If he seriously intends to enforce the basic policy (first sentence), he will have to police the equipment, and that raises the question of costs all over again.

11   Also the memo states that he will maintain an open-door policy (second sentence)—and surely there will be some, probably a good many, who will stroll in and offer to pay for what they use. His secretary has enough to do without keeping track of affairs of that kind.

12   Finally, the first and second sentences are at odds with each other. The first says that personal copying is out, and the second implies that it can be arranged.

13   The facts of organizational life thus force Sam to clarify in his own mind exactly what his position on the use of copiers is going to be. As he sees the problem now, what he really wants to do is put the copiers on a pay-as-you-go basis. After making the decision, he begins anew:

> To: All Employees
> From: Samuel Edwards, General Manager
> Subject: Use of Copiers
>
> We are revamping our policy on the use of copiers . . .

This is the draft that goes into distribution and now allows him to turn his attention to other problems.

The Chicken or the Egg?

14   What are we to make of all this? It seems a rather lengthy and tedious report of what, after all, is a routine writing task created by a problem of minor importance. In making this kind of analysis, have I simply labored the obvious?

15   To answer this question, let's drop back to the original draft. If you read it over, you will see that Sam began with this kind of thinking:

- ■ "The employees are taking advantage of the company."
- ■ "I'm a nice guy, but now I'm going to play Dutch uncle."
- ∴ "I'll write them a memo that tells them to shape up or ship out."

In his final version, however, his thinking is quite different:

- ■ "Actually, the employees are pretty mature, responsible people. They're capable of understanding a problem."
- ■ "Company policy itself has never been crystallized. In fact, this is the first memo on the subject."

■ "I don't want to overdo this thing—any employee can make an error in judgment."

∴ "I'll set a reasonable policy and write a memo that explains how it ought to operate."

Sam obviously gained a lot of ground between the first draft and the final version, and this implies two things. First, if a manager is to write effectively, he needs to isolate and define, as fully as possible, all the critical variables in the writing process and scrutinize what he writes for its clarity, simplicity, tone, and the rest. Second, after he has clarified his thoughts on paper, he may find that what he has written is not what has to be said. In this sense, writing is feedback and a way for the manager to discover himself. What are his real attitudes toward that amorphous, undifferentiated gray mass of employees "out there"? Writing is a way of finding out. By objectifying his thoughts in the medium of language, he gets a chance to see what is going on in his mind.

16   In other words, *if the manager writes well, he will think well.* Equally, the more clearly he has thought out his message before he starts to dictate, the more likely he is to get it right on paper the first time round. In other words, *if he thinks well, he will write well.*

17   Hence we have a chicken-and-the-egg situation: writing and thinking go hand in hand; and when one is good, the other is likely to be good.

Revision Sharpens Thinking

18   More particularly, rewriting is the key to improved thinking. It demands a real openmindedness and objectivity. It demands a willingness to cull verbiage so that ideas stand out clearly. And it demands a willingness to meet logical contradictions head on and trace them to the premises that have created them. In short, it forces a writer to get up his courage and expose his thinking process to his own intelligence.

19   Obviously, revising is hard work. It demands that you put yourself through the wringer, intellectually and emotionally, to squeeze out the best you can offer. Is it worth the effort? Yes, it is—if you believe you have a responsibility to think and communicate effectively.

Questions on Content

1. In paragraph 1, Swift makes an assumption about words. What is that assumption?

2. Identify the metaphor in paragraph 19, and comment on its effectiveness. Can you think of another metaphor that could work here?

3. Swift seems to concentrate on the use of language in business communications. Why, however, does his advice apply to all writing regardless of setting?

**Questions
on Structure
and Style**

4. What is the purpose of paragraphs 2 and 14?

5. What is the topic sentence of paragraph 15, and how effective is it?

6. How would you describe the tone of this essay? Cite five expressions Swift uses that help create this tone.

7. Swift's essay is carefully organized. List his key points. How important is their order? Try to change this order. Will your new order work?

Assignments

1. Compose a memo to the president of your college or university. In the memo, recommend changes in parking regulations for students and staff. Be sure to (1) identify specific changes, (2) create the appropriate tone, and (3) be brief.

2. Assume that you have received the following letter. Rewrite it, following Swift's recommendations for revision.

Dear Students:

The Financial Aid Office is in a position to be of help to all students. Many students mistakenly believe that financial aid is given only to students in dire need, but this is not true. Scholarships, grants, and loans are available to a wide range of students, and it is in your best interests to seek information from us about how we can help you.

An uninformed student is his own worst enemy. We have the information. Why not see us and make the most of the financial resources available to you? Anyone is welcome in our office in Benning Hall, Room 218. Stop by and make school life easier for yourself.

Yours truly,

Martin Reynolds

Financial Aid Officer

Simplicity

William Zinsser

As a critic, editor, writer, and teacher of writing, William Zinsser
has devoted most of his professional life to words. In "Simplicity," a chapter from his book *On Writing Well*, Zinsser shows that
simplicity is not synonymous with simple-mindedness. Instead,
he links simplicity with clarity, a quality that is impossible if
"some fuzz has worked its way into the machinery."

1   Clutter is the disease of American writing. We are a society strangling in
unnecessary words, circular constructions, pompous frills and meaningless jargon.

2   Who can understand the viscous language of everyday American
commerce and enterprise: the business letter, the interoffice memo, the
corporation report, the notice from the bank explaining its latest "simplified" statement? What member of an insurance or medical plan can decipher the brochure that tells him what his costs and benefits are? What
father or mother can put together a child's toy—on Christmas Eve or
any other eve—from the instructions on the box? Our national tendency
is to inflate and thereby sound important. The airline pilot who wakes us
to announce that he is presently anticipating experiencing considerable weather wouldn't dream of saying that there's a storm ahead and
it may get bumpy. The sentence is too simple—there must be something
wrong with it.

3   But the secret of good writing is to strip every sentence to its cleanest
components. Every word that serves no function, every long word that
could be a short word, every adverb which carries the same meaning that is
already in the verb, every passive construction that leaves the reader unsure of who is doing what—these are the thousand and one adulterants
that weaken the strength of a sentence. And they usually occur, ironically,
in proportion to education and rank.

4   During the late 1960s the president of a major university wrote a letter
to mollify the alumni after a spell of campus unrest. "You are probably
aware," he began, "that we have been experiencing very considerable
potentially explosive expressions of dissatisfaction on issues only partially
related." He meant that the students had been hassling them about different things. I was far more upset by the president's English than by the
students' potentially explosive expressions of dissatisfaction. I would have
preferred the presidential approach taken by Franklin D. Roosevelt when
he tried to convert into English his own government's memos, such as this
blackout order of 1942:

> Such preparations shall be made as will completely obscure all Federal buildings and non-Federal buildings occupied by the Federal government during an air raid for any period of time from visibility by reason of internal or external illumination.

5   "Tell them," Roosevelt said, "that in buildings where they have to keep the work going to put something across the windows."

6   Simplify, simplify. Thoreau said it, as we are so often reminded, and no American writer more consistently practiced what he preached. Open *Walden* to any page and you will find a man saying in a plain and orderly way what is on his mind:

> I love to be alone. I never found the companion that was so companionable as solitude. We are for the most part more lonely when we go abroad among men than when we stay in our chambers. A man thinking or working is always alone, let him be where he will. Solitude is not measured by the miles of space that intervene between a man and his fellows. The really diligent student in one of the crowded hives of Cambridge College is as solitary as a dervish in the desert.

7   How can the rest of us achieve such enviable freedom from clutter? The answer is to clear our heads of clutter. Clear thinking becomes clear writing: one can't exist without the other. It is impossible for a muddy thinker to write good English. He may get away with it for a paragraph or two, but soon the reader will be lost, and there is no sin so grave, for he will not easily be lured back.

8   Who is this elusive creature the reader? He is a person with an attention span of about twenty seconds. He is assailed on every side by forces competing for his time: by newspapers and magazines, by television and radio and stereo, by his wife and children and pets, by his house and his yard and all the gadgets that he has bought to keep them spruce, and by that most potent of competitors, sleep. The man snoozing in his chair with an unfinished magazine open on his lap is a man who was being given too much unnecessary trouble by the writer.

9   It won't do to say that the snoozing reader is too dumb or too lazy to keep pace with the train of thought. My sympathies are with him. If the reader is lost, it is generally because the writer has not been careful enough to keep him on the path.

10   This carelessness can take any number of forms. Perhaps a sentence is so excessively cluttered that the reader, hacking his way through the verbiage, simply doesn't know what it means. Perhaps a sentence has been so shoddily constructed that the reader could read it in any of several ways. Perhaps the writer has switched pronouns in mid-sentence, or has switched tenses, so the reader loses track of who is talking or when the

5 --

is too dumb or too lazy to keep pace with the
~~writer's~~ train of thought. My sympathies are
~~entirely~~ with him. ~~He's not so dumb.~~ If the reader
is lost, it is generally because the writer ~~of the
article~~ has not been careful enough to keep him
on the ~~proper~~ path.

This carelessness can take any number of
~~different~~ forms. Perhaps a sentence is so
excessively ~~long and~~ cluttered that the reader,
hacking his way through ~~all~~ the verbiage, simply
doesn't know what *it* ~~the writer~~ means. Perhaps a
sentence has been so shoddily constructed that
the reader could read it in any of *several* ~~two or three
different~~ ways. ~~He thinks he knows what the
writer is trying to say, but he's not sure.~~ Perhaps
the writer has switched pronouns in mid-sentence,
or ~~perhaps he~~ has switched tenses, so the reader
loses track of who is talking *to whom,* or ~~exactly~~
when the action took place. Perhaps Sentence B is
not a logical sequel to Sentence A--the writer, in
whose head the connection is ~~perfectly~~ clear, has
not *bothered to provide* ~~given enough thought to providing~~ the missing
link. Perhaps the writer has used an important
word incorrectly by not taking the trouble to
look it up ~~and make sure.~~ He may think that
"sanguine" and "sanguinary" mean the same thing,
but ~~I can assure you that~~ the difference is a
bloody big one ~~to the reader.~~ *The reader* ~~He~~ can only ~~try to~~
infer ~~word~~ (speaking of big differences) what the
writer is trying to imply.

Faced with *these* ~~such a variety of~~ obstacles, the
reader is at first a remarkably tenacious bird.
He ~~tends to~~ blames himself. He obviously missed

52

something, ~~he thinks,~~ and he goes back over the mystifying sentence, or over the whole paragraph, piecing it out like an ancient rune, making guesses and moving on. But he won't do this for long. ~~He will soon run out of patience.~~ The writer is making him work too hard, ~~harder than he should have to work~~ and the reader will look for one ~~a writer~~ who is better at his craft.

The writer must therefore constantly ask himself: What am I trying to say? ~~in this sentence?~~ Surprisingly often, he doesn't know. ~~And~~ Then he must look at what he has ~~just~~ written and ask: Have I said it? Is it clear to someone encountering ~~who is coming upon~~ the subject for the first time? If it's not, ~~clear,~~ it is because some fuzz has worked its way into the machinery. The clear writer is a person ~~who is~~ clear-headed enough to see this stuff for what it is: fuzz.

I don't mean ~~to suggest~~ that some people are born clear-headed and are therefore natural writers, whereas others ~~other people~~ are naturally fuzzy and will ~~therefore~~ never write well. Thinking clearly is a ~~an entirely~~ conscious act that the writer must force ~~keep~~ ~~forcing~~ upon himself, just as if he were embarking ~~starting out~~ on any other ~~kind of~~ project that requires ~~calls for~~ logic: adding up a laundry list or doing an algebra problem, ~~or playing chess.~~ Good writing doesn't ~~just~~ come naturally, though most people obviously think it does. ~~it's as easy as walking.~~ The professional

Two pages of the final manuscript for this article. Although they look like a first draft, they have already been rewritten and retyped—like almost every other page—four or five times. With each rewrite I try to make what I have written tighter, stronger and more precise, eliminating every element that is not doing useful work, until at last I have a clean copy for the printer. Then I go over it once more, reading it aloud, and am always amazed at how much clutter can still be profitably cut.

action took place. Perhaps Sentence B is not a logical sequel to Sentence A—the writer, in whose head the connection is clear, has not bothered to provide the missing link. Perhaps the writer has used an important word incorrectly by not taking the trouble to look it up. He may think that "sanguine" and "sanguinary" mean the same thing, but the difference is a bloody big one. The reader can only infer (speaking of big differences) what the writer is trying to imply.

11   Faced with these obstacles, the reader is at first a remarkably tenacious bird. He blames himself—he obviously missed something, and he goes back over the mystifying sentence, or over the whole paragraph, piecing it out like an ancient rune, making guesses and moving on. But he won't do this for long. The writer is making him work too hard, and the reader will look for one who is better at his craft.

12   The writer must therefore constantly ask himself: What am I trying to say? Surprisingly often, he doesn't know. Then he must look at what he has written and ask: Have I said it? Is it clear to someone encountering the subject for the first time? If it's not, it is because some fuzz has worked its way into the machinery. The clear writer is a person clear-headed enough to see this stuff for what it is: fuzz.

13   I don't mean that some people are born clear-headed and are therefore natural writers, whereas others are naturally fuzzy and will never write well. Thinking clearly is a conscious act that the writer must force upon himself, just as if he were embarking on any other project that requires logic: adding up a laundry list or doing an algebra problem. Good writing doesn't come naturally, though most people obviously think it does. The professional writer is forever being bearded by strangers who say that they'd like to "try a little writing sometime" when they retire from their real profession. Good writing takes self-discipline and, very often, self-knowledge.

14   Many writers, for instance, can't stand to throw anything away. Their sentences are littered with words that mean essentially the same thing and with phrases which make a point that is implicit in what they have already said. When students give me these littered sentences I beg them to select from the surfeit of words the few that most precisely fit what they want to say. Choose one, I plead, from among the three almost identical adjectives. Get rid of the unnecessary adverbs. Eliminate "in a funny sort of way" and other such qualifiers—they do no useful work.

15   The students look stricken—I am taking all their wonderful words away. I am only taking their superfluous words away, leaving what is organic and strong.

16   "But," one of my worst offenders confessed, "I never can get rid of anything—you should see my room." (I didn't take him up on the offer.) "I have two lamps where I only need one, but I can't decide which one I like better, so I keep them both." He went on to enumerate his duplicated

or unnecessary objects, and over the weeks ahead I went on throwing away his duplicated and unnecessary words. By the end of the term—a term that he found acutely painful—his sentences were clean.

17   "I've had to change my whole approach to writing," he told me. "Now I have to *think* before I start every sentence and I have to *think* about every word." The very idea amazed him. Whether his room also looked better I never found out.

18   Writing is hard work. A clear sentence is no accident. Very few sentences come out right the first time, or the third. Keep thinking and rewriting until you say what you want to say.

Questions on Content

1.   The author cites an example of cluttered language and then says, "The sentence is too simple—there must be something wrong with it" (paragraph 2). What is Zinsser implying at this point?

2.   Zinsser says, "Clear thinking becomes clear writing" (paragraph 7). Find other terms that, in the context of this essay, become synonyms for *clear*.

3.   According to the author, what are two personal qualities of a good writer?

4.   In paragraph 14, Zinsser refers to *qualifiers*. He gives one example. Suggest at least five similar qualifiers that he could have cited.

Questions on Structure and Style

5.   What is the topic sentence of paragraph 2, and how effective is it?

6.   Zinsser discusses the reader and says, "My sympathies are with him." Does Zinsser oversimplify at this point (paragraphs 8–11)? How effective is his discussion of the reader?

7.   What signs are there that the author is addressing students in this essay?

8.   Choose three adjectives to describe the author's tone.

Assignments   1. Locate a copy of a recent political speech, perhaps in
                       a newspaper or a national magazine. Choose a pas-
                       sage of about one hundred words, and "simplify"
                       the prose, shortening the passage by at least 10 per-
                       cent (without distorting its meaning) and making
                       the speaker's meaning clearer.

                   2. In an essay, compose your own definition of sim-
                       plicity. You need not restrict yourself to simplicity
                       in writing, but keep in mind what Zinsser says
                       about simplicity. Be sure to include carefully chosen
                       examples to illustrate your definition.

In Praise of the
Humble Comma

Pico Iyer

Punctuation means rules. However, as Pico Iyer explains with
style and imagination, the rules of punctuation allow us to express much more than we could without them. Moreover, the
rules often express the spirit of an entire culture. Iyer has traveled
widely and now serves as a contributor to *Time* magazine. Although he concentrates on the comma, he reminds us throughout
his essay of the intimate, complex, and often overlooked relationship between punctuation and the human voice.

1   The gods, they say, give breath, and they take it away. But the same could
be said—could it not?—of the humble comma. Add it to the present
clause, and, of a sudden, the mind is, quite literally, given pause to think;
take it out if you wish or forget it and the mind is deprived of a resting
place. Yet still the comma gets no respect. It seems just a slip of a thing, a
pedant's tick, a blip on the edge of our consciousness, a kind of printer's
smudge almost. Small, we claim, is beautiful (especially in the age of
the microchip). Yet what is so often used, and so rarely recalled, as the
comma—unless it be breath itself?

2   Punctuation, one is taught, has a point: to keep up law and order.
Punctuation marks are the road signs placed along the highway of our
communication—to control speeds, provide directions and prevent head-
on collisions. A period has the unblinking finality of a red light; the comma
is a flashing yellow light that asks us only to slow down; and the semicolon
is a stop sign that tells us to ease gradually to a halt, before gradually
starting up again. By establishing the relations between words, punctuation establishes the relations between the people using words. That may be
one reason why schoolteachers exalt it and lovers defy it ("We love each
other and belong to each other let's don't ever hurt each other Nicole let's
don't ever hurt each other," wrote Gary Gilmore to his girlfriend). A
comma, he must have known, "separates inseparables," in the clinching
words of H. W. Fowler, King of English Usage.

3   Punctuation, then, is a civic prop, a pillar that holds society upright. (A
run-on sentence, its phrases piling up without division, is as unsightly as a
sink piled high with dirty dishes.) Small wonder, then, that punctuation
was one of the first proprieties of the Victorian age, the age of the corset,
that the modernists threw off: the sexual revolution might be said to have
begun when Joyce's Molly Bloom spilled out all her private thoughts in 36

pages of unbridled, almost unperioded and officially censored prose; and another rebellion was surely marked when E. E. Cummings first felt free to commit "God" to the lower case.

4   Punctuation thus becomes the signature of cultures. The hot-blooded Spaniard seems to be revealed in the passion and urgency of his doubled exclamation points and question marks ("¡Caramba! ¿Quien sabe?"), while the impassive Chinese traditionally added to his so-called inscrutability by omitting directions from his ideograms. The anarchy and commotion of the '60s were given voice in the exploding exclamation marks, riotous capital letters and Day-Glo italics of Tom Wolfe's spray-paint prose; and in Communist societies, where the State is absolute, the dignity—and divinity—of capital letters is reserved for Ministries, Sub-Committees and Secretariats.

5   Yet punctuation is something more than a culture's birthmark; it scores the music in our minds, gets our thoughts moving to the rhythm of our hearts. Punctuation is the notation in the sheet music of our words, telling us when to rest, or when to raise our voices; it acknowledges that the meaning of our discourse, as of any symphonic composition, lies not in the units but in the pauses, the pacing and the phrasing. Punctuation is the way one bats one's eyes, lowers one's voice or blushes demurely. Punctuation adjusts the tone and color and volume till the feeling comes into perfect focus: not disgust exactly, but distaste; not lust, or like, but love.

6   Punctuation, in short, gives us the human voice, and all the meanings that lie between the words. "You aren't young, are you?" loses its innocence when it loses the question mark. Every child knows the menace of a dropped apostrophe (the parent's "Don't do that" shifting into the more slowly enunciated "Do not do that"), and every believer, the ignominy of having his faith reduced to "faith." Add an exclamation point to "To be or not to be . . ." and the gloomy Dane has all the resolve he needs; add a comma, and the noble sobriety of "God save the Queen" becomes a cry of desperation bordering on double sacrilege.

7   Sometimes, of course, our markings may be simply a matter of aesthetics. Popping in a comma can be like slipping on the necklace that gives an outfit quiet elegance, or like catching the sound of running water that complements, as it completes, the silence of a Japanese landscape. When V. S. Naipaul, in his latest novel, writes, "He was a middle-aged man, with glasses," the first comma can seem a little precious. Yet it gives the description a spin, as well as a subtlety, that it otherwise lacks, and it shows that the glasses are not part of the middle-agedness, but something else.

8   Thus all these tiny scratches give us breadth and heft and depth. A world that has only periods is a world without inflections. It is a world without shade. It has a music without sharps and flats. It is a martial music. It has a

jackboot rhythm. Words cannot bend and curve. A comma, by comparison, catches the gentle drift of the mind in thought, turning in on itself and back on itself, reversing, redoubling and returning along the course of its own sweet river music; while the semicolon brings clauses and thoughts together with all the silent discretion of a hostess arranging guests around her dinner table.

9   Punctuation, then, is a matter of care. Care for words, yes, but also, and more important, for what the words imply. Only a lover notices the small things: the way the afternoon light catches the nape of a neck, or how a strand of hair slips out from behind an ear, or the way a finger curls around a cup. And no one scans a letter so closely as a lover, searching for its small print, straining to hear its nuances, its gasps, its sighs and hesitations, poring over the secret messages that lie in every cadence. The difference between ''Jane (whom I adore)'' and ''Jane, whom I adore,'' and the difference between them both and ''Jane—whom I adore—'' marks all the distance between ecstasy and heartache. ''No iron can pierce the heart with such force as a period put at just the right place,'' in Isaac Babel's lovely words; a comma can let us hear a voice break, or a heart. Punctuation, in fact, is a labor of love. Which brings us back, in a way, to gods.

Questions on Content

1. Look closely at sentence 3 in paragraph 1. What does the sentence say? What is the relationship between what Iyer says in this sentence and how he says it?

2. Explain how the "law and order" metaphor works in paragraph 6.

3. Explain the following quotations:
   A. "Punctuation, then, is a civic prop, a pillar that holds society upright" (paragraph 3).
   B. "Punctuation thus becomes the signature of cultures" (paragraph 4).
   C. ". . . the noble sobriety of 'God Save the Queen' becomes a cry of desperation bordering on double sacrilege" (paragraph 6).

4. How does the comma change the meaning of this sentence: "He was a middle-aged man, with glasses" (paragraph 7)?

5. Discuss the tone of this essay. Is it appropriate for Iyer's audience? (Of course, you'll need to identify the audience.)

6. What is the purpose of all the figurative and hyperbolic language? How does it affect the tone?

7. Comment on the opening and closing sentences.

8. Do you feel that this essay is so carefully wrought that art has taken charge? In other words, is the essay crafted too carefully to really do what it attempts?

9. Why does Iyer use so many short, simple sentences in paragraph 8?

Assignments

1. Read this essay very carefully, and then compile a list of rules for the comma, the semicolon, and the period. Compare your rules with those in a handbook.

2. Write a summary of this essay in which you discuss the main purposes of punctuation as Iyer sees them.

3. Write an essay in response to question 8 above.

An Ethic of Clarity

Donald Hall

Donald Hall is both a noted poet and an author of textbooks on expository writing that are used in many colleges and universities. In "An Ethic of Clarity," Hall explains why "good" writing is not merely efficient; rather, it displays the moral quality of honesty that respected writers and thinkers have always cherished. Hall also explains how writing can make us better people by teaching us to know ourselves better.

1   Ezra Pound, George Orwell, James Thurber, and Ernest Hemingway don't have much in common: a great poet who became a follower of Mussolini, a disillusioned left-wing satirist, a comic essayist and cartoonist, and a great novelist. If anything, they could represent the diversity of modern literature. Yet one thing unites them. They share a common idea of good style, an idea of the virtues of clarity and simplicity. This attitude toward style was not unknown to earlier writers, but never before has it been so pervasive and so exclusive.

2   Style is the manner of a sentence, not its matter. But the distinction between manner and matter is a slippery one, for manner affects matter. When *Time* used to tell us that President Truman slouched into one room, when General Eisenhower strode into another, their manner was trying to prejudice our feelings. The hotel that invites me to enjoy my favorite beverage at the Crown Room is trying not to sound crass: "Have a drink at the bar." One linguist, in discussing this problem, took Caesar's "I came; I saw; I conquered," and revised it as, "I arrived on the scene of the battle; I observed the situation; I won the victory." Here, the matter is the same, but Caesar's tone of arrogant dignity disappears in the pallid pedantry of the longer version. It is impossible to say that the matter is unaffected. But, let us say that this kind of difference, in the two versions of Caesar, is what we mean by style.

3   In the expression "good writing" or "good style," the word "good" has usually meant "beautiful" or "proficient"—like a good Rembrandt or a good kind of soap. In our time it has come to mean honest as opposed to fake. Bad writing happens when the writer lies to himself, to others, or to both. Probably, it is usually necessary to lie to oneself in order to lie to others; advertising men use the products they praise. Bad writing may be proficient; it may persuade us to buy a poor car or vote for an imbecile, but it is bad because it is tricky, false in its enthusiasm, and falsely motivated. It appeals to a part of us that wants to deceive itself. I am encouraged to tell myself that I am enjoying my favorite beverage when, really, I am only getting sloshed.

4   "If a man writes clearly enough anyone can see if he fakes," says Hemingway. Orwell reverses the terms: "The great enemy of clear language is insincerity. . . . When there is a gap between one's real and one's declared aims, one turns as it were instinctively to long words and exhausted idioms, like a cuttlefish squirting out ink." Pound talks about the "gap between one's real and one's declared aims" as the distance between expression and meaning. In "The New Vocabularianism," Thurber speaks of the political use of clichés to hide a "menacing Alice in Wonderland meaninglessness."

5   As Robert Graves says, "The writing of good English is thus a moral matter." And the morality is a morality of truth-telling. Herbert Read declares that "the only thing that is indispensable for the possession of a good style is personal sincerity." We can agree, but we must add that personal sincerity is not always an easy matter, nor is it always available to the will. Real aims, we must understand, are not necessarily conscious ones. The worst liars in the world may consider themselves sincere. Analysis of one's own style, in fact, can be a test of one's own feelings. And certainly, many habits of bad style are bad habits of thinking as well as of feeling.

6   There are examples of the modern attitude toward style in older writers. Jonathan Swift, maybe the best prose writer of the language, sounds like George Orwell when he writes:

> Our English tongue is too little cultivated in this kingdom, yet the faults are nine in ten owing to affectation, not to want of understanding. When a man's thoughts are clear, the properest words will generally offer themselves first, and his own judgment will direct him in what order to place them, so as they may be best understood.

Here Swift appears tautological; clear thoughts only *exist* when they are embodied in clear words. But he goes on: "When men err against this method, it is usually on purpose," purposes, we may add, that we often disguise from ourselves.

7   Aristotle in his *Rhetoric* makes a case for plainness and truth-telling. "The right thing in speaking really is that we should be satisfied not to annoy our hearers, without trying to delight them; we ought in fairness to fight our cause with no help beyond the bare facts." And he anticipates the modern stylist's avoidance of unusual words: "Clearness is secured by using the words . . . that are current and ordinary." Cicero attacks the Sophists because they are "on the lookout for ideas that are neatly put rather than reasonable. . . ."

8   Yet, when we quote Cicero, the master rhetorician, on behalf of honest clarity, we must remember that the ancients did not really think of style as we do. Style until recent times has been a division of rhetoric. To learn

style, one learned the types of figures of speech, and the appropriateness of each to different levels of discourse—high, middle, and low. The study of style was complex, but it was technical rather than moral. For some writers, Latin was high and the vernacular low, but in the Renaissance the vernacular took in all levels. It is only in modern times that style divorces itself from rhetoric—rhetoric belongs to the enemy, to the advertisers and the propagandists—and becomes a matter of ethics and introspection.

9   Ezra Pound, like some French writers before him, makes the writer's function social. "Good writers are those who keep the language efficient. That is to say, keep it accurate, keep it clear." We must ask why this idea of the function of good style is so predominantly a modern phenomenon. Pound elsewhere speaks of the "assault," by which he means the attack upon our ears and eyes of words used dishonestly to persuade us, to convince us to buy or to believe. Never before have men been exposed to so many words—written words, from newspapers and billboards and paperbacks and flashing signs and the sides of buses, and spoken words, from radio and television and loudspeakers. Everyone who wishes to keep his mind clear and his feelings his own must make an effort to brush away these words like cobwebs from the face. The assault of the phoney is a result of technology combined with a morality that excuses any technique which is useful for persuasion. The persuasion is for purposes of making money, as in advertising, or winning power, as in war propaganda and the slogans of politicians. Politicians have always had slogans, but they never before had the means to spread their words so widely. The cold war of rhetoric between communism and capitalism has killed no soldiers, but the air is full of the small corpses of words that were once alive: "democracy," "freedom," "liberation."

10   It is because of this assault, primarily, that writers have become increasingly concerned with the honesty of their style to the exclusion of other qualities. Concentration on honesty is the only way to exclude the sounds of the bad style that assault us all. These writers are concerned finally *to be honest about what they see, feel, and know.* For some of them, like William Carlos Williams, we can only trust the evidence of our eyes and ears, our real knowledge of our immediate environment.

11   Our reading of good writers and our attempt to write like them can help to guard against the dulling onslaught. But we can only do this if we are able to look into ourselves with some honesty. An ethic of clarity demands intelligence and self-knowledge. Really, the ethic is not only a defense against the assault (nothing good is ever merely defensive), but is a development of the same inwardness that is reflected in psychoanalysis. One cannot, after all, examine one's motives and feelings carefully if one takes a naïve view that the appearance of a feeling is the reality of that feeling.

12   Sometimes, the assault is merely pompous. Some people say "wealthy" instead of "rich" in order to seem proper, or "home" instead of "house" in order to seem genteel. George Orwell translates a portion of *Ecclesiastes*

into academic-pompous, for example; Quiller-Couch does something similar with Hamlet's soliloquy. Years ago, James Russell Lowell ridiculed the newspapers that translated "A great crowd came to see . . ." into "A vast concourse was assembled to witness. . . ." None of these examples is so funny as a colonel's statement on television that one of our astronauts "has established visual contact" with a piece of his equipment. He meant that the astronaut had *seen* it.

13   Comic as these pomposities are, they are signs that something has gone wrong somewhere. (My father normally spoke a perfectly good plain English, but, occasionally, when he was unhappy with himself, he would fall off dreadfully; I remember him once admonishing me at dinner, "It is necessary to masticate thoroughly.") The colonel must have been worried about the intellectual respectability of the space program when he resorted to phrases like "visual contact." The lady who speaks of "luncheon" instead of "lunch" is worried about her social status. She gives herself away. Something has gone wrong, and it has gone wrong inside her mind and emotions.

14   The style is the man. Again and again, the modern stylists repeat this idea. By a man's metaphors you shall know him. When a commencement orator advises students to enrich themselves culturally, chances are that he is more interested in money than in poetry. When a university president says that his institution turned out 1,432 B.A.s last year, he tells us that he thinks he is running General Motors. The style is the man. Remy de Gourmont used the analogy that the bird's song is conditioned by the shape of the beak. And Paul Valery said, ". . . what makes the style is not merely the mind applied to a particular action; it is the whole of a living system extended, imprinted and recognizable in expression." These statements are fine, but they sound too deterministic, as if one expresses an unalterable self and can no more change the style of that self than a bird can change the shape of its beak. Man is a kind of bird that can change his beak.

15   A writer of bad prose, to become a writer of good prose, must alter his character. He does not have to become good in terms of conventional morality, but he must become honest in the expression of himself, which means that he must know himself. There must be no gap between expression and meaning, between real and declared aims. For some people, some of the time, this simply means *not* telling deliberate lies. For most people, it means learning when they are lying and when they are not. It means learning the real names of their feelings. It means not saying or thinking, "I didn't *mean* to hurt your feelings," when there really existed a desire to hurt. It means not saying "luncheon" or "home" for the purpose of appearing upper-class or well-educated. It means not using the passive mood to attribute to no one in particular opinions that one is unwilling to call one's own. It means not disguising banal thinking by polysyllabic writing or the lack of feeling by clichés that purport to display feeling.

16   The style is the man, and the man can change himself by changing his style. Prose style is the way you think and the way you understand what you feel. Frequently, we feel for one another a mixture of strong love and strong hate; if we call it love and disguise the hate to ourselves by sentimentalizing over love, we are thinking and feeling badly. Style is ethics and psychology; clarity is a psychological sort of ethic, since it involves not general moral laws, but truth to the individual self. The scrutiny of style is a moral and psychological study. By trying to scrutinize our own style, perhaps with the help of people like Orwell and Pound, Hemingway and Thurber, we try to understand ourselves. Editing our own writing, or going over in memory our own spoken words, or even inwardly examining our thought, we can ask *why* we resorted to the passive in this case or to clichés in that. When the smoke of bad prose fills the air, something is always on fire somewhere. If the style is really the man, the style becomes an instrument for discovering and changing the man. Language is expression of self, but language is also the instrument by which to know that self.

Questions on Content

1. According to Hall, what is "bad" writing, and why is it bad?

2. Why may people sometimes have difficulty judging how honest their writing is?

3. Why is the "assault of the phoney" a modern phenomenon?

4. Hall says that "nothing good is ever merely defensive" (paragraph 11). What does he mean by this? How can you apply this statement to honesty in your own writing?

5. In paragraph 16, Hall links language and knowledge. Explain this link.

Questions on Structure and Style

6. Parallel construction makes following ideas and information easier. Locate a clear example of parallel construction in the essay.

7. Why does Hall quote historical figures going back into antiquity? Why not quote only modern figures? Why is the use of so many quotations from historical figures *not* simply a stylistic maneuver on Hall's part?

8. The author cites many examples of what he considers common, everyday violations of sincerity that are related to the use of language. How effective are his examples? Can you think of others that are equally common, perhaps so common that we seldom recognize them?

9. What is Hall's purpose in writing this essay? Is he merely discussing the use of language, or do you believe he is recommending something? For students? Voters? Shoppers? Everyone?

Assignments

1. Write three paragraphs. In the first, demonstrate the ethic of clarity in a description of the place where you live. In the second paragraph, describe the same place as you would if you were trying to sell it to strangers. In the third, explain why you made changes in the first paragraph when writing the second.

2. Hall states, "Style is the manner of a sentence, not its matter" (paragraph 2). Write an essay in which you discuss what he means by this. Examine prose samples by writers with distinct styles, perhaps two writers you admire. Remember to focus your discussion on the *manner* rather than the *matter;* that is, focus on how the writers say something rather than on what they say.

Additional Assignments and Research Topics

1. Some faculty members at your college no doubt have written for publication. There may also be other writers in your community. Find one of these writers, and in an interview, ask the following questions (and others).

    A. Why do you write? For money? Professional advancement? Personal satisfaction?
    B. What aspect of writing was most difficult to master? What aspect is still most difficult?
    C. What aspects of writing seemed difficult at first but now come naturally?
    D. Who gave you the greatest help in learning to write well?
    E. Does reading other people's work play a role in your own writing?
    F. What writing habits do you follow? (For example, at what time of day do you most often write; do you write first drafts in longhand or on a typewriter?)
    G. What role does revision play in your writing process?
    H. Who is your most reliable critic?
    I. Is there a type of writing you have never tried but would like to try?
    J. What advice can you give to a student of writing?

    Report your findings either in an essay or in an oral report to your class.

2. Interview three classmates, asking them to describe their writing processes. Then compose an essay comparing the processes, referring to the authors in this chapter.

3. Peter Elbow ("Freewriting") and Marvin H. Swift ("Clear Writing Means Clear Thinking Means . . .") emphasize different steps in the writing process. Their advice might seem contradictory. Swift urges careful revision, whereas Elbow warns against premature editing. Compose a hypothetical ten-minute dialogue between these two writers, in which they argue the merits of their approaches.

4. Write an essay analyzing your own writing habits. Find papers you wrote in high school or in previous college courses, and use them as research material. How do the papers exemplify the writing process you relied on in the past? How would you proceed differently now?

Names
and Naming

P eople with a gloomy view of the future predict that someday our names will be replaced by numbers. Even today, social security numbers often seem as important as names. Why is there such concern about threats to our names, which, after all, can be untidy and cumbersome, difficult to spell, and awkward to pronounce? Numbers, by contrast, are neat, efficient, and in desirably infinite supply—and they eliminate the problem of asking or answering the question, "Which Michael?" or "Which Jennifer?"

Our appalled response is easy to understand, however. To be identified by a number instead of by a name implies a dehumanized future—a future in which human life is not valued as we believe it deserves to be. We identify ourselves with names and not numbers *because* we're human. We give names to other people as well as to places and things, and this impulse to name everything we live with also is uniquely human. The names we have and give are the subject of this chapter, which examines what names reveal about our understanding of the world and our reactions to it.

Surnames are a storehouse of history, and the first selection, J. N. Hook's "From a World without Surnames," looks at the origins of surnames and their value in tracing historical change. In "Women and Names," Casey Miller and Kate Swift examine the psychological implications of names and naming, paying particular attention to first names. Both selections show the significance of the many ways in which we name people.

The names we give to places and things are equally important and revealing. W. F. Bolton's "Putting American English on the Map" discusses toponymics—the study of place names—and the apparently clean slate our country presented to its new inhabitants in the eighteenth and nineteenth centuries. John Leo looks at sports teams and asks, "What's in a Nickname?" His answer shows how much we can infer from nicknames and how amusing the subject can be. The chapter concludes with Paul Dickson's "Smile, Dr. Fuchs, Your Fuchsia Is Bright," an essay on many of the proper names that have become household words (to the delight or chagrin of those so honored).

A Chinese proverb declares, "The beginning of wisdom is to call things by their right names." Names identify, reveal, and classify our experience of the world, and the wise person learns to respect their significance and to use them with care. When identity seems threatened by anonymity, this is the declaration we hear: "I'm not a number. I have a name."

From a World without Surnames

J. N. Hook

Imagine trying to function without a surname in our complex modern society. For many centuries in Europe, however, people had no surnames; these developed only as changes in society made them necessary. This is one of many issues examined in this richly detailed selection by J. N. Hook, co-author of twenty-one textbooks about English. Hook shows that surnames reveal history, geography, and the unique character of nationalities.

1 When the world's population was small and even a city might hold only a few thousand people, and when most folks never got more than ten or fifteen miles from their birthplace (usually walking), and when messages were sent by personal messenger rather than by impersonal post, there was hardly a necessity for more than one name. Even kings got by with a single name. When someone referred to King David, there was no need to ask David who?

2 No one knows who first felt the need to apply any name at all to himself or any of his fellows. According to Pliny, some ancient tribes were *anonymi* (nameless) and it is barely possible that a few *anonymi* may still exist in remote corners of the world. But for the most part personal names of some sort exist wherever there are human beings. As British onomatist C. L. Ewen has said,

> The most general custom among the savage tribes was to give a child the name of a deceased ancestor, but any descriptive word which might indicate sex, order of birth, race, caste, office, physical feature, god, historical fact, or a more fanciful concept, served the purpose of a distinguishing label.

3 "A distinguishing label"—that of course is what a name is. It differentiates one person from another, allowing a mother to single out one child's attention, helping an officer to address a command to an individual, assisting any of us to carry out our daily tasks that depend on distinguishing one person from another.

4 Customs in naming have varied considerably, and some seem strange to us. Ewen mentioned an African tribe in which young boys had names that

71

were changed to something else at puberty, and another tribe in which a father took a new name when his first child was born, his virility having thus been confirmed. Members of other tribes change their names after serious illness or when they get old. Some American Indians had different names for different seasons. People of Dahomey, in East Africa, once had several names, including some that named guardian spirits and others that were kept secret except from intimates. Some names have been very long: *The Encyclopedia of Religion and Ethics* mentions a Babylonian name that can be translated "O Ashur, the lord of heaven and earth, give him life." To this day, the Balinese have no surnames, and as youngsters many often change their personal names. They do have caste and birth-order designations that stay with them all their lives.

5   The ancient Greeks generally used only single names (Sophocles and Plato, for example), but occasionally employed additional phrases for further identification. Thus Alexander, whom we describe as "the Great," was Alexandros o Philippon, Alexander the son of Phillip.

6   During Rome's centuries of greatness, Romans—especially those of the upper classes—were likely to have three names, like Gaius Julius Caesar. The *praenomen* (Gaius) corresponded to our given names. The *nomen* or *nomen gentilium* (Julius) identified the clan or tribe (*gens*), which usually consisted of a number of families sharing this name. The *cognomen* (Caesar) designated the particular family within the *gens*. There might even be a fourth name, called an *agnomen*, which could be a mark of distinction (like "Africanus" bestowed on Scipio after military victories in Africa), or just an additional mark of identification (for instance, Emperor Octavian, born Gaius Octavius, added the name Julius Caesar after Gaius, but retained Octavianus as an *agnomen*). During the period of Rome's decline, some persons adopted or were given even more names—as many as thirty-six.

7   In Roman times the *cognomens* were most like our surnames. They were hereditary, and they usually fell into the same classifications as English and Continental names. Some indicated the place from which the family had come or with which it was associated: Gnaeus Marcius Coriolanus, about whom Shakespeare wrote a play, is said to have won the battle of Corioli in 493 B.C. A few names are those of ancestors: Agrippa, the family name of some of the descendants of Herod the Great. Some plebeians bore *cognomens* that named their occupations, as Metellus (servant), Missor (archer). The Romans especially liked descriptive *cognomens*, as Sapiens (the wise), Crassus (the fat), or Marcellus (the little hammer).

8   After the fall of Rome, multiple names largely disappeared for a few centuries throughout Europe, although compound names were fairly frequent in some places. Thus Irish Faolchadh was a compound of *wolf* and *warrior*, and the German Gerhard was compounded of *spear* and *firm*.

9   In the tenth century Venetian noblemen began to adopt hereditary family names. This custom was to be followed later by the Irish, the French, the English, and then the Germans and other Europeans.

10   Suppose that you were living in England in the Middle Ages. Suppose further that your name was John. Not John Something—just John. The Somethings did not yet exist in England. King or commoner, you were just John.

11   Your male ancestors had also been John, or Thomas, Robert, Harold, Richard, William, or more anciently Eadgar or Eadwine or Aelfred, and their wives may have been Alice, Joan, Berthe, Blanche, Beatrice, Margaret, Marie, Inga, or Grette. Most names of your day were Norman French, since the descendants of William the Conqueror and his followers ruled the land. Huntingdon, for instance, had only 1 percent recognizably Anglo-Saxon names in A.D. 1295.

12   The number of different names was not large. The same Huntingdon list shows that 18 percent of all males in that county were called William, 16 percent John, 10 percent Richard, and 7 percent Robert, and that only 28 other names made up the remainder. So over half of these men shared only 4 names. In Yorkshire in the fourteenth century, in a list of 19,600 mixed male and female names, C. L. Ewen found that John accounted for 17 percent of the total, followed by William, Thomas, and Robert, with Alice (5 percent) and Joan (4 percent in various spellings) the most popular names for women. There were some biblical names other than John— almost 2 percent Adam, for example—but the popularity of Peter, Paul, Abraham, David, and others was still in the future.

13   England, like other countries in the Middle Ages, was mainly a rural and male-dominated society. There were no large cities. Some groups of people lived within the walls of a castle or nearby; still others clustered in villages from which workers trudged short distances each day to tend the crops or the livestock, or where they remained to do their smithing, wagon making, tailoring, or other tasks. Women often worked beside the men in the fields, and in a family wealthy enough to have its own cow or a few pigs or sheep, the women were likely to be responsible for the animals' care. Women's liberation was centuries away and largely undreamed of—although older England had had some strong queens, and Shakespeare's plays would later reflect some influence of women on medieval national affairs. In general, women were subservient, and their subservience was to be shown in the naming processes getting under way.

14   Almost all the occupational names, for example, refer to work done mainly or entirely by men in the Middle Ages, and countless fathers but few mothers were memorialized in names that would become family names. Had women's prestige been higher we would today have many persons with names like Milkmaid, Buxom, and Margaretson.

15   If the Middle Ages had been urbanized, no doubt the use of second names would have accelerated. If a city has three thousand Williams, ways must be found to indicate which William one talks about. A typical medieval village, though, might have had only five or ten Williams, a similar number of Johns, and maybe two or three Roberts or Thomases.

16   Even so, distinctions often needed to be made. If two villagers were talking about you (John, you remember, is who you are), misunderstandings would arise if each had a different John in mind. So qualifications were added, as in imaginary bits of conversation like these:

> "A horse stepped on John's foot."
> "John from the hill?"
> "No. John of the dale."
>
> "John the son of William?"
> "No. John the son of Robert."
>
> "John the smith?"
> "No. John the tailor."
>
> "John the long?"
> "No. John the bald."

17   In the rush of conversation the little, unimportant words could drop out or be slurred over so that John from the hill became John hill, and the other persons could be John dale, John William's son, John Robert's son, John smith, John tailor, John long, and John bald (or ballard, which means *the bald one*). The capital letters that we now associate with surnames are only scribal conventions introduced later on.

18   Distinctions like those illustrated in the conversations were a step toward surnames. But the son of John the smith might be Robert the wainwright (wagon maker). That is, he did not inherit the designation *smith* from his father. There were no true English surnames—family names—until Robert the son of John smith became known as Robert smith (or Smith) even though his occupation was a wainwright, a fletcher (arrow maker), a tanner or barker (leather worker), or anything else. Only when the second name was passed down from one generation to the next did it become a surname.

19   That step did not occur suddenly or uniformly, although throughout most of Europe it was a medieval development. Ewen has described the details of the development in England, basing his scholarly analysis on thousands of entries in tax rolls, court records, and other surviving documents. He has pointed out that before the fourteenth century most of the differentiating adjuncts were prefaced by *filius* (son of), as in Adam fil' Gilberti (Adam, son of Gilbert), by *le* (the), as in Beaudrey le Teuton, by *de* (of, from), as in Rogerius de Molis (Roger from the mills), or by *atta* (at the), as in John atte Water (John at the water), which later might be John

Atwater. These particles often dropped out. Thus a fourteenth-century scribe began writing his name as David Tresruf, but other evidence shows that Tresruf was simply a place name and that David de Tresruf was the way the scribe earlier wrote his name.

20   Almost all English and Continental surnames fall into the four categories I have illustrated:

Place Names	John Hill, John Atwater
Patronyms (or others based on personal names)	John Robertson, John Williams, John Alexander
Occupational Names	John Smith, John Fletcher
Descriptive Names	John Long, John Armstrong

21   With a few exceptions the million-plus surnames that Americans bear are of these four sorts. If we were mainly an Oriental or an African nation, the patterns would be different. But we are primarily European in our origins, and in Europe it seemed natural to identify each person during the surname-giving period according to location, parentage, occupation, appearance or other characteristics.

22   It never used to occur to me that my name and almost everyone else's name has a meaning, now often unknown even to its possessors. My own name, I found, is a place name. A *hook* is a sharp bend in a stream or a peninsula or some odd little corner of land. My paternal ancestors, who came from Somerset in southern England, lived on such a hook, probably one of the many irregularly shaped bits of land in Somerset. The numerous Hookers, like General Joseph Hooker in the Civil War, lived in similar places in the name-giving period. Hocking(s), Hoke(r), Horn(e), and Horman(n) are other English or German names that share the meaning of Hook, so they are my cousins, by semantics though not by blood. So are the Dutch Hoekstra, van Hoek, and Haack, who lived in their own odd little corners in the Netherlands.

23   By coincidence, my mother's father (part Finnish, mostly German) bore a name that also referred to a bend or angle. He was Engel, and his ancestors had lived in Angeln, in Schleswig in northern Germany. The Angles who came in the fifth century to the British Isles with the Saxons, Jutes, and Frisians to help the Celts against the savage Picts (but eventually drove their hosts to the western and northern reaches of the islands) took their name from the same German area, and England—Angle-land historically—is named for them. Angeln got its name because it was shaped somewhat like a fishhook; the word is obviously related to *angle* and the sport of *angling*.

24   The fourfold identification of people by place, ancestry, occupation, or description has worked well, and only science fiction writers today ever

suggest that our names may or should be replaced by numbers or number-letter combinations. Even an ordinary name like William Miller, George Rivers, or Anne Armstrong can acquire an individuality and a rememberable quality hard to imagine for 27-496-3821 or Li94T8633. I'd probably not enjoy a love affair with American names that looked like mere license plate identifications.

25   The proportion in each category of names may vary from one European language to another. Thus 70 percent or more of Irish, Welsh, and Scandinavian surnames are patronyms. Spanish families have also preferred patronyms, but place names are not far behind. In France patronyms lead once more, but names of occupations are in second place. In Germany, however, patronyms of the simple English sort are relatively few, although hereditary combinative descriptions like the previously mentioned Gerhard are common, occupational names are frequent, and place names not uncommon. In most countries personal descriptive surnames lag behind the others.

26   Elsdon Smith analyzed seven thousand of our most common American surnames and found these proportions:

	Percentage
Place names	43.13
Patronyms	32.23
Occupational names	15.16
Nicknames (descriptives)	9.48

27   In an analysis that I made of several hundred American surnames of English origin, I obtained the following percentages:

	Percentage
Place names	35.49
Patronyms	32.37
Occupational names	19.66
Personal descriptors	12.47

The fact that large numbers of American surnames are derived from England is reflected in the similarities between Smith's percentages and mine.

28   Often, superficially different American surnames turn out to be essentially the same name in meaning when translated from the foreign language into English. . . . Place names, often unique or nearly so, are not likely to be internationally duplicated except when they refer to geographically common features like bodies of water or land masses. We may illustrate the possibilities with the English surname Hill, whose German

equivalent may be Buhl, Buehler, Knor(r), or Piehl, paralleled by Dutch Hoger and Hoogland (literally *high land*), French Depew and Dumont, Italian Costa and Colletti, Finnish Maki (one of Finland's most common names), Hungarian Hegi, Scandinavian Berg, Bergen, Bagge, and Haugen, and Slavic Kopec, Kopecky, and Pagorak, all of which mean *hill* or *small mountain*.

29   Differences in size or in skin or hair coloration are international, as many of our personal descriptive surnames confirm. English Brown and Black, for instance, may refer to either dark skin or brown or black hair. (*Black*, however, sometimes comes from the Old English *blac*, related to our *bleach* and meaning *white* or *light*, so Mr. Black's ancestors may have been either fair or dark.) Blake is a variant of Black. The French know the dark person as Le Brun or Moreau, the Germans as Braun, Brun, Mohr, or Schwartz, the Italians as Bruno, the Russians as Chernoff. Pincus refers to a dark-skinned Jew, Mavros to a dark Greek. Dark Irishmen may be named, among other possibilities, Carey, Duff, Dunn(e), Dolan, Dow, or Kearns. Hungarian Fekete has a dark skin. Czechoslovakian Cerny or Czerny (black) reveals his linguistic similarity to Polish Czarnik, Czarniak, or Czarnecki and Ukrainian Corney. Spanish Negron is a very dark person.

30   Many names spelled identically are common to two or more languages, and a considerable number of such names have more than a single meaning. So Gray, although usually an English name meaning *gray haired*, in a few instances is French for a person from Gray (the estate of Gradus) in France. Gray must therefore be classified both as a personal descriptor and a place name. Hoff is usually German for a farm or an enclosed place, but less often is English for Hoff (pagan temple), a place in Westmoreland. Many Scandinavian names are identical in Denmark, Norway, and Sweden, although spelling variants such as *-sen* and *-son* suggest the likelihood of one country rather than another. In general a person must know at least a little about his or her ancestry before determining with assurance the nationality and most likely meaning of his or her name.

31   A small percentage of names, few of them common in the United States, is derived from sources other than the basic four. For example, a few Jewish names are based on acronyms or initials. Thus Baran or Baron sometimes refers to *Ben Rabbi Nachman*, and Brock to *Ben Rabbi Kalman*. Zak, abbreviating *zera kedoshim* (the seed of martyrs), is often respelled Sack, Sacks, or Sachs, although these may also be place names for people from Saxony. Katz is sometimes based on *kohen tzedek* (priest of righteousness), and Segal (in several spellings) can be *segan leviyyah* (member of the tribe of Levi).

32   Other Jewish names are somewhat arbitrary German or Yiddish pairings, usually with pleasant connotations, like Lowenthal (lions' valley), Gottlieb (God's love), or Finkelstein (little finch stone). Some modern Swedes have replaced their conventional patronyms (Hanson, Jorgenson, etc.) with nature words or pairings of nature words, like Lind

(linden), Lindstrom (linden stream), Asplund (aspen grove), or Ekberg (oak mountain).

33   Numerous Norwegian surnames are a special variety of place names called farm names. Many Norwegian farms have held the same name for hundreds of years, and people from a given farm have come to be known by its name. So Bjornstad, for instance, means *Bjorn's farm*, and Odega(a)rd means *dweller on uncultivated land*.

34   Japanese names are comparable to some of the Jewish and Swedish names mentioned a moment ago, in that they frequently combine two words, one or both of which may refer to nature. So Fujikawa combines two elements meaning *wisteria* and *river*, Hayakawa is *early, river*, Tanaka is *ricefield, middle*, Inoue is *well* (noun), *upper*, and Kawasaki is *river, headland*.

35   Chinese surnames are very few—perhaps nine or ten hundred in all— and endlessly repeated. A few dozen of them are especially widely used, like the familiar Wong, which may mean either *field* or *large body of water*, Chin (the name of the first great dynasty, of more than two thousand years ago), Wang (*yellow* or *prince*), Le (*pear tree*), and Yee (*I*).

36   The names given foundlings could readily provide material for a full chapter. Bastard as an appellation was once freely applied to foundlings or any illegitimate children even among royalty and the nobility, but today the name is opprobrious and there are few if any Bastards listed in American directories. Italian Esposito is the same as Spanish Exposita, for which the Italian spelling is generally substituted. Other Italian names suggest the blessedness or holiness of the foundling: De Benedictis, De Angelis, De Santis, and della Croce (one who lives near the cross).

37   The English Foundling Hospital authorities once conferred noble or famous names on foundlings, who thus might be named Bedford, Marlborough, Pembroke, or the like, or sometimes Geoffrey Chaucer, John Milton, Francis Bacon, Oliver Cromwell, or even Peter Paul Rubens. Some names were taken from fiction: Tom Jones, Clarissa Harlowe, Sophia Western. Other foundlings were given the names of places where they were found: e.g., Lawrence because the infant was found in St. Lawrence. A little girl in a waiting room of the Southern Railway was named Frances Southern.

38   Not more than one American surname in twenty, however, can be classified with assurance in any category other than the big four: places, patronyms, occupations, and descriptors.

Questions on Content

1. According to Hook, what is the single most important function of a person's name?

2. For many centuries in Europe, multiple names were unusual. Most people went by single names—*John* and *Eadgar* and *Alice* and *Inga*. Why did surnames finally become necessary?

3. Hook points out that the subservient position of women in the Middle Ages was reflected in the naming process. Explain how this is true.

4. Nearly all English and continental surnames fall into one of four categories. What are they?

5. Explain the origin of the name *England*.

6. What do Japanese names have in common with Jewish and Swedish names?

7. Hook discusses the origin of his own surname. What does this add to his presentation?

Questions on Structure and Style

8. Why does Hook begin by discussing naming customs in ancient Greece and Rome and in certain African tribes?

9. Why do you think Hook wrote his book *Family Names* (from which this selection is taken)? What audience did he have in mind? Was the book designed as a reference tool or as something else?

10. The selection is filled with examples. Are they confusing or interesting? Could Hook have written this selection effectively with fewer examples?

Assignments

1. In his book *Listening to America*, Stuart Berg Flexner lists the eighteen most common surnames in the United States:

Smith	Taylor
Johnson	Thomas
Williamson	Moore
Brown	White
Jones	Martin
Miller	Thompson
Davis	Jackson
Wilson	Harris
Anderson	Lewis

All of these are English names, but not all the people bearing them are English. For example, *Schmidt, Smeds, Goldsmith,* and *Smidnovics* may have become *Smith*. Nevertheless, they are all English names; in fact, the forty most common names in America are English. This string is finally broken by the forty-first most common name, *Cohen*. This list is for the country as a whole, and it tells us a great deal about how the United States was settled. In many areas, however, other names are more common, and these names provide a history of how a particular region was settled. Study the surnames in your region, and write an essay showing how they reflect the history of that region.

2. Make a family tree for your family, tracing its history back several generations. What do the surnames tell you about your family? Write an essay discussing these names. Identify the nationalities they reflect, and tell whether the names are derived from place names, patronyms, occupations, or descriptions. (You probably won't be able to do this with every name, but gather as much information as possible. Interviewing relatives or people with the same surnames may help in difficult cases.)

Women and Names

Casey Miller and Kate Swift

▬▬▬▬▬▬

Our names are not mere designations, like street addresses. In many ways, they determine how people treat us (and how we see ourselves). In this excerpt from their book *Words and Women*, Casey Miller and Kate Swift look closely at the psychology of names, examining how given names often signal parental expectations that children act on. They look, too, at the "first-and-last-name mix," at the effect on women of the expectation that they will give up their last names when they marry, and at how society's attitudes toward women are reflected in and result from their names. Miller and Swift—freelance writers, editors, and photographers—assert that in our society women's names are less important than men's, a status that has far-reaching consequences.

▬▬▬▬▬▬

1 The photograph of the three bright, good-looking young people in the Army recruitment ad catches the eye. All three have a certain flair, and one knows just by looking at the picture that they are enjoying life and glad they joined up. They are typical Americans, symbols of the kind of people the modern Army is looking for. The one closest to the camera is a white male. His name, as can be seen from the neat identification tag pinned to the right pocket of his regulation blouse, is Spurgeon. Behind him and slightly to the left is a young black man. He is wearing a decoration of some kind, and his name is Sort—. Perhaps it is Sorter or Sortman—only the first four letters show. A young woman, who is also white, stands behind Spurgeon on the other side. She is smiling and her eyes shine; she looks capable. She is probably wearing a name tag too, but because Spurgeon is standing between her and the camera, her name is hidden. She is completely anonymous.

2 The picture is not a candid shot; it was carefully posed. The three models were chosen from thousands of possible recruits. They are the same height; they all have dark hair and are smiling into the camera. They look like students, and the copy says the Army will pay 75 percent of their tuition if they work for a college degree. It is no accident that two are white, one black, or that two are male, one female. Nor is it an accident that Spurgeon stands in front of the others at the apex of a triangle, or that, since someone had to be anonymous, the woman was chosen.

3 In our society women's names are less important than men's. The reasons why are not hard to identify, but the consequences for both men and women are more far-reaching than members of either sex, with a few notable exceptions, have been prepared to admit or even, until recently, to

examine. Like other words, names are symbols; unlike other words, what they symbolize is unique. A thousand John Does and Jane Roes may live and die, but no bearer of those names has the same inheritance, the same history, or the same fears and expectations as any other. It therefore seems legitimate to ask what effect our naming customs have on girls and boys and on the women and men they grow into. Are the symbol-words that become our names more powerful than other words?

4   Few people can remember learning to talk. The mystery of language is rarely revealed in a single moment of electrifying insight like Helen Keller's, when suddenly, at the age of seven, the deaf and blind child realized for the first time the connection between the finger signals for w-a-t-e-r her teacher was tapping into her palm and "the wonderful cool something" that flowed from the pump spout onto her other hand.

5   From what scholars report about the way children normally acquire speech, it seems probable that "learning to talk" is actually the measured release, in conjunction with experience, of an innate capacity for language that is common to all human beings. We are no more likely to remember the process than we are to remember growing taller. What one may remember is a particular moment—seeing the yardstick exactly even with the latest pencil line marking one's height on the door jamb or learning a word for some particular something one had been aware of but could not name: tapioca, perhaps, or charisma, or a cotter pin. Anyone who has ever said, "So *that's* what those things are called," knows the experience.

6   When children are first learning to talk they go through a series of similar experiences. The very act of learning what a person or thing is called brings the object into the child's ken in a new way. It has been made specific. Later, the specific will also become general, as when the child calls any small, furry animal a "kitty." Words are symbols; their meanings can be extended.

7   Amanda, who is twenty months old, has spurts of learning names. "Mum," she says to her mother while pointing to the box. "Mum," she says again, pointing to the doorknob. "What is it?" she is asking without using words. "Tell me its name." When she calls her mother by a name, she knows her mother will respond to it. She knows that she, Amanda, has a name. It is important to her, for she has already become aware of herself as a thing different from everything else. As a psychologist might put it, her ego is emerging. Hearing her name, being called by it, is part of the process.

8   Amanda makes certain sounds, naming food or her bottle, that tell her parents she is hungry or thirsty. Before long she will speak of herself in the third person: "'Manda want apple." "'Manda come too." She may repeat her name over and over, perhaps mixing it with nonsense syllables. It is like a charm. It may be the first word she learns to spell. She will delight in seeing the letters of her name, this extension of herself, on her toothbrush

or drinking mug. They belong to her, not to her brother or to her mother or father.

9   When children begin to play with other children and when they finally go to school, their names take on a public dimension. The child with a "funny" name is usually in for trouble, but most kids are proud of their names and want to write them on their books and pads and homework. There was a time when older children carved their names or initials on trees. Now that there are so many people and so few trees, the spray can has taken over from the jackknife, but the impulse to put one's identifying mark where all the world can see it is as strong as ever. The popularity of commercially produced name-on objects of every kind, from tee-shirts to miniature license plates, also attests to the importance youngsters (and a lot of grown-ups too) place on claiming and proclaiming their names.

10   Given names are much older than surnames, of course, probably as old as language itself. One can imagine that as soon as our ancient forebears started using sounds to represent actions or objects, they also began to distinguish each other in the same way. One might even speculate that the people who most often assigned sounds to others were those who produced and cared for the group's new members. Commenting on the assumption of philologists that the exchange of meaningful vocal sounds began among males as they worked and hunted together—hence the so-called "yo-heave-ho" and "bow-wow" theories of language origin—Ethel Strainchamps, a psycholinguist, notes that most philologists have in the past been men. Considering the importance to human survival of communication between mother and child when open fires, venomous reptiles, and other hazards were everywhere, "it might have occurred to a woman that a 'no-no' theory was more likely," Strainchamps says. Perhaps her suggestion should be taken a step further: who knows that it was not the creative effort of women, striving to communicate with each new baby, calling it by a separate and distinguishing sound, that freed the primordial human mind from the prison of animal grunts and led in time to the development of language?

11   Inevitably, some people dislike the names they have been given, and many children go through a phase of wanting to be called something else. For no apparent reason Anne announces that her name is really Koko and she will not answer to any other. For months nothing will change her resolve. She is Koko—and then one day she is Anne again. But if Cecil decides he wants to be called Jim, or Fanny elects to be known as Jill, the reasons may be less obscure: names do seem to give off vibrations of a sort, and other people's response to your name becomes a part of their response to you. Some psychologists think that given names are signals of parental expectations; children get the message and act on it either positively or negatively. One study claims to show, for example, that names can be "active" or "passive." If you call your son Mac or Bart he will become a

more active person than if you call him Winthrop or Egbert. Your daughter is more likely to be outgoing and confident, according to this theory, if you call her Jody rather than Letitia. It follows, though, that if Jody prefers to be called Letitia, she is letting it be known that she sees herself in a more passive and dependent way than you anticipated.

12   Last names, too, can be positive or negative. Some carry a mystique of greatness or honor: Randolph, Diaz, Morgenthau, Saltonstall. Others are cumbersome, or they invite cruel or tasteless jokes. Many people decide, for one reason or another, to change their last names, but a great many more take pride today in being identified as a Klein or a Mackenzie, a Giordano or a Westervelt. The first-and-last-name mix which a person grows up with—that combination of particular and general, of personal and traditional—is not lightly exchanged for another.

13   Whether a name is self-chosen or bestowed at birth, making it one's own is an act of self-definition. When a former Cabinet member who had been involved in the Watergate scandal asked the Senate investigating committee to give back his good name, he was speaking metaphorically, for no one had taken his name away. What he had lost, justly or unjustly, was his public image as a person of integrity and a servant of the people. One's name also represents one's sense of power and self-direction. "I'm so tired I don't know my own name" is a statement of confusion and fatigue. *Your* name, the beginning of your answer to "Who am I?" is the outermost of the many layers of identity reaching inward to the real you. It is one of the significant differences between you and, let's say, a rose, which is named but does not know it. Yet it is one of the things a little girl grows up knowing she will be expected to lose if she marries.

14   The loss of women's last names may seem compensated for by a custom in first-naming that allows girls to be called by a version of their fathers' names, so that—after a fashion, at least—continuity is restored. In this post-Freudian age it would be bad form to give a boy a version of his mother's first name. Nevertheless, if a couple named Henrietta and Frank should decide to call their son Henry, chances are an earlier Henry, after whom Henrietta was named, provides the necessary male for him to identify with. In any case, the name has come back into its own; it stands foursquare and solid, which is seldom true of the derivative names given to girls. The strength of John is preserved in Joan and Jean, but these are exceptions. Names like Georgette and Georgina, Josephine, Paulette and Pauline, beautiful as they may sound, are diminutives. They are copies, not originals, and like so many other words applied to women, they can be diminishing.

15   A man in most Western societies can not only keep his name for his lifetime but he can pass it on intact to his son, who in turn can pass it on to *his* son. The use of a surname as a given name is also usually reserved for

males, presumably on the grounds that such names do not have a sufficiently "feminine" sound for the "weaker sex." When tradition permits the
giving of a family surname to daughters, as in the American South, a
woman can at least retain her identification with that branch of her family.
Once a surname has gained popularity as a girl's name, however, it is
likely to face extinction as a boy's name. Shirley, for example, an old
Yorkshire family name meaning "shire meadow," was once given as a first
name only to boys. Not until Charlotte Brontë wrote *Shirley*—a novel published in 1849, whose central character, Shirley Keeldar, was modeled on
Charlotte's sister Emily—was it used for a girl. Since then, Shirley has
become popular as a girl's name but has dropped out of use as a boy's.
Names like Leslie, Beverly, Evelyn, and Sidney may be traveling the same
route. Once they have become popular as women's names, their histories
as surnames are forgotten, and before long they may be given to girls
exclusively.

16   In English, names like Charity, Constance, Patience, Faith, Hope, Pru-
dence, and Honor no longer have popular equivalents for males, as they
often do in other languages. The qualities described are not limited to
females, of course, and yet to name a son Honor or Charity, even if doing
so breaks no objective rule, would somehow run counter to social expectations. This may be true in part because such names are subjective, expressing more intimately than would seem appropriate for a boy the parents'
expectations for their offspring. Or the principle that applied in the case of
Shirley may apply here, for once a name or a word becomes associated
with women, it is rarely again considered suitable for men.

17   One of the most useful functions of a given name is to serve as a quick
identifier of sex. Nearly everyone, whether they admit it or not, is interested in knowing what sex an unknown person is. You get a postcard from
a friend saying he will be stopping by to see you next week with someone
named Lee, and chances are the first question that pops into your mind is
not whether Lee is young or old, black or white, clever or dull, but whether
Lee will turn out to be female or male. Still, natural curiosity does not
entirely explain the annoyance or embarrassment some people seem to feel
when women have names that are not specifically female by tradition or
why names that become associated with women are thenceforth out of
bounds for men.

18   If quick sex identification were the only consideration, the long male
tradition of using initials in place of first names would not have come
about. People with names like J. P. Morgan, P. T. Barnum, or L. L. Bean
were always male—or were they? No one could stop women from sneak-
ing under the flap of *that* tent, and in fact so many did that the practice had
to be disallowed. In the early years of this century Columbia University,
which in its academic bulletins identified male faculty members only

by their surnames and initials, wrote out the names of women faculty members in full—lest anyone unintentionally enroll in a course taught by a woman.

19   Perhaps it is because of the transience of women's last names that their first names seem often to be considered the logical, appropriate, or even polite counterpart of men's surnames, and the news media frequently reflect this feeling. When Secretary of State Henry Kissinger and Nancy Maginnis were married, many news stories called them "Kissinger and Nancy" after the first paragraph. The usage is so accepted, and its belittling implications so subliminal, that it often persists in defiance of changes taking place all about it. In a magazine story on the atypical career choices of six graduate students, the subhead read "Stereotypes fade as men and women students . . . prepare to enter fields previously dominated almost exclusively by the opposite sex." Three women going into dentistry, business administration, and law were introduced by their full names, as were three men whose fields of study were nursing, library science, and primary education. The men were then referred to as Groves, White, and Fondow, while the women became Fran, Carol, and Pam.

20   Children, servants, and other presumed inferiors are apt to be first-named by adults and employers and by anyone else who is older, richer, or otherwise assumed to be superior. In turn, those in the first category are expected to address those in the second by their last names prefixed with an appropriate social or professional title. People on a fairly equal footing, however, either first-name each other or by mutual if unspoken agreement use a more formal mode of address.

21   As it happens, even though the average full-time working woman in the United States is slightly older than the average man who is employed full-time, she makes only slightly more than half the salary he makes. This may explain why a great many more women than men are called by their first names on the job and why, in offices where most of the senior and junior executives are men and most of the secretaries and clerks are women, the first-naming of all women—including executives, if any—easily becomes habitual. Or it could be that women are at least slightly less impressed by the thought of their own importance, slightly more inclined to meet their colleagues and employees on equal terms. When a reporter asked newly elected Governor Ella Grasso of Connecticut what she wanted to be called and she answered, "People usually call me Ella," a new benchmark for informality must have been set in the other forty-nine state capitals. Unless men respond in the same spirit, however, without taking advantage of what is essentially an act of generosity, women like Governor Grasso will have made a useless sacrifice, jeopardizing both their identity and their prestige.

22   In the whole name game, it is society's sanction of patronymy that most diminishes the importance of women's names—and that sanction is social

only, not legal. In the United States no state except Hawaii legally requires a woman to take her husband's name when she marries, although social pressures in the other states are almost as compelling. The very fact that until recently few women giving up their names realized they were not required to do so shows how universal the expectation is. Any married couple who agree that the wife will keep her own name are in for harassment, no matter how legal their stand: family, friends, the Internal Revenue Service, state and local agencies like motor vehicle departments and voter registrars, hotels, credit agencies, insurance companies are all apt to exert pressure on them to conform. One judge is quoted as saying to a married woman who wanted to revert to her birth name, "If you didn't want his name, why did you get married? Why didn't you live with him instead?" To thus equate marriage with the desire of some women to be called "Mrs." and the desire of some men to have "a Mrs." is insulting to both sexes; yet the equation is so widely accepted that few young people growing up in Western societies think in any different terms.

23   The judge just quoted was, in effect, defining what a family is in a patronymical society like ours where only males are assured permanent surnames they can pass on to their children. Women are said to "marry into" families, and families are said to "die out" if an all-female generation occurs. The word family, which comes from the Latin *famulus*, meaning a servant or slave, is itself a reminder that wives and children, along with servants, were historically part of a man's property. When black Americans discard the names of the slaveholders who owned their forebears, they are consciously disassociating their sense of identity from the property status in which their ancestors were held. To adopt an African name is one way of identifying with freedom and eradicating a link to bondage. The lot of married women in Western society today can hardly be called bondage, but to the degree that people's names are a part of themselves, giving them up, no matter how willingly, is tantamount to giving up some part of personal, legal, and social autonomy.

▬▬▬▬▬▬

**Questions
on Content**

1. Do you agree that "other people's response to your name becomes a part of their response to you" (paragraph 11)? If so, cite examples demonstrating this tendency.

2. Why do Miller and Swift refer to the ideas of Ethel Strainchamps (paragraph 10)?

3. Do you agree that "one of the most useful functions of a given name is to serve as a quick identifier of sex" (paragraph 17)? What do Miller and

Swift say about names that are given to both men and women?

4. The authors refer to a study that claims that "names can be 'active' or 'passive'" (paragraph 11). Do you agree? What examples can you give?

5. Miller and Swift say that many more women than men are called by their first names on the job. Why does this happen?

6. The authors say that some last names "carry a mystique of greatness or honor" (paragraph 12) and offer four examples. They then say that some last names "are cumbersome, or they invite cruel or tasteless jokes," but they provide no examples of these names. Why not?

Questions on Structure and Style

7. Why do Miller and Swift devote their opening paragraph to an anecdote? Is this an appropriate introduction?

8. Where do the authors state their thesis? Is it adequately developed?

9. Outline the selection. Are the topics logically related?

10. Miller and Swift usually provide unmistakable topic sentences. Identify the topic sentences of paragraphs 4 through 6 and of paragraphs 17 through 22.

Assignments

1. How do you feel about your own name? Does it reflect your personality? Does it *affect* your personality? Why did your parents choose your particular name? Does it perhaps reveal their expectations? Write an essay on what your name means to you, and respond to some of these questions.

2. In an essay, describe some of the names you like and/or dislike. What special qualities do these

names have? What kind of "vibrations" do they give off for you?

3. To highlight the connotations certain names can carry for many people, match each name below with the "most appropriate" description.

Floyd	cheerleader
Emily	doctor
Florence	steelworker
Bobbi	accountant
Robert	child genius
Theodore	librarian
Bertha	farmer
Katherine	hairdresser
Bruno	overweight cook
Morris	nurse

Of course there are no right or wrong answers, but compare your choices with those of your classmates. How much variation do you see?

Putting American English on the Map

W. F. Bolton

What happens when "a whole new nation . . . composed of literally millions of places—states, counties, cities and towns, rivers, mountains, even swamps—. . . [awaits] new names from its new inhabitants"? W. F. Bolton, a writer and philologist at Rutgers University, answers this question with wit and scholarship, concluding that place names are a major factor in defining the linguistic character of our nation. For Bolton, toponymics, the study of place names, is essential to a grasp of American English.

1   American English came of age in the nineteenth century when it accomplished the naming of places and naming of persons. For while the name for a native American plant or animal may be distinctive, it is usually no more so than its referent, and often rather less. The change of meaning for an ancient English word such as *robin*, for example, adds nothing to the resources of the vocabulary, although it does adjust them a trifle. Even the outright borrowing of a word like *boss* from a foreign language is only a minuscule addition. Most important of all, such adjustment or addition takes place unsystematically and anonymously.

2   But when a whole new nation, and a huge one at that, is composed of literally millions of places—states, counties, cities and towns, rivers, mountains, even swamps—all awaiting new names from its new inhabitants, then the consequence, whatever else it is, will be of equally huge importance in defining the linguistic character of the nation. So the study of toponymics—placenames—is essential to a grasp of American English.

3   When, furthermore, the nation's new inhabitants arrive in their millions from hundreds of other nations, and become parents in their new country to hundreds of millions more new inhabitants, then the patterns of personal name giving that they develop here are hundreds of millions of times more significant than the designation of an unfamiliar bird as a *robin*. So the study of onomastics—personal names—like the study of toponymics assumes an importance to be measured by nothing less than the nation into which America grew during the nineteenth century.

Names of Places

4   Twenty-seven of the fifty United States—over half—have names of native American origin. Eleven of the others have names that come from personal

names; five are named after other places; five are from common words in Spanish or French; and two are from common words in English. These five categories (native words, personal names, other placenames, common words in other European languages, and common words in English) account for most other American placenames as well, although not always in the same proportions.

5   The state names based on native words range from *Alabama* and *Alaska* to *Wisconsin* and *Wyoming*. They include the names of tribes (*Arkansas, Dakota*), descriptions (*Mississippi*, "big river"; *Alaska*, "mainland"), and words of long-lost meaning (*Hawaii, Idaho*). Many of them are now very far from the form they had in the native language, and some seem to be simply a mistake. The native *Mescousing* or *Mesconsing*, of uncertain meaning, was written *Ouisconsing* by the French who first heard it, and *Wisconsin* by the English. One map had the French form misspelled as *Ouariconsint* and broke the word before the last syllable, so a reader who did not notice the *sint* on the line below would take the name—here of the river—to be *Ouaricon*. At length, that became *Oregon*. The Spanish heard the Papago word *Arizonac* (little spring) as *Arizona;* Spanish and American alike now think it is from the Spanish for "arid zone."

6   The confusion is not surprising. The native Americans themselves often did not know what the placenames meant because the names had been around since time out of memory, perhaps given by a tribe that had long ago disappeared, taking its language and leaving the names. Many placenames were invented on the spot for the benefit of curious white settlers where the native Americans lacked a name; that was especially true of large features in the landscape like mountains. When a Choctaw chief was asked the name of his territory, he replied with the words for "red people"—*Oklahoma*. The names were transcribed in so many different forms that it is usually sheer accident, and often unhelpful, that one has survived as the "official" form rather than another. Delaware *Susquehanna* (a tribal name) became something quite indecipherable in Huron, from which the French got their version *Andastoei;* the English made this *Conestoga* (ultimate source of the name *Conestoga wagon*) and used the word to name a branch of the Susquehanna River, a toponymic variant of the "I'm my own grandpa" song. And careful study of native American languages did not begin until long after many of these names had become settled—indeed until many of the native speakers too had become settled in six feet of earth and were beyond unraveling the placename mysteries they had left behind. Maybe that is just as well, at least for delicate readers; native Americans had a vocabulary rich in abusive terms, and they were not above using them as a joke when a white inquired the name of a local river or neighboring tribe.

7   All that is true of state names from native sources is also true of other such placenames. *Chicago* appears to mean "the place of strong smells,"

but exactly *which* strong smells is not clear. *Mohawk* is a familiar name, but its derivation—apparently from the Iroquois for "bear"—is obscured by its early spellings in no fewer than 142 different forms, the most authentic seeming to be something like *mahaqua*. A single expedition might bring back many new names—the Frenchmen Joliet and Marquette, for example, brought back *Wisconsin, Peoria, Des Moines, Missouri, Osage, Omaha, Kansas, Iowa, Wabash,* and *Arkansas.* The story of *Des Moines* is typical. The Frenchmen found a tribe, the Moingouena, who lived on a river. It was the explorers who named the river Rivière des Moingouenas and later shortened it to Rivière des Moings. Now *moines* is "monks" in French, so by folk etymology *des Moings,* which is nothing in particular, became *des Moines,* which is at least something. But the French pronunciation /de mwan/ is far from what an American makes of the spelling *Des Moines,* and so we have /də mɔin/. It is a long way from the Moingouena tribe—too long for us to trace by the normal process of historical reconstruction back through Americanization, folk etymology, shortening, and the European transfer of a tribal name to a river, if we did not have the documents to help us. In most other cases, we do not have the documents, and the native names speak in a lost language.

8   Many of the earlier native placenames became disused among the descendants of the settlers who adopted them: *Powhatan's River* became the *James,* the *Agiochook Mountains* became the *White Mountains.* Fashion in these matters followed the fashion in the native Americans' prestige, some whites thinking them fine in an exotic and primitive way, others scorning them as crude and even barbaric. Frontier people were often among the latter, people in the settled regions among the former; but of course the frontier turned into the settled region, which sometimes brought about a return to a native name or the imposition of a new one. In New England, *Agawam* became *Ipswich* (after the English town), and later *Agawam* again. The names settlers chose were not always tribally appropriate; unlike the frontier people, settlers were insensitive to the differences among tribes about whom they knew next to nothing anyway, so that—for example— the name of a Florida chief would be given to some seventeen places, many of them far from his Florida habitat.

9   The vogue for native American placenames was supported by literary models like Longfellow's *Hiawatha.* But the native names did not always meet the demands of American literary taste or English poetic forms, and when they clashed it was the placenames that were reworked. As a result, the "beauty" of such names is sometimes in the pen of the poet and not on the lip of the native speaker. The same is true of translations: *Minnesota* is approximately "muddy river," but *muddy* could also be "cloudy," and skies are "cloudy" too. Clouds pass, skies remain, and what have you? *Minnesota* translated as "the sky-blue water." The nineteenth-century

American fad for native placenames falsified the native American words in both form and meaning, and often imposed a native name where none had been before. Ironically, the travestied native name is often more recent than the English or other European placenames it replaced.

10   Native American names in their least native American form appear not only in places like *Indian Bottom, Indian Creek, Indian Harbour, Indian Head, Indian Lake, Indian Peak, Indian River,* but also *Cherokee River, Cherokee Strip, Chippewa River* (two), *Chippewa Village, Chippewa County* (three), *Chippewa Falls,* and *Chippewa Lake.*

Placenames from Personal Names and Other Words

11   The states named after persons stretch from *Pennsylvania* (after William Penn, the English Quaker who founded it) in the east to *Washington* (after George Washington) in the west. Three were named after one royal couple: Charles I named the two *Carolinas* after himself (Latin *Carolus* means Charles), and *Maryland* after his wife, Queen Henrietta Maria. Queen Elizabeth I named *Virginia* both after herself (the virgin queen) and after the New World (the virgin land); *West Virginia* followed naturally. Other royal names remain in *Georgia* (King George II of England) and *Louisiana* (King Louis XIV of France). The governor, Lord de la Warr, supplied the name for *Delaware.* Just as *Arizona* seems to stem from the Spanish for "arid zone," so *California* seems to represent the Spanish for "hot oven." It figures. It figures, but it is wrong. When Cortés came to the place around 1530, he thought he had found a legendary land entirely peopled by women—his soldiers must have loved that—teeming in gold and jewels and ruled by the fabled Queen Calafia. He named it, accordingly, *California,* and California, accordingly, is a state named after a person.

12   The Americanization of placenames involves not only folk etymology, translation, and loan translation, but the distinctive rendition of words pronounced quite differently elsewhere. To English ears our pronunciation of *Birmingham* (Alabama) may or may not contain a giveaway /r/, depending on the regional dialect of the American who says it. If he is from the place itself, the /r/ will probably be absent, as it is in England. But almost any American will make the last syllable much more distinct than would an English resident of Birmingham (England), where the last three letters get no more than a syllabic [m]. This tendency is also observable in the local pronunciation of a place like *Norwich* (NJ), approximately "nor witch"; in England the place of the same name rhymes with "porridge." The tendency is not always present in common nouns, however; for example, the noun *record* is pronounced with two distinct syllables in Britain but not in America. The careful spelling-pronunciation seems to be a consistent Americanism only when it comes to placenames.

NAMES OF DISCONTINUED POSTAL UNITS

Name Discontinued	Attached to	Mail to
Arapaho	Richardson	Richardson
Big Town	Mesquite	Mesquite
Blue Mound	Fort Worth	Fort Worth
Broadway	Mesquite	Mesquite
Camp San Saba		Brady
Canyon Creek Square	Richardson	Canyon Creek
Cedar Bayou	Baytown	Baytown
Cleo		Menard
Cottonwood	Baird	Baird
Dal-Rich	Richardson	Richardson
Easter	Hereford	Hereford
Edom	Brownsboro	Brownsboro
Field Creek		Pontotoc
Franklin	Houston	Houston
Freestone	Teague	Teague
Gay Hill		Brenham
Gilliland	Truscott	Truscott
Great SW Airport	Fort Worth	Fort Worth
Grit		Mason
Lake Air	Waco	Waco
Leary	Texarkana	Texarkana
McNair	Baytown	Baytown
Mount Sylvan	Lindale	Lindale
Oakalla		Killeen
Olmos Park	San Antonio	San Antonio
Pandale		Ozona
Patricia		Lamesa
Patroon		Shelbyville
Postoak		Bowie
Possum Kingdom	Graford	Graford
Raymond A. Stewart, Jr.	Galveston	Galveston

(continued)		
Name Discontinued	**Attached to**	**Mail to**
Richland Hills	Fort Worth	Greater Richlands Area
Sachse	Garland	Garland
Salt Gap		Lohn
Six Flags Over Texas	Arlington	Arlington
Slocum	Elkhart	Elkhart
Spring Hill	Longview	Longview
Stacy		Coleman
Startzville	New Braunfels	Canyon Lake
Sunnyvale	Mesquite	Mesquite
Telico	Ennis	Ennis
Town Hall	Mesquite	Mesquite
Weldon		Lovelady
Woodlands	Spring	The Woodlands
Washburn	Claude	Claude

Ghost "Postal Units" in Texas. The discontinued offices include native American names, Spanish names, British names, personal names, and still others for which there is no obvious category. Adapted from the *U.S. Directory of Post Offices* (1977). Copyright by the United States Postal Service.

13   If the placename is not an English one, American pronunciation will vary even more. We have already seen that many native American placenames changed beyond all recognition in the white settlers' vocal apparatus. The same is often true of names from European languages other than English. *Los Angeles* is a notorious case—the common pronunciation contains several sounds not in Spanish, and the first word is liable to sound like *las* in Americanized form. But no matter; the city was not, in any case, named after the angels, but after the mother of Christ, "the Queen of the Angels."

Other Placenames

14   The five states that are named after other places show, in four of them, the origins of their settlers: *New Mexico* by Spanish explorers coming northward from "Old" Mexico; *New Hampshire, New Jersey,* and *New York* by Britons who remembered an English county, an island in the English Channel, and a northern English city, respectively. But *Rhode Island* is named after the Mediterranean island of Rhodes, where the famous Colossus once bestrode the entrance to the port, a statue of a man so huge that it

gives us our adjective *colossal* today. Why the smallest state should struggle under a name associated with the largest statue is, all the same, a
colossal mystery.

15   Spanish words for common things remain in the state names *Mon-
tana* (mountainous), *Colorado* ([colored] red), *Nevada* (snowed on), *Florida*
(flowered, because it had many flowers, and because it was discovered a
few days after Easter, called "the Easter of flowers" in Spanish), and—in
an unorthodox form—the French *Vermont* (green mountain). English common words remain in *Maine* (great or important, as in *mainland* or *main sea*,
from which comes *the billowing main* or *the Spanish main*); and in *Indiana*,
from the Indiana Company that was formed by land speculators to settle
the former Indian Territory.

16   All these patterns, like the pattern of naming with native American
words, are repeated in the patterns of naming places other than states.
Washington names not only a state but, at one count, 32 counties; 121 cities,
towns, and villages; 257 townships; 18 lakes and streams; 7 mountains; and
no end of streets. Many saints' names appear in Spanish, French, and
English placenames. With suitable suffixes on secular names we get *Pittsburgh, Jacksonville,* and many more. Common things remain in *Oil City* and
in *Carbondale,* as well as in the rather less common Canadian *Moose Jaw* and
Medicine Hat. Placenames are transferred from abroad—the English *Boston*
supplied the name for the well-known city in Massachusetts and eighteen
more *Bostons* and *New Bostons*—or from the east of the United States, re-
producing *Princetons* (fifteen municipalities and, in Colorado, a peak) and
Philadelphias across the American landscape with no more than a zip code
of difference among them.

17   So what is true of the state names is true of other placenames. But the
other placenames have a few features that, probably fortunately, never got
put on the map in letters quite so large as those employed for states. Some
of these are European words from languages other than the staple of Spanish, French, and English. Some are names from classical or biblical lore.
Some describe the place or its animals or plants. And some seem to be
inspired by nothing more serious than verbal playfulness, nothing more
reverent than onomastic cussedness. Placenames such as these, especially
the last category, have attracted the disproportionate attention of many
otherwise judicious investigators of American English, and they have inspired poetic encomiums such as Stephen Vincent Benét's "American
Names."* They are colorful, it is true, but you can scan the average gasoline company map for hours before you will find anything more than the
usual, usually colorless, run of American placenames.

18   Dutch names are among the most important following the native American, French, Spanish, and English. Like the others, the Dutch had a way

---

* Benét's poem is reprinted on page 110.

with native names, and their way gave us *Hackensack* and *Hoboken* (the latter from *Hopoakanhacking*) and other names too. They named New World places after Old World places, like *New Amsterdam* and *Haarlem*; their *Breukelyn* born anew on these shores became *Brooklyn*. They gave their personal names to places as well, so that Jonas Bronck (actually a Dane in a Dutch settlement) gave his to the *Bronx*, and Jonkheer (squire) Donck gave his title to *Yonkers*. And they gave the name of their language and culture to places like *Dutch Neck* (NJ). Many of the Dutch names did not survive the occupation of their settlements by the English—Nieuw Amsterdam became *New York*, for example—and in this as in the other Dutch placenames, only the language in question is different: the patterns of naming are the same as they were for the languages that named thousands of other places.

19   A somewhat more novel trait of American placenames is their reference to classical and biblical lore. *Philadelphia* may "mean" City of Brotherly Love, in approximate translation from the Greek, but it was probably named (by William Penn) after an Asian city of the same name, with the additional warrant of the words of Saint Paul, "Be kindly affectionate one to another with brotherly love." Both the classical and the scriptural had singular importance in a country that, unlike Britain, had millions of new places awaiting names, places as often as not settled by those (again like Penn) whose wanderings had a religious impetus. When we today have a new product, we may invent a neoclassical name for it: *television* is the most common example. But when we want such a name, it is to the classical scholar that we turn. The early settlers likewise turned to the schoolteacher or to the minister who was, frequently, the same person. And they got just what they might have expected: in central New York there is a *Troy,* a *Utica,* a *Rome,* an *Ithaca,* and a *Syracuse.* (Troy was not the first name the place had; under the Dutch, it had been *Vanderheyden* or *Vanderheyden's Ferry.*) State names like the *Carolinas* and *Virginia* took a Latin-like form, and when the Virginia town near the Alexander plantation got its name, it was more than a happy coincidence that it was called *Alexandria* after the great city of the ancient world. The practice is most notable in the east, but that has not stopped placenames farther west like *Cincinnati* (Ohio), *Cairo* (Illinois), *Tempe* and *Phoenix* (Arizona), and many others from achieving permanence.

20   The Bible too had an influence beyond the Philadelphia city limits. Mencken counted eleven *Beulahs,* nine *Canaans,* eleven *Jordans,* and twenty-one *Sharons.* The pattern is general: a preference for the Old Testament over the New as a toponymic source. Most of the American placenames with *St.-* are taken over from the French or the Spanish, as are the frequent placenames still untranslated from those languages: *Sacramento, San Francisco,* and so many more that Whitman grew angry at their number and demanded their renaming in secular terms. It didn't come about.

Placenames very quickly lose their referential content beyond the place they name. They "mean" nothing more than the place, and so *Phoenix* (AZ), for example, becomes a different word from the phoenix that was a legendary bird. By the same process, *Sacramento* has no religious overtones for those who know it as a place, even though they may also know something of the sacrament it was originally meant to recall. And folk etymology often made oblivion certain. The place the Spanish called *El Río de las Animas Perdidas en Purgatorio* (River of the Souls Lost in Purgatory) was translated and shortened by the French into *Purgatoire,* and the Americans who followed them imitated this as *Picketwire.* Any resemblance between purgatory and picketwire is purely coincidental.

21   A name like the one the Spanish gave this river is a reference to something else not present, as is most naming for persons and places. But some placenames refer to the place itself by describing it: *Sugarloaf Mountain,* for example, which looked like a sugarloaf to those who had to name it, and *Cedar Mountain,* which was covered with trees. Nowadays no one knows what a sugarloaf looks like, so the name of the mountain is as abstract as if it had been Algonquian; and chances are the cedars have all been cut down as well to make shingles for houses where no sugarloaf will enter. No high school French course will enable the American pupil to see in the *Grand Teton* mountains the original comparison to "big breasts," which may be why the name has been left untranslated. Descriptive placenames have made a great comeback since World War II, for they appear to lend a quaint and historical air to new subdivision developments. *Oak Dell* certainly sounds worth a down payment, even if no oaks ever grew within miles of the spot and the terrain is perfectly flat; and *Miry Run* has the same reassuring sound, at least until the customer remembers what *miry* means.

22   The most colorful names are the rarest. They are found mostly in old accounts of the frontier and in books like this one. Many of the most colorful have been civilized out of existence: in Canada, *Rat Portage* became *Kenora.* But *King of Prussia* and *Intercourse* still survive in Pennsylvania, *Tombstone* in Arizona, and others elsewhere. Mencken claims that West Virginia is "full" of such placenames, giving as proof *Affinity, Bias, Big Chimney, Bulltown, Caress, Cinderella, Cowhide,* and *Czar,* just for the ABCs. But some of his examples are more madcap than others, and they do not really "fill" the state. *Truth or Consequences* (NM) is a recent alteration that needs no explanation. Almost self-explanatory are the portmanteau or blendword placenames such as *Calexico* (on the California side of the Mexican border; *Mexicali* is on the other side), *Penn Yan* (settled by Pennsylvanians and Yankees), *Delmarva* (a common though unofficial name for the peninsula that is partly in Delaware, partly in Maryland, partly in Virginia). The blend process is relatively common in all varieties of the English language, but as a source of placenames it seems to be distinctively American.

Questions
on Content

1. Why is toponymics "essential to a grasp of American English" (paragraph 2)?

2. What five categories of American place names does Bolton identify?

3. Explain the origins of the names *Wisconsin* and *Minnesota*.

4. Which states are named after famous persons?

5. Identify some of the Dutch influences on American place names.

6. Which source do you think accounts for the most colorful place names?

Questions
on Structure
and Style

7. Examine the relationship between paragraphs 1 and 2. What is the function of paragraph 2?

8. What kind of transitions are used in the first three paragraphs? Are those in the rest of the selection similar?

9. We note Bolton's sense of humor in paragraph 6. Find other examples of his humor. What do they tell us about him and about his attitude toward his subject?

10. Are Bolton's examples appropriate? Does he include enough examples?

Assignments

1. Study Bolton's five categories for the names of the fifty states. Then write an essay classifying the place names in your region. (You may have to devise new categories to be accurate.)

2. Write an essay discussing the history of your region as reflected in its place names.

What's in a Nickname?

John Leo

"Sports teams must have nicknames," says John Leo. *Generals, Raiders, Tigers, Jets*—these names identify qualities we expect from athletes, especially from our hometown athletes. The names also identify the times during which such names were chosen. Leo, a contributor to *Time* magazine, makes this point, too: The right nickname sometimes can be quirky, silly, or simply funny. If the students at one university believe that the right name for their school team is the *Banana Slugs*, are they necessarily wrong?

1   Everyone knows that sports teams must have nicknames, but selecting an appropriate one is fraught with peril. Alabama, for instance, may be proud of the Crimson Tide, but it sounds like a bloodbath or a serious algae problem. Notre Dame's famous jocks are ossified as the Fighting Irish, though Hibernian-American athletes are about as rare in South Bend as they are on the Boston Celtics. Nothing exposed the nickname crisis more starkly than the 1982 NCAA basketball championship game played between the Georgetown Hoyas and the North Carolina Tar Heels. Even if you know what a hoya or a tarheel is, the only sensible strategy is to forget it. (For those overwhelmed by a need to know, hoya is short for *Hoya saxa!*, a garbled Greek and Latin cheer meaning "What rocks!," and tarheel originated during the Civil War as a disparaging term for folks from the Carolina pine forests.) Few knew what the Fort Wayne Zollner Pistons were when a pro basketball team played under that name. (They were players owned by Fred Zollner, who also happened to own a piston factory in Fort Wayne.) The early vogue of naming a team for a person seems to have come to an end with Paul Brown, the original coach of the Cleveland Browns. Fans who found the cult of personality distasteful at least were grateful that he wasn't named Stumblebrenner.

2   The Zollner Pistons eventually became the Detroit Pistons, showing that some nicknames travel well. The Brooklyn Dodgers, named for the difficulty of evading trolley cars in the famous borough, are now the Los Angeles Dodgers, where evading mayhem on the freeways is equally hard. The name Los Angeles Lakers, however, makes no sense at all, though it did when the team was in Minnesota. Utah, with its Mormon tradition, could easily have accepted the New Orleans football team (the Saints, as in Latter-Day Saints and saints who go marching in). Instead it got the New Orleans basketball team, now known as the Utah Jazz, which makes about as much sense as the New Orleans Tabernacle Choir.

3   In general, nicknames are supposed to come from two categories: animals that specialize in messy predation (lions, sharks, falcons and so forth)

or humans famous for rapine and pillage (pirates, buccaneers, Vikings, conquistadors, bandits, raiders, etc.). The image of mangled flesh must be evoked, but tastefully, one reason why there are no teams named the Massacres or the Serial Murderers. The aim, of course, is to borrow ferocity, but there are signs of change. Some years ago, students at Scottsdale Community College in Arizona voted to name their team the Artichokes and picked pink and white as the team colors. Authorities balked, but three years later students got half a loaf: the team is the Artichokes, but the colors are blue and white. Last year a similar nickname struggle took place. By 5 to 1, students at the University of California at Santa Cruz voted to call school teams the Banana Slugs in honor of a slimy yellow gastropod that swarms over the seaside campus on rainy days. Lest anyone miss the message, pro-Slug students said they meant to twit the "football mentality" of other California schools.

4   Not every team, of course, can be accused of seeking overly aggressive names. The New York University Violets or the Swarthmore Little Quakers do not induce terror. At Transylvania College, the team nickname is not the Neck Biters but the Pioneers. Women's teams are caught between the quaint feminine names of the old days (Colleens, Lassies) and the carnage-producing names of male teams. The defunct Women's Pro Basketball League had the Fillies and the Does, but leaned toward unisex names (Pioneers, Stars, Pride, Diamonds and Hustle). Most colleges, however, simply put the word lady in front of the men's nickname: the Lady Dragons or the Lady Monarchs. The Midwest Christian Lady Conquerors are deeply awe-inspiring, perhaps a bit more so than the Hofstra Flying Dutchwomen or the Iowa Wesleyan Tigerettes.

5   In major league baseball, most of the aggressive nicknames, like Pirates and Tigers, are attached to older franchises. Now that the game is played by college-trained millionaires, the newer teams have been more sedately named after seagoers and spacegoers (Mariners, Astros), birds (Blue Jays), religious figures (Angels, Padres) or a dimly remembered world's fair (Expos).

6   While the nicknames of many older pro football teams enshrine civic boosterism (Packers, Steelers, Oilers), newer names include most of the violent ones. The United States Football League produced the Invaders, Maulers, Gamblers, Gunslingers and Outlaws. As one irritated analyst put it, this group "sounds like the roster from a Hell's Angels' convention."

7   The growth areas for team names are the military-industrial complex (Jets, Supersonics, Generals, Astros, Bombers, Rockets) and the more nostalgic violence of cowboys and Indians (Braves, Redskins, Chiefs, Indians, Outlaws, Cowboys, Wranglers and Rangers).

8   Copycat names (Oakland Raiders, Oakland Invaders) are also popular. After the New York Mets came the football Jets, basketball Nets, the team-tennis Sets and the Off-Track Betting Bets (known locally as the Debts). There was even some loose talk of a water-polo squad to be known,

inevitably, as the Wets, and a women's basketball team, the Pets. This sort of secondhand glory is an old story in sports, dating back at least to football's Detroit Lions' and Chicago Bears' attempting to identify with the established baseball teams, the Detroit Tigers and Chicago Cubs. Another kind of identity problem forced the Cincinnati Reds, America's oldest professional sports team, to change their name to the Redlegs during the height of the cold war. One Cincinnati sportswriter objected on the ground that since the Moscow Reds were the newcomers, they should be asked to change *their* name.

9   Every now and then a franchise attempts a punning name. A hockey team in Georgia was known as the Macon Whoopees, and the Los Angeles Rams cheerleaders were once called the Embraceable Ewes. The name Buffalo Bills is a pun of sorts. So was the name of the late American Basketball Association team, the St. Louis Spirits. (Get it? *The Spirit of St. Louis?*) Perhaps one day we will have the Norman (Okla.) Conquests or the Greenwich Village Idiots.

10   One trend is to name teams for malevolent forces, such as the Blast, Sting, Blizzard and Blitz. Three team names celebrate disasters that destroyed much of their native locale: the Golden Bay Earthquakes, Chicago Fire and Atlanta (now Calgary) Flames. Such a breakthrough in reverse civic pride may yet induce other cities to celebrate their local disasters. Just think. The Boston Stranglers, the New York Muggers, the Washington Scams, the Los Angeles Smog . . .

Questions on Content

1. According to Leo, why was the "nickname crisis" (paragraph 1) exposed in a 1982 NCAA basketball championship game?

2. Leo believes that nicknames come from two categories. What are they? Do these categories seem correct?

3. What differences does Leo note between the nicknames of the older and the newer major league baseball teams?

4. Which team is the oldest American professional sports team? What happened to its nickname during the Cold War? What does this historical detail demonstrate about names and naming in general?

5. How does Leo classify the following nicknames: *Cleveland Browns, Seattle Supersonics, Detroit Tigers, Chicago Bears?* How would he classify Miami's entry into the NBA: the *Miami Heat?*

Questions on Structure and Style

6. Discuss how the first paragraph is developed. Is it unified? Is it coherent?

7. Discuss Leo's use of transitions between each paragraph. Does Leo use transitions successfully?

8. How would you describe the tone of this essay? Can you find examples of humor? If so, what type of humor do you find—exaggeration, irony, understatement?

9. Ending an essay with ellipsis marks is certainly irregular. Why does Leo do this?

Assignments

1. In paragraph 9, Leo has fun with names that pun—the *St. Louis Spirits,* for example. Invent other names that pun, such as the *Australian Crawlers* or the *Wisconsin Cheddars.* What type of "sport" would you expect each team to play?

2. Make a list of nicknames of high school sports teams in your region. Look for ways to group the names. Write a classification essay based on your findings.

3. Make a topic outline for this essay, and in a paragraph, explain Leo's method of organization.

Smile, Dr. Fuchs, Your Fuchsia Is Bright

Paul Dickson

Think how pleased you'd be if you, Chris Davis, invented a machine so useful that owning a "davis" became as common as owning a car. Think, too, of inventing a machine that you introduce to the world during a live television broadcast, a machine that promptly explodes. Such a davis would enrich language but not your bank account, even though thereafter your name would be identified with any invention equipped with a big surprise. As Paul Dickson points out in the following essay, the English language contains a large stock of eponymous words. What noun or verb would you like to be some day?

1   The odds against your name becoming a household word, or any word at all, must be positively mind-boggling. About as likely as your living to be 115 years old.

2   Nevertheless, some men might have preferred that the honor pass them by. Britain's great Prime Minister William Ewart Gladstone, for instance, is better remembered for the baggage he carried than for his statesmanship. By contrast, the Earl of Cardigan probably did better than he should have, for the choleric commander who ordered the ill-fated Charge of the Light Brigade is remembered, if at all, in the name of the woolen jacket (a button-up sweater to us) that his troops wore in the Crimea.

3   Then there are those whose names get attached to unpleasant things. Think of Dr. Joseph-Ignace Guillotin, a man who went to his grave protesting the fact that *they* had put his name on that machine which he did *not* invent. All the poor doctor had done was to give a speech advocating that this more "merciful" means of execution replace the noose and ax in use at the time. And thanks to Thomas A. Edison, who was then trying to discredit alternating current, his archrival George Westinghouse only narrowly missed having electrocution referred to as Westinghousing.

4   According to word expert Robert Hendrickson, author of *Human Words*, there are about 3,000 eponymous words in general use. Despite the possible pitfalls, for most of us becoming a noun or verb is as near immortality as we can ever hope to get. And the best helpful hint for anyone who wishes to acquire this ultimate accolade: your odds improve if you hang around people who name, breed or discover plants. Consider: Michel

Bégon (begonia), Maj. John Bibb (Bibb lettuce), Anders Dahl (dahlia), Dr. Alexander Garden (gardenia), Timothy Hanson (timothy grass), Pierre Magnol (magnolia) and, in a slightly different connection, Leonhard Fuchs, the German botanist who became both a flower and the color fuchsia.

5   Eponymous words like these obviously can refer to people, or even, very occasionally, to places. Some of the more famous examples: Louis Braille, Rudolf Diesel, Gabriel Daniel Fahrenheit and Vidkun Quisling, not to mention Amelia Jenks Bloomer, the abolitionist, temperance crusader and women's rights advocate who did not invent but wore bloomers and spoke in favor of them as an alternative to hoopskirts.

6   Another item of feminine apparel has an even more tenuous connection to the source of its eponymous moniker. The skimpy, two-piece, bare-midriff bikini got its name because it was introduced at a Paris fashion show soon after the atomic explosion that took place on Bikini Atoll in the Pacific on July 1, 1946. That was one of the oddest and quirkiest jumps in the history of eponyms. But no odder than its sequel, for when the topless bathing suit was invented, the French, with that quickness of wit for which they are infamous, instantly dubbed it the monokini.

7   French, in fact, seems to lend itself to eponymy. There is Johnny Crapaud, a nickname of one Bernard Marigny, a New Orleans gambler who, so it is said, brought the first pair of dice to that city, thus making possible the first craps game. (Crapaud means "toad"—an epithet that 19th-century Americans often applied to the French.) Jean Martinet, a colonel in the service of Louis XIV, who insisted that military discipline be maintained by making soldiers march till they practically dropped. And Jules Léotard, the Gallic trapeze artist who urged a "more natural garb that does not hide your best features." Somewhere along the line, though, the name for that revealing garb became pluralized. Superman, for example, wears leotards, not a leotard.

8   These men at least had words formed from names they regularly used. But Emperor Haile Selassie of Ethiopia is unwittingly remembered for a name he had shed when he became Emperor, Ras Tafari. This designation has been incorporated into the word Rastafarian because the Jamaican cult venerates Selassie's memory and advocates a return to Africa. Whereas Britain's crusty old Adm. Edward Vernon fell victim to a double pun. He got *his* nickname, Old Grog, for his cloak made of grogram, a coarse mix of silk and wool. But he is memorable, eponymously speaking, only because he ordered his sailors to dilute their ration of rum with water, which became known as grog.

9   New eponymous words are constantly being suggested in hopes they will somehow stick in the language. Edsel is showing strength as a noun meaning a commercial disaster. The noun Armstrong has gained some credence

as a word for a high and sustained trumpet note. And Sam Gold-
wyn (Goldwynism), George Orwell (Orwellian) and the Reverend Moon
(Moonie) are well in the running.

10   Others' names have been nominated with, it must be admitted, only
mixed results. Wilfred Espy, word gamesman par excellence, offers Cronkite to denote a heavy-duty anchor, immobile in the fiercest storms. Kurt
Vonnegut has proposed the word Stowe, from abolitionist Harriet Beecher
Stowe, to designate units of socially useful activity.

11   And just imagine what it would be like if eponymous people had been
switched in their cradles. In that case a guillotine might be a sweater and a
cardigan a big blade. Which leads to the Liberty Cabbage vs. Sauerkraut
(or would-a-rose-by-any-other-name-smell-as-sweet) debate. What if the
French countryside near the town of Roquefort abounded in grapes instead
of ewes' milk, and the Champagne region was long on sheep and short on
vineyards? Wine experts might praise its "nose," but would a bubbly glass
of Roquefort taste as good as a bubbly glass of Champagne?

Questions on Content

1. Explain the following terms: *eponymous words, mono-kini, Rastafarian, grog*.

2. If you want your name to become a household word, with whom should you "hang around," according to Dickson?

3. Explain the derivations of the following eponyms: *cardigan, craps, leotards, dahlia, Edsel*. What do we gain by knowing their derivations?

4. What point is Dickson making in the final paragraph with his discussion of Roquefort and Champagne?

Questions on Structure and Style

5. Identify the audience for this essay, which originally appeared in *Smithsonian* magazine. How would you describe the essay's tone? How does the tone relate to the audience?

6. Discuss Dickson's use of three sections to structure his essay. Why does Dickson use such divisions?

7. Defend the author's use of a sentence fragment in the opening paragraph.

8. Dickson obviously delights in his subject. How is this delight reflected in his writing?

9. Discuss the effectiveness of the conclusion. Is the tone of the final paragraph consistent with the rest of the essay?

Assignments

1. Make a topic outline for the essay, and in a paragraph, discuss Dickson's organizational method. Compare the organization of this essay with the organization of the John Leo essay that appears earlier in this chapter.

2. Eponymous words make up part of the private (as opposed to the public) languages of families and groups of friends. In an essay, identify some of the eponymous words in your own private language. Discuss their derivation and use. (In your introduction, you may want to consider why eponymous words are popular with families or other closed groups.)

3. Take assignment 2 one step further by discussing some of the other elements that make your family's private language unique. Carefully use classification and illustration as you develop the essay.

Additional Assignments and Research Topics

1. Examine the following table of names of things compiled by
    W. F. Bolton.

Dishes and recipes (Eggs Benedict, cherries jubilee)
Sports teams (Philadelphia Flyers, Pittsburgh Penguins)
State nicknames (Garden State, Blue Hen State)
Street names (The Midway, Wall Street)
Former telephone exchanges (now superseded by num-
    bered exchanges)
Apartment houses and housing developments (Olympic
    Towers, Co-Op City)
Railroad cars, airplanes, naval and other ships (*USS
    Midway*)
Houses of worship (St. Paul's, First Congregational,
    Temple Beth-El)
Newspapers, magazines (*Town Topics, Road & Track*)
Pets, race horses (Bowser, Court Fleet)
Natural disasters (Hurricane Cora, the Hayward Fault)
Novels, motion pictures (*Amok, The French Connection*)
Consumer products (Vaseline, Touch and Go)
Ailments (Legionnaires' disease, psoriasis, influenza)
Garments (Fairisle sweater, miniskirt, Docksiders)
Schools, colleges, universities (Arizona State, Oral
    Roberts)
Car makes, models, names (Buick, Mustang, Draggin'
    Wagon)
Government agencies (Small Business Administration)
Charitable and nonprofit organizations (Nader's Raiders)
Theatres and cinemas (Lyceum, Palace)
Medicines (Kaopectate, aspirin)
Plants and flowers (moneywort, mandrake, fuchsia)
Weapons (bayonet, bazooka)
Eras and generations (the age of anxiety, the "me"
    generation)

And Things. Place names are easy to collect with the aid of a good road map.
Other proper names will repay study, too—almost every business name in the
Yellow Pages of the telephone directory will provide a good starting place, as
will the categories listed above (with a few examples in parentheses).

Choose a category such as names of professional baseball teams, street names, or names of automobiles, and write an essay in which you classify the names in this category and discuss what they reveal.

2. In an essay, respond to one or more of the following quotations:

    . . . for as his name is, so is he . . .

    I Samuel 25:25

    A name is sound and smoke.

    Goethe

    The renaming of things is the essence of conquest.

    William Broyles

    . . . a rose by any other name would smell as sweet.

    Shakespeare

    A good name is better than riches.

    Cervantes

    The beginning of wisdom is to call things by their right names.

    Chinese proverb

3. Many authors carefully select their characters' names to reflect their personalities. Charles Dickens's Mr. Murdstone and Mr. Gradgrind, and Ralph Ellison's Jim Trueblood and Dr. Bledsoe are examples of this tactic. Think of novels or short stories you've read in which the authors send such obvious messages with their characters' names, and in an essay, discuss the importance of these names.

4. The following is from the *Interpreter's Bible:*

    In biblical thought a name is not a mere label of identification; it is an expression of the essential nature of the bearer. A man's name reveals his character. Adam was able to give names to beasts and birds because, as Milton says, he understood their nature.

    Write an essay explaining your own ideas about the importance of names. Consider the quotation from the *Interpreter's Bible,* and keep in mind the ideas presented in this chapter.

5. Write a research paper examining the meaning and importance of some type of name. You might, for example, write
about American place names or surnames. Be certain to
narrow your topic carefully.

6. The American poet Stephen Vincent Benét was so consumed by the power of American names that he wrote the
following poem about them.

AMERICAN NAMES

I have fallen in love with American names,
The sharp names that never get fat,
The snakeskin-titles of mining claims.
The plumed war-bonnet of Medicine Hat.
Tucson and Deadwood and Lost Mule Flat.

Seine and Piave are silver spoons,
But the spoonbowl-metal is thin and worn,
There are English counties like hunting-tunes
Played on the keys of a postboy's horn.
But I will remember where I was born.

I will remember Carquinez Straits,
Little French Lick and Lundy's Lane,
The Yankee ships and the Yankee dates
And the bullet-towns of Calamity Jane.
I will remember Skunktown Plain.

. . . .

Rue des Martyrs and Bleeding-Heart-Yard,
Senlis, Pisa, and Blindman's Oast,
It is a magic ghost you guard
But I am sick for a newer ghost,
Harrisburg, Spartanburg, Painted Post.

Henry and John were never so
And Henry and John were always right?
Granted, but when it was time to go
And the tea and the laurels had stood all night,
Did they never watch for Nantucket Light?

I shall not rest quiet in Montparnasse.
I shall not lie easy at Winchelsea.
You may bury my body in Sussex grass,
You may bury my tongue at Champmedy.
I shall not be there. I shall rise and pass.
Bury my heart at Wounded Knee.

In an essay, compare your own reaction to American names with Benét's reaction. Do you share his fascination? What names do you find most intriguing? Most revealing? Most meaningful?

7. "Sniglets" are nonsense words—words that don't exist and that sound strange and funny to us. Perhaps many of them should exist, and maybe someday some will. Our language is constantly changing, and words enter and leave virtually every day. We do not have an academy to monitor new words. If we need a word, we form one; if enough people use it, then the word becomes part of the language.

New words are structured in several different ways. Some of the "sniglets" below are based on what the word sounds like (onomatopoeia) or looks like; some are combinations of two or more words or parts of words; some are new combinations of a familiar word (root) with a familiar prefix or suffix; and some are combinations of familiar foreign words and word parts. Have a look at these "sniglets," created by Rich Hall and Friends, and do the exercises that follow.

(1)   ALPOPUCK (al' po puk) *n:* Any empty dish pushed around the kitchen floor by a dog trying to get the last morsel.

(2)   BANECTOMY (bah nek' to mee) *n:* The removal of bruises on a banana.

(3)   BEAVO (bee' vo) *n:* A pencil with teeth marks all over it.

(4)   CHUBBLE (chuh' bul) *n:* The aerobic movement combining deep knee bends and sideward hops used when trying to fit into pantyhose.

(5)   DIMP (dimp) *n:* A person who insults you in a cheap department store by asking, "Do you work here?"

(6)   DOWNPAUSE (down' pawz) *n:* The split second of dry weather experienced when driving under an overpass during a storm.

(7)   GLUTE (glewt) *v:* To shake sugar packets vigorously so as to move the contents to the bottom before tearing open.

(8) MIMOIDS (mim' oydz) *n:* People addicted to the smell of newly mimeographed test papers.

(9) OPUP (op' uhp) *v:* To push one's glasses back on the nose.

(10) PREMADERCI (pree muh dayr' chi) *n:* The act of saying goodbye to someone, then running into him again moments later (usually accompanied by a lame quip, such as "You following me?").

A. Determine the structure of each "sniglet." For example, is the word based on sight or sound recognition, on compounding of familiar words, on joining familiar roots with prefixes and suffixes, or on familiar foreign words?

B. Look around your environment—dormitory, cafeteria, parking lot—and try to find needs for "sniglets." Once you find a need, make up a new "sniglet." For example, what can you call the crevice on an ashtray where a cigarette rests or a person who orders chocolate cheesecake and a diet drink?

C. Look at the existing names of places and things, and determine how they are structured. How about words like *silent butler, Kool Aid,* or *cockatoo?*

8. In the *B.C.* cartoon on page 113, the name *mammoth shrimp* is an oxymoron. Warren S. Blumenfeld provides an entertaining collection of such expressions in his book *Jumbo Shrimp and Other Almost Perfect Oxymorons.* Blumenfeld defines *oxymoron* this way: "An oxymoron is two concepts (usually two words) that do *not* go together but are used together. It is the bringing together of contradictory expressions." A sampling of oxymorons (some of them from Blumenfeld's book) includes *freezer burn, civil war, vaguely aware, clearly confused, dry ice, working vacation, old news, undecided major, divorce court, cardinal sin, good loser.*

A. Obviously, oxymorons are all around us—*almost everywhere.* Look for them in restaurants, in stores, on television, in books and magazines, in advertisements. Collect as many oxymorons as you can, and invent some of your own. You will *almost suddenly* and *essentially agree* that such *important trivia* will keep you *slightly preoccupied—almost totally.* Share your collection with your classmates.

By permission of Johnny Hart and Creators Syndicate, Inc.

B. The oxymoron, although entertaining in its own right, has evolved into a type of joke in which a name serves as an insult or caustic commentary. *Military intelligence* is a familiar example, as are *criminal justice system, Amtrak schedule,* and *faculty party.* As a classroom project, compose a list of similar terms.

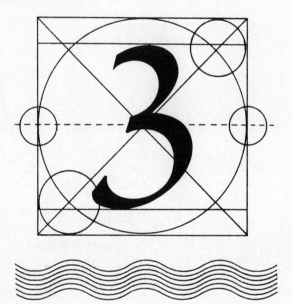

Dictionaries

A common attitude toward dictionaries goes something like this: A dictionary is a big spelling book. We're supposed to know how to spell correctly, so when someone (usually a teacher) says that we've misspelled a word, we look it up in a dictionary. Aside from this use, dictionaries make handy book ends or doorstops.

Saying that dictionaries exist to check spelling is like saying that supermarkets exist to sell bread. Such oversimplifications actually distort the truth. The truth is that dictionaries are important reference tools that contain a wide variety of carefully chosen information. The information is accessible from dictionaries that are inexpensive, readily available, and produced by reputable authorities—unlike the earliest English "dictionaries." Dictionaries also reflect the beliefs of both society and lexicographers and can affect individuals, groups, and sometimes society itself. In short, it is possible to check your spelling with a dictionary, but it is also possible to obtain much more from dictionaries if we understand what they *are* and what they sometimes *do*.

The first English dictionaries appeared in the seventeenth century, long after English entered what is usually called its "modern" period. (For a discussion of the evolution of English, see Paul Roberts's "A Brief History of English," beginning on page 182.) However, these books were not like the dictionaries we use today. Rather, they were vocabularies devoted to "hard words," words that common, unsophisticated people were supposed to need to learn if they aspired to a higher social status. The titles of two such works denote their limited contents: Cockeram's *English Dictionarie: or, an Interpreter of Hard English Words* (1623) and Elisha Coles's *An English Dictionary Explaining Difficult Terms* (1676). These works are far removed from the dictionaries we accept today.

In 1755, Samuel Johnson published his *English Dictionary*, and the English language had its first truly modern dictionary. Johnson toiled virtually alone for nine years to produce this massive work. To his credit, it remained the standard for over a hundred years. Although its definitions sometimes reflected Johnson's idiosyncrasies and biases, the *English Dictionary* was the first to follow two principles that we now expect in any dictionary: It sought to include *all* important words, not just "hard" words, and it reflected the language itself, not merely the editor's own beliefs or storehouse of knowledge. Johnson studied how English was used by English-speaking people—first; then he wrote his definitions. Thus, the dictionary served as a report of findings. This is the general procedure lexicographers follow today, but Johnson was the first to use it consistently. In doing so, he secured his place as the pre-eminent English lexicographer. In the two hundred years since Johnson's contribution, many other well-respected dictionaries have appeared, including the monumental *Oxford English Dictionary* (completed in 1928) and in America, Noah Webster's *An American Dictionary of the English Language* (1828). Today, the name *Webster* is nearly synonymous with the word *dictionary*. We owe a great debt to Johnson, Webster, and others for the work they accomplished.

The dictionaries we now use are produced by committees and editorial boards (and even computers have a role in lexicography), so no one person can take sole credit for a dictionary's contents. Lexicography is less personal, but we like to think, it gives us dictionaries that are more authoritative—more reliable in their choice of words and in what they say about those words. A dictionary's authority results, in part, from the principles that guide those who write the dictionary, and those principles form one of the issues addressed by the reading selections in this chapter.

Dictionaries can produce profound effects. We see in Malcolm X's "Get Hold of a Dictionary" how one man's life was transformed because of a dictionary. Dictionaries result from a process of study and evaluation. Anne H. Soukhanov describes this process in "Welcome to the Web of Words: The Lexicographer's Role in Observing and Recording the Changing Language." Michael Olmert's "Points of Origin" conveys one man's delight with the treasury of information available in *The Oxford English Dictionary*, among the best known, most often cited reference works in English. The chapter concludes with Robert Burchfield's "Dictionaries and Ethnic Sensibilities," an essay detailing how whole societies and nations can react to a dictionary's contents, and we see, once again, how dictionaries can have enormous (and often unexpected) ramifications.

The importance of dictionaries can be subtle and spectacular, going far beyond merely telling us how to distinguish *imply* from *infer*. Because they contain carefully selected information, dictionaries are a record of changes in our society. Dictionaries also express beliefs—ours and those of lexicographers; understanding this fact helps us to use dictionaries wisely. And, dictionaries do list standard spellings, too.

Get Hold of a Dictionary

Malcolm X

Many famous people have claimed that books changed their lives. Some cite the Bible; others name literary or philosophical works. But someone saying that a dictionary changed his life might surprise us. That, however, is what Malcolm X asserts in this passage from *The Autobiography of Malcolm X*. Malcolm X spent years in prison for a variety of serious crimes, but, as he explains, he finally found a special freedom in prison—because of a dictionary. He later became a well-known Black Muslim leader, devoting himself to politics and social change; he was murdered in 1965 while giving a speech.

1 I've never been one for inaction. Everything I've ever felt strongly about, I've done something about. I guess that's why, unable to do anything else, I soon began writing to people I had known in the hustling world, such as Sammy the Pimp, John Hughes, the gambling house owner, the thief Jumpsteady, and several dope peddlers. I wrote them all about Allah and Islam and Mr. Elijah Muhammad. I had no idea where most of them lived. I addressed their letters in care of the Harlem or Roxbury bars and clubs where I'd known them.

2 I never got a single reply. The average hustler and criminal was too uneducated to write a letter. I have known many slick sharp-looking hustlers, who would have you think they had an interest in Wall Street; privately, they would get someone else to read a letter if they received one. Besides, neither would I have replied to anyone writing me something as wild as "the white man is the devil."

3 What certainly went on the Harlem and Roxbury wires was that Detroit Red was going crazy in stir, or else he was trying some hype to shake up the warden's office.

4 During the years that I stayed in the Norfolk Prison Colony, never did any official directly say anything to me about those letters, although, of course, they all passed through the prison censorship. I'm sure, however, they monitored what I wrote to add to the files which every state and federal prison keeps on the conversion of Negro inmates by the teachings of Mr. Elijah Muhammad.

5 But at that time, I felt that the real reason was that the white man knew that he was the devil.

6 Later on, I even wrote to the Mayor of Boston, to the Governor of Massachusetts, and to Harry S Truman. They never answered; they probably never even saw my letters. I handscratched to them how the white

man's society was responsible for the black man's condition in this wilderness of North America.

7   It was because of my letters that I happened to stumble upon starting to acquire some kind of a homemade education.

8   I became increasingly frustrated at not being able to express what I wanted to convey in letters that I wrote, especially those to Mr. Elijah Muhammad. In the street, I had been the most articulate hustler out there—I had commanded attention when I said something. But now, trying to write simple English, I not only wasn't articulate, I wasn't even functional. How would I sound writing in slang, the way I would *say* it, something such as, "Look, daddy, let me pull your coat about a cat. Elijah Muhammad—"

9   Many who today hear me somewhere in person, or on television, or those who read something I've said, will think I went to school far beyond the eighth grade. This impression is due entirely to my prison studies.

10   It had really begun back in the Charlestown Prison, when Bimbi first made me feel envy of his stock of knowledge. Bimbi had always taken charge of any conversation he was in, and I had tried to emulate him. But every book I picked up had few sentences which didn't contain anywhere from one to nearly all of the words that might as well have been in Chinese. When I just skipped those words, of course, I really ended up with little idea of what the book said. So I had come to the Norfolk Prison Colony still going through only book-reading motions. Pretty soon, I would have quit even these motions, unless I had received the motivation that I did.

11   I saw that the best thing I could do was get hold of a dictionary—to study, to learn some words. I was lucky enough to reason also that I should try to improve my penmanship. It was sad. I couldn't even write in a straight line. It was both ideas together that moved me to request a dictionary along with some tablets and pencils from the Norfolk Prison Colony school.

12   I spent two days just riffling uncertainly through the dictionary's pages. I'd never realized so many words existed! I didn't know *which* words I needed to learn. Finally, just to start some kind of action, I began copying.

13   In my slow, painstaking, ragged handwriting, I copied into my tablet everything printed on that first page, down to the punctuation marks.

14   I believe it took me a day. Then, aloud, I read back, to myself, everything I'd written on the tablet. Over and over, aloud, to myself, I read my own handwriting.

15   I woke up the next morning, thinking about those words—immensely proud to realize that not only had I written so much at one time, but I'd written words that I never knew were in the world. Moreover, with a little effort, I also could remember what many of these words meant. I reviewed

the words whose meanings I didn't remember. Funny thing, from the dictionary first page right now, that "aardvark" springs to my mind. The dictionary had a picture of it, a long-tailed, long-eared burrowing African mammal, which lives off termites caught by sticking out its tongue as an anteater does for ants.

16   I was so fascinated that I went on—I copied the dictionary's next page. And the same experience came when I studied that. With every succeeding page, I also learned of people and places and events from history. Actually the dictionary is like a miniature encyclopedia. Finally the dictionary's A section had filled a whole tablet—and I went on into the B's. That was the way I started copying what eventually became the entire dictionary. It went a lot faster after so much practice helped me pick up handwriting speed. Between what I wrote in my tablet, and writing letters, during the rest of my time in prison I would guess I wrote a million words.

17   I suppose it was inevitable that as my word-base broadened, I could for the first time pick up a book and read and now begin to understand what the book was saying. Anyone who has read a great deal can imagine the new world that opened. Let me tell you something: from then until I left that prison, in every free moment I had, if I was not reading in the library, I was reading on my bunk. You couldn't have gotten me out of books with a wedge. Between Mr. Muhammad's teachings, my correspondence, my visitors . . . and my reading of books, months passed without my even thinking about being imprisoned. In fact, up to then, I never had been so truly free in my life.

**Questions
on Content**

1. Why did Malcolm X begin writing letters to people he had known in the hustling world?

2. Malcolm X says that not only wasn't he articulate, he wasn't even functional (paragraph 8). What distinction is he making between *articulate* and *functional?*

3. What motivated Malcolm X to turn to a dictionary? What two goals did he hope the dictionary would help him achieve?

4. Malcolm X says that he finally, paradoxically, achieved freedom while in prison. What does he mean?

Questions
on Structure
and Style

5. The point of view often controls the tone and style of a piece of writing. What features of the tone and style are influenced by Malcolm X's use of the first person?

6. Why is the relatively simple level of diction appropriate for this selection?

7. What does this selection suggest to you about learning to write more effectively? Are any of Malcolm X's experiences relevant for most writing students?

8. The author refers to such people as Bimbi and Jumpsteady. These references mean little to most readers, but they strengthen the essay. Why?

Assignments

1. Malcolm X suggests that a dictionary is like a miniature encyclopedia. Locate *Webster's Third International Dictionary* (found in most libraries) and two reputable desk dictionaries, and examine the entries for the following words:

   fool   lacrosse   ottoman

   Then check a good encyclopedia to see what it reveals about these words. How does the dictionary information compare with that found in the encyclopedia? What do the dictionaries reveal that the encyclopedia does not? What about the reverse?

2. This essay dramatizes something we have all felt: frustration because of inadequate language skills. Write about a time when you were frustrated because your language skills seemed inadequate.

3. Clearly, the dictionary had a significant effect on Malcolm X's life. Write an essay describing how a single book, incident, or person changed the way you think about your own life.

Welcome to the Web of Words: The Lexicographer's Role in Observing and Recording the Changing Language

Anne H. Soukhanov

Anne Soukhanov is executive editor of the American Heritage dictionaries and author of the "Word Watch" column in the *Atlantic*. In the following selection, prepared exclusively for this edition of *About Language*, Soukhanov explains some of the ways that lexicographers gather evidence of how English speakers and writers are using the language over time—evidence that forms the bedrock of dictionary development.

1   *These are revolutionary times, not only in terms of threats of nuclear war, hijackings, terrorism, inner-city violence and all the rest, but in attitudes to language.*[1]

We see our function as marshalling, recording, setting down the good, the bad, the indifferent, the sacred and the profane, for ourselves and for future generations.[2]

—*Robert W. Burchfield*
Chief Editor
The OED Supplements

2   One of the questions most often asked of dictionary editors is this: How do you decide whether or not to enter a word in the dictionary? Since it is the editors' responsibility to record the language as it is actually used over the long term by a broad group of educated native English speakers and writers in diverse sources, the editors' decisions to include or exclude words or senses of words depend largely on the number of printed citations at hand, citations attesting to the use of the words over a considerable length of time in various sources.

[1] "The Long Trek to *Zyrian*," *The Bookseller*, 22 March 1986.

[2] "The Art of the Lexicographer," a paper given to the Royal Society, 26 February 1975.

3   As we all know, the English language is not a static entity; it changes through the years, and at times from day to day. New words and new senses of existing words come and go, patterns of usage change, spellings can and do vary, and frequency of occurrence fluctuates. In order to stay abreast of linguistic change, dictionary editors maintain ongoing citation-accrual programs. At Houghton Mifflin we have a combined electronic and manual citation program, and it is with the manual side that we are concerned here.

A Web of Words . . . Old and New

4   lobola . . . death-qualify . . . homeschooler . . . greenfield site . . . infotainment . . . jogger's paw . . . narcokleptocracy . . . liger . . . colposcope . . . mahosker . . . accessory apartment . . . blurgit . . . camelback . . . glaciation . . . Marfan's Syndrome . . . WORM . . . electronic anklet . . . go-fast . . . crack . . . inscape . . . liberation theology . . . secular humanism . . . motor mall . . . netback . . . open adoption . . . psychographics . . . retro-futurist . . . rubber mirror . . . thalassotherapy . . . airturbo-ramjet . . . doo-doo . . . Laffer curve . . . privatize . . . trivialize . . . fictionalize . . . fetishize . . . finalize . . . hopefully . . . disemploy . . . zebu . . . Arctic haze . . . birthparent . . . gastric balloon . . . Memphis . . . phreak . . . punch perm . . . durance vile . . . urban wind . . . agrimation . . . steel-collar . . . robotics . . . gerontocrat . . . technopeasant . . . prequel . . . back-story . . . genetic engineering . . . bumfuzzle . . . urgi-center . . . factoid . . . zine . . . gimme cap . . . newszak . . . inter-feron . . . interleukin . . . overargue . . . performance medicine . . . sandhog . . . sneezeweed . . . buffalo grass . . . space law . . . sull up . . . tamperable . . . yob . . . wholistic . . . ashcake . . . bio-dot . . . boiled baby . . . erumpent . . . façadism . . . kanban . . . maglev . . . heresthetics . . . plutography . . . Quannie . . . ruburb . . . scramjet . . . slitz . . . wonky . . . ustulate . . . widdershins . . . lerp . . . contragestive . . .

This random sampling typifies the kinds of words the Houghton Mifflin dictionary editors marked for insertion in the dictionary citation files during the year 1986. Some words are new; others have been in the language since the nineteenth century or earlier. Some words are to be found in our dictionary; others are not. Some words are British; others are examples of American regional English. Some words will be entered in future editions of *The American Heritage Dictionary;* others will not.

What Is a Citation?

5   A citation is an example of a word or phrase along with its surrounding context. Appended to the citation are the name of the writer or speaker, the

title of the source in which the word or phrase appears, the page number of the source, the name of the publishing house if the source is a book, and the publication date. Here is a citation illustrating use of the word *kerblam* by Anne Tyler. This word is not yet entered in *Webster's Third New International Dictionary* (an unabridged book of over 400,000 entries), nor is it to be found in *The American Heritage Dictionary, Second College Edition; Webster's New World Dictionary;* or *Webster's Ninth New Collegiate Dictionary.*

```
kerblam v.


And didn't he think her hair was
hopeless, kerblamming out the
way it did in the slightest bit
of humidity?

Anne Tyler, The Accidental
Tourist
New York: Knopf, 1985 p. 211
```

6   This citation, taken from *Harper's*, illustrates the use of *inscape*, a word not to be found in our dictionary but entered in some others:

```
inscape n.


Aha, the reader may remark, here
is the inscape, the epiphany,
the moment of truth.

Harper's
4/86
p. 64
Madison Bell
```

7   Not only is the citation informative of meaning; it is also an example of what we call a "quotable illustration."

How Do We Accrue Citations?

8   Our editors read and mark a broad group of newspapers, magazines, books, and catalogues for designated periods of time each week. Included in the program are specialist and general publications, fiction and non-fiction, and nationally circulated and regional periodicals.

9   These titles are read and marked on a regular basis: *New Age, American Demographics, New York Times, Wall Street Journal, Newsweek, Time, Business Week, People, Boston, New York, Atlantic, Harper's, Food & Wine, Valley Advocate, TV Guide, Dial, Boston Globe, Christian Science Monitor, Musician, Artist's Magazine, US, Science, Byte, Gourmet, Modern Maturity, Bon Appétit, Foreign Affairs, Town & Country, Vanity Fair, New Republic, National Observer, New England Business, Boston Business, Times Literary Supplement, Smithsonian, New Yorker,* and *Cook's,* among others.

10   Other publications read on a more sporadic basis are: *Berkeley* (CA) *Monthly, Washington Post, New York Daily News, Congressional Quarterly, National Law Journal, ABA Journal, Scientific American, Key Reporter, Academic American, Sports Illustrated, Economist, Saturday Night, American Film, Pace, US Air, Ithaca Journal, Charleston* (SC) *News & Courier, Columbia* (SC) *State, Richmond* (VA) *Times-Dispatch, Chicago Tribune,* and *Los Angeles Times.* When our editors travel they will often read and mark local papers, in-flight magazines, and other material to which we do not have regular access.

11   Here are the titles of some of the books our editors read and marked during the past twelve months. Each book in the list has generated high-quality citations: John Fowles's *A Maggot,* John Le Carré's *A Perfect Spy,* John Updike's *The Witches of Eastwick,* Garrison Keillor's *Lake Wobegon Days,* Jimmy Breslin's *Table Money,* Margaret Atwood's *The Handmaid's Tale,* Louis Auchincloss's *Honorable Men,* Robertson Davies's *What's Bred in the Bone,* Anne Tyler's *The Accidental Tourist,* Nicholas Proffitt's *The Embassy House,* Mario Puzo's *The Sicilian,* Bobbie Ann Mason's *In Country,* Padgett Powell's *Edisto,* Carolyn Chute's *The Beans of Egypt, Maine,* and *Afro-American Folktales: Stories from Black Traditions in the New World* edited by Roger D. Abrahams.

What Kinds of Lexical Items Are Marked in Context?

12   Here is a short list of the types of items we watch for when reading:

- new words not entered in *The American Heritage Dictionary, Second College Edition* (an example is *bazuko,* a cheap cocaine by-product, highly addictive);
- new sense(s) of existing words (an example is *graze,* meaning to make a meal of hors d'oeuvres);
- contexts appropriate to quoted illustration in the dictionary (an example is this quotation from Benno Schmidt: "Yale's greatness carries an urgent need to guard against the fall of excellence into <u>exclusivity</u>, of

refinement into preciousness, of elegance into class and convention," in which the underscored term is the one of prime interest);

- regional American words (*bodacious, tump*);
- examples of new foreign borrowings (*nomenklatura, kanban*);
- meanings delineated within the context of the citations (for example, we look for citations that provide us with information useful later when we must define new or unfamiliar words, especially in technical fields such as medicine);
- usage problems (as an example, if the President of the United States says *squoze* instead of *squeezed* or if a professor of English uses *snuck* instead of *sneaked* in a *New York Times Book Review* piece, we want printed evidence of these and other usage anomalies);
- variations in usage;
- stigmatized words (e.g., words labeled *Slang* and *Informal* in the dictionary; words hitherto regarded as archaic or obsolete; words considered offensive, vulgar, or obscene);
- new abbreviations (e.g., *PAC*);
- prefixes and suffixes;
- variant spellings of the same word (e.g., *withershins* or *widdershins*);
- styling of compounds (solid, hyphened, or open);
- phrasal verb use (e.g., the use and occurrence of two-word verbs such as *back down*);
- idioms (e.g., new and old idiomatic phrases such as *on a roll* and *bite the dust*);
- derived forms (e.g., the adverb *entrepreneurially* and the adjective *entrepreneurial* derived from the noun *entrepreneur*);
- pronunciations, especially of unfamiliar words;
- etymologies (at times the citation will give the known or supposed origin of a word or words).

What Sources Do We *Not* Mark When We Look for These Items?

13   We generally avoid poetry, drama, advertisements, translations, English texts written by nonnative English speakers, ghostwritten material, multi-authored material, and the classics (e.g., Joyce, Hawthorne, Miller). The language of poetry more often than not reflects poetic license, and the language of plays and advertising can be contrived for special effects. Translations may not always reflect the content of the original material. Nonnative English speakers' use of the language can be unidiomatic. With ghosted material and multiauthored matter, the question arises: Who is the real writer? Finally, there is no need to read and mark the classics, for ample citational evidence from them is already to be found in the *OED*,* comprehensive quotation books, and various concordances.

* *Oxford English Dictionary*

The Atlantic [FRANCIS DAVIS]

polystylistic adj.
boisterous adj.
motivic adj.
tintinnabulation n.

zenship in jazz and classical music. Significantly, Ganelin is the musical director for the Russian Dramatic Theater in Vilnius, Lithuania; Chekasin teaches music at the Vilnius Conservatory; and Tarasov, though self-taught, works full time with the Lithuanian State Symphony Orchestra. These are jobs of the sort that vanguard musicians in the West either have or covet. [Vyacheslav] Ganelin has described the music he outlines for the trio as "polystylistic," a way of saying that he juxtaposes not only jazz from various eras but classical and world folk music as well, in harmony with the recent eclectic tendencies of Western avant-garde composers. Ganelin, Chekasin, and Tarasov are said to have declined an invitation to jam with American musicians at a reception at Gracie Mansion during their tour, apparently fearful of being misjudged for their lack of intimacy with bebop and the blues. I know many younger American musicians who might also have declined the invitation, for the same reason.

Although the Ganelin Trio's music has a boisterous, at times even bellicose, tone, in all of the sets I heard them play the emphasis was on disciplined motivic exposition rather than spontaneous expression. Each set consisted of one Ganelin opus that blurred the distinction between composition and improvisation, much as do the works that Cecil Taylor and his disciples play. As a pianist, Ganelin resembled Taylor in stamina, speed, and intensity, though his lyrical passages were unabashedly rhapsodic, more akin to the musings of Keith Jarrett or the Romantic flourishes of Ganelin's countrymen Sergei Rachmaninoff and Vladimir Horowitz. Ganelin's percussive density freed Tarasov to concentrate on tintinnabulation rather than propulsion, and the drummer tapped out bewitching rhythms on every object he laid his hands on—bells, shakers, chimes, even a tin water cup, in addition to his traps. From time to time Ganelin and Chekasin also picked up small percussion instruments and a variety of pots and pans, in a manner reminiscent of the Art Ensemble of Chicago and the other black groups affiliated with the Association for the Advancement of Creative Musicians, albeit without the African signification.

Like most of these Chicagoans, Ganelin and Chekasin are multi-instrumentalists. In fact, they often play two or more instruments simultaneously,

Ganelin producing chimerical bass lines and atmospheric special effects from a variety of small electronic keyboards that he keeps stacked atop the piano, à la Sun Ra, and Chekasin creating skewered overtones by blowing through two saxophones at once, à la Rahsaan Roland Kirk. (Chekasin plays with a crazed vehemence suggestive of the late Albert Ayler and the German avant-gardist Peter Brötzmann.)

There is an air of post-Beckett theatricality to the Ganelin Trio's multi-instrumentalism, a suggestion of mime in Chekasin's arm-waving and arrhythmic foot-stomping, and a touch of buffoonery in their send-up of "Mack the Knife," the tune that they offered as an encore both times I heard them. In this last respect, as in many others, they bear greater similarity to European outfits like the Willem Breuker Kollektief and the Misha Mengelberg–Han Bennink Duo than to musically comparable black American groups, many of whom still associate broad humor with Uncle Tom. back=number v. Despite these many points of comparison to Western counterparts, there was nothing back-numbered or secondhand about the Ganelin Trio's brand of jazz. The source of the trio's inventiveness is hard to place. In the absence of recognizable Soviet folk interpolations or statements of purpose from the musicians themselves, one has to accept on faith the contention of Leo Feigin and the Ganelin Trio's other champions that their music owes its special fervor to its courageous, if tacit, rejection of Soviet social realism in favor of the suppressed Slavic penchant for abstraction.

THE GANELIN TRIO'S North American tour received more publicity than any other event in jazz this summer, with the possible exception of Benny Goodman's death. There was even attention from *The Today Show* and *Entertainment Tonight*, two television programs not usually hospitable to the jazz avant-garde. As a result of this coverage and the natural curiosity surrounding any Soviet export, the Ganelin Trio's concerts drew many ticket buyers previously unexposed to avant-garde jazz, which probably explains why—in Philadelphia in particular, but even in San Francisco, where the Rova Saxophone Quartet, an avant-garde group with its own local following, was also on the bill—there were audible sighs of relief followed by loud bursts of applause

free-form adj.
whitey n. [note occurrence]

whenever the musicians happened into a steady four beats per measure.

Some American jazz critics suggested in their reviews of the concerts that the Ganelin Trio might pique interest in homegrown avant-gardists. This is an outcome much to be desired but one that strikes me as improbable, for reasons summed up in the reaction of a friend of mine, who thinks of herself as liking jazz though she rarely buys records or visits clubs. "I'm glad I heard them, but I wouldn't want to hear them again, and I do wish they had played a little more American jazz," she told me—and I could guess that her response to Cecil Taylor, Anthony Braxton, or the Art Ensemble of Chicago might have been much the same. Inasmuch as novice listeners often mistake passion for anger in free-form jazz, many of those in the predominantly white crowds who showed up to hear the Ganelin Trio probably felt less threatened in the presence of comrades (perceived target: Soviet bureaucracy) than they would have in the presence of brothers (perceived target: whitey).

Less than a week after the Ganelin Trio returned to the USSR, an episode of the BBC series *Comrades*, shown here on PBS last summer, was devoted to the tribulations of Sergei Kuryokhin, a self-absorbed Leningrad-based avant-garde jazz musician who has begun to toy with rock-and-roll. Much was made of the fact that Kuryokhin was "unofficial"—that is, not a sanctioned member of the Composers' Union (unlike Ganelin), and therefore not permitted to record for Melodiya or to advertise his concerts, except by word of mouth.

What was not mentioned but perhaps should have been, if only in the panel discussion that followed, was that jazz visionaries are also unofficial in the United States, at least in the sense that they are caught between popular culture and the fine arts, unequipped to compete for the consumer dollar yet allocated a fraction of the institutional funding lavished on avant-gardists in other disciplines. Kuryokhin probably has a better chance of eventually recording for Melodiya than the typical American avant-garde jazz musician has of recording for CBS or any of the other corporate labels. If anything, the Ganelin Trio's example proves that the Soviet jazz avant-garde has been more successful in locating a mass following. It is impossible to imagine an album by David Murray or the World Saxophone Quartet

[NOVEMBER 1986]   [P. 127]

An example of marked text.

The Mechanics of Marking

14 Our editors always try to mark with a copy of *The American Heritage Dictionary, Second College Edition* close at hand. In this way they can determine whether a word or a sense of a word is in the dictionary, whether a particular idiom is entered in the dictionary and where, whether a particular spelling variant is entered and how, among other things.

15 When we decide to mark a particular item, we

- underscore the term in question;
- put a check mark in the margin beside each underscored term;
- write the base form of the term in the margin with the correct part of speech (e.g., if *squoze* has been underscored in the text, the editor writes *squeeze v.—squoze* in the margin);
- surround the selected context with angle brackets <>;
- ensure the inclusion of all publication data;
- ensure that the speaker's name as well as the author's name is included on the citation if it is a quoted illustration.

Word Watching at Work

16 Here are some examples of trial definitions of relatively new words and senses, written on the basis of citational evidence. These entries, representing a cross-section of productive linguistic processes such as compounding, blending, borrowing, eponymy, back-formation, and functional shift, appeared at various times in the "Word Watch" column of the *Atlantic*:

agita *noun*, acid indigestion: "He wrote funny songs. . . . One was about cooking scungilli, or conch, an Italian delicacy. Another was about the acid indigestion, *agita*, that can afflict those who indulge in too much good Italian food" (*New York Times*). "No wonder Christopher Columbus sailed to America—why get *agita* with Alitalia?" (*Adweek*). BACKGROUND: Our earliest citation for *agita* is a 1982 article in *The New York Times* in which Arthur Perfall, a spokesman for the MTA, was quoted thus: "Boring, maybe, but nice. . . . No running around, no *agita*. Nice." Professor Luigi Ballerini, of the Department of Italian at New York University, believes that *agita*, an Italian-American word, comes from the Italian *acidità*, a technical term meaning "acidity." Apparently, the word is gaining popularity: "Enid is going to give them such *agita*! I would tell them to change their telephone number and not give her the new one," Carol Burnett said in the February 20, 1984, issue of *People*, forecasting events on the soap opera *All My Children*. In Woody Allen's *Broadway Danny Rose*, an entertainer speaks of "*agita* in the panza*," which can be translated as "acid in the paunch." *Agita* is pronounced äj′·ĭ·tǝ.

blaff *noun,* a West Indian stew consisting of fish or, occasionally, pork, seasonings such as lime and garlic, and often fruits and vegetables: "Stuffed crabs, crayfish dishes, a fish stew called *blaff*, and acras, or hot fish fritters, are among the specialties served in the Creole restaurants [of the Caribbean]" (*The New York Times*).
BACKGROUND: Blaff is of interest not only because it is beginning to appear on American menus but also because it illustrates the dangers inherent in basing etymological judgments solely on printed citational evidence. Our citation from the *Times,* and another from the *Washington Post,* suggests that the word, used chiefly in Guadeloupe (French West Indies), is "imitative"—spelled to reflect the sound made when a fish is plunged into boiling water or oil. Professor S. R. R. Allsopp, of the University of the West Indies at Cave Hill, Bridgetown, Barbados, disagrees. Allsopp, who is the coordinator of the Caribbean Lexicography Project and the compiler of the *Dictionary of Caribbean English & Usage,* writes that "*blaff* is likely formed from *braff* by way of a shift from *r* to *l*, a common linguistic occurrence. *Braff* is the form that occurs in Dominica, a neighbor of Guadeloupe. . . . In Grenada the same is called *fish-broff*." Allsopp adds: "Both *braff* and *broff* derive from English *broth* [and show] the influence of London cockney (i.e., the shift from *th* to *f*), of which some examples occur in Dickens."

death qualify *or* **death-qualify** *verb,* to exclude, during the process of jury selection, opponents of the death penalty from impanelment on a jury. "We are constrained to point out what we believe to be several serious flaws in the evidence upon which the courts below reached the conclusion that 'death qualification' produces conviction-prone juries. . . . We hold, nonetheless, that the Constitution does not prohibit the states from *death-qualifying* juries in capital cases" (Supreme Court Justice William H. Rehnquist).
BACKGROUND: This compound is one of a class formed by juxtaposing a noun with a verb, as is the case with the terms *plea bargain, board certify, judge shop, profit take,* and *income switch.* It exhibits strong signs of making its way into the language, for we already have examples of the use of adjectival and noun forms.

dis *verb, slang,* to exhibit disrespect toward: "The victim, according to detectives, made the mistake of irritating Nuke at a party. 'He *dissed* him,' Sergeant Croissant said, using the street term for acting disrespectfully" (*The New York Times*).
BACKGROUND: Much has happened to the verb *disrespect* since the time of its first attested appearance, in 1614, seventeen years before the emergence of the noun. One might reasonably assume that *dis,* a clipped form of this verb, would never gain entry in a reputable dictionary. But consider *sus* (also spelled *suss*), a chiefly British

slang word that has worked its way into both the Supplement to the *Oxford English Dictionary* and *12,000 Words,* a supplement to *Webster's Third New International Dictionary.* The noun *sus,* abbreviated from *suspicion* or from *suspect,* depending on context, goes back to the mid-1930s and can mean "suspicion of criminal behavior" or "a criminal suspect." It has sustained widespread attributive use by the British in locutions such as *sus law, sus case,* and *sus charge.* The verb, now most often spelled *suss* and going back only as far as the mid-1950s, can mean "to suspect (someone) of a crime," "to feel that an event is likely to occur; surmise," or, in combination with *out,* "to discover the truth about; figure out." We have citations for the noun and the verb from *Vanity Fair,* the *Los Angeles Times, People, The Economist,* and the *Manchester Guardian Weekly.* This 1987 citation from *The Financial Times* is typical: "We had the inveterate gambler *sussed* out: he was a self-punishing neurotic who played in order to lose." Another indicator of the staying power of *sus* is the emergence of the adjective *sussy,* defined as "suspicious" by Jonathon Green in his *Slang Thesaurus.* Another noun and verb, formed in the same manner as *sus* and *dis,* and now a fixture in English, is *sub,* meaning "a substitute" or "to act as a substitute."

impitoyable *noun,* a large, typically lead-crystal wine-tasting glass configured so

as to enhance taste and amplify aroma: "The new *impitoyable* . . . lead crystal glasses are weirdly shaped indeed. At a recent private tasting nearly half the guests showed up with *impitoyables*" (*Valley Advocate*, Hatfield, Mass.).
BACKGROUND: For those who are ruthlessly honest in their judgments about wine, this French borrowing is particularly apropos. In French the adjective *impitoyable*, pronounced /ēpitwájabl/, means "pitiless, unpitying, unmerciful, unsparing." In French, as well as in English, the word can be used as a noun: "You'll want *Les impitoyables* ('the pitiless'), designed to concentrate odors" (*New York Times*). The *Valley Advocate*'s wine adviser, Richard M. Gold, explains that the glasses are made in four shapes for four kinds of wine: a giant brandy snifter for young red wines, an enormous tulip-shaped glass for old red wines, a flute with a rippled interior surface that stimulates bubble formation for champagnes, and a tall chimney-shaped glass for white wines. The great size of the glasses allows more oxygen to reach the wine when it is swirled. All the glasses have narrow mouths, to concentrate aroma during tasting. The word *impitoyable* is not yet completely naturalized into English, and usually appears either in italics or within quotation marks.

incent *verb*, to stimulate to action; provide incentive for or to: "The government felt that we needed to *incent* activity which

is highly risky" (Edmund Pratt, the CEO of Pfizer, on *The MacNeil/Lehrer NewsHour*).
BACKGROUND: The verb *incent* is a back-formation from *incentive*. A back-formation is a new word created by removing from an existing word a true affix or an element mistakenly thought to be an affix. This process, which reverses the more usual trend of word formation by deleting, rather than adding, elements, is frowned upon by many linguistic conservatives—sometimes, as perhaps in this case, for good reason. But as Roy Copperud writes in *Usage and Style: The Consensus*, "Usefulness is what wins back-formation acceptance" over time. Examples of back-formations that have gained widespread acceptance are *edit*, formed from *editor*; *sedate*, from *sedative*; *televise*, from *television*; *diagnose*, from *diagnosis*; and *donate*, from *donation*. Strangely enough, *incentive* has spawned yet another verb, *incentivize*, which is sure to offend the sensibilities of many English-speakers. Overuse of the very productive suffix -*ize* to create coinages such as *concretize*, *envisionize*, and *audiblize* may offend both the eye and the ear. Nevertheless, critics would not turn a hair at *symbolize, criticize, formalize, hospitalize, publicize, nationalize, popularize, modernize, epitomize,* or *rationalize*, ten words that have been extant for a combined total of 2,505 years.

jogger's paw *noun*, sore pads on dogs that accom-

pany their owners while jogging, caused by hot surfaces and preventable by keeping the dogs off asphalt and concrete in hot weather: "In addition to their ankle sprains and shinsplints, joggers have a new affliction they can commiserate about: the heartbreak of *jogger's paw*. As more runners take Fido along to relieve the boredom of long jaunts through the city, veterinarians report a surge in painful burns on the foot pads of jogging dogs" (*The Wall Street Journal*).
BACKGROUND: The term *jogger's paw* is an example of a relatively small subclass of English compounds made up of a possessive noun (the one experiencing a condition, which is often but not always a malady) and another noun (the physiological site or a characteristic sign or symptom of the condition). This compounding process is evident especially in the language of medicine, particularly sports and performance medicine: *pitcher's arm, swimmer's ear, athlete's foot, guitarist's nipple, diver's palsy, runner's high,* and *harpist's cramp* are but a few examples, not to mention *gin-drinker's liver, smoker's cough, writer's cramp,* and *housemaid's knee.*

mahosker *noun*, money, especially a paycheck: " 'The *mahosker* isn't here. It don't come until later.' 'The what?' 'The checks. The company don't bring them here until after two' " (Jimmy Breslin, *Table Money*, Ticknor & Fields, 1986).

BACKGROUND: Jimmy Breslin says that *mahosker* means essentially "anything heavy—power, money, even a badge— or anything conferring power. . . . If a cop goes into a bar and holds up a badge, saying, 'This is the real mahosker,' he might mean 'Here's the power, the badge. Now where's the drink?' " He also suggested a Hebrew or a Yiddish origin for the word. Dr. Joseph Malone, of the Department of Linguistics, Barnard College, who is a well-known authority on New York dialects and a specialist in Gaelic, originally suspected that *mahosker*, with a silent *r* (exhibiting the New Yorker's *r*-dropping pronunciation), "might reflect Irish *mo thosca*, literally 'my business,' with connotations not far from those that the Italian *cosa nostra*, 'our thing,' has developed." Malone later encountered the word *makhzoke* in *Harkavy's Pocket Dictionary*, a lexicon of New York Yiddish terms, published in 1900. This word means "business; dealings." The similar pronunciations and the not too divergent meanings of the separate Irish and Yiddish words seem to have converged in the English form *mahosker*. Malone says the odds are "around 85 percent that either the Irish or the Yiddish etymology is right on the nose, or at least glancing one nostril" and that the odds for a dual Irish-Yiddish etymology are "better than 15 percent but worse than 85 percent," given the social mingling among the two groups of speakers.

mamou *noun,* something very big or important, such as a key objective or a crucial maneuver fraught with risk. "It was becoming clear that we needed to do something bigger— much bigger. It was time for the big *mamou*" (T. Boone Pickens, Jr., *Boone*). BACKGROUND: It is possible that the meaning of *mamou* in this sense is derived from the name of the Louisiana town Mamou, which is renowned as the Cajun Music Capital of the World and calls itself the home of the first and most authentic Mardi Gras. The town was immortalized as "the Big Mamou" in "La Chanson des Mardi-Gras." The origin of *mamou* itself is unknown. An article that appeared in *The Mamou Acadian Press* in 1986 states, "There are many stories about the name MAMOU. One was the legendary Indian, Chief Mamou. It is certain that [the] vast prairie [in southwestern Louisiana, consisting of more than 1.2 million acres] was known as Mamou Prairie as far back as the 1700s and that the Anglo-Americans first called it the 'Mammouth Prairie' because of its immense size. And when the Frenchmen came they called it 'Mamou' for mammouth." There is also a line of possible connection between *mamou* and the French words *mammouth* for "mammoth" and *mamelu*, meaning a person with sharply pronounced breasts, as in *une grosse mamelue*. Frederic G. Cassidy, the chief editor of the *Dictionary of American Regional English*, said in a letter that he was "pretty

sure that *mamou* is French." He added, "To me, *mamou* is a baby-talk [hypocristic] variant of French *maman*, parallel to our *mamma*, British *mummy*, etc. Used by adults, these terms of affection often become ironic or even satiric, as in our use of 'What a mamma,' 'She's a big mamma.' The French do this too. I'd easily dismiss *mammouth* and *mamelu*, which would make *big* redundant."

playtza *noun,* a method of body toning and relaxation in which a person is beaten gently with oak leaves and then usually takes a few minutes of steam followed by a sauna: "After a Turkish bath, have any remaining cares driven away by a Shiatsu massage, a Swiss needle shower, or the Bulgarian oak *playtza*" (*Business Week*). BACKGROUND: Here is a retrospective on a word that appeared in this column in March of 1987. At the time, we said that the background of *playtza* was "obscure" and that the context of the single citation in our files suggested the possibility of a Bulgarian connection. A number of readers subsequently suggested that *playtza* comes from a Yiddish word meaning variously "shoulder," "the shoulders," "the upper back." Several others suggested Polish and Russian etymologies. We asked Marvin Herzog, a professor of Yiddish studies and linguistics at Columbia University and the editor-in-chief of *The Great Dictionary of the Yiddish*

Language, to adjudicate the matter. Here is his response:

"The word *playtza* is surely derived directly from Yiddish *pleytse*—'back,' 'shoulder.' The Yiddish word, in turn, is derived from the Polish plural form *plecy*, meaning i) 'back,' 'shoulders,' and ii) 'protection' (i.e., 'pull') and 'patronage.'

"What of possible Slavic sources other than Polish? Most, or perhaps all, of the Slavic languages have a form cognate with Polish *plecy*. They are all presumed to derive from the reconstructed Common Slavic *pletje*. Nevertheless, Bulgarian is the least likely source of Slavic influence on Yiddish and an unlikely source of the word in English, as well. Russian influence on Yiddish is relatively late and really quite meager. It's no rival for Polish.

"The Yiddish expression *untershteln a pleytse* means 'to lend a hand.' I'm pleased to have been able to do that in this case."

skosh *noun,* a small amount; a little bit. "This is a well-plotted, economical thriller. Although the beginning is a *skosh* slow, [the author] picks up the pace" (*Los Angeles Times*). BACKGROUND: This word, borrowed from the Japanese term *sukoshi,* meaning "a tiny amount," goes back in English at least to the Korean War. *Skosh* (pronounced skōsh), has been used by a major clothing manufacturer in its advertising, as is indicated by this citation from a 1982 issue of *U.S. News & World Report:*

"Levi Strauss, which offers adults a '*skosh* more room' in jeans, is one firm taking aim at the maturing market." A recent citation from *Red Storm Rising*, by Tom Clancy, attests to a new, prepositional use of *skosh*, the meaning being "without or almost without": "O'Malley didn't have enough fuel to pursue. 'Stand by, Romeo, we're coming in *skosh* fuel.' "

snide *noun,* a slyly disparaging character, tone, or outlook: " 'Of course,' says Dorothy Sarnoff, an image consultant in New York, . . . 'I changed him [Senator Robert Dole]. He was the best student I ever had. A nice, nice man. I took away his *snide*' " (*Life*). BACKGROUND: *The Oxford English Dictionary* records the noun use of *snide* as far back as 1885, when it meant "counterfeit jewelry; a base coin." Other senses, meaning variously "a swindler, cheat, or liar" and "hypocrisy; pretense; malicious gossip," go back to 1874 and 1902, respectively. The process of "functional shift" from adjective to noun is discussed at some length by Hans Marchand in his book *The Categories and Types of Present-Day English Word-Formation*. Marchand explains that most such changes involve elliptical constructions where the substantive (noun) is absent but can always be readily supplied, as in *advisory* (an advisory *report*), *facial* (a facial *treatment*), *spectacular* (a spectacular *performance, show,* or *program*), *local* (a local *resident*), and *hopeful* (a

hopeful *candidate*). Marchand points out that "some of these elliptic expressions have gained complete independence . . . , as is the case with *musical.* The word is no longer thought of as a shortening of *musical comedy* but has become a substantive in its own right." Still other examples, called "de-adjectivals" by Randolph Quirk, are *natural, final, regular, comic, roast, perennial, annual, monthly, weekly,* and *daily.* Sarnoff's use of *snide* is equivalent to the use of the noun *cool* in the sentence "Don't lose your *cool.*"

Thucydides syndrome *noun,* a symptom complex that begins with influenza and develops into staphylococcal tracheitis, pneumonia, or toxic-shock syndrome, and that often results in death. "MacDonald et al and Sperber and Francis report the emergence (or re-emergence) of *Thucydides syndrome*. . . . it now behooves physicians to be aware of this new entity and to consider quickly the diagnosis of TSS [toxic-shock syndrome] in a patient with influenza whose condition suddenly worsens" (*Journal of the American Medical Association*). BACKGROUND: In October of 1985 Alexander Langmuir, M.D., a former chief of epidemiology at the Centers for Disease Control, postulated in *The New England Journal of Medicine* that the catastrophic plague of Athens (430–427 B.C.), heretofore a medical mystery, and described in detail by Thucydides, was actually influenza complicated by a "toxin-producing strain of non-invasive staphylococcus." Langmuir, the coiner of this new eponym, also predicted that the syndrome might appear again, perhaps as an adjunct to a major flu epidemic. Shortly after Langmuir's article was published, patients exhibiting similar symptoms were seen in a Minnesota epidemic. The symptoms noted by Thucydides included high fever, hoarseness, coughing, sneezing, thirst, vomiting, blisters, amnesia, and peripheral gangrene. It is believed that the Athenians, having been debilitated by the influenza, succumbed to staphylococcal "superinfections" through small cuts or irritated nasal passages. Dr. Langmuir does not maintain that the plague reported by Thucydides was identical to toxic-shock syndrome as we know it; he does think that the "same basic pathogenetic mechanisms were involved."

wallyo *noun,* a young man; a fellow, usually of Italian descent: "I swung open the heavy glass doors. Everywhere I looked was marble and the Great Food hush. I wanted to back out and get a steak and *pommes frites,* but it was too late. I had been seen by the *wallyo* and the madame in the black jeweled sweater" (*New York*). BACKGROUND: This colloquialism, which is used in our one citation to refer to a Parisian wine steward, is often heard in communities with large Italian populations. It is a phonetic respelling into English of the Neapolitan *guaglione,* "street urchin; corner boy." Although some etymologists point to the French *voyou,* "street bum; urchin," from *voie,* "street; road," as the root of *wallyo,* Luigi Ballerini, the director of New York University's department of French and Italian, disagrees. Ballerini firmly believes that the ultimate origin of *guaglione,* and hence *wallyo,* is Latin *ganeo, ganeonis,* "a dissolute man; a frequenter of disreputable inns." If this is so, amelioration has occurred during the word's development from Latin to Italian to English, for, according to Robert Chapman's *New Dictionary of American Slang, wallyo* is "nearly always used affectionately," like "young squirt." Ballerini adds that "*Guaglione*" is the title of a popular 1950s Italian tune in which a young man with a crush on a girl is discouraged from further pursuit of her because of his tender age.

Questions on Content

1. Because she is explaining a process unfamiliar to most of her readers, Soukhanov must sometimes define terms. What is the first term that she defines in her article?

2. The author presents many examples of new words and their proposed definitions. Identify the words that are the result of the following linguistic processes:

   back-formation   eponymy

   borrowing   functional shift

   compounding   regionalism

   corruption   truncation

3. Are you surprised by the complexity of the process that lexicographers use in researching new words? Before reading the selection, what process did you

believe they used? How is the process you imagined different from the actual one?

4. Soukhanov's article does not follow strict essay form as it describes the process of lexicographical research. However, the article is clearly organized. According to what method of development is it organized?

5. How would you describe the author's style in presenting her material?

6. What role does the author play in this article? What role *should* an author play in an article like this one?

1. Scan a newspaper that is distributed only in your geographic area. Look for and mark those terms that appear to be part of your regional dialect. Check the dictionary to see whether or not the terms you've marked are labeled in the dictionary as being regional.

2. Write a one-page "lexical autobiography" in which you describe your past relationship with dictionaries. Explain how Soukhanov's article may have changed your attitude toward dictionaries and how they are compiled.

3. After reading about the process used by lexicographers, what type of person do you believe would be attracted to lexicography? Respond in an essay, being sure to cite evidence from Soukhanov's article to support your inferences.

Points of Origin

Michael Olmert

━━━━━━━━

The Oxford English Dictionary is a monumental work of scholarship (and perseverance). In this article, Michael Olmert discusses the dictionary's origin, contents, and uniqueness, but this is more than a report on the *OED*; he also describes how language delights and surprises him. Through Olmert's experiences, we can see why the *OED* is indispensable for "the congenitally curious," as well as for scholars and writers.

━━━━━━━━

1   On January 18, 1884, at the Clarendon Press, Oxford, appeared the first volume of a work that has become the indispensable tool of writers and wordsmiths, scholars, critics and the congenitally curious for nearly a century. The work's title page proclaimed it as *A New English Dictionary on a Historical Basis,* of which this was to be the first part, covering "A" through "Ant-." Truly, this was a modest start for a project that appeared at the same time as *Huckleberry Finn,* Brahms' Symphony No. 3 and Rodin's *The Burghers of Calais.*

2   The "Historical Basis" noted in the title is what aroused so much interest in the work and what keeps it alive today. That means each word is not only described in all of its meanings, but is also presented in its original context, with a line or two for poetry, a phrase or sentence for prose. Further, the listing for each sense is continued, through time, from the first appearance of the word in the English language to the close of the 19th century.

3   For example, the dictionary begins with the first English use of the word "A," in its meaning as a letter of the alphabet. It appeared around the year 1340, in a poem called "The Pricke of Conscience" by the English mystical writer Richard Rolle of Hampole. The text presents the belief that you can determine a newborn's sex by the sound of its first cry:

> If it be man it says a!a!,
> That the first letter is of the name
> of our forme-fader Adam.
> And if the child a woman be,
> When it is born it says e!e!
> E. is the first letter and the head
> Of the name of Eve. . . .

4   Here is no bland start for the dictionary but a riveting one, reflecting an ancient custom obviously promulgated by nervous fathers outside the

birthing chambers. The entry continues with other significant uses for the letter "A"—Chaucer in 1386, Samuel Butler in 1678, Tennyson in 1842.

5   Each such entry in the dictionary—known today as the *Oxford English Dictionary*, or more simply the *OED*—gives, in addition to the year and author, the quoted work's title and a line or page reference, so the interested reader can fill out the complete context of the passage (although it takes a rather full library).

6   Actually the need for such a dictionary had been seriously discussed since 1857, when the work was first sponsored by Britain's fledgling Philological Society and its early director, F. J. Furnivall. Right off, Furnivall recognized the importance of having reliable texts for the dictionary's quotations and so founded the Early English Text Society in 1864 (which is still publishing more than a century later) and the Chaucer Society in 1868 (now moved to America and the University of Oklahoma in Norman).

7   But a projected work of this scale needed a full-time editor and, by degrees, the job was turned over to a 42-year-old schoolmaster, James A. H. Murray, in 1879. Murray directed the project until his death in 1915. Still, the *OED* was not complete until April 1928, when the last section, "Wise" through "Wyzen," was printed (an easier task, "XYZ," had been completed in October 1921). A catchall supplementary volume for words missed the first time round appeared in 1933.

8   The continuity alone is impressive—54 years of production and 44 years of continuous publication. It is rumored that one of the Oxford University Press compositors set nothing else in type for the whole of his working life. Murray himself gave 38 years of labor to the dictionary and was knighted for his trouble—and achievement—in 1908.

9   One reason the *OED* is so valuable to us today is that so much unalloyed hard work went into its production. Under the direction of the indefatigable Murray and his editorial staff at Oxford, a corps of readers from around the globe undertook to read the entire body of English literature, as well as legal and historical documents, private papers, tracts and other ephemera. Five million such excerpts were collected on thin slips of paper that constantly engulfed the staff; about 1.8 million of those quotations appear in print. The result is a 12-volume work of 15,487 oversize pages, nearly half of them written by Murray.

10   And, oh, what you can do with those pages, where the outcome is so much more than just looking up words! Take as a test case my favorite passage in the films of W. C. Fields. There is a point in *The Bank Dick* where Fields' patience wears thin and he is forced to scowl at his great lummox of a prospective son-in-law (played to insouciant perfection by Grady Sutton): "Don't be a mooncalf. Don't be a jobbernowl. You're not one of those, are you?" Mooncalf. Jobbernowl. We can hear in Fields' intonation that those are terms of derision, but what is their linguistic heritage? Who first capitalized on their load of derisive meaning?

Language (læ·ŋgwĕdӡ), *sb.*[1] Forms: 3-6 lan-gage, (3 langag, 4 longage, langwag, 5 lang-wache, langegage), 3, 5- language. [a. F. *lan-gage* (recorded from 12th c.) = Pr. *leng(u)atge*, *len-gage*, Sp. *lenguaje*, Pg. *linguage(m*, It. *linguaggio* :—pop. L. type **linguāticum*, f. *lingua* tongue, lan-guage (F. *langue*: see LANGUE).
The form with *u*, due to assimilation with the F. *langue*, occurs in AF. writings of the 12th c., and in Eng. from about 1300.]

1. The whole body of words and of methods of combination of words used by a nation, people, or race; a 'tongue'. *Dead language*: a language no longer in vernacular use.

c **1290** *S. E. Leg.* I. 108/55 With men þat onder-stoden hire langage. **1297** R. GLOUC. (Rolls) 1569 Vor in þe langage of rome rane a frogge is. *a* **1300** *Cursor M.* 247 (Gött.) Seldom was for ani chance Englis tong preched in france, Gif we þaim ilkan þair language [*MS. Cott.* langage], And þan do we na vtetrage. *Ibid.*, 6384 (Gött.) Þis mete..þai called it in þair langag man. **1387** TREVISA *Higden* (Rolls) II. 157 Walsche men and Scottes, þat beeþ nouӡt i-medled wiþ oþer nacions, holdeþ wel nyh hir firste longage and speche. *c* **1400** *Apol. Loll.* 32 In a langwag vnknowun ilk man and womman mai rede. *c* **1449** PECOCK *Repr.* I. xii. 66 Thei.. han vsid the hool Bible..in her modris langage. *c* **1450** *Mirour Saluacioun* 3650 Wymmen spak these diuerse lange-gages. **1588** SHAKS. *L. L. L.* v. i. 40 They haue beene at a great feast of Languages, and stolne the scraps. **1589** PUTTENHAM *Eng. Poesie* III. iv. (Arb.) 156 After a speach is fully fashioned to the common vnderstanding, and accepted by consent of a whole countrey and nation, it is called a language. **1699** BENTLEY *Phal.* xiii. 392 Every living Language .. is in perpetual motion and alteration. **1769** *De Foe's Tour Gt. Brit.* (ed. 7) IV. 303 It is called in the Irish Language, I-colm-kill; some call it Iona. **1779-81** JOHNSON *L. P., Addison* Wks. III. 44 A dead language, in which nothing is mean because nothing is familiar. **1823** DE QUINCEY *Lett. Yng. Man* Wks. 1860 XIV. 37 On this Babel of an earth..there are said to be about three thousand languages and jargons. **1845** M. PATTISON *Ess.* (1889) I. 13 In fact, Bede is writing in a dead language, Gregory in a living. **1875** STUBBS *Const. Hist.* II. 414 The use of the English language in the Courts of law was ordered in 1362. *fig.* **1720** GAY *Prol. Dione* 4 Love, devoid of art, Spoke the consenting langutge of the heart. **1812** W. C. BRYANT *Thanatopsis* 3 To him who in the love of Nature holds Com-munion with her visible forms, she speaks A various language.

b. *transf.* Applied to methods of expressing the thoughts, feelings, wants, etc., otherwise than by words. *Finger language* = DACTYLOLOGY. *Lan-guage of flowers*: a method of expressing sentiments by means of flowers.

1606 SHAKS. *Tr. & Cr.* IV. v. 55 Ther's a language in her eye, her cheeke, her lip. **1697** COLLIER *Ess. Mor. Subj.* II. 120 As the language of the Face is universal so 'tis very comprehensive. **1711** STEELE *Spect.* No. 66 ▶ 2 She is utterly a Foreigner to the Language of Looks and Glances. **1827** WHATELY *Logic* (1850) Introd. § 6 A Deaf-mute, before he has been taught a Language, either the Finger-language, or Reading, cannot carry on a train of Reasoning. **1837** *Penny Cycl.* VIII. 282/2 Dactylology must not be confounded with the natural language of the deaf and dumb, which is purely a language of mimic signs. **1876** MOZLEY *Univ. Serm.* vi. 134 All action is .. besides being action, language. **1880** *Times* 23 June 9/5 Teaching the deaf by signs and by finger language. **1894** H. DRUMMOND *Ascent Man* 212 A sign Language is of no use when one savage is at one end of a wood and his wife at the other.

c. *transf.* Applied to the inarticulate sounds used by the lower animals, birds, etc.

1601 SHAKS. *All's Well* IV. i. 22 Choughs language, gabble enough, and good enough. **1667** MILTON *P. L.* VIII. 373 Is not the Earth With various living creatures, and the Aire Replenisht, .. know'st thou not Thir language and thir wayes? **1797** BEWICK *Brit. Birds* (1847) I. p. xxvii, The notes, or as it may with more propriety be called, the language of birds.

2. In generalized sense: Words and the methods of combining them for the expression of thought.

1599 SHAKS. *Much Ado* IV. i. 98 There is not chastitie enough in language, Without offence to vtter them. **1644** MILTON *Educ.* Wks. (1847) 98/2 Language is but the instru-ment conveying to us things useful to be known. **1781** COWPER *Conversat.* 15 So language in the mouths of the adult, .. Too often proves an implement of play. **1841** TRENCH *Parables* ii. (1877) 25 Language is ever needing to be recalled, minted and issued anew. **1862** J. MARTINEAU *Ess.* (1891) IV. 104 Language, that wonderful crystallization of the very flow and spray of thought. **1892** WESTCOTT *Gospel of Life* 186 Language must be to the last inadequate to express the results of perfect observation.

b. Power or faculty of speech; ability to speak a foreign tongue. Now *rare*.

1526 WOLSEY *Let. to Tayler* in Strype *Eccl. Mem.* I. v. 66 A gentleman..who had knowledge of the country and good language to pass. **1601** SHAKS. *All's Well* IV. i. 77, I shall loose my life for want of language. If there be heere German or Dane, Low Dutch, Italian, or French, let him speake to me. **1610** — *Temp.* II. ii. 86 Here is that which will giue language to you Cat; open your mouth. **1790** COWPER *Receipt Mother's Pict.* 1 Oh that those lips had language!

3. The form of words in which a person expresses himself; manner or style of expression. *Bad language*: coarse or vulgar expressions. *Strong language*: expressions indicative of violent or excited feeling.

a **1300** *Cursor M.* 3743 Iacob .. þat es to sai wit right langage, Supplanter als of heritage. *c* **1384** CHAUCER *H. Fame* II. 353 With-outen any subtilite Of speche .. For harde langage and hard matere Is encombrouse for to here Attones. *c* **1425** LYDG. *Assembly Gods* 368 In elo-quence of langage he passyd all the pak. **1430-40** — *Bochas* II. xiii. (1554) 53 a, Though some folke wer large of their langage Amisse to expoune by report. *c* **1489** CAXTON *Blanchardyn* i. 14 For it is sayde in comyn lan-gage, that the goode byrde affeyteth hirself. *a* **1533** LD. BERNERS *Huon* lxix. 236 Come to yᵉ poynt, and vse no more such langage nor suche serymonyes. **1593** SHAKS. *2 Hen. VI*, IV. ix. 45 Be not to rough in termes, For he is fierce, and cannot brooke hard Language. **1611** BIBLE *Ecclus.* vi. 5 Sweet language will multiply friends. **1643** SIR T. BROWNE *Relig. Med.* I. § 5 By his sentence I stand excommunicated: Heretick is the best language he affords me. **1694** PENN *Pref. to G. Fox's Jrnl.* (1827) I. 15 They also used the plain language of Thou and Thee. **1770** *Junius Lett.* 187 They suggest to him a language full of severity and reproach. **1809-10** COLERIDGE *Friend* (1865) 135 These pretended constitutionalists recurred to the language of in-sult. **1849** MACAULAY *Hist. Eng.* vi. II. 118 He lived and died, in the significant language of one of his countrymen, a bad Christian, but a good Protestant. **1855** MOTLEY *Dutch Rep.* II. ii. (1856) 155 In all these interviews he had uniformly used one language: his future wife was to 'live as a Catholic'. **1875** JOWETT *Plato* (ed. 2) V. 348 The language used to a servant ought always to be that of a command.

b. The phraseology or terms of a science, art, profession, etc., or of a class of persons.

1502 *Ord. Crysten Men* (W. de W. 1506) Prol. 4 The swete and fayre langage of theyr phylosophy. **1596** SHAKS. *1 Hen. IV,* II. iv. 21, I can drinke with any Tinker in his owne Language. **1611** — *Cymb.* III. iii. 74 This is not Hunters Language. **1651** HOBBES *Leviath.* III. xxxiv. 207 The words Body, and Spirit, which in the language of the Schools are termed Substances, Corporeall and Incorporeall. **1747** SPENCE *Polymetis* VIII. xv. 243 Those attributes of the Sword, Victory, and Globe, say very plainly (in the language of the statuaries) that [etc.]. **1841** J. R. YOUNG *Math. Dissert.* i. 10 Thus can be expressed in the language of algebra, not only distance but position. **1891** *Speaker* 2 May 532/1 In it metaphysics have again condescended to speak the language of polite letters.

c. The style (of a literary composition); also, the wording (of a document, statute, etc.).

1712 ADDISON *Spect.* No. 285 ¶ 6 It is not therefore sufficient that the Language of an Epic Poem be Perspicuous, unless it be also Sublime. **1781** COWPER *Conversat.* 236 A tale should be judicious, clear, succinct, The language plain. **1886** SIR J. STIRLING in *Law Times Rep.* LV. 283/2 There are two remarks which I desire to make on the language of the Act.

d. *Long language:* † (*a*) verbosity (tr. Gr. μακρολογία; (*b*) language composed of words written in full, as opposed to cipher.

1589 PUTTENHAM *Eng. Poesie* III. xxii. (Arb.) 264 *Macrologia,* or long language, when we vse large clauses or sentences more than is requisite to the matter. **1823** J. BADCOCK *Dom. Amusem.* 34 Those Greeks did not use cypher, but the long language of the country.

e. *vulgar.* Short for *bad language* (see above).

1886 BESANT *Childr. Gibeon* II. xxv, That rude eloquence which is known in Ivy Lane as 'language'. **1893** SELOUS *Trav. S. E. Africa* 3 The sailor..had never ceased to pour out a continuous flood of 'language' all the time.

†4. The act of speaking or talking; the use of speech. *By language:* so to speak. *In language with:* in conversation with. *Without language:* not to make many words. *Obs.*

a **1400** *Cov. Myst.* iv. Noah's *Flood* ii, Affyr Adam without̄yn langage, The secunde fadyr am I [Noe] in fay. *a* **1450** *Knt. de la Tour* (1868) 18 M.˙ fader sette me in langage with her. **1461** *Paston Lett.* No. 393 II. 17, I said I dwelled uppon the cost of the see here, and be langage hit were more necessare to with hold men here than take from hit. **1477** EARL RIVERS (Caxton) *Dictes* 57 One was surer in keping his tunge, than in moche speking, for in moche langage one may lightly erre. **1490** CAXTON *Eneydos* xxviii. 107 Wythout eny more langage dydo .. seased thenne the swerde. **1514** BARCLAY *Cyt. & Uplondyshm.* (Percy Soc.) p. xviii, To morowe of court we may have more language.

†b. That which is said, words, talk, report; *esp.* words expressive of censure or opprobrium. Also *pl.* reports, sayings. *To say language against:* to talk against, speak opprobriously of. *Obs.*

a **1450** *Knt. de la Tour* (1868) 2 And so thei dede bothe deseiue ladies and gentilwomen, and bere forthe diuerse langages on hem. **1465** MARG. PASTON in *P. Lett.* No. 502 II. 188, I hyre moch langage of the demenyng betwene you and herre. **1467** *Mann. & Househ. Exp.* (Roxb.) 172 3e haue mekel on setenge langwache a3enste me, were of I mervel gretely for I have 3effen 3owe no schwsche kawse. **1470–85** MALORY *Arthur* II. xl, Euery daye syre Palomydes

brauled and sayd langage ageynst syr Tristram. **1485** CAXTON *Chas. Gt.* 225 Feragus said in this manere...The valyaunt Rolland was contente ryght wel, & accepted hys langage. **1636** SIR H. BLUNT *Voy. Levant* 33 A Turke .. gave such a Language of our Nation, and threatning to all whom they should light upon, as made me upon all demands profe-se my selfe a Scotchman.

5. A community of people having the same form of speech, a nation. *arch.* [A literalism of translation.]

1388 WYCLIF *Dan.* v. 19 Alle puplis, lynagis, and langagis [1382 tungis]. **1611** BIBLE *Ibid.* **1653** URQUHART *Rabelais* I. x, All people, and all languages and nations.

b. A national division or branch of a religious and military Order, *e. g.* of the Hospitallers.

1727–52 CHAMBERS *Cycl., Language* is also used, in the order of Malta, for *nation.* **1728** MORGAN *Algiers* I. v. 314 Don Raimond Perellos de Roccapoul, of the Language of Aragon,..was elected Grand Master. **1885** *Catholic Dict.* (ed. 3) 413/2 The order [of Hospitallers] ..was divided into eight 'languages', Provence, Auvergne, France, Aragon, Castile, England, Germany, and Italy.

6. *attrib.* and *Comb.* **a.** simple attributive, as *language-capacity, -family, -history, -turn*; **b.** objective, as *language-maker, -teacher*; **language-master,** a teacher of language or languages.

1875 WHITNEY *Life Lang.* 281 Every division of the human race has been long enough in existence for its *language-capacities to work themselves out.* **1891** *Tablet* 29 Aug. 331 The rank it holds among the *language-families of the world.* **1875** WHITNEY *Life Lang.* Pref. 5 Scholars .. versed in the facts of *language-history.* **1607** BREWER *Lingua* III. v. F 2, These same *language makers haue the very quality of colde in their wit, that freezeth all Heterogeneall languages together.* **1712** ADDISON *Spect.* No. 305 ¶ 11 The Third is a sort of *Language-Master,* who is to instruct them in the Style proper for a Foreign Minister in his ordinary Discourse. **1831** T. MOORE *Mem.* (1854) VI. 190 It turned out that what his friend, the language-master, had..been teaching him was Bas-Breton! **1826** PUSEY *Let. to Lloyd* in *Life* (1893) I. v. 97 A *language-teacher gives me lectures .. five times a week. **1803** SOUTHEY *Let. to C. W. W. Wynn* 9 June, In all these modern ballads there is a modernism of thought and *language-turns* to me very perceptible.

Language (læˑŋgwĕdʒ), *v.* [f. LANGUAGE *sb.*] *trans.* To express in language, put into words.

1636 ABP. WILLIAMS *Holy Table* (1637) 95 Learn, Doctour, learn to language this Sacrament from a Prelate of this Church. *a* **1652** J. SMITH *Sel. Disc.* VI. xiii. (1821) 294 The style and manner of languaging all pieces of prophecy. **1655** FULLER *Ch. Hist.* VI. v. False Miracles § 11 Predictions..were languaged in such doubtful Expressions, that they bare a double sense. **1667** WATERHOUSE *Fire Lond.* 185 Seneca has languaged this appositely to us.

b. *transf.* To express (by gesture).

1824 *New Monthly Mag.* X. 196 'Twas languaged by the tell-tale eye.

Hence **Laˑnguaging** *vbl. sb.* In quot. *attrib.*

1875 LOWELL in *N. Amer. Rev.* CXX. 395 It is very likely that Daniel had only the thinking and languaging parts of a poet's outfit.

Language, variant of LANGUID *sb.* (sense 2).

11   Jobbernowl, the *OED* advises us, signifies "a blockish or stupid head; a ludicrous term for the head, usually connoting stupidity." Its first use was in 1599, when John Marston used it in his collection of verse satires called *The Scourge of Villanie*. There, he characterized the very type of a phony poet, the simpleton ballad maker whose "guts are in his brains, huge Jobbernoul,/ Right gurnet's-head; the rest without all soul." Gurnet's-head, we learn elsewhere in the *OED*, is a term of contempt, used with reference to the disproportionate head of a certain fish, the gurnard (of the genus *Trigla*, typically with a large spiny head and armored cheeks).

12   And mooncalf? Shakespeare used it in Act II of *The Tempest* (1611) to mean a misshapen child, a monstrosity, as was his character Caliban: "How now, mooncalf!" Shakespeare's contemporary Ben Jonson used it in a play of 1620 to signify a born fool: "Moone Calves! what Monster is that . . . ?/ Monster? none at all; a very familiar thing, like our foole here on earth." The extension of the word's meaning to suggest one who gazes at the moon, a "mooning," absentminded person, was made by Thomas Middleton in his 1613 play, *No Wit like Woman's:* "One Weatherwise . . . Observes the full and change [of the moon], an arrant moon-calf."

13   The great advantage of the *OED*, of course, is that it shows, dramatically, how some words have been transformed from their former meanings. Pedagogue, for example, originally meant a type of Roman slave who accompanied patrician youths on their walks to school each day. The *OED* derives the word from Greek roots meaning "child-leader." Yet the original pedagogues were in no sense leaders or tutors, but merely escorts who drilled the children as they walked and who often sat in on the day's classes in a vain attempt to improve themselves. Such men became boring, moralistic, platitudinous dolts. In the *OED* entries, one can watch the early use of the English word connoting contempt and hostility (1735: "Cow'd by the ruling Rod, and haughty Frowns of Pedagogues severe"), watered down to the point in comparatively recent times when some educators would actually seek to have the practice of education called "pedagogy."

14   Conversely, the *OED* can make us feel good about the way we use our language. It is comforting to see that the word "decimate," a derivation from the Roman custom of executing every tenth man in a mutinous legion (and a current bête noire of popular commentators on "the decline of the English language," who claim we use the word too loosely) has in fact been very loosely applied since the beginning. In the 17th century, Oliver Cromwell "decimated" the Royalist Cavaliers, the losers in the Great Civil War, merely by forcing them to give up a tenth of their estates to the victorious government. Decimate seems only to have been used "properly" when it was cited by historians referring to the original Roman custom. Only a "scowling pedagogue" would insist that it be strictly reserved for that historical purpose.

15   A particularly attractive word category is represented by the so-called onomatopoetic words, those that imitate actual sounds in nature. Such words had early appearances: mum (1377), buzz (1530), ding-dong (about 1560), to name a few. But my particular favorite is bow-wow, which was not used to stand for the dog itself—only its bark—until around 1800 in a poem by William Cowper, the rural poet. Cowper had earlier written a slight bit of verse that he entitled "On a Spaniel Called Beau, Killing a Young Bird." He then responded with "Beau's Reply," which coined the new usage and still gives us a smile in the bargain:

> Sir, when I flew to seize the bird
>   In spite of your command,
> A louder voice than yours I heard,
>   And harder to withstand . . .
>
> Well knowing him a sacred thing,
>   Not destined to my tooth,
> I only kiss'd his ruffled wing
>   And lick'd the feathers smooth.
>
> Let my obedience then excuse
>   My disobedience now,
> Nor some reproof yourself refuse
>   From your aggrieved bow-wow. . . .

16   In the face of this wealth of detail, the *OED*'s editors were constantly aware that their work would be closely followed by future dictionaries. And it has been. But to put off the truly sedulous apes, the editors, it is rumored, concocted a single spurious word, complete with false etymology and meanings. It may even lie somewhere in those 15,487 pages to this day, a lexicographic time bomb waiting to catch a slavish imitator (as indeed it may already have done). A scholar could spend a lifetime hunting down that word with no more chance of success than a Boy Scout on a "snipe hunt."

**Questions
on Content**

1. What is the single most important feature of the *OED*, and why has it kept the dictionary from becoming obsolete?

2. Olmert says that each quotation in the *OED* includes the author, the year, the quoted work's title, and a line or page reference. This information is included, says Olmert, so that the reader can look

up the quoted source, "although it takes a rather full library" (paragraph 5). What does he mean?

3. The author says that in checking the pages of the *OED*, "the outcome is so much more than just looking up words!" (paragraph 10). What *is* the outcome?

4. Why will the "spurious word" supposedly included in the *OED* serve to "catch" any "slavish imitator" (paragraph 16)?

**Questions
on Structure
and Style**

5. Why does Olmert mention *Huckleberry Finn*, Brahms, and Rodin in the first paragraph?

6. Identify the transitions that link paragraphs 1 to 7.

7. Olmert says that the poem by William Cowper (quoted in paragraph 15) shows us a new usage of the word *bow-wow* and also gives us "a smile in the bargain." Why do we smile?

8. Comment on Olmert's choice of examples of what the *OED* offers. Do you see reasons for choosing *A, mooncalf, pedagogue,* and the others?

Assignments

1. The author says that "the need for such a dictionary [as the *OED*] had been seriously discussed since 1857" (paragraph 6). List three hypothetical but specific instances in which the *OED*, because it traces a word's historical meanings, would be indispensable. For example, if a legal document written in 1750 were discovered to have some present-day importance, the *OED* could help in determining the real intentions of the people who wrote the document.

2. Using *The Oxford English Dictionary*, answer the following questions about the word *murder:*
   A. What are some of the various spellings for the word throughout its history in English?

B.   What is the first recorded use of the word?
C.   Was the word first used as a noun or a verb?
D.   What was the role of secrecy in early defi-
     nitions of *murder?*
E.   What is the earliest recorded figurative use of
     the word?

3.   James A. H. Murray became editor of the *OED* in
     1879. He devoted thirty-eight years to the dictionary
     and wrote nearly half of its 15,487 pages. Think
     about the people you know, and identify someone
     who has worked for years to achieve a personal
     goal, such as training for athletic competition, de-
     veloping an artistic talent, establishing a small busi-
     ness, or attending college at night in pursuit of a
     degree. Write an essay explaining what the person
     did and why he or she persisted for so long. What
     sustains someone in such an undertaking?

Dictionaries and Ethnic Sensibilities

Robert Burchfield

Robert Burchfield is the chief editor of the Oxford English dictionaries. In the following essay, he describes several controversies generated by dictionaries. The most obvious controversies center on words that are considered vulgar or obscene. But definitions themselves carry great social importance, and as Burchfield explains, they can create anger that lexicographers don't anticipate.

1   At the beginning of *Macbeth*, a bleeding sergeant describes how brave Macbeth killed the "merciless" rebel, Macdonwald: "he unseamed him from the nave to th' chaps," that is, from the navel to the jaws, "and fixed his head upon our battlements." It may seem a far cry from the rebellious "kerns and gallow-glasses" of Macdonwald to the persevering scholarship involved in dictionary editing, but the connection will be made clear as I proceed.

2   The head some want to display on the battlements is that of a dictionary, or of its publishers, and, especially, any dictionary that records a meaning that is unacceptable or at best unwelcome to the person or group on the warpath. The ferocity of such assaults is almost unbelievable except as a by-product of what Professor Trevor-Roper calls the twentieth-century "epidemic fury of ideological belief." Key words are *Jew, Palestinian, Arab, Pakistan, Turk, Asiatic, Muhammadan,* and *Negro,* and there are others.

3   It is impossible to discover exactly when the battle cry was first heard, but certainly by the 1920s a pattern of protest existed. In the *Jewish Chronicle* of 24 October 1924, a leading article expressed "no small gratification" that, in deference to complaints that had been published in the *Jewish Chronicle,* the delegates of the Clarendon Press had decided that the "sinister meaning" attached to the word *Jew* (that is, the meaning "unscrupulous usurer or bargainer," and the corresponding verb meaning "to cheat, overreach") should be labelled to make it clear that it was a derogatory use. The *Jewish Chronicle* had maintained that users of the *Pocket Oxford Dictionary* would conclude that "every Jew is essentially the sort of person thus described." Mr. R. W. Chapman, who at that time was the head of the section of OUP which publishes dictionaries, replied that "it is no part of the duty of a

lexicographer to pass judgement on the justice or propriety of current usage." The editor of the *Pocket Oxford Dictionary*, the legendary H. W. Fowler, in a letter to Chapman declared:

> The dictionary-maker has to record what people say, not what he thinks they can politely say: how will you draw the line between this insult to a nation and such others as 'Dutch courage', 'French leave', 'Punic faith', the 'Huns', 'a nation of shopkeepers', and hundreds more? The real question is not whether a phrase is rude, but whether it is current.

4   The *Pocket Oxford* and other Oxford dictionaries, and dictionaries elsewhere, labelled the "sinister meaning" of the word *Jew* "derogatory," "opprobrious," or the like, and an uneasy peace was established. But not for long. Some other "Sinister" meanings in the *Pocket Oxford* were pointed out. "*Turk*: Member of the Ottoman race; unmanageable child." "*Tartar*: native of Tartary (etc.); intractable person or awkward customer." "*Jesuit*: member of Society of Jesus (etc.); deceitful person."

5   Fowler felt that he was being incited, as he said, "to assume an autocratic control of the language and put to death all the words and phrases that do not enjoy our approval." He maintained that the *POD* was not keeping the incriminated senses alive but that, unfortunately, they were not in danger of dying. In a letter to Kenneth Sisam in September 1924, he insisted: "I should like to repeat that I have neither religious, political, nor social antipathy to Jews"—nor, by implication, to Turks, Tartars, or Jesuits. The episode passed, but was not forgotten. The *Jewish Chronicle* at that time appeared to be satisfied by an assurance that the unfavorable senses would be labelled as such. They did not ask for, far less demand, the exclusion of the disapproved meanings.

6   In the United States in the 1920s, a parallel protest movement aimed at the compulsory capitalization of the initial letter of the word *Negro* and the abandonment, except among black inhabitants of the States, of the word *nigger*. Again, dictionaries were among the main targets, and here, too, the lexicographers replied that if writers, including the editors of newspapers, used a capital initial for *Negro,* they would themselves be happy to include this form in their dictionaries, and to give it priority if it became the dominant form in print.

7   A half-century later, it is easy to see that the lexicographers had "scotch'd the snake, not killed it." Resentment smoldered away in certain quarters, and the issues were brought out into the open again after the 1939–1945 war. But this time there was a difference. Dictionaries remained a prime target, but the protesters brought new assault techniques to bear, especially the threat of sanctions if the lexicographers did not come to heel.

Now, dictionary editors, judged by the standards of the broad world, are a soft target. With little personal experience of the broil that forms the daily experience of, for example, politicians, newspaper editors, and psychiatrists, editors of dictionaries tend to be too unworldly and too disdainfully scholarly to recognize the severity of an assault made on them. What is this assault and what form does it take? Quite simply, it is a concerted attempt by various pressure groups to force dictionary editors to give up recording the factual unpleasantnesses of our times and to abandon the tradition of setting down the language as it is actually used, however disagreeable, regrettable, or uncongenial the use.

8   Two definitions in the *Concise Oxford Dictionary*, one in the early fifties and the other in 1976, exacerbated things. One concerned the word *Pakistan*, and the other, the word *Palestinian*. The editor of the *Concise Oxford Dictionary* unwisely entered the word *Pakistan* in his dictionary in 1951— unwisely, because names of countries as such do not qualify for an entry in Oxford dictionaries—and defined it as "a separate Moslem State in India, Moslem autonomy; (from 1947) the independent Moslem Dominion in India."

9   It lay apparently unnoticed until 1959, when somebody must have pointed it out. The Pakistanis, understandably, were outraged, and called for a ban on the *COD* in Pakistan and for all unsold copies in Pakistan to be confiscated. The OUP admitted that the definition was "tactless" and "locally irritating," but pointed out that the intention had been to show that Pakistan was in the familiar, triangular section of territory which had always been called India on maps and in geography books. No political motive was in question. The Karachi police raided bookstalls in the city and seized 215 copies of the fourth edition of the *COD*. They also raided the Karachi office of the OUP, and seized the only copy of the dictionary on the premises, which was, in fact, the typist's copy. Copies in government offices were commandeered by the police, and apparently hundreds of copies were collected from public offices, schools, and colleges.

10   After high-level discussion, the Pakistan government decided to lift its ban on the *COD* in November 1959, after receiving an undertaking by the OUP to issue a correction slip for insertion in all copies of *COD* sold in Pakistan, and to enter a new definition in the next impression of the dictionary. Later, a more permanent solution was found when the word *Pakistan* was dropped from the main-line Oxford dictionaries altogether, as a proper name with no other meanings. It remains in the semi-encyclopedic *Oxford Illustrated Dictionary*, where it is defined as "Muslim State in SE Asia, formed in 1947 from regions where Muslims predominated."

11   This was a striking example of the serious consequences arising from a simple error of judgement by a lexicographer. There were other minor

skirmishes, for example, when it was noticed that the definition of the word *American* in some of the Oxford dictionaries failed to allow for the existence of black Americans and of Latin Americans. The dictionary editors gladly revised the definitions and brought them up to date with a minimum of fuss and with no heat generated on either side.

12   However, the problem of the word *Jew* kept returning in an increasingly dramatic way. Some correspondents contrasted the derogatory definitions of *Jew* with the colloquial senses of the word *Christian. Christian* is defined as "a human being, as distinguished from a brute," for example, in Shaftesbury (1714): "The very word Christian is, in common language, us'd for Man, in opposition to Brute-beast." It is also recorded with the colloquial sense, "a decent, respectable, or presentable person," as in Dickens (1844): "You must take your passage like a Christian; at least as like a Christian as a fore-cabin passenger can."

13   One correspondent, in 1956, said that she was concerned with the way in which stereotypes about groups of people became formulated, and she argued that the preservation of derogatory definitions in dictionaries did nothing to prevent the persistence of such stereotypes. Others drew attention to the cultural and scholarly achievements of Jews, for example, that thirty-eight Nobel prizes had been awarded to Jews by 1960. A representative of the American Conference of Businessmen came to the OED Department in Oxford in March 1966, and he and I discussed the problem amicably. "Men of good will," he said, "should unite to do everything possible not to give any appearance of acceptance to unfavorable applications of the word *Jew* if they exist." If they exist? But we knew from our quotation files that unfavorable applications of the word *Jew* did and do exist, both in speech and in print, deplorable though they are. All I could do was to repeat the familiar lexicographical arguments. It is the duty of lexicographers to record actual usage, as shown by collected examples, not to express moral approval or disapproval of usage; dictionaries cannot be regulative in matters of social, political, and religious attitudes; there is no question of any animus on the part of the lexicographers against the Jews, or the Arabs, or anyone else.

14   In 1969, a Jewish businessman from Salford came on the scene and claimed that the definitions of *Jew* were "abusive and insulting and reflected a deplorable attitude toward Jewry." He turned the screw more forcibly by releasing the text of his letters to the national newspapers, who by now realized that the matter was an issue of public controversy. He also wrote to politicians, church leaders, including the chief rabbi and the archbishop of Canterbury, to the commissioner of police, and to other instruments of the church and state.

15   In 1972, this Salford businessman brought an action against the Clarendon Press, claiming that the secondary definitions of the word *Jew* were

"derogatory, defamatory, and deplorable." He lost the case in the High Court in July 1973. Mr. Justice Goff held that, in law, the plaintiff had no maintainable cause of action because he could not, as required by English law, show that the offending words in the dictionary entries "referred to him personally or were capable of being understood by others as referring to him."

16   The next episode occurred on the other side of the world. Toward the end of 1976, Mr. Al Grassby, Australia's commissioner for community relations, called for the withdrawal of the *Australian Pocket Oxford Dictionary* from circulation because it contained a number of words applied in a derogatory way to ethnic or religious groups: words like *wog, wop,* and *dago.*

17   Knowing very little, if anything, about lexicographical policy, he thought it deplorable that there was no entry for *Italy* but one for *dago,* none for Brazil as a country but one for *Brazil nut,* and so on. This wholly simplistic notion was rejected with humor and scorn by the Australian press. A cartoon in the *Australian* showed two European migrants looking very unhappy, and the caption read: "Did you hear what those ignorant Aussie dingoes called us?" And a headline in the *Melbourne Sunday Press* makes its point quite simply: "You are on a loser, pal Grassby."

18   The most recent example of hostility toward dictionary definitions occurred a short time ago. On this occasion, as with *Pakistan,* the criticized definition was inadequate, and, curiously, the concession of its inadequacy merely transferred the attack from one quarter to another. In the sixth edition of the *Concise Oxford Dictionary,* published in July 1976, the word *Palestinian* was defined as "(native or inhabitant) of Palestine; (person) seeking to displace Israelis from Palestine." Early in 1977, the definition provoked angry editorial comment in newspapers in the Middle East, and threats were made that if the Oxford University Press did not agree to amend it at once, the matter would be brought to the attention of the Arab League, with a proposal to place the OUP on the Arab boycott list.

19   Each day's post brought fresh evidence of what appeared to be a severe reaction throughout Arabic-speaking countries, if the newspapers were anything to go by. The sales records for the *Concise Oxford Dictionary* in Egypt showed that all of eleven copies had been sold there in the financial year 1976–1977! But, sales apart, what was clear was that the Arabs considered the definition to be partisan, and that, in my opinion, would have been the attitude of the man on the Clapham omnibus, too.

20   In two lines of the *COD*—because that was all the space available in such a small dictionary—we concluded that it was not possible to arrive at other than a formulaic definition of *Palestinian.* Any form of words ascribing motives to "Palestinians" simply failed by one test or another

when the space available was so limited. We therefore decided to adopt another type of definition, one of the type that is used in every desk dictionary in the world, and the new definition reads as follows: "*n.* Native or inhabitant of Palestine. *a.* Of, pertaining to, or connected with Palestine."

21   The Arabs were satisfied ("it represents a victory for truth and objectivity," declared the *Egyptian Gazette* of 3 May 1977) and, had the matter rested there, without further publicity, that would probably have been the end of it. Not content with severing the head, however, the Arabs wished to fix it upon the battlements. A press statement was issued to British national newspapers by a London-based Arab organization, and even though this statement was factually and unemotionally expressed, it brought an instant reaction from the other side.

22   Letters of protest began to arrive from various Jewish organizations, and the scholarly lexicographers of the OUP had to endure the kind of concerted campaign with which politicians have always been familiar. The letters expressed "profound distress" and declared that the lexicographers "had departed from their usual standards of scholarly objectivity in yielding to pro-Arab pressure groups." The "selfsame tune and words" came from several directions. "We consider this an encroachment on traditional British integrity and on British values," "Political appeasement for commercial considerations," "I wish to register the strongest protest against such abject and cowardly behaviour on the part of your organization," and so on. It dawned on us, as the letters arrived, that we were dealing with an organized petition. The individuals and groups writing to us had been urged to write to us by some central body. The same phrases occurred in several of the letters; for example: "In describing a Palestinian as a native or inhabitant of Palestine, you impliedly deny the existence of the State of Israel." That "impliedly" rather gave the game away.

23   This Palestinian affair is for all practical purposes over, though not without bruises on all sides. Dictionary editors are now at last aware that they must give maximum attention to sensitive words, like *Palestinian, Jap,* and so on. Politically sensitive words like *Palestine* and *Kashmir* can be entered only as geographical, and not as political entities unless there is adequate space to describe the claims and counterclaims and there are facilities for the frequent updating of the entries.

24   For the most part lexicographers are agreed about the necessity of recording derogatory applications of words even if some sections of the general public are not. Since the 1960s or so most dictionaries (other than the smallest ones and those prepared for the use of children) have also included most of the more commonly heard expressions used in contexts describing sexual or excretory matters. A different practice, which I believe to be mistaken, is defended in classical manner by David B. Guralnik in the

foreword to his *Webster's New World Dictionary of the American Language* (Second College Edition, 1972), p. viii:

> The absence from this dictionary of a handful of old, well-known vulgate terms for sexual and excretory organs and functions is not due to a lack of citations for these words from current literature. On the contrary, the profusion of such citations in recent years would suggest that the terms in question are so well known as to require no explanation. The decision to eliminate them as part of the extensive culling process that is the inevitable task of the lexicographer was made on the practical grounds that there is still objection in many quarters to the appearance of these terms in print and that to risk keeping this dictionary out of the hands of some students by introducing several terms that require little if any elucidation would be unwise. In a similar vein, it was decided in the selection process that this dictionary could easily dispense with those true obscenities, the terms of racial or ethnic opprobrium, that are, in any case, encountered with diminishing frequency these days.

25   In respect of such vocabulary, inclusion or exclusion should be governed by the size of the dictionary or by the educational market envisaged for it. In large dictionaries like the *OED*, the *Shorter Oxford English Dictionary* and *Webster's Third New International Dictionary*, such vocabulary should be automatically included, with suitable indications of the status of each item. In desk dictionaries like the *Concise Oxford Dictionary* and *Webster's New Collegiate Dictionary* the editors normally have sufficient space to include such words: a wide range of suitable status labels is available to indicate the degree of vulgarity of words like *crap, cunt, fart, fuck, turd*, and so on; and for terms of racial abuse a special symbol meaning "regarded as offensive in varying degrees by a person to whom the word is applied" is long overdue. Such dictionaries should aim to be regulative or normative in such matters only by the use of cautionary labels and/or symbols and not by censorship. In smaller dictionaries, and in school dictionaries, the absence of such vocabulary needs no defense.

26   In the end, in their function as "marshallers of words," lexicographers responsible for the compilation of the larger dictionaries must aim to include vocabulary from the disputed areas of vocabulary as well as from safe or uncontroversial subject areas, words that are gracefully formed as well as those that are not, words from sets of religious, political, or social beliefs with which one has no sympathy beside those that one finds acceptable. And to the list of words that must not be excluded I should add those that are explosive and dangerous, like words of ethnic abuse, as well.

Questions
on Content

1. What were the "new assault techniques" lexicographers faced "after the 1939–1945 war"?

2. Why were the Pakistanis outraged by the definition of *Pakistan* in the 1951 edition of *The Concise Oxford Dictionary*?

3. Why does Burchfield use the word *instruments* in paragraph 14? What is he implying?

4. What is the "lexicographical policy" referred to in paragraph 17, and why is it so important to the incident described in paragraphs 16 and 17?

5. Explain the controversy over the definition of *Palestinian* in the 1976 edition of *The Concise Oxford Dictionary*.

Questions
on Structure
and Style

6. This essay can be divided into two sections. What is the topic of each, and where does one end and the other begin?

7. Burchfield first discusses controversy over the definition of the word *Jew* in paragraph 3. He then moves on to comment on other words, but he returns to the word *Jew* in paragraph 12. Why does Burchfield *not* make all his comments on *Jew* at one time? Your answer should reveal one of the essay's organizational principles.

8. The author often uses metaphors in his discussion, and many of them are alike in one way. What is this similarity that helps make them consistent?

Assignments

1. Burchfield recommends the use of "cautionary labels and/or symbols" for words that some people would object to seeing included in dictionaries. Write an essay in which you either agree or disagree with Burchfield on this point. Should a source of information professing to be unbiased offer warnings about usage?

2. Burchfield gives many examples of words whose dictionary definitions have offended certain groups. Write a paragraph (or essay) explaining why people should or should never be offended by dictionary definitions.

Additional Assignments and Research Topics

1. In "Welcome to the Web of Words" (page 121), Anne H. Soukhanov describes the process lexicographers use in tracking changes in our language. Using the methods she describes, read and mark a section of a daily newspaper, a magazine, or a book with a view toward recording new words and new meanings of existing words. Mark only those words and meanings that are absent from your dictionary. Then compose entries for the new words and meanings that are similar to the entries Soukhanov prepares for her "Word Watch" column.

2. Explain in an essay why no dictionary that has been published can be a complete record of the English language. (Many of the reading selections in Chapter 4 can help you form ideas on this topic, as well as providing material that you can cite to substantiate your claims.)

3. Turn to the front pages of your desk dictionary, and make a list of the usage labels that the dictionary uses, along with their meaning. There are, for example, seven usage labels in *Webster's New World Dictionary:* colloquial, slang, obsolete, archaic, poetic, dialect, and British (or Canadian, Scottish, etc.). Then study your dictionary to find three entries exemplifying each of the usages. As you consider the usage issue, think about what is meant by the term "standard American English."

4. Assume that certain members of Congress hope to pass a law saying, in effect, that meanings of words should be fixed so as to eliminate confusion.
    A. Assume that you agree with the proposed law, and write a letter to your representative in Congress giving reasons for permanently standardizing the meanings of words.
    B. Assume that you are outraged by the proposed law, and write a letter to your representative in Congress urging opposition to any such measure. Give specific reasons why such a law would be dangerous. Feel free to cite Soukhanov and Burchfield.

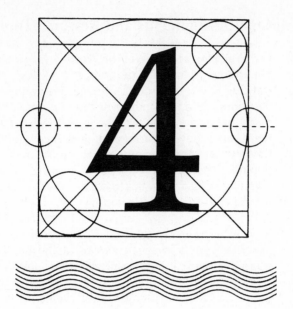

Language
Development

Just what *is* language? Briefly stated, language is a set of agreements we make. We agree that certain symbols (letters, numbers, words, and other less obvious symbols) will mean certain things to us. Any short definition like this one, however, can never reveal how important—how profoundly human—language is. The best way to approach that deeper significance is to answer these two questions: Why did language develop? How does it go on developing even today? The selections in this chapter seek answers to these basic yet highly revealing questions.

Thinking of ourselves within the larger context of social animals, we know that we are different essentially because of our language. Lewis Thomas's "Just That One Thing" shows us some implications of this "single human trait that marks us all genetically, setting us apart from the rest of life." Understanding the nature of this human trait is easier if we look back at its beginnings. Charles Barber, in "The Origin of Language," reviews the many theories about how prehistoric humans invented language. Barber's presentation illustrates how appropriate it is to examine at the same time both *what* language is and *why* it developed.

Development implies change, and the remaining readings in this chapter examine how a language, in this case, English, can change. In her lively article, "English Spoken Here . . . Sort Of," Susan Trausch discusses the rapid rate of change in the language we take for granted. "A Brief History of English," by Paul Roberts, presents a historical sketch and demonstrates both how and why the English language we use today seems so different from that of the people who first used "English." H. L. Mencken focuses on the English language as it is spoken in America. In "American English: The Period of Growth," Mencken's informative, intriguing details emphasize how quickly the American language developed in the nineteenth century.

Finally, if our language has changed, and is changing, what version of the English language will our children and grandchildren take for granted? Lane Jennings speculates on this topic in "Brave New Words." In the future that Jennings envisions, the English language both endures and evolves.

Jennings reaffirms an idea about the nature of language development that underlies all of the readings in this chapter: Language is integral to what we are as humans. It's an energy running throughout humanity. If our relationship to language is difficult to appreciate and easy to underestimate, it is only because that relationship is so intense and compelling.

Just That One Thing

Lewis Thomas

What distinguishes humans from other living creatures? This ancient question is both scientific and philosophical, and in the following excerpt from his book *The Lives of a Cell*, Lewis Thomas offers an answer. Thomas is a medical doctor and president of the Memorial Sloan-Kettering Cancer Center in New York (that is, a scientist and an administrator), and he clearly understands the profound emotional implications of defining our uniqueness. His answer to such a difficult question takes both a scientific and a personal approach to explaining language development and what it means for us.

1   Not all social animals are social with the same degree of commitment. In some species, the members are so tied to each other and interdependent as to seem the loosely conjoined cells of a tissue. The social insects are like this; they move, and live all their lives, in a mass; a beehive is a spherical animal. In other species, less compulsively social, the members make their homes together, pool resources, travel in packs or schools, and share the food, but any single one can survive solitary, detached from the rest. Others are social only in the sense of being more or less congenial, meeting from time to time in committees, using social gatherings as *ad hoc* occasions for feeding and breeding. Some animals simply nod at each other in passing, never reaching even a first-name relationship.

2   It is not a simple thing to decide where we fit, for at one time or another in our lives we manage to organize in every imaginable social arrangement. We are as interdependent, especially in our cities, as bees or ants, yet we can detach if we wish and go live alone in the woods, in theory anyway. We feed and look after each other, constructing elaborate systems for this, even including vending machines to dispense ice cream in gas stations, but we also have numerous books to tell us how to live off the land. We cluster in family groups, but we tend, unpredictably, to turn on each other and fight as if we were different species. Collectively, we hanker to accumulate all the information in the universe and distribute it around among ourselves as though it were a kind of essential foodstuff, ant-fashion (the faintest trace of real news in science has the action of a pheromone, lifting the hairs of workers in laboratories at the ends of the earth), but each of us also builds a private store of his own secret knowledge and hides it away like untouchable treasure. We have names to label each as self, and we believe without reservation that this system of taxonomy will guarantee the entity, the absolute separateness of each of us, but the mechanism has

155

no discernible function in the center of a crowded city; we are essentially nameless, most of our time.

3   Nobody wants to think that the rapidly expanding mass of mankind, spreading out over the surface of the earth, blackening the ground, bears any meaningful resemblance to the life of an anthill or a hive. Who would consider for a moment that the more than three billion of us are a sort of stupendous animal when we become linked together? We are not mindless, nor is our day-to-day behavior coded out to the last detail by our genomes, nor do we seem to be engaged together, compulsively, in any single, universal, stereotyped task analogous to the construction of a nest. If we were ever to put all our brains together in fact, to make a common mind the way ants do, it would be an unthinkable thought, way over our heads.

4   Social animals tend to keep at a particular thing, generally something huge for their size; they work at it ceaselessly under genetic instructions and genetic compulsion, using it to house the species and protect it, assuring permanence.

5   There are, to be sure, superficial resemblances in some of the things we do together, like building glass and plastic cities on all the land and farming under the sea, or assembling in armies, or landing samples of ourselves on the moon, or sending memoranda into the next galaxy. We do these together without being quite sure why, but we can stop doing one thing and move to another whenever we like. We are not committed or bound by our genes to stick to one activity forever, like the wasps. Today's behavior is no more fixed than when we tumbled out over Europe to build cathedrals in the twelfth century. At that time we were convinced that it would go on forever, that this was the way to live, but it was not; indeed, most of us have already forgotten what it was all about. Anything we do in this transient, secondary social way, compulsively and with all our energies but only for a brief period of our history, cannot be counted as social behavior in the biological sense. If we can turn it on and off, on whims, it isn't likely that our genes are providing the detailed instructions. Constructing Chartres was good for our minds, but we found that our lives went on, and it is no more likely that we will find survival in Rome plows or laser bombs, or rapid mass transport or a Mars lander, or solar power, or even synthetic protein. We do tend to improvise things like this as we go along, but it is clear that we can pick and choose.

6   For practical reasons, it would probably be best for us not to be biologically social, in the long run. Not that we have a choice, of course, or even a vote. It would not be good news to learn that we are all roped together intellectually, droning away at some featureless, genetically driven collective work, building something so immense that we can never see the outlines. It seems especially hard, even perilous, for this to be the burden of a species with the unique attribute of speech, and argument. Leave this kind of life to the insects and birds, and lesser mammals, and fish.

7   But there is just that one thing. About human speech.

8   It begins to look, more and more disturbingly, as if the gift of language is the single human trait that marks us all genetically, setting us apart from the rest of life. Language is, like nest-building or hive-making, the universal and biologically specific activity of human beings. We engage in it communally, compulsively, and automatically. We cannot be human without it; if we were to be separated from it our minds would die, as surely as bees lost from the hive.

9   We are born knowing how to use language. The capacity to recognize syntax, to organize and deploy words into intelligible sentences, is innate in the human mind. We are programmed to identify patterns and generate grammar. There are invariant and variable structures in speech that are common to all of us. As chicks are endowed with an innate capacity to read information in the shapes of overhanging shadows, telling hawk from other birds, we can identify the meaning of grammar in a string of words, and we are born this way. According to Chomsky, who has examined it as a biologist looks at live tissue, language "must simply be a biological property of the human mind." The universal attributes of language are genetically set; we do not learn them, or make them up as we go along.

10   We work at this all our lives, and collectively we give it life, but we do not exert the least control over language, not as individuals or committees or academies or governments. Language, once it comes alive, behaves like an active, motile organism. Parts of it are always being changed, by a ceaseless activity to which all of us are committed; new words are invented and inserted, old ones have their meaning altered or abandoned. New ways of stringing words and sentences together come into fashion and vanish again, but the underlying structure simply grows, enriches itself, expands. Individual languages age away and seem to die, but they leave progeny all over the place. Separate languages can exist side by side for centuries without touching each other, maintaining their integrity with the vigor of incompatible tissues. At other times, two languages may come together, fuse, replicate, and give rise to nests of new tongues.

11   If language is at the core of our social existence, holding us together, housing us in meaning, it may also be safe to say that art and music are functions of the same universal, genetically determined mechanism. These are not bad things to do together. If we are social creatures because of this, and therefore like ants, I for one (or should I say we for one?) do not mind.

Questions on Content

1. Thomas begins by discussing social animals. How would you define this term?

2. In paragraph 6, the author states, "It would not be good news to learn that we are all roped together intellectually." Why not? Is Thomas speaking as a scientist at this point?

3. Thomas says that "it begins to look, more and more disturbingly, as if the gift of language is the single human trait" that makes us unique (paragraph 8). Why is this belief disturbing?

4. We give language life, the author says, "but we do not exert the least control over language" (paragraph 10). Do you think we would be better off if we could control language? Who might benefit? Who might suffer?

Questions on Structure and Style

5. Thomas uses many comparisons in this selection. Mark two or three paragraphs in which this rhetorical device is most obvious.

6. What is the topic sentence of paragraph 5?

7. Why is paragraph 7 so short?

8. What effect does Thomas create with the metaphor "nests of new tongues" in paragraph 10? What structural reason is there for the placement of this metaphor?

9. Thomas is both a scientist and a popular author. In this selection, when do we clearly hear the scientist's voice, and when do we hear the popular author's? Make two lists of words and expressions that denote each role.

Assignments

1. Thomas says that we cannot be human without language. Choose one of the following human activities, and write an essay describing the role of language in making that activity human.

   playing basketball or football

   cooking a meal

   conducting a romance

2. List five daily activities in which language seems least important. In an essay, discuss what they reveal about being human.

The Origin of Language

Charles Barber

In the following selection from his book *The Story of Speech and Language*, Charles Barber reviews the many theories about how language originated. Because language began in prehistory, all discussion of its origin relies on educated guesswork. Barber, a professor at the University of Leeds (England), thus proceeds cautiously as he guides us through this "realm of more or less plausible speculation," in which ideas seem as conflicting as they are illuminating.

1   We are profoundly ignorant about the origins of language, and have to content ourselves with more or less plausible speculations. We do not even know for certain when language arose, but it seems likely that it goes back to the earliest history of man, perhaps half a million years. We have no direct evidence, but it seems probable that speech arose at the same time as tool making and the earliest forms of specifically human cooperation. In the great Ice Ages of the Pleistocene period, our earliest human ancestors established the Old Stone Age culture: they made flint tools, and later tools of bone, ivory, and antler; they made fire and cooked their food; they hunted big game, often by methods that called for considerable cooperation and coordination. As their material culture gradually improved, they became artists, and made carvings and engravings on bones and pebbles, and wonderful paintings of animals on the walls of caves. It is difficult to believe that the makers of these Palaeolithic cultures lacked the power of speech. It is a long step, admittedly, from the earliest flint weapons to the splendid art of the late Old Stone Age: the first crude flints date back perhaps to 500,000 B.C., while the finest achievements of Old Stone Age man are later than 100,000 B.C.; and in this period we can envisage a corresponding development of language, from the most primitive and limited language of the earliest human groups to a fully developed language in the flowering time of Old Stone Age culture.

Evidence about the Origins of Language

2   How did language arise in the first place? There are many theories about this, based on various types of indirect evidence, such as the language of children, the language of primitive societies, the kinds of changes that have taken place in languages in the course of recorded history, the behavior of higher animals like chimpanzees, and the behavior of people

159

suffering from speech defects. These types of evidence may provide us with useful pointers, but they all suffer from limitations, and must be treated with caution.

3   When we consider the language of children we have to remember that their situation is quite different from that of our earliest human ancestors, because the child is growing up in an environment where there is already a fully developed language, and is surrounded by adults who use that language and are teaching it to him. For example, it has been shown that the earliest words used by children are mainly the names of things and people ("Doll," "Spoon," "Mummy"): but this does not prove that the earliest words of primitive man were also the names of things and people. When the child learns the name of an object, he may then use it to express his wishes or demands: "Doll!" often means "Give me my doll!" or "I've dropped my doll: pick it up for me!"; the child is using language to get things done, and it is almost an accident of adult teaching that the words used to formulate the child's demands are mainly nouns, instead of words like "Bring!"; "Pick up!"; and so on.

4   One thing that we can perhaps learn from the small child is the kind of articulated utterance that comes easiest to a human being before he has learned the sound system of one particular language. The first articulate word pronounced by a child is often something like *da, ma, na, ba, ga,* or *wa*. The vowel is most commonly a short *ah* sound, and the consonant a nasal or a plosive. Nearly always, these early "words" consist of a consonant followed by a vowel or of a sequence of syllables of this type (*dadada,* etc.). When the child attempts to copy words used by adults, he at first tends to produce words of this form, so that "grandfather" may be rendered as *gaga,* "thank you" as *tata,* and "water" as *wawa*. This explains why, in so many languages, the nursery words for mother and father are *mama* or *dada* or *baba* or something similar: there is no magic inner connection between the idea of parenthood and words of this form: these just happen to be the first articulated sounds that the child makes, and the proud parent attributes a suitable meaning to them. Such words may also have been the first utterances of primitive man, though hardly with this meaning.

5   The languages of primitive peoples, and the history of languages in literate times, may throw some light on the origin of language by suggesting what elements in it are the most archaic. But again we have to be careful, because the language of the most primitive people living today is still a very ancient and sophisticated one, with half a million years of history behind it; and the earliest written records can take us back only a few thousand years. It is probable, of course, that in early times language changed more slowly than in historical times. The whole history of human culture has been one of an accelerating rate of change: it took man about half a million years to develop through the Old Stone Age to the higher material culture of the Middle and New Stone ages, but a mere 5,000 years

or so for these to give way to the Bronze Age, and perhaps 1,000 for the Bronze Age to develop into the Iron Age; and since the Industrial Revolution, the pace has become dizzying. It is perhaps arguable that the rate of change in language has been parallel to that in material culture, and in that case the gap of half a million years between the origin of language and the first written records becomes a little less daunting. It remains daunting enough, however, and we must obviously be careful in theorizing about the remote past.

6   Still, we may be able to pick up some hints. For example, it is noticeable among primitive peoples how closely their languages are adapted to their material needs: in Eskimo, there is no single word for "snow," but a whole series of words for "new fallen snow," "hard snow," and so on; and in general a primitive people tends to have words for the specific things that are materially important to it (like the particular birds or plants that it eats), and to lump together other things (like birds or plants that it does not eat) under some generic expression. We may also find some evidence about the types of word and the types of expression which are oldest: there is a good deal to suggest that words of command (like "Give!"; "Strike!") are very archaic, since in the earliest known forms of many languages these imperative forms are identical with the simple stem of the verb, without any special ending added. Compare, for example, Latin *dic* ("say!") with *dicit* ("he says"), *dicunt* ("they say"), or *dicere* ("to say"): the form used for giving a command is the shortest, the most elementary. Some of the personal pronouns, like *me,* also seem to be very archaic, and so do vocatives (the forms of words used in addressing people).

7   A study of the higher animals can help us by suggesting what man was like in the prelinguistic stage, immediately before he became man. The expressive noises, signals, and gestures of the higher apes show us what man started from in his creation of language; but they cannot show us how he created language, for it is man alone who has broken through to the use of symbols: the apes, however expressive their signals may be, remain on the other side of language. Apes, of course, have smaller brains than men; and man's development, as part of his adaptive evolution, of a larger and more complex brain than any other creature was undoubtedly a prerequisite for the emergence of language.

8   The last source of evidence, the behavior of people suffering from speech defects, is probably the least helpful. The condition which has especially been referred to is *aphasia,* in which the power of speech is wholly or partially lost, often as a result of a brain injury. In recovering from aphasia, the patient to some extent repeats the process gone through by a child in learning to speak for the first time, and some psychologists have suggested that he also repeats the history of the human race in inventing language. It is difficult, however, to see the grounds for this belief, since language, though it uses inherited biological skills and aptitudes, is not itself a biological inheritance but a cultural one; and the kind of prehistory of language

which has been constructed on evidence of this kind is not a very convincing one.

9   Emphasis on one type of evidence or another has led to rather different theories of the origin of language. Different authors, too, seem to mean different things when they talk about the origin of language: some are thinking especially of the prelanguage situation, and of the basic human skills and equipment that were a prerequisite for the invention of language; others are thinking more of the actual situations in which the first truly linguistic utterances took place; others again are thinking of the very early stages of language after its invention, and the ways in which it expanded its resources.

The Bow-wow Theory

10   One theory is that primitive language was an imitation of natural sounds, such as the cries of animals. This has been called the bow-wow theory. Supporters of the theory point to the large number of words in any language which are, it seems, directly imitative of natural sounds—words like *quack, cuckoo, peewit.* They add that many other words show a kind of "sound symbolism," enacting in sound whatever it is that they denote; examples of such words in English would be *splash, sludge, slush, grumble, grunt, bump,* and *sneeze.* It is certainly plausible to believe that a primitive hunter, wishing to tell his companions what kind of game he had found, may have imitated in gesture and sound whatever kind of animal it was— horse, or elephant, or quail; and this may well have played a part in the development of vocal symbols.

11   This theory, however, does not explain how language obtained its articulated structure. When we invent an imitative word like *whizzbang* or *crump,* we use an already existing language system, with its vowels and consonants, its laws of word structure, and so on, and we make our imitative word conform to this pattern. But man in the prelinguistic stage had no such language system, and his imitation of a horse or an elephant would simply be a whinnying or trumpeting sound, without the articulation characteristic of speech. Imitation of this kind may explain part of the primitive vocabulary, and it may have played a part in the transition from expressive cry to vocal symbol, but it cannot by itself account satisfactorily for the rise of language.

12   Moreover, we probably deceive ourselves about the extent and importance of sound symbolism in language. Because of our intimate knowledge of our language since our early years, and the way it is bound up with our whole emotional and intellectual life, the words that we use inevitably *seem* appropriate to what they mean, simply by constant association. It may be retorted that some groups of sounds really are appropriate to certain meanings, and this is shown by their occurrence in a number of words of similar

meaning: for example, in English we find initial *fl-* in a number of words connected with fire and light (e.g., *flame, flare, flash*) and in an even larger number of words connected with a flying or waving kind of motion (e.g., *flail, flap, flaunt, flay, flicker, flog, fluctuate, flurry, flutter*). But it is difficult to see any *inherent* appropriateness in the *fl-* sound for expressing ideas of flame or flickering motion: the sense of appropriateness surely arises from the fact that it occurs in all these words, not vice versa. And once a group of words like this exists in the language, new words may be coined on the same model (as perhaps happened with *flash* and *flap*), and words of similar form may develop new meanings on analogy with the members of the group (as has perhaps happened with *flourish*). But there are many other words in English which begin with *fl-*, which have nothing to do with flames or flickering, and yet which by long familiarity sound equally appropriate to their meanings, like *flange, flank, flannel, flask, flat, flesh, flimsy, flinch, flock,* and so on. It is noticeable that, when you learn a foreign language, the words that strike you as particularly appropriate in sound (or, sometimes, as grotesquely inappropriate) are very often ones that do not strike a native speaker in this way.

The Pooh-pooh Theory

13   A second theory of the origins of language has been called the pooh-pooh theory. This argues that language arose from instinctive emotional cries, expressive for example of pain or joy. On this view, the earliest linguistic utterances were interjections, simple exclamations expressive of some emotional state. This theory, it seems to me, suggests some of the material which language may have used, rather than the process by which it arose. The theory does nothing to explain the articulated nature of language, and it does little to bridge the gap between expressive cry and symbol. We can, indeed, imagine how, by association, an emotional cry may have become a signal: a cry of fear or of pain, for example, could easily become a signal which warned the group of danger; but this level has already been reached by the higher animals, which react to signals of this kind; the further step from trigger stimulus to symbol must also be explained. And the theory does not suggest any motivation for this development; a tremendous task like the creation of language would surely have been undertaken only under the pressure of man's needs.

The Ding-dong Theory

14   A third theory is the so-called nativistic theory, nicknamed the ding-dong theory. This begins from a fact we have already noticed, namely, that there is an apparently mysterious harmony between sound and sense in a

language. On this basis, the theory argues that primitive man had a peculiar instinctive faculty, by which every external impression that he received was given vocal expression. Every sensory impression was like the striking of a bell, producing a corresponding utterance. The trouble with this theory is that it explains nothing: it merely describes the facts in a different terminology, and so is only a pseudotheory.

The Yo-he-ho Theory

15   A fourth theory, put forward by the nineteenth-century scholar Noiré, has been called the yo-he-ho theory. This envisages language arising from the noises made by a group of men engaged in joint labor or effort—moving a tree trunk, lifting a rock. We all know from experience that, while performing work of this kind, we make involuntary vocal noises. While exerting powerful muscular effort we trap the breath in our lungs by tightly closing the glottis (the vocal cords); in the intervals of relaxation between the bursts of effort, we open the glottis and release the air, making various grunting and groaning noises in the process; since a stop is released, these noises often contain a consonantal sound as well as a vowel. Vocal noises of this kind might then develop into words meaning such things as "heave!"; "rest!"; "lift!" This theory has two great virtues: it gives a plausible explanation for the origin of the consonant-vowel structure of language, and it envisages the origin of language in a situation involving human cooperation, with adequate motivation. It also envisages the earliest speech utterances as commands, and we have already seen that there is some linguistic evidence for the antiquity of such imperative forms. Against the theory, it has been argued that it postulates too advanced a form of social cooperation: language, it is argued, would be necessary *before* men could embark on the kind of complex communal labor that the theory demands. I am not sure that this objection is very compelling: we must surely envisage language and cooperative human labor arising *simultaneously*, each making the other possible; they would continually react on one another, so that there would be a progressive development from the simplest utterances and acts of cooperation to the most complex speech and division of labor.

16   A variant of the theory has recently been elaborated by A. S. Diamond. He agrees that the first articulated words were commands, uttered simultaneously with the execution of violent arm movements, but argues that all the evidence shows that the most primitive words did not mean such things as "Haul!" but rather such things as "Strike!"; "Cut!"; "Break!"; he therefore envisages the rise of language in requests for assistance from one man to another in situations where maximum bodily effort was required. He does not speculate on the exact nature of these situations, but

presumably they might be such things as tool making, the breaking off of tree branches, and the killing of animals during hunting. Such things might occur at a more primitive stage of human society than the communal heaving suggested by Noiré.

The Gesture Theory

17   A fifth theory of the origins of language takes the view that gesture language preceded speech. Supporters of this theory point to the extensive use of gestures by animals of many different kinds, and the highly developed systems of gesture used by some primitive peoples. One of the popular examples is the sign language formerly used by the Indians of North America; this was an elaborate system of gestures which was used for negotiations between tribes that spoke different languages. It is certainly true that speech and gesture are closely intertwined; the centers in the brain which control hand movements are closely linked with those that control the vocal organs, and it seems highly probable that speech and gesture grew up together. This does not prove, however, that gesture came *first*. And, while it is true that animals use gestures, it is also true that they use cries: the chimpanzee makes signals and expresses its feelings both by bodily movements and by vocal noises, and the same was probably true of early man.

18   An extreme form of the gesture theory argues that speech arose very late (round about 3500 B.C.) and was derived from early pictorial writing; this writing itself, it is argued, was derived from gesture language. I must say that I find this incredible. We are asked to believe that man lacked speech right through the Old and New Stone ages, and did not develop it until the time of the city civilizations of the early Bronze Age. But it is difficult to believe that man could have built up the elaborate cultural apparatus of the New Stone Age (agriculture, pottery, weaving, house building, religious burial) without the aid of speech; for a gesture language, however highly developed, has grave disadvantages compared with a spoken language. To use a gesture language you have to have your hands free; but as soon as man becomes a tool maker and a craftsman his hands cease to be free; and the times when primitive man needed to communicate most urgently must have been precisely the times when he had a tool or a weapon in his hand. It is in fact arguable that it was just this preoccupation of man's hands with tools and weapons that led to the increased importance of vocal language compared with gestures; and this would support the view that spoken language goes right back to the beginning of man's career as tool maker. Gesture, too, has the disadvantage that it cannot be used in the dark, or when the users are separated by obstructions like trees—a serious disadvantage for a hunting band, which would surely develop hunting calls and

similar cries. Nor can a gesture be used to attract the attention of somebody who is looking in another direction, and so it has very limited value as a warning of the approach of danger. None of these disadvantages of gesture can *prove* that early man had a spoken language, but they do suggest that he had very powerful motives for creating one.

19   A more attractive version of the gesture theory is the *mouth gesture* theory, which was strongly argued by Sir Richard Paget and has recently been supported by an Icelandic professor, Alexander Jóhannesson. Paget argues that primitive man at first communicated by gestures; as his intelligence and technique developed he needed more exact gestures, but at the same time found that his eyes and hands were more occupied by his arts and crafts. But the gestures of the hands were unconsciously copied by movements of the tongue, lips, and mouth; and when the man was unable to go on gesturing with his hands because of their other uses, the mouth gestures continued without them, and he discovered that if air was blown through the mouth or nose the gesture became audible as whispered speech; if he simultaneously sang or roared or grunted, he produced voiced speech. To support his theory of the sympathetic movements of the speech organs, Paget quotes a passage from Darwin's book *The Expression of the Emotions:*

> There are other actions which are commonly performed under certain circumstances independently of habit, and which seem to be due to imitation or some kind of sympathy. Thus, persons cutting anything with a pair of scissors may be seen to move their jaws simultaneously with the blades of the scissors. Children learning to write often twist about their tongue as their fingers move, in a ridiculous fashion!

20   Language was thus produced by a sort of pantomime, the tongue and lips mimicking the movements of the hands in a gesture. As an elementary example, Paget takes the movement of the mouth, tongue, and jaws as in eating, as a gesture sign meaning "eat." If, while making this sign, we blow air through the vocal cavities and switch on voice, we produce the sounds *mnyum mnyum* or *mnya mnya,* which, Paget says, would be universally understood. Similarly, the action of sucking a liquid in small quantities into the mouth produces words like *sip* or *sup.* Paget goes on to analyze large numbers of words in terms of mouth gestures of this kind, and this work has been continued by Jóhannesson, who has examined large numbers of the basic words of the earliest known languages. Some of these analyses strike me as fanciful, and there are times when one feels that, with sufficient ingenuity, any movement of the tongue could be construed as a gesture representing anything one liked. Nevertheless, the theory has considerable plausibility, and must be taken seriously. It has

the merit of accounting for the articulated nature of speech, and of giving an explanation for the way the linkage was effected between sound and meaning.

The Musical Theory

21   A sixth theory sees the origin of language in song, or at any rate sees speech and music as emerging from something earlier that included both. This theory was put forward by the great Danish linguist Otto Jespersen. He thought that the bow-wow, pooh-pooh, and yo-he-ho theories could all explain the origins of parts of language, but that none of them could explain the whole of it. His own method was to trace the history of language backwards, to see what the long-term trends were, and then to assume that these same trends had existed since the beginning of language. By this means he arrived at the view that primitive language consisted of very long words, full of difficult jaw-breaking sounds; that it used tone and pitch more than later languages, and a wider range of musical intervals; and that it was more passionate and more musical than later languages. Earlier still, language was a kind of song without words; it was not communicative, but merely expressive; the earliest language was not matter-of-fact or practical, but poetic and emotional, and love in particular was the most powerful emotion for eliciting outbursts of music and song. "Language," he writes, "was born in the courting days of mankind; the first utterances of speech I fancy to myself like something between the nightly love-lyrics of puss upon the tiles and the melodious love-songs of the nightingale." A romantic picture.

22   It may be doubted, however, whether the trends in language are as constant and universal as Jespersen thinks. His theory assumes that the same kinds of general change have taken place in all languages throughout their history. But we know nothing of languages before the Bronze Age; even if there has been a universal trend in language since the beginnings of Bronze Age civilization (which is by no means certain), it does not follow that the same trend occurred in the Old Stone Age, when man's circumstances were entirely different. Moreover, we have a historical knowledge of relatively few of the world's languages: of the two thousand languages spoken today, only a handful have records going back to the pre-Christian era.

The Contact Theory

23   Finally, mention may be made of the contact theory, which has recently been advanced by G. Révész, a former professor of psychology at Amsterdam.

He sees language as arising through man's instinctive need for contact with his fellows, and he works out a series of stages by which language may have developed. First comes the contact sound, which is not communicative, but merely expresses the individual's need for contact with his fellows; such as the noises made by gregarious animals. Next comes the cry, which is communicative, but which is directed to the environment generally, not to an individual; examples are mating calls and the cries of young nestlings in danger. Then there is the call, which differs from the cry in being directed to an individual; it is the demand for the satisfaction of some desire, and is found in domestic animals (begging) and speechless infants (crying for their mother); the call is seen as the starting point for both music and language. Finally comes the word, which has a symbolic function and is found only in man. Révész thinks that the earliest speech was an "imperative language," consisting only of commands; this later developed into mature human language, which contains also statements and questions. Révész's sequence of stages is carefully worked out, and is made very plausible. He does not, however, explain how human language came to be articulated; and he places undue emphasis on the instinctive need for contact as a motive for the invention of language, while rather neglecting the urgent practical motives in cooperative labor which must surely have impelled early man.

The Probabilities

24   What are we to make of this welter of theories? It is plain that no finality is possible at present, and that it is merely a matter of weighing the probabilities. It seems to me that we should attach great weight to the question of motivation in the origin of language, since such a great intellectual achievement would hardly have been possible except under the pressure of definite needs. Since the basic function of language is to influence the behavior of our fellow men, this would favor theories that emphasize the origins of language in situations of social cooperation: such for example are the yo-he-ho theory and Diamond's variant of it. However, other theories, such as the bow-wow theory and the mouth gesture theory, can also be adapted to views of this kind. In the second place, I think we should attach great importance to the articulatedness of language, as seen for example in its vowel and consonant structure; and it seems to me the weakness of many theories that they do nothing to explain this structure; the theories that come off best on this count are the yo-he-ho theory and the mouth gesture theory. But at present we cannot reach absolute certainty.

25   We must also remain in doubt about the nature of the earliest language, and we do not even know if there was one original language or whether language was invented independently at several different times and places. Jespersen, we have seen, postulates a primitive language that was

musical and passionate; he believes that it was very irregular; that it dealt with the concrete and particular rather than the abstract and general; that it contained very long words full of difficult combinations of sounds; and indeed that the earliest utterances consisted of whole sentences rather than single words. Somewhat similar views have been advanced by investigators who have attached great significance to the babbling stages of child speech. But Révész thinks that the earliest language consisted solely of commands; so does Diamond, who argues that these were single words and had the structure consonant-vowel-consonant-vowel (like *bada* or *taka*). The bow-wow theory, on the other hand, demands a primitive language full of imitative sounds like the howling of wolves or the trumpeting of elephants. In the absence of certainty about the origins of language, we must obviously lack certainty about the form which that language took (though the kind of language envisaged by Révész or Diamond seems more plausible than that envisaged by Jespersen).

26   Inevitably we remain in the realm of more or less plausible speculation as long as we are dealing with a period which has left us no record of its language. [Only when] we reach periods in which writing was practiced [are we] on much firmer ground.

Questions on Content

1. How can the language of children be used as indirect evidence to explain how language evolved in the first place? How can the languages of primitive peoples be used for this purpose? The language of higher animals? People with speech defects?

2. What is meant by *imperative language*? How does this concept help to explain one possible origin of language?

3. What is aphasia, and how is it related to language development?

4. Barber has this to say about the yo-he-ho theory: "It also envisages the earliest speech utterances as commands, and we have already seen that there is some linguistic evidence for the antiquity of such imperative forms" (paragraph 15). What is his linguistic evidence?

5. How does the quotation from Darwin (paragraph 19) support the theory that language was first produced as a sort of pantomime?

6. How is Barber's presentation organized? How do the section titles help to simplify the presentation?

7. Consider the author's language. For what audience is he writing? How can we tell?

8. How does Barber inject his own opinions into his discussion? In this method effective, or does it detract from the objectivity we expect in a discussion of a topic such as Barber's?

9. Discuss the use of transitions among the first nine paragraphs.

10. What does the last section, "The Probabilities," allow the author to do?

1. Choose one of the theories about the origin of language, and in a paragraph, explain why you consider it believable or unbelievable. Be sure to cite specific reasons for your opinion.

2. Observe a child who is acquiring language. In an essay, discuss how the child's experiences can help explain the origin of language.

3. Barber points out that "the expressive noises, signals, and gestures of the higher apes show us what man started from in his creation of language" (paragraph 7).

   A. Observe the gestures and body language of people in similar situations, such as two candidates for the same office, two teachers, or two news broadcasters. In an essay, compare how the two people express themselves non-verbally.

   B. Observe the different ways in which people greet each other, perhaps in a cafeteria, classroom, or office. Do you notice any patterns to the gestures and body language used by people of different age groups, genders, or social positions? Discuss your findings in an essay.

English Spoken Here . . .
Sort Of

Susan Trausch

Changes in the English language are often rapid, chaotic, and difficult to track. In the following essay, Susan Trausch, a staff writer for the *Boston Globe Magazine,* describes the reactions of dictionary editors, writers, and other language lovers as they watch English evolve. Trausch's presentation illustrates the journalistic style of writing, but her tone is not that of a reporter; instead, she speaks as an amazed but entertained witness to the actions of "the language god . . . [who] just lets words rip at will."

1   There is a god that rules the English language, and he, she, or it is a real wacko. Probably the same force in the universe created fruit cake, Robin Williams, and hula-hoops.

2   No disrespect is intended toward God with a capital G. It's just that the big boss contracts out sometimes during the busy season, and that's how bugs get in the system. Oh, sure, Keats and Shelley wrote some good stuff with English. So did Shakespeare and Joyce and a lot of other folks. The language certainly has its moments and can be powerful, timeless, and exquisitely beautiful to the eye and ear. But in its everyday state, say on a Wednesday afternoon with no particular place to go, as spoken by you and me in the elevator, or the gang on the corner, or the bureaucrats, or, Lord help us, the grammarians, it is often less than noble and tends to come up with weirdies like *impacted.*

3   Remember when *impacted* used to be relegated to a depressing little corner of the dentist's office reserved for bad wisdom teeth? Now the word is doing guest spots on *Donahue.* The economy is being *impacted* by the value of the dollar overseas. The election is being *impacted* by the economy. And the dollar is being *impacted* by the election. Where will it end? Who said *impacted* first and why? We want names; we want home phone numbers.

4   We won't get them, of course, because the language god doesn't do business that way. The Old Verbalizer just lets the words rip at will, zapping them into our brains and shooting them out of our mouths like cannon fire. This usually happens so quickly or when we are so intently involved in a conversation that we don't even notice a new word being minted or an old one being changed. Suddenly, there it is—*impacted,* followed by *parenting* and *hopefully* and *exacerbated* and *number crunching* and

hacker and *significant other* and *awesome* and *totally awesome* and *hog heaven* and *gifting* and *yuppie* and *condo* and *ditz* and *gridlock* and *big mo* and *little mo* and *power lunch* and *fajitas* and *couch potato,* to name a few.

5   Zap, zap, zap and the words are carried off on the wind and into TV stations throughout the land as The Old Verbalizer chuckles maniacally from atop the mighty Funk & Wagnalls in the sky.

6   Some people think dictionary editors create new words. They don't. They simply study the ebb and flow of words, sort of in the same way state officials watch a river during a flood. What happens at Merriam-Webster, Random House, the American Heritage department of Houghton Mifflin, and other dictionary shops is that editors spend the day reading everything they can get their hands on. They look at popular magazines, newspapers, scientific journals, and books. When they see a new word or an old word used in a new way or a subtle shift in the meaning of a word, they note the citation on a 3-by-5-inch card and put it in a file. Eventually these citations find their way into dictionaries, although when and how that happens depends on the publishing house and the editor. Just as one government official looking at a rising river will call the scene a disaster area while another will figure the flood is somewhere between a normal and heavy spring rain, while a third will want to watch the water a while longer before making up his or her mind, dictionary editors deal in judgment calls.

7   "This is not an exact science," says James Lowe, senior editor at Merriam-Webster Inc., in Springfield, which is considered to be the most liberal word watcher in the business. Editors there put the language in the book more or less the way people talk and don't care if the purists consider a word to be really off-the-wall slang. *The American Heritage Dictionary*, on the other hand, is the most conservative book on the shelf and has a "usage panel" that rules on the entries and decides whether something should be labeled "slang" or "nonstandard." Editors at both ends of the spectrum, however, emphasize that language has a life of its own and pays absolutely no attention to how it is labeled in a dictionary.

8   "We have no control over the language," says Anne Soukhanov, executive editor of *The American Heritage Dictionary* and author of the "Word Watch" column in *The Atlantic Monthly* magazine. "We are reactive. Back in the 1960s our usage panel said the word *tycoon* was bad form. Now it is hard to imagine anybody having an objection to that word. Language is a living thing. It is constantly changing."

9   Soukhanov's *Atlantic* column is a romp through the citation files, or a canoe trip down the raging river of words with The Old Verbalizer, if you want to thoroughly mix the metaphors in a blender here. The words she writes about haven't been entered in the dictionary yet. They're raw, hot, new to the tongue, and beg to be read out loud: *blaff, blendo,*

populuxe, glowboy, buildering, mamou, egoboo, warmedy, ear candy, cocooning. Any guesses on meanings? *Blaff* (noun): a West Indian stew; *blendo* (noun): a mixed-bag interior-decorating style; *populuxe* (adjective): of or referring to the blatantly consumer-oriented 1950s; *glowboy* (noun): nuclear power plant worker exposed to radiation; *buildering* (noun): the wild and crazy sport of climbing tall buildings; *mamou* (noun): something really major and often risky, as in "the big *mamou*"; *egoboo* (noun): an ego boost; *warmedy* (noun): a TV sitcom that oozes warmth and traditional family values; *ear candy* (noun): a short, pleasing piece of music; *cocooning* (noun): relaxing in the coziness of one's own living room instead of battling the crowds in the big bad world.

10   Soukhanov's latest discovery is *zorched out*—a phrase found in the business pages of a newspaper in February. It means to really bomb, as in "I *zorched out* on the exam."

11   "I had never seen that word before, and it just jumped off the page," she says. "It's probably been used by computer hackers for years. They have a language all their own."

12   A word can be in the language a long time before a dictionary editor will see it in print and start considering it for entry in the lexicon. That's why tracing words to their original source is usually impossible unless you're looking at something like Catch-22, from Joseph Heller's novel of the same name. (Just for the record, Heller had wanted to call his work *Catch-18*, but an editor changed the title. Would Catch-18 have caught on in the same way? Only the language god knows for sure.) Such obvious connections between a person and a word are rare, however, because language moves around in the same untraceable way jokes do.

13   "You can tell a good joke in Boston today, and it'll be in New Mexico next week," says Paul Dickson, author of the book *Words,* who writes out of his home in Garrett Park, Maryland. "Jokes and words have always traveled that way, even before television and advanced telecommunications. A light-bulb joke can arrive inside a maximum-security prison and a TV newsroom on the same day. It's a mystery how it gets there."

14   He and other word mavens say language always springs up out of whatever people are doing, which means words of the '70s and '80s reflect such developments as the health craze (*fitness walking, aerobics, pasta primavera*), the moving and shaking of big business (*leveraged buyout, bottom line, hostile takeover*), the women's movement (*chairperson, sexism, unisex*), drugs (*uppers, downers, ludes*), and the widespread use of computers (*high tech, Atari Democrats, daisy-wheel printer*). Computer-think has become so pervasive that personality traits are sometimes referred to now as being *hard-wired* (deeply ingrained and probably permanent) or *soft-wired* (easily changeable). This constant talk about *hardware* and *software* has inspired some MIT scientists to start calling the human brain *wetware.*

15   The English language is constantly adapting, realigning, borrowing word endings and beginnings, and moving them around. It has a long history of turning nouns into verbs, for instance, which explains *impacted*. Dickson says people in the last century used the word *poulticed* when they talked about applying a poultice, or hot cloth soaked in medication, to a wound. Some 600 years ago the noun *dance* two-stepped its way into usage as a verb, which scandalized the purists for a while, until they got used to it. The New York grapevine reports that billionaire real estate developer Donald Trump is well on his way to becoming a noun and a verb. People refer to "doing a *Donald Trump*" when making a major purchase, or simply "*Trumping*," which, when you think about it, is a bit like what happens in card games with a small *t*.

16   "Yesterday's atrocity becomes commonplace today," Dickson says, citing the word *irregardless*, which has been considered an assault on the language in many quarters but which is becoming acceptable anyway. "Language is a river moving through a canyon. It goes where it wants to go and wears down the landscape."

17   Dickson, who is in the *Guinness Book of World Records* for having thought up the most synonyms for describing drunkenness, is finishing a book called *Family Words* that will be published by Addison Wesley Publishing Co. Inc. this fall. In it he has collected all those words not found in dictionaries that families invent for use within the tribe. Dickson's family, for instance, has always said *pflurgg* for *thing*, as in, "Hand me that *pflurgg* over there." Other families say *woofler* when they're talking about clumps of dust under the bed; *yolke* when referring to the gunk in the corner of one's eye in the morning; and *show towel* for the guest towel nobody is supposed to touch in the bathroom.

18   Then there's *FHB*, meaning "family hold back" when company is at the table and there isn't enough food for everybody to have seconds. Another acronym is *XYZ*, a signal to "examine your zipper," because if you don't you'll embarrass the whole family. Dickson collected these words and phrases by appearing on talk shows around the country and having people call in with their favorites. Had I heard him in Boston I would have given him *gazinta*, my husband's word for plastic containers used to hold leftovers. It's a shortened form of "goes into." A *gazinta* gets its name because stuff *gazinta* it.

19   "I think people are very comfortable with the language today," says Dickson. "In the '60s there was this fear that individuality was going to disappear and that everybody would start sounding like Walter Cronkite. This hasn't happened."

20   He feels that regional accents are becoming more evident on national television and that advertising in particular reflects jargon and regionalisms. He notes that lobstermen with Massachusetts accents are featured

in a national ad for a cold medicine and that the "Wang makes it work" ads for Wang Laboratories Inc. are full of computerese—*integration, connectivity, PBX, VS, IBM iron*—that no one but a high-tech marketing person can understand.

21   "The ads tell the listener, 'This is a private club, and too bad if you can't understand what's going on,' " says Dickson. "One hundred years from now those ads will be a sociological treasure trove of life and language in the '80s."

22   Rap music will offer sociologists another pot of gold. The language of rap makes up the private club of school corridors and the streets. It's the verbal place kids can go to create their own world far from the comprehension of adults. Magnus Johnstone, who does a Saturday night rap show on WZBC out of Boston College, offers this vocabulary list: *def:* incredibly great, as in, "That's really *def,* man"; *stupid:* loose, as in "get stupid," meaning, you are so cool you are not afraid of looking ridiculous; *word!:* indicates that whatever has been said is profoundly correct and agreed with; *chill out:* relax; *dope:* very hip, as in, "That's a *dope* beat"; *perpetrating:* doing something rotten, telling lies about somebody, or actually committing a crime; *hip-hop:* rap music; *hip-hop gangster:* somebody who is really cool; *flex:* to leave, as in, "I'm going to *flex.*"

23   Anthony Mosley, a 10th-grader at the Cambridge Rindge and Latin School, adds some more: *My bag:* It's my fault; *Don't put me on the loud:* Don't single me out; *dis:* cut someone off, as in disinherit; *fake from sucker state:* a fraud; *square from Delaware:* a nerd; *rebel without a pause:* someone who can't be stopped; *crib:* home; *mugged* or *dogged:* really ugly, as in, "He's mugged"; *livin' large:* the best; *fat:* to be nice to somebody; *treacherous treach:* really good.

24   "Anybody who is into rap music talks this way—black kids, white kids, it doesn't matter," says Johnstone, who notes that the lingo comes directly from the stories in the music. The songs tell long, involved sagas of love, hurt, jail, dope, and growing up fast. "This is the folk music of the '80s. Those people playing sweet guitar music in the subway stations are not where it's at anymore. Life is not sweet."

25   No, it's not, say Edwin Newman and William Lutz, and language should do something about it. Newman, retired NBC correspondent and author of several books on the deterioration of the mother tongue, feels that the country is beginning to see a swing back to more conservative English usage and to stricter adherence to the rules of grammar.

26   "People are realizing how far the decline in education has gone," says Newman. "The nation's competitiveness is being affected. Business is worried about getting people they need, and companies are providing courses in English. Thirteen percent of the US work force is made up of functioning

illiterates. The Army has begun to give courses to recruits to bring them up to the ninth-grade level. I think all of this suggests why a change is coming. It used to be that anyone who thought correct language mattered was considered an elitist and a snob, but now people are seeing how vital it is."

27   Newman cringes at the widespread use of *irregardless* and *hopefully*, as in *"Hopefully*, it won't rain," and *squoze* for the past tense of squeeze, and *snuck* instead of sneaked.

28   "The question is, where do you draw the line?" says Newman.

29   "If you let the barriers down here, where else will they collapse? You have to maintain standards. The correct way is usually more precise." He feels jargon used in the Wang computer ads "shouldn't be permitted to spread" and adds, "Think of what it would do to conversation in this country."

30   William Lutz, a professor of English at Rutgers University and editor of the *Quarterly Review of Doublespeak*, feels that the bureaucratic jargon should also be stopped in the interests of a better America. His publication was established in 1971 by members of the National Council of Teachers of English, who wanted to make a statement about the duplicitous govern-ment language surrounding the Vietnam War and Watergate. But the jour-nal hasn't had much luck changing the way Washington talks, says Lutz, who thinks government gobbledygook has gotten even more convoluted in the past two decades.

31   "With Watergate we got words or phrases that the public could latch onto and make fun of," says Lutz, citing such gems as *surreptitious entry*, *plumbers, at this point in time*, and *expletive deleted*. "But in the Iran-contra scandal [Lt. Col. Oliver] North and [former national security adviser John] Poindexter have created a whole web of language that is impossible to penetrate." Both men were given the journal's 1987 Doublespeak Awards. North was honored for his statements "cleaning up the historical record" and "providing additional input that was radically different from the truth" instead of saying he lied. Poindexter got the barbed kudos for say-ing, among other things, that he didn't authorize the arms shipment to Iran but rather *acquiesced* to it. He also said he was not responsible for the way underlings testified before Congress because he did not *micromanage* the testimony.

32   "What's frightening about this language is that it shows how these men view the world," says Lutz. "They have imposed their reality on the world." Lutz feels that the public should challenge any officials who talk that way by laughing in their faces whenever possible, writing letters, and calling their offices.

33   "People have to learn to be aggressive," he says. "Maybe we should have little stickers made up that say 'garbage language' so that we can slap them on form letters and memos and anything else that comes across our

desks. This is a terrible, ugly way to use language and it's offensive to all of us."

34 And speaking of politics, 'tis the season [1988] for that inevitable crush of presidential campaign blah-blah to hit us right between the ears and other parts. In addition to *mo, big mo, little mo,* and *no mo,* all of which refer to a candidate's *momentum,* or lack of it, we now have *spin, spin control,* and *spin patrol. Spin* is the good face a campaign manager puts on a candidate's poor showing in a caucus or a primary.

35 Obviously this takes great skill, or *spin control,* not to mention the quick-footed efforts of campaign staffers, known as the *spin patrol.* Meanwhile, all the maneuvering may inspire staffers of an opposing candidate to marshal a *truth squad* to inform the public of exactly how much *spinning* is going on over in the other camp.

36 In addition to squads and patrols, every candidate has a *body man,* some-one who fulfills a kind of mothering role on the trail. The *body man* makes sure the candidate's tie is straight for the TV debate, keeps his mood up, and makes sure he gets his favorite cereal for breakfast.

37 If the candidate has done well, he is said to have been given a *bump* or a *bounce,* which means he got at least 15 percent of the vote. The politician who appears to be about to take off is considered to have *surge potential.* He is also *viable* and a hot prospect for *Super Tuesday.* The term *Super Tuesday* has been around since the 1976 campaign, by the way, but this year 20 primaries and caucuses, more than ever before, were scheduled on March 8. This caused a few people to start calling it *Super Duper Tuesday,* although that hasn't really caught on. Yet.

38 It's enough to make Noah Webster *plotz.* That's Yiddish for being so over-whelmed one could burst, which is what Webster would probably do were he to see that the 70,000 words he put in his two-volume dictionary, pub-lished in 1828, had grown to 470,000 in the unabridged *Webster's Third New International Dictionary,* published in 1976. Merriam-Webster also put out a supplement to that tome last year, adding 12,000 words to the lexicon.

39 Noah Webster was the first person to get American English into a dic-tionary, noting how spellings and usage here differed from those in Great Britain. He began by publishing a small compendium of 40,000 words in 1806 and then worked up to the larger, two-volume collection 22 years later.

40 He often allowed his biases to surface in his definitions, according to editor Lowe at Merriam-Webster, defining the word *cat,* for instance, as "a mean, spiteful animal." Webster's big dictionary didn't sell well, maybe because it offended cat lovers. Also, it cost $20, which for 1828 was exorbi-tant. After Webster died in 1843, his heirs sold the dictionary rights to

printers George and Charles Merriam in Springfield. They re-bound the book and began selling it for $6 a copy in 1847. And the rest, as they say, is history. Today Merriam-Webster publishes more than 30 dictionaries and handbooks. Their latest, *Webster's Ninth New Collegiate Dictionary*, has sold five million copies.

41   A lot of other companies publish Webster's dictionaries, too. There were no copyright laws back in 1843 to allow the Merriam brothers to put a lock on the famous moniker, so the name became part of the public domain.

42   Lowe, like other dictionary editors, says the public has a love affair with words. His company gets 2,000 letters a year from people reporting errors in the dictionary, suggesting new words, or asking questions about usage.

43   "Some people actually think we pay for words," says Lowe. "We don't, of course. But we put their letters in the files. We don't throw anything away."

44   The love of language has people working crossword puzzles into the night, solving jumbles and other word games at breakfast, buying books of puns, jokes, bloopers, and funny newspaper headlines, and even going to word conventions. Gloria Rosenthal of Long Island has been organizing a Wonderful World of Words gathering in upstate New York every November since 1982 and says that about 100 people usually attend. They spend a weekend playing team Scrabble, solving puzzles, having discussions on language, and listening to guest speakers. Rosenthal says the convention brings in everybody from publishers to bridge builders.

45   "People are fascinated by words," says Rosenthal, author of the book *In 25 Words or Less*, which tells of her success as a slogan and jingle writer. "Words really have power. They can kindle a romance or kill a deal. They set us apart from the animals."

46   Richard Lederer of Concord, New Hampshire, a language historian, New Hampshire Public Radio commentator, and author of the book *Anguished English*, says one linguistic theory has it that people actually didn't become human until they could speak. "People began emitting sounds from the holes in their faces around 1 million BC," notes Lederer, who writes the column "Looking at Language" for papers in New England and overseas. "This meant they were able to have words for the past and the future, which gave them an identity." He says the first words may have developed when man imitated the sounds of nature or the sounds made when dragging a tree, moving a rock, or killing an animal. As life became more complex, the language evolved.

47   Lederer says English is a "three-stringed instrument" because it was molded by the Anglo-Saxon invasion of the British Isles in 449, the Norse invasion in 1066, which brought the French influence, and finally by the Renaissance, which contributed Latin and Greek. He notes that the word

ask (Anglo-Saxon) has a French counterpart, *question*, and a Latin-based equivalent, *interrogate*. The same is true for *rise, mount,* and *ascend* as well as a whole host of other words.

48   "This makes English incredibly rich," says Lederer, "because you have three meanings for one idea, each slightly different from the other." He adds that in addition to these three basic roots, English has borrowed words from every corner of the Earth. He counts at least 100 languages represented in our everyday speech. The word *camel,* for instance, is Hebrew, *boondocks* is from the Philippines, *kindergarten* is German, *tattoo* is from the Caribbean, and *chimpanzee* is African.

49   Lederer sees two contradictory movements at work in the language today—"expansion" and "meltdown." Expansion is good, he says, because that accounts for all the new words being created. He feels meltdown is bad, however, because the meanings of too many words are "melting into each other." He points out that *disinterested,* which in the past has meant "impartial," is used interchangeably with *uninterested,* which traditionally meant "not interested."

50   "I think it was George Will who wrote that anybody who doesn't know the difference between *disinterested* and *uninterested* should have to come before an *uninterested* judge in court," notes Lederer.

51   He says the words *lie* (to recline) and *lay* (to place) are also merging, as are *compliment* (expression of admiration) and *complement* (something that completes or makes up a whole). "There's a local fast-food chain here with a sign on the wall that says, 'Try our salad to compliment your meal.' Every time I see it, I picture the lettuce saying, 'Hey, great-looking burger and fries.' When these kinds of things happen, I think we darken the windows on the house of language. But then, language laughs at logic all the time."

52   The Old Verbalizer, ever chuckling, ever unpredictable, has given us New Englanders some *wicked good* turns of phrase. We say *frappe* for *milkshake, cunning,* pronounced *cunnin',* for *sweet* or *cute, keeping room* for *family room,* and *so don't I* when we mean *so do I.*

53   Somebody says, "I have the flu." Then somebody else says, "So don't I," or "So doesn't Mary," which, according to logic, would mean that Mary and the person speaking *do not* have the flu. We speak of *down Maine,* which is up north, and going *down the Cape,* which isn't. We take *day trips,* sometimes still driving a *beach wagon,* or we ride *the T.*

54   In New York, commuters simply ride *the subway,* while people in Washington take the *Metro,* San Franciscans travel on *BART,* and Clevelanders board the *Rapid Transit.* This can get confusing, or cause a person to be *flusterated* if he or she happens to be from Maryland. A person from the deep South would be *bumfuzzled* and somebody from Boston might be plain old *discombobulated.* Meals cause further frustrations because a

Northerner orders a *sub*, while a Southerner calls for a *poor boy*, a guy from Wisconsin asks for a *garibaldi*, and everybody else wants *heroes*, *grinders*, and *hoagies*.

55   Remember the Tower of Babel story in the Bible? People were building a huge tower to heaven so that they could see what God was up to. He didn't care much for the project and scotched it by making everybody involved speak in different tongues. (Sounds like a typical day in the office, doesn't it?) That's where The Old Verbalizer came in, and we've been babbling ever since. In other words: You say *tomato*, I say *love apple*—let's call the whole thing off.

Questions on Content

1. Why does Trausch devote a paragraph to *impacted* (paragraph 3)? Why does she do this so early in the essay?

2. According to Trausch, how do words enter the dictionary?

3. Anne Soukhanov, executive editor of *The American Heritage Dictionary*, describes this dictionary as "reactive" (paragraph 8). What does she mean?

4. Paul Dickson believes that "language always springs up out of whatever people are doing" (paragraph 14). What does he mean? Discuss this idea in light of your own activities and their effects on your language.

5. Why, in this age of instant communication, are regional accents becoming more evident in television commercials?

6. About "rap," Magnus Johnstone says, "This is the folk music of the '80s" (paragraph 24). Do you agree? In answering, devise definitions for both *rap music* and *folk music*.

7. What are the differences between linguistic expansion and linguistic meltdown?

Questions on Structure and Style

8. Trausch's article follows journalistic style. Transitions are often intentionally weak so that the article can be easily cut to meet length requirements. Identify places in this article where transitions facilitate cutting.

9. Discuss the effectiveness of the short introductory paragraph. How well does it work with the concluding paragraph?

10. Where does Trausch state her thesis?

11. This essay's lively tone reflects the author's love of language. Identify specific places where her enthusiasm is obvious.

Assignments

1. Examine copies of *Webster's Ninth New Collegiate Dictionary* and *The American Heritage Dictionary*. Discuss your findings in an essay comparing the two reference works. (Paragraphs 6 through 11 of Trausch's essay should prove helpful as you begin.)

2. In paragraphs 9 through 11, Trausch points to new words that haven't yet entered a dictionary. Try to find as many such words as you can by examining the language of your own private groups. Describe your findings in a paragraph or an essay.

3. Trausch addresses the issue of private, family language—"words not found in dictionaries that families invent for use within the tribe" (paragraph 17). Look at the examples she offers. Then examine your own family language. In an essay, explain what makes your family language unique and also what purposes a private, family language serves for the people who invent it.

A Brief History of English

Paul Roberts

███████████

This well-known essay by Paul Roberts makes it clear that language development is determined by historical change. What
people do contributes to the language they speak. Thus, to understand English, we must understand English history, and
Roberts approaches his subject with history in mind. The resulting essay, remarkable for its brevity, takes a complex subject and
makes it accessible—and engaging, thanks to Roberts's skill at
storytelling.

███████████

1   No understanding of the English language can be very satisfactory without
a notion of the history of the language. But we shall have to make do with
just a notion. The history of English is long and complicated, and we can
only hit the high spots.

2   The history of our language begins a little after A.D. 600. Everything
before that is pre-history, which means that we can guess at it but can't
prove much. For a thousand years or so before the birth of Christ our
linguistic ancestors were savages wandering through the forests of northern Europe. Their language was a part of the Germanic branch of the Indo-
European family.

3   At the time of the Roman Empire—say, from the beginning of the Christian Era to around A.D. 400—the speakers of what was to become English
were scattered along the northern coast of Europe. They spoke a dialect of
Low German. More exactly, they spoke several different dialects, since
they were several different tribes. The names given to the tribes who got to
England are *Angles, Saxons*, and *Jutes*. For convenience, we can refer to
them all as Anglo-Saxons.

4   Their first contact with civilization was a rather thin acquaintance with
the Roman Empire on whose borders they lived. Probably some of the
Anglo-Saxons wandered into the Empire occasionally, and certainly Roman merchants and traders traveled among the tribes. At any rate, this
period saw the first of our many borrowings from Latin. Such words as
kettle, wine, cheese, butter, cheap, plum, gem, bishop, church were borrowed at
this time. They show something of the relationship of the Anglo-Saxons
with the Romans. The Anglo-Saxons were learning, getting their first taste
of civilization.

5   They still had a long way to go, however, and their first step was to help
smash the civilization they were learning from. In the fourth century the
Roman power weakened badly. While the Goths were pounding away at
the Romans in the Mediterranean countries, their relatives, the Anglo-
Saxons, began to attack Britain.

6   The Romans had been the ruling power in Britain since A.D. 43. They had subjugated the Celts whom they found living there and had succeeded in setting up a Roman administration. The Roman influence did not extend to the outlying parts of the British Isles. In Scotland, Wales, and Ireland the Celts remained free and wild, and they made periodic forays against the Romans in England. Among other defense measures, the Romans built the famous Roman Wall to ward off the tribes in the north.

7   Even in England the Roman power was thin. Latin did not become the language of the country as it did in Gaul and Spain. The mass of people continued to speak Celtic, with Latin and the Roman civilization it contained in use as a top dressing.

8   In the fourth century, troubles multiplied for the Romans in Britain. Not only did the untamed tribes of Scotland and Wales grow more and more restive, but the Anglo-Saxons began to make pirate raids on the eastern coast. Furthermore, there was growing difficulty everywhere in the Empire, and the legions in Britain were siphoned off to fight elsewhere. Finally, in A.D. 410, the last Roman ruler in England, bent on becoming emperor, left the islands and took the last of the legions with him. The Celts were left in possession of Britain but almost defenseless against the impending Anglo-Saxon attack.

9   Not much is surely known about the arrival of the Anglo-Saxons in England. According to the best early source, the eighth-century historian Bede, the Jutes came in 449 in response to a plea from the Celtic king, Vortigern, who wanted their help against the Picts attacking from the north. The Jutes subdued the Picts but then quarreled and fought with Vortigern, and, with reinforcements from the Continent, settled permanently in Kent. Somewhat later the Angles established themselves in eastern England and the Saxons in the south and west. Bede's account is plausible enough, and these were probably the main lines of the invasion.

10   We do know, however, that the Angles, Saxons, and Jutes were a long time securing themselves in England. Fighting went on for as long as a hundred years before the Celts in England were all killed, driven into Wales, or reduced to slavery. This is the period of King Arthur, who was not entirely mythological. He was a Romanized Celt, a general, though probably not a king. He had some success against the Anglo-Saxons, but it was only temporary. By 550 or so the Anglo-Saxons were firmly established. English was in England.

11   All this is pre-history, so far as the language is concerned. We have no record of the English language until after 600, when the Anglo-Saxons were converted to Christianity and learned the Latin alphabet. The conversion began, to be precise, in the year 597 and was accomplished within thirty or forty years. The conversion was a great advance for the Anglo-Saxons, not only because of the spiritual benefits but because it reestablished contact with what remained of Roman civilization. This civilization

didn't amount to much in the year 600, but it was certainly superior to anything in England up to that time.

12   It is customary to divide the history of the English language into three periods: Old English, Middle English, and Modern English. Old English runs from the earliest records—i.e., seventh century—to about 1100; Middle English from 1100 to 1450 or 1500; Modern English from 1500 to the present day. Sometimes Modern English is further divided into Early Modern, 1500–1700, and Late Modern, 1700 to the present.

13   When England came into history, it was divided into several more or less autonomous kingdoms, some of which at times exercised a certain amount of control over the others. In the century after the conversion the most advanced kingdom was Northumbria, the area between the Humber River and the Scottish border. By A.D. 700 the Northumbrians had developed a respectable civilization, the finest in Europe. It is sometimes called the Northumbrian Renaissance, and it was the first of the several renaissances through which Europe struggled upward out of the ruins of the Roman Empire. It was in this period that the best of the Old English literature was written, including the epic poem *Beowulf*.

14   In the eighth century, Northumbrian power declined, and the center of influence moved southward to Mercia, the kingdom of the Midlands. A century later the center shifted again, and Wessex, the country of the West Saxons, became the leading power. The most famous king of the West Saxons was Alfred the Great, who reigned in the second half of the ninth century, dying in 901. He was famous not only as a military man and administrator but also as a champion of learning. He founded and supported schools and translated or caused to be translated many books from Latin into English. At this time also much of the Northumbrian literature of two centuries earlier was copied in West Saxon. Indeed, the great bulk of Old English writing which has come down to us is in the West Saxon dialect of 900 or later.

15   In the military sphere, Alfred's great accomplishment was his successful opposition to the Viking invasions. In the ninth and tenth centuries, the Norsemen emerged in their ships from their homelands in Denmark and the Scandinavian peninsula. They traveled far and attacked and plundered at will and almost with impunity. They ravaged Italy and Greece, settled in France, Russia, and Ireland, colonized Iceland and Greenland, and discovered America several centuries before Columbus. Nor did they overlook England.

16   After many years of hit-and-run raids, the Norsemen landed an army on the east coast of England in the year 866. There was nothing much to oppose them except the Wessex power led by Alfred. The long struggle ended in 877 with a treaty by which a line was drawn roughly from the northwest of England to the southeast. On the eastern side of the line Norse rule was to prevail. This was called the Danelaw. The western side was to be governed by Wessex.

17   The linguistic result of all this was a considerable injection of Norse into the English language. Norse was at this time not so different from English as Norwegian or Danish is now. Probably speakers of English could understand, more or less, the language of the newcomers who had moved into eastern England. At any rate, there was considerable interchange and word borrowing. Examples of Norse words in the English language are *sky, give, law, egg, outlaw, leg, ugly, scant, sly, crawl, scowl, take, thrust*. There are hundreds more. We have even borrowed some pronouns from Norse—*they, their,* and *them*. These words were borrowed first by the eastern and northern dialects and then in the course of hundreds of years made their way into English generally.

18   It is supposed also—indeed, it must be true—that the Norsemen influenced the sound structure and the grammar of English. But this is hard to demonstrate in detail.

19   We may now have an example of Old English. The favorite illustration is the Lord's Prayer, since it needs no translation. This has come to us in several different versions. Here is one:

> Fæder ure þuðe eart on heofonum si þin nama gehalgod. To-
> becume þin rice. Gewurðe þin willa on eorðan swa swa on
> heofonum. Urne gedæghwamlican hlaf syle us to dæg. And for-
> gyf us ure gyltas swa swa we forgyfaþ urum gyltendum. And ne
> gelæd þu us on costnunge ac alys us of yfele. Soðlice.

20   Some of the differences between this and Modern English are merely differences in orthography. For instance, the sign æ is what Old English writers used for a vowel sound like that in modern *hat* or *and*. The *th* sounds of modern *thin* or *then* are represented in Old English by þ or ð. But of course there are many differences in sound too. *Ure* is the ancestor of modern *our*, but the first vowel was like that in *too* or *ooze*. *Hlaf* is modern *loaf*; we have dropped the *h* sound and changed the vowel, which in *hlaf* was pronounced something like the vowel in *father*. Old English had some sounds which we do not have. The sound represented by *y* does not occur in Modern English. If you pronounce the vowel in *bit* with your lips rounded, you may approach it.

21   In grammar, Old English was much more highly inflected than Modern English is. That is, there were more case endings for nouns, more person and number endings for verbs, a more complicated pronoun system, various endings for adjectives, and so on. Old English nouns had four cases—nominative, genitive, dative, accusative. Adjectives had five—all these and an instrumental case besides. Present-day English has only two cases for nouns—common case and possessive case. Adjectives now have no case system at all. On the other hand, we now use a more rigid word order and more structure words (prepositions, auxiliaries, and the like) to express relationships than Old English did.

22   Some of this grammar we can see in the Lord's Prayer. *Heofonum*, for instance, is a dative plural; the nominative singular was *heofon*. *Urne* is an accusative singular; the nominative is *ure*. In *urum gyltendum* both words are dative plural. *Forgyfaþ* is the third person plural form of the verb. Word order is different: "urne gedæghwamlican hlaf syle us" in place of "Give us our daily bread." And so on.

23   In vocabulary Old English is quite different from Modern English. Most of the Old English words are what we may call native English: that is, words which have not been borrowed from other languages but which have been a part of English ever since English was a part of Indo-European. Old English did certainly contain borrowed words. We have seen that many borrowings were coming in from Norse. Rather large numbers had been borrowed from Latin, too. Some of these were taken while the Anglo-Saxons were still on the Continent (*cheese, butter, bishop, kettle,* etc.); a large number came into English after Conversion (*angel, candle, priest, martyr, radish, oyster, purple, school, spend,* etc.). But the great majority of Old English words were native English.

24   Now, on the contrary, the majority of words in English are borrowed, taken mostly from Latin and French. Of the words in *The American College Dictionary* only about 14 percent are native. Most of these, to be sure, are common, high-frequency words—*the, of, I, and, because, man, mother, road,* etc.; of the thousand most common words in English, some 62 percent are native English. Even so, the modern vocabulary is very much Latinized and Frenchified. The Old English vocabulary was not.

25   Sometime between the year 1000 and 1200 various important changes took place in the structure of English, and Old English became Middle English. The political event which facilitated these changes was the Norman Conquest. The Normans, as the name shows, came originally from Scandinavia. In the early tenth century they established themselves in northern France, adopted the French language, and developed a vigorous kingdom and a very passable civilization. In the year 1066, led by Duke William, they crossed the Channel and made themselves masters of England. For the next several hundred years, England was ruled by kings whose first language was French.

26   One might wonder why, after the Norman Conquest, French did not become the national language, replacing English entirely. The reason is that the Conquest was not a national migration, as the earlier Anglo-Saxon invasion had been. Great numbers of Normans came to England, but they came as rulers and landlords. French became the language of the court, the language of the nobility, the language of polite society, the language of literature. But it did not replace English as the language of the people. There must always have been hundreds of towns and villages in which French was never heard except when visitors of high station passed through.

27   But English, though it survived as the national language, was profoundly changed after the Norman Conquest. Some of the changes—in

sound structure and grammar—would no doubt have taken place whether there had been a Conquest or not. Even before 1066 the case system of English nouns and adjectives was becoming simplified; people came to rely more on word order and prepositions than on inflectional endings to communicate their meanings. The process was speeded up by sound changes which caused many of the endings to sound alike. But no doubt the Conquest facilitated the change. German, which didn't experience a Norman Conquest, is today rather highly inflected compared to its cousin English.

28   But it is in vocabulary that the effects of the Conquest are most obvious. French ceased, after a hundred years or so, to be the native language of very many people in England, but it continued—and continues still—to be a zealously cultivated second language, the mirror of elegance and civilization. When one spoke English, one introduced not only French ideas and French things but also their French names. This was not only easy but socially useful. To pepper one's conversation with French expressions was to show that one was well-bred, elegant, *au courant*. The last sentence shows that the process is not yet dead. By using *au courant* instead of, say, *abreast of things*, the writer indicates that he is no dull clod who knows only English but an elegant person aware of how things are done in *le haut monde*.

29   Thus French words came into English, all sorts of them. There were words to do with government: *parliament, majesty, treaty, alliance, tax, government*; church words: *parson, sermon, baptism, incense, crucifix, religion*; words for foods: *veal, beef, mutton, bacon, jelly, peach, lemon, cream, biscuit*; colors: *blue, scarlet, vermilion*; household words: *curtain, chair, lamp, towel, blanket, parlor*; play words: *dance, chess, music, leisure, conversation*; literary words: *story, romance, poet, literary*; learned words: *study, logic, grammar, noun, surgeon, anatomy, stomach*; just ordinary words of all sorts: *nice, second, very, age, bucket, gentle, final, fault, flower, cry, count, sure, move, surprise, plain*.

30   All these and thousands more poured into the English vocabulary between 1100 and 1500, until at the end of that time many people must have had more French words than English at their command. This is not to say that English became French. English remained English in sound structure and in grammar, though these also felt the ripples of French influence. The very heart of the vocabulary, too, remained English. Most of the high-frequency words—the pronouns, the prepositions, the conjunctions, the auxiliaries, as well as a great many ordinary nouns and verbs and adjectives—were not replaced by borrowings.

31   Middle English, then, was still a Germanic language, but it differed from Old English in many ways. The sound system and the grammar changed a good deal. Speakers made less use of case systems and other inflectional devices and relied more on word order and structure words to express their meanings. This is often said to be a simplification, but it isn't really. Languages don't become simpler; they merely exchange one kind of

complexity for another. Modern English is not a simple language, as any foreign speaker who tries to learn it will hasten to tell you.

32   For us Middle English is simpler than Old English just because it is closer to Modern English. It takes three or four months at least to learn to read Old English prose and more than that for poetry. But a week of good study should put one in touch with the Middle English poet Chaucer. Indeed, you may be able to make some sense of Chaucer straight off, though you would need instruction in pronunciation to make it sound like poetry. Here is a famous passage from the *General Prologue to the Canterbury Tales*, fourteenth century:

> Ther was also a nonne, a Prioresse,
> That of hir smyling was ful symple and coy,
> Hir gretteste oath was but by Seinte Loy,
> And she was cleped Madam Eglentyne.
> Ful wel she song the service dyvyne,
> Entuned in hir nose ful semely.
> And Frenshe she spak ful faire and fetisly,
> After the scole of Stratford-atte-Bowe,
> For Frenshe of Parys was to hir unknowe.

33   Sometime between 1400 and 1600 English underwent a couple of sound changes which made the language of Shakespeare quite different from that of Chaucer. Incidentally, these changes contributed much to the chaos in which English spelling now finds itself.

34   One change was the elimination of a vowel sound in certain unstressed positions at the end of words. For instance, the words *name, stone, wine, dance* were pronounced as two syllables by Chaucer but as just one by Shakespeare. The *e* in these words became, as we say, "silent." But it wasn't silent for Chaucer; it represented a vowel sound. So also the words *laughed, seemed, stored* would have been pronounced by Chaucer as two-syllable words. The change was an important one because it affected thousands of words and gave a different aspect to the whole language.

35   The other change is what is called the Great Vowel Shift. This was a systematic shifting of half a dozen vowels and diphthongs in stressed syllables. For instance, the word *name* had in Middle English a vowel something like that in the modern word *father; wine* had the vowel of modern *mean; he* was pronounced something like modern *hey; mouse* sounded like *moose; moon* had the vowel of *moan*. Again the shift was thoroughgoing and affected all the words in which these vowel sounds occurred. Since we still keep the Middle English system of spelling these words, the differences between Modern English and Middle English are often more real than apparent.

36   The vowel shift has meant also that we have come to use an entirely different set of symbols for representing vowel sounds than is used by

writers of such languages as French, Italian, or Spanish, in which no such vowel shift occurred. If you come across a strange word—say, *bine*—in an English book, you will pronounce it according to the English system, with the vowel of *wine* or *dine*. But if you read *bine* in a French, Italian, or Spanish book, you will pronounce it with the vowel of *mean* or *seen*.

37   These two changes, then, produced the basic differences between Middle English and Modern English. But there were several other developments that had an effect upon the language. One was the invention of printing, an invention introduced into England by William Caxton in the year 1475. Where before books had been rare and costly, they suddenly became cheap and common. More and more people learned to read and write. This was the first of many advances in communication which have worked to unify languages and to arrest the development of dialect differences, though of course printing affects writing principally rather than speech. Among other things it hastened the standardization of spelling.

38   The period of Early Modern English—that is, the sixteenth and seventeenth centuries—was also the period of the English Renaissance, when people developed, on the one hand, a keen interest in the past and, on the other, a more daring and imaginative view of the future. New ideas multiplied, and new ideas meant new language. Englishmen had grown accustomed to borrowing words from French as a result of the Norman Conquest; now they borrowed from Latin and Greek. As we have seen, English had been raiding Latin from Old English times and before, but now the floodgates really opened, and thousands of words from the classical languages poured in. *Pedestrian, bonus, anatomy, contradict, climax, dictionary, benefit, multiply, exist, paragraph, initiate, scene, inspire* are random examples. Probably the average educated American today has more words from French in his vocabulary than from native English sources, and more from Latin than from French.

39   The greatest writer of the Early Modern English period is of course Shakespeare, and the best-known book is the King James Version of the Bible, published in 1611. The Bible (if not Shakespeare) has made many features of Early Modern English perfectly familiar to many people down to present times, even though we do not use these features in present-day speech and writing. For instance, the old pronouns *thou* and *thee* have dropped out of use now, together with their verb forms, but they are still familiar to us in prayer and in Biblical quotation: "Whither thou goest, I will go." Such forms as *hath* and *doth* have been replaced by *has* and *does;* "Goes he hence tonight?" would now be "Is he going away tonight?"; Shakespeare's "Fie on't, sirrah" would be "Nuts to that, Mac." Still, all these expressions linger with us because of the power of the works in which they occur.

40   It is not always realized, however, that considerable sound changes have taken place between Early Modern English and the English of the present day. Shakespearean actors putting on a play speak the words, properly

enough, in their modern pronunciation. But it is very doubtful that this pronunciation would be understood at all by Shakespeare. In Shakespeare's time, the word *reason* was pronounced like modern *raisin; face* had the sound of modern *glass;* the *l* in *would, should, palm* was pronounced. In these points and a great many others the English language has moved a long way from what it was in 1600.

41   The history of English since 1700 is filled with many movements and countermovements, of which we can notice only a couple. One of these is the vigorous attempt made in the eighteenth century, and the rather half-hearted attempts made since, to regulate and control the English language. Many people of the eighteenth century, not understanding very well the forces which govern language, proposed to polish and prune and restrict English, which they felt was proliferating too wildly. There was much talk of an academy which would rule on what people could and could not say and write. The academy never came into being, but the eighteenth century did succeed in establishing certain attitudes which, though they haven't had much effect on the development of the language itself, have certainly changed the native speaker's feeling about the language.

42   In part a product of the wish to fix and establish the language was the development of the dictionary. The first English dictionary was published in 1603; it was a list of 2500 words briefly defined. Many others were published with gradual improvements until Samuel Johnson published his *English Dictionary* in 1755. This, steadily revised, dominated the field in England for nearly a hundred years. Meanwhile in America, Noah Webster published his dictionary in 1828, and before long dictionary publishing was a big business in this country. The last century has seen the publication of one great dictionary: the twelve-volume *Oxford English Dictionary*, compiled in the course of seventy-five years through the labors of many scholars. We have also, of course, numerous commercial dictionaries which are as good as the public wants them to be if not, indeed, rather better.

43   Another product of the eighteenth century was the invention of "English grammar." As English came to replace Latin as the language of scholarship it was felt that one should also be able to control and dissect it, parse and analyze it, as one could Latin. What happened in practice was that the grammatical description that applied to Latin was removed and superimposed on English. This was silly, because English is an entirely different kind of language, with its own forms and signals and ways of producing meaning. Nevertheless, English grammars on the Latin model were worked out and taught in the schools. In many schools they are still being taught. This activity is not often popular with school children, but it is sometimes an interesting and instructive exercise in logic. The principal harm in it is that it has tended to keep people from being interested in English and has obscured the real features of English structure.

44   But probably the most important force in the development of English
in the modern period has been the tremendous expansion of English-
speaking peoples. In 1500 English was a minor language, spoken by a few
people on a small island. Now it is perhaps the greatest language of the
world, spoken natively by over a quarter of a billion people and as a second
language by many millions more. When we speak of English now, we
must specify whether we mean American English, British English, Australian English, Indian English, or what, since the differences are considerable. The American cannot go to England or the Englishman to America
confident that he will always understand and be understood. The Ala-
baman in Iowa or the Iowan in Alabama shows himself a foreigner every
time he speaks. It is only because communication has become fast and easy
that English in this period of its expansion has not broken into a dozen
mutually unintelligible languages.

**Questions
on Content**

1. What is the significance of each of the following
    in the development of the English language:

    Alfred the Great   William Caxton

    Norman Conquest   English Renaissance

    Great Vowel Shift

2. What are the three major periods in the history of
    the English language? What does Roberts suggest
    were the major characteristics of the language dur-
    ing each period?

3. What does Roberts mean when he calls Old
    English a more inflected language than Mod-
    ern English?

4. Are structure words more important in Old Eng-
    lish or Modern English? Why?

5. What are some of the problems with the system of
    grammar that was imposed on the English lan-
    guage in the eighteenth century?

6. Why is the vocabulary of Modern English so differ-
    ent from that of Old English?

7. Why was the printing press so important to the
    development of English?

Questions
on Structure
and Style

8. What audience does Roberts have in mind for this essay? Mark three paragraphs that clearly show this audience.

9. Where does Roberts state the thesis of his essay?

10. How does Roberts organize his material? Is this method effective? What other methods might he have used?

11. There are forty-four relatively short paragraphs in this selection. Obviously, Roberts has to be conscious of transitions. Discuss his use of transitions in one section of the essay.

Assignments

1. Choose a short passage of modern prose written for a general audience. Look up in a dictionary at least ten of the words in the passage. Do your findings substantiate some of the major points that Roberts makes about the development of English?

2. List five words that have recently become part of the English lexicon. (You might look in the field of technology to find such words, or look for slang terms or foreign influences.)

3. Study some of the place names in your geographic area. What do they tell you about the language history of your region?

4. Roberts feels that "no understanding of the English language can be very satisfactory without a notion of the history of the language" (paragraph 1). Write an essay explaining why Roberts says this and why you agree or disagree.

5. Each family has its own language and/or dialect history. Look back two or three generations in your own family, and discuss the personal linguistic history of your ancestors (both immediate and distant).

American English:
The Period of Growth

H. L. Mencken

We don't speak English. We speak American English, and in this essay, H. L. Mencken shows how this came about. Mencken, journalist, editor, and essayist, was particularly interested in our language. The selection is from *The American Language*, a monumental work of scholarship that is still respected more than fifty years after its original publication. The term *scholarship* often implies dullness and pedantry, but Mencken's work is lively and informative as it paints a detailed picture of the development of our "native" language.

1   Though the American language had begun its dizzy onward march before the Revolution, it did not begin to show its vigor and daring until the Nineteenth Century. Until then its free proliferation was impeded by the lack of a consequential national literature and by an internal political disharmony. Conflicting interests, suppressed during the Revolution by common aims and common dangers, reappeared with peace and yielded suspicions and hatreds which often came near wrecking the new Confederation. Few Americans of the period were able to detach themselves from the struggle for domination then going on in Europe. Not only the surviving Loyalists—perhaps a third of the population in 1776—but also many propertied patriots were ardently in favor of England, and such patriots as Jefferson were as ardently in favor of France. This engrossment in the rivalries of foreign nations made it difficult for the people of the new nation to think of themselves, politically and culturally, as Americans. Soon after the Treaty of Paris was signed, someone referred to the late struggle, in Franklin's hearing, as the War for Independence. "Say, rather, the War of the Revolution," said Franklin. "The War for Independence is yet to be fought."

2   "That struggle," adds B. J. Lossing in "Our Country" (1873), "occurred, and that independence was won, by the Americans in the War of 1812." In the interval the new Republic had passed through a period of *Sturm und Drang* whose gigantic perils and passions we have begun to forget. The poor debtor class was fired by the French Revolution to demands which threatened the country with bankruptcy and anarchy, and the class of property owners, in reaction, went far to the other extreme. On all sides flourished a strong British party, particularly in New England, where the codfish aristocracy exhibited an undisguised Anglomania, and looked

forward to a *rapprochement* with the mother country. This Anglomania showed itself, not only in ceaseless political agitation, but also in an elaborate imitation of English manners.

3   The first sign of the dawn of a new national order came with the election of Thomas Jefferson to the Presidency in 1800; he was the man who introduced the bugaboo of English plots into American politics. His first acts after his inauguration were to abolish all ceremonial at the court of the Republic, and to abandon spoken discourses to Congress for written messages. Both reforms met with wide approval; the exactions of the English, particularly on the high seas, were beginning to break up the British party. But confidence in the solidarity and security of the new nation was still anything but universal. Democracy was still experimental, doubtful, full of gunpowder. Jefferson, its protagonist, was the hero of the populace, but he was not a part of the populace himself, nor did he ever quite trust it.

4   It was reserved for Andrew Jackson to lead the rise of the lower orders with dramatic effectiveness. Jackson was the archetype of the new American who appeared after 1814—ignorant, pushful, impatient of restraint and precedent, an iconoclast, a Philistine, an Anglophobe in every fiber. He came from the extreme backwoods, and his youth was passed, like that of Abraham Lincoln after him, amid surroundings but little removed from savagery. Thousands of other young Americans of the same sort were growing up at the same time. They swarmed across the mountains and down the great rivers, wrestling with the naked wilderness and setting up a casual, impromptu sort of civilization where the Indian still menaced. Schools were few and rudimentary; any effort to mimic the amenities of the East, or of the mother country, in manner or even in speech, met with instant derision. In these surroundings at this time the thoroughgoing American of tradition was born. America began to stand for something new in the world—in government, in law, in public and private morals, in customs and habits of mind. And simultaneously the voice of America began to take on its characteristic tone colors, and the speech of America began to differentiate itself unmistakably from that of England. The Philadelphian or Bostonian of 1790 had no difficulty in making himself understood by a visiting Englishman. But the Ohio boatman of 1810 or plainsman of 1815 was already speaking a dialect that the Englishman would have shrunk from as barbarous and unintelligible, and before long it began to leave its marks upon a distinctively national literature. The same year, 1828, which saw Jackson elected for his first term also saw the publication of Noah Webster's "American Dictionary of the English Language," and a year later followed Samuel Lorenzo Knapp's "Lectures on American Literature," the first formal treatise on the national letters. Knapp, by that time, had enough material at hand to make a very creditable showing— Bryant's "Thanatopsis" (1817); Irving's "Knickerbocker" (1809), "Sketch Book" (1819), and "Columbus" (1828); Cooper's "The Spy" (1821), "The

Pilot" (1823), and "The Prairie" (1826); Hawthorne's "Fanshaw" (1828); and Poe's "Tamerlane and Other Poems" (1827); not to mention School-craft's "Through the Northwest" (1821) and "Travels in the Mississippi Valley" (1825), Kent's "Commentaries" (1826), Marshall's "Washington" (1804) and Audubon's "Birds of America" (1827).

5   The national feeling, long delayed in appearing, leaped into being at last in truly amazing vigor. "One can get an idea of the strength of that feel-ing," says R. O. Williams,

> by glancing at almost any book taken at random from the Ameri-can publications of the period. Belief in the grand future of the United States is the keynote of everything said and done. All things American are to be grand—our territory, population, products, wealth, science, art—but especially our political in-stitutions and literature. Unbounded confidence in the material development of the country . . . prevailed throughout the . . . Union during the first thirty years of the century, and over and above a belief in, and concern for, materialistic progress, there were enthusiastic anticipations of achievements in all the moral and intellectual fields of national greatness.

6   Nor was that vast optimism wholly without warrant. With the memory of old wrongs shutting them off from England, the new American writers turned to the Continent for inspiration and encouragement. Irving had already drunk at Spanish springs; Emerson and Bayard Taylor were to receive powerful impulses from Germany, following Ticknor, Bancroft and Everett before them; Bryant was destined to go back to the classics. More-over, Irving, Cooper, John P. Kennedy and many another had shown the way to native sources of literary material, and Longfellow was making ready to follow them; the ground was preparing for "Uncle Tom's Cabin." Finally, Webster himself worked better than he knew. His American Dic-tionary was not only thoroughly American; it was superior to any of the current dictionaries of the English.

7   Thus all hesitations disappeared, and there arose a national conscious-ness so soaring and so blatant that it began to dismiss every British usage and opinion as puerile and idiotic. The debate upon the Oregon question gave a gaudy chance to the new breed of super-patriots who raged un-checked until the Civil War. Thornton quotes a typical speech in Congress:

> The proudest bird upon the mountain is upon the American en-sign, and not one feather shall fall from her plumage there. She is American in design, and an emblem of wildness and freedom. I say again, she has not perched herself upon American standards to die there. Our great Western valleys were never scooped out for her burial place. Nor were the everlasting, untrodden

mountains piled for her monument. Niagara shall not pour her endless waters for her requiem; nor shall our ten thousand rivers weep to the ocean in eternal tears. No, sir, no! Unnumbered voices shall come up from the river, plain, and mountain, echoing the songs of our triumphant deliverance, wild lights from a thousand hilltops will betoken the rising of the sun of freedom.

8   This tall talk was not reserved for occasions of state; it decorated everyday speech, especially in the Jackson country to the southward and beyond the mountains. It ran to grotesque metaphors and farfetched exaggerations, and out of it came a great many Americanisms that still flourish. A noble example comes from Mark Twain's "Life on the Mississippi," the time being *c.* 1852:

Whoo-oop! I'm the old original iron-jawed, brass-mounted, copper-bellied corpse-maker from the wilds of Arkansaw! Look at me! I'm the man they call Sudden Death and General Desolation! Sired by a hurricane, dam'd by an earthquake, half-brother to the cholera, nearly related to the smallpox on the mother's side! . . . Blood's my natural drink, and the wails of the dying is music to my ear! Cast your eye on me, gentlemen, and lay low and hold your breath, for I'm 'bout to turn myself loose!

9   This extravagance of metaphor, with its naïve bombast, was borrowed eagerly by the humorous writers and was to leave its marks upon Whitman and Mark Twain, but the generality of American authors eschewed it. "Whatever differences there may be," says Sir William Craigie, "between the language of Longfellow and Tennyson, of Emerson and Ruskin, they are differences due to style and subject, to a personal choice or command of words, and not to any real divergence in the means of expression." But meanwhile, says Sir William, there was going on

a rise and rapid growth within the United States of new types of literature which would either give fuller scope to the native element by mingling it with the conventional, or would boldly adopt it as a standard in itself.

10   On the levels below the Olympians a wild and lawless development of the language went on, and many of the uncouth words and phrases that it brought to birth gradually forced themselves into more or less good usage. The old hegemony of the Tidewater gentry, North and South, had been shaken by the revolt of the frontier under Jackson, and what remained of an urbane habit of mind and utterance began to be confined to the narrowing feudal areas of the South and the still narrower refuge of the Boston Brahmins. The typical American, in Paulding's satirical phrase, became "a

bundling, gouging, impious" fellow, without either "morals, literature, religion, or refinement." Next to the savage struggle for land and dollars, party politics was the chief concern, and with the entrance of pushing upstarts from the backwoods, political controversy sank to an incredibly low level. First the enfranchised mob, whether in the city wards or along the Western rivers, invented fantastic slang words and turns of phrase; then they were "seized upon by stump-speakers at political meetings"; then they were heard in Congress; then they got into the newspapers; and finally they came into more or less good repute. W. C. Fowler, in listing "low expressions" in 1850, described them as "chiefly political." "The vernacular tongue of the country," said Daniel Webster, "has become greatly vitiated, depraved and corrupted by the style of the congressional debates." This flood of racy and unprecedented words and phrases beat upon and finally penetrated the austere retreat of the literati, but the dignity of speech cultivated there had little compensatory influence upon the vulgate. The newpaper was enthroned, and belles-lettres were cultivated almost in private, and as a mystery. "Uncle Tom's Cabin" and "Ten Nights in a Barroom," both published in the early 1850s, were probably the first contemporary native books, after Cooper's day, that the American people, as a people, ever really read. Nor did the pulpit lift a corrective voice; it joined the crowd, and contributed to the vernacular such treasures as *to doxologize* and *to funeralize.*

11   This pressure from below eventually broke down the defenses of the purists, and forced the new national idiom upon them. "When it comes to *talking*," wrote Charles Astor Bristed for Englishmen in 1855, "the most refined and best educated American, who has habitually resided in his own country, the very man who would write, on some serious topic, volumes in which no peculiarity could be detected, will in half a dozen sentences, use at least as many words that cannot fail to strike the inexperienced Englishman who hears them for the first time."

12   American slang, says Krapp, was "the child of the new nationalism, the spirit of joyous adventure that entered American life after the close of the War of 1812." He goes on:

> One will search earlier colonial literature in vain for any flowering of those verbal ingenuities which ornament the colloquial style of Americans so abundantly in the first great period of Western expansion, and which have ever since found their most favorable conditions along the shifting line of the frontier.

The old American frontier vanished by the end of the Nineteenth Century, but to the immigrants who poured in after 1850, even the slums of the great Eastern cities presented essentially frontier conditions, and there are still cultural, if not geographic, frontiers at Las Vegas and Miami, not to mention Alaska and Mississippi. From 1814 to 1861 the influence of the great open spaces was immediate and enormous, and during those gay and hopeful and melodramatic days all the traditional characteristics of American English were developed—its disdain of all scholastic rules and precedents, its tendency toward bold and often bizarre tropes, its rough humors, its not infrequent flights of what might almost be called poetic fancy, its love of neologisms for their own sake. Recently most neologisms have come from the East, not a few of them painfully artful, but before the Civil War the great reservoir was the West, which then still included a large part of the South, and they showed a gaudy innocence.

13   "American humor," says Thomas Low Nichols, "consists largely of exaggeration, and of strange and quaint expressions. . . . Much that seems droll to English readers in the extravagances of Western American is very seriously intended. The man who described himself as 'squandering about permiscuous' had no idea that his expression was funny. When he boasted of his sister that 'she slings the nastiest ankle in old Kentuck' he only intended to say that she was a good dancer." Yet, however much this may have been true in the earliest days, among the loutish fur trappers and mountain men who constituted the first wave of pioneers, it had ceased to be so by the time the new West began to develop recorders of its speech. The identity of its first recorders has been forgotten, but some of them were professional humorists, for by the end of the 1840s the stars of the craft were beginning to turn from the New England Yankee to the trans-Allegheny American, often a Southerner and usually only theoretically literate. The discovery of gold in California attracted not only fortune seekers but also journalists, and out of their ranks came a large number of satirical historians of the rise of Western civilization, with Mark Twain, in the end, overshadowing all the rest. These wags really made "tall talk" the fearful and wonderful thing that it became during the two pre-war decades, though no doubt its elements were derived from authentic folk speech. It was, said William F. Thompson,

> a form of utterance ranging in composition from striking concoctions of ingeniously contrived epithets, expressing disparagement or encomium, to wild hyperbole, fantastic simile and metaphor, and a highly bombastic display of oratory, employed to impress the listener with the physical prowess or general superiority of the speaker or of his friends.

14   It survives more or less in Western fiction, and there are even traces of it remaining in real life, but the best of it belongs to the Jackson era, when it first burgeoned: *to absquatulate, bodaciously, to obflisticate, to ramsquaddle, ringtailed roarer* and *screamer*. *To absquatulate*, meaning to depart stealthily, is traced by the DA to 1830, and *bodaciously*, meaning completely, to 1837; in the form *body-aciously* it was used by James Hall in his "Legends of the

West" (second edition, 1832). *To obflisticate,* meaning to eclipse or obliterate, is traced to 1832, with *to obflusticate* and *to obfusticate* as variants. *To ramsquaddle,* which dates from 1830, seems to have been a synonym for its contemporary *to exflunct, i.e.,* to beat, which soon developed a host of variants and derivatives. *Ringtailed roarer,* a big and hearty fellow, is traced to 1830, and *screamer,* a strong man, to 1831. Many other similar coinages date from the period. *Rip-roaring,* now almost standard American, is traced to 1834, and *rip-snorter* to 1840. The DAE's first example of *teetotal* is dated 1837, three years later than the date of the first English example, but *teetotaciously* had appeared in 1833, and *tetotally* (soon *teetotally*) in the letters of the celebrated Parson Weems (1807). *Conbobberation,* a disturbance, is traced to 1835; *to hornswoggle,* to cheat, to 1829; *rambunctious,* uncontrollable, to 1830; and *peedoodles,* a nervous disorder, to 1835.

15   Some of the Western terms of the 1812–61 era remain mysterious, *e.g.,* *bogus* and *burgoo.* The noun *bogus* first signified an apparatus for making counterfeit money. By 1839 it was being applied to counterfeit money, and had become an adjective with the general sense of not genuine. *Burgoo* was borrowed originally from the argot of British sailors, to whom it meant a thick oatmeal porridge. It came to designate a meat-and-vegetable stew in the West in the early 1830s, and since then it has been generally associated with Kentucky, especially with the Derby. Arthur H. Deute, a culinary authority, says that it is composed of a mixture of rabbit or squirrel meat, chicken, beef, salt pork, potatoes, string beans, onions, lima beans, corn, okra, carrots and tomatoes, and is made in two pots, the meats in a small one and the vegetables in a large. The two are well stirred together, and the *burgoo* is ready. [*Charivari* seems to have been adopted from the French in the Mississippi Valley, to replace a variety of Eastern terms.] It signifies, primarily, a rowdy serenade of a newly married couple, but it is also used to designate any noisy demonstration. In various spellings, it dates from the early Nineteenth Century. The *shivaree* (the simplest phonetic spelling) still survives in many rural areas, East and West, under such other names as *belling, warmer, serenade, horning, rouser, wake-up, jamboree, tin-pan shower, skim-melton* and *callithumpian. Callithumpian* was once used "in New York as well as other parts of the country" to designate a noisy parade on New Year's Eve, but such parades have gone out of fashion; [in the Midwest a *callithumpian band* or *parade,* of children in false faces, was often a part of Independence Day festivities down to World War I].

16   *Stogy,* in the sense of a crude cigar, made with a simple twist at the mouthward end instead of a fashioned head, is not traced beyond 1893, but it must be very much older. It is a shortened form of *Conestoga,* the name for a heavy covered wagon with broad wheels, much in use in the early days for transport over the Alleghenies. This name came from that of the Conestoga Valley in Lancaster County, Pa., which came in turn from that of a long-extinct band of Iroquois Indians. The term *Conestoga wagon* was used in Pennsylvania before 1750, but it was apparently but little

known to the country at large until the westward migrations after 1800. Many of the Conestoga wagoners were Pennsylvanians, and they prepared the tobacco of Lancaster County for smoking on their long trips by rolling it into what soon became known as *Conestogies* and then *stogies*. The commercial manufacture of these pseudo-cigars is now centered, not in Pennsylvania, but at Wheeling, W. Va. The *Conestoga wagon* survived until the Twentieth Century, not only in the Pennsylvania German country, but in the southern Appalachians. The covered wagon of the Western pioneer was often a *Conestoga*. . . .

17   Today it is no longer necessary for an American writer to apologize for writing American. Indeed, he seems a bit stiff and academic if he doesn't make some attempt to add to the stock of neologisms himself. In 1926 a lexicographer of experience reported that "the accepted language grows at the rate of 3,000 words a year—of sufficient currency to be inserted in the dictionary." "In days of stress, in times of war, in an era of discovery and invention," he continued, "5,000 or more words will win the favor of the public so that their inclusion in the dictionary is demanded by scholar and layman." So many novelties swarm in that it is quite impossible for the dictionaries to keep up with them; indeed, a large number come and go without the lexicographers so much as hearing of them. We Americans live in an age and society given over to enormous word-making—the most riotous seen in the world since the break-up of Latin. It is an extremely wasteful process, for with so many newcomers to choose from, large numbers of pungent and useful words and phrases must be discarded and in the end forgotten by all save linguistic paleontologists. But all the great processes of nature are wasteful, and it is by no means assured that the fittest always survive.

**Questions
on Content**

1. Why didn't the American language begin to develop significantly until the nineteenth century?

2. Mencken says that the codfish aristocracy in New England exhibited "an undisguised Anglomania" (paragraph 2). What does he mean?

3. What contributions did Thomas Jefferson and Andrew Jackson make to the development of American English?

4. What is unique about the humor of the American West?

5. What is the origin of the word *stogies*?

Questions on Structure and Style

6. Is a thesis sentence clearly stated in the opening paragraph? If so, where? How does the rest of the paragraph function in relation to the thesis?

7. Comment on the use of transitions within and among paragraphs 6 through 9.

8. Comment on the use of figurative language in paragraph 7. In the quotation from a "typical" patriotic speech in Congress, what gives the language an "oratorical" style?

9. Mencken makes many classical and mythological allusions in this essay. What purpose, for example, does the allusion to "the Olympians" serve in paragraph 10? Look for other such allusions, and comment on their purposes.

10. Mencken quotes directly from many sources. How do these quotations, such as the quotation from Twain's *Life on the Mississippi* (paragraph 8), contribute to Mencken's writing?

11. In his monumental work on American English (from which this selection is taken), Mencken chronicles the development of a language that is uniquely American. He clearly loves this language and is enthusiastic about its break from England, but at times he is irritated by the course of its development. Mark passages that convey Mencken's strong personal feelings. (The last paragraph is a good example.)

Assignments

1. Mencken points out that a major cause of change in a language is the slang and "uncouth words and phrases" of people who are not in the mainstream of society. This surely is still true. Examine the modern slang and/or language of a particular group. (Age, race, ethnic background, and geographical region are characteristics that can define a group.) Then in an essay, use your findings to discuss this issue. One topic to address might be the reasons why the group has adopted this particular language.

2. The *Dictionary of American English (DAE)* and the *Dictionary of Americanisms (DA)* are full of words that are uniquely American. Use one of these dictionaries to find the origins of the following terms:

blue laws	dicker
carpetbagger	dude
clambake	ranch
conniption	sidewinder

Browse in the dictionary, and find ten other examples of interesting Americanisms that reveal our special history, culture, prejudices, and values.

3. Give the American equivalent of the following British terms. (You may have to do some detective work to find all the answers.)

accumulator	public house
biscuit	bonnet (of a car)
boot (of a car)	wing (of a car)
chips	dustbin
silencer	drawing pin
plimsolls	lorry

Can you think of other examples? What other differences are there between British and American English? Can you think of differences other than vocabulary and pronunciation?

Brave New Words

Lane Jennings

By the year 2000, the language you speak and write today will be old-fashioned, and Lane Jennings explains why. Language changes continuously, and faster than we realize. Predicting what will change, and how, is risky, but Jennings (who is research director for the World Future Society) uses history as a guide to what will happen to English. His essay is both informative and intriguing for what it reveals about language development and those who use—and will use—English.

1   Imagine, as you read these words, that alien scientists on a planet 600 light-years out in space are listening to the earth. Using sensitive instruments that can pick up the sound of a single human voice, this is what they might hear:

> Whanne that Aprille with his shoures soote
> The droghte of March hath perced to the roote
>
> . . . .
>
> Thanne longen folk to goon on pilgrimages
> And palmers for to seken straunge strondes. . . .

2   These lines, from *The Canterbury Tales,* were written by the poet Geoffrey Chaucer some 600 years ago. Chaucer was writing English, but many of his words look odd and sound still odder to English-speakers of the twentieth century. Clearly, English has changed a lot since the 1380s.

3   But our imaginary eavesdroppers in outer space won't know this. For any message from Earth arriving on their planet today—even if it traveled at the speed of light—must have begun its journey 600 years ago. The only English they can know is the English of Chaucer's time. If these same alien scientists try using what they know to send a message back to us "in our own language," it will take another 600 years traveling at the speed of light to reach us. By the year 2581, the English we speak and write today may seem as odd to people living then as Chaucer's language does to us. And only an archeologist might recognize that the mysterious radio message just received from outer space was actually phrased in ancient English.

4   Change is the natural state of any living language. In the past 200 years, scholars and scientists have learned to trace the signs of change through written records, and to measure differences in speech and usage in the present with great precision. However, they still are unable to pinpoint

why a language changes in a particular way at a particular time. Most language changes appear to take place unconsciously as writers and speakers gradually adopt new habits over long periods of time.

5   It may never be possible to predict with certainty how a language will look or sound at a given moment in the future. But today, for the first time in history, we do know enough to suggest where changes in language use are likely to occur, and to speculate with some assurance on how new social norms and new technologies might affect the way we use words to express our feelings and convey information.

6   New words and expressions are constantly coming into fashion and going out of style. But the language changes that last are generally those that make communication faster, simpler, or more effective for large numbers of people. In the case of English, future changes are likely to occur where the language seems awkward or inadequate today. Such "trouble spots" may result from new inventions and discoveries, changing needs, or altered perceptions of reality.

The Shape of Sounds to Come

7   Do you say toMAYto, toMAHto, or toMYto? How you pronounce the word *tomato* will probably depend on whether you learned your English in New York City, Cambridge, England, or Sydney, Australia. But in spite of local variations, the sounds of English are surprisingly uniform the world around.

8   More than 300 million people consider English their native language, and millions more speak or write it as a second language. English-speaking communities are found in every corner of the globe, yet the standard pronunciation used in radio broadcasts, television programs, and films from England or the United States is understood even in places where local residents speak to one another in a heavy dialect.

9   In the twentieth century, world-wide exposure to British and American speech via the mass media has helped tie the English-speaking world together, and particularly encouraged the growth of English as a second language. But cable television systems and prerecorded videotapes and videodiscs could change this in the years ahead by breaking up today's mass TV audience into smaller groups. A greater focus on locally produced programs and on advertising "personalized" to appeal to one specific ethnic or regional community could accentuate existing dialect differences and erode the national standards of acceptable pronunciation established and reinforced by the mass media.

10   Another emerging communications technology has the potential to influence English in a different way. The use of satellites to relay voice or TV signals directly to homes and offices over any distance could make two-

way radio or television service available everywhere. Regular users of these services might rapidly evolve into new language groups based on common interests rather than geography.

11   Ham radio operators and CB enthusiasts have already adopted special jargons that are seldom if ever used in face-to-face conversations. In a fuel-short world of limited travel, these "radio-dialects" of English could develop into full-fledged "electronic language communities" spanning continents and linking together individuals from many scattered locations who rely on electronic communication to conduct business and exchange information.

Fast Talking/Speed Listening

12   "Talk is cheap," they say; but "time is money." And during the past few years, several companies have developed machines that compress re-corded speech for faster listening. Although most English-speakers talk at a rate of between 100 and 180 words per minute, the brain can process speech sounds at rates as high as 400 words per minute. This is one reason why our minds often wander when we listen to a slow speaker. The speech-compressing tape recorder works by speeding up the sound of a recorded speech without altering its pitch. In this way, it becomes possible to listen to a two-hour lecture in 40 minutes without missing a word.

13   Widespread use of speech-compressing tape recorders (by students at-tending university lectures, for example) could sharpen people's listening skills. It might even encourage faster speech in ordinary conversation as people come to accept compressed speech rates as "normal" and try to save their listeners' time and hold their attention better with faster talk. Listen for early signs of this trend to appear in political speeches and in radio and TV commercials, where fast-talking salespeople are already common.

14   Though people spend much of their waking hours talking or listening, the status of spoken language as a reliable medium of communication seems to be declining throughout the industrialized world. The problem may be that we are losing our memories—and with them, our faith in one another's "word." Studies of cultures where few people read and write suggest that, in general, as literacy improves, the ability to remember information conveyed by sound alone declines. The ability to listen and report accurately what was heard without using pictures or writing may be on the "endangered skills" list as this century ends.

15   Fewer and fewer important exchanges of information take place by word of mouth alone. Business deals are almost always based on written con-tracts so complexly worded that even those who sign them prefer to let their lawyers do the actual drafting and interpretation. Rarely does a

government leader venture a policy statement without a written text to read from. Even at press conferences, reporters depend on written notes or machine recordings to keep their facts straight. And while the words "Will you live with me?" are probably still most persuasive when spoken, modern couples often make the answer "Yes" conditional on a written agreement spelling out responsibilities and expectations.

16   Decreased emphasis on teaching children such skills as careful listening, persuasive rhetoric, entertaining conversation, and even story-telling may have made reading and writing appear more necessary to education than they really are. But without some special effort to teach better speaking and listening, the average citizen of the future may be an "oral illiterate."

Listening Ahead

17   What will English sound like in the future? Historical evidence suggests that different types of sound will change at different rates. By comparing rhyme words in poetry written at different periods, and looking at how foreign names have been reproduced in English, scholars can reconstruct the sounds of spoken English in the past. It seems that consonants and unstressed vowels have changed very little in the past 1,000 years. But a major change affecting stressed vowels occurred in English between Chaucer's time and that of Shakespeare 200 years later. In fact, Shakespeare's English sounded more like Chaucer's than like English today, but the modern spelling adopted in most editions of Shakespeare's works since the nineteenth century largely conceals this difference.

18   The so-called "Great English Vowel Shift" has had the effect of transforming stressed vowel sounds that were once made at the back of the mouth into sounds made closer to the front and top of the mouth. Thus, a word that Chaucer pronounced as "coo" we now pronounce "cow." But the sound of the word *milk* has hardly changed at all.

19   Language scholars disagree about which trends in pronunciation will have the greatest influence on English in the future. But here are a few examples of sound change at work today:

- *Lost sounds.* In ordinary conversation, unstressed syllables and even whole words or phrases are often dropped. *Ham and eggs* becomes *ham 'n' eggs, laboratory* becomes *lab'ratory,* and *Why don't you come?* becomes *Wyncha come?*
- *Tongue-untwisters.* Difficult-to-pronounce consonant clusters like the "ndf" and "ndm" in "grandfather" and "grandmother" change to simpler sounds, as in "granfather" or "grammah."
- *Combinations.* Two old words may join to form a new word with a meaning related to both the old ones. Newspaper writers and

advertisers have coined many trendy or comic words in this manner, such as "sexploitation," "alcoholiday," "funtastic," etc., few of which survive for long. But other, more serious combination words appear when people encounter new phenomena or experiences that have similarities but no exact parallels to those past language has equipped them to describe. One good example is "smog" from the combination of "smoke" and "fog."

■ *Acronyms, initialisms, and abbreviations.* The trend toward inventing words built up from the first letters or syllables of other words has spread rapidly from science and government to all parts of society. In the future, we can expect more words like ZIP code (originally the letters stood for Zone Improvement Plan), and ICBM (short for Intercontinental Ballistic Missile).

Writing or Wronging English?

20   Writing was invented as a way to communicate reliably across barriers of space and time. Today, we have other means for accomplishing this purpose. Radio, TV, telephones, and the computer could replace books, letters, and documents, some communication experts argue, and in the future people may no longer need to read and write. Nevertheless, print and writing offer some unique advantages for accumulating, storing, and displaying information.

21   Compared to electronic media, the equipment required for writing or reading is simple to manufacture and inexpensive to operate. An acceptable "information system" might consist of no more than a pencil, a pad of paper, a book, and the light of the sun. Written texts are convenient for dealing with abstract concepts that would be difficult or impossible to dramatize using sound or pictures alone. The single word *chair* is better than 1,000 pictures of things-to-sit-upon if you want to focus attention on what this piece of furniture *does* rather than what it might look like. Even the fact that reading is one-way communication from author to reader is not necessarily a disadvantage when your goal is to understand someone else's thoughts rather than to reveal your own. Sometimes it is far more instructive to overhear a conversation than to take part in one. In short, it is hard to imagine a future without the written word in which people would not be poorer for the loss.

22   But if writing does not disappear, it will certainly change. In the case of English, one change that many would welcome is spelling reform. There are approximately 45 different "phonemes" or "meaningful sounds" in the English language as it is spoken today in the United States. To record those sounds on paper, we use 26 letter symbols (often in combinations), 14 common punctuation marks, and a number of stylistic conventions,

including upper- and lower-case letters, different typestyles, and blank spaces inserted between words, sentences, and paragraphs. Unfortunately, the system in its present form is hopelessly inadequate to its task.

23   When the Roman alphabet we use today was first devised, each of its symbols represented one—and only one—sound in the Latin language. Texts could be written without division into words or sentences because each written letter was meant to be pronounced out loud as it was read so that words became recognizable from their sound. For centuries in Europe, "reading out loud" was the only kind of reading anyone could do.

24   It was not until the practice of inserting spaces between words began in the early Middle Ages that people came to think of words as clumps of letters independent of their sound. This new habit, combined with the use of Roman letters to record languages (like English) that contained sounds not found in Latin, led to the breakdown of one-sound/one-letter spelling. The result is a quagmire of alternative written forms for the same sound. To cite just one example, the English sound "sh," which does not occur in Latin, is symbolized by 14 different letter combinations in modern English (SHoe, SUgar, naTIon, oCEan, miSSIon, etc.). Clearly, a logical future for written English should include phonetic spelling.

25   At least one system of phonetic spelling is already available and is taught at universities throughout the world. It is called the International Phonetic Alphabet, or IPA. It was originally devised by a group of European language scholars in 1888, and has been expanded over the years until today it contains several hundred symbols for recording human speech sounds in minute detail.

26   Anthropologists and language scholars have used the IPA to transcribe every known language and dialect on earth. But the symbols are also used by newscasters to standardize the pronunciation of foreign words and names; by actors taking the role of a character who speaks in dialect or with a foreign accent; and by speech therapists and language teachers to help their students learn to reproduce and recognize word sounds with precision.

27   Although the sounds commonly found in English can be represented using only a small portion of the symbols available in the IPA, the system is too complicated for convenient use in everyday writing and printing. Moreover, the IPA was devised to record sounds exactly as they are heard, so that unless one "ideal" pronunciation is accepted as standard, the visual representation of a given word will change depending on who is speaking it.

28   The British playwright, George Bernard Shaw, who died in 1950, left money in his will to be used for the purpose of devising an entirely new phonetic alphabet for English. The standard he specified for English pronunciation was to be the recorded voice of King George V. Shaw specified

that this new alphabet should have at least 40 symbols so that there would be no need to use more than one symbol to represent a single sound, or to employ extra accent marks at any time. About 450 different designs were submitted, and the winning design, designated as "the Shaw alphabet," was first used by Penguin Books in 1962 to publish an edition of Shaw's play *Androcles and the Lion*.

29   Shaw never intended that anyone be forced to abandon the existing alphabet, but hoped that by making texts available in both old and new formats, the handier symbols might gradually become the new standard. In just this way, Arabic numerals have gained worldwide acceptance, although Roman numerals continue to be used for decoration and other special purposes.

Making Sense of Sounds

30   In addition to letters, punctuation marks are used to help make the sense of spoken words clear on paper. Punctuation marks first came into systematic use in the fifteenth and sixteenth centuries when the printing press began to make written material available to a wide audience for the first time. The basic forms—commas, periods, apostrophes, quotation marks, etc.—have changed very little in the last 400 years. But the enormous growth in printed advertising and colloquial journalism in the twentieth century, both of which put a premium on attention-grabbing and instantly memorable words and phrases, has worked to destandardize punctuation and to awaken interest in new alternatives to traditional grammar and spelling.

31   A few modern writers have experimented with the use of punctuation marks in unexpected ways to create startling visual effects and suggest additional meanings in a text. But only one new punctuation mark has been added to English in this century. This mark, called the "interrobang," was originally devised by the American Type Founders Company, Inc. It combines the exclamation point and question mark, and is used to express both doubt and surprise at the same time, as in the sentence "Did he really tell you *that*?"

32   The interrobang has not been followed by a host of new innovations in punctuation. Apparently authors and readers alike are generally satisfied with the existing signs and symbols. But this situation may change in the near future, thanks to the spread of personal computer networks. These networks enable two or more individuals, using terminals linked by telephone lines or satellite relays to a large central computer, to pass written messages back and forth as fast as they can type. At first glance, these "written conversations" or "chats" may seem like nothing more than a

throwback to the early days of the telegraph. But in fact, they represent an entirely new way to use the written word—one that is certain to develop its own conventions and protocols in time.

33   For example, one problem with computer chats today is that it is hard to know when one chatter has completed a statement and is waiting to be answered. A new punctuation mark may be needed here to convey the same sense as the aircraft pilot's radio exclamation "Over." Another problem is that there is no way to know, when a line of print begins appearing on your computer terminal's video screen or printer, how soon it will end. Since every second of computer time costs money, considerate chatters might want to indicate by a special sign that they are about to send a long text, and offer their co-chatter the option of refusing it or holding it in the central computer's memory file, where it could be picked up at a more convenient time.

New Worlds of Words and Meanings

34   The fastest and most obvious changes taking place in the English language are in the words we use and the meanings we give them. For instance, growing sensitivity to sexual bias is leading many authors and publishers to avoid words like "mankind" and "businessman" and to take great pains to avoid using the pronoun "he" in contexts where gender is not specified.

35   Prospects for the immediate future of space exploration remain in doubt, despite the successful flight of America's space shuttle. But other areas of science and technology seem certain to add many new words and phrases to English during the 1980s. Two especially promising areas for word-creation are holistic health and genetic engineering. As biofeedback devices become more popular, people will want new words to describe the state of being "in tune" or "out of sync" with one's own pulse rate, brain-wave rhythms, or blood pressure. New advances in medicine have blurred the meanings of familiar words like "alive" and "sane," and more exact descriptive terms are needed now. The new products and new life forms emerging from genetic engineering labs will also need names to distinguish them from their counterparts (if any) in nature. Already, specially cloned bacteria can produce chemical facsimiles of human interferon (a substance that ordinary human cells make only in tiny quantities to combat a virus infection). But soon it may be possible to produce hormones, fresh blood, bone tissue—perhaps even grow lumber or beefsteaks to order without need to saw down a tree or slaughter a cow. As long as the products remain "artificial equivalents" or "imitations" of familiar substances, the problem of finding names for them may be mostly one of public relations and advertising. But how will we deal with wholly new

substances—or hybrid plants and animals that have no counterparts in human experience? We will need new nouns to identify them and perhaps new verbs as well to describe what they do.

Machine Language

36   So far, the impact of computers on vocabulary has generally been to add technical terms that gradually come to be applied in contexts that have nothing to do with computers. Such phrases as "This article includes *input* from many sources" or "I want you to *access* that information for me right away" are already widely understood, although as yet few dictionaries list "input" as a noun or "access" as a verb.

37   But there is growing interest today in equipment that permits a computer to recognize and respond to spoken words and to generate its own spoken messages. The quirks and characteristics of computer speech synthesis and voice recognition devices could alter the way human beings talk and even affect their choice of words in the future. If voice-activated 24-hour banking machines replace human tellers; if a spoken password opens and locks your house door or starts your car instead of a key; if the telephone order you place from the Sears catalog is taken by a talking computer—it could quickly become worthwhile to change your habits of speech so as to avoid confusing the machine.

38   Today, for instance, most voice recognition equipment has trouble separating words from the normal flow of human speech. As a result, humans who work with this equipment have to speak more distinctly than they would to a human listener, and will often insert longer pauses between words. In time, this speech pattern might become a habit that would carry over into normal conversations and not be found distracting or odd. Computers also have trouble distinguishing between words that sound alike but have different meanings—or words whose meaning differs greatly depending on the context. Attempts at computer translation from one language to another tend to break down completely when confronted by multiple meanings and the general illogic of human colloquial speech and writing. But here, computers' great speed and enormous memory capacity may provide a way out of their dilemma—and our own.

39   In his book *The Miracle of Language,* language scholar Charlton Laird pointed out that it is possible to define each word in the sentence "*Civilized man can not live without religion*" in several different ways. To make the sentence unambiguous, its author would need to label each word in some way that would identify the particular definition he intended. Laird suggested checking all the possible definitions in a standard dictionary (he used the 12-volume Unabridged Oxford English Dictionary, or OED) and

appending the number of the definition preferred in this context as a subscript. The sentence would then look like this:

$$\text{Civilized}_{10} \ \text{man}_8 \ \text{can}_2 \ \text{not}_1 \ \text{live}_{14} \ \text{without}_3 \ \text{religion}_9.$$

40   Its meaning would now be established beyond any doubt and could be verified by anyone who cared to check the original definitions in the OED.

41   Laird was quick to add that such a method of composition, however precise it might be, was totally impractical since it would require constant references back and forth between dictionary and text. "All of us," he warned, "would have to wheel monumental dictionaries about with us, using something like a self-service grocery cart."

42   Laird's judgment was undoubtedly correct for the time in which he wrote (the early 1950s). But today, or at most within the next few years, a computer small enough to fit inside a shirt pocket should be able to hold the entire OED and, wired to a desk-top printer, could produce standard forms, contracts, and other documents to order, adding definition subscripts automatically to every word. Such a process, though clumsy for casual use, could eliminate many legal problems and simplify the job of translating form letters, government policy statements, and international treaties into foreign languages.

To Grow Is Not to Die

43   New technologies, new values, and the endless search for greater convenience, novelty, or impact in communication all work to change the way we speak and write English. Teachers lament the fact that children are reading less. Pundits and grammarians complain that the art of conversation is being lost, as people talk more and think less about what they say. There is no shortage of voices proclaiming the imminent downfall of Western culture and gleefully citing the abandonment of grammar and spelling to prove their case.

44   But change is not necessarily "change for the worse," and in the case of language, distinguishing "good" changes from "bad" ones is largely a matter of personal taste. No less an authority than Robert Burchfield, chief editor of the Oxford dictionaries, warns against concluding that our language is being corrupted or that this somehow produces the decline many people perceive in the quality of life. It is not the use of words like "ain't" or "right on" that people really object to, Burchfield argues, but rather "the highjackings, the drugs, the things that your middle class doesn't like because they constitute a threat to the stability of life as they've known it." People are afraid of change, and they express that fear by condemning

changes in language—particularly language as it is used by people from another age or ethnic group than their own.

45   Much can be done to improve the skill with which people use words to convey information, express an emotion, or attract attention to their needs, hopes, and ideas. But any language that gets the job done is "right language." And English, for all its trouble spots, is still very much alive, well, and growing to meet the future.

Questions on Content

1. A. Why has English become an almost world-wide second language? Discuss the consequences of this fact.
    B. If there are international students in your class, ask them about the use of English in their home countries. What effect has the popularity of English had on these students?

2. Jennings discusses the speech-compressing tape recorder (paragraphs 12 and 13). Do you think this invention is always beneficial? What problems might it create?

3. According to Jennings, why is written language unlikely to disappear entirely? What are the advantages of written, rather than spoken, language?

4. What is the International Phonetic Alphabet? What are its benefits and limitations?

5. To what does Jennings attribute the changes in punctuation during this century? Does this de-standardization create problems? If so, what kind, and for whom?

6. What are some of the effects that computers might have on our everyday language?

7. Jennings is generally optimistic about our use of language in the future. Given what he describes in his essay, are you equally optimistic?

8. Where does Jennings state the thesis of his essay? Is the thesis effectively placed?

9. Jennings uses topic sentences very carefully. In which paragraphs is this deliberate use of topic sentences especially obvious? (Paragraph 15 is one example.)

10. Identify the topic sentence of paragraph 21.

11. Paragraph 35 is complex but clearly organized. Compose an outline of the paragraph.

12. Circle the transitional words and phrases in paragraph 38.

13. For what audience is Jennings writing? How do we know?

Assignments

1. Jennings points out that we rely heavily on punctuation marks to make our writing clear. We use capital letters for the same reason. As an exercise, write a fifty-word paragraph in which you use no capital letters or punctuation marks of any sort. Then have a classmate read the paragraph aloud— quickly.

2. Jennings discusses Charlton Laird's proposal for labeling words in sentences to make them unambiguous (paragraphs 39–41). He states that new technology might soon make such a system practical. Even if it is practical, do you think such a system would be advisable? In all cases? Would we lose anything by using it? Explain your answer in an essay.

Additional Assignments and Research Topics

1. If you're interested in or speak another language, write an essay examining the ways in which that language has influenced English. How has knowing English helped you learn the other language? How has being a speaker of English presented problems in learning another language?

2. The best-known ancient theory on the origin of the world's different languages is the story of the Tower of Babel in Genesis II: 1–9. Read this passage in the 1611 King James version of the Bible and in a modern translation, such as *The Way*. Write an essay discussing some of the differences in the English language as reflected in the two translations of this passage.

3. Rewrite the first two paragraphs of the Declaration of Independence in contemporary English. Pay attention not only to vocabulary and tone but also to sentence length.

4. Write an essay explaining your personal language history. What languages did your ancestors speak? Try to show how these languages have affected English. If your own family tree is difficult to trace, interview a non-native speaker, and write a paper describing his or her language history.

5. Choose one of the following, and write a research paper explaining why this person or event is important to the development of English:

   Alfred the Great
   William the Conqueror
   The Norman Conquest
   William Caxton

6. Most communities have their own language histories, language features that make the community different from a community of similar size in a neighboring state. Write a paper exploring the language history of your community. A good way to begin is by examining geographic place names in your region and interviewing long-time residents of your community.

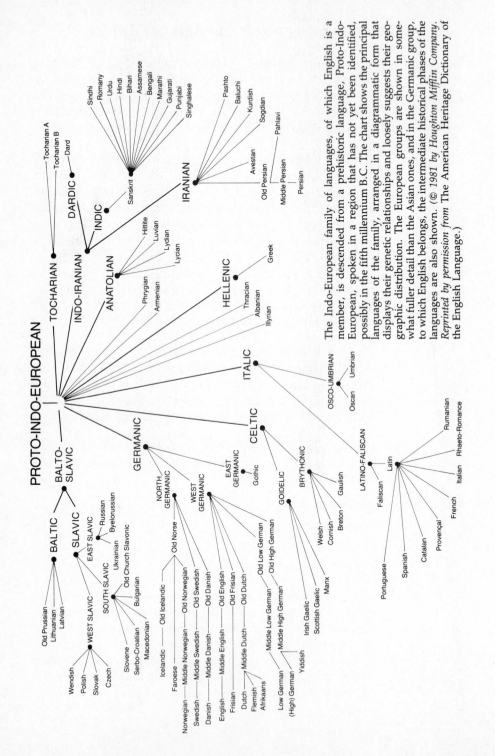

The Indo-European family of languages, of which English is a member, is descended from a prehistoric language, Proto-Indo-European, spoken in a region that has not yet been identified, possibly in the fifth millennium B.C. The chart shows the principal languages of the family, arranged in a diagrammatic form that displays their genetic relationships and loosely suggests their geographic distribution. The European groups are shown in somewhat fuller detail than the Asian ones, and in the Germanic group, to which English belongs, the intermediate historical phases of the languages are also shown. (© 1981 by Houghton Mifflin Company. Reprinted by permission from The American Heritage Dictionary of the English Language.)

7. Think about the different ways in which animals communicate. Observe, if possible, parrots, mynah birds, chimpanzees, your own pets, or even the dancing of bees. Drawing freely from research in this area, write an essay discussing the differences among these types of communication.

8. The Indo-Europeans were the speakers of the original language from which most of the languages of Europe and Asia are derived. Evidence suggests that these speakers began in a compact homeland and then migrated. Over the centuries, distances separated the immigrants, and new languages evolved. Where do you feel the homeland might have been, and why do you feel this? (To answer this question, you'll need to study the chart on page 216 to determine where the languages are spoken today, if they are.)

9. Most scholars accept the theory that English developed from the Indo-European language family. In a research paper, discuss the Indo-European family, and show how English is related to the modern languages of Europe. In your paper, you might want to define *Romance languages* and show how these languages are related to English.

Slang, Taboo,
and Euphemism

Before the job interview, you stare into the closet, deciding which clothes will make the right impression. Jeans won't do. Neither will the elaborate outfit you bought for the semiformal dinner last winter—and maybe that blouse or tie is just *too* red. So what's appropriate? What's right?

Such planning is not unusual. We try to choose clothing that fits the occasion because we know how effectively clothes can reveal our perceptions of both ourselves and those we associate with. We think jeans make us seem casual and relaxed so they're fine at the supermarket or movie theater. A suit announces something else: a more formal approach befitting contact with people who expect formality and whose expectations we're willing to fulfill. If none of this were true, we'd wear bathing suits to weddings and tuxedos to funerals, and no one would notice. Language "rightness" operates the same way. Our response to circumstances dictates which words are right. The selections in this chapter examine the links between words and contexts—the ways in which what is appropriate depends on who we are, where we are, what we value, what we fear, and what we want to accomplish with language.

Jeff Kunerth's "Sometimes the Liveliest Words" provides an overview of slang, defining it, identifying its origins and users, and exploring its sociological implications. Next, John Updike's short story "A&P" illustrates the slang of one young person and his desire to use language to identify himself as an adult. Both of these selections confirm that slang sometimes allows people to differentiate themselves from others. Because it's initially restricted to specific groups or situations, slang can be private, and if used skillfully, it adds energy and color to language.

Taboo language and euphemisms can also affect the appropriateness of the language used in a particular context. Geoffrey Wagner and Sanford R. Radner explain the complex psychological forces behind taboo language in "Taboo: The Sacred and the Obscene." The authors link taboo with euphemisms, showing how both serve important purposes that are sometimes difficult to see. Two selections then concentrate on euphemisms. In his essay "Euphemisms," Hugh Rawson examines the many ways in which words can be used to avoid ideas that are considered unpleasant, and in "Of Words That Ravage, Pillage, Spoil," Otto Friedrich focuses on the ways and reasons that governments find euphemisms so useful. The chapter concludes with "Good-bye to All T___t!" in which Wallace Stegner asserts his belief that the power of taboo language has been dulled by irresponsible use—and what he, a writer, intends to do as a result.

Slang, taboo, and euphemism allow us to show respect for circumstances and to recognize strengths and weaknesses, ours and those of other people. Circumstances differ. Contexts change. A word is right if it's appropriate to the circumstances and to the speaker's intentions in those circumstances, and skilled speakers and writers know the importance of both.

Sometimes the Liveliest Words

Jeff Kunerth

When students use slang in their writing, instructors often advise them not to. But when is slang appropriate and useful—and actually necessary? In the following article, originally published in the *Orlando Sentinel*, Jeff Kunerth examines slang as a social phenomenon that allows one group to distinguish itself from others. Kunerth also focuses on American slang, demonstrating how what is true for a small group can also be true for an entire nation. A slang vocabulary is unique; it is the result of identifiable social forces; and it mirrors those who devise it.

1   Today he is a successful, middle-aged businessman, but a youth spent on the beatnik fringes of Greenwich Village has left a permanent residue on his speech. While other men of his age and stature might say, "Do you understand?" he says, "You dig?"

2   Of the estimated 10,000 to 20,000 words that make up the average American's vocabulary, slang constitutes about 10 percent, according to the authors of the *Dictionary of American Slang*. Although slang words represent a rather small segment of our English language (about 10,000 of more than 600,000 words), they are often the liveliest, most innovative and most colorful words we use.

3   There is something sensual and tactile about many slang words, which borrow heavily from the vocabularies associated with food. Hands are called meat hooks; loved ones are called honey, sweetie pie or sugar; someone whose intellect is suspect is a fruitcake, cabbage head or just plain nuts.

4   Among the young, the current slang words for "intoxicated" sound like kitchen conversation: fried, baked and toasted. Their parents spoke of being juiced, stewed and basted.

5   Slang, wrote British lexicographer Eric Partridge, is more than mere self-expression. It connotes personality, a method of distinguishing ourselves by virtue of our linguistic virtuosity.

6   "The primary function of slang is to adorn your speech, to be lively, witty and new. Newness is the essence of slang," says David Pharies, professor of linguistics at the University of Florida.

7   Slang is the verbal equivalent of fashion. When they lose their freshness, most slang words are discarded as casually as lime-colored leisure suits and white belts. Some people, at the risk of appearing outdated, continue

wearing leisure suits because they feel comfortable in them. Likewise, some people may cling to slang words that fit their self-images or fill the voids of their vocabularies.

8   One of the main purposes of using slang is to solidify one's identification with a group. Slang is most prevalent among the young and among such disfranchised groups as blacks, teen-agers, drug users, criminals, carnival workers, hobos and the uneducated. Often, slang is used as a code language to fortify the group and to exclude outsiders. Some criminal slang, called cant, is so highly developed that pickpockets, for example, can carry on a conversation in front of a victim without the person's realizing that they are discussing which pocket to pick.

9   Slang also is used by the majority to refer, usually in a derogatory manner, to minorities. The majority uses slang as racial and ethnic slurs to reinforce power or status.

10   "To generate slang, a group must either be very large and in constant contact with the dominant culture or be small, closely knit, and removed enough from the dominant culture to evolve an extensive, highly personal, and vivid vocabulary," writes linguist Stuart Berg Flexner in his preface to the *Dictionary of American Slang*.

11   Slang, Flexner notes, tends toward degradation rather than elevation. There are more derogatory slang terms than complimentary ones.

12   In some societies, slang is considered a class distinction, but in the United States it is more often an indication of education. The use of slang tends to decrease as one's educational and social status increases.

13   "I think educated people are not as playful and inventive with language as uneducated people," says Connie C. Ebley, associate professor of English at the University of North Carolina. "Uneducated people also overlap with people who don't have access to power in society. They rely on verbal [oral] rather than written strategies."

14   Slang is essentially oral, which contributes to the short life span of most slang terms. Before slang terms gain acceptance into standard dictionaries, they must prove their durability by lasting more than four years and finding their way into print, preferably in hard-cover books, says David Guralnik, editor of *Webster's New World Dictionary*. Of the 225,000 meanings contained in *Webster's New World Dictionary*, only about 15,000 are designated as slang, Guralnik says.

15   But because of their short lives, slang words offer linguists a unique opportunity to study how new words are formed and disseminated, says Ebley.

16   "In some ways, we can see slang as a miniature language-change laboratory. We generally think of language change as being gradual and taking a long time, but with slang we have an example of language change taking place very rapidly," Ebley says. "We still poorly understand the nature of slang. It has to do very much with how we get new words into language."

17   In America, slang has been generated predominantly by males, according to Flexner. American men traditionally have had more group associations, in which slang becomes the common language, than have women. With more women leaving the home for the workplace, however, that may change, Ebley says.

18   Flexner also contends that Americans, in general, use more slang than other nationalities because of our diversity, emphasis on free speech, immigrant heritage and lack of a formal, national language academy. The mobility of Americans has further spread regional expressions that have become general slang.

19   Pharies speculates that our society's future-mindedness also contributes to our acceptance of slang. Our appetite for something new and novel is fed, in part, by the constant generation of slang expressions. In societies that are very traditional and heritage-oriented, slang does not flourish, says Pharies.

20   Spain, which historically has been the most conservative and least forward-looking country in Europe, produced very little slang until the death of Franco. Since then, the use of slang has spread among Spanish young people.

21   "Only recently with the death of Franco has there emerged something called *cacheli,* which is a drug-, youth-, rock music-oriented slang," says Pharies. "It is condemned by the vast majority of the population because it is so new and youthful and future-oriented."

22   Young people, fascinated with anything new and intolerant of anything old, are the primary contributors to slang, says Pharies. Slang appeals to teen-agers and college students because it is, by nature, irreverent and slightly rebellious. Young people are also an emotional group, and slang conveys that emotion. Slang gives their language its color and flavor.

23   "You can talk about any particular object with standard English, but you can't use the emotional coloring without slang," says Pharies. "Slang is necessary because we are a highly emotional species."

24   For advertisers who want to appeal to young people, speaking their language is essential. And that includes keeping up with the latest teen-age slang. Pharies says he has received requests from New York ad agencies for lists of college-student slang: "A lot of advertising agencies are desperate to know the absolutely latest words so that their products will be seen as totally up to date."

25   Similarly, some teachers trying to relate more closely to their students will adopt the slang of young people. Because of the exclusive nature of slang, however, most attempts by adults to use teen-age slang are doomed. A teacher dressing his or her speech with the slang of students can be as comical as a grandmother dressed in a miniskirt.

26   And like the miniskirt, slang has a way of fading for a while and then returning when it is rediscovered by another group or generation.

"Groovy" was first used by jazz musicians in the 1930s, was resurrected in the mid-1950s, and has been reintroduced by the young people of the '80s.

27   Slang also serves the linguistic purpose of identifying new concepts and social trends. Getting "drunk" or "juiced" was appropriate when intoxication involved drinking liquids. But when large numbers of people began getting high by inhaling or ingesting substances that were not liquid, other slang descriptions became necessary. Today, one expression for intoxication is getting "lit," which probably is derived from the lighting of a marijuana cigarette, says Pharies.

28   Young people are the most prolific producers of slang as an age group, but California is probably the most fertile geographical area for slang. The surfer slang of the 1960s, the "upscale" slang of the 1970s and the Valley Girl talk of the 1980s all originated on the West Coast and moved eastward.

29   "All countries have cultural centers. In our culture, for the last 20 to 30 years, all the new stuff has started on the West Coast and moved to the East Coast and then to the middle," says Pharies. "The productive center of the culture is California. The last place to get it is the Midwest."

30   As a verbal fad, slang is susceptible to the same influences as other fads. The dissemination of slang words through newspapers, television and movies hastens the spread of slang and, ultimately, quickens their demise, says Pharies.

31   In some ways, slang words closely follow the course of other fads. When the popularity of Izod shirts began to wane, and they were no longer the status symbol for the young that they once were, the clothing gave birth to a new teen-age slang term for someone who is out of date. In teen slang, that person is a "zod."

A Sampling of Slang

Here is a glossary of slang in use early in 1985. The social group in which the usage began is given in parentheses.

> **Bagging Z's**   sleeping (teen-agers)
>
> **Bag your faith**   to leave (teen-agers)
>
> **Big time**   severely, as in "I flunked that exam big time" (teen-agers)
>
> **Blinker**   a police helicopter (blacks)
>
> **Blow groceries, blow chunks, blow chow, blow oats**   to vomit (teen-agers)
>
> **Bogus, gnarly, beige**   bad (teen-agers)
>
> **Boojie, bojie, boochie**   an upwardly mobile black person (blacks)
>
> **Chill out, chill your jets**   calm down, relax (teen-agers)
>
> **Dizzbrain, wastecase**   a stupid person (teen-agers)

Dog juice   cheap liquor (blacks)

Double $20 (carnival workers)

Dr. Thomas   a black who has taken on white, middle-class values (blacks)

Dweeb, feedbag, wally, dexter, deebie, eunice   a nerd (teen-agers)

Flying cow, tuna, whale pup   a fat female (teen-agers)

Get chomped   to be rejected (teen-agers)

Grab joints   food concession booths (carnival workers)

Graspless, clueless   stupid (teen-agers)

Grounder   a partly smoked cigarette found on the street (hobos)

Hammered, twisted   intoxicated (teen-agers)

Jazz, boogie   sexual intercourse (blacks)

Juice man   an electrician (carnival worker)

Kennel   a house or rented room (hobos)

Life-boat   a commuted sentence (criminals)

Main squeeze   a girlfriend (blacks)

Mawsquaw   mother (blacks)

One on the city   a glass of water (restaurant workers)

Porsche   a short, round, compact female (blacks)

Put it in the wind   to leave (blacks)

Punk   a child (carnival workers)

Rents, parental units   parents (teen-agers)

Slum   cheap prizes (carnival lingo)

Smoke   marijuana cigarette (drug users)

Space bandit   press agent (show people)

Spam cluster   the shoulder patch of the Army Service Forces (military personnel)

Spanking monkeys, parallel parking   having sexual intercourse (teen-agers)

Suck face   to kiss (teen-agers)

T-bones   virile men (teen-agers)

Toot, nose candy   cocaine (drug users)

Yard $100 (carnival workers)

Wicked, unreal, choice, golden   good (teen-agers)

Worms   ugly men (teen-agers)

Zod   a person who is out of style (teen-agers)

1. According to Kunerth, what purposes does slang serve for those who use it?

2. Kunerth says that slang is often "a code language" (paragraph 8). How would he define this term?

3. Why does slang change so quickly? What helps it spread and die? How does the speed with which it changes help those who study language?

4. Why do Americans in particular use so much slang?

5. Why are some advertisers especially interested in teenage slang?

6. When is slang counterproductive for those who use it?

7. In what geographic area of the United States does slang most often originate? Why?

8. The list of slang expressions starting on page 224 is probably dated. Which expressions are still in use, and which are not?

9. This article, which originally appeared in a newspaper, seems far less cohesive than most of the other reading selections thus far. Where is this particularly true?

10. What is the function of paragraph 20?

11. Is paragraph 31 an effective conclusion? Why or why not?

12. In paragraph 7, Kunerth states that "slang is the verbal equivalent of fashion," and he returns to this analogy in paragraphs 25 and 26. Why does Kunerth employ this analogy? How effective is it?

13. The author quotes several sources of information for his article. How do these sources add to (or detract from) his presentation?

Assignments

1. According to this article, "Young people, fascinated with anything new and intolerant of anything old, are the primary contributors to slang" (paragraph 22). Make a list of slang terms that are currently popular among young people. Then examine the list to see whether it confirms the author's assertion about young people's attitudes toward the new and the old.

2. This article originally appeared in a newspaper, and it follows newspaper style. Compare Kunerth's manner of presentation with that of Otto Friedrich in "Of Words That Ravage, Pillage, Spoil" (page 257). How do the two essays differ?

A&P

John Updike

In this short story, John Updike examines a teenager during the transition from adolescence to adulthood. At some points, the main character's language is filled with the exaggeration, carica- ture, and slang we associate with teenagers speaking informally. At other times, we hear a more serious, carefully considered lan- guage—that of the emerging adult. Sammy is concerned with his place in the world. His language as well as his actions reflect that concern about what has been and is now appropriate for him.

1   In walks these three girls in nothing but bathing suits. I'm in the third checkout slot, with my back to the door, so I don't see them until they're over by the bread. The one that caught my eye first was the one in the plaid green two-piece. She was a chunky kid, with a good tan and a sweet broad soft-looking can with those two crescents of white just under it, where the sun never seems to hit, at the top of the backs of her legs. I stood there with my hand on a box of HiHo crackers trying to remember if I rang it up or not. I ring it up again and the customer starts giving me hell. She's one of these cash-register-watchers, a witch about fifty with rouge on her cheek- bones and no eyebrows, and I know it made her day to trip me up. She'd been watching cash registers for fifty years and probably never seen a mistake before.

2   By the time I got her feathers smoothed and her goodies into a bag—she gives me a little snort in passing, if she'd been born at the right time they would have burned her over in Salem—by the time I get her on her way the girls had circled around the bread and were coming back, without a pushcart, back my way along the counters, in the aisle between the check- outs and the Special bins. They didn't even have shoes on. There was this chunky one, with the two-piece—it was bright green and the seams on the bra were still sharp and her belly was still pretty pale so I guessed she just got it (the suit)—there was this one, with one of those chubby berry-faces, the lips all bunched together under her nose, this one, and a tall one, with black hair that hadn't quite frizzed right, and one of these sunburns right across under the eyes, and a chin that was too long—you know, the kind of girl other girls think is very "striking" and "attractive" but never quite makes it, as they very well know, which is why they like her so much— and then the third one, that wasn't quite so tall. She was the queen. She kind of led them, the other two peeking around and making their shoul- ders round. She didn't look around, not this queen, she just walked

straight on slowly, on these long white prima-donna legs. She came down a little hard on her heels, as if she didn't walk in her bare feet that much, putting down her heels and then letting the weight move along to her toes as if she was testing the floor with every step, putting a little deliberate extra action into it. You never know for sure how girls' minds work (do you really think it's a mind in there or just a little buzz like a bee in a glass jar?) but you got the idea she had talked the other two into coming in here with her, and now she was showing them how to do it, walk slow and hold yourself straight.

3   She had on a kind of dirty-pink—beige maybe, I don't know—bathing suit with a little nubble all over it and, what got me, the straps were down. They were off her shoulders looped loose around the cool tops of her arms, and I guess as a result the suit had slipped a little on her, so all around the top of the cloth there was this shining rim. If it hadn't been there you wouldn't have known there could have been anything whiter than those shoulders. With the straps pushed off, there was nothing between the top of the suit and the top of her head except just *her*, this clean bare plane of the top of her chest down from the shoulder bones like a dented sheet of metal tilted in the light. I mean, it was more than pretty.

4   She had sort of oaky hair that the sun and salt had bleached, done up in a bun that was unravelling, and a kind of prim face. Walking into the A&P with your straps down, I suppose it's the only kind of face you *can* have. She held her head so high her neck, coming up out of those white shoulders, looked kind of stretched, but I didn't mind. The longer her neck was, the more of her there was.

5   She must have felt in the corner of her eye me and over my shoulder Stokesie in the second slot watching, but she didn't tip. Not this queen. She kept her eyes moving across the racks, and stopped, and turned so slow it made my stomach rub the inside of my apron, and buzzed to the other two, who kind of huddled against her for relief, and then they all three of them went up the cat-and-dog-food-breakfast-cereal-macaroni-rice-raisins-seasonings-spreads-spaghetti-soft-drinks-crackers-and-cookies aisle. From the third slot I look straight up this aisle to the meat counter, and I watched them all the way. The fat one with the tan sort of fumbled with the cookies, but on second thought she put the package back. The sheep pushing their carts down the aisle—the girls were walking against the usual traffic (not that we have one-way signs or anything)—were pretty hilarious. You could see them, when Queenie's white shoulders dawned on them, kind of jerk, or hop, or hiccup, but their eyes snapped back to their own baskets and on they pushed. I bet you could set off dynamite in an A&P and the people would by and large keep reaching and checking oatmeal off their lists and muttering "Let me see, there was a third thing, began with A, asparagus, no, ah, yes, applesauce!" or

whatever it is they do mutter. But there was no doubt, this jiggled them. A few houseslaves in pin curlers even looked around after pushing their carts past to make sure what they had seen was correct.

6   You know, it's one thing to have a girl in a bathing suit down on the beach, where what with the glare nobody can look at each other much anyway, and another thing in the cool of the A&P, under the fluorescent lights, against all those stacked packages, with her feet paddling along naked over our checkerboard green-and-cream rubber-tile floor.

7   "Oh Daddy," Stokesie said beside me. "I feel so faint."

8   "Darling," I said. "Hold me tight." Stokesie's married, with two babies chalked up on his fuselage already, but as far as I can tell that's the only difference. He's twenty-two, and I was nineteen this April.

9   "Is it done?" he asks, the responsible married man finding his voice. I forgot to say he thinks he's going to be manager some sunny day, maybe in 1990 when it's called the Great Alexandrov and Petrooshki Tea Company or something.

10   What he meant was, our town is five miles from a beach, with a big summer colony out on the Point, but we're right in the middle of town, and the women generally put on a shirt or shorts or something before they get out of the car into the street. And anyway these are usually women with six children and varicose veins mapping their legs and nobody, including them, could care less. As I say, we're right in the middle of town, and if you stand at our front doors you can see two banks and the Congregational church and the newspaper store and three real-estate offices and about twenty-seven old freeloaders tearing up Central Street because the sewer broke again. It's not as if we're on the Cape; we're north of Boston and there's people in this town haven't seen the ocean for twenty years.

11   The girls had reached the meat counter and were asking McMahon something. He pointed, they pointed, and they shuffled out of sight behind a pyramid of Diet Delight peaches. All that was left for us to see was old McMahon patting his mouth and looking after them sizing up their joints. Poor kids, I began to feel sorry for them, they couldn't help it. . . .

12   Now here comes the sad part of the story, at least my family says it's sad, but I don't think it's so sad myself. The store's pretty empty, it being Thursday afternoon, so there was nothing much to do except lean on the register and wait for the girls to show up again. The whole store was like a pinball machine and I didn't know which tunnel they'd come out of. After a while they come around out of the far aisle, around the light bulbs, records at discount of the Caribbean Six or Tony Martin Sings or some such gunk you wonder they waste the wax on, sixpacks of candy bars, and plastic toys done up in cellophane that fall apart when a kid looks at them anyway. Around they come, Queenie still leading the way, and holding a little gray jar in her hand. Slots Three through Seven are unmanned and I

could see her wondering between Stokes and me, but Stokesie with his usual luck draws an old party in baggy gray pants who stumbles up with four giant cans of pineapple juice (what do these bums *do* with all that pineapple juice? I've often asked myself) so the girls come to me. Queenie puts down the jar and I take it into my fingers icy cold. Kingfish Fancy Herring Snacks in Pure Sour Cream: 49¢. Now her hands are empty, not a ring or a bracelet, bare as God made them, and I wonder where the money's coming from. Still with that prim look she lifts a folded dollar bill out of the hollow at the center of her nubbled pink top. The jar went heavy in my hand. Really, I thought that was so cute.

13   Then everybody's luck begins to run out. Lengel comes in from haggling with a truck full of cabbages on the lot and is about to scuttle into that door marked MANAGER behind which he hides all day when the girls touch his eye. Lengel's pretty dreary, teaches Sunday school and the rest, but he doesn't miss that much. He comes over and says, "Girls, this isn't the beach."

14   Queenie blushes, though maybe it's just a brush of sunburn I was noticing for the first time, now that she was so close. "My mother asked me to pick up a jar of herring snacks." Her voice kind of startled me, the way voices do when you see the people first, coming out so flat and dumb yet kind of tony, too, the way it ticked over "pick up" and "snacks." All of a sudden I slid right down her voice into her living room. Her father and the other men were standing around in ice-cream coats and bow ties and the women were in sandals picking up herring snacks on toothpicks off a big glass plate and they were all holding drinks the color of water with olives and sprigs of mint in them. When my parents have somebody over they get lemonade and if it's a real racy affair Schlitz in tall glasses with "They'll Do It Every Time" cartoons stencilled on.

15   "That's all right," Lengel said. "But this isn't the beach." His repeating this struck me as funny, as if it had just occurred to him, and he had been thinking all these years the A&P was a great big dune and he was the head lifeguard. He didn't like my smiling—as I say he doesn't miss much—but he concentrates on giving the girls that sad Sunday-school-superintendent stare.

16   Queenie's blush is no sunburn now, and the plump one in plaid, that I liked better from the back—a really sweet can—pipes up, "We weren't doing any shopping. We just came in for the one thing."

17   "That makes no difference," Lengel tells her, and I could see from the way his eyes went that he hadn't noticed she was wearing a two-piece before. "We want you decently dressed when you come in here."

18   "We *are* decent," Queenie says suddenly, her lower lip pushing, getting sore now that she remembers her place, a place from which the crowd that runs the A&P must look pretty crummy. Fancy Herring Snacks flashed in her very blue eyes.

19   "Girls, I don't want to argue with you. After this come in here with your shoulders covered. It's our policy." He turns his back. That's policy for you. Policy is what the kingpins want. What the others want is juvenile delinquency.

20   All this while, the customers had been showing up with their carts but, you know, sheep, seeing a scene, they had all bunched up on Stokesie, who shook open a paper bag as gently as peeling a peach, not wanting to miss a word. I could feel in the silence everybody getting nervous, most of all Lengel, who asks me, "Sammy, have you rung up their purchase?"

21   I thought and said "No" but it wasn't about that I was thinking. I go through the punches, 4, 9, GROC, TOT—it's more complicated than you think, and after you do it often enough, it begins to make a little song, that you hear words to, in my case "Hello (*bing*) there, you (*gung*) hap-py *pee-pul* (*splat*)!"—the *splat* being the drawer flying out. I uncrease the bill, tenderly as you may imagine, it just having come from between the two smoothest scoops of vanilla I had ever known were there, and pass a half and a penny into her narrow pink palm, and nestle the herrings in a bag and twist its neck and hand it over, all the time thinking.

22   The girls, and who'd blame them, are in a hurry to get out, so I say "I quit" to Lengel quick enough for them to hear, hoping they'll stop and watch me, their unsuspected hero. They keep right on going, into the electric eye; the door flies open and they flicker across the lot to their car, Queenie and Plaid and Big Tall Goony-Goony (not that as raw material she was so bad), leaving me with Lengel and a kink in his eyebrow.

23   "Did you say something, Sammy?"

24   "I said I quit."

25   "I thought you did."

26   "You didn't have to embarrass them."

27   "It was they who were embarrassing us."

28   I started to say something that came out "Fiddle-de-doo." It's a saying of my grandmother's, and I know she would have been pleased.

29   "I don't think you know what you're saying," Lengel said.

30   "I know you don't," I said. "But I do." I pull the bow at the back of my apron and start shrugging it off my shoulders. A couple customers that had been heading for my slot begin to knock against each other, like scared pigs in a chute.

31   Lengel sighs and begins to look very patient and old and gray. He's been a friend of my parents for years. "Sammy, you don't want to do this to your Mom and Dad," he tells me. It's true, I don't. But it seems to me that once you begin a gesture it's fatal not to go through with it. I fold the apron, "Sammy" stitched in red on the pocket, and put it on the counter, and drop the bow tie on top of it. The bow tie is theirs, if you've ever wondered. "You'll feel this for the rest of your life," Lengel says, and I know that's true, too, but remembering how he made that pretty girl blush

makes me so scrunchy inside I punch the No Sale tab and the machine whirs "pee-pul" and the drawer splats out. One advantage to this scene taking place in summer, I can follow this up with a clean exit, there's no fumbling around getting your coat and galoshes, I just saunter into the electric eye in my white shirt that my mother ironed the night before, and the door heaves itself open, and outside the sunshine is skating around on the asphalt.

32   I looked around for my girls, but they're gone, of course. There wasn't anybody but some young married screaming with her children about some candy they didn't get by the door of a powder-blue Falcon station wagon. Looking back in the big windows, over the bags of peat moss and aluminum lawn furniture stacked on the pavement, I could see Lengel in my place in the slot, checking the sheep through. His face was dark gray and his back stiff, as if he'd just had an injection of iron, and my stomach kind of fell as I felt how hard the world was going to be to me hereafter.

**Questions
on Content**

1. How does Sammy characterize each of the three girls?

2. Why does Sammy refer to customers in the A&P as "sheep" (paragraph 20) and "pigs" (paragraph 30)?

3. Identify the major difference Sammy sees between himself and Stokesie.

4. What does Sammy allow us to infer about his family? What does he infer about Queenie's family?

5. Why does Sammy refer to himself as "their unsuspected hero" (paragraph 22)? Is his behavior heroic?

6. In what ways is Sammy surprised at his own behavior?

**Questions
on Structure
and Style**

7. What effect does Updike achieve by beginning his story so abruptly?

8. In describing one of the girls, Sammy refers to "this clean bare plane of the top of her chest down from the shoulder bones like a dented sheet of

metal tilted in the light" (paragraph 3). This is one of several uses of figurative language in the story. How does the use of figurative language contribute to Sammy's voice?

9. The tone of the story changes at paragraph 12. How does Updike signal this change? Do you notice a change in Sammy's language?

10. Find examples of caricature and exaggeration in Sammy's language.

Assignments

1. In "Sometimes the Liveliest Words" (page 221), Jeff Kunerth quotes Eric Partridge, who defines slang as "more than mere self-expression. It connotes personality, a method of distinguishing ourselves by virtue of our linguistic virtuosity" (paragraph 5). Write an essay discussing this "linguistic virtuosity" as it applies to Sammy.

2. In Sammy's first-person account, Updike captures the rhythms of adolescent language. Much of the story's success is attributable to the authenticity of this voice. In an essay, discuss how Sammy's language captures the essence of teenage speech.

3. In an essay, examine how Sammy's language mirrors his attitudes and values.

4. "A&P" is as popular today as it was in 1962, when it was written. Write an essay suggesting possible reasons for its continuing popularity.

Taboo: The Sacred and the Obscene

Geoffrey Wagner and Sanford R. Radner

There is much that we choose *not* to say, and taboo and euphemism are both language tools designed for this avoidance. They are, however, as revealing as any other utterances. In the following selection from *Language and Reality*, Geoffrey Wagner and Sanford R. Radner define *taboo* and *euphemism*, show their relationship, and explain why we have invented these methods for acknowledging "the space where no language is."

1   *Taboo* is a Tongan word (sometimes spelled *tabu*) supposedly adopted from Polynesian culture by Captain Cook, an eighteenth-century English explorer. Today most Americans probably associate it with the perfume of that name showing, in the celebrated Kreisler Sonata ad, the longest kiss on record. Freud, however, assured us of the double, or "ambivalent," meaning of taboo: (1) as sacred, (2) as forbidden-unclean. The unutterable pair form a sort of self-complementary antithesis—"so that," as he writes, "the objects of veneration become objects of aversion." If this dynamic were understood, we should not be supporting by our taxes small armies of official snoopers all trying to detect something called obscenity in our midst, and world statesmen would not be making damn fools of themselves in public by calling pornography the origin of Communism.

2   The way in which taboo collects this strange semantic pair-bond in our culture is curious. Until not too long ago in England, at any rate, authors who had infringed laws governing sexual purity were sometimes also prosecuted for profanity or blasphemy. Relatively recently, Gerard-Kornelis Van Het Reve was prosecuted under Article 147 of the Dutch Penal Code concerning blasphemy, when it was considered likely that he would get off on the score of obscenity.

3   Here, in the neat phrasing of Kenneth Burke, "scatology and eschatology overlap." The objects of aversion and the objects of veneration illide (*veneration* itself is close to *venery*). We are all familiar with G-d avoidances. Totemism was the ritual preservation of taboo, and not to write God's name in full, or that of Yahweh (a protective tetragrammaton meaning *I am who shall be*), was avoiding visually identifiable blasphemy. Moses was rebuked for wanting to know God's name—"the Lord will not hold him guiltless that taketh his name in vain" (Exodus 21:7).

4   *Gee, Jeepers* for Jesus, *heck* for hell, the *deuce* for the devil, *shucks* for shit, and *bloody* (in England) for By Our Lady are all examples of Freud's point,

as well as Kenneth Burke's extension of it. Taboo involved the "blindness" of a sense: *Holy Tchee!* thus fulfills the source of the taboo for the ear, while making no verbal infringement, but it is a "dirty" word, one for which an excremental alias could well be (and often is) substituted.

5   A few years ago an enterprising West German marketed a toilet paper, rather appropriately bearing the trade name *Adios.* For a while the product sold pretty well. Then it was brought to the attention of the Bishop of Munich, who protested violently (*Der Spiegel*, March 14, 1962). A less sacrilegious name had to be, and was in fact, found. Generically, what the good bishop was saying in his objection was that the sacred and the fecal are both exceptional, and exceptionally nonutterable. There was even a hint of this taboo when Rolls Royce marketed their revered Silver Mist model in Germany, and had hastily to retitle it; *Mist* is German shit, or at any rate manure.

6   Egyptian pyramidal tombs are supposed to have mimicked dung piles, while it is said that the Dalai Lamas believed their excrement to be notably holy (cp. U.S. *head*). That the organs of sex are also those of excretion has been called God's final joke on man. Privacy taboos resulting from the vetoes available in this area proliferated in Puritanism, of course, and repeatedly crisscrossed the tracks of capitalism. For money has been called a kind of dung, and there is still a great deal of touchiness about bank balances and the like ("May we anticipate an early remittance?"); in fact, this sometimes reaches the point of real confusion.*

7   Essentially we must remember, however, that the savages studied in Freud's *Totem and Taboo* were living in small societies literally threatened by uncleanness. Dead bodies putrefied and carried disease. They were actually unclean and so cast out—"untouchable."

8   Such could be called behavioral taboo (with its relic in our charges of "indecent behavior"). Linguistic taboo ("insulting language") involves phonemic situations, and Edmund Leach shows us the same Freudian pair-bond operating in *quim*, one of the most taboo terms (*the* most, he claims) for the feminine pudenda—euphemism! euphemism!—yet one etymologically associated with *queen*.

9   God-dog, dog collar, God damn, son of a bitch (one doesn't say, You son of a kangaroo)—the area of taboo rests on social valuation of animals and, if Leach is correct, the classifying of animals as regards their edibility involves sex. It is well known that we cringe from consuming dog—or even horse, which the French eat—and are yet surprised by the Indians' similar fastidiousness about cow (or the pious Jews about pork).

---

* This kind of confusion was best highlighted by the boy who was told by his mother to avoid his schoolmates' synonyms for urination and substitute *whisper.*

"Daddy," he said that evening to his father, who was not yet in on the code, "I want to whisper."

"Sure, son," came the answer. "Do it in my ear."

Subjects of Taboo in Our Culture

10   The social environment of a child is a continuum which is then broken up into discrete entities. The gaps between these naturally form the taboo part of the environment since they are full of uncertainty. The same anxiety must pertain, too, about the human body itself. The child needs to find itself finite, to identify itself as apart from its surroundings, with the result that nearly all exudations of the body come under some sort of taboo. This certainly varies in degree, excreta being more tabooed than menstrual flow, say, and the latter more than mere tears; but even hair and nails are often subject to ritual fears.

11   The greatest outlaw of all, here, is not unnaturally death, the binary antithesis of life in most world religions. This is understandable. In small Royal Air Force squadrons during the Battle of Britain of World War II, the casualty rate was so high that fighter pilots had, for the sake of some sort of sanity, to invent a death-diminishing slang. This touching jargon, with its terms like *gone for a burton* (a special kind of beer) to replace "blown to smithereens," was later made the subject of an illuminating article by Eric Partridge. But this was essentially a private, protective slang; it was not used for hiding reality, and it was not disseminated beyond the group using it.

12   There is no doubt that death taboos are universal. Only a year or so ago, a village in central Italy called Camposanto, successfully petitioned to change its name because of its connotations of cemetery. Yet it is significant that it did so only recently. In our own technological society, death is a living criticism and a reiterated public defeat. Consequently, our terms for neutralizing this event can become truly absurd, as in certain California mortuaries.

13   It is not simply that we coin *passed on, joined the majority, no longer with us,* and the like; I defy anyone who has lost a close and dear relative to not want to grope for some such expression directly thereafter. All cultures euphemize death, even those, like the Japanese, where the dead are sometimes conceived as still present.

14   But when the reluctance grossly exceeds the human need, something is afoot, and the semanticist takes note. No one wants to die. And stink. But when the "leave-taking" in Forest Lawn of millionaire mortician Hubert Eaton resembles, verbally and physically, a minor Fascist ceremony, taboo turns into phobia. The concealment becomes so much social rococo.

15   Similarly, when military shorthand refers to dead Marines as H.R.'s, meaning is demeaned if this term is passed on to the American public as a verbal antiseptic. It may be that it is easier for combat troops to talk about *horizontally repatriated* rather than dead, or to call wounded *W.I.A.'s* (wounded in action), but to tell press reporters, as has been the case, "The

weeklies are on the rack" for *Dead and wounded figures have been posted* looks close to obfuscation of the type that tried to turn napalm into *incendigel*. Euphemisms are not intended to hide; they are, rather, transparent veils to soften the starkness of our human existences.

16   Taboo is a reluctance to utter which is not necessarily an inhibition; it may be a kind of linguistic self-protection, which is to say that it is, in Anatol Rapoport's sense, "operational." It may of course be either oral or written, and the meeting of these twain can be, in our semantic society, a very bloody crossroad indeed.

17   Excremental taboos are, in fact, so extreme in American society—the deodorant society, after all—that they form as good a place as any at which to come to grips with some of the most glaring conflicts about taboo. For instance: a ladies' REST ROOM (or LOUNGE) scarcely describes "operationally" what goes on inside it. Yet even this euphemism, REST ROOM, does not apparently anesthetize sufficiently the reality, and thousands of dollars have been spent reshooting sequences of movies so that the supposedly more innocuous POWDER ROOM will appear.

18   Despite decades of "liberation," sex is still the area in American life where taboo operates most powerfully. According to Professor H. J. Eysenck, Freud's true importance with regard to sex lay in his formulation (and subsequent popularization) of a language which contained ideas people could use—so that what was previously unutterable could be uttered. The Kinsey Report, whatever its failings, undoubtedly showed that elementary sexual matters were not being rendered into a vocabulary in our culture. Since they were not, parents had scant terms with which to discuss such matters with their children—much to the derision of the latter.

19   To *sleep with* or *go to bed with* has been shown up as a seriously inadequate language deputy for the sexual act. Naturally there are many other such, ranging from *having relations* to the (legal) *sexual congress*. Partridge found a virtual dictionary of such in his *Shakespeare's Bawdy*. Ozark women used to *lay down* for the same activity. There is the Biblical *know*.

20   A few years ago a British lawyer put a prostitute on the stand in a famous case and asked her if she had *slept with* the accused. She replied that she had not. This considerably disconcerted counsel, since the lady involved had frankly admitted that she had indeed had sexual intercourse with the man identified. The question had to be rephrased in sterner terms so that she might understand that *sleeping with* meant "sleeping with," not merely sleeping with. A hoary chestnut of British colonial days has it that a district administrator of the pukka sahib type enjoyed for years the sexual services of a native concubine; but when asked by his friends, who knew of this, whether he had ever *gone to bed with* the woman, he fervently denied having done so. On being pressed, over cups, to come clean, he got out stertorously the three words, "On the mat!"

Euphemism: Use and Abuse

21   We have already defined euphemism as a less direct symbol for the tabooed word, and we have discussed examples in various areas of taboo in our culture. Sometimes the original euphemism does not do the job of sufficiently quieting anxiety about the taboo, and a further step of *re-euphemizing* is necessary: *manure* gets dumped as *fertilizer* which then gets too closely attached to its stink so that it has to be called *plant food*. Similarly, *face-lifting* is disguised as *cosmetic surgery* which then turns into *skin sculpture*. A *garbage man* becomes a *sanitation engineer* who is now talked about in some parts as an *environmental expert*.

22   Euphemism certainly performs a serious function in survival—cancer is genuinely easier to bear when it is called a *tumor,* and some addicts prefer to have a fix known as *inoculation;* but it clearly loses all purpose when it so clouds reality that no one knows what is happening at all. In such extreme cases, symbol loses all contact with referent.

23   Lincoln, Nebraska's Hospital for the Crippled and Deformed is now the Nebraska Orthopedic Hospital, and New York's Hospital for the Society for the Relief of the Ruptured and Crippled has become the Hospital for Special Surgery. In this same spirit, artificial limbs are sometimes termed *prosthetic devices.*

24   This has been shown genuinely to help, rather than hinder. Reality can, after all, become so unpleasant as to be unbearable. Someone who is called *crippled* by one society may be assisted by being reclassified *handicapped* or *disabled* by another. Are not sports players in the best of health also "handicapped"? To be blind is, surely, to be *visually handicapped* rather than *crippled,* since the blind are capable of extraordinary tactile and auditory sensitivity. An expert typist or concert pianist may well lack the use of eyes.

25   Where, then, comes the borderline or breaking point at which the taboo totem gets worshiped for itself, as a kind of verbal golden calf? Of course, it is hard to be semantically specific. Since the renaming of a reality cannot change that reality, calling gelled gasoline fluid which is being dropped on Asiatic peasantry *napalm* is merely so much verbalized shame.

26   Napalm was a technological neologism drawn from naphthenic and palmitic acids; but it soon became so closely attached to the dreadful reality that *incendigel,* even more technically neutral, it was hoped, was coined, and South Vietnamese newspapers were instructed to use the term. To the rice-paddy peasant anointed with one or the other, such subtleties of semantics must have seemed the luxury of a very rich and callous society indeed.

27   The same attempt at reality-concealment of course proceeds on a more mundane level. At a point in our unsaying, we reach a moment when we

hinder, rather than help, by such terms. The *environmental expert* is still shifting trash and the *grief therapist* (for which read funeral director) is still burying bodies—or *stiffs*. Ladies who do not want to mention *nose jobs* have been known to refer to them as *deviated septum operations;* however, a plain and simple deviated septum is a serious matter and should certainly not be confused with a *nose job*.

28   Society gets the euphemisms it wants. The White House tried to induce journalists to eschew the term *escalation* and rename it *supplementary bombing,* without notable success. You might say—the way in which our lies are told us is important. The motive of the user is well revealed in a euphemism.

29   Take our reiterated importation of the term *engineer*. Surely here the totem-creature is in danger of becoming more sacred than the being in reality. The plumber becomes a *household engineer,* the ditchdigger a *construction engineer,* a salesman a *sales engineer,* and a moving truck has *Moving Engineers* emblazoned on its flanks. Mencken unearthed a bedding manufacturer terming himself a *sleep-engineer,* and also an *exterminator-engineer*. The list could be continued indefinitely, and has been in fact; in 1935 the National Society of Professional Engineers protested against all these pseudo-engineers in our midst, in an action to try to get American railroads to call their locomotive engineers *enginemen*.

30   Once again science admires itself in a mirror. There is a reflection, as we write, of the same tendency in the common substitution on all sides of *technologist* for technician. The Laverne-Pisani Bill was the result of one of these very contentions in the field of nursing; it was aimed at precisely defining what a *nurse* was, in the inclusion or exclusion of certain medical regimens. The American Medical Association now wants to reclassify all GPs as *specialists*.

31   The neologisms of technology, which artificially swell our dictionaries every year, are generally emotion-poor and depriving in effect. The man in the street still has problems using simple terms like amps and ohms. Now words like *polyunsaturates, quasars, rhochromatics,* and the like spatter our breakfast-food semantic, and to tell the layman that he has *agrypnia* or *cephalalgia* or *pyrexia* in lieu of the complaints they actually stand for (insomnia, headache, fever) is simply to confuse and probably alarm him. A *cold* is a *respiratory infection*. Most people would probably rather have a cold.

32   Once again, it should be emphasized that the use of these terms often depends on context. They may be genuinely helpful. Thus a doctor can discuss a cancer innocently enough in front of an alarmed patient by referring to it as *neoplasia;* alcoholism may be called *extensive two-carbon fragment intake,* or just *etch* (from ethanol). Yet all too often technological euphemism can merely turn into another Humpty Dumpty. The effect of continual euphemism is really to make everything rather foggily similar

and in the end to work against individuality and eccentricity. "The smatterer in science," Herman Melville has a character in *White Jacket* say, "thinks that by mouthing hard words he proves that he understands hard things."

33   To conclude the entire subject, we should see that taboo stands for a stage in language. It is not mutism, nor is it substitute physical activity. It is essentially a semantic transaction, and to utter an unutterable in the form of euphemism is perhaps an important pace forward in communication and makes certain dialogues easier and more "normal." But the *space where no language is* remains constant—the gap between symbol and reality.

Questions on Content

1. What stand do the authors take on the issues of obscenity and pornography?

2. Why would a bishop protest naming a toilet paper *Adios* (paragraph 5)?

3. Define the behavioral taboo. How does it differ from the linguistic taboo?

4. Why do "nearly all exudations of the body come under some sort of taboo" (paragraph 10)?

5. Why is taboo sometimes "a kind of linguistic self-protection" (paragraph 16)?

6. The authors call *sleep with* or *go to bed with* a "language deputy for the sexual act" (paragraph 19). What do they mean by "language deputy"? Why do they employ the term *the sexual act* rather than some other term?

7. Why are some euphemisms valuable? Why are some *not* valuable?

8. What do taboo and euphemism have in common?

Questions on Structure and Style

9. Some paragraphs of the essay consist entirely of examples; they have no apparent topic sentences. Identify three of these paragraphs, and explain how they function.

10. For what audience are Wagner and Radner writing? How can we tell?

11. Describe the authors' tone, and circle at least five places where language helps set this tone.

12. If Wagner and Radner want their study of language to be taken seriously, why do they employ humor so often? Is *humor* an accurate term here?

Assignments

1. Wagner and Radner describe excremental taboos as "extreme" in our society—which explains why, when speaking with their children, parents often employ euphemisms to describe bodily functions. Write down the euphemisms for these functions that you were taught as a child. Then have one person collect the lists from all the students in your class, and have that person review the results. How many different euphemisms did students name? What were they, and which were most (and least) common?

2. We all know people for whom any discussion of sex seems taboo. Think of one such person whom you know. In an essay, explain, first, various circumstances in which this person is probably uncomfortable. (Watching certain television programs? At a newsstand?) Then explain how this person has (or has not) adapted to those circumstances. Be sure to consider the role of language in the person's discomfort and adaptability.

3. Has a euphemism ever become important for you? Think of a time when someone close to you died or became seriously ill. In an essay, describe the role that a euphemism played (or perhaps, failed to play) in helping you deal with your feelings.

Euphemisms

Hugh Rawson

▓▓▓▓▓▓▓▓▓▓▓▓▓▓▓▓

The following selection appears as the introduction to Hugh Rawson's *A Dictionary of Euphemisms and Other Doubletalk*. Rawson describes in rich detail types of euphemisms, their ways of entering our speech, their origins, and their purposes. Moreover, Rawson's voice makes his analysis as entertaining as it is precise.

▓▓▓▓▓▓▓▓▓▓▓▓▓▓▓▓

1   Mr. Milquetoast gets up from the table, explaining that he has to go to the *little boys' room* or *see a man about a dog;* a young woman announces that she is *enceinte.* A secretary complains that her boss is a pain in the *derrière;* an undertaker (or *mortician*) asks delicately where to ship the *loved one.* These are euphemisms—mild, agreeable, or roundabout words used in place of coarse, painful, or offensive ones. The term comes from the Greek *eu,* meaning "well" or "sounding good," and *phēmē,* "speech."

2   Many euphemisms are so delightfully ridiculous that everyone laughs at them. (Well, almost everyone: The people who call themselves the National Selected Morticians usually manage to keep from smiling.) Yet euphemisms have very serious reasons for being. They conceal the things people fear the most—death, the dead, the supernatural. They cover up the facts of life—of sex and reproduction and excretion—which inevitably remind even the most refined people that they are made of clay, or worse. They are beloved by individuals and institutions (governments, especially) who are anxious to present only the handsomest possible images of themselves to the world. And they are embedded so deeply in our language that few of us, even those who pride themselves on being plainspoken, ever get through a day without using them.

3   The same sophisticates who look down their noses at *little boys' room* and other euphemisms of that ilk will nevertheless say that they are going to the *bathroom* when no bath is intended; that Mary has been *sleeping* around even though she has been getting precious little shut-eye; that John has *passed away* or even *departed* (as if he'd just made the last train to Darien); and that Sam and Janet are *friends,* which sounds a lot better than "illicit lovers."

4   Thus, euphemisms are society's basic *lingua non franca.* As such, they are outward and visible signs of our inward anxieties, conflicts, fears, and shames. They are like radioactive isotopes. By tracing them, it is possible to see what has been (and is) going on in our language, our minds, and our culture.

5   Euphemisms can be divided into two general types—positive and negative. The positive ones inflate and magnify, making the euphemized items seem altogether grander and more important than they really are. The

243

negative euphemisms deflate and diminish. They are defensive in nature, offsetting the power of tabooed terms and otherwise eradicating from the language everything that people prefer not to deal with directly.

6   Positive euphemisms include the many fancy occupational titles, which salve the egos of workers by elevating their job status: *custodian* for janitor (itself a euphemism for caretaker), *counsel* for lawyer, the many kinds of *engineer* (*exterminating engineer, mattress engineer, publicity engineer,* ad infinitum), *help* for servant (itself an old euphemism for slave), *hooker* and *working girl* for whore, and so forth. A common approach is to try to turn one's trade into a profession, usually in imitation of the medical profession. *Beautician* and the aforementioned *mortician* are the classic examples, but the same imitative instinct is responsible for social workers calling welfare recipients *clients,* for football coaches conducting *clinics,* and for undertakers referring to corpses as *cases* or even *patients.*

7   Other kinds of positive euphemisms include personal honorifics such as *colonel,* the *honorable,* and *major,* and the many institutional euphemisms, which convert madhouses into *mental hospitals,* colleges into *universities,* and small business establishments into *emporiums, parlors, salons,* and *shoppes.* The desire to improve one's surroundings also is evident in geographical place names, most prominently in the case of the distinctly nongreen *Greenland* (attributed to an early real estate developer named Eric the Red), but also in the designation of many small burgs as *cities,* and in the names of some cities, such as *Troy,* New York (*née* Vanderheyden's Ferry, its name-change in 1789 began a fad for adopting classical place names in the United States).

8   Negative, defensive euphemisms are extremely ancient. It was the Greeks, for example, who transformed the Furies into the *Eumenides* (the Kindly Ones). In many cultures, it is forbidden to pronounce the name of God (hence, pious Jews says *Adonai*) or of Satan (giving rise to the *deuce,* the *good man,* the *great fellow,* the generalized *Devil,* and many other roundabouts). The names of the dead, and of animals that are hunted or feared, may also be euphemized this way. The bear is called *grandfather* by many peoples and the tiger is alluded to as the *striped one.* The common motivation seems to be a confusion between the names of things and the things themselves: The name is viewed as an extension of the thing. Thus, to know the name is to give one power over the thing (as in the Rumpelstiltskin story). But such power may be dangerous: "Speak of the Devil and he appears." For mere mortals, then, the safest policy is to use another name, usually a flattering, euphemistic one, in place of the supernatural being's true name.

9   As strong as—or stronger than—the taboos against names are the taboos against particular words, especially the infamous *four-letter words.* (According to a recent Supreme Court decision, the set of *four-letter words* actually contains some words with as few as three and as many as 12 letters, but the

logic of Supreme Court decisions is not always immediately apparent.) These words form part of the vocabulary of practically everyone above the age of six or seven. They are not slang terms, but legitimate Standard English of the oldest stock, and they are euphemized in many ways, typically by conversion into pseudo-Latin (e.g., *copulation, defecation, urination*), into slang (*make love, number two, pee*), or into socially acceptable dashes (*f___, s___, p___,* etc.). In the electronic media, the function of the dash is fulfilled by the *bleep* (sometimes pronounced *blip*), which has completed the circle and found its way into print.

10   The taboo against words frequently degenerates into mere prudery. At least—though the defensive principle is the same—the primitive (or *preliterate*) hunter's use of *grandfather* seems to operate on a more elemental level than the excessive modesty that has produced *abdomen* for belly, *afterpart* for ass, *bosom* for breast, *limb* for leg, *white meat* for breast (of a chicken), and so on.

11   When carried too far, which is what always seems to happen, positive and negative euphemisms tend finally to coalesce into an unappetizing mush of elegancies and genteelisms, in which the underlying terms are hardly worth the trouble of euphemizing, e.g., *ablutions* for washing, *bender* for knee, *dentures* for false teeth, *expectorate* for spit, *home* for house, *honorarium* for fee, *ill* for sick, *libation* for drink, *perspire* for sweat, *position* for job, etc., etc., etc.

12   All euphemisms, whether positive or negative, may be used either unconsciously or consciously. Unconscious euphemisms consist mainly of words that were developed as euphemisms, but so long ago that hardly anyone remembers the original motivation. Examples in this category include such now-standard terms as *cemetery* (from the Greek word for "sleeping place," it replaced the more deathly "graveyard"), and the names of various barnyard animals, including the *donkey* (the erstwhile ass), the *sire* (or studhorse), and the *rooster* (for cock, and one of many similar evasions, e.g., *haystack* for haycock, *weather vane* for weathercock, and Louisa May *Alcott*, whose father changed the family name from the nasty-sounding Alcox). Into this category, too, fall such watered-down swear words as *cripes, Jiminy Cricket, gee,* and *gosh,* all designed to avoid taking holy names in vain and now commonly used without much awareness of their original meaning, particularly by youngsters and by those who fill in the balloons in comic strips. Then there are the words for which no honest *Anglo-Saxon* (often a euphemism for "dirty") equivalents exist, e.g., *brassiere,* which has hardly anything to do with the French *bras* (arm) from which it derives, and *toilet,* from the diminutive of *toile* (cloth).

13   Conscious euphemisms constitute a much more complex category, which is hardly surprising, given the ingenuity, not to say the deviousness, of the human mind. This is not to imply that euphemisms cannot be

employed more or less honestly as well as knowingly. For example, garbage men are upgraded routinely into *sanitation men*, but to say "Here come the sanitation men" is a comparatively venial sin. The meaning does come across intelligibly, and the listener understands that it is time to get out the garbage cans. By the same token, it is honest enough to offer a woman condolences upon "the loss of her husband," where *loss* stands for death. Not only are amenities preserved: By avoiding the troublesome term, the euphemism actually facilitates social discourse.

14   Conscious euphemisms also lead to social double-thinking, however. They form a kind of code. The euphemism stands for "something else," and everyone pretends that the "something else" doesn't exist. It is the essentially duplicitous nature of euphemisms that makes them so attractive to those people and institutions who have something to hide, who don't want to say what they are thinking, and who find it convenient to lie about what they are doing.

15   It is at this point, when speakers and writers seek not so much to avoid offense as to deceive, that we pass into the universe of dishonest euphemisms, where the conscious elements of circumlocution and doubletalk loom large. Here are the murky worlds of the CIA, the FBI, and the military, where murder is translated into *executive action*, an illegal break-in into a *black bag job*, and napalm into *soft* or *selective ordnance*. Here are the Wonderlands in which Alice would feel so much at home: advertising, where small becomes *medium* if not *large*, and politics, where gross errors are passed off as *misspeaking* and lies that won't wash anymore are called *inoperative*. Here, too, are our great industries: the prison business, where solitary confinement cells are disguised as *adjustment centers*, *quiet cells*, or *seclusion;* the atomic power business, where nuclear accidents become *core rearrangements* or simply *events;* the death business, where *remains* (not bodies) are *interred* (not buried) in *caskets* (not coffins); and, finally, of murder on its largest scale, where people are put into *protective custody* (imprisonment) in *concentration camps* (prison camps) as a first step toward achieving the *Final Solution* (genocide). George Orwell wrote in a famous essay ("Politics and the English Language," 1946) that "political language . . . is designed to make lies sound truthful and murder respectable, and to give an appearance of solidity to pure wind." His dictum applies equally through the full range of dishonest euphemisms.

16   Such doubletalk is doubly dangerous: Besides deceiving those on the receiving end, it helps the users fool themselves. As John W. Dean III has noted: "If . . . Richard Nixon had said to me, 'John, I want you to do a little crime for me. I want you to obstruct justice,' I would have told him he was crazy and disappeared from sight. No one thought about the Watergate coverup in those terms—at first, anyway. Rather, it was 'containing' Watergate or keeping the defendants 'on the reservation' or coming up with the right public relations 'scenario' and the like" (*New York Times,*

4/6/75). And as the Senate Intelligence Committee observed in 1975, after wading through a morass of euphemisms and circumlocutions in its investigation of American plots to kill foreign leaders: "'Assassinate,' 'murder,' and 'kill' are words many people do not want to speak or hear. They describe acts which should not even be proposed, let alone plotted. Failing to call dirty business by its rightful name may have increased the risk of dirty business being done." It is probably no coincidence that the conversations and internal memos of the Nixon White House were liberally studded with terms that had been popularized in the underworld and in the cloak-and-dagger business, where few, if any, holds are barred, e.g., *caper* (burglary), *covert operation* (burglary), *launder* (cleaning dirty money), *neutralize* (murder or, as used in the White House, character assassination), *plausible denial* (official lying), and so forth.

17   Euphemisms are in a constant state of flux. New ones are created almost daily. Many of them prove to be nonce terms—one-day wonders that are never repeated. Of those that are ratified through reuse as true euphemisms, some may last for generations, even centuries, while others fade away or develop into unconscious euphemisms, still used, but reflexively, without thought of their checkered origins. The ebb and flow of euphemisms is governed to a large extent by two basic rules: Gresham's Law of Language and the Law of Succession.

18   In monetary theory, where it originated, Gresham's Law can be summarized as "bad money drives out good"—meaning that debased or underweight coins will drive good, full-weight coins out of circulation. (By the by: Though Sir Thomas Gresham, 1519–1579, has gotten all the credit, the effect was noticed and explained by earlier monetary experts, including Nicolaus Koppernick, 1473–1543, who doubled as an astronomer and who is better known as Copernicus.) In the field of language, on the same principle, "bad" meanings or associations of words tend to drive competing "good" meanings out of circulation. Thus, *coition, copulation,* and *intercourse* once were general terms for, respectively, coming together, coupling, and communication, but after the words were drawn into service as euphemisms, their sexual meanings became dominant, so that the other senses are hardly ever encountered nowadays except in very special situations. The same thing happened to *crap* (formerly a general term for chaff, residue, or dregs), *feces* (also dregs, as of wine or salad oil), and *manure* (literally: "to work with the hands").

19   Gresham's Law remains very much in force, of course. Witness what has happened to *gay*, whose homosexual meaning has recently preempted all others. The law is by no means limited to euphemisms, and its application to other words helps explain why some euphemisms are formed. Thus, the incorrect and pejorative uses of "Jew" as a verb and adjective caused many people, Jews as well as Gentiles, to shift to *Hebrew* even though that term

should, in theory, be reserved for the Jews of ancient times or their language. A similar example is "girl," whose pejorative meanings have recently been brought to the fore, with the result that anxiety-ridden men sometimes fall into the worse error of referring to their *lady* friends.

20   Gresham's Law is the engine that powers the second of the two great euphemistic principles: the Law of Succession. After a euphemism becomes tainted by association with its underlying "bad" word, people will tend to shun it. For example, the seemingly innocent *occupy* was virtually banned by polite society for most of the seventeenth and eighteenth centuries because of its use as a euphemism for engaging in sex. (A man might be said to *occupy* his wife or to go to an *occupying* house.) Once people begin to shun a term, it usually is necessary to develop a new euphemism to replace the one that has failed. Then the second will become tainted and a third will appear. In this way, chains of euphemisms evolve. Thus, "mad" has been euphemized successively as *crazy, insane, lunatic, mentally deranged,* and just plain *mental.* Then there are the poor and backward nations that have metamorphosed from *underdeveloped* to *developing* to *emergent.* (*Fledgling* nations never really took hold despite the imprimatur of Eleanor Roosevelt.) A new chain seems to be evolving from the FBI's *black bag job,* which has fallen into sufficient disrepute that agents who condone break-ins are more likely now to talk in terms of *surreptitious entries, technical trespasses, uncontested physical searches,* or *warrantless investigations.*

21   Extraordinary collections of euphemisms have formed around some topics over the years as a result of the continual creation of new terms, and it seems safe to say that the sizes of these collections reflect the strength of the underlying taboos. Nowhere is this more evident than in the case of the *private parts,* male and female, whose Anglo-Saxon names are rarely used in mixed company, except by those who are on intimate terms. Thus, the monumental *Slang and Its Analogues* (J. S. Farmer and W. E. Henley, 1890–94) lists some 650 synonyms for *vagina,* most of them euphemistic, and about half that number for *penis.* (These are just the English synonyms; for *vagina,* for example, Farmer and Henley include perhaps another 900 synonyms in other languages.) Other anatomical parts that have inspired more than their share of euphemisms include the *bosom, bottom, limb,* and *testicles.* All forms of sexual *intercourse* and the subjects of *defecation, urination,* and the *toilet* also are richly euphemistic, as are *menstruation* (well over 100 terms have been noted), all aspects of death and dying, or *passing away,* and disease (it used to be *TB* and the sexual, *social diseases* that were euphemized; now it is cancer, usually referred to in *obituaries,* or death notices, as a *long illness*).

22   The incidence of euphemisms may also reflect society's ambivalent feelings on certain subjects. Alcohol, for example, is responsible for a great many euphemisms: There are 356 synonyms for "drunk"—more than for

any other term—in the appendixes to the *Dictionary of American Slang* (Harold Wentworth and Stuart Berg Flexner, 1976). The practice of punishing criminals with death (*capital punishment*) also makes many people uncomfortable, judging from the number of linguistic evasions for it, both in the United States, where the electric chair may be humorously downplayed as a *hot seat*, and in other countries, such as France, where the condemned are introduced to *Madame, la guillotine*. Meanwhile, the so-called victimless crime of prostitution has inspired an inordinate number of euphemisms, with some 70 listed in this book under *prostitute* (a sixteenth-century Latinate euphemism for "whore," which itself may have begun life as a euphemism for some now-forgotten word, the Old English *hōre* being cognate with the Latin *cara*, darling). The precarious position of *minorities* (a code term for blacks and/or Hispanics) and other oft-oppressed groups (e.g., homosexuals, servants, women) also is revealed by the variety of terms that have been devised to characterize them.

23   Just as the clustering of euphemisms around a given term or topic appears to reflect the strength of a particular taboo, so the unusual accumulation of euphemisms around an institution is strongly indicative of interior rot. Thus, the Spanish Inquisition featured an extensive vocabulary of words with double meanings (e.g., *auto-da-fé* for act of faith, and the *question* for torture). In our own time, the number of euphemisms that have collected around the CIA and its attempts at *assassination*, the FBI and its reliance on break-ins and *informants*, and the prison business and its noncorrectional *correctional facilities*, all tend to confirm one's darker suspicions. This is true, too, of the *Defense* (not War) *Department*, with its *enhanced radiation weapons* (neutron bombs) and its *reconnaissance in force* (search-and-destroy) missions. The military tradition, though, is very old. As long ago as ca. 250 B.C., a Macedonian general, Antigonus Gonatas, parlayed a "retreat" into a *strategic movement to the rear*. And, finally, there is politics, always a fertile source of doubletalk, but especially so during the Watergate period when euphemisms surfaced at a rate that is unlikely (one hopes) ever to be matched again; *Deep six, expletive deleted, inoperative, sign off,* and *stonewall* are only a few of the highpoints (or lowpoints, depending upon one's perspective) of this remarkably fecund period.

24   Watergate aside, it is usually assumed that most of our greatest euphemisms come from the Victorian era, but this is not quite correct. Many of the euphemisms that are associated most closely with the Victorians—*bosom* and *limb*, for instance—actually came into use prior to the start of Victoria's reign in 1837.

25   The beginning of the period of pre-Victorian prudery is hard to date—as are most developments in language. Normally, it is only possible to say, on the basis of a quotation from a book, play, poem, letter, newspaper, and so forth, that such-and-such word or phrase was being used in such-and-such

way when the particular work was written. But there is no guarantee that the dictionary-maker—or compiler of euphemisms—has found the earliest example. Also, many words, especially slang words, may be used informally for a long time, perhaps centuries, before they are committed to writing. As a result, one can only say that fastidiousness in language became increasingly common from about 1750, and that this trend accelerated around the turn of the century, almost as if the incipient Victorians were frantically cleaning up their act in preparation for her ascent to the throne.

26   One of the first indications of the new niceness of the eighteenth century is the taint that was attached to "ass" after it became a euphemism for *arse* (the real term is now used cutely but quite mistakenly as a euphemism for the euphemism!). As early as 1751, polite ladies, whose equally polite grandmothers had thought it clever to say "arse," were shying clear of "ass" no matter what the occasion, with the result that a new euphemistic name had to be devised for the four-legged kind; hence, the appearance of *donkey*. The first *rooster* and the first *drumstick* (to avoid "leg") seem to date from the 1760s, while *darn* comes from the 1770s. By 1813, some farmers were speaking of the *bosom* of their plows, meaning the forward part of the moldboard, formerly called the "breast." And at about this time, too, begins the nineteenth-century sentimentalization of death, as recorded on tombstones of the period, which start to report that people, instead of dying, have *fallen asleep, gone to meet their Maker, passed over the river*, etc.

27   The two great landmarks in the development of pre-Victorian thought are the expurgations of the Bard and the Bible, with *The Family Shakespeare*, by the Bowdlers, appearing in 1807, and Noah Webster's version of the word of God ("with Amendments of the language"), coming out in 1833. The objective of the Bowdlers, as stated in the preface to the enlarged second edition of 1818, was to omit "those words and expressions . . . which cannot with propriety be read aloud in a family." (Note that "family" here has essentially the same meaning as when television executives speak of *family* time.) Though Dr. Thomas Bowdler has usually been given all the credit, the expurgation was primarily the work of his sister, Henrietta Maria. She has only herself to blame, however, for the lack of recognition: She didn't sign her name to the book probably because, as a maiden lady, she didn't want to admit publicly to understanding all the things she was censoring. As for Noah Webster, he carefully took out of the Bible every "whore," every "piss," and even every "stink," while making a great many other curious changes, such as *idolatries* for whoredom, *lewd deeds* for fornication (itself a Latinate evasion for an Anglo-Saxon word), and *nurse* for the apparently too animalistic "suck." In his introduction, Webster justified his rewrite of the King James Version of 1611, saying "Purity of mind is a Christian virtue that ought to be carefully guarded; and purity of language is one of the guards which protect this virtue."

28   The precise causes of this pre-Victorian linguistic revolution, whose leg-
acy remains with us, are difficult to pinpoint, involving as they do a combination of religious revival, industrialization, an emerging middle class,
increasing literacy, and an improvement in the status of women. Bench
marks of change include the Great Awakening, the religious revival that
shook New England in the late 1730s and soon spread to the rest of the
colonies; the near-simultaneous development of Methodism in England;
the beginnings of the factory system (Samuel Slater emigrated to America
in 1789, bringing with him most of the secrets of the English textile industry); the invention of the steam-powered press (the *Times* of London
installed two in 1814 that made 1,100 impressions per hour, a great technological advance); and, especially in the United States, a spirit of egalitari-
anism that extended to women and affected the language that men used in
front of them. As Alexis de Tocqueville noted: "It has often been remarked
that in Europe a certain degree of contempt lurks even in the flattery which
men lavish upon women; although a European frequently affects to be the
slave of a woman, it may be seen that he never sincerely thinks her his
equal. In the United States men seldom compliment women, but they . . .
constantly display an entire confidence in the understanding of a wife and
a profound respect for her freedom. . . . their conduct to women always
implies that they suppose them to be virtuous and refined; and such is the
respect entertained for the moral freedom of the sex that in the presence of
a woman the most guarded language is used lest her ear should be offended by an expression" (*Democracy in America*, 1835, 1840).

29   The ancient Egyptians called the deadhouse, where bodies were turned
into mummies, the *beautiful house*, and the ways of expunging offensive
expressions from language have not changed since. Simplest is to make a
straight substitution, using a word that has happier connotations than the
term one wishes to avoid. Frequently, a legitimate synonym will do. Thus,
agent, speculator, and *thrifty* have better vibes than "spy," "gambler," and
"tight," although the literal meanings, or denotations, of each pair of
words are the same. On this level, all the euphemist has to do is select
words with care. Other principles may be applied, however, a half dozen
of which are basic to creating—and deciphering—euphemisms. They are:

30   *Foreign Languages Sound Finer.*   It is permissible for speakers and writers of
English to express almost any thought they wish, as long as the more
risqué parts of the discussion are rendered in another language, usually
French or Latin. The versatility of French (and the influence of French
culture) is evident in such diverse fields as love (*affair, amour, liaison*), war
(*matériel, personnel, sortie, triage*), women's underwear (*brassiere, chemise,
lingerie*), and dining (goat, cow, deer, and other animals with English
names when they are alive and kicking are served up on the dinnertable as

the more palatable *chevon, filet mignon,* and *venison*). *French* itself is a euphemistic prefix word for a variety of "wrong" and/or "sexy" things, such as the *French disease* (syphilis) and one of the methods of guarding against it, the *French letter* (condom). Latin is almost equally popular as a source of euphemisms, especially for the body's sexual and other functions. Thus, such words as *copulation, fellatio, masturbation, pudendum,* and *urination* are regarded as printable and even broadcastable by people (including United States Supreme Court justices) who become exercised at the sight and sound of their English counterparts. Other languages have contributed. For example, the Dutch *boss* (master), the Spanish *cojones* (balls), and the Yiddish *tushie* (the ass). Not strictly speaking a foreign language is potty talk, a distinct idiom that has furnished many euphemisms, i.e., *number one, number two, pee, piddle,* and other relics of the nursery, often used by adults when speaking to one another as well as when addressing children.

31   **Bad Words Are Not So Bad When Abbreviated.**   Words that otherwise would create consternation if used in mixed company or in public are acceptable when reduced to their initial letters. Essentially, such abbreviations as *BS* and *SOB* work the same way as the dash in *f*___ : Everyone knows what letters have been deleted, but no one is seriously offended because the taboo word has not been paraded in all its glory. Dean Acheson even got away with *snafu* when he was secretary of state, though the acronym did cause some comment among the British, not all of whom felt this to be a very diplomatic way of apologizing for an American—er—*foul up*. This acronym also is noteworthy for spawning a host of picturesque albeit short-lived descendants, including *fubar* (where *bar* stands for Beyond All Recognition), *janfu* (Joint Army-Navy), *tarfu* (Things Are Really), and *tuifu* (The Ultimate In). Abbreviations function as euphemisms in many fields, e.g., the child's *BM*, the advertiser's *BO*, the hypochondriac's *Big C*, and the various shortenings for offbeat sex, such as *AC/DC* for those who swing both ways, *bd* for bondage and discipline, and *S/M*.

32   **Abstractions Are Not Objectionable.**   The strength of particular taboos may be dissipated by casting ideas in the most general possible terms; also, abstractions, being quite opaque to the uninformed eye (and meaningless to the untrained ear), make ideal cover-up words. Often, it is only a matter of finding the lowest common denominator. Thus, *it, problem, situation,* and *thing* may refer to anything under the sun: the child who keeps playing with *it* and the girl who is said to be doing *it; problem* days and *problem* drinking; the *situation* at the Three Mile Island, Pennsylvania, nuclear power plant; an economic *thing* (slump, recession, or depression), *our thing* (i.e., the Cosa Nostra), or the Watergate *thing* (elaborated by the president himself into the *prething* and the *postthing*). The American tendency toward

abstraction was noted early on by Tocqueville, who believed that democratic nations as a class were "addicted to generic terms and abstract expressions because these modes of speech enlarge thought and assist the operation of the mind by enabling it to include many objects in a small compass." The dark side of this is that abstractions are inherently fuzzy. As Tocqueville also noted: "An abstract term is like a box with a false bottom; you may put in what ideas you please, and take them out again without being observed" (*op. cit.*). Bureaucrats, engineers, scientists, and those who like to be regarded as scientists, are particularly good at generalizing details out of existence. They have produced such expressions as *aerodynamic personnel decelerator* for parachute, *energy release* for radiation release (as from a nuclear reactor), *episode* and *event* for disasters of different sorts and sizes, *impact attenuation device* for a crash cushion, and *Vertical Transportation Corps* for a group of elevator operators.

33 *Indirection Is Better Than Direction.*   Topics and terms that are too touchy to be dealt with openly may be alluded to in a variety of ways, most often by mentioning one aspect of the subject, a circumstance involving it, a related subject, or even by saying what it is not. Thus, people really do come together in an *assembly center* and soldiers do stop fighting when they *break off contact with the enemy*, but these are indirect euphemisms for "prison" and "retreat," respectively. *Bite the dust* is a classic of this kind, and the adjective is used advisedly, since the expression appears in Homer's *Iliad*, circa 750 B.C. Many of the common anatomical euphemisms also depend on indirection—the general, locational, it's-somewhere-back-there allusions to the *behind*, the *bottom*, and the *rear*, for example. A special category of anatomical euphemisms are those that conform to the Rule of the Displaced Referent, whereby "unmentionable" parts of the human body are euphemized by referring to nearby "mentionable" parts, e.g., *chest* for breasts; *fanny*, a word of unknown origin whose meaning has not always been restricted to the back end of a person; *tail*, which also has had frontal meanings (in Latin, *penis* means "tail"), and *thigh*, a biblical euphemism for the balls. Quaintest of the indirect euphemisms are those that are prefaced with a negative adjective, telling us what they are not, such as *unnatural*, *unthinkable*, and *unmentionable*. (The latter also appears as a noun in the plural; some women wear *upper unmentionables* and *lower unmentionables*.) An especially famous negative euphemism is the dread *love that dare not speak its name*, but the phrase was not totally dishonest in the beginning, since it dates to 1894 (from a poem by Oscar Wilde's young *friend*, Alfred, Lord Douglas), when "homosexual" was still so new a word as not to be known to many people, regardless of their *sexual orientation*.

34 *Understatement Reduces Risks.*   Since a euphemism is, by definition, a mild, agreeable, or roundabout word or phrase, it follows logically that its real

meaning is always worse than its apparent meaning. But this is not always obvious to the uninitiated, especially in constructions that acknowledge part of the truth while concealing the extent of its grimness. Thus, a nuclear reactor that is said to be *above critical* is actually out of control, *active defense* is attack, *area bombing* is terror bombing, *collateral damage* is civilian damage (as from nuclear bombs), and so on. The soft sell also is basic to such euphemisms as *companion, partner,* and *roommate,* all of which downplay "lover"; to *pro-choice* for pro-abortion, and to *senior citizen* for old person. The danger with understatement is that it may hide the true meaning completely. As a result, euphemists often erect signposts in front of the basic term, e.g., *close personal friend, constant companion, criminal conversation* (a legalism for adultery), *meaningful relationship,* etc. The signposts ensure that even dullards will get the message.

35 *The Longer the Euphemism the Better.*   As a rule, to which there are very few exceptions (*hit* for murder, for instance), euphemisms are longer than the words they replace. They have more letters, they have more syllables, and frequently, two or more words will be deployed in place of a single one. This is partly because the tabooed Anglo-Saxon words tend to be short and partly because it almost always takes more words to evade an idea than to state it directly and honestly. The effect is seen in euphemisms of every type. Thus, *Middle Eastern* dancing is what better "belly" dancers do; more advertisers agree that *medication* gives faster relief than "medicine"; the writers of financial reports eschew "drop" in favor of *adjustment downward,* and those poor souls who are required to give testimony under oath prefer *at this point in time* to "now." The list is practically endless. Until this very point in time, however, it was impossible for anyone to say exactly *how much* longer was *how much* better. That important question has now been resolved with the development of the Fog or Pomposity Index (FOP Index, for short).

36   The FOP Index compares the length of the euphemism or circumlocution to the word or phrase for which it stands, with an additional point being awarded for each additional letter, syllable, or word in the substitute expression. Thus, "medicine" has 8 letters and 3 syllables, while *medication* has 10 letters and an extra, fourth syllable, giving it a point count of 11. Dividing 8 into 11 produces a FOP Index of 1.4. By the same token, *adjustment downward* has a FOP Index of 5.75 compared to "drop" (18 letters, plus 4 extra syllables, plus 1 extra word, for a total of 23, divided by the 4 letters of the euphemized term).

37   Like most breakthroughs in the social (or soft) sciences, the FOP Index doesn't really tell you anything you didn't already know. Everyone (well, almost everyone) has always sensed that *medication* is on the pretentious side. The index, however, arms users with a number to back up their

intuition, thus enabling them to crush opponents in debate. It can now be said authoritatively that *lower extremity* (FOP Index of 6.6) outdoes *limb* (1.3) as a euphemism for leg. In much the same way, *prostitute* (2.4) improves upon *harlot* (1.4) for whore. In another field: *Oval Office* (2.6) is better than *Presidency* (2.4) is better than "Nixon," but both pale in comparison to the 17.8 of former HEW Secretary Joe Califano's *Personal Assistant to the Secretary (Special Activities)*, who was a "cook." (Califano's *Personal Assistant* illustrates a basic rule of bureaucracies: the longer the title, the lower the rank.) And so it goes: *Active defense* has a FOP Index of 2.5 for attack; *benign neglect* rates 2.3 for neglect (the "benign" being an example of a Meaningless Modifier); *categorical inaccuracy* is a whopping 10.3 compared to lie; *intestinal fortitude* is 6.5 for guts.

38   With quantification, the study of euphemisms has at last been put on a firm scientific footing. FOP Indexes have been included for a number of the entries in this dictionary and it is hoped that readers will enjoy working out indexes for themselves in other instances. As they proceed, given the nature of the terms for which euphemisms stand, they may also wish to keep in mind Shakespeare's advice (*Henry IV*, Part 2, 1600):

> 'Tis needful that the most immodest word
> Be looked upon and learned.

**Questions
on Content**

1. In paragraph 2, Rawson says that euphemisms have "very serious reasons for being." What are those serious reasons?

2. How does the author distinguish between positive and negative euphemisms? Are his own terms *positive* and *negative* perhaps euphemisms, or are they the right words for what he means?

3. Rawson says that "the common motivation seems to be a confusion between the names of things and the things themselves" (paragraph 8). What does he mean?

4. How do conscious and unconscious euphemisms differ?

5. According to Rawson, what are dishonest euphemisms (paragraph 15)?

6. Why does Rawson create what he calls "Gresham's Law of Language" and the "Law of Succession" (paragraph 17)? How do these terms help his explanations?

7. What was once objectionable about *occupy* (paragraph 20)? Why do you believe Rawson cites this particular term to illustrate his point?

8. The author claims that "the clustering of euphemisms around a given term or topic appears to reflect the strength of a particular taboo" (paragraph 23). What does this mean?

Questions on Structure and Style

9. What effect does Rawson create with his use of parallel structure in paragraph 2?

10. How would you identify Rawson's tone? Where is that tone particularly noticeable?

11. What audience is Rawson addressing?

12. What does Rawson's FOP Index tell us about Rawson himself? Why does he use it as the basis for his conclusion?

Assignments

1. For a day, be alert for positive euphemisms, noting their role in what you say and what others say to you. In a short essay, identify the most important of these euphemisms, and discuss why they proved important to you.

2. Repeat Assignment 1, this time with negative euphemisms as your subject.

3. Rawson writes, "The common motivation seems to be a confusion between the names of things and the things themselves: The name is viewed as an extension of the thing" (paragraph 8). Shakespeare says that "a rose by any other name would smell as sweet." In an essay, discuss the correctness of these beliefs. Which of the two does your own experience seem to confirm?

Of Words That Ravage, Pillage, Spoil

Otto Friedrich

Otto Friedrich is a senior writer for *Time* magazine. In the following essay, Friedrich presents ample evidence of the ways that political decisions often require the truth to serve political purposes, and he shows how euphemisms serve governments well by transforming unpleasant and unpopular truths. Controlling language means controlling everything else. For this reason, when governments use language to "invoke a kind of magic to guard their authority," even mass murder can become "the final solution."

1   When the Federal Government launched a program last fall to gas chickens—more than 7 million so far—in an effort to contain an influenza virus in Pennsylvania, it said it had "depopulated" the birds. "We use that terrible word depopulation to avoid saying slaughter," explained a federal information officer, David Goodman.

2   Actually, it is not a terrible word but a rather distinguished one, derived from the Latin *depopulare* and meaning, according to the *Oxford English Dictionary*, "to lay waste, ravage, pillage, spoil." Shakespeare used it in *Coriolanus* when he had the tribune Sicinius ask, "Where is this viper/That would depopulate the city?" John Milton's *History of England* referred to military forces "depopulating all places in their way," and Shelley wrote in *Lines Written Among the Euganean Hills* of "thine isles depopulate."

3   As with many words, though, the original meaning has faded, and *Webster's* now defines *depopulate* only as "to reduce greatly the population of." Even that is probably too clear and specific. When Goodman uses the word not as something done to an area but as something done to the victims, then its only function is to be long and Latinate and abstract. That makes it suitable as a euphemism for a blunter word, like kill.

4   All governments deal in euphemisms, of course, since the purpose of a euphemism is to make anything unpleasant seem less unpleasant. And since killing is the most unpleasant of government functions, the result is linguistic legerdemain. Killing reached its apotheosis in Nazi Germany, and so did the language used to avoid saying so. Prisoners sent to concentration camps in the east carried identity papers marked *"Rückkehr unerwünscht,"* meaning "return unwanted," meaning death. Whole carloads of such prisoners were assigned to *"Sonderbehandlung,"* meaning "special treatment," also meaning death. The totality of persecutions and killings

was called *"die Endlösung,"* meaning "the final solution," that too meaning death.

5   Though the Nazis have never been outdone in applying seemingly harmless labels to the most hideous practices, most governments sooner or later find euphemism an indispensable device. "Pacification" has become a popular term for war ("War is peace," as the Ministry of Truth says in *Nineteen Eighty-Four*), but the Romans meant much the same thing by the term Pax Romana. "Where they make a desert, they call it peace," protested an English nobleman quoted in Tacitus. Viet Nam brought us new words for the old realities: soldiers "wasted" the enemy, some "fragged" their own officers, bombers provided "close air support." Even the CIA contributed a verbal novelty: "termination with extreme prejudice."

6   By changing the language that describes their actions, governments implicitly deny those actions. They invoke a kind of magic to guard their own authority. Language has always been a partly magical process, and the power to give names to things has always seemed a magical power. The *Book of Genesis* reports that when God created the lesser animals, every beast of the field and every fowl of the air, he "brought them unto Adam to see what he would call them." In China too, Confucius taught that the root of good government lies in the principle of *cheng ming,* or precise definition.

7   Ah, but what is precise definition? One nation's freedom fighter is another nation's terrorist. Ronald Reagan is by no means the first President to put bright words on dark realities; Jimmy Carter, for example, called his aborted helicopter raid on Iran "an incomplete success." But Reagan seems to bring an exceptional dedication to the process. The term MX does not mean very much (the letters stand for "missile experimental"), but everybody knew the weapon under that name until Reagan began calling it the "peace keeper." After the Grenada invasion, which Reagan himself had first called an "invasion," he bristled at reporters for "your frequent use of the word invasion. This was a rescue mission." For such a small place, in fact, Grenada proved a richly fertile territory for linguistic flowering. The laurels go to Admiral Wesley L. McDonald, who, in trying to avoid admitting that the Navy had not known exactly what was happening on the island just before the U.S. landing, took a deep breath and declared, "We were not micromanaging Grenada intelligencewise until about that time frame."

8   Occasionally, of course, the military gets so carried away in its passion to rename things that it cannot persuade anyone to use its most imaginative terms. Resisting any mention of retreat, it devised the word "exfiltration," but even its own spokesmen find that hard to say. A "combat emplacement evacuator" is a splendidly resonant euphemism for a shovel, but somehow it has never caught on. It was only public ridicule, however, that

persuaded the Pentagon to abandon the term "sunshine units" as a measure of nuclear radiation.

9   Government does not involve only military affairs, to be sure. Every aspect of economic policy attracts similar expressions of right thinking. When Reagan was convinced that taxes had to be increased, after he had promised to cut them, he began referring not to taxes but to "revenue enhancements," a term apparently invented by Lawrence Kudlow, formerly of the Office of Management and Budget. The tendency seems to be spreading. A spokesman for Budget Director David Stockman won special recognition for declaring that the Administration was not considering a means test for Medicare but a "layering of benefits according to your income." The poor, in fact, are regularly euphemized into invisibility by being given new names such as "disadvantaged." One of the oddities of euphemisms, though, is that they tend to reacquire the unpleasant connotations of the words they supplant, like a facelift that begins to sag, and so they have to be periodically replaced. The world's poor nations have changed over the years from underdeveloped nations to developing nations to emerging nations.

10   Does the spread of such phrases—if they are indeed spreading—mean that the Government is becoming increasingly deceptive, or that it has more to hide? That would be uncharitable, perhaps unfair. Consider it instead a perfectly understandable desire to think well of oneself and of one's work. Isn't everyone counseled to think positively, to look on the bright side, to observe the doughnut rather than the hole, to see that a half-empty glass is really half full? In a time of uncertainty, it is possible to give the Government the benefit of the doubt, just as any citizen customarily gives the same benefit to himself. After all, as the saying goes, nothing is certain except death and taxes. Or rather depopulation and revenue enhancement.

**Questions
on Content**

1. Why does Friedrich object to the use of *depopulate* as a euphemism? Why does he cite the etymology of the word?

2. Why does Friedrich devote almost an entire paragraph (paragraph 4) to the language of Nazi Germany?

3. Friedrich states, "By changing the language that describes their actions, governments implicitly deny those actions" (paragraph 6). How does this

assertion illustrate the author's attitude toward governments in general? What *is* the author's attitude toward governments?

4. Why do you believe Friedrich focuses on these euphemisms: *pacification, exfiltration,* and *revenue enhancement?*

5. Friedrich uses this evidence in paragraph 9: "The world's poor nations have changed over the years from underdeveloped nations to developing nations to emerging nations." What is he implying?

Questions on Structure and Style

6. The first three paragraphs constitute the essay's introduction. Examine the relationship among the three paragraphs. What effect does Friedrich achieve with this introduction?

7. How does paragraph 4 contribute to both the content and the structure of the essay?

8. How effective are the last two sentences as a closing for the essay?

9. Is Friedrich's tone in paragraph 10 consistent with his tone elsewhere in the essay? How would you describe the tone of paragraph 10?

Assignments

1. Friedrich's essay is carefully organized. Prepare a topic outline of the essay, and discuss the author's organizational strategy.

2. Examine the language used in advertisements for a particular product, such as cars, cosmetics, or beer. Then write an essay about that language, using Friedrich's organization as a model.

3. Using *The Oxford English Dictionary* as your reference tool, write a one-paragraph definition of one of the

following words. Model your paragraph on Friedrich's second paragraph.

atom   kale

card   pig

daughter   rosary

4. Friedrich focuses on the ways that governments use
    euphemisms to hide the truth. What recent exam-
    ples have you noted in government efforts to use
    language, as Friedrich puts it, "to look on the bright
    side"? In a paragraph, describe one such example.

Good-bye to All T___t!

Wallace Stegner

Can taboo language be used responsibly? Wallace Stegner asserts that it can and explains in the following argument the link between restraint and emphasis in the use of language. If used properly, taboo language has power. Stegner, a novelist as well as a teacher, believes that this power evaporates with the "impropriety" of using "a loaded word in the wrong place or in the wrong quantity." Any fault lies not in taboo language but in its misuse.

1   Not everyone who laments what contemporary novelists have done to the sex act objects to the act itself, or to its mention. Some want it valued higher than fiction seems to value it; they want the word "climax" to retain some of its literary meaning. Likewise, not everyone who has come to doubt the contemporary freedom of language objects to strong language in itself. Some of us object precisely because we value it.

2   I acknowledge that I have used four-letter words familiarly all my life, and have put them into books with some sense that I was insisting on the proper freedom of the artist. I have applauded the extinction of those d----d emasculations of the Genteel Tradition and the intrusion into serious fiction of honest words with honest meanings and emphasis. I have wished, with D. H. Lawrence, for the courage to say shit before a lady, and have sometimes had my wish.

3   Words are not obscene: naming things is a legitimate verbal act. And "frank" does not mean "vulgar," any more than "improper" means "dirty." What vulgar does mean is "common"; what improper means is "unsuitable." Under the right circumstances, any word is proper. But when any sort of word, especially a word hitherto taboo and therefore noticeable, is scattered across a page like chocolate chips through a toll-house cookie, a real impropriety occurs. The sin is not the use of an "obscene" word; it is the use of a loaded word in the wrong place or in the wrong quantity. It is the sin of false emphasis, which is not a moral but a literary lapse, related to sentimentality. It is the sin of advertisers who so plaster a highway with neon signs that you can't find the bar or liquor store you're looking for. Like any excess, it quickly becomes comic.

4   If I habitually say shit before a lady, what do I say before a flat tire at the rush hour in Times Square or on the San Francisco Bay Bridge? What do I say before a revelation of the inequity of the universe? And what if the lady takes the bit in her teeth and says shit before *me*?

5   I have been a teacher of writing for many years and have watched this problem since it was no bigger than a man's hand. It used to be that with some Howellsian notion of the young-girl audience one tried to protect tender female members of a mixed class from the coarse language of males trying to show off. Some years ago Frank O'Connor and I agreed on a system. Since we had no intention whatever of restricting students' choice of subject or language, and no desire to expurgate or bowdlerize while reading their stuff aloud for discussion, but at the same time had to deal with these young girls of an age our daughters might have been, we announced that any stuff so strong that it would embarrass us to read it aloud could be read by its own author.

6   It was no deterrent at all, but an invitation, and not only to coarse males. For clinical sexual observation, for full acceptance of the natural functions, for discrimination in the selection of graffiti, for boldness in the use of words that it should take courage to say before a lady, give me a sopho-more girl every time. Her strength is as the strength of ten, for she assumes that if one shocker out of her pretty mouth is piquant, fifty will be litera-ture. And so do a lot of her literary idols.

7   Some acts, like some words, were never meant to be casual. That is why houses contain bedrooms and bathrooms. Profanity and so-called ob-scenities are literary resources, verbal ways of rendering strong emotion. They are not meant to occur every ten seconds, any more than—Norman Mailer to the contrary not withstanding—orgasms are.

8   So I am not going to say shit before any more ladies. I am going to hunt words that have not lost their sting, and it may be I shall have to go back to gentility to find them. Pleasant though it is to know that finally a writer can make use of any word that fits his occasion, I am going to investigate the possibilities latent in restraint.

9   I remember my uncle, a farmer who had used four-letter words ten to the sentence ever since he learned to talk. One day he came too near the circular saw and cut half his fingers off. While we stared in horror, he stood watching the bright arterial blood pump from his ruined hand. Then he spoke, and he did not speak loud. "Aw, the dickens," he said.

10   I think he understood, better than some sophomore girls and better than some novelists, the nature of emphasis.

Questions on Content

1. Stegner deals with the use of taboo language in general and his own use of it in particular. What central point does he make about each use?

2. In paragraph 3, Stegner says, "naming things is a legitimate verbal act." Why does he use the word

legitimate? What other adjectives could he have used?

3. The author refers to "the sin of false emphasis" and cites the example of "advertisers who . . . plaster a highway with neon signs" (paragraph 3). Have you yourself encountered similar examples of false emphasis? What were they?

4. Stegner calls taboo expressions "literary resources" (paragraph 7). What does he mean? What other resources might he name?

5. Stegner often refers to his own life as a writer. If we consider this essay an argument, how do these references strengthen Stegner's position?

Questions on Structure and Style

6. Identify the topic sentences of paragraphs 6, 7, and 8.

7. In a periodic sentence, the speaker's meaning is not fully revealed until the end of the sentence. Identify the periodic sentence in paragraph 6.

8. Mark at least three places in which Stegner uses parallel construction. What effects does he create at these places?

9. Does paragraph 10 serve well as a conclusion? Why or why not?

10. Describe Stegner's tone. Where does he establish it? Does he maintain it consistently?

11. Stegner often shifts his focus from one paragraph to the next; yet he seldom uses the stock transitional words and expressions (*also, however, therefore*). What effect does he achieve by avoiding these standard devices?

Assignments

1. Stegner claims that "under the right circumstances, any word is proper" (paragraph 3). Do you agree? Respond in a paragraph.

2. "Words are not obscene" (paragraph 3), according to Stegner. If you agree that words can never be obscene, what can be? Write a paragraph or essay in which you define the word *obscene* and provide specific examples.

3. Stegner argues for restraint in the use of language. Think of a specific incident you witnessed in which someone failed to exercise restraint in the use of language. Write an essay describing the event and explaining why restraint would have been wiser. Be sure not to confuse lack of restraint with anger.

Additional Assignments and Research Topics

1. In the *Dictionary of American Slang* (1975), Harold Wentworth and Stuart Berg Flexner state, "The concept having the most slang synonyms is *drunk*" (page 652). Wentworth and Flexner provide a long list of these synonyms (pages 653–655), many of which are included in the *Dictionary* itself. Use the *Dictionary of American Slang* to demonstrate the wide variety of origins for these synonyms. Consider both where the terms originated and when.

2. In "Sometimes the Liveliest Words" (page 221), Jeff Kunerth quotes Stuart Berg Flexner as saying that slang "tends toward degradation rather than elevation" (paragraph 11). Using the *Dictionary of American Slang,* examine the origins of ten slang expressions for *unintelligent.* In an essay, explain what these expressions reveal about our concept of intelligence.

3. As Jeff Kunerth's article on slang reveals, advertisers believe that using teenage slang will help ads appeal to this particular market. Review advertisements aimed at teenagers (in magazines, newspapers, and other places), and find examples of slang used as a marketing tool. In an essay, summarize your findings, and comment on how effectively (or ineffectively) this tactic works in the ads you discuss.

4. Slang always reflects the lifestyle of the group that employs it. Make a list of slang expressions currently popular with teenagers. In a short essay, explain what this slang vocabulary reveals about the lifestyles of teenagers.

5. In "Taboo: The Sacred and the Obscene" (page 235), Geoffrey Wagner and Sanford R. Radner identify death as our primary taboo subject—"the greatest outlaw of all" (paragraph 11). We have a great many words and expressions that we substitute for *death* and *die,* some softer (*expire*) and some coarser (*kick the bucket*). As a classroom project, list all the expressions you can think of that are sometimes substituted for *death* and *die.* Then do the same for *life* and *live.*

6. Assume that you work as secretary to the academic dean of your college. The dean gives you the following task: "Write a form letter I can send to students who've flunked out this

semester. Tell them that I have bad news, and I can't do anything about it. I'll sign the letter." Write the letter, using whatever euphemisms seem appropriate. Follow the letter with a paragraph explaining why you chose the language you used.

7. In an essay, respond to one of the following statements:
    A. "[Euphemisms] are outward and visible signs of our inward anxieties, conflicts, fears, and shames" (Hugh Rawson, "Euphemisms," paragraph 4).
    B. "Language has always been a partly magical process, and the power to give names to things has always seemed a magical power" (Otto Friedrich, "Of Words That Ravage, Pillage, Spoil," paragraph 6).

8. Choose five euphemisms from the list below. Identify the people most likely to employ each euphemism, and explain possible reasons why the euphemism might be used.

friendly fire	incarcerated offender
nuclear exchange	civil servant
terminal illness	*persona non grata*
special-needs child	adult reading material
the physically challenged	irregularity
golden agers	fib
security system	facial blemishes
the economically disadvantaged	water closet
revenue enhancement	the departed
authoritarian government	put to sleep

9. From the list of euphemisms in Assignment 8, choose three that you consider acceptable and three that you disapprove of, and in a short essay, explain the reasons for your reactions.

Language,
Identity, and
Discrimination

We all belong to groups, often by choice. When we attend school, we are "students." If we seek admission to a fraternity or sorority, we hope to become "brothers" or "sisters." A move to Texas makes us "Texans" or "southerners." However, there are times when we belong to groups because of qualities we have that are beyond our control, such as our race, age, height, ethnic background, sex, or innate talents—the list is almost endless. Moreover, often we are *identified*—rightly or wrongly—by the qualities of the group, and one of the most important of these qualities is language. As Chapter 4 pointed out, the human use of language itself distinguishes us from other living creatures, but *which* language we use and how we use it distinguishes one group from another.

This chapter is about language identities—the ways in which our language identifies us as members of certain groups: black, white, Hispanic, male, and female. The chapter also looks at the relationship between language and discrimination—that is, at the ways in which language can be used to identify a group so as to unfairly set it apart from others. Ossie Davis's "The English Language Is My Enemy!" provides a powerful introduction to the topic of discrimination through language as Davis condemns what he considers the English language's inherent bias against blacks. Dorothy Z. Seymour then examines this bias through the issue of black English in "Black Children, Black Speech." Hispanics and bilingualism are the subjects of three selections. Richard Rodriguez's "Aria: A Memoir of a Bilingual Childhood" sensitively argues against bilingualism by explaining what it meant in his own life, and Thomas Palmer reviews some specific details of the national debate over bilingualism in "Spanglish: Hispanics and the Bilingual Dilemma." George Will's "In Defense of the Mother Tongue" provides a concise argument in favor of English as the official American language.

Just as language often identifies members of racial or ethnic groups, it can reveal male or female identities. Alfie Kohn examines this phenomenon in "Sex and Status and a Manner of Speaking." The sexist qualities of English come under attack in Francine Frank and Frank Anshen's "Of Girls and Chicks," and William

Safire, in "Hypersexism and the Feds," cautions against using legal means to correct discriminatory language. The chapter concludes with Muriel R. Schulz's "Is the English Language Anybody's Enemy?" a rebuttal to many points raised by the other selections.

Although our identity doesn't lie entirely in the language we use, our language does have immense power to declare who we are (and were, and sometimes who we want to be). Such declarations shouldn't work against us; that is, our language shouldn't be used against us. However, language is a convenient indicator for anyone who wants simple ways to include or exclude us from a group of job applicants, loan applicants, renters, candidates for promotion or public office, or any of the countless groups to which we sometimes belong. Unfair efforts like these will probably persist forever, but by understanding the power of our language to identify us, we can at least remain alert and ready to resist.

The English Language Is My Enemy!

Ossie Davis

In this brief argument, Ossie Davis makes his point quickly, confidently, and without qualification: English is biased against black people, who victimize themselves merely by speaking it. Davis, a well-known actor and playwright, here explains what a thesaurus tells him about "blackness" in our language, emphasizing how vital and revealing connotations are.

1   A superficial examination of Roget's *Thesaurus of the English Language* reveals the following facts: the word WHITENESS has 134 synonyms, 44 of which are favorable and pleasing to contemplate, i.e., purity, cleanness, immaculateness, bright, shining, ivory, fair, blonde, stainless, clean, clear, chaste, unblemished, unsullied, innocent, honorable, upright, just, straightforward, fair, genuine, trustworthy (a white man's colloquialism). Only ten synonyms for WHITENESS appear to me to have negative implications—and these only in the mildest sense: gloss over, whitewash, gray, wan, pale, ashen, etc.

2   The word BLACKNESS has 120 synonyms, 60 of which are distinctly unfavorable, and none of them even mildly positive. Among the offending 60 were such words as: blot, blotch, smut, smudge, sully, begrime, soot, becloud, obscure, dingy, murky, low-toned, threatening, frowning, foreboding, forbidden, sinister, baneful, dismal, thundery, evil, wicked, malignant, deadly, unclean, dirty, unwashed, foul, etc. . . . not to mention 20 synonyms directly related to race, such as: Negro, Negress, nigger, darky, blackamoor, etc.

3   When you consider the fact that *thinking* itself is sub-vocal speech—in other words, one must use *words* in order to think at all—you will appreciate the enormous heritage of racial prejudgment that lies in wait for any child born into the English Language. Any teacher good or bad, white or black, Jew or Gentile, who uses the English Language as a medium of communication is forced, willy-nilly, to teach the Negro child 60 ways to despise himself, and the white child 60 ways to aid and abet him in the crime.

4   Who speaks to me in my Mother Tongue damns me indeed! . . . the English Language—in which I cannot conceive my self as a black man without, at the same time, debasing myself . . . my enemy, with which to survive at all I must continually be at war.

**Questions
on Content**

1. Davis begins by referring to "a superficial examination of Roget's *Thesaurus of the English Language*" (paragraph 1). Why does Davis use the word *superficial?*

2. Does Davis believe that schools can correct the prejudice he sees in the English language?

3. What does Davis mean when he says, "Who speaks to me in my Mother Tongue damns me indeed!" (paragraph 4).

**Questions
on Structure
and Style**

4. Where does Davis state his thesis? Why does he position it as he does? Why is the placement of the thesis important in an argument such as this one?

5. Is Davis's argument based on reason, emotion, or both?

6. This is a brief treatment of an important topic. Is Davis's discussion too short to be effective, or is brevity a strength here?

Assignments

1. Davis makes many points about the connotative values of *white* and *black*. Although he doesn't make specific suggestions, Davis would probably prefer a more neutral English. Write an essay describing what our society might do to make English more neutral. Can society do anything to change English this way, or will society's values have to change first?

2. Read Chapter 42 of Melville's *Moby Dick*, "The Whiteness of the Whale," and examine how the author uses the color white.

3. American blacks have been given many different labels in our society. The labels *Negroes, colored people,* and *Afro-Americans* have been used at different times. Discuss the connotations of such labels. Do white Americans have similar experiences with

labels such as *Caucasians* and *whites?* Explain your ideas in an essay.

4. Many people believe that the English language is both sexist and racist. If this is true, the problem is serious. What can correct it? Time? Education? Laws? Something else? Respond in an essay.

Black Children, Black Speech

Dorothy Z. Seymour

Black English has been a controversial topic among educators, linguists, and even politicians. In this essay, first published in 1972, when the debate over black English was greatest, Dorothy Z. Seymour, formerly a reading teacher, maintains that black English "is not just 'sloppy talk' but a dialect with a form and structure of its own." The debate goes beyond linguistics; it involves the implications of standard English for people whose culture does not recognize it as standard. (For another viewpoint, see the selection by Richard Rodriguez, beginning on page 283.)

1   "Cmon, man, les git goin'!" called the boy to his companion. "Dat bell ringin'. It say, 'Git in rat now!' " He dashed into the school yard.

2   "Aw, f'get you," replied the other. "Whe' Richuh? Whe'da' muvvuh? He be goin' to schoo'."

3   "He in de' now, man!" was the answer as they went through the door.

4   In the classroom they made for their desks and opened their books. The name of the story they tried to read was "Come." It went:

> Come, Bill, come
> Come with me.
> Come and see this.
> See what is here.

The first boy poked the second. "Wha' da' wor'?"

5   "Da' wor' *is*, you dope."

6   "*Is?* Ain't no wor' *is*. You jivin' me? Wha' da' wor' mean?"

7   "Ah dunno. Jus' *is*."

8   To a speaker of Standard English, this exchange is only vaguely comprehensible. But it's normal speech for thousands of American children. In addition it demonstrates one of our biggest educational problems: children whose speech style is so different from the writing style of their books that they have difficulty learning to read. These children speak Black English, a dialect characteristic of many inner-city Negroes. Their books are, of course, written in Standard English. To complicate matters, the speech they use is also socially stigmatized. Middle-class whites and Negroes alike scorn it as low-class poor people's talk.

9   Teachers sometimes make the situation worse with their attitudes toward Black English. Typically, they view the children's speech as "bad
English" characterized by "lazy pronunciation," "poor grammar," and
"short, jagged words." One result of this attitude is poor mental health on
the part of the pupils. A child is quick to grasp the feeling that while school
speech is "good," his own speech is "bad," and that by extension he
himself is somehow inadequate and without value. Some children react to
this feeling by withdrawing; they stop talking entirely. Others develop the
attitude of "F'get you, honky." In either case, the psychological results are
devastating and lead straight to the dropout route.

10   It is hard for most teachers and middle-class Negro parents to accept the
idea that Black English is not just "sloppy talk" but a dialect with a form
and structure of its own. Even some eminent black educators think of it as
"bad English grammar" with "slurred consonants" (Professor Nick Aaron
Ford of Morgan State College in Baltimore) and "ghettoese" (Dr. Kenneth
B. Clark, the prominent educational psychologist).

11   Parents of Negro school children generally agree. Two researchers of
Columbia University report that the adults they worked with in Harlem
almost unanimously preferred that their children be taught Standard English in school.

12   But there is another point of view, one held in common by black militants and some white liberals. They urge that middle-class Negroes stop
thinking of the inner-city dialect as something to be ashamed of and re-
pudiated. Black author Claude Brown, for example, pushes this view.

13   Some modern linguists take a similar stance. They begin with the premise that no dialect is intrinsically "bad" or "good," and that a non-standard
speech style is not defective speech but different speech. More important,
they have been able to show that Black English is far from being a careless
way of speaking the Standard; instead, it is a rather rigidly constructed set
of speech patterns, with the same sort of specialization in sounds, structure, and vocabulary as any other dialect.

The Sounds of Black English

14   Middle class listeners who hear black inner-city speakers say "dis" and
"tin" for "this" and "thin" assume that the black speakers are just being
careless. Not at all; these differences are characteristic aspects of the
dialect. The original cause of such substitutions is generally a carryover
from one's original language or that of his immigrant parents. The interfer-
ence from that carryover probably caused the substitution of /d/ for the
voiced *th* sound in *this*, and /t/ for the unvoiced *th* sound in *thin*. (Linguists
represent language sounds by putting letters within slashes or brackets.)

Most speakers of English don't realize that the two *th* sounds of English are lacking in many other languages and are difficult for most foreigners trying to learn English. Germans who study English, for example, are surprised and confused about these sounds because the only Germans who use them are the ones who lisp. These two sounds are almost nonexistent in the West African languages which most black immigrants brought with them to America.

15   Similar substitutions used in Black English are /f/, a sound similar to the unvoiced *th*, in medial word-position, as in *birfday* for *birthday*, and in final word-position, as in *roof* for *Ruth* as well as /v/ for the voiced *th* in medial position, as in *bruvver* for *brother*. These sound substitutions are also typical of Gullah, the language of black speakers in the Carolina Sea Islands. Some of them are also heard in Caribbean Creole.

16   Another characteristic of the sounds of Black English is the lack of /l/ at the end of words, sometimes replaced by the sound /w/. This makes words like *tool* sound like *too*. If /l/ occurs in the middle of a Standard English word, in Black English it may be omitted entirely: "I can hep you." This difference is probably caused by the instability and sometimes interchangeability of /l/ and /r/ in West African languages.

17   One difference that is startling to middle-class speakers is the fact that Black English words appear to leave off some consonant sounds at the end of words. Like Italian, Japanese and West African words, they are more likely to end in vowel sounds. Standard English *boot* is pronounced *boo* in Black English. *What* is *wha*. *Sure* is *sho*. *Your* is *yo*. This kind of difference can make for confusion in the classroom. Dr. Kenneth Goodman, a psycholinguist, tells of a black child whose white teacher asked him to use *so* in a sentence—not "sew a dress" but "the other *so*." The sentence the child used was "I got a *so* on my leg."

18   A related feature of Black English is the tendency in many cases not to use sequences of more than one final consonant sound. For example, *just* is pronounced *jus'*, *past* is *pass*, *mend* sounds like *men* and *hold* like *hole*. *Six* and *box* are pronounced *sick* and *bock*. Why should this be? Perhaps because West African languages, like Japanese, have almost no clusters of consonants in their speech. The Japanese, when importing a foreign word, handle a similar problem by inserting vowel sounds between every consonant, making *baseball* sound like *besuboru*. West Africans probably made a simpler change, merely cutting a series of two consonant sounds down to one. Speakers of Gullah, one linguist found, have made the same kind of adaptation of Standard English.

19   Teachers of black children seldom understand the reason for these differences in final sounds. They are apt to think that careless speech is the cause. Actually, black speakers aren't "leaving off" any sounds; how can you leave off something you never had in the first place?

20   Differences in vowel sounds are also characteristic of the nonstandard language. Dr. Goodman reports that a black child asked his teacher how to spell rat. "R-a-t," she replied. But the boy responded "No ma'am, I don't mean rat mouse, I mean rat now." In Black English, *right* sounds like *rat*. A likely reason is that in West African languages, there are very few vowel sounds of the type heard in the word *right*. This type is common in English. It is called a glided or diphthongized vowel sound. A glided vowel sound is actually a close combination of two vowels; in the word *right* the two parts of the sound "eye" are actually "ah-ee." West African languages have no such long, two-part, changing vowel sounds; their vowels are generally shorter and more stable. This may be why in Black English, *time* sounds like *Tom*, *oil* like *all*, and *my* like *ma*.

Language Structure

21   Black English differs from Standard English not only in its sounds but also in its structure. The way the words are put together does not always fit the description in English grammar books. The method of expressing time, or tense, for example, differs in significant ways.

22   The verb *to be* is an important one in Standard English. It's used as an auxiliary verb to indicate different tenses. But Black English speakers use it quite differently. Sometimes an inner-city Negro says "He coming"; other times he says "He be coming." These two sentences mean different things. To understand why, let's look at the tenses of West African languages; they correspond with those of Black English.

23   Many West African languages have a tense which is called the habitual. This tense is used to express action which is always occurring and it is formed with a verb that is translated as *be*. "He be coming" means something like "He's always coming," "He usually comes," or "He's been coming."

24   In Standard English there is no regular grammatical construction for such a tense. Black English speakers, in order to form the habitual tense in English, use the word *be* as an auxiliary: *He be doing it. My Momma be working. He be running.* The habitual tense is not the same as the present tense, which is constructed in Black English without any form of the verb *to be: He do it. My Momma working. He running.* (This means the action is occurring right now.)

25   There are other tense differences between Black English and Standard English. For example, the nonstandard speech does not use changes in grammar to indicate the past tense. A white person will ask, "What did your brother say?" and the black person will answer, "He say he coming." (The verb *say* is not changed to *said*.) "How did you get here?" "I walk."

This style of talking about the past is paralleled in the Yoruba, Fante, Hausa, and Ewe languages of West Africa.

26   Expression of plurality is another difference. The way a black child will talk of "them boy" or "two dog" makes some white listeners think Negroes don't know how to turn a singular word into a plural word. As a matter of fact, it isn't necessary to use an *s* to express plurality. In Chinese and Japanese, singular and plural are not generally distinguished by such inflections; plurality is conveyed in other ways. For example, in Chinese it's correct to say "There are three book on the table." This sentence already has two signals of the plural, *three* and *are;* why require a third? This same logic is the basis of plurals in most West African languages, where nouns are often identical in the plural and the singular. For example, in Ibo, one correctly says *those man,* and in both Ewe and Yoruba one says *they house.* American speakers of Gullah retain this style; it is correct in Gullah to say *five dog.*

27   Gender is another aspect of language structure where differences can be found. Speakers of Standard English are often confused to find that the nonstandard vernacular often uses just one gender of pronoun, the masculine, and refers to women as well as men as *he* or *him.* "He a nice girl," even "Him a nice girl" are common. Thus usage probably stems from West African origins, too, as does the use of multiple negatives, such as "Nobody don't know it."

28   Vocabulary is the third aspect of a person's native speech that could affect his learning of a new language. The strikingly different vocabulary often used in Negro Nonstandard English is probably the most obvious aspect of it to a casual white observer. But its vocabulary differences don't obscure its meaning the way different sounds and different structure often do.

29   Recently there has been much interest in the African origins of words like *goober* (peanut), *cooter* (turtle), and *tote* (carry), as well as others that are less certainly African, such as *to dig* (possibly from the Wolof *degan,* "to understand"). Such expressions seem colorful rather than low-class to many whites; they become assimilated faster than their black originators do. English professors now use *dig* in their scholarly articles, and current advertising has enthusiastically adopted *rap.*

30   Is it really possible for old differences in sound, structure, and vocabulary to persist from the West African languages of slave days into present-day inner city Black English? Easily. Nothing else really explains such regularity of language habits, most of which persist among black people in various parts of the Western Hemisphere. For a long time scholars believed that certain speech forms used by Negroes were merely leftovers from archaic English preserved in the speech of early English settlers in America and copied by their slaves. But this theory has been greatly weakened,

largely as the result of the work of a black linguist, Dr. Lorenzo Dow Turner of the University of Chicago. Dr. Turner studied the speech of Gullah Negroes in the Sea Islands off the Carolina coast and found so many traces of West African languages that he thoroughly discredited the archaic-English theory.

31   When anyone learns a new language, it's usual to try speaking the new language with the sounds and structure of the old. If a person's first language does not happen to have a particular sound needed in the language he is learning, he will tend to substitute a similar or related sound from his native language and use it to speak the new one. When Frenchman Charles Boyer said "Zees ees my heart," and when Latin American Carmen Miranda sang "Souse American way," they were simply using sounds of their native languages in trying to pronounce sounds of English. West Africans must have done the same thing when they first attempted English words. The tendency to retain the structure of the native language is a strong one, too. That's why a German learning English is likely to put his verb at the end: "May I a glass beer have?" The vocabulary of one's original language may also furnish some holdovers. Jewish immigrants did not stop using the word *bagel* when they came to America; nor did Germans stop saying *sauerkraut*.

32   Social and geographical isolation reinforces the tendencies to retain old language habits. When one group is considered inferior, the other group avoids it. For many years it was illegal to give any sort of instruction to Negroes, and for slaves to try to speak like their masters would have been unthinkable. Conflict of value systems doubtless retards changes, too. As Frantz Fanon observed in *Black Skin, White Masks*, those who take on white speech habits are suspect in the ghetto, because others believe they are trying to "act white." Dr. Kenneth Johnson, a black linguist, put it this way: "As long as disadvantaged black children live in segregated communities and most of their relationships are confined to those within their own subculture, they will not replace their functional nonstandard dialect with the nonfunctional standard dialect."

33   Linguists have made it clear that language systems that are different are not necessarily deficient. A judgment of deficiency can be made only in comparison with another language system. Let's turn the tables on Standard English for a moment and look at it from the West African point of view. From this angle, Standard English: (1) is lacking in certain language sounds, (2) has a couple of unnecessary language sounds for which others may serve as good substitutes, (3) doubles and drawls some of its vowel sounds in sequences that are unusual and difficult to imitate, (4) lacks a method of forming an important tense, (5) requires an unnecessary number of ways to indicate tense, plurality and gender, and (6) doesn't mark negatives sufficiently for the result to be a good strong negative statement.

34   Now whose language is deficient?

35   How would the adoption of this point of view help us? Say we accepted the evidence that Black English is not just a sloppy Standard but an organized language style which probably has developed many of its features on the basis of its West African heritage. What would we gain?

36   The psychological climate of the classroom might improve if teachers understood why many black students speak as they do. But we still have not reached a solution of the main problem. Does the discovery that Black English has pattern and structure mean that it should not be tampered with? Should children who speak Black English be excused from learning the Standard in school? Should they perhaps be given books in Black English to learn from?

37   Any such accommodation would surely result in a hardening of the new separatism being urged by some black militants. It would probably be applauded by such people as Roy Innis, Director of C.O.R.E., who is currently recommending dual autonomous education systems for white and black. And it might facilitate learning to read, since some experiments have indicated that materials written in Black English syntax aid problem readers from the inner city.

38   But determined resistance to the introduction of such printed materials into schools can be expected. To those who view inner-city speech as bad English, the appearance in print of sentences like "My mama, he work" can be as shocking and repellent as a four-letter word. Middle-class Negro parents would probably mobilize against the move. Any stratagem that does not take into account such practicalities of the matter is probably doomed to failure. And besides, where would such a permissive policy on language get these children in the larger society, and in the long run? If they want to enter an integrated America they must be able to deal with it on its own terms. Even Professor Toni Cade of Rutgers, who doesn't want "ghetto accents" tampered with, advocates mastery of Standard English because, as she puts it, "if you want to get ahead in this country, you must master the language of the ruling class." This has always been true, wherever there has been a minority group.

39   The problem then appears to be one of giving these children the ability to speak (and read) Standard English without denigrating the vernacular and those who use it, or even affecting the ability to use it. The only way to do this is to officially espouse bidialectism. The result would be the ability to use either dialect equally well—as Dr. Martin Luther King did—depending on the time, place, and circumstances. Pupils would have to learn enough about Standard English to use it when necessary, and teachers would have to learn enough about the inner-city dialect to understand and accept it for what it is—not just a "careless" version of Standard English but a different form of English that's appropriate in certain times and places.

40   Can we accomplish this? If we can't, the result will be continued alienation of a large section of the population, continued dropout trouble with
consequent loss of earning power and economic contribution to the nation,
but most of all, loss of faith in America as a place where a minority people
can at times continue to use those habits that remind them of their link
with each other and with their past.

**Questions
on Content**

1. How are black schoolchildren affected by the attitude that black English is "bad English"?

2. Many modern linguists argue that black English is
not merely a careless way of speaking standard
English. How do they explain black English?

3. Below are some examples characteristic of black
English. Explain them, using Seymour's evidence.

    "dat" (that), "tin" (thin)

    "birfday" (birthday)

    "schoo" (school)

    "mo" (more)

    "col" (cold)

    "rat" (right)

4. According to Seymour, in what ways are West African languages similar to Japanese?

5. Account for the substitution of *be* for *is* in black
English.

6. Explain the origin of the verb *to dig*.

7. Why has the archaic-English theory been discredited?

8. What is bidialectism?

**Questions
on Structure
and Style**

9. What is the function of paragraph 21?

10. Are the first seven paragraphs an effective introduction? Why or why not?

11. Seymour uses several rhetorical questions in this essay. (A rhetorical question is one that does not call for a response; rather, it creates an effect.) The first sentence of paragraph 30 is an example. Find other examples, and discuss their purpose and effectiveness.

12. Paragraph 34 consists of one sentence. What purpose does it serve? What is the function of paragraph 35?

13. Specifically, what is Seymour's conclusion? Where does she make it? Explain why her timing is effective or ineffective.

Assignments

1. This essay is a fine example of an inductive argument. Seymour provides a number of examples, which she uses as evidence to support the conclusion she eventually draws. Prepare an outline demonstrating the arrangement of ideas and examples.

2. Seymour points out that "when anyone learns a new language, it's usual to try speaking the new language with the sounds and structure of the old" (paragraph 31). This phenomenon creates dialects. Listen carefully to a speaker for whom English is a second language. Then write a paragraph describing the dialect as accurately and vividly as possible.

3. According to Seymour, bidialectism is the only solution that will give black children the ability to speak standard English without demeaning their own black English. This position is controversial among both blacks and whites. Write an essay examining the advantages and disadvantages of bidialectism in a pluralistic society. Use the inductive approach; that is, draw a conclusion after presenting your evidence. (You may want to read the next selection, "Aria," by Richard Rodriguez, before answering this question.)

Aria: A Memoir of a Bilingual Childhood

Richard Rodriguez

Growing up usually means growing away—away from child-hood, away from home, and sometimes away from family. Language plays a role in this growth. In this selection from *Hunger of Memory*, his collection of autobiographical essays, Richard Rodriguez explains how being bilingual intensified his own "growing away" and how, in his opinion, those who advocate bilingual education in schools "equate mere separateness with individuality." Bilingualists "simplistically scorn the value and necessity of assimilation" into public society, but for the author, assimilation is part of growth, and public language should be part of our inescapable public identity.

1   I remember to start with that day in Sacramento—a California now nearly thirty years past—when I first entered a classroom, able to understand some fifty stray English words.

2   The third of four children, I had been preceded to a neighborhood Roman Catholic school by an older brother and sister. But neither of them had revealed very much about their classroom experiences. Each afternoon they returned, as they left in the morning, always together, speaking in Spanish as they climbed the five steps of the porch. And their mysterious books, wrapped in shopping-bag paper, remained on the table next to the door, closed firmly behind them.

3   An accident of geography sent me to a school where all my classmates were white, many the children of doctors and lawyers and business executives. All my classmates certainly must have been uneasy on that first day of school—as most children are uneasy—to find themselves apart from their families in the first institution of their lives. But I was astonished.

4   The nun said, in a friendly but oddly impersonal voice, "Boys and girls, this is Richard Rodriguez." (I heard her sound out: *Rich-heard Road-ree-guess.*) It was the first time I had heard anyone name me in English. "Richard," the nun repeated more slowly, writing my name down in her black leather book. Quickly I turned to see my mother's face dissolve in a watery blur behind the pebbled glass door.

5   Many years later there is something called bilingual education—a scheme proposed in the late 1960s by Hispanic-American social activists, later endorsed by a congressional vote. It is a program that seeks to permit

non-English-speaking children, many from lower-class homes, to use their family language as the language of school. (Such is the goal its supporters announce.) I hear them and am forced to say no: It is not possible for a child—any child—ever to use his family's language in school. Not to understand this is to misunderstand the public uses of schooling and to trivialize the nature of intimate life—a family's "language."

6   Memory teaches me what I know of these matters; the boy reminds the adult. I was a bilingual child, a certain kind—socially disadvantaged—the son of working-class parents, both Mexican immigrants.

7   In the early years of my boyhood, my parents coped very well in America. My father had steady work. My mother managed at home. They were nobody's victims. Optimism and ambition led them to a house (our home) many blocks from the Mexican south side of town. We lived among *gringos* and only a block from the biggest, whitest houses. It never occurred to my parents that they couldn't live wherever they chose. Nor was the Sacramento of the fifties bent on teaching them a contrary lesson. My mother and father were more annoyed than intimidated by those two or three neighbors who tried initially to make us unwelcome. ("Keep your brats away from my sidewalk!") But despite all they achieved, perhaps because they had so much to achieve, any deep feeling of ease, the confidence of "belonging" in public was withheld from them both. They regarded the people at work, the faces in crowds, as very distant from us. They were the others, *los gringos*. That term was interchangeable in their speech with another, even more telling, *los americanos*.

8   I grew up in a house where the only regular guests were my relations. For one day, enormous families of relatives would visit and there would be so many people that the noise and the bodies would spill out to the backyard and front porch. Then, for weeks, no one came by. (It was usually a salesman who rang the doorbell.) Our house stood apart. A gaudy yellow in a row of white bungalows. We were the people with the noisy dog. The people who raised pigeons and chickens. We were the foreigners on the block. A few neighbors smiled and waved. We waved back. But no one in the family knew the names of the old couple who lived next door; until I was seven years old, I did not know the names of the kids who lived across the street.

9   In public, my father and mother spoke a hesitant, accented, not always grammatical English. And they would have to strain—their bodies tense—to catch the sense of what was rapidly said by *los gringos*. At home they spoke Spanish. The language of their Mexican past sounded in counterpoint to the English of public society. The words would come quickly, with ease. Conveyed through those sounds was the pleasing, soothing, consoling reminder of being at home.

10   During those years when I was first conscious of hearing, my mother and father addressed me only in Spanish; in Spanish I learned to reply. By

contrast, English (*inglés*), rarely heard in the house, was the language I came to associate with *gringos*. I learned my first words of English overhearing my parents speak to strangers. At five years of age, I knew just enough English for my mother to trust me on errands to stores one block away. No more.

11   I was a listening child, careful to hear the very different sounds of Spanish and English. Wide-eyed with hearing, I'd listen to sounds more than words. First, there were English (*gringo*) sounds. So many words were still unknown that when the butcher or the lady at the drugstore said something to me, exotic polysyllabic sounds would bloom in the midst of their sentences. Often, the speech of people in public seemed to me very loud, booming with confidence. The man behind the counter would literally ask, . "What can I do for you?" But by being so firm and so clear, the sound of his voice said that he was a *gringo*; he belonged in public society.

12   I would also hear then the high nasal notes of middle-class American speech. The air stirred with sound. Sometimes, even now, when I have been traveling abroad for several weeks, I will hear what I heard as a boy. In hotel lobbies or airports, in Turkey or Brazil, some Americans will pass, and suddenly I will hear it again—the high sound of American voices. For a few seconds I will hear it with pleasure, for it is now the sound of *my* society—a reminder of home. But inevitably—already on the flight headed for home—the sound fades with repetition. I will be unable to hear it anymore.

13   When I was a boy, things were different. The accent of *los gringos* was never pleasing nor was it hard to hear. Crowds at Safeway or at bus stops would be noisy with sound. And I would be forced to edge away from the chirping chatter above me.

14   I was unable to hear my own sounds, but I knew very well that I spoke English poorly. My words could not stretch far enough to form complete thoughts. And the words I did speak I didn't know well enough to make into distinct sounds. (Listeners would usually lower their heads, better to hear what I was trying to say.) But it was one thing for *me* to speak English with difficulty. It was more troubling for me to hear my parents speak in public: their high-whining vowels and guttural consonants; their sentences that got stuck with 'eh' and 'ah' sounds; the confused syntax; the hesitant rhythm of sounds so different from the way *gringos* spoke. I'd notice, moreover, that my parents' voices were softer than those of *gringos* we'd meet.

15   I am tempted now to say that none of this mattered. In adulthood I am embarrassed by childhood fears. And, in a way, it didn't matter very much that my parents could not speak English with ease. Their linguistic difficulties had no serious consequences. My mother and father made themselves understood at the county hospital clinic and at government offices. And yet, in another way, it mattered very much—it was unsettling

to hear my parents struggle with English. Hearing them, I'd grow nervous, my clutching trust in their protection and power weakened.

16   There were many times like the night at a brightly lit gasoline station (a blaring white memory) when I stood uneasily, hearing my father. He was talking to a teenaged attendant. I do not recall what they were saying, but I cannot forget the sounds my father made as he spoke. At one point his words slid together to form one word—sounds as confused as the threads of blue and green oil in the puddle next to my shoes. His voice rushed through what he had left to say. And, toward the end, reached falsetto notes, appealing to his listener's understanding. I looked away to the lights of passing automobiles. I tried not to hear anymore. But I heard only too well the calm, easy tones in the attendant's reply. Shortly afterward, walking toward home with my father, I shivered when he put his hand on my shoulder. The very first chance that I got, I evaded his grasp and ran on ahead into the dark, skipping with feigned boyish exuberance.

17   But then there was Spanish. *Español:* my family's language. *Español:* the language that seemed to me a private language. I'd hear strangers on the radio and in the Mexican Catholic church across town speaking in Spanish, but I couldn't really believe that Spanish was a public language, like English. Spanish speakers, rather, seemed related to me, for I sensed that we shared—through our language—the experience of feeling apart from *los gringos*. It was thus a ghetto Spanish that I heard and I spoke. Like those whose lives are bound by a barrio, I was reminded by Spanish of my separateness from *los otros, los gringos* in power. But more intensely than for most barrio children—because I did not live in a barrio—Spanish seemed to me the language of home. (Most days it was only at home that I'd hear it.) It became the language of joyful return.

18   A family member would say something to me and I would feel myself specially recognized. My parents would say something to me and I would feel embraced by the sounds of their words. Those sounds said: *I am speaking with ease in Spanish. I am addressing you in words I never use with los gringos. I recognize you as someone special, close, like no one outside. You belong with us. In the family.*

19   (*Ricardo.*)

20   At the age of five, six, well past the time when most other children no longer easily notice the difference between sounds uttered at home and words spoken in public, I had a different experience. I lived in a world magically compounded of sounds. I remained a child longer than most; I lingered too long, poised at the edge of language—often frightened by the sounds of *los gringos*, delighted by the sounds of Spanish at home. I shared with my family a language that was startlingly different from that used in the great city around us.

21   For me there were none of the gradations between public and private society so normal to a maturing child. Outside the house was public

society; inside the house was private. Just opening or closing the screen door behind me was an important experience. I'd rarely leave home all alone or without reluctance. Walking down the sidewalk, under the canopy of tall trees, I'd warily notice the—suddenly—silent neighborhood kids who stood warily watching me. Nervously, I'd arrive at the grocery store to hear there the sounds of the *gringo*—foreign to me—reminding me that in this world so big, I was a foreigner. But then I'd return. Walking back toward our house, climbing the steps from the sidewalk, when the front door was open in summer, I'd hear voices beyond the screen door talking in Spanish. For a second or two, I'd stay, linger there, listening. Smiling, I'd hear my mother call out, saying in Spanish (words): "Is that you, Richard?" All the while her sounds would assure me: *You are home now; come closer; inside. With us.*

22   "*Sí*," I'd reply.

23   Once more inside the house I would resume (assume) my place in the family. The sounds would dim, grow harder to hear. Once more at home, I would grow less aware of that fact. It required, however, no more than the blurt of the doorbell to alert me to listen to sounds all over again. The house would turn instantly still while my mother went to the door. I'd hear her hard English sounds. I'd wait to hear her voice return to soft-sounding Spanish, which assured me, as surely as did the clicking tongue of the lock on the door, that the stranger was gone.

24   Plainly, it is not healthy to hear such sounds so often. It is not healthy to distinguish public words from private sounds so easily. I remained cloistered by sounds, timid and shy in public, too dependent on voices at home. And yet it needs to be emphasized: I was an extremely happy child at home. I remember many nights when my father would come back from work, and I'd hear him call out to my mother in Spanish, sounding relieved. In Spanish, he'd sound light and free notes he never could manage in English. Some nights I'd jump up just at hearing his voice. With *mis hermanos* I would come running into the room where he was with my mother. Our laughing (so deep was the pleasure!) became screaming. Like others who know the pain of public alienation, we transformed the knowledge of our public separateness and made it consoling—the reminder of intimacy. Excited, we joined our voices in a celebration of sounds. *We are speaking now the way we never speak out in public. We are alone—together,* voices sounded, surrounded to tell me. Some nights, no one seemed willing to loosen the hold sounds had on us. At dinner, we invented new words. (Ours sounded Spanish, but made sense only to us.) We pieced together new words by taking, say, an English verb and giving it Spanish endings. My mother's instructions at bedtime would be lacquered with mock-urgent tones. Or a word like *sí* would become, in several notes, able to convey added measures of feeling. Tongues explored the edges of words, especially the fat vowels. And we happily sounded that military

drum roll, the twirling roar of the Spanish *r*. Family language: my family's sounds. The voices of my parents and sisters and brother. Their voices insisting: *You belong here. We are family members. Related. Special to one another. Listen!* Voices singing and sighing, rising, straining, then surging, teeming with pleasure that burst syllables into fragments of laughter. At times it seemed there was steady quiet only when, from another room, the rustling whispers of my parents faded and I moved closer to sleep.

25   Supporters of bilingual education today imply that students like me miss a great deal by not being taught in their family's language. What they seem not to recognize is that, as a socially disadvantaged child, I considered Spanish to be a private language. What I needed to learn in school was that I had the right—and the obligation—to speak the public language of *los gringos*. The odd truth is that my first-grade classmates could have become bilingual, in the conventional sense of that word, more easily than I. Had they been taught (as upper-middle-class children are often taught early) a second language like Spanish or French, they could have regarded it simply as that: another public language. In my case such bilingualism could not have been so quickly achieved. What I did not believe was that I could speak a single public language.

26   Without question, it would have pleased me to hear my teachers address me in Spanish when I entered the classroom. I would have felt much less afraid. I would have trusted them and responded with ease. But I would have delayed—for how long postponed?—having to learn the language of public society. I would have evaded—and for how long could I have afforded to delay?—learning the great lesson of school, that I had a public identity.

27   Fortunately, my teachers were unsentimental about their responsibility. What they understood was that I needed to speak a public language. So their voices would search me out, asking me questions. Each time I'd hear them, I'd look up in surprise to see a nun's face frowning at me. I'd mumble, not really meaning to answer. The nun would persist, "Richard, stand up. Don't look at the floor. Speak up. Speak to the entire class, not just to me!" But I couldn't believe that the English language was mine to use. (In part, I did not want to believe it.) I continued to mumble. I resisted the teacher's demands. (Did I somehow suspect that once I learned public language my pleasing family life would be changed?) Silent, waiting for the bell to sound, I remained dazed, diffident, afraid.

28   Because I wrongly imagined that English was intrinsically a public language and Spanish an intrinsically private one, I easily noted the difference between classroom language and the language of home. At school, words were directed to a general audience of listeners. ("Boys and girls.") Words were meaningfully ordered. And the point was not self-expression alone but to make oneself understood by many others. The teacher quizzed:

"Boys and girls, why do we use that word in this sentence? Could we think of a better word to use there? Would the sentence change its meaning if the words were differently arranged? And wasn't there a better way of saying much the same thing?" (I couldn't say. I wouldn't try to say.)

29   Three months. Five. Half a year passed. Unsmiling, ever watchful, my teachers noted my silence. They began to connect my behavior with the difficult progress my older sister and brother were making. Until one Saturday morning three nuns arrived at the house to talk to our parents. Stiffly, they sat on the blue living room sofa. From the doorway of another room, spying the visitors, I noted the incongruity—the clash of two worlds, the faces and voices of school intruding upon the familiar setting of home. I overheard one voice gently wondering, "Do your children speak only Spanish at home, Mrs. Rodriguez?" While another voice added, "That Richard especially seems so timid and shy."

30   *That Rich-heard!*

31   With great tact the visitors continued, "Is it possible for you and your husband to encourage your children to practice their English when they are home?" Of course, my parents complied. What would they not do for their children's well-being? And how could they have questioned the Church's authority which those women represented? In an instant, they agreed to give up the language (the sounds) that had revealed and accentuated our family's closeness. The moment after the visitors left, the change was observed. "*Ahora,* speak to us *en inglés,*" my father and mother united to tell us.

32   At first, it seemed a kind of game. After dinner each night, the family gathered to practice "our" English. (It was still then *inglés,* a language foreign to us, so we felt drawn as strangers to it.) Laughing, we would try to define words we could not pronounce. We played with strange English sounds, often over-anglicizing our pronunciations. And we filled the smiling gaps of our sentences with familiar Spanish sounds. But that was cheating, somebody shouted. Everyone laughed. In school, meanwhile, like my brother and sister, I was required to attend a daily tutoring session. I needed a full year of special attention. I also needed my teachers to keep my attention from straying in class by calling out, *Rich-heard*—their English voices slowly prying loose my ties to my other name, its three notes, *Ri-car-do.* Most of all I needed to hear my mother and father speak to me in a moment of seriousness in broken—suddenly heartbreaking—English. The scene was inevitable: One Saturday morning I entered the kitchen where my parents were talking in Spanish. I did not realize that they were talking in Spanish however until, at the moment they saw me, I heard their voices change to speak English. Those *gringo* sounds they uttered startled me. Pushed me away. In that moment of trivial misunderstanding and profound insight, I felt my throat twisted by unsounded grief. I turned quickly and left the room. But I had no place to escape to with Spanish. (The spell

was broken.) My brother and sisters were speaking English in another part of the house.

33   Again and again in the days following, increasingly angry, I was obliged to hear my mother and father: "Speak to us *en inglés.*" (*Speak.*) Only then did I determine to learn classroom English. Weeks after, it happened: One day in school I raised my hand to volunteer an answer. I spoke out in a loud voice. And I did not think it remarkable when the entire class understood. That day, I moved very far from the disadvantaged child I had been only days earlier. The belief, the calming assurance that I belonged in public, had at last taken hold.

34   Shortly after, I stopped hearing the high and loud sounds of *los gringos.* A more and more confident speaker of English, I didn't trouble to listen to *how* strangers sounded, speaking to me. And there simply were too many English-speaking people in my day for me to hear American accents anymore. Conversations quickened. Listening to persons who sounded eccentrically pitched voices, I usually noted their sounds for an initial few seconds before I concentrated on *what* they were saying. Conversations became content-full. Transparent. Hearing someone's *tone* of voice—angry or questioning or sarcastic or happy or sad—I didn't distinguish it from the words it expressed. Sound and word were thus tightly wedded. At the end of a day, I was often bemused, always relieved, to realize how "silent," though crowded with words, my day in public had been. (This public silence measured and quickened the change in my life.)

35   At last, seven years old, I came to believe what had been technically true since my birth: I was an American citizen.

36   But the special feeling of closeness at home was diminished by then. Gone was the desperate, urgent, intense feeling of being at home; rare was the experience of feeling myself individualized by family intimates. We remained a loving family, but one greatly changed. No longer so close; no longer bound tight by the pleasing and troubling knowledge of our public separateness. Neither my older brother nor sister rushed home after school anymore. Nor did I. When I arrived home there would often be neighborhood kids in the house. Or the house would be empty of sounds.

37   Following the dramatic Americanization of their children, even my parents grew more publicly confident. Especially my mother. She learned the names of all the people on our block. And she decided we needed to have a telephone installed in the house. My father continued to use the word *gringo.* But it was no longer charged with the old bitterness or distrust. (Stripped of any emotional content, the word simply became a name for those Americans not of Hispanic descent.) Hearing him, sometimes, I wasn't sure if he was pronouncing the Spanish word *gringo* or saying gringo in English.

38   Matching the silence I started hearing in public was a new quiet at home. The family's quiet was partly due to the fact that, as we children learned

more and more English, we shared fewer and fewer words with our parents. Sentences needed to be spoken slowly when a child addressed his mother or father. (Often the parent wouldn't understand.) The child would need to repeat himself. (Still the parent misunderstood.) The young voice, frustrated, would end up saying, "Never mind"—the subject was closed. Dinners would be noisy with the clinking of knives and forks against dishes. My mother would smile softly between her remarks; my father at the other end of the table would chew and chew at his food, while he stared over the heads of his children.

39   My *mother!* My *father!* After English became my primary language, I no longer knew what words to use in addressing my parents. The old Spanish words (those tender accents of sound) I had used earlier—*mamá* and *papá*—I couldn't use anymore. They would have been too painful reminders of how much had changed in my life. On the other hand, the words I heard neighborhood kids call *their* parents seemed equally unsatisfactory. *Mother* and *Father; Ma, Papa, Pa, Dad, Pop* (how I hated the all-American sound of that last word especially)—all these terms I felt were unsuitable, not really terms of address for *my* parents. As a result, I never used them at home. Whenever I'd speak to my parents, I would try to get their attention with eye contact alone. In public conversations, I'd refer to "my parents" or "my mother and father."

40   My mother and father, for their part, responded differently, as their children spoke to them less. She grew restless, seemed troubled and anxious at the scarcity of words exchanged in the house. It was she who would question me about my day when I came home from school. She smiled at small talk. She pried at the edges of my sentences to get me to say something more. (What?) She'd join conversations she overheard, but her intrusions often stopped her children's talking. By contrast, my father seemed reconciled to the new quiet. Though his English improved somewhat, he retired into silence. At dinner he spoke very little. One night his children and even his wife helplessly giggled at his garbled English pronunciation of the Catholic Grace before Meals. Thereafter he made his wife recite the prayer at the start of each meal, even on formal occasions, when there were guests in the house. Hers became the public voice of the family. On official business, it was she, not my father, one would usually hear on the phone or in stores, talking to strangers. His children grew so accustomed to his silence that, years later, they would speak routinely of his shyness. (My mother would often try to explain: Both his parents died when he was eight. He was raised by an uncle who treated him like little more than a menial servant. He was never encouraged to speak. He grew up alone. A man of few words.) But my father was not shy, I realized, when I'd watch him speaking Spanish with relatives. Using Spanish, he was quickly effusive. Especially when talking with other men, his voice would spark, flicker, flare alive with sounds. In Spanish, he expressed ideas

and feelings he rarely revealed in English. With firm Spanish sounds, he conveyed confidence and authority English would never allow him.

41   The silence at home, however, was finally more than a literal silence. Fewer words passed between parent and child, but more profound was the silence that resulted from my inattention to sounds. At about the time I no longer bothered to listen with care to the sounds of English in public, I grew careless about listening to the sounds family members made when they spoke. Most of the time I heard someone speaking at home and didn't distinguish his sounds from the words people uttered in public. I didn't even pay much attention to my parents' accented and ungrammatical speech. At least not at home. Only when I was with them in public would I grow alert to their accents. Though, even then, their sounds caused me less and less concern. For I was increasingly confident of my own public identity.

42   I would have been happier about my public address had I not sometimes recalled what it had been like earlier, when my family had conveyed its intimacy through a set of conveniently private sounds. Sometimes in public, hearing a stranger, I'd hark back to my past. A Mexican farmworker approached me downtown to ask directions to somewhere. "¿Hijito . . . ?" he said. And his voice summoned deep longing. Another time, standing beside my mother in the visiting room of a Carmelite convent, before the dense screen which rendered the nuns shadowy figures, I heard several Spanish-speaking nuns—their busy, singsong overlapping voices—assure us that yes, yes, we were remembered, all our family was remembered in their prayers. (Their voices echoed faraway family sounds.) Another day, a dark-faced old woman—her hand light on my shoulder—steadied herself against me as she boarded a bus. She murmured something I couldn't quite comprehend. Her Spanish voice came near, like the face of a never-before-seen relative in the instant before I was kissed. Her voice, like so many of the Spanish voices I'd hear in public, recalled the golden age of my youth. Hearing Spanish then, I continued to be a careful, if sad, listener to sounds. Hearing a Spanish-speaking family walking behind me, I turned to look. I smiled for an instant, before my glance found the Hispanic-looking faces of strangers in the crowd going by.

43   Today I hear bilingual educators say that children lose a degree of "individuality" by becoming assimilated into public society. (Bilingual schooling was popularized in the seventies, that decade when middle-class ethnics began to resist the process of assimilation—the American melting pot.) But the bilingualists simplistically scorn the value and necessity of assimilation. They do not seem to realize that there are *two* ways a person is individualized. So they do not realize that while one suffers a diminished sense of *private* individuality by becoming assimilated into public society, such assimilation makes possible the achievement of *public* individuality.

44   The bilingualists insist that a student should be reminded of his difference from others in mass society, his heritage. But they equate mere separateness with individuality. The fact is that only in private—with intimates—is separateness from the crowd a prerequisite for individuality. (An intimate draws me apart, tells me that I am unique, unlike all others.) In public, by contrast, full individuality is achieved, paradoxically, by those who are able to consider themselves members of the crowd. Thus it happened for me: Only when I was able to think of myself as an American, no longer an alien in *gringo* society, could I seek the rights and opportunities necessary for full public individuality. The social and political advantages I enjoy as a man result from the day that I came to believe that my name, indeed, is *Rich-heard Road-ree-guess*. It is true that my public society today is often impersonal. (My public society is usually mass society.) Yet despite the anonymity of the crowd and despite the fact that the individuality I achieve in public is often tenuous—because it depends on my being one in a crowd—I celebrate the day I acquired my new name. Those middle-class ethnics who scorn assimilation seem to me filled with decadent self-pity, obsessed by the burden of public life. Dangerously, they romanticize public separateness and they trivialize the dilemma of the socially disadvantaged.

45   My awkward childhood does not prove the necessity of bilingual education. My story discloses instead an essential myth of childhood—inevitable pain. If I rehearse here the changes in my private life after my Americanization, it is finally to emphasize the public gain. The loss implies the gain: The house I returned to each afternoon was quiet. Intimate sounds no longer rushed to the door to greet me. There were other noises inside. The telephone rang. Neighborhood kids ran past the door of the bedroom where I was reading my schoolbooks—covered with shopping-bag paper. Once I learned public language, it would never again be easy for me to hear intimate family voices. More and more of my day was spent hearing words. But that may only be a way of saying that the day I raised my hand in class and spoke loudly to an entire roomful of faces, my childhood started to end

---

**Questions
on Content**

1. In paragraph 4, Rodriguez says of his teacher, "I heard her sound out: *Rich-heard Road-ree-guess*." Why is this memory so strong for him?

2. What important distinction does Rodriguez make between public and private language?

3. When did the author stop concentrating on how *los gringos* sounded and begin concentrating on what they were saying?

4. How did knowing English affect the author's family life? Did this Americanization affect all members of his family similarly? Explain.

5. Rodriguez still has difficulty using the words *Mother* and *Father*. Why?

Questions on Structure and Style

6. This essay is both an argument and a memoir, and its tone shifts as the author moves between the two rhetorical methods. When do you notice the first shift? Is there a thesis to the argument? Is it directly stated or implied?

7. Characterize the tone of the memoir and that of the argument. Do the two complement each other?

8. Rodriguez's use of italics, parentheses, and extremely short paragraphs (sometimes single words) is characteristic of his style and consistent throughout the essay. Why does he use these devices? Are they merely ways to be different, or are they systematic, serving identifiable purposes?

9. How effective is the concluding paragraph? Does it clearly relate to the opening? If so, how? Does it pull the argument and the memoir together?

10. In paragraph 16, Rodriguez makes this simile: "At one point his words slid together to form one word—sounds as confused as the threads of blue and green oil in the puddle next to my shoes." Find other examples of figurative language in the essay. What does the figurative language contribute to Rodriguez's presentation?

11. Rodriguez describes bilingual education as a "scheme" (paragraph 5). What effect does the word *scheme* create? What other terms could he have used, and what effects would they create?

Assignments

1. Later in *Hunger of Memory*, Rodriguez again discusses his childhood and says, "The great change in my life was not linguistic but social." Using "Aria" as evidence, write an essay explaining this assertion.

2. Dorothy Seymour (in "Black Children, Black Speech") and Richard Rodriguez hold very different views on "speaking English." Seymour discusses bidialectism, and Rodriguez discusses bilingualism. In an essay, summarize the two issues, and discuss the similar and different problems that they present to native and non-native speakers of English.

3. Many people, even native speakers, have had to change their language habits. Write an account of such a change that you or someone close to you had to make. Explain both what changed and why it had to change.

4. Rodriguez focuses on public language and its effect on private language, which in this case could be called family language. Think of how the language you use with your family differs from your public language—the language you use at school, at work, and with strangers. Write an essay describing the differences and explaining why they exist.

Spanglish: Hispanics and the Bilingual Dilemma

Thomas Palmer

████████████

Debate over bilingualism has become especially intense because of organized efforts to declare English the official language of the United States. In the following newspaper article, journalist Thomas Palmer reports on some specific elements of the debate—the people involved and their arguments in the "linguistic war [that] will affect voting materials and ballots, public signs and courtrooms, and, perhaps most immediately, bilingual education."

████████████

1   Willcox, Ariz.—When Manny Gonzales spotted a friend with a new truck, he noted the purchase: *"Ah, compraste a pickup."* "You bought a pickup," he had said, planting the English word for the vehicle at the end of an otherwise Spanish sentence. Gonzales tells his wife, *"Vamanos a lunchay,"* using a slightly Spanish form of the word "lunch" instead of *almuerzo.*

2   Holda Villanueva and Dolores Ramos, secretaries in a small Miami law firm, also speak what is known as Spanglish. Their sentences, in casual conversation, are patchworks of words from the two predominant languages in the United States.

3   These Hispanic-Americans live in two regions—one tiny and rural, one a dense metropolis—that are intensely bilingual, where a large percentage of the population speaks Spanish—some to the exclusion of English. After a long period of growth and even encouragement, however, bilingualism is being looked on by increasing numbers as a scourge.

4   The first long strides have been taken in the march to make English the "official" language of the country.

5   "Our basic assertion is that English is essential for a feeling of nationhood, a feeling of cohesiveness, of social understanding," said Gerda Bikales, executive director of U.S.English, a four-year-old organization dedicated to securing the place of English as premier language of the land. She said she considers the use of English especially important "in places of the country settled by immigrants recently."

A Charge of Racism

6   That position incenses many in Hispanic and other foreign-speaking communities, who consider U.S.English, its younger counterpart English First, and the groups' supporters poorly disguised racists and xenophobes.

7   "Those that want the primacy of English . . . they want the suppression of anything in their view that is not American," said Maurice Ferre, former mayor of Miami and a leader in the Hispanic community.

8   The outcome of this linguistic war will affect voting materials and ballots, public signs and courtrooms, and, perhaps most immediately, bilingual education.

9   Initially it is being waged over legislation that, state-by-state, is declaring English the "official" language. The 10th state, North Dakota, adopted such a law on March 20 [1987]. It followed Arkansas in February, California last November, and before that Nebraska (the first, having included it in 1920 as an amendment to the state's constitution), Georgia, Illinois, Indiana, Kentucky, Tennessee and Virginia.

10   One of the major objectives to such legislation is that it is vague and its effects debatable—likely to be argued out in protracted, expensive court battles for years hence. State legislatures are invited—obliged, many believe—to construct enacting legislation that would specify how English will be enshrined as the official tongue.

11   Californians enthusiastically (71 percent to 29 percent) adopted English as their official language in November with a constitutional amendment, though under its enforcement section the measure specifies only that "The Legislature shall make no law which diminishes or ignores the role of English as the common language of the State of California."

12   No law has yet been enacted.

13   As Mississippi, South Carolina, Massachusetts and more than 25 other states consider such legislation—and five bills await action in Congress to make English the official national language—opponents snipe at each other over whether it is necessary or even desirable. And large numbers of US residents are speaking Spanish. According to the Census Bureau's 1980 figures, 11 million US residents speak Spanish, and more than 1 million persons living here speak a foreign language to the exclusion of any English.

14   A US law that requires "an understanding of the English language" for new residents is sometimes ignored, according to an Immigration and Naturalization Service official in Boston.

Little Willcox and Little Havana

15   Little Willcox, in southeast Arizona, once a cattle-shipping center of the nation, is 24 percent Hispanic today, and most of that population has arrived in the last 25 years. Some of the residents, mostly only older ones, speak Spanish exclusively.

16   "They bring their children to town to translate for them—to interpret," said Mayor Jonnie Belle Bethel, a lifetime resident of Willcox. Few signs in

town indicate the presence of a Hispanic population, though, in an unusual act of ethnic activism, someone had recently scribbled "Alto" on
several stop signs with a white marker.

17   Miami's Little Havana area is in vast contrast to Willcox. Commercial
signs are exclusively in Spanish, English is seldom heard on the street, and
there are periodic debates over whether to rename streets and public places
after Hispanic heroes. Thirteen of 47 radio stations received there broadcast in Spanish.

18   But bilingual communities as diverse as Miami and Willcox have this in
common: According to language specialists and members of the Hispanic
community, the young tend to speak both English and Spanish. In other
words, not only is the community bilingual, but so are most of the individuals within it.

19   "Their dominant language is English, or it should be," said Isabel M.
Castellanos, a sociolinguist at Florida International University. "But they
take great pride in their Spanish."

20   Like others who oppose official-English initiatives, Castellanos believes a
US resident must speak English. "If you don't, you are condemning people
to being second- or third-class citizens," she said. "English is the most
important language in the nation and in the world right now."

21   In fact, none of more than two dozen people interviewed held that
encouraging a person to speak only Spanish—or any other foreign language—to the exclusion of English is wise.

22   "It would be an asinine, ridiculous, unbelievable statement for anyone to
say they want their children to be more proficient in their own cultural
language than English," said Ferra, "because how in the world do you
survive? Nobody wants to be out of the mainstream."

Transitional vs. "Immersion"

23   Some in the pro-English movement, however, question the motives of
their opposition. And the specific issue on which the sides most disagree
most concretely appears to be bilingual education.

24   Lawrence D. Pratt, president of English First, a lobbying group with
the same goals as U.S.English, is skeptical of the statements by Hispanic leaders that they do not seek a society in which some speak Spanish
exclusively.

25   If they want their children to speak English also, Pratt said, "they've
chosen a way to make it come about that's producing in almost every case,
if not a reduced proficiency, a total failure."

26   "The most damaging statistic I can think of to corroborate that statement," he said, "is the Hispanic dropout rate, which is about 50 percent."

27   How to instruct children who speak little or no English has been the
subject of a long debate but few widely shared conclusions.

28   A fixture of school systems nationwide in recent years has been so-called transitional bilingual education, in which students learn various subjects in their own language and are shifted, over a period of years, into classes with the rest of the pupils, where English is spoken.

29   U.S. English and English First representatives say transitional bilingual education is a failure. They prefer what is known as English-as-a-second-language, or ESL, programs, if not "immersion." ESL classes instruct primarily in English, but the teacher may assist students in their native languages. Immersion is a system in which students are forced to learn English because no other language is spoken.

30   Bilingualism is opposed on cultural grounds. The divisive experiences of Canada, Belgium, Spain and South Africa, it is argued, must be avoided because they threaten national spirit and heritage. The monetary costs of bilingualism also are cited, but they are not paramount.

31   "This society is so complex already," said Bikales, "that we don't need another level of complexity, which is translation and retranslation. Those are the real costs."

32   "What we're in danger of getting is language ghettos, like the Lower East Side, which was almost completely Yiddish-speaking. They were temporary. I think the ones now have the potential for being permanent. People are basically going to be trapped into lives of no opportunity."

The Reagan Stance

33   The Voting Rights Act required that 375 electoral jurisdictions in the nation provide bilingual voting materials, and U.S. English seeks to sweep that out of existence through an amendment to the act. The group got a boost late last month when President Reagan, who supports allowing states to choose how to spend their federal bilingual-education funds, said, "Let's get everybody to talk in our language."

34   Enos Schera, secretary of Citizens of Dade United, in Miami, and his group successfully fought the use of Spanish in local government. "We thought it was a terrible atrocity to take the taxpayers' money and sponsor . . . the transcribing of county meetings," Schera said.

35   "What has happened here is an almost takeover by foreign people," he said. "I believe people are waking up to the fact that, if you lose your language, it won't be very far down the road till you lose your country."

Questions on Content

1. What is Spanglish? What are some of its characteristics?

2. Palmer draws many examples from two Hispanic-American regions. What are they? How are they similar? How are they different?

3. Is this article an argument, or does it objectively discuss two sides of a controversial issue?

4. Palmer refers to a "linguistic war" (paragraph 8). What are the two sides? List the major issues for each side.

5. Discuss the differences between transitional bilingual education and English as a second language (ESL) education.

Questions on Structure and Style

6. Where does Palmer state his thesis?

7. Discuss Palmer's introductory technique in paragraph 1; then examine his closing technique in the final paragraph. How do the two work together?

8. What is the purpose of paragraph 12, a one-sentence paragraph?

Assignments

1. Choose one of the two sides of the "linguistic war" that Palmer describes, and argue in its favor. (This topic may be more approachable after a classroom debate.)

2. Interview two people for whom English is not a primary language, perhaps people who live in your community or attend your school. Ask about bilingualism in their lives and about language-related problems they may have encountered. Present your findings to the class in a report or an essay.

In Defense
of the Mother Tongue

George Will

One of America's best-known political conservatives, George Will writes regularly for *Newsweek* and other publications, and he often appears as a guest commentator on television network news broadcasts. He was awarded the Pulitzer Prize for distinguished commentary in 1977. In the following essay, Will explains why he believes English should become our officially designated national language. As he points out, a shared language characterizes any nation, and "bilingualism . . . dilutes the idea of citizenship."

1   On the Fourth of July the corn, rhetorical as well as agricultural, should be as high as an elephant's eye. But while enjoying the rhetoric of liberty, consider the connection between the English language and American liberty.

2   A proposed amendment to the Constitution would declare "the English language shall be the official language of the United States" and "neither the United States nor any state shall require . . . the use in the United States of any language other than English." It would prohibit governments from mandating multilingual publications and from establishing bilingual education as a general entitlement. It would end the pernicious practice of providing bilingual ballots, a practice that denies the link between citizenship and shared culture. Bilingual ballots, says Richard Rodriguez, proclaim that people can exercise the most public of rights while keeping apart from public life.

3   Rodriguez's autobiography, "Hunger of Memory," is an elegant and eloquent evocation of the modern immigrant's experience. A son of Mexican immigrants, he grew up in Sacramento in the 1950s. He was so "cloistered" by family sounds, so long "poised at the edge of language" that he was timid in public—too timid to be at home outside his home, in his community. Language is an instrument of intimacy, and Rodriguez's book is a hymn to the poignant bravery of immigrant parents. Such parents often launch children toward a cultural divide the parents cannot cross, the passage into linguistic fluency and social ease.

Urgent Issue

4   Rodriguez's intelligent and unsentimental opposition to bilingual education makes his opposition to the constitutional amendment interesting.

301

Writing today, he notes that bilingualism became part of the agenda of the left in the late 1960s, when there was "a romantic surrender to the mystique of the outsider." Those people who considered the culture diseased naturally thought the culture should be shunned. Bilingualism is an urgent issue because so much of current immigration comes from the Spanish-speaking Western Hemisphere and because the availability of Spanish-language news and entertainment broadcasting encourages the notion that English is merely a marginally important option.

5   "Those who have the most to lose in a bilingual America," Rodriguez says, "are the foreign-speaking poor, who are being lured into a linguistic nursery." However, he considers the constitutional amendment divisive because many Hispanics will regard it as aimed "against" them. Such sensitivity should not be decisive, especially given the reasons, which Rodriguez gives, why bilingualism is injurious to Hispanics.

6   "Our government," he says, "has no business elevating one language above all others, no business implying the supremacy of Anglo culture." He is wrong, twice. The government has a constitutional duty to promote the general welfare, which Rodriguez himself says is linked to a single shared language. Government should not be neutral regarding something as important as language is to the evolution of the culture. Furthermore, it should not be bashful about affirming the virtues of "Anglo culture"— including the political arrangements bequeathed by the men of July 4, 1776, a distinctly Anglo group. The promise of America is bound up with the virtues and achievements of "Anglo culture," which is bound up with English. Immigrants, all of whom come here voluntarily, have a responsibility to reciprocate the nation's welcome by acquiring the language that is essential for citizenship, properly understood.

7   Citizenship involves participation in public affairs, in the governance and hence the conversation of the community. In ancient Greece, from which the political philosophy of "Anglo culture" directly descends, such participation was considered natural and hence essential to normal life. When government nurtures a shared language it is nurturing a natural right—the ability to live in the manner that is right for human nature.

8   Nowadays this nation is addicted to a different rhetoric of rights—including, for a few specially entitled minorities, the right to a publicly assisted dispensation from learning the language of public life. This age defines self-fulfillment apart from, even against, the community. The idea of citizenship has become attenuated and now is defined almost exclusively in terms of entitlements, not responsibilities. Bilingualism, by suggesting that there is no duty to acquire the primary instrument of public discourse, further dilutes the idea of citizenship.

9   Rodriguez wants America to "risk uncertainty" and "remain vulnerable," "between fixity and change." Obviously America cannot freeze its culture. But another way of saying that human beings are social animals is

to say they are language-users. To be sociable they must share a language. America has always been (in Rodriguez's nifty phrase) "a marinade of sounds." But it would be wrong to make a romance of linguistic diversity. Americans should say diverse things, but in a language that allows universal participation in the discussion. Acceptance of considerable pluralism is a precondition of a free society; but so, too, is a limit to pluralism. Yes, *e pluribus unum*. But also: one national language is a prerequisite for the sort of pluralism that is compatible with shared national identity.

Linguistic Unity

10   Teddy Roosevelt's life was one long Fourth of July, a symphony of fireworks and flamboyant rhetoric. He embodied the vigor of the nation during the flood tide of immigration. He said: "We have room for but one language here and that is the English language, for we intend to see that the crucible turns our people out as Americans, of American nationality, and not as dwellers in a polyglot boarding house." American life, with its atomizing emphasis on individualism, increasingly resembles life in a centrifuge. Bilingualism is a gratuitous intensification of disintegrative forces. It imprisons immigrants in their origins and encourages what Jacques Barzun, a supporter of the constitutional amendment, calls "cultural solipsism."

11   On the Fourth of July, when we are full of filial piety toward the Founding Fathers, we should not lightly contemplate tampering with their Constitution. But a change may be necessary to preserve the linguistic unity that is as important as the Constitution to a harmonious national life.

Questions on Content

1. If Richard Rodriguez's position on the constitutional amendment issue contrasts with that of Will, why does Will devote so much attention to Rodriguez? (Answering this question may be easier after reading the Rodriguez selection, which begins on page 283.)

2. Where does Will make his own position clear?

3. Why does Rodriguez consider the constitutional amendment "divisive" (paragraph 5)? Why does Will disagree?

4. How does Will define citizenship? How does he use this definition to support his position?

5. Explain the following statement: "The idea of citizenship has become attenuated and now is defined almost exclusively in terms of entitlements, not responsibilities" (paragraph 8).

Questions on Structure and Style

6. The opening paragraph is effective. Discuss in detail what Will accomplishes in this paragraph. How does the opening paragraph relate to the conclusion of Will's essay?

7. Is the short second sentence in paragraph 9 effective? Why or why not?

8. Describe Will's tone in this essay. If you have heard George Will on a network news program, does his tone (or position on this issue) surprise you?

Assignments

1. In an essay, respond to this statement from Will: "Government should not be neutral regarding something as important as language is to the evolution of the culture" (paragraph 6).

2. Read Richard Rodriguez's "Aria: A Memoir of a Bilingual Childhood," beginning on page 283. Are you surprised to learn from Will that Rodriguez opposes the constitutional amendment declaring English to be the "official" language of the United States? Answer in a paragraph or essay.

3. In an essay, explain why you do or do not believe that Will is insensitive to the feelings of those for whom English is not the native language. As you write, be careful to avoid purely emotional claims, and also avoid simply describing your own feelings for or against the people involved. Look calmly and carefully at the issue itself. (Richard Rodriguez's argument, beginning on page 283, may help you clarify your own thoughts.)

Sex and Status
and a Manner of Speaking

Alfie Kohn

▬▬▬▬▬▬

Language always reveals those who use it, often in unexpected—and unintended—ways. One example involves men and women and their apparently different ways of using language in conversation. In the following newspaper article, Alfie Kohn reviews contemporary research on these differences. Moreover, Kohn's sources theorize that these differences exist because relative status always affects how people talk to each other, and in relative status, too, men and women are different.

▬▬▬▬▬▬

1   *Hey, y'know what?*

2   *Mmmm?*

3   *I was walking near that, um, new construction site? Near the bank?*

4   *Yah.*

5   *Well, this kinda scuzzy guy comes up to me, you know? I'm, like, ready to run for the bank.*

6   *Huh.*

7   *It's really aMAZing that these people approach you in broad daylight, don't you think?*

8   *I know. I was at the movies once and some bum started asking me for money.*

9   *Really? What happened?*

10   A sociolinguist who read this imaginary dialogue would probably conclude that it was a woman who opened the conversation, and that she was talking to a man.

11   That judgment is supported by a decade's worth of research in sociolinguistics, the study of the interaction of social behavior and language. The research has found that men and women in our culture exhibit distinctive styles of speech and also tend to play different roles in conversation.

12   The reasons for the differences are a matter of debate. Some sociolinguists, in fact, now explain such speech patterns as a function of social status and occupation—rather than gender. But studies in many settings have repeatedly confirmed that, whatever their origins, there are clear-cut differences in the ways men and women engage in conversation.

13   The differences cluster into two patterns. On the one hand, men's speech more often sounds authoritative, while women's is perceived as tentative. On the other hand, men tend to dominate rather than simply

participate in conversations; women play a more supportive role, listening to others and encouraging them to participate.

14   In one of the earlier studies of the subject, sociologist Charles Derber of Boston College recorded and analyzed 100 dinner conversations of acquaintances and friends. He found that men often shift conversations to their own preferred topics—barely responding to what the last speaker has said. Women, by contrast, are more apt to offer "support responses" that draw others out.

15   In a larger analysis of 1500 interactions in a variety of settings, Derber also examined the conversations of married couples. He found that, in general, "the wife gave more . . . active encouragement to her husband's talk about himself, while the husband listened less well and was less likely to actively 'bring her out' about herself and her own topics."

16   In fact, men often interrupt outright, and they do it far more frequently than women, as several studies have shown. In the 1970s, Candace West and Don Zimmerman, sociologists at the University of California, recorded 31 public two-party conversations. In the two-thirds of these that involved men talking with men or women with women, there were only seven interruptions altogether. But in the 11 mixed-sex conversations, there were 48 interruptions, and 46 of them—96 percent—were men interrupting women.

17   After doing doctoral research on the topic at the University of California at Santa Barbara, Pamela Fishman wrote in a 1978 article: "Both men and women regarded topics introduced by women as tentative [while] topics introduced by the men were treated as topics to be pursued. The women . . . did much of the necessary work of interaction, starting conversations and then working to maintain them."

18   Gender differences are not limited to conversational roles, however; they show up also in styles of speech. In her pioneering work "Language and Women's Place," Robin Lakoff, professor of linguistics at the University of California at Berkeley, found—like Fishman, West and Zimmerman—that questioning is a distinctive characteristic of women's speech.

19   Fishman analyzed 52 hours of taped conversations between three professional couples in their homes and found the women asked nearly three times as many questions as the men.

20   Women were also twice as likely as men to start off a conversation with a question ("Hey, y'know what?"). Fishman notes that children use the same strategy when talking to adults as a way of "ensuring [their] rights to speak."

21   Lakoff went a step further, suggesting that women not only ask more questions but also tend to use a questioning tone when making statements ("I was walking near that, um, new construction site?"). "The rising inflection . . . is as though one were seeking confirmation, though . . .

the speaker may be the only one who has the requisite information," Lakoff wrote.

22   Lakoff also observed that women use more "hedges" or qualifiers in their speech ("kinda") and also rely on intensifiers ("really"). The latter, which can refer not only to the choice of words but to the emphasis with which certain words are pronounced ("aMAZing"), does not contradict other findings. Speaking "in italics" tells the listener "how to react, since my saying something by itself is not likely to convince you," Lakoff wrote. "I'd better use double force to make sure you see what I mean."

23   If women's speech often "sounds unsure," Lakoff says, this can be explained by social norms. Women are "ostracized as unfeminine by both men and women" if they speak directly and assertively, she argues. On the other hand, adopting the traditional style and role can cause a woman to be dismissed as "someone not to be taken seriously, of dim intelligence, frivolous. . . . A woman is damned if she does and damned if she doesn't."

24   That women express their thoughts more tentatively and work harder to get someone's attention may say something about their experiences with male listeners—experiences along the lines of what West and Zimmerman, Derber and Fishman have documented.

25   Many researchers emphasize the value of women's conversational patterns; requesting rather than commanding, attending to others' needs in a conversation and listening carefully. Conversely, says Lakoff, "the male style has so many bad aspects of its own that nobody is advised to acquire it."

26   Sally McConnell-Ginet, associate professor of linguistics at Cornell University, said in an interview that the issue is not just "how women should change the way they speak, but how men should change the way they listen."

27   She urges women to "look for a style that doesn't give up [sensitivity] but nevertheless doesn't make you sound as if you have less commitment to your beliefs than you have."

28   Recently, researchers have begun to talk less about abstract features of men's and women's speech and more about what happens in particular settings. "There's been a change from looking at discrete elements of language [and toward] interaction—the whole situation," said Cheris Kramerae, professor of speech communication at the University of Illinois, in a telephone interview. "[We're] studying language in context."

29   Such situational studies have led some observers to argue that speech patterns are a function of social status at least as much as of gender. Anthropologist William O'Barr of Duke University pored over 10 weeks' worth of trial transcripts and concluded that a witness's occupation and experience on the stand told more about speech patterns than whether the witness was male or female.

30   "So-called women's language is neither characteristic of all women nor limited only to women," O'Barr wrote in his 1982 book, "Linguistic Evidence." If women generally use "powerless" language, he added, this may be due largely "to the greater tendency of women to occupy relatively powerless social positions" in American society.

31   Occupation—or at least situation—also proved to be the dominant factor in a study of day-care workers by Jean Berko Gleason, professor of psychology at Boston University. "Male day-care teachers' speech to young children is more like the language of female day-care teachers than it is like that of fathers at home," she wrote.

32   In another attempt to separate the effects of occupation and gender, Candace West spent three months exploring conversational dynamics among male and female doctors and patients at a family medicine practice. Because the doctor-patient relationship is a clear model of an unequal status relationship, she expected to determine whether interruptions reflected status or gender.

33   The answer: Both played a part. Overall, doctors interrupted patients more often than the reverse, but female physicians were interrupted more when they had male patients. "It appears that gender can take precedence over occupational status in conversation," she said.

34   To some, gender differences in speech simply reflect male-female power relations in general. Maryann Ayim, who teaches education at the University of Western Ontario, put it this way in 1984: "If females are more polite and less aggressive than males in their language practices, if they are more supportive and less dominant, this is hardly shocking, for it simply reflects the reality in every other sphere of life."

Questions on Content

1.   What is sociolinguistics?

2.   According to Kohn, male-female speech differences cluster into two patterns. What are they?

3.   Kohn's report is essentially a mustering of authorities and their research. How does he use the authorities? Are his own ideas important?

4.   Summarize the findings of Robin Lakoff of the University of California at Berkeley. Do her claims surprise you?

5.   About women's speech, Lakoff says, "A woman is damned if she does and damned if she doesn't" (paragraph 23). What does she mean by this?

6. What are some of the characteristics of the male listener? Do any of these characteristics surprise you?

Questions
on Structure
and Style

7. Examine the dialogue that Kohn uses to open the article. How does it serve as an introduction? Where does Kohn present his thesis?

8. Because he is writing a newspaper article, Kohn does not use transitions in the same way that an essayist would. How is his use of transitions different?

9. Why is the concluding paragraph of this essay particularly effective?

Assignments

1. After reading Kohn's article, and after considering relevant examples of language use in your own experience, do you believe that speech is influenced more by gender or by occupation? Is there perhaps a link between gender and occupation that is also important in explaining the differences between male-female language use? Defend your opinion in an essay.

2. Much recent research suggests that "men and women in our culture exhibit distinctive styles of speech and also tend to play different roles in conversation" (paragraph 11). In an essay, respond to this assertion, presenting evidence from Kohn's article and other relevant sources.

Of Girls and Chicks

Francine Frank and Frank Anshen

No one wants to sound sexist, yet anyone who uses English probably does. Francine Frank and Frank Anshen, both teachers of linguistics, here examine how English subtly but consistently denigrates women as it identifies them. English reflects society's attitudes, and as those attitudes change, so will English. In this chapter from their book *Language and the Sexes*, Frank and Anshen show how far-ranging those changes are likely to be.

1   English is a sexist language! Angry women have often been driven to make such a statement. But is it accurate? Can we really label some languages as more sexist than others? In a recent movie, a rather obnoxious adolescent described his favorite pastime as "cruising chicks." If the adolescent had been female, she would not have had a parallel term to refer to finding boys. This asymmetry in vocabulary is a linguistic reflection of sexism in our society.

2   One of the more intriguing and controversial hypotheses of modern linguistics is the idea that the grammatical structure of a language may influence the thought processes of speakers of that language. Regardless of the truth of that idea, known among linguists as the Sapir-Whorf hypothesis, it seems clear that we can gain insights into the culture and attitudes of a group by examining the language of that group. Eskimos live in an environment in which the condition of snow is vital to survival, and they therefore have a large number of distinct words for different kinds of snow. Most Hindi speakers live in areas of India where it does not snow and, as a result, Hindi has only a single word equivalent to the two English words *snow* and *ice*. In Modern English, the plethora of words such as *road, avenue, freeway, highway, boulevard, street, turnpike, expressway, parkway, lane,* and *interstate,* might lead one to conclude that automobiles are very important to Americans, while the relative scarcity of words for various types of kinfolk would suggest that extended familial relationships are not very important to Americans. (We do not, for example, have separate words for our mother's brother and our father's brother.) In this chapter, we will look at the linguistic treatment of women in English for clues to the attitudes towards women held by speakers of English.

3   First let us consider what the last members of the following groups have in common: Jack and Jill, Romeo and Juliet, Adam and Eve, Peter, Paul and Mary, Hansel and Gretel, Roy Rogers and Dale Evans, Tristan and Isolde, Guys and Dolls, Abelard and Heloise, man and wife, Dick and Jane, Burns and Allen, Anthony and Cleopatra, Sonny and Cher, Fibber Magee and

Molly, Ferdinand and Isabella, Samson and Delilah, and Stiller and Meara. That's right, it is a group of women who have been put in their place. Not that women must always come last: Snow White gets to precede all seven of the dwarfs, Fran may follow Kukla, but she comes before Ollie, Anna preceded the King of Siam, although it must be noted that, as colonialism waned, she was thrust to the rear of the billing in "The King and I." Women with guns are also able to command top billing, as in Frankie and Johnny, and Bonnie and Clyde. The moral is clear: a woman who wants precedence in our society should either hang around with dwarfs or dragons, or shoot somebody. "Women and children first" may apply on sinking ships, but it clearly doesn't apply in the English language.

4   Not only are women put off, they are also put down, numerically and otherwise. In the real world, women slightly outnumber men. But the world created for American schoolchildren presents a different picture. In an article describing the preparation of a dictionary for schoolchildren, Alma Graham recounts the imbalance discovered in schoolbooks in all subjects in use in the early 1970s. A computer analysis of five million words in context revealed many subtle and not-so-subtle clues to the status of women in American society. The numbers alone tell us a lot: men outnumber women seven to one, boys outnumber girls two to one; girls are even in the minority in home economics books, where masculine pronouns outnumber feminine ones two to one. In general, the pronouns *he, him,* and *his* outnumber *she, her,* and *hers,* by a ratio of four to one.

5   When the linguistic context of the above pronouns was analyzed to see if they were generics, referring to people regardless of sex, it was found that of 940 examples, almost eighty percent clearly referred to male human beings; next came references to male animals, to persons such as sailors and farmers, who were assumed to be male, and only thirty-two pronouns were true generics. In another set of words, we do find more women: mothers outnumber fathers, and wives appear three times as often as husbands. However, children are usually labelled by referring to a male parent (Jim's son rather than Betty's son), most mothers have sons rather than daughters, and so do most fathers. There are twice as many uncles as aunts and every first born child is a son. It is not altogether clear from all this how the race reproduces itself without dying out in a few generations. Notice further that, although the word *wife* is more frequent, expressions like *the farmer's wife, pioneers and their wives,* etc., indicate that the main characters are male.

6   Consider now another area of our language. English has a large number of nouns which appear to be neutral with regard to sex, but actually are covertly masculine. Although the dictionary may define *poet* as one who writes poetry, a woman who writes poetry appears so anomalous or threatening to some, that they use the special term *poetess* to refer to her. There is no corresponding term to call attention to the sex of a man who

writes poetry, but then we find nothing remarkable in the fact that poetry is written by men. Of course, if a woman is sufficiently meritorious, we may forgive her her sex and refer to her as a poet after all, or, wishing to keep the important fact of her sex in our consciousness, we may call her a *woman poet*. However, to balance the possible reward of having her sex overlooked, there remains the possibility of more extreme punishment; we may judge her work so harshly that she will be labelled a *lady poet*. Once again, the moral is clear: people who write poetry are assumed to be men until proven otherwise, and people identified as women who write poetry are assumed to be less competent than sexually unidentified (i.e., presumably male) people who write poetry.

7   If the phenomenon we have been discussing were limited to poetry, we might not regard it as very significant; after all, our society tends to regard poets as somewhat odd anyway. But, in fact, it is widespread in the language. There is a general tendency to label the exception, which in most cases turns out to be women. Many words with feminine suffixes, such as *farmerette, authoress,* and *aviatrix,* have such a clear trivializing effect, that there has been a trend away from their use and a preference for *woman author* and the like. The feminines of many ethnic terms, such as *Negress* and *Jewess,* are considered particularly objectionable. Other words, such as *actress* and *waitress,* seem to have escaped the negative connotations and remain in use. However, we note that waiters often work in more expensive establishments than do waitresses, that actresses belong to "Actor's Equity," and that women participants in theatrical groups have begun to refer to themselves as "actors." On rare occasions, this presumption of maleness in terms which should be sexually neutral, works to women's advantage. If someone is called a *bastard,* either as a general term of abuse, or as a statement of the lack of legal marital ties between that person's parents, we assume that person is a male. While an illegitimate child may be of either sex, only men are bastards in common usage. Although the dictionary seems to regard this as a sex-neutral term, a recent dictionary of slang gives the term *bastarda* as a "female bastard/law, Black/."

8   Sometimes the feminine member of a pair of words has a meaning which is not only inferior to the masculine one, but also different from it. Compare, for instance, a *governor* with a *governess* or a *major* with a *majorette*. Ella Grasso was the governor of Connecticut, and a high ranking woman in the U.S. Army would certainly not be a majorette. In a large number of cases, the supposed feminine form does not even exist to refer to a woman occupying a "male" position. Women, for example, may be United States Senators, but there is no such thing as a *Senatress*. Often, where the feminine noun does exist, it will acquire sexual overtones not found in the original: compare a *mistress* with a *master*.

9   The last effect even spills over to adjectives applied to the two sexes. A *virtuous* man may be patriotic or charitable or exhibit any one of a number

of other admirable traits; a *virtuous* woman is chaste. (The word *virtue* is, itself, derived from the Latin word for *man*.) Similarly, consider the different implications involved in saying *He is a professional* versus *She is a professional*. Although adjectives also may come in seemingly equivalent pairs like *handsome* and *pretty*, they prove not to be equivalent in practice; it is a compliment to call a woman *handsome* and an insult to call a man *pretty*. In other cases, where pairs of adjectives exist, one term covers both sexes and the other one tends to refer only to one sex, usually females. So, members of both sexes may be *small*, but only women seem to be *petite*; both boys and girls may have a *lively* personality, but when did you last meet a *vivacious* boy?

10   In addition to this use of certain adjectives almost exclusively to refer to women, descriptions of women typically include more adjectives and expressions referring to physical appearance than do descriptions of men. The media clearly reflect this tendency; a report on an interview with a well-known woman rarely fails to mention that she is *attractive* or *stylish*, or to say something about her clothes or the color of her hair or eyes, even if the context is a serious one like politics or economics, where such details have no importance. Readers are also likely to be informed of the number and ages of her children. Men are not treated in a parallel fashion.

11   Verbs turn out to be sex-differentiated also. Prominent among such verbs are those which refer to women's linguistic behavior and reflect stereotypes. Women, for example, may *shriek* and *scream*, while men may *bellow*. Women and children (girls?) hold a virtual monopoly on *giggling*, and it seems that men rarely *gossip* or *scold*. There are also a large number of sex-marked verbs which refer to sexual intercourse. In their article, "Sex-marked Predicates in English," Julia P. Stanley and Susan W. Robbins note the abundance of terms which describe the male role in sexual intercourse, and the lack of parallel terms for women's role. Women are thus assigned a passive role in sex by our language.

12   Another set of words which are presumably sex-neutral are the ones that end in *-man*. This suffix, which is pronounced with a different vowel from the one in the word *man*, supposedly indicates a person of either sex. It is commonly found in words designating professions—*salesman, postman, congressman*, for example—and in some other expressions such as *chairman* and *freshman*. However, the very fact that there exist female counterparts for many of these words, such as *chairwoman* and *congresswoman*, indicates that they are thought of as typically male and, as in the case of poets, when a woman is referred to, her sex must be clearly indicated. In the case of *salesman*, there are a variety of feminine forms: *saleswoman, saleslady*, and *salesgirl*. Although they appear to be synonymous, they convey significant social distinctions; someone referred to as a *saleslady* or a *salesgirl* probably works in a retail establishment such as a department store or a variety store. A woman who sells mainframe computers to large corporations

would be called a *saleswoman,* or even a *salesman.* The more important the position, the less likely it is to be held by a *-girl* or a *-lady,* and the more likely it is to be the responsibility of a *-man.*

13   If speakers of English often have a choice of using separate words for men and women, of pretending that a single word with a male marker like *chairman* refers to both sexes, or of using a truly sex-neutral term like *chairperson* or *chair,* speakers of some other languages do not enjoy such freedom. They are constrained by the grammar of their languages to classify the nouns they use according to something called gender. Grammatical gender is a feature of most European languages and of many others as well. Depending on the language, nouns may be classified according to whether they are animate or inanimate, human or non-human, male or female, or, in the case of inanimate objects, the class may depend on shape or some other characteristic. In some languages, meaning plays little part in determining noun class or gender; it may be predictable from the phonetic shape of the words, or it may be completely arbitrary. In the European tradition, genders are labelled *masculine* and *feminine* and, if there is a third noun class, *neuter.* This is in spite of the fact that most words included in all three of these classes represent inanimate objects like *tables* and *doors,* abstract concepts like *freedom,* or body parts like *head, toe, nose,* etc. Some of us English speakers may begin to wonder about the strange world view of speakers of languages which classify books as masculine and tables as feminine, especially when we notice that the word for nose is feminine in Spanish, but masculine in French and Italian. It turns out, however, that they are not following some animistic practice whereby inanimate objects are thought of as having sexual attributes; in the modern European languages at least, grammatical gender is, for most nouns, a purely arbitrary classification, often the result of linguistic tradition and of a number of historical accidents. The labels come from the fact that most nouns referring to males belong to one class and most nouns referring to females belong to another class and, following the human practice of classifying everything in terms of ourselves, we extend the distinguishing labels to all nouns. There are, not surprisingly, exceptions to this prevalent mode of classification, which lead to the oddity of such words as the French *sentinelle,* "guard," being grammatically feminine, although most guards are men, while two German words for "young woman," *Fräulein* and *Mädchen,* are grammatically neuter.

14   Are speakers of languages with grammatical gender completely strait-jacketed by their grammar and forced to be sexist? We note that in these languages, the masculine forms usually serve as generics and are considered the general forms, in much the same way as the *-man* words are in English. Just as there are often alternatives to these masculine words in English, other languages also have many words that are potentially neutral and can belong to either gender, depending on the sex of the person

referred to—French *poète* and Spanish *poeta* are examples, despite the dictionaries' classification of them as masculine. Yet speakers often insist on signalling the sex of women poets by adding suffixes parallel to the English *-ess*, *poétesse* and *poetisa* being the French and Spanish equivalents, or by tacking on the word for woman, as in *médecin femme*, one term for a "woman doctor" in French.

15   Although it is true that the masculine forms serve as the unmarked or neutral terms in many languages, this does not seem to be a universal feature of human languages, as some have claimed. Iroquoian languages use feminine nouns as unmarked or generic terms; however, in the case of Iroquoian occupational terms, which are composed of a pronoun and a verb (literally translated as "she cooks" or "he cooks"), the sex-typing of the job determines whether the masculine or feminine pronoun is used. In Modern Standard Arabic many nouns switch to the feminine gender when they are pluralized. In many European languages, abstract nouns are predominantly in the feminine gender.

16   English nouns no longer exhibit grammatical gender, but the language does have a large number of words that refer to members of one sex only. In addition, when we do not know the sex of the person referred to by a noun such as *writer* or *student,* the choice of the pronoun will, as in Iroquois, often depend on culturally defined sex roles. *Teacher,* therefore, is usually *she,* while *professor, doctor,* and *priest* usually go with *he.* This brings us to the question of the "generic" use of *he* and the word *man.*

17   In the case of the word *man,* as in *Man is a primate,* it has been argued that this usage is independent of sex, that it refers to all members of the species, and that it is just an etymological coincidence that the form for the species is the same as that for the male members of the species. Certainly, using the same form for the entire species and for half the species creates the possibility of confusion, as those colonial women discovered who rashly thought that the word *man* in the sentence "All men are created equal" included them. More confusion may come about when we use phrases like *early man.* Although this presumably refers to the species, notice how easy it is to use expressions like *early man and his wife* and how hard it is to say things like *man is the only animal that menstruates* or even *early woman and her husband.* As with the poetical examples discussed earlier, the common theme running through these last examples is that the male is taken as the normal, that masculine forms refer both to the sex and the species, while women are the exception, usually absorbed by the masculine, but needing special terms when they become noticeable.

18   If the above examples have not convinced you that *man* as a generic is at best ambiguous, consider the following quote from Alma Graham:

> If a woman is swept off a ship into the water, the cry is "Man
> overboard!" If she is killed by a hit-and-run driver, the charge is

"manslaughter." If she is injured on the job, the coverage is "workmen's compensation." But if she arrives at a threshold marked "Men Only," she knows the admonition is not intended to bar animals or plants or inanimate objects. It is meant for her.

19   Historically, *man* did start out as a general term for human beings, but Old English also had separate sex-specific terms: *wif* for women and *wer* or *carl* for men. The compound term *wifman* (female person) is the source for today's *woman*, but the terms for males were lost as *man* came to take on its sex-specific meaning, thus creating the confusion we have been discussing. For an authoritative opinion on the modern meaning of this word, we could turn to the *Oxford English Dictionary*, which notes that the generic use of *man* is obsolete: "in modern apprehension *man* as thus used primarily denotes the male sex, though by implication referring also to women." We note that the "modern apprehension" referred to was the late nineteenth century. If anything, the situation is even clearer today.

20   An even shorter word which is supposed to include women but often excludes them is the pronoun *he*. Observers have long pointed out the inconvenience of the ambiguity of this form and the advantages of having a true generic singular pronoun, which would be sex-neutral. In the absence of such a sex-neutral pronoun, speakers of English have been expected to utter sentences such as *Everybody should bring his book tomorrow*, where the *everybody* referred to includes forty women and just one man. For centuries, speakers and writers of English have been happily getting around this obstacle by using *they* in such situations, yielding sentences such as *Everybody should bring their book tomorrow*. Unfortunately, since the middle of the eighteenth century, prescriptive grammarians have been prescribing the use of *he* in these situations and attacking the use of *they*, by arguing that the use of *they* is a violation of the rule for pronoun agreement, i.e., a singular noun such as *everybody* should not take a plural pronoun such as *they*.

21   Although the prescriptive grammarians have not explained why it is all right for a female person such as *Mary* to be referred to by a masculine pronoun such as *he*, they have managed to make many people feel guilty about breaking the law when they use *they* in such sentences. As a result, many of us consciously avoid the use of *they* in these contexts, and some of us avoid the use of such sentences at all. Ann Bodine quotes a writer of a grammatical handbook advocating the latter course when faced with the need to formulate the sentence, "Everyone in the class worried about the midyear history exam, but he all passed." In 1850, an actual law was passed on the subject when the British Parliament, in an attempt to shorten the language in its legislation, declared: "in all acts words importing the masculine gender shall be deemed and taken to include females. . . ." The importance of shortening the language of legislation can clearly be seen by

Parliament's use of "deemed and taken." Statements similar to Parliament's are found in leases and other legal contracts today, but, as Casey Miller and Kate Swift point out in *The Handbook of Nonsexist Writing for Writers, Editors, and Speakers,* "it was often conveniently ignored. In 1879, for example, a move to admit female physicians to the all-male Massachusetts Medical Society was effectively blocked on the grounds that the society's by-laws describing membership used the pronoun *he.*" Julia Stanley is one of a number of writers who have discredited the "myth of generics" in English. Her essay contains many examples of ambiguous and "pseudogeneric" usages.

22   Rather than rely on authority or opinion, some scholars have conducted experiments to determine whether or not today's speakers of English perceive the forms *man* and *he* as generic. In one study, Joseph Schneider and Sally Hacker asked some students to find appropriate illustrations for an anthropology book with chapter headings like "Man and His Environment," and "Man and His Family"; another group of students was given titles like "Family Life" and "Urban Life." The students who were assigned titles with the word *man* chose more illustrations of men only, while the second group chose more pictures showing men, women, and children. Other studies have confirmed our tendency to interpret *he* and *man* as masculine unless the context clearly indicates they are meant generically, the contrary of what is usually claimed. One experiment, conducted by Wendy Martyna, that tested the usage and meaning of these words among young people, found that women and men may be using the terms quite differently. The men's usage appears to be based on sex-specific (male) imagery, while the women's usage is based instead on the prescription that *he* should be used when the sex of the person is not specified. Things can now run smoothly with women believing that they are included while men know otherwise.

23   Being treated as a trivial exception, being made to go to the rear linguistically, or even being made to disappear, are not the worst things that happen to women in the English language. Our lopsided lexicon is well supplied with unpleasant labels for women. Many, although by no means all of these, are slang words. The editor of the 1960 edition of the *Dictionary of American Slang* writes that "most American slang is created and used by males." This observation may be prejudiced by the fact that most collectors of American slang are males, but in any case, the words referring to women should give us an idea of the attitudes of American men towards women. The dictionaries reveal an unpleasant picture indeed.

24   Disregarding the obscene terms, and that is quite a task, since the list of obscene words for women is long, if monotonous, we still find term after term referring to women in a sexually derogatory way. Consider the following small sample: *chick, hussy, tart, broad, dame,* and *bimbo.* In one study, "The Semantic Derogation of Women," Muriel Schulz found over one

thousand words and phrases which put women in their place in this way. She analyzes a long series of words which started out as harmless terms or had a positive meaning, and gradually acquired negative connotations. It would seem that men find it difficult to talk about women without insulting them. The opposite is not true—few of the words have masculine counterparts. After going through the lists compiled by Schulz and other writers, one may begin to wonder about the popular belief that men talk about more serious topics than do women. Unless, of course, sexual jokes and insults constitute a serious topic, men should scarcely need so many derogatory terms. An interesting, if depressing, party game is to try to think of positive labels which are used for women.

25   Let's examine a few examples of words for women, their meanings and their histories. The woman of the house, or *housewife*, became a *hussy* with the passage of time, and eventually the word had to be reinvented with its original meaning. So much for the dignity of housewives. *Madam* and *mistress* did not change in form, but they took on new sex-related meanings, while *Sir* and *master* participate in no double entendres. Many of the most insulting words began life as terms of endearment and evolved into sexual slurs. *Tart*, originally a term of endearment like *sweetie-pie*, came to mean a sexually desirable woman and then a prostitute, while *broad* originally meant a young woman. *Girl* started out meaning a child of either sex, then took on the following meanings at various stages: a female child, a servant, a prostitute, and a mistress. The process then seemed to reverse itself and *girl* has gone back to meaning a female child most of the time, although some of the other meanings remain. *Whore*, which has the same root as Latin *carus*, "dear," referred at first to a lover of either sex, then only to females, and finally came to mean prostitute. Almost all the words for female relatives—*mother, aunt, daughter*, and the like—have at one time or another been euphemisms for prostitute. Stanley analyzes 220 terms used to describe sexually promiscuous women. This is just a sample of a much larger group, although there are relatively few words to describe sexually promiscuous men. Even though most of the derogatory terms for women originated as positive words, some of them did not: *shrew*, for example, never had a favorable connotation.

26   There are many animal metaphors used to insult both men and women, *dog* being an example. However, here too, there seem to be more terms of abuse for women: *chick* is one example, another is *cow*, which has been "a rude term for a woman" since the mid 1600s according to one recent dictionary of slang. Side by side with *dog*, which can be used for both sexes, we find *bitch*, limited to women. We know of no animal terms of abuse which are limited to men. In another semantic area, there is the large group of terms used both to label and to address women as objects to be consumed: *tomato, honey, cookie, sweetie-pie*, and *peach* are but a few examples. These are not necessarily derogatory and some of them, like *honey*,

can be used by women to address men, but most refer largely or exclusively to women, and there is no parallel set used to refer to men. The food terms have not escaped the process of pejoration which commonly afflicts words for women, as is shown by the example of *tart*, which was included in our discussion of derogatory words. . . .

27   We discussed some of the similarities between stereotypes about the way women speak and beliefs about the speech of other powerless groups. Not surprisingly, there are also many derogatory labels for such groups in the form of ethnic and racial slurs and, like women, they are the butt of many jokes. Once again we find that Black women are doubly insulted. In the words of Patricia Bell Scott, "the English language has dealt a 'low-blow' to the self-esteem of developing Black womanhood." After consulting the 1960 *American Thesaurus of Slang*, Scott states: "From a glance at the synonyms used to describe a Black person, especially a Black woman, one readily senses that there is something inherently negative about 'being Black' and specifically about being a Black woman. The words listed under the heading 'Negress,' in itself an offensive term, have largely negative and sexual connotations." Some of the milder terms listed include *Black doll*, *femmoke*, and *nigger gal*. Black women do not seem to be treated much better by Black English. Scott also examined handbooks of Black language and found "a preoccupation with physical attractiveness, sex appeal, and skin color, with the light-skinned Black women receiving connotations of positiveness." She concludes that "much of Black English has also dealt Black Womanhood a 'low-blow.' "

28   At the beginning of this chapter we asserted that one can determine a great deal about the attitudes of a group of speakers by examining their linguistic usage. At the end of this chapter we must conclude that the attitudes towards women reflected in the usage of English speakers are depressing indeed. They have sometimes been belittled and treated as *girls*; at other times, they have been excluded or ignored by the pretense of "generic" terms; they have frequently been defined as sex objects or insulted as prostitutes, or, on the contrary, placed on a pedestal, desexed, and treated with deference, as *ladies*. It is no wonder that many women have rebelled against being the object of such language and have become creators and advocates of new usages designed to bring equity to the English language.

Questions on Content

1.   What is the Sapir-Whorf hypothesis as Frank and Anshen describe it? How does it apply to sexism in the English language?

2.   Why do the authors object to such groupings as Hansel and Gretel, Bonnie and Clyde, Sonny and

Cher, Ike and Tina Turner, Frankie and Johnny, and Samson and Delilah (paragraph 3)?

3. What are some of the many nouns in English that appear to be sexually neutral but are in fact covertly masculine?

4. The authors suggest that one source of sexism in English is the "general tendency to label the exception" (paragraph 7). What do they mean? Give three examples.

5. Why do such adjectives as *virtuous* and *professional* create problems for Frank and Anshen? Can you think of other examples that illustrate the authors' point?

6. Why do the authors object to words like *chairwoman, saleswoman,* and *congresswoman?*

7. Is there a generic singular pronoun in English that is sexually neutral?

8. Why do the authors argue that "Black women are doubly insulted" by derogatory labels (paragraph 27)?

**Questions
on Structure
and Style**

9. How effectively does the first paragraph introduce this essay? Does it successfully catch the reader's attention and state a thesis?

10. Frank and Anshen pay close attention to transitions between ideas and paragraphs. Mark five especially smooth and strong transitions.

11. Do Frank and Anshen generalize without providing specific evidence? Do they always provide *enough* evidence?

12. Is the final paragraph an effective conclusion?

1. The authors point out that elementary school text-books "put off . . . and put down" women (paragraph 4). Examine some of your college textbooks. Do you see any effort to treat the sexes equally? Explain your findings in a paragraph or essay.

2. List five specific instances in which the generic use of *he* and *man* might be inaccurate, misleading, or confusing.

3. Analyze the persuasive strategy in this essay. Is it convincing as an argument?

4. Listen carefully to a local or network news pro-gram, paying attention to whether the broad-casters use sexually neutral language. Compare your findings with those of your classmates.

5. It may be difficult to see the problems created by using *he* generically. To highlight them, write a fifty-word paragraph describing the qualities needed to be a successful politician, using *she* generically in the paragraph. Then read the para-graph aloud to someone who is unaware of your intentions. What is this person's reaction? How do you answer if the person says, "Why is it a woman?"

Hypersexism and the Feds

William Safire

In his regular column for the *New York Times Magazine*, William Safire writes about language, often about the use (and abuse) of language by government officials. In the following argument, Safire declares that sexism is wrong, but "spirited public debate" is the proper way to abolish sexist language. Governmental action against such language is simply "a big fat mistake."

1 Some people take sexism in language very seriously.

2 A few weeks ago, it was pointed out here that it was O.K. to say "Everyone should watch his pronoun agreement," that it was not necessary to say "Everyone should watch his *or her* pronoun agreement." Nor was it required that, in the name of equality, we drop *mankind* and substitute *humankind;* historically, the male usage has embraced the female, and such expressions as "the family of man" is no put-down of women. I don't get worked up over Mother Earth and don't expect women to get worked up over Father Time.

3 "It seems to me that inequality is so morally unacceptable," writes Iva E. Deutchman, assistant professor of political science at Vassar College, "that one cannot be 'too excited' about inequality." She believes that using the pronoun *their* would be better than *his* in referring back to the singular-construed *everyone,* despite the lack of agreement in number.

4 "Perhaps, however, you provide an inadvertent autobiographical clue to this," adds Professor Deutchman, "in your empirically incorrect and grossly sexist observation that 'male always embraces the female,' rather than the reverse. Having never known (I surmise) the warmth of a female-initiated embrace, you no doubt came to the astounding conclusion that women were socially and linguistically inferior."

5 Wow. I have frequently been engaged in *ad hominem* exchanges, but have never before come under *ad mulierien* attack. "Such nonsense as sexism masquerading simply as concern for linguistic purity," snaps the professor, "must stop at once."

6 My first reaction to that is disappointment that anyone would surmise that I, a lifelong member of the Sadie Hawkins Day committee, have never known the warmth—nay, the all-consuming passion—of a female-initiated embrace. My second reaction is ungrudging admiration: as a professional polemicist who draws vitality from vituperation, I not only respect but also enjoy the sight and sound of a straight, hard shot, delivered with zest and good-natured venom, by an opponent who knows where they stand. (Somehow, the sexless pronoun *they* doesn't sound right as a

substitute for *he* or *she* in that sentence, but I'll try anything once.) In my view, the professor goes overboard, but I like the form of her dive.

7   Academics and journalists can merrily, or even savagely, joust about language: it's a fair field and no favor, with nobody coerced. Not so when a government official enters the fray in his official capacity.

8   A couple of weeks ago, a seemingly sex-crazed agency that Ronald Reagan long ago promised to abolish—the United States Department of Education—leaned on a university for daring to use such sexist terms as *man-made* in one of its catalogues.

9   Paul D. Grossman, chief regional attorney for the department's office for civil rights, first called the office of the chancellor of the University of California to report a complaint that the school was using sexist language in course descriptions. When university officials asked him to be specific, the Government lawyer then sent a hit list of words, which Mr. Grossman contended "may be perceived by some persons as subtly discouraging female student interest in the courses to which the phrases pertain." Alongside each word to be deleted by Federal diktat was what the lawyer called "a viable alternative."

10   I have the departmental hit list. In the business-administration courses, the phrase *manpower development* was deemed outside the pale: in the Government's sexlesspeak, the acceptable version is *human resource development*.

11   In the education section of the catalogue, the lawyer zeroed in on the colloquial term "Grantsmanship" in a course called "The Role of Experts in Social Services." The word *grantsmanship* is an extension of Stephen Potter's *one-upmanship* and *gamesmanship*; it is a mocking coinage, meaning "one who plays the game of getting Federal or foundation money." No matter; it has the word *man* in it, and the power of the Federal Government, wielded by one earnest lawyer, demands that the substitute be *grant acquisition* or *grantwriting*; for no apparent reason, he eschewed *grantpersonship*.

12   In other courses, the university was directed—"informally," as the lawyer put it—to scrap *mankind*, substituting *the human species, humankind* or *humanity*. In biochemistry, "Of Molecules and Man: A View for the Layman," the school was told to kill the two mentions of "man" and change the course title to "Of Molecules and Human Beings: A View for the Lay Person." In the history department, a reference to *Man on Horseback*—a phrase about the heroic "solitary horseman" who often led to military rule—was ordered watered down by our Federal bureaucrat to a meaningless *combatant*. (Try this for size: "Gaullists are seeking a new Combatant on Horseback. . . .")

13   To its credit, and to the relief of believers in academic freedom, the university told the Federal attorney to get lost. Vice Chancellor Roderic B. Park bucked the matter to Prof. David Littlejohn of the journalism school,

who shrewdly circulated the lawyer's objections to 15 journalists for comment before answering. Highlights of his report:

14   On *mankind:* "The argument against the long-accepted universal use of *man* and *mankind* is political, not linguistic or logical. It may be compared to the mandated universal use of *comrade* . . . in 'classless' societies. . . . Pretending, or asserting, that the syllable *man* signifies males exclusively can lead one into such barbarisms as *ombudsperson* or *freshperson.*"

15   On pronouns: "*His* as the appropriate (and neutral) pronoun to follow *one* or *a person* is an English usage of similar longstanding acceptance, although some writers—especially in state institutions—have lately taken to substituting the cumbersome and unnecessary *his or her.*" (Person-oh-person, are they going to hear from Vassar, which is not even a state institution.)

16   On hypersensitivity: "In no case should good English words, which are a part of our common history and heritage, simply be legislated in and out of usage according to the whims of persons or groups who suddenly declare themselves 'offended.' " Mr. Littlejohn, who calls himself *chairman* and not *chair*, accepts some changes in the name of clarity, as in changing *workman's compensation* to *worker's compensation*.

17   On freedom: "In no case should the University accept the idea that the office for civil rights is a better judge of appropriate language in its publications, or descriptions of its courses, than the University itself."

18   I tried to reach Mr. Grossman, the taxpayer's new Anti-Sexist Language Czar (which includes *czarina*), but was told gruffly that he was "in travel status," which is Federalese for junketing or vacationing. The Department of Education's regional director in San Francisco, John Palomino, won't come to the phone: presumably, he has dived under his desk and barricaded himself with blotters until the storm passes.

19   The Secretary of Education in Washington, William J. Bennett, did return my call: "The minute I saw this story in The Times," he said, referring to Wallace Turner's account of the brouhaha, "I said 'Good grief—I want to know how this happens.' " And how would he characterize the action of his attorney in San Francisco, presently on travel status in Japan? "Intrusive, meddlesome, unwarranted and wrong. My assistant secretary has counseled the regional directors that this should not happen again."

20   We then discussed the synonymy of his adjectives: *intrusive* implies forcing entrance without right, and *meddlesome* suggests a milder interposition without right; another adjective in this vein is *officious*, connoting authority where none exists. *Unwarranted* is stronger than *unapproved* and both more disapproving than and closer in meaning to *uncalled-for*; *wrong* imputes a moral or ethical error or, in this case, a big fat mistake. Sexism is *wrong*; the imposition of language change by Government fiat, rather than by spirited private debate, is—as the Secretary of Education likes to say—intrusive, meddlesome, unwarranted and wrong.

1. Safire quotes and paraphrases Iva E. Deutchman in paragraphs 2 through 4. Explain the point Deutchman makes in paragraphs 2 and 3. How would you describe her tone in paragraphs 2, 3, and 4? Is Safire's response appropriate?

2. Safire has two reactions to Deutchman's comments. What are they?

3. How does Safire finally resolve the issue of whether to use *his*, *his or her*, or *their* in a sentence like "Everyone must hang up ____ coat"? Do you agree?

4. What is Safire's attitude toward Paul Grossman's response to the university that uses sexist language in its catalogue? How does Safire convey his attitude?

5. Why does the author mix terms like *polemicist* and *vituperation* with *hard shot* in the same paragraph (paragraph 6)? Can you find other similar examples?

6. Can you find examples of humor in this essay? What type of humor? Be specific in answering.

1. Assume the role of William Safire, and write a letter responding to Frank and Anshen's "Of Girls and Chicks" (which begins on page 310). As you proceed, carefully summarize Frank and Anshen's position on specific language issues. If you wish, try to capture Safire's tone and style in your own prose.

2. William Safire's tone in "Hypersexism and the Feds" certainly makes the essay stand apart from many others in this chapter. In an essay, identify the tone, and discuss why you believe the tone is appropriate or offensive.

Is the English Language
Anybody's Enemy?

Muriel R. Schulz

In this chapter, several authors have accused the English language of being biased against women and racial groups. Is our language guilty as charged? Not everyone believes so, and the following essay presents a rebuttal. Muriel R. Schulz maintains that "language is nobody's enemy." Language merely reflects human feelings, and it can't be held responsible for those feelings. Language, she maintains, doesn't sometimes denigrate as it identifies. *We* do.

1   Ossie Davis started it. In an article, "The English Language Is My Enemy," he complained that in English we equate the word *white* with good things and *black* with evil. *White* is associated with pleasant, favorable attributes (pure, innocent, clean), while *black* is associated with feared, unfavorable ones (foul, sinister, dismal). Mixed in among the synonyms for *black* are words denoting race (*Black, Nigger, Darky*), and this association with evil is just one more burden that Blacks are forced to carry in our society. He suggested that if we were to compare the connotations of the word *Jew* (unfavorable) with those of the word *Hebrew* (neutral), we would understand why he was fighting to stop using the word *Negro* (unfavorable) and to substitute *Afro-American* (neutral).

2   We were not very far into the Women's Movement of the Sixties before women, too, discovered the English language to be their enemy. It is contemptuous of them, having a great wealth of derogatory labels like *whore, slut, slattern, hag, bag*, and *witch*. It derides female characteristics by the easy insult, using feminine terms, such as *sissy, old maidish*, and *effeminate*, as scornful slurs. It implies that some qualities (*weakness, frivolity, timidity*, and *passivity*, for example) are appropriate only to women, while others (like *courage, power, forcefulness*, and *bravery*) are available only to men. It renders women invisible, by considering masculine to be the norm for such terms as *doctor, professor, lawyer*, and *worker*, by subsuming women under the cover terms *man* and *mankind*, and by using the masculine pronoun whenever sex is unknown or unspecified (as in "Everyone must have his ticket punched"). Women wonder, with some justice, just what the effect is upon the female child, who is forming a sense of her own identity, when she finds herself alternately abused and ignored by her own language.

3 But is our language so one-sided? Are Blacks and women dealt with more harshly than men? Have race and sex provided categories subject to a kind of linguistic abuse that doesn't operate against White Anglo-Saxon males?

4 Not at all! English is rich in scathing terms for men. Consider, for example, the synonyms for *scoundrel* "a bold, selfish man who has very low ethical standards." We have *cur, dog, hound, mongrel, reptile, viper, serpent, snake, swine, skunk, polecat, insect, worm, louse,* and *rat* in animal metaphors, as well as *bounder, knave, rotter, rascal, rogue, villain, blackguard, shyster, heel, stinker, son of a bitch, bastard,* and many more. Our language enables us to make fine distinctions in describing villainy, and English attributes this quality to the male. When the grizzled old prospector curls his lip and snarls, "You dirty, low-down varmint," we automatically assume that his adversary is a man.

5 Our terms for people who drink too much are also primarily masculine in reference. Statistics argue that a large percentage of our alcoholics are women, but English doesn't carry such a message. The synonyms for *inebriate,* whether happy or obnoxious, habitual or temporary, seem to be coded primarily "male": for example, *boozer, drunkard, tippler, toper, swiller, tosspot, guzzler, barfly, drunk, lush, boozehound, souse, tank, stew, rummy,* and *bum.*

6 In a similar way, our words for law-breakers seem to have masculine reference: *crook, felon, criminal, conspirator, racketeer, gangster, outlaw, convict, jailbird, desperado,* and *bookie* all designate males. And when used figuratively, the reference remains masculine. Any man who bests another in a money transaction may earn the epithet of "dirty crook," and when we hear the phrase, we have no doubt of the sex of the person so named.

7 We are most venomous in characterizing men sexually. Women complain of the richness of vocabulary denoting them as sex objects, but at least many of these are positive, admiring terms. Not so the words which designate a man as a sexual being. Of *rapist, debaucher, despoiler, seducer, rip, betrayer, deceiver, ravisher, ravager, violator, defiler, rake,* and *dirty old man,* perhaps only the last two can be said to have positive connotations. In an article, "Our Sexist Language," Ethel Strainchamps has pointed out an ironic double standard which operates against men in our society: "If a man watches a woman undressing before a window, he can be arrested as a Peeping Tom. If a woman watches a man undressing before a window, the man can be arrested for indecent exposure." *Voyeur* and *exhibitionist* are both masculine terms.

8 Thus, men come in for a share of abuse in English, too. What we see operating is a natural function of language, one which Stuart Flexner noticed when he was gathering materials for his *Dictionary of American Slang.* There is no rich vocabulary of slang for attractive, chaste women, nor for good amiable wives and mothers, for sober, hardworking men, nor

for intelligent, attractive older people. Commenting on these impoverished areas, he remarked, "Slang—and it is frequently true for all language levels—always tends toward degradation rather than elevation." It may not be an admirable quality, but it does appear to be human nature. The chant "Sticks and stones may break my bones, but names can never hurt me" is acknowledgment that we can use names in an attempt to get at others, to categorize them as Other, to label what we dislike in them (and in ourselves). Language is potentially everyone's enemy, whether he or she is old (*geezer, old fool, codger, fogey, crone*) or young (*squirt, young punk, hippie*), whether a farmer (*yokel, hick, rube, bumpkin, clod*) or a laborer (*menial, flunky, hack, drudge*), whether a physician (*quack, croaker, pill pusher, butcher*) or an attorney (*shyster, ambulance chaser*).

9   Can we eliminate this use of language? The slogan "Black is Beautiful" seems to have succeeded in de-mythicizing the word *Black*, removing from it our associations with evil, as well as removing from it the suggestions it carried when used as a label by a White Southerner in the Fifties. Having neither the euphemistic qualities of *Colored Person* nor the stigma of *Nigger*, it has given us a fairly neutral label, relatively free of the associations and stereotypes of the past. Women have introduced *Ms.* and *chairperson* and have suggested new neutral pronouns as a means of escaping from under the cloak of masculine reference. And they have urged us all to become aware of the unfavorable connotations of many of the words we use denoting women and to avoid abusive terms. But if Whites continue to think of Blacks as Other, and if men continue to think of women as Other, we will find the old associations drifting to the new terminology. As Simone de Beauvoir says in *The Second Sex*, "The category of the *Other* is as primordial as consciousness itself. In the most primitive societies, in the most ancient mythologies, one finds the expression of a quality—that of Self and the Other." We should not be surprised to find this opposition expressed in language. Language is nobody's enemy. It is simply used to express the hostility and fear we feel toward others. Whether the difference is one of race, or sex, or religion, or behavior does not matter. The human responds to differences with suspicion and distrust, and those responses are going to be expressed in language.

**Questions
on Content**

1. Schulz maintains that English is just as slanted against white males as it is against blacks and women. She uses synonyms for *scoundrels, drinkers, lawbreakers,* and *sexual deviants* to support her contention (paragraphs 4 to 8). Is this the same issue discussed by Davis (in "The English Language Is My Enemy!") and by Frank and Anshen (in "Of Girls and Chicks")? Why or why not?

2. The essay quotes Stuart Flexner as saying, "Slang . . . always tends toward degradation rather than elevation" (paragraph 8). Do you agree? Can you think of slang expressions that do not degrade?

3. Schulz believes that the English language is not prejudiced; rather, she believes, it enables us to make fine distinctions. Is this an answer that would satisfy Davis or Frank and Anshen?

Questions on Structure and Style

4. The opening paragraph suggests that this essay is a direct response to Ossie Davis's "The English Language Is My Enemy!" (page 271). Is this really true? Is this opening misleading, or is it an effective introduction?

5. What is the function of the short third paragraph?

6. Where does the author state her thesis?

7. Discuss Schulz's use of quotations and specific examples. Whom does she quote, and why does she choose these particular sources? Why does she choose the examples she includes?

Assignments

1. Write an essay addressing the question "Is the English language anybody's enemy?" Use the reading selections in this chapter as source material.

2. In an essay, respond to the following quotation from Simone de Beauvoir: "The category of the *Other* is as primordial as consciousness itself. In the most primitive societies, in the most ancient mythologies, one finds the expression of a quality— that of Self and the Other." Explain what de Beauvoir means, and provide examples from your own experiences.

3. Assume the role of Muriel R. Schulz, and write a letter responding to either Ossie Davis ("The English Language Is My Enemy!") or Francine Frank and Frank Anshen ("Of Girls and Chicks").

Additional Assignments and Research Topics

1. Ossie Davis declares that the English language is his enemy (p. 271). Is the English language *your* enemy? Before answering, consider whether you are male, female, short, tall, fat, thin, young, old, athletic, completely unathletic, a member of a particular ethnic, religious, or racial group— in any way "noteworthy," as far as language is sometimes concerned. Research the language that is your enemy. Then in an essay, describe the language and its effects on you.

2. The issue of sexist language has presented special problems for teachers of English. They often find themselves choosing between what is grammatically acceptable and what is socially acceptable. For example, here is how one writing handbook presents the issue of the plural *their* with singular antecedents such as *each* or *every:*

   > Some writers prefer to use the pronoun *their* because it includes *his* and *her*. Although this is acceptable in informal writing, you should consult with your instructor before using this device. It is probably most desirable to change both the pronoun and antecedent to plural whenever possible.
   >
   > It is unfortunate that the English language does not have a singular pronoun that can stand for *his* or *her*. Constructions like *his/her* and *his or her* are cumbersome and should be avoided. Generally the consistent use of *their* is preferable to these constructions.*

   What do you feel should be done about this issue? Do you favor grammatical or social propriety? Must we actually choose between the two at all?

3. In his essay "Hypersexism and the Feds," William Safire quotes David Littlejohn, a journalism professor, as follows: "In no case should good English words, which are a part of our common history and heritage, simply be legislated in and out of usage according to the whims of persons or groups who suddenly declare themselves 'offended' " (paragraph 16). Think about the selections by Frank and Anshen, Kohn, Safire, and Schulz. Also consider your own experiences. Then in an essay or even a letter, respond to Littlejohn's comments.

---

* William H. Roberts, *The Writer's Companion* (Boston: Little, Brown and Company, 1985), p. 143.

4. Select an occupation in which both men and women are well represented—health care workers or teachers, for example. Interview people of each sex in the same occupation, or just listen carefully to their use of language. What differences do you note in the ways in which men and women speak? Report your findings, being sure to establish a consistent basis for your comparison.

5. Listen carefully to a local or network news program, paying attention to whether or not the broadcasters use sexually neutral language. Write down specific examples of what you discover, and compare your findings with those of your classmates. Overall, can you identify one television station or network that seems particularly conscious of sexist language as an issue—or one that seems oblivious to the issue?

6. Muriel R. Schulz ("Is the English Language Anybody's Enemy?") believes that language reflects what we feel. If we're hostile and fearful, language reflects those feelings. Other authors in this chapter obviously believe that language itself can generate hostility and fear, and to improve human relationships, we should correct elements of language that cause discrimination. In short, two views clash; and the central question becomes, Does *language* cause bias, or do *people* cause bias that language merely reflects? Respond to this question in an essay, using the reading selections in this chapter as source material.

Jargon

Language is "right" if it is appropriate to our needs and desires, as Chapter 5 points out. Slang, taboo language, and euphemisms can all be appropriate at times, and so can language like this:

> "The flyer goes out Sunday, so do the counts Saturday night."
>
> "Where do we put the extras?"
>
> "Redo the endcap across from the register. Oh—one other thing. The new A.M. said we can have someone from up front to ring if we get busy."

If you've worked in retailing, you may recognize this language. Without experience in retailing, however, you may find the language confusing, and maybe even silly. "The counts" refers to inventory counts of stock on hand—in this case, of stock scheduled to go on sale and be advertised in the store's newspaper supplement (the "flyer"). "Extras" refers to additional goods, brought in specifically for the sale and for which there is no room with the regular stock. The extras are to be placed on an "endcap," the shelves that "cap" the end of a gondola (another retailing term, this one identifying the long shelves placed along store aisles). The "register" is, of course, the cash register; the "A.M." is the store's assistant manager; and "someone from up front to ring" means a cashier who normally operates one of the cash registers located at the front of the store—and who will temporarily operate the register in the department in which the conversation is taking place.

This language is an example of *jargon*, specialized language devised and used by professional and occupational groups. Jargon makes working easier because it's often a verbal shorthand. "The counts" is simpler to say than "the inventory counts." Jargon can also be specific, denoting objects and ideas that are unique to the job. An "endcap," for example, is used in a store but in few other environments. Despite its utility, however, jargon can also create problems. If you've never worked in retailing, you most likely didn't fully understand the dialogue quoted earlier. While this in itself is unlikely to create trouble, suppose you *needed* to understand the people being quoted. Their jargon would amount to a foreign language for you. While only a relative few of us may *need* to understand the jargon of retailing, other jargon confronts us often enough, and with sufficiently important consequences, so that the use of jargon deserves attention. Thus, the selections in this chapter allow us to look at specific examples of jargon, and perhaps more importantly, at how jargon can serve those who use it.

The chapter begins with Philip Howard's "The Two Sides of Jargon," in which the author defines his subject and illustrates in detail his assertion that jargon isn't necessarily faulty language. The next three essays express the bewilderment, frustration, and even laughter that jargon sometimes causes. In "Doctor Talk," Diane Johnson discusses the public's difficulty with medical jargon that helps no one, except perhaps doctors. John Leo takes a light approach to presenting his findings in "Journalese: A Ground-breaking Study," and Florence Miller, in "Why EdSpeak Endures," speculates about the motives of educators and others for whom the irritating jargon of education actually comforts (while it obscures the truth). "Legal Trees," by Frances Norris, concludes the chapter with a humorous re-invention of Joyce Kilmer's famous poem—a revision in which legal jargon flourishes even if the tree dies.

Jargon is specialized language created by some professional and occupational groups to meet their own needs. If jargon causes problems, we should remember that the words themselves aren't at fault. Usually, someone has simply forgotten that the audience consists of "them," not "us."

Jargon can be a useful tool. However, when it is used intentionally to keep "outsiders" from understanding, it becomes a tool for deception. We then need to cut through to the truth. Someone armed with jargon hopes to hide it.

The Two Sides of Jargon

Philip Howard

Jargon has a bad name, or we may say, jargon *is* a bad name. In the following excerpt (titled "Jargon" in the original) from his book *The State of the Language: English Observed*, Philip Howard acknowledges this opinion of jargon. He goes further, however, and asserts that jargon isn't always the "linguistic flatulence" that most people think of. An author, columnist, and literary editor of the *Times* of London, Howard believes that jargon can actually serve well by facilitating communication.

1
> '*Il n'y a bête ni oiseau*
> *Qu'en son jargon ne chante ou crie . . .*'

> '*What's a' your jargon o' your schools,*
> *Your Latin names for horns and stools;*
> *If honest Nature made you fools,*
> *   What sairs your grammars?*'
> *   Robert Burns (1759–1796)*
> *   First Epistle to John Lapraik*

Jargon is a complex descriptive and value word: its meaning depends on the context, and the opinions and judgements of the person using it.

2   Originally, as illustrated in the first quotation at the head of this chapter, *jargon* was a delightful Old French word, meaning the twittering of birds. By the fifteenth century in French *jargon* had come to mean the *argot des malfaisants*. In most languages thieves and other *malfaisants* develop secret languages that they can twitter in the hearing of outsiders without being understood.

3   In English jargon has come to mean language that sounds ugly and is hard to understand for various reasons. It has been used to describe a hybrid speech of different languages. This meaning is otiose and obsolescent. We have pidgin for a hybrid language made up of elements of two or more other languages, and used for trading and other contacts between the speakers of other languages. When a pidgin becomes the mother tongue of a speech community, as in parts of the West Indies and West Africa, it is called a creole. We do not need jargon to describe these mixed languages; especially since we have lingua franca in the cupboard as well.

4   Second, in English jargon is used to describe the sectional vocabulary and register of a science, art, trade, class, sect, or profession, full of technical terms and codes, and consequently difficult, or often incomprehensible, for those who are not in the know. Professionals are usually writing

and speaking for other professionals, and can accordingly use their private jargon as a form of shorthand, not needing to take the time, trouble, and space to spell everything out in simple English that the man in the Clapham omnibus or the woman on the New York subway can understand.

5   When addressing other research chemists, a scientist can say: 'Chlorophyll makes food by photo-synthesis', and they will all understand the platitude he is expressing in simple jargon. When addressing a class of non-scientists, the research chemist could translate his statement into, 'Green leaves build up food with the help of light', without oversimplifying his meaning excessively or begging too many questions. But for a professional audience the jargon is more exact.

6   A recent and, I dare say, important American research paper concerning the habits of racoons included the passage: 'Although solitary under normal prevailing circumstances, racoons may congregate simultaneously in certain situations of artificially enhanced nutrient resource availability.' I am not a biologist specializing in the Procyonidae, and I do not understand the jargon. But I have an uncharitable suspicion that the sentence means no more than that racoons live alone, but gather at bait. Presumably the simple version was considered not impressive enough for a research paper.

7   This use of technical jargon to blind outsiders with science has led to the third modern meaning of jargon in English: viz. pompous use of long words, circumlocution, and other linguistic flatulence in order to impress hoi polloi. Various other pejorative names have been invented for the long-winded jargon for which the civil service is, rather unfairly these days, blamed as the principal propagator: gibberish, gobbledygook, barnacular, pudder, gargantuan. It would be tidier if we could select one of these for the pretentious gibberish, and reserve jargon to describe the specialized technical vocabularies of science and the professions, the arts and the services, sports and games, trades and crafts, and all other such groups that develop esoteric languages as a form of shorthand. But, alas and dammit, language is not tidy. And the two kinds of jargon, the specialist vocabulary and the gobbledygook, continually trespass into each other's territory, so that the well-meaning outsider is hard put to it to tell which is which.

8   Take the following scientific report:

—'This day I shot a condor. It measured from tip to tip of the wings eight and a half feet and from beak to tail four feet. Captain Fitz Roy took the Beagle no further up the river, and at Valparaiso I saw a living condor sold for sixpence. The Chilenos destroy and catch numbers. At night they climb the trees in which the condors roost, and noose them. They are such heavy sleepers, as I have myself witnessed, that this is not a difficult task.'

9   Charles Darwin wrote that when his science was still pristine, and before its jargon had solidified into complex codes and shorthands. If he wanted to publish that report today in a scientific journal, he would have to rewrite it something like: 'As can be observed from tables 3 and 4, the mean wingspan and length of 132 condors taken at night or purchased (ACME Poultry Inc, Old Market Street, Valparaiso, Chile VP3 7BZ) were 2590.8mm and 1219.2mm respectively.'

10   I prefer the former version. But I am not a scientist. It is possible that professionals find the tables and the millimetric exactitude and the references more useful than the gripping narrative of Darwin. But I think that we should resist accepting as an axiom that scientific jargon has to be unreadable gobbledygook. . . .

11   The social sciences are comparatively new; and it usually takes a century or two for the jargon of a new science to settle down. Most sciences deal with matters beyond the ken of the rest of us. Sociology deals with the everyday affairs of everyday people. Accordingly, we have the unworthy suspicion that they prefer an abstruse jargon to make their everyday subject sound more scientific. Sociologese has certainly been partly responsible for the proliferation of such pretentious vogue abstractions as constructions with 'situation', which have become a laughing-stock, and are dying of shame.

12   Nevertheless, if you are looking for a rich example of gobbledygook-jargon, you could do worse than look in the professional journals of sociologists, where you will find such jargon as, 'a relatively unstructured conversational interaction', which is a pompous description of what the ordinary man would call an informal chat.

13   Here's a piece:

> 'The examples given suggest that the multiformity of environmental apprehension and the exclusivity of abstract semantic conceptions constitute a crucial distinction. Semantic responses to qualities, environmental or other, tend to abstract each individual quality as though it were to be experienced in isolation, with nothing else impinging. But in actual environmental experience, our judgements of attributes are constantly affected by the entire milieu, and the connectivities such observations suggest reveal this multiform complexity. Semantic response is generally a consequence of reductive categorization, environmental response or synthesizing holism.'

14   We can detect bits of meaning, as if by flashes of lightning, in that monstrous cloud of jargon. 'The multiformity of environmental apprehension' must mean that we are aware of our surroundings in a number of different ways; 'semantic responses' are the words we use to describe what

we see; and 'environmental experience' is our observation of our surroundings. But I should not care to give a plain translation of that paragraph, nor try the patience of the printer by attempting one.

15   Faced with such gobbledygook-jargon, it is tempting to dismiss all sociology as a pseudo-science, the principal purpose of which is laboriously to redefine everyday platitudes in pompous jargon. That would be an understandable, impatient reaction, but it would be a mistake. Over the past century sociology has discovered important new truths about us and our world. As in any other discipline, there are brilliant and lucid scholars working in it, and brilliant scholars who are not lucid (Talcott Parsons), and pseuds and charlatans who give the trade a bad name. But the proper sociologist can present truth without gobbledygook. Here is a typical passage from Émile Durkheim, a founding father of sociology, translated from French:

> 'Instead of stopping at the exclusive consideration of events that lies at the surface of social life, there has arisen the need for studying the less obvious points at the base of it—internal causes and impersonal, hidden forces that move individuals and collectivities. A tendency to this sort of study has already been manifested by some historians; but it is up to sociology to increase consciousness of it, to illuminate and develop it.'

16   Durkheim, Weber, and their best successors demonstrated that it is possible to explain the ways in which society works without sending up clouds of impenetrable jargon.

17   Psychology is another new science that has the same sort of trouble with its jargons as sociology. It has not had time to establish its vocabulary. In any case the Freudians, Jungians, Adlerians, and other later disputing sects of the science, that is part medical, part social, part metaphysical, and part gobbledygook, cannot agree on what the simplest terms are to mean. Its jargon has been widely plagiarized and picked up by the general public, which lives in a scientific age, and is anxious to sound scientific. And very often the general public gets hold of the wrong end of the stick, even if the psychologists can agree among themselves as to what is the right end of the stick. As a consequence the jargon of psychology has been widely abused in Freudian English. In it somebody who is a nervous traveller, worried about missing the train, is described as neurotic or even paranoid. Somebody who cannot make up her or his mind is called schizophrenic. Somebody else refuses fish, for example, on the exaggerated grounds that he is allergic to it. The jargon adds to the gaiety of nations. But it confuses the serious work of psychology and psychiatry; and occasionally it wounds the feelings of those, or the friends of those, who are really suffering from the conditions so lightly bandied about.

18   In parts of the world much given to analysis and psychiatry, such as California, Freudian English has developed into a secondary jargon, described as Psychobabble. In Psychobabble, analysts' terms are mixed with the latest slang, misunderstandings of the other social sciences, and the jargons of the cults and other charlatanries that infect that fair State. 'Upfront' means honest; 'heavy' means serious or grave; people say things like: 'She and Harry hadn't finalized the parameters of their own interface.' And California is where it's at, you know, in the jargon situation.

19   But the latest and fastest growing of the technical jargons, as we move into the age of the silicon chip, is Computerese. It has already given us such popularized technicalities as 'interface' and 'input'. Like many new jargons, deficient of vocabulary, it converts nouns into verbs, as 'to access' and 'to format'. It then converts the verb back into a gerund noun again by adding -ing. For example, 'window' is a vogue word and metaphor of Computerese. It refers to the latest technology that allows a computerist to keep a dozen or more items on his screen at the same time, as on a crowded desk. This has created the verb 'to window', and then the gerund 'windowing', or keeping a cluttered VDU screen. The bright new word has already been picked up by the bower-birds of marketing, who have, characteristically, got the jargon slightly wrong. 'Our window for this product is very small' is used to mean that the product will be obsolete very quickly.

20   Other terms of Computerese from Silicon Valley in California are:

> 'A Gating Event' means a crux or turning-point: the gate on a silicon microprocessor chip is a key element in controlling its logic.
>
> 'Bandwidth' means the amount of information exchanged in a conversation. It is derived from the jargon for the breadth of information in certain computer devices. You would not want to have a protracted conversation with somebody whose bandwidth was small.
>
> 'He's pushing things on the stack' means he is getting overwhelmed: one stacks trays of circuit boards in a computer.
>
> 'To core dump' means to get everything off one's chest: it comes from the jargon for emptying out a computer's central memory.
>
> 'He's a read-only memory' is unkind. It means that, as a courtier said of Louis XVIII, *il n'a rien oublié et n'a rien appris*. It comes from read-only memory, or ROM, a computer part that cannot be altered by the user. A more sophisticated version is PROM, or programmable read-only memory. You can even get EPROMS, E standing for erasable.
>
> 'I'm interrupt driven' means that my life is frantic and disorganized. Computers are designed to avoid such human failings.

21   *InfoWorld Magazine*, which deals with computer science and Computerese, has devised a language mingled from the two latest Californian jargons, Psychobabble and Computerese.

> Babbler 1: 'I'm starting to relate to what you're saying. At first I was as down as my computer is when power spikes and bad vibes surge through the lines and don't go with the data flow, but now I think I'm beginning to feel a sense of wellness about this thing.'

> Babbler 2: 'Yeah, and you know, if you think of bad vibes on a power line as an analogue to bad vibes in the central nervous system, you've really accessed something important. People are really computers. They feel good; they feel bad—just like you and me. They relate to each other and interface with each other; people interface with each other; people interface with computers. Really cosmic parameters.'

> Babbler 1: 'Wow! I'm accessing it!'

22   Computerese is an instructive example of how fast jargon is changing in the present English revolution. Computers are a field where technology is moving extremely fast: too fast, in fact, for language to keep up with it. You frequently hear computer people talking about 'Core Store'. They are referring to the memory of the computer, that is, the part of the computer that holds data that *is* being processed. (Note, in passing, how Computerese has turned *data* into a singular. Computers deal with such prodigious numbers of data that computer people cannot think of their raw material as one datum, plus another datum, plus another datum . . . , but rather as numerous as the sands of the desert or the stars in the sky. So they treat *data* as an aggregate noun, like sugar, in which the essential point of the noun is choosing to ignore the individual grains or components, and considering the collection as though it were a packaged unit. In Computerese small numbers of *data* are as embarrassing to enumerate as wild oats. *Data* is. Purists need not repine. A similar process of translating an original Latin plural into an eventual English singular has happened before, to words such as *agenda* and *stamina*. It is happening to *media*.) Computerese still widely uses the term Core Store for the memory of a computer, even though it has become an anachronism in ten years. Since the early seventies the ferrite cores that were the basis of memory have become obsolete, and are no longer used. They have been replaced by silicon chips.

23   In the same way, one still regularly hears the users of Computerese refer to the Processor as the CPU (Central Processor Unit). This is another instant anachronism. CPU is an obsolete echo from the far-off days, all of ten years

ago, when all computers were large computers, and the processing unit or CPU stood in the middle of a large computer room, surrounded by the peripheral units, i.e., the devices that supplied input data, and printed output *data* as it poured like sugar out of the CPU. In those days central and peripheral were precise descriptions of the lay-out of a computer room. *Nous avons changé tout cela:* or rather the advent of the silicon chip and the microcomputer (in which both processor and input/output can be housed in one small device) has destroyed the descriptive validity of the terms. However, they are still widely used.

24   Computerese is a classic example of how the vast and hurried strides of modern science and technology are changing the English language. The strides are so fast that even that swift runner, language, cannot keep up. . . .

25   English today is a language encrusted with layers of new jargon. This is a result of the explosion of knowledge rather than a fundamental change in the language. It means that there are many lexicons of technical terms that the ordinary English-speaker cannot understand, and need not trouble to learn. It means that more popularized technicalities are adopted, pla-giarized, and misunderstood by the ordinary speaker than ever before. In particular, English towards the end of the twentieth century has a pro-pensity to abstract and impressive-sounding blanket-words from the social sciences.

26   But jargon is a source of strength in the language. It enables those with a particular interest to talk to each other in a sort of code or sub-language, without bothering the rest of us in the crowded and noisy world. If their knowledge is true and important, and their jargon sound, we shall cer-tainly pick up the best bits of it, like magpies, to decorate our discourse. We may get it a bit wrong. In which case the specialists may need to invent a new jargon. Neurosis is a term that has been so widely popularized that psychiatrists are having to invent new words.

27   Along with the hard, shiny new technical jargon, inevitably comes the tinsel language of gobbledygook-jargon. For every quark and quasar you will have any number of situations and parameters of interaction. But the fastidious and the purist need not throw their hands in the air in despair at the decay of the language because of the proliferation of gargantuan pudder-jargon. Language purifies itself in the same sort of way that the ocean does. Popularized technicality goes in impatient vogues. It has a brief life. As a dead body or other decaying matter does not last long in the sea, so meaningless jargon does not last long in the language. Anybody with any sensitivity for language already finds some other way of speaking about what would have been called, ten years ago, the environment situa-tion. There is a lot of jargon around, and it increases every day. But you do not have to learn it unless you want to. That is the point of jargon.

Questions
on Content

1. In what ways is jargon like pidgin and creole? How is it different?

2. Summarize the etymology of the word *jargon*.

3. Explain Howard's use of the quotation from Charles Darwin in paragraph 8. Why does he choose Darwin, and why does he choose that particular passage?

4. What does Howard imply when he states, in paragraph 10, "But I think we should resist accepting as an axiom that scientific jargon has to be unreadable gobbledygook"?

5. Howard suggests that the jargon of sociology and psychology has been widely abused. Why may this be true?

6. What is the latest and fastest growing jargon?

7. What point is Howard making in discussing *data* in paragraph 22? What are the implications of the change that Howard discusses?

8. Howard states in his conclusion, "But the fastidious and the purist need not throw their hands in the air in despair at the decay of language because of the proliferation of gargantuan pudder-jargon" (paragraph 27). Do you agree? Why or why not?

Questions
on Structure
and Style

9. Why does Howard begin with a definition of jargon? Why does he order the three modern meanings of jargon as he does?

10. Why does the author employ the running metaphor in paragraph 24?

11. Examine Howard's choice of words. Many of them are obviously British, but Howard's unique voice guides them throughout. What specific words and phrases reveal Howard, the man, most clearly?

1. Review Howard's presentation carefully, and respond in a paragraph to the following statement: "Language purifies itself in the same sort of way that the ocean does" (paragraph 27). As you think about how this idea applies to Howard's thesis, think also about how it may apply to your own use of language.

2. We are all members of "in-groups," sometimes just because of our age, where we live, the type of work we do, or the social or economic class we belong to. Choose one of the several in-groups to which you belong, and in an essay, describe its private language.

3. From one of your textbooks, choose a passage rich with jargon. First, rewrite the passage in conventional English. Then in a paragraph, discuss the differences between the original and your revision, and also explain which version performs its task better.

Doctor Talk

Diane Johnson

We've all talked with doctors, either as patients or as the relatives
of patients. The language of doctors is unique, and in this essay,
Diane Johnson, a professor of English (and wife of a medical
doctor), offers reasons why "doctor talk" exists. Johnson looks at
doctors' jargon much as we would (that is, *not* as a doctor), and
her opinions, though one-sided and not reassuring, do articulate
many people's feelings—and suspicions.

1   In Africa or the Amazon, the witch doctor on your case has a magic language to say his spells in. You listen, trembling, full of hope and dread and
mystification; and presently you feel better or die, depending on how
things come out. In England and America too, until recent times, doctors
talked a magic language, usually Latin, and its mystery was part of your
cure. But modern doctors are rather in the situation of modern priests;
having lost their magic languages, they run the risk of losing the magic
powers too.

2   For us, this means that the doctor may lose his ability to heal us by our
faith; and doctors, sensing powerlessness, have been casting about for new
languages in which to conceal the nature of our afflictions and the ingredients of cures. They have devised two main dialects, but neither seems
quite to serve for every purpose—this is a time of transition and trial for
them, marked by various strategies, of which the well-known illegible
handwriting on your prescription is but one. For doctors themselves seem
to have lost faith too, in themselves and in the old mysteries and arts. They
have been taught to think of themselves as scientists, and so it is first of all
to the language of science that they turn, to control and confuse us.

3   Most of the time scientific language can do this perfectly. We are terri-
fied, of course, to learn that we have "prolapse of the mitral valve"—we
promise to take our medicine and stay on our diet, even though these
words describe a usually innocuous finding in the investigation of an innocent heart murmur. Or we can be lulled into a false sense of security
when the doctor avoids a scientific term: "you have a little spot on your
lung"—even when what he puts on the chart is "probable broncho-
genic carcinoma."

4   With patients, doctors can use either scientific or vernacular speech but
with each other they speak Science, a strange argot of Latin terms, new
words, and acronyms, that yearly becomes farther removed from everyday
speech and is sometimes comprised almost entirely of numbers and letters:
"His pO_2 is 45; pCO_2, 40; and pH, 7.4." Sometimes it is made up of peculiar

verbs originating from the apparatus with which they treat people: "Well, we've bronched him, tubed him, bagged him, cathed him, and PEEPed him," the intern tells the attending physician. ("We've explored his airways with a bronchoscope, inserted an endotrachial tube, provided assisted ventilation with a resuscitation bag, positioned a catheter in his bladder to monitor his urinary output, and used positive end-expiratory pressure to improve oxygenation.") Even when discussing things that can be expressed in ordinary words, doctors will prefer to say "he had a pneumonectomy" to saying "he had a lung removed."

5   One physician remembers being systematically instructed, during the 1950s, in scientific-sounding euphemisms to be used in the presence of patients. If a party of interns were examining an alcoholic patient, the wondering victim might hear them say that he was "suffering from hyperingestation of ethynol." In front of a cancer victim they would discuss his "mitosis." But in recent years such discussions are not conducted in front of the patient at all, because, since Sputnik, laymen's understanding of scientific language has itself increased so greatly that widespread ignorance cannot be assumed.

6   Space exploration has had its influence, especially on the *sound* of medical language. A CAT-scanner (computerized automated tomography), *de rigueur* in an up-to-date diagnostic unit, might be something to look at the surface of Mars with. The resonance of physical, rather than biological, science has doubtless been fostered by doctors themselves, who, mindful of the extent to which their science is really luck and art, would like to sound astronomically precise, calculable and exact, even if they cannot be so.

7   Acronyms and abbreviations play the same part in medical language that they do in other walks of modern life: We might be irritated to read on our chart that "this SOB patient complained of DOE five days PTA." (It means "this Short Of Breath patient complained of Dyspnea On Exertion five days Prior To Admission.") To translate certain syllables, the doctor must have yet more esoteric knowledge. Doctor A, reading Dr. B's note that a patient has TTP, must know whether Doctor B is a hematologist or a chest specialist in order to know whether the patient has thrombotic thrombocytopoenic puerpura, or traumatic tension pneumothorax. That pert little word *ID* means identification to us, but Intradermal to the dermatologist, Inside Diameter to the physiologist, Infective Dose to the bacteriologist; it can stand for our inner self, it can mean *idem* (the same), or it can signify a kind of rash.

8   But sometimes doctors must speak vernacular English, and this is apparently difficult for them. People are always being told to discuss their problems with their doctors, which, considering the general inability of doctors to reply except in a given number of reliable phrases, must be some of the worst advice ever given. Most people, trying to talk to the doctor—trying

to pry or to wrest meaning from his evasive remarks ("I'd say you're coming along just fine")—have been maddened by the vague and slightly inconsequential nature of statements which, meaning everything to you, ought in themselves to have meaning but do not, are noncommittal, or unengaged, have a slightly rote or rehearsed quality, sometimes a slight inappropriateness in the context ("it's nothing to worry about really"). This is the doctor's alternative dialect, phrases so general and bland as to communicate virtually nothing.

9   This dialect originates from the emotional situation of the doctor. In the way passers-by avert their eyes from the drunk in the gutter or the village idiot, so the doctor must avoid the personality, the individuality, any involvement with the destiny, of his patients. He must not let himself think and feel with them. This shows in the habit doctors have of calling patients by the names of their diseases: "put the pancreatitis in the other ward and bring the chronic lunger in here." In order to retain objective professional judgment, the doctor has long since learned to withdraw his emotions from the plight of the patient and has replaced his own ability to imagine them and empathize with them, with a formula language—the social lie and the understatement—usually delivered with the odd jocularity common to all gloomy professions.

10   "Well, Mrs. Jones, Henry is pretty sick. We're going to run a couple of tests, have a look at that pump of his." ("Henry is in shock. We're taking him to the Radiology Department to put a catheter in his aorta and inject contrast material. If he has what I think he has, he has a forty-two percent chance of surviving.") We might note an apparent difference of style in English and American doctors, with the English inclined to drollery in such situations. One woman I know reported that her London gynecologist said to her, of her hysterectomy, "We're taking out the cradle, but we're leaving in the playpen!" Americans on the other hand often affect tough talk: "Henry is sick as hell."

11   The doctor's *we*, by the way, is of especial interest. Medical pronouns are used in special ways that ensure that the doctor is never out alone on any limb. The referents are cleverly vague. The statement "we see a lot of that" designates him as a member of a knowledgeable elite, "we doctors"; while "how are we today" means you, or him and you, if he is trying to pass himself off as a sympathetic alter ego. Rarely does he stand up as an *I*. Rarely does he even permit his name to stand alone as Smith, but affixes syllables before and after—the powerful abbreviation *Dr.* itself, which can even be found on his golf bags or skis; or the letters *M.D.* after, or sometimes the two buttressing his name from both sides, like bookends: "Dr. Smart Smith, M.D."; in England a little train of other letters may trail behind: *F.R.C.P.* In America another fashionable suffix has been observed recently: *Inc.* Dr. Smart Smith, M.D., Inc. This stands for Incorporated, and indicates that the doctor has made himself into a corporation, to minimize his income taxes. A matrix of economic terms already evident in the

vocabulary of some doctors is expected to become more pervasive as time goes on.

12   We may complain even of how the doctor talks to us; doctors will say, on the other hand, that it is we who do not listen. Very likely this is true. Our ears thunder with hope and dread. We cannot hear the doctor. He says "bone marrow test," we think he says "bow and arrow test." We have all been struck with disbelief, listening to an account by a friend or family member of his trip to the doctor; the doctor cannot possibly have said it was okay to go on smoking, that she doesn't need to lose weight, that he must never eat carrots. This is the case. According to doctors, patients hear themselves. The patient says, "I can't even look at a carrot," and then imagines the doctor has interdicted them. Doctors' sense of our inability to understand things may increase their tendency to talk in simple terms to us, or not to speak at all. Nonetheless, we all hear them talking, saying things they say they never say.

Questions on Content

1. In paragraphs 1 and 2, what relationship does Johnson describe between language and power?

2. What does Johnson mean when she compares doctors to "modern priests" who have "lost their magic languages" (paragraph 1)?

3. Why has "the language of science" (paragraph 2) become important for doctors?

4. Why do doctors have difficulty speaking vernacular English?

5. According to the author, why do doctors resort to the vague *we* so often?

6. Johnson examines the language of doctors almost entirely from the nonmedical point of view. Where in the essay does she explain the doctor's point of view? What transitional term signals the shift in point of view?

Questions on Structure and Style

7. What effect does Johnson create by beginning her essay with a discussion of witch doctors?

8. Where does the author state her thesis?

9. What effect is Johnson seeking when she capitalizes *Science* in paragraph 4?

10. Explain the organizational plan of paragraphs 4 through 10.

11. What is Johnson's overall point about the language of doctors? If she is condemning this language, is she, by extension, condemning doctors themselves?

12. Johnson's husband is a professor of medicine. Does knowing this have any effect on your reading of her essay?

Assignments

1. Think of a time when something a doctor said was important to you, perhaps because you were a patient or the relative of a patient. What do you remember about the doctor's language? Write an essay describing what happened and the role of the doctor's language in your understanding of events.

2. In paragraph 9, Johnson says that a doctor "must avoid the personality, the individuality, any involvement with the destiny, of his patients. He must not let himself think and feel with them."
   A. If you agree with Johnson on this point, write an essay explaining why doctors must adopt this attitude.
   B. If you disagree with Johnson's claim, write an essay explaining why she is mistaken.

Journalese:
A Ground-breaking Study

John Leo

Anyone who cares about language yet still listens carefully to the six o'clock news will appreciate the following lament from John Leo. As a contributor to *Time* magazine (and previously, as a newswriter and editor), Leo surely qualifies as a journalist. Moreover, his precision and wit make him an engaging essayist. In his "Ground-breaking Study," Leo skewers his colleagues (and perhaps himself) for relying on "journalese," a jargon that is stale, often illogical, and sometimes unintentionally humorous.

1   Unbeknown to an unsuspecting public, Boy George's drug troubles touched off a severe crisis in the journalese-speaking community. How should reporters and pundits, all fluent in journalese as well as English, refer to the suddenly woozy singer? Naturally enough, conventions of the language demanded a hyphenated modifier. "Much-troubled" might have been acceptable, but that adjective is reserved, as are "oil-rich" and "war-torn," for stories about the Middle East. One tabloid, apparently eager to dismiss the celebrity as a wanton hussy, called him "gender-confused pop star Boy George." This was a clear violation of journalese's "most-cherished tenet": while doing in the rich and famous, never appear to be huffy. One magazine settled for "cross-dressing crooner," and many newspapers temporarily abandoned the hyphenated tradition to label George "flamboyant," a familiar journalese word meaning "kinky" or "one who does not have all of his or her paddles in the water."

2   Few readers realize how much effort is devoted to meshing the disparate tongues of journalese and English. In journalese, for example, the word chilling is an omnibus adjective modifying "scenario" in nuclear-weapons stories, "evidence" and "reminder" in crime stories and "effect" in any story on threats to the First Amendment. In English it is merely something one does with white wine. Reforms and changes can only be "sweeping" and investigations "widening," especially on days when the investigators have no actual news to report. "Mounting" is always followed by pressures or deficits. All arrays are "bewildering," whereas all contrasts are either "striking" or, if the story is weak, "startling."

3   Many sociologists have speculated (widely, of course) about the love affair between journalese-users and hyphenated modifiers. The gist of all this celebration seems to be that readers cannot stand the shock of an unmodified noun, at least on first reference. Thus we have Libyan-sponsored terrorism, Ping-Pong diplomacy, debt-laden Brazil and the two

most popular hyphenated modifiers of the 1980s, "financially-troubled" and "financially-plagued," which can fairly be used to describe most Latin American nations, many banks and the United States Football League. The Syrian-backed P.L.O., an earlier hyphenated champion, had to be retired when the Syrian backers began shooting at the P.L.O. backs. Any dictator who leaves his homeland hastily, with or without his bullion and wife's shoe collection, is not fleeing in disgrace, merely heading into self-imposed exile.

4   Some multiple modifiers in journalese have no known meaning, much like "clinically-tested" in headache-remedy advertising. Many seem to have been invented solely for their soothing rhythm: "Wide-ranging discussions" refers to any talks at all, and "award-winning journalist" to any reporter employed three or more years who still has a pulse. A totally disappointing report, containing nothing but yawn-inducing truisms, can always be described as a "ground-breaking study." The most exciting news on the hyphen front is that adventurous journalese users, like late-medieval theologians, are experimenting with new forms, to wit, multi-hyphen adjectives. So far, "actor-turned-politician," which can be found just to the left of Clint Eastwood's name in any story about Carmel, Calif., is the most beloved two-hyphen entry, while "state-of-the-art" is such a successful three-hyphen innovation that it may be used several times a week without risking reproof from an editor.

5   Though of lower wattage, nonhyphenated modifiers also count for something in journalese. Since "buxom blond" and "leggy redhead" are no longer in fashion, journalese has evolved alternate descriptions of females, like a "handsome woman" (virtually any female over 50) or an "attractive woman" (any woman at all). Negative journalese, a strong branch of the language, combines a complimentary word with an apparently innocent but actually murderous modifier. "She is still pretty," for instance, means, "She is long in the tooth" or "Good grief! Is she still around?" Other useful adjectives include "crusty" (obnoxious), "unpredictable" (bonkers), "experienced" (ancient) and "small but well-financed" (don't invest in this turkey).

6   A subcategory of journalese involves the language used to indicate a powerful or celebrated person who is about to self-destruct or walk the plank. Anyone referred to as an "American institution," for example, is in trouble. In politics, two or more stories in the same week referring to a power person as clever or, worse, brilliant indicate that the end is near. Soon Mr. Brilliant will be labeled a "loose cannon" and transmute himself into an adviser, the Washington version of self-imposed exile. In business journalism, the phrase "one of the most respected managers in his field" informs knowing readers that envy is unnecessary—the respected manager is on the way out. Before long, there will be hints that his managerial ferocity is insufficient, and perhaps a profile mentioning that he drinks

decaffeinated coffee, collects porcelain miniatures or loves San Francisco. This means that in a week he will be "leaving to pursue outside interests." In sports, it is understood that all such rapid declines are drug-related, and sportswriters, the original masters of journalese, are constantly casting about for nonlibelous ways of suggesting that Johnny Jumpshot is deeply in love with controlled substances. The current code words are "listless" and "lacking motivation or concentration." If the reporter writes that the athlete "occasionally misses the team bus," the astute reader understands that Jumpshot is a walking pharmacy who no longer knows where or who he is, though his body still turns up for games.

7   One of the many challenges in journalism is turning out serious articles about celebrities who say they served in Joan of Arc's army or strolled through Iran with Jesus Christ. "Free spirit," "flamboyant" and "controversial" are not really up to the task. In a profile of a well-known woman who insists that she has lived several times before, one journalese speaker came up with this deft line: "More than most people on this earth, she has found spiritual answers." In crime journalese, the top thug in any urban area is always referred to as a "reputed Mafia chieftain" and generally depicted as an untutored but charismatic leader of a successful business operation. The chieftain's apprentice thugs are his "associates." This sort of coverage reflects the automatic respect and dignity accorded crime figures who know where reporters live and recognize the understandable desire of journalists everywhere to keep their kneecaps in good working order.

8   As all users know, journalese is a formidable bulwark against libel, candor and fresh utterance. Any threat to its state-of-the-art ground-breaking terminology would have a chilling effect on everybody, especially us award-winning journalists.

Questions on Content

1. In developing his essay, Leo uses comparison, classification, and definition—as well as abundant examples of journalese. Identify places where Leo uses each rhetorical approach.

2. Leo's humor makes his discussion as entertaining as it is precise in arguing its point. Which statements seem particularly effective at using humor to reveal the absurdity and silliness of journalese?

3. Leo states in paragraph 5, "Though of lower wattage, nonhyphenated modifiers also count for something in journalese." Why does Leo choose the

word *wattage?* What does this particular word contribute to Leo's topic sentence for the paragraph?

4. What does Leo imply in his final paragraph? Why does the paragraph work well as a conclusion?

Questions on Structure and Style

5. In opening his essay, Leo withholds stating his thesis and presents something else instead. What does he present? Why do you believe he opens the essay as he does?

6. Transitions between paragraphs seem weak. Why does the essay function smoothly without strong, clear transitional expressions between paragraphs?

7. Listen carefully to Leo as he describes both journalese and his reaction to it. What sort of person do you imagine him to be? What specific features of Leo's style account for the impression he creates?

Assignments

1. Choose a newspaper or magazine article that clearly exemplifies journalese. From the article, choose one paragraph and rewrite it, using fresh language that Leo would appreciate.

2. Compose a news story riddled with journalese. For example, report on the arrival of your new roommate, a recent argument at home, a noteworthy event at your college or university, last Saturday's date, or any "news item" that you believe deserves public attention. Present your report to the class.

Why EdSpeak Endures

Florence Miller

Education is a field rich with jargon, a fact that parents criticize as they struggle to decipher the language of teachers, school administrators, and guidance counselors—various people now called "educators." Parents aren't the only group affected (and dismayed), but as Florence Miller explains, parents themselves and the public in general "talk EdSpeak fluently under the right circumstances." When communicating clearly is less important than other objectives, EdSpeak becomes useful for everyone involved. Miller is an elementary school teacher and guidance counselor in New York City.

1   There are groans mixed with laughter at the high school faculty meeting as the staff is briefed on new state guidelines on occupational education. "I know," sighs the assistant principal. " 'Futuring process' sounds idiotic. But if that's what they call it, that's what we have to call it."

2   There's no laughter at all in the parking lot after a tense parent-teacher conference, however. "What was that about 'delayed language learner'?" the mother asks the father. "Were they saying she's retarded? Did they mean her lisping? I told you she needed speech therapy."

3   Oh, that EdSpeak! Depending on where you sit, it's a joke, a burden or a menace, as anxiety-provoking as I.R.S.-Speak or as obstructive as U.N.-Speak. It's a hodgepodge of jargon, euphemisms and stock phrases, the lingua franca of ed biz, as irritating as chalk dust. Teachers despise it. The public makes fun of it or is wounded by it. No one defends it. Why, then, doesn't it just blow away? Could it be that EdSpeak, like all insider languages, thrives because it is useful, even necessary? Could it be that teachers, parents and administrators can be closet EdSpeakers when it suits them?

4   Teachers talk EdSpeak defensively. Despite emotional graduation-day applause for speeches about children as the future of our nation and teachers as the guardians of the flame, the complex, fascinating work that teachers actually do is of yawning uninterest to the public. People are bored hearing about teacher complaints—humiliating working conditions; poor salaries; a new top priority every semester; accountability to everyone, from little Joan's father's latest girlfriend to the Secretary of Education. Teachers, teachers say, get no respect, and so even the gentlest primary-grade teacher will say "age-appropriate" and "task-oriented" now and then. Talking EdSpeak doesn't raise a teacher's salary, but it

sounds technical, almost professional, and that can make a teacher feel better for a while.

5   The public likes to lean against the old hitching post when it complains about EdSpeak: "What's wrong with you people? Can't you say 'suitable' instead of 'age-appropriate'? You have something against plain American English, pardner?" Yet the public talks EdSpeak fluently enough under the right circumstances. Parents who want their kids to be taught in classrooms restricted to children they approve of have no trouble pronouncing "tracking" or "homogeneous grouping to maximize potential." And though there is no evidence that sifting children like gravel maximizes anything, parents want their children's progress through the grades ever more quantified and calibrated. The public has faith in facts, even if facts aren't true, and that's why it embraces the rich EdSpeak vocabulary of testing.

6   Administrators parry public criticism of their schools with EdSpeak. The argument is, "If I ran my business the way you people run the schools . . ." and the schools respond by generating more EdSpeak—providing flashy or obscure names for programs, policies and procedures designed to satisfy the public clamor. "Exit requirement," for example, is the latest EdSpeak for what used to be called promotion standard. It fits the current mood for rigorous quality control over the tax dollar.

7   In Florida, there are now exit requirements for 5-year-olds to get out of kindergarten. If a child satisfies the requirements for kindergarten achievement, on to first grade. If not, another year in kindergarten. This may seem straightforward, but it is EdSpeak. Exit requirements sound as if there is some statewide consensus on what 5-year-olds are supposed to accomplish in what was once a paradise of Play Dough and blocks. Not so. The consensus is that the term be used. Some Florida districts administer expensive testing programs to score children on scales of maturity, socialization and physical development. But in other districts there are no such tests; a child's presence in kindergarten from September to June is thought a good enough reason to send him on to first grade. In this way "exit requirements" becomes classic EdSpeak—new jargon replacing but not improving on old jargon, the ring of education policy but oh, how hollow the sound, the real meaning critical to the lives of children in schools but never said straight.

Questions on Content

1. Why does Miller use the term "closet Edspeakers" (paragraph 3)? What other term could she have chosen?

2. The author argues that "teachers talk EdSpeak defensively" (paragraph 4). What does she mean?

Why does she say that EdSpeak makes teachers "feel better for a while" (paragraph 4)?

3. Miller suggests that one reason for the existence of EdSpeak is that "the public has faith in facts, even if the facts aren't true . . ." (paragraph 5). Although at first such a statement seems like nonsense, it does make sense. Why?

4. Florence Miller is a teacher and guidance counselor. Are you surprised by her attitude toward the jargon of her own profession?

Questions on Structure and Style

5. Miller's essay is carefully organized. Compose an outline for it.

6. Discuss the relationship between paragraphs 1 and 2. Why is balance between them so important?

7. What does Miller accomplish with the use of figurative language, most specifically, hyperbole and similes such as "irritating as chalk dust"? Locate other examples of such language. How do they contribute to Miller's tone?

Assignments

1. In a short essay, poke fun at the "in-speak" of another profession or business that is rich with jargon, for example, the jargon of insurance salespeople or of morticians. To research the jargon of the group you choose, either speak with a group member, or examine professional journals published for the group.

2. On page 356 is a humorous but sharply pointed glossary of EdSpeak, which Miller appends to her essay. Interview a member of another professional group—a psychologist, economist, computer scientist, or meteorologist, for example, and compose a short glossary based on the language of that profession. (Faculty members at your school most likely make up a pool of possible subjects to interview.)

There are no EdSpeak handbooks or dictionaries for easy reference because the terms change faster than the state of the art. The glossary that follows offers a sampling of current usage, but read fast: "A" may be obsolete by the time you get to "W."

Attention deficit   Your daughter is a world-class pain who draws hearts and arrows on her notebook cover while I'm up there reviewing the Articles of Confederation. By the way, if D.D. is who I think he is, you've *really* got a problem.

Controlled language texts   Quasi-stories written neither to instruct nor delight but to "introduce words of increasing difficulty" and to "reinforce learning by repetition." Some children are so numbed by plowing through these simulacra that they never read real books unless threatened.

Decertification   The final step in shifting the special-education child (certified) back into the regular classes from which he was earlier removed (decertified). Since in 1983–84 this happened to only 2 percent of New York City's special-education children, decertification might be considered a term that is becoming almost obsolete as a result of atrophy.

Eye-hand coordination   An "excellent" eye-hand coordination rating is usually earned by neat spelling papers. A "poor" rating results when the snowflake cutouts are considered too raggedy to tack on the "Winter Is Here" bulletin board. A poor rating is sure to evoke nightmare images of neurologicals and lapsed medical coverage.

Gifted child   A nice kid who came to school already reading, catches on quickly, and looks alert when adults talk. A gifted child often brings pretty shells from Sanibel for the science corner.

Immature   An all-purpose fallback used to describe any child who isn't succeeding.

Needs improvement   Report card terminology similar to the numerical grade 70 or the letter grade C. Favored by schools that have gerbil cages in classrooms and teach "the whole child." Back-to-basics schools feed no gerbils and favor 70 or C.

Special-needs child   Basically, your child doesn't fit into our program here. He's too fast, too slow, too clumsy, too annoying, too angry, too different. No, I didn't say he's not normal, but he'll be much happier somewhere else.

Thinking skills   A curriculum without content popular where teachers are not thought bright enough to teach. Takes the form of expensively priced exercises in "observing, comparing, imaging, hypothesizing, interpreting, and criticizing."

Word-attack skills   A synonym for decoding; what your grandmother called "sounding out the words." A child may rate high in word-attack skills yet fail reading comprehension. By the time she has changed the written code "business" to the spoken code "buh-uh-ss-uh-ene-uh-ss," she's so tired of huffing, puffing, and hissing that she's forgotten what she was reading about.

Legal Trees

Frances Norris

▬▬▬▬▬▬▬▬

Joyce Kilmer's poem "Trees," below, is the starting point for
Frances Norris's "Legal Trees."

> I think that I shall never see
> A poem lovely as a tree.
>
> A tree whose hungry mouth is pressed
> Against the earth's sweet flowing breast;
>
> A tree that looks at God all day,
> And lifts its leafy arms to pray;
>
> A tree that may in summer wear
> A nest of robins in her hair;
>
> Upon whose bosom snow has lain;
> Who intimately lives with rain.
>
> Poems are made by fools like me,
> But only God can make a tree.
>
> [1914]

In the following humorous parody, Frances Norris presents the
poem that Joyce Kilmer might have written had Kilmer looked at
a tree with a lawyer's eyes—and written about it armed with a
lawyer's jargon. Norris is managing editor of *Equity and Choice*, a
journal devoted to examining public education.

▬▬▬▬▬▬▬▬

(In homage to Joyce Kilmer, pursuant to Section 103 of Copyright Laws—Title 17,
U.S. Code—heretofore referenced under the pains and penalties of plagiarism.)

> I think that I shall never see,
> Notwithstanding any past, present, or future visions,
> A poem lovely as a tree—the word *tree*
> Used herein to include her, his, or its respective
> Limbs, leaves, bark, roots,
> Sap (if said tree proves maple), knotholes,
> Birds, squirrels, insects, agents, and servants.
> If more than one tree is mentioned herein,
> The images, similes, metaphors, and allusions

5

10   Shall be the joint and several obligations of each such tree
     Through no fault of its own.

     A tree whose hungry mouth is prest [sic]
     Against the earth's sweet flowing breast
     In the event that no receptacles, vehicles, baby carriages,
15   Or other like equipment
     Obstruct the common ground as heretofore described.

     A tree that, pursuant to religious beliefs
     Not set forth herein, looks at God all day,
     And lifts her, his, or its leafy arms, in a manner authorized
20   Under lawful convenant, to pray.

     A tree that may in Summer wear,
     To the most practical extent under the circumstances,
     A nest of robins in her, his, or its hair;
     Provided that the aforementioned birds,
25   Their spouses, friends, relatives, invitees, visitors,
     Agents, servants, and any offspring born to them
     Shall neither make nor suffer any noisy, unclean,
     Or otherwise offensive use of said tree.

     Upon whose bosom snow has lain;
30   Who intimately lives with rain, hereupon and until
     The reasonable cessation of said rain,
     Or until the expiration and termination of said tree
     By exercise of the power of eminent terrain,
     Or by the action and authority of strong wind, lightning,
35   Chain saw, Dutch elm disease (if said tree proves elm),
     Or any other natural or unnatural force,
     Unless otherwise stipulated in writing.

     Poems are made by fools like me,*
     But only God,
40   And no other instrument of like tenor,
     Can make a legal tree.

     * Subject to applicable law

━━━━━━━━━━━

**Questions
on Content**

1. Lines 1 through 7 present a laborious definition.
    What term is being defined? Can you think of any
    context in which such a term may actually need a
    definition like this one?

2. Lawyers claim that legal jargon exists in part because lawyers must be precise in what they say and write. Where in Norris's parody do we sense the deliberately misguided and humorous effort to be precise?

3. The term *heretofore* usually signals a lawyer at work. What other terms and language constructions in "Legal Trees" immediately identify the legal profession?

4. What is Norris's intention? To ridicule lawyers or Joyce Kilmer? To offer a warning? Something else?

Questions on Structure and Style

5. Although a logical structure is not necessary to create the humor that Norris intends, this "poem" is structured logically. Describe why this is true.

6. We can make inferences about the author of this parody by considering her subject, language, and tone. What can we infer about Norris—her attitudes, values, skills, and knowledge? What kind of person is she?

Assignments

1. In a single paragraph, identify the differences in the language of Kilmer's poem and Norris's parody of it. Be sure your wording is specific. In another paragraph, you may also consider the contrasting attitudes that are evident in Kilmer's original and in Norris's skillfully exaggerated version of a lawyer's reaction to trees.

2. On page 361 is another famous poem. Compose your own version of it, using the specialized vocabulary you're probably learning in one of your college courses—psychology, biology, economics, college writing, or any other.

HOW DO I LOVE THEE?
LET ME COUNT THE WAYS

Elizabeth Barrett Browning

How do I love thee? Let me count the ways.
I love thee to the depth and breadth and height
My soul can reach, when feeling out of sight
For the ends of Being and ideal Grace.
I love thee to the level of every day's
Most quiet need, by sun and candlelight.
I love thee freely, as men strive for right;
I love thee purely, as they turn from praise.
I love thee with the passion put to use
In my old griefs, and with my childhood's faith.
I love thee with a love I seemed to lose
With my lost saints—I love thee with the breath,
Smiles, tears, of all my life!—and, if God choose,
I shall but love thee better after death.

[1850]

Additional Assignments and Research Topics

1. This chapter has focused on the use of jargon by various professional and occupational groups. Another type of group is defined by its special interests. Some groups enjoy motorcycles, some collect stamps, and so on. Many special-interest magazines are published to appeal to these various groups. Locate issues of five different magazines aimed at such groups. (*Motorhome Life, Fishing World,* and *Model Railroader* are just a few examples.) Using the magazines as your sources, find at least five words or expressions that seem to typify the language of each group. Write an essay comparing the languages and showing what they reveal about the people who use them.

2. Diane Johnson's "Doctor Talk" discusses the problem we often have in trying to understand doctors. We're especially frustrated because we depend on doctors for crucial help. However, we all have "linguistic blind spots" in other, less vital areas. If we are not interested in sports, sports jargon can be mystifying. If we know little about cars, speaking with an auto mechanic can be baffling (and worrisome). Think of some linguistic blind spot of your own. Locate a piece of writing that exemplifies this language that you find inscrutable. Write an essay that (a) describes the language accurately and identifies the group associated with it, (b) explains your own reaction to the language (anger? fascination? admiration?), and (c) analyzes your feelings about being excluded from the group. (If you wish to discuss sports jargon, the sports section of your local newspaper is a good place to find source material. If business and finance are a mystery to you, a newspaper's business section and magazines like *Forbes* and *Business Week* could be useful. No matter what subject you choose, you can be sure that source material does exist—in the library, at a newsstand or elsewhere.)

3. In "Doctor Talk," Diane Johnson points out why a special, almost private language has proven valuable for a particular group. Write an essay in which you consider the social implications of jargon—the specialized language of professional and occupational groups or the private languages devised by prisoners, adolescents, or other groups. Do such

languages weaken a society or strengthen it? Should "outsiders" study such languages, and if so, can you see any danger in the conclusions that may be drawn about the people who use the languages? Are there times when a private language should *intentionally* be constructed? What do you think prompts jargon and private languages to develop? Is it prejudice? Treachery? Fear? Simple necessity? The need to be separate and special? The need to be efficient? You obviously cannot consider all these topics in one essay, so choose one or two topics for which you can find evidence to substantiate your claims.

4. Advertisers often rely on jargon to signal their intended audience, saying, in effect, "We speak your language." Examine ads for running shoes, audio equipment, motorcycles, office copiers—any product aimed at a specific audience. How often do the advertisers rely on jargon? Conversely, which products or services would *not* likely be marketed with a lot of jargon?

Language and
Advertising

H is car having lurched and died minutes earlier, a man hurried through the residential section of a city, searching for a service station or public telephone and cursing his car, his bad luck, and the mounting gray clouds signaling rain. He took heart, however, at the sound of approaching children, perhaps eight or nine years old, singing as they walked. Thoughts of childish innocence and spontaneous gaiety provided him with unexpected, welcome relief—until the children were close enough for their song to be clearly audible: "You deserve a break today, so get up and get away . . . to McDonald's."

Children today accept and sing commercial jingles as though they were nursery rhymes. We're startled, and perhaps saddened, by this sign of how advertising pervades our lives and colors our culture in ways that are often too subtle to be seen clearly. Like language, advertising is ubiquitous, part of the background of everyday experiences for Americans, but it affects us so often and so significantly that examining it teaches us much about our perceptions, values, and motives. Advertisers, knowing well our needs and weaknesses and how effectively words can influence behavior, manipulate language to manipulate us. This chapter's reading selections reveal some of the ways and reasons why language and advertising are linked, reminding us throughout that both words and ads are too powerful to take for granted.

In "The Rhetoric of Democracy," Daniel J. Boorstin emphasizes the central role of advertising in American folk culture. With clarity and precision, Boorstin analyzes advertising's six rhetorical qualities. The resulting essay is a model of skillful exposition. Attention then shifts to ads themselves. Carl P. Wrighter, in his article "Weasel Words: God's Little Helpers," presents us with a compilation of words that "help" us do whatever advertisers want us to do. "It's Natural! It's Organic! Or Is It?" examines how advertisers have capitalized on the word *natural*. Prepared by Consumers Union, publisher of *Consumer Reports,* the article concludes that although it "does not have to be synonymous with 'ripoff,' " the word *natural* today serves too often as one of the most versatile of deceptive marketing tools. In "A Consumer's Guide to Social Offenses," Stuart Berg

Flexner highlights the use of language in manipulating emotions for profit. Six ads for analysis conclude the chapter.

American corporations and businesses spend over fifty billion dollars a year on advertising. (See that figure as $50,000,000,000, and its magnitude is clearer.) Advertisers do so because advertising works. It persuades, convinces, motivates, seduces, suggests, entices, intimidates, and promotes—and much of its power comes from language itself.

The Rhetoric of Democracy

Daniel J. Boorstin

▬▬▬▬▬▬▬

We've all heard the cliché "As American as apple pie and mother-hood," but to be accurate, and honest, we should include advertising in this short list. As Daniel J. Boorstin explains in this chapter from his book *Democracy and Its Discontents,* advertising is at the heart of our culture, a phenomenon uniquely American. In an essay notable for its clarity, Boorstin analyzes the historical reasons for this phenomenon, the qualities of our advertising, and the implications of these qualities. Boorstin is well qualified to speak on the American character. One of our country's best-respected historians, he has written more than fifteen books on American history and has served, in the course of a distinguished career, as Senior Historian of the Smithsonian Institution and as Director of the Library of Congress.

▬▬▬▬▬▬▬

1   Advertising, of course, has been part of the mainstream of American civilization, although you might not know it if you read the most respectable surveys of American history. It has been one of the enticements to the settlement of this New World, it has been a producer of the peopling of the United States, and in its modern form, in its world-wide reach, it has been one of our most characteristic products.

2   Never was there a more outrageous or more unscrupulous or more ill-informed advertising campaign than that by which the promoters for the American colonies brought settlers here. Brochures published in England in the seventeenth century, some even earlier, were full of hopeful overstatements, half-truths, and downright lies, along with some facts which nowadays surely would be the basis for a restraining order from the Federal Trade Commission. Gold and silver, fountains of youth, plenty of fish, venison without limit, all these were promised, and of course some of them were found. It would be interesting to speculate on how long it might have taken to settle this continent if there had not been such promotion by enterprising advertisers. How has American civilization been shaped by the fact that there was a kind of natural selection here of those people who were willing to believe advertising?

3   Advertising has taken the lead in promising and exploiting the new. This was a new world, and one of the advertisements for it appears on the dollar bill on the Great Seal of the United States, which reads *novus ordo seclorum,* one of the most effective advertising slogans to come out of this country. "A new order of the centuries"—belief in novelty and in the desirability of opening novelty to everybody has been important in our lives throughout our history and especially in this century. Again and

again advertising has been an agency for inducing Americans to try any-thing and everything—from the continent itself to a new brand of soap. As one of the more literate and poetic of the advertising copywriters, James Kenneth Frazier, a Cornell graduate, wrote in 1900 in "The Doctor's Lament":

> This lean M.D. is Dr. Brown
> Who fares but ill in Spotless Town.
> The town is so confounded clean,
> It is no wonder he is lean,
> He's lost all patients now, you know,
> Because they use *Sapolio.*

4   The same literary talent that once was used to retail Sapolio was later used to induce people to try the Edsel or the Mustang, to experiment with Lifebuoy or Body-All, to drink Pepsi-Cola or Royal Crown Cola, or to shave with a Trac II razor.

5   And as expansion and novelty have become essential to our economy, advertising has played an ever-larger role: in the settling of the continent, in the expansion of the economy, and in the building of an American standard of living. Advertising has expressed the optimism, the hyperbole, and the sense of community, the sense of reaching which has been so important a feature of our civilization.

6   Here I wish to explore the significance of advertising, not as a force in the economy or in shaping an American standard of living, but rather as a touchstone of the ways in which we Americans have learned about all sorts of things.

7   The problems of advertising are of course not peculiar to advertising, for they are just one aspect of the problems of democracy. They reflect the rise of what I have called Consumption Communities and Statistical Com-munities, and many of the special problems of advertising have arisen from our continuously energetic effort to give everybody everything.

8   If we consider democracy not just as a political system, but as a set of institutions which do aim to make everything available to everybody, it would not be an overstatement to describe advertising as the characteristic rhetoric of democracy. One of the tendencies of democracy, which Plato and other antidemocrats warned against a long time ago, was the danger that rhetoric would displace or at least overshadow epistemology; that is, *the temptation to allow the problem of persuasion to overshadow the problem of knowledge.* Democratic societies tend to become more concerned with what people believe than with what is true, to become more concerned with credibility than with truth. All these problems become accentuated in a large-scale democracy like ours, which possesses all the apparatus of mod-ern industry. And the problems are accentuated still further by universal

literacy, by instantaneous communication, and by the daily plague of words and images.

9   In the early days it was common for advertising men to define advertisements as a kind of news. The best admen, like the best journalists, were supposed to be those who were able to make their news the most interesting and readable. This was natural enough, since the verb to "advertise" originally meant, intransitively, to take note or to consider. For a person to "advertise" meant originally, in the fourteenth and fifteenth centuries, to reflect on something, to think about something. Then it came to mean, transitively, to call the attention of another to something, to give him notice, to notify, admonish, warn or inform in a formal or impressive manner. And then, by the sixteenth century, it came to mean: to give notice of anything, to make generally known. It was not until the late eighteenth century that the word "advertising" in English came to have a specifically "advertising" connotation as we might say today, and not until the late nineteenth century that it began to have a specifically commercial connotation. By 1879 someone was saying, "Don't advertise unless you have something worth advertising." But even into the present century, newspapers continued to call themselves by the title "Advertiser"—for example, the Boston *Daily Advertiser*, which was a newspaper of long tradition and one of the most dignified papers in Boston until William Randolph Hearst took it over in 1917. Newspapers carried "Advertiser" on their mastheads, not because they sold advertisements but because they brought news.

10   Now, the main role of advertising in American civilization came increasingly to be that of persuading and appealing rather than that of educating and informing. By 1921, for instance, one of the more popular textbooks, Blanchard's *Essentials of Advertising*, began: "Anything employed to influence people favorably is advertising. The mission of advertising is to persuade men and women to act in a way that will be of advantage to the advertiser." This development—in a country where a shared, a rising, and a democratized standard of living was the national pride and the national hallmark—meant that advertising had become the rhetoric of democracy.

11   What, then, were some of the main features of modern American advertising—if we consider it as a form of rhetoric? First, and perhaps most obvious, is *repetition*. It is hard for us to realize that the use of repetition in advertising is not an ancient device but a modern one, which actually did not come into common use in American journalism until just past the middle of the nineteenth century.

12   The development of what came to be called "iteration copy" was a result of a struggle by a courageous man of letters and advertising pioneer, Robert Bonner, who bought the old New York *Merchant's Ledger* in 1851 and turned it into a popular journal. He then had the temerity to try to change the ways of James Gordon Bennett, who of course was one of the

most successful of the American newspaper pioneers, and who was both a sensationalist and at the same time an extremely stuffy man when it came to things that he did not consider to be news. Bonner was determined to use advertisements in Bennett's wide-circulating New York *Herald* to sell his own literary product, but he found it difficult to persuade Bennett to allow him to use any but agate type in his advertising. (Agate was the smallest type used by newspapers in that day, only barely legible to the naked eye.) Bennett would not allow advertisers to use larger type, nor would he allow them to use illustrations except stock cuts, because he thought it was undignified. He said, too, that to allow a variation in the format of ads would be undemocratic. He insisted that all advertisers use the same size type so that no one would be allowed to prevail over another simply by presenting his message in a larger, more clever, or more attention-getting form.

13   Finally Bonner managed to overcome Bennett's rigidity by leasing whole pages of the paper and using the tiny agate type to form larger letters across the top of the page. In this way he produced a message such as "Bring home the New York Ledger tonight." His were unimaginative messages, and when repeated all across the page they technically did not violate Bennett's agate rule. But they opened a new era and presaged a new freedom for advertisers in their use of the newpaper page. Iteration copy—the practice of presenting prosaic content in ingenious, repetitive form—became common, and nowadays of course is commonplace.

14   A second characteristic of American advertising which is not unrelated to this is the development of *an advertising style.* We have histories of most other kinds of style—including the style of many unread writers who are remembered today only because they have been forgotten—but we have very few accounts of the history of advertising style, which of course is one of the most important forms of our language and one of the most widely influential.

15   The development of advertising style was the convergence of several very respectable American traditions. One of these was the tradition of the "plain style," which the Puritans made so much of and which accounts for so much of the strength of the Puritan literature. The "plain style" was of course much influenced by the Bible and found its way into the rhetoric of American writers and speakers of great power like Abraham Lincoln. When advertising began to be self-conscious in the early years of this century, the pioneers urged copywriters not to be too clever, and especially not to be fancy. One of the pioneers of the advertising copywriters, John Powers, said, for example, "The commonplace is the proper level for writing in business; where the first virtue is plainness, 'fine writing' is not only intellectual, it is offensive." George P. Rowell, another advertising pioneer, said, "You must write your advertisement to catch damned fools—not college professors." He was a very tactful person. And he

added, "And you'll catch just as many college professors as you will of any other sort." In the 1920's, when advertising was beginning to come into its own, Claude Hopkins, whose name is known to all in the trade, said, "Brilliant writing has no place in advertising. A unique style takes attention from the subject. Any apparent effort to sell creates corresponding resistance. . . . One should be natural and simple. His language should not be conspicuous. In fishing for buyers, as in fishing for bass, one should not reveal the hook." So there developed a characteristic advertising style in which plainness, the phrase that anyone could understand, was a distinguishing mark.

16   At the same time, the American advertising style drew on another, and what might seem an antithetic, tradition—the tradition of hyperbole in tall talk, the language of Davy Crockett and Mike Fink. While advertising could think of itself as 99.44 percent pure, it used the language of "Toronado" and "Cutlass." As I listen to the radio in Washington, I hear a celebration of heroic qualities which would make the characteristics of Mike Fink and Davy Crockett pale, only to discover at the end of the paean that what I have been hearing is a description of the Ford dealers in the District of Columbia neighborhood. And along with the folk tradition of hyperbole and tall talk comes the rhythm of folk music. We hear that Pepsi-Cola hits the spot, that it's for the young generation—and we hear other products celebrated in music which we cannot forget and sometimes don't want to remember.

17   There grew somehow out of all these contradictory tendencies—combining the commonsense language of the "plain style," and the fantasy language of "tall talk"—an advertising style. This characteristic way of talking about things was especially designed to reach and catch the millions. It created a whole new world of myth. A myth, the dictionary tells us, is a notion based more on tradition or convenience than on facts; it is a received idea. Myth is not just fantasy and not just fact but exists in a limbo, in the world of the "Will to Believe," which William James has written about so eloquently and so perceptively. This is the world of the neither true nor false—of the statement that 60 percent of the physicians who expressed a choice said that our brand of aspirin would be more effective in curing a simple headache than any other leading brand.

18   That kind of statement exists in a penumbra. I would call this the "advertising penumbra." It is not untrue, and yet, in its connotation it is not exactly true.

19   Now, there is still another characteristic of advertising so obvious that we are inclined perhaps to overlook it. I call that *ubiquity*. Advertising abhors a vacuum and we discover new vacuums every day. The parable, of course, is the story of the man who thought of putting the advertisement on the other side of the cigarette package. Until then, that was wasted space and a society which aims at a democratic standard of living, at

extending the benefits of consumption and all sorts of things and services to everybody, must miss no chances to reach people. The highway billboard and other outdoor advertising, bus and streetcar and subway advertising, and skywriting, radio and TV commercials—all these are of course obvious evidence that advertising abhors a vacuum.

20   We might reverse the old mousetrap slogan and say that anyone who can devise another place to put another mousetrap to catch a consumer will find people beating a path to his door. "Avoiding advertising will become a little harder next January," the *Wall Street Journal* reported on May 17, 1973, "when a Studio City, California, company launches a venture called StoreVision. Its product is a system of billboards that move on a track across supermarket ceilings. Some 650 supermarkets so far are set to have the system." All of which helps us understand the observation attributed to a French man of letters during his recent visit to Times Square. "What a beautiful place, if only one could not read!" Everywhere is a place to be filled, as we discover in a recent *Publishers Weekly* description of one advertising program: "The $1.95 paperback edition of Dr. Thomas A. Harris' million-copy best seller 'I'm O.K., You're O.K.' is in for full-scale promotion in July by its publisher, Avon Books. Plans range from bumper stickers to airplane streamers, from planes flying above Fire Island, the Hamptons and Malibu. In addition, the $100,000 promotion budget calls for 200,000 bookmarks, plus brochures, buttons, lipcards, floor and counter displays, and advertising in magazines and TV."

21   The ubiquity of advertising is of course just another effect of our uninhibited efforts to use all the media to get all sorts of information to everybody everywhere. Since the places to be filled are everywhere, the amount of advertising is not determined by the *needs* of advertising, but by the *opportunities* for advertising which become unlimited.

22   But the most effective advertising, in an energetic, novelty-ridden society like ours, tends to be "self-liquidating." To create a cliché you must offer something which everybody accepts. The most successful advertising therefore self-destructs because it becomes cliché. Examples of this are found in the tendency for copyrighted names of trademarks to enter the vernacular—for the proper names of products which have been made familiar by costly advertising to become common nouns, and so to apply to anybody's products. Kodak becomes a synonym for camera, Kleenex a synonym for facial tissue, when both begin with a small *k*, and Xerox (now, too, with a small *x*) is used to describe all processes of copying, and so on. These are prototypes of the problem. If you are successful enough, then you will defeat your purpose in the long run—by making the name and the message so familiar that people won't notice them, and then people will cease to distinguish your product from everybody else's.

23   In a sense, of course, as we will see, the whole of American civilization is an example. When this was a "new" world, if people succeeded in

building a civilization here, the New World would survive and would reach the time—in our age—when it would cease to be new. And now we have the oldest written Constitution in use in the world. This is only a parable of which there are many more examples.

24   The advertising man who is successful in marketing any particular product, then—in our high-technology, well-to-do democratic society, which aims to get everything to everybody—is apt to be diluting the demand for his particular product in the very act of satisfying it. But luckily for him, he is at the very same time creating a fresh demand for his services as advertiser.

25   And as a consequence, there is yet another role which is assigned to American advertising. This is what I call "erasure." Insofar as advertising is competitive or innovation is widespread, erasure is required in order to persuade consumers that this year's model is superior to last year's. In fact, we consumers learn that we might be risking our lives if we go out on the highway with those very devices that were last year's lifesavers but without whatever special kind of brakes or wipers or seat belt is on this year's model. This is what I mean by "erasure"—and we see it on our advertising pages or our television screen every day. We read in the *New York Times* (May 20, 1973), for example, that "For the price of something small and ugly, you can drive something small and beautiful"—an advertisement for the Fiat 250 Spider. Or another, perhaps more subtle example is the advertisement for shirts under a picture of Oliver Drab: "Oliver Drab. A name to remember in fine designer shirts? No kidding. . . . Because you pay extra money for Oliver Drab. And for all the other superstars of the fashion world. Golden Vee [the name of the brand that is advertised] does not have a designer's label. But we do have designers. . . . By keeping their names *off* our label and simply saying Golden Vee, we can afford to sell our $7 to $12 shirts for just $7 to $12, which should make Golden Vee a name to remember. Golden Vee, you only pay for the shirt."

26   Having mentioned two special characteristics—the self-liquidating tendency and the need for erasure—which arise from the dynamism of the American economy, I would like to try to place advertising in a larger perspective. The special role of advertising in our life gives a clue to a pervasive oddity in American civilization. A leading feature of past cultures, as anthropologists have explained, is the tendency to distinguish between "high" culture and "low" culture—between the culture of the literate and the learned on the one hand and that of the populace on the other. In other words, between the language of literature and the language of the vernacular. Some of the most useful statements of this distinction have been made by social scientists at the University of Chicago—first by the late Robert Redfield in his several pioneering books on peasant society, and then by Milton Singer in his remarkable study of Indian civilization, *When a Great Tradition Modernizes* (1972). This distinction between the great

tradition and the little tradition, between the high culture and the folk culture, has begun to become a commonplace of modern anthropology.

27   Some of the obvious features of advertising in modern America offer us an opportunity to note the significance or insignificance of that distinction for us. Elsewhere I have tried to point out some of the peculiarities of the American attitute toward the *high* culture. There is something distinctive about the place of thought in American life, which I think is not quite what it has been in certain Old World cultures.

28   But what about distinctive American attitudes to *popular* culture? What is our analogue to the folk culture of other peoples? Advertising gives us some clues—to a characteristically American democratic folk culture. Folk culture is a name for the culture which ordinary people everywhere lean on. It is not the writings of Dante and Chaucer and Shakespeare and Milton, the teachings of Machiavelli and Descartes, Locke or Marx. It is, rather, the pattern of slogans, local traditions, tales, songs, dances, and ditties. And of course holiday observances. Popular culture in other civilizations has been for the most part both an area of continuity with the past, a way in which people reach back into the past and out to their community, and at the same time an area of local variations. An area of individual and amateur expression in which a person has his own way of saying, or notes his mother's way of saying or singing, or his own way of dancing, his own view of folk wisdom and the cliché.

29   And here is an interesting point of contrast. In other societies outside the United States, it is the *high* culture that has generally been an area of centralized, organized control. In Western Europe, for example, universities and churches have tended to be closely allied to the government. The institutions of higher learning have had a relatively limited access to the people as a whole. This was inevitable, of course, in most parts of the world, because there were so few universities. In England, for example, there were only two universities until the early nineteenth century. And there was central control over the printed matter that was used in universities or in the liturgy. The government tended to be close to the high culture, and that was easy because the high culture itself was so centralized and because literacy was relatively limited.

30   In our society, however, we seem to have turned all of this around. Our high culture is one of the least centralized areas of our culture. And our universities express the atomistic, diffused, chaotic, and individualistic aspect of our life. We have in this country more than twenty-five hundred colleges and universities, institutions of so-called higher learning. We have a vast population in these institutions, somewhere over seven million students.

31   But when we turn to our popular culture, what do we find? We find that in our nation of Consumption Communities and emphasis on Gross National Product (GNP) and growth rates, advertising has become the heart

of the folk culture and even its very prototype. And as we have seen, American advertising shows many characteristics of the folk culture of other societies: repetition, a plain style, hyperbole and tall talk, folk verse, and folk music. Folk culture, wherever it has flourished, has tended to thrive in a limbo between fact and fantasy, and of course, depending on the spoken word and the oral tradition, it spreads easily and tends to be ubiquitous. These are all familiar characteristics of folk culture and they are ways of describing our folk culture, but how do the expressions of our peculiar folk culture come to *us*?

32   They no longer sprout from the earth, from the village, from the farm, or even from the neighborhood or the city. They come to us primarily from enormous centralized self-consciously *creative* (an overused word, for the overuse of which advertising agencies are in no small part responsible) organizations. They come from advertising agencies, from networks of newspapers, radio, and television, from outdoor-advertising agencies, from the copywriters for ads in the largest-circulation magazines, and so on. These "creators" of folk culture—or pseudo-folk culture—aim at the widest intelligibility and charm and appeal.

33   But in the United States, we must recall, the advertising folk culture (like all advertising) is also confronted with the problems of self-liquidation and erasure. These are by-products of the expansive, energetic character of our economy. And they, too, distinguish American folk culture from folk cultures elsewhere.

34   Our folk culture is distinguished from others by being discontinuous, ephemeral, and self-destructive. Where does this leave the common citizen? All of us are qualified to answer.

35   In our society, then, those who cannot lean on the world of learning, on the high culture of the classics, on the elaborated wisdom of the books, have a new problem. The University of Chicago, for example, in the 1930's and 1940's was the center of a quest for a "common discourse." The champions of that quest, which became a kind of crusade, believed that such a discourse could be found through familiarity with the classics of great literature—and especially of Western European literature. I think they were misled; such works were not, nor are they apt to become, the common discourse of our society. Most people, even in a democracy, and a rich democracy like ours, live in a world of popular culture, our special kind of popular culture.

36   The characteristic folk culture of our society is a creature of advertising, and in a sense it *is* advertising. But advertising, our own popular culture, is harder to make into a source of continuity than the received wisdom and commonsense slogans and catchy songs of the vivid vernacular. The popular culture of advertising attenuates and is always dissolving before our very eyes. Among the charms, challenges, and tribulations of modern life, we must count this peculiar fluidity, this ephemeral character of that very

kind of culture on which other peoples have been able to lean, the kind of culture to which they have looked for the continuity of their traditions, for their ties with the past and with the future.

37   We are perhaps the first people in history to have a centrally organized mass-produced folk culture. Our kind of popular culture is here today and gone tomorrow—or the day after tomorrow. Or whenever the next semiannual model appears. And insofar as folk culture becomes advertising, and advertising becomes centralized, it becomes a way of depriving people of their opportunities for individual and small-community expression. Our technology and our economy and our democratic ideals have all helped make that possible. Here we have a new test of the problem that is at least as old as Heraclitus—an everyday test of man's ability to find continuity in his experience. And here democratic man has a new opportunity to accommodate himself, if he can, to the unknown.

**Questions
on Content**

1. Why does Boorstin use the term *natural selection* in discussing the settling of America (paragraph 2)?

2. Explain the historical link between advertising and news. Why is this important to an understanding of what advertising is today?

3. Boorstin titles his essay "The Rhetoric of Democracy"; he uses the term *rhetoric* again in paragraph 10. Define this term as Boorstin uses it.

4. Boorstin states in paragraph 14 that "many unread writers . . . are remembered today only because they have been forgotten." What does he mean?

5. Why is plainness traditional in American advertising language?

6. Why does Boorstin use the word *parable* in paragraph 23? Is he using the word conventionally, or does he have a special meaning for it?

7. What is folk culture? How does American folk culture differ from that found in Western Europe? Why is folk culture so important to Boorstin's analysis?

**Questions
on Structure
and Style**

8. Where does Boorstin state his thesis? Why doesn't he state it immediately?

9. Explain how paragraphs 14 through 18 are related. Why do they function as a short essay in themselves?

10. Boorstin is always careful to provide smooth, strong transitions. Circle the transitions in paragraphs 14 through 18.

11. Describe Boorstin's tone. How does this tone affect our impression of him as an authority on his subject?

Assignments

1. Boorstin's essay is a model of careful structure. Outline the essay, revealing its parts and their relationships.

2. Boorstin identifies six qualities of American advertising. List these qualities, and then cite two or three specific examples of each. (Finding examples is easy; as Boorstin points out, one quality of American advertising is ubiquity.) An effective way to conduct research is to work in groups, perhaps dividing up the search for examples.

3. According to Boorstin, American folk culture originates in advertising, and this separates us from other societies. What constitutes the folk culture of your own life? (Review Boorstin's analysis of this term before answering.) Do the elements of your personal folk culture originate in advertising, as Boorstin claims? Respond in an essay.

Weasel Words:
God's Little Helpers

Carl P. Wrighter

The following selection is from Carl P. Wrighter's *I Can Sell You Anything*. The book title sets an unmistakable tone, one that Wrighter, an ad writer, maintains consistently as he argues that advertising language "makes you hear things that aren't being said, accept as truths things that have only been implied, and believe things that have only been suggested." We're manipulated, Wrighter claims, because we allow ourselves to be, and he offers his detailed catalogue of weasels to prove his point.

---

1   First of all, you know what a weasel is, right? It's a small, slimy animal that eats small birds and other animals, and is especially fond of devouring vermin. Now, consider for a moment the kind of winning personality he must have. I mean, what kind of a guy would get his jollies eating rats and mice? Would you invite him to a party? Take him home to meet your mother? This is one of the slyest and most cunning of all creatures; sneaky, slippery, and thoroughly obnoxious. And so it is with great and warm personal regard for these attributes that we humbly award this King of All Devious the honor of bestowing his name upon our golden sword: the weasel word.

2   A weasel word is "a word used in order to evade or retreat from a direct or forthright statement or position" (Webster). In other words, if we can't say it, we'll weasel it. And, in fact, a weasel word has become more than just an evasion or retreat. We've trained our weasels. They can do anything. They can make you hear things that aren't being said, accept as truths things that have only been implied, and believe things that have only been suggested. Come to think of it, not only do we have our weasels trained, but they, in turn, have got you trained. When *you* hear a weasel word, you automatically hear the implication. Not the real meaning, but the meaning *it* wants *you* to hear. So if you're ready for a little reeducation, let's take a good look under a strong light at the two kinds of weasel words.

378

Words That Mean Things They Really Don't Mean

Help

3   That's it. "Help." It means "aid" or "assist." Nothing more. Yet, "help" is the one single word which, in all the annals of advertising, has done the most to say something that couldn't be said. Because "help" is the great qualifier; once you say it, you can say almost anything after it. In short, "help" has helped help us the most.

Helps keep you young.
Helps prevent cavities.
Helps keep your house germ-free.

4   "Help" qualifies everything. You've never heard anyone say, "This product will keep you young," or "This toothpaste will positively prevent cavities for all time." Obviously, we can't say anything like that, because there aren't any products like that made. But by adding that one little word, "help," in front, we can use the strongest language possible afterward. And the most fascinating part of it is, you are immune to the word. You literally don't hear the word "help." You only hear what comes after it. And why not? That's strong language, and likely to be much more important to you than the silly little word at the front end.

5   I would guess that 75 percent of all advertising uses the word "help." Think, for a minute, about how many times each day you hear these phrases:

Helps stop . . .
Helps prevent . . .
Helps fight . . .
Helps overcome . . .
Helps you feel . . .
Helps you look . . .

I could go on and on, but so could you. Just as a simple exercise, call it homework if you wish, tonight when you plop down in front of the boob tube for your customary three and a half hours of violence and/or situation comedies, take a pad and pencil, and keep score. See if you can count how many times the word "help" comes up during the commercials. Instead of going to the bathroom during the pause before Marcus Welby operates, or raiding the refrigerator prior to witnessing the Mod Squad wipe out a nest of dope pushers, stick with it. Count the "helps," and discover just how dirty a four-letter word can be.

Like

6 Coming in second, but only losing by a nose, is the word "like," used in comparison. Watch:

It's like getting one bar free.
Cleans like a white tornado.
It's like taking a trip to Portugal.

7   Okay. "Like" is a qualifier, and is used in much the same way as "help." But "like" is also a comparative element, with a very specific purpose; we use "like" to get you to stop thinking about the product per se, and to get you thinking about something that is bigger or better or different from the product we're selling. In other words, we can make you believe that the product is more than it is by likening it to something else.

8   Take a look at that first phrase, straight out of recent Ivory Soap advertising. On the surface of it, they tell you that four bars of Ivory cost about the same as three bars of most other soaps. So, if you're going to spend a certain amount of money on soap, you can buy four bars instead of three. Therefore, it's like getting one bar free. Now, the question you have to ask yourself is, "Why the weasel? Why do they say 'like'? Why don't they just come out and say, 'You get one bar free'?" The answer is, of course, that for one reason or another, you really don't. Here are two possible reasons. One: sure, you get four bars, but in terms of the actual amount of soap that you get, it may very well be the same as in three bars of another brand. Remember, Ivory has a lot of air in it—that's what makes it float. And air takes up room. Room that could otherwise be occupied by more soap. So, in terms of pure product, the amount of actual soap in four bars of Ivory may be only as much as the actual amount of soap in three bars of most others. That's why we can't—or won't—come out with a straightforward declaration such as, "You get 25 percent more soap," or "Buy three bars, and get the fourth one free."

9   Reason number two: the actual cost and value of the product. Did it ever occur to you that Ivory may simply be a cheaper soap to make and, therefore, a cheaper soap to sell? After all, it doesn't have any perfume or hexachlorophene, or other additives that can raise the cost of manufacturing. It's plain, simple, cheap soap, and so it can be sold for less money while still maintaining a profit margin as great as more expensive soaps. By way of illustrating this, suppose you were trying to decide whether to buy a Mercedes-Benz or a Ford. Let's say the Mercedes cost $7,000, and the Ford $3,500. Now the Ford salesman comes up to you with this deal: as long as you're considering spending $7,000 on a car, buy my Ford for

$7,000 and I'll give you a second Ford, free! Well, the same principle can apply to Ivory: as long as you're considering spending 35 cents on soap, buy my cheaper soap, and I'll give you more of it.

10   I'm sure there are other reasons why Ivory uses the weasel "like." Perhaps you've thought of one or two yourself. That's good. You're starting to think.

11   Now, what about that wonderful white tornado? Ajax pulled that one out of the hat some eight years ago, and you're still buying it. It's a classic example of the use of the word "like" in which we can force you to think, not about the product itself, but about something bigger, more exciting, certainly more powerful than a bottle of fancy ammonia. The word "like" is used here as a transfer word, which gets you away from the obvious—the odious job of getting down on your hands and knees and scrubbing your kitchen floor—and into the world of fantasy, where we can imply that this little bottle of miracles will supply all the elbow grease you need. Isn't that the name of the game? The whirlwind activity of the tornado replacing the whirlwind motion of your arm? Think about the swirling of the tornado, and all the work it will save you. Think about the power of that devastating windstorm; able to lift houses, overturn cars, and now, pick the dirt up off your floor. And we get the license to do it simply by using the word "like."

12   It's a copywriter's dream, because we don't have to substantiate anything. When we compare our product to "another leading brand," we'd better be able to prove what we say. But how can you compare ammonia to a windstorm? It's ludicrous. It can't be done. The whole statement is so ridiculous it couldn't be challenged by the government or the networks. So it went on the air, and it worked. Because the little word "like" let us take you out of the world of reality, and into your own fantasies.

13   Speaking of fantasies, how about the trip to Portugal? Mateus Rosé is actually trying to tell you that you will be transported clear across the Atlantic Ocean merely by sipping their wine. "Oh, come on," you say. "You don't expect me to believe that." Actually, we don't expect you to believe it. But we do expect you to get our meaning. This is called "romancing the product," and it is made possible by the dear little "like." In this case, we deliberately bring attention to the word, and we ask you to join us in setting reality aside for a moment. We take your hand and gently lead you down the path of moonlit nights, graceful dancers, and mysterious women. Are we saying that these things are all contained inside our wine? Of course not. But what we mean is, our wine is part of all this, and with a little help from "like," we'll get you to feel that way, too. So don't think of us as a bunch of peasants squashing a bunch of grapes. As a matter of fact, don't think of us at all. Feel with us.

14   "Like" is a virus that kills. You'd better get immune to it.

Other Weasels

15   "Help" and "like" are the two weasels so powerful that they can stand on their own. There are countless other words, not quite so potent, but equally effective when used in conjunction with our two basic weasels, or with each other. Let me show you a few.

16   *Virtual* or *virtually.*   How many times have you responded to an ad that said:

Virtually trouble-free . . .
Virtually foolproof . . .
Virtually never needs service . . .

Ever remember what "virtual" means? It means "in essence or effect, but not in fact." Important—"but not in fact." Yet today the word "virtually" is interpreted by you as meaning "almost or just about the same as. . . ." Well, gang, it just isn't true. "Not," in fact, means not, in fact. I was scanning, rather longingly I must confess, through the brochure Chevrolet publishes for its Corvette, and I came to this phrase: "The seats in the 1972 Corvette are virtually handmade." They had me, for a minute. I almost took the bait of that lovely little weasel. I almost decided that those seats were just about completely handmade. And then I remembered. Those seats were not, *in fact*, handmade. Remember, "virtually" means "not, in fact," or you will, in fact, get sold down the river.

17   *Acts* or *works.*   These two action words are rarely used alone, and are generally accompanied by "like." They need help to work, mostly because they are verbs, but their implied meaning is deadly, nonetheless. Here are the key phrases:

Acts like . . .
Acts against . . .
Works like . . .
Works against . . .
Works to prevent (or help prevent) . . .

You see what happens? "Acts" or "works" brings an action to the product that might not otherwise be there. When we say that a certain cough syrup "acts on the cough control center," the implication is that the syrup goes to this mysterious organ and immediately makes it better. But the implication here far exceeds what the truthful promise should be. An act is simply a deed. So the claim "acts on" simply means it performs a deed on. What that deed is, we may never know.

18   The rule of thumb is this: if we can't say "cures" or "fixes" or use any other positive word, we'll nail you with "acts like" or "works against," and get you thinking about something else. Don't.

Miscellaneous Weasels

19   *Can be.*   This is for comparison, and what we do is to find an announcer who can really make it sound positive. But keep your ears open. "Crest can be of significant value when used in . . . ," etc., is indicative of an ideal situation, and most of us don't live in ideal situations.

20   *Up to.*   Here's another way of expressing an ideal situation. Remember the cigarette that said it was aged, or "cured for up to eight long, lazy weeks"? Well, that could, and should, be interpreted as meaning that the tobaccos used were cured anywhere from one hour to eight weeks. We like to glamorize the ideal situation; it's up to you to bring it back to reality.

21   *As much as.*   More of the same. "As much as 20 percent greater mileage" with our gasoline again promises the ideal, but qualifies it.

22   *Refreshes, comforts, tackles, fights, comes on.*   Just a handful of the same action weasels, in the same category as "acts" and "works," though not as frequently used. The way to complete the thought here is to ask the simple question, "How?" Usually, you won't get an answer. That's because, usually, the weasel will run and hide.

23   *Feel* or *the feel of.*   This is the first of our subjective weasels. When we deal with a subjective word, it is simply a matter of opinion. In our opinion, Naugahyde has the feel of real leather. So we can say it. And, indeed, if you were to touch leather, and then touch Naugahyde, you may very well agree with us. But that doesn't mean it is real leather, only that it feels the same. The best way to handle subjective weasels is to complete the thought yourself, by simply saying, "But it isn't." At least that way you can remain grounded in reality.

24   *The look of* or *looks like.*   "Look" is the same as "feel," our subjective opinion. Did you ever walk into a Woolworth's and see those $29.95 masterpieces hanging in their "Art Gallery"? "The look of a real oil painting," it will say. "But it isn't," you will now reply. And probably be $29.95 richer for it.

Words That Have No Specific Meaning

25   If you have kids, then you have all kinds of breakfast cereals in the house. When I was a kid, it was Rice Krispies, the breakfast cereal that went snap, crackle, and pop. (One hell of a claim for a product that is supposed to offer nutritional benefits.) Or Wheaties, the breakfast of champions, whatever that means. Nowadays, we're forced to a confrontation with Quisp, Quake, Lucky-Stars, Cocoa-Puffs, Clunkers, Blooies, Snarkles, and Razzmatazz. And they all have one thing in common: they're all "fortified." Some are simply "fortified with vitamins," while others are specifically "fortified with vitamin D," or some other letter. But what does it all mean?

26   "Fortified" means "added on to." But "fortified," like so many other weasel words of indefinite meaning, simply doesn't tell us enough. If, for instance, a cereal were to contain one unit of vitamin D, and the manufacturers added some chemical which would produce two units of vitamin D, they could then claim that the cereal was "fortified with twice as much vitamin D." So what? It would still be about as nutritional as sawdust.

27   The point is, weasel words with no specific meaning don't tell us enough, but we have come to accept them as factual statements closely associated with something good that has been done to the product. Here's another example.

Enriched

28   We use this one when we have a product that starts out with nothing. You mostly find it in bread, where the bleaching process combined with the chemicals used as preservatives renders the loaves totally void of anything but filler. So the manufacturer puts a couple of drops of vitamins into the batter, and presto! It's enriched. Sounds great when you say it. Looks great when you read it. But what you have to determine is, is it really great? Figure out what information is missing, and then try to supply that information. The odds are, you won't. Even the breakfast cereals that are playing it straight, like Kellogg's Special K, leave something to be desired. They tell you what vitamins you get, and how much of each in one serving. The catch is, what constitutes a serving? They say, one ounce. So now you have to whip out your baby scale and weigh one serving. Do you have an idea how much that is? Maybe you do. Maybe you don't care. Okay, so you polish off this mound of dried stuff, and now what? You have ostensibly received the minimum, repeat, minimum dosage of certain vitamins for the day. One day. And you still have to go find the vitamins you didn't get. Try looking it up on a box of frozen peas. Bet you won't find it. But do be alert to "fortified" and "enriched." Asking the right questions will prove beneficial.

29   Did you buy that last sentence? Too bad, because I weaseled you, with the word "beneficial." Think about it.

Flavor and *Taste*

30   These are two totally subjective words that allow us to claim marvelous things about products that are edible. Every cigarette in the world has claimed the best taste. Every supermarket has advertised the most flavorful meat. And let's not forget "aroma," a subdivision of this category. Wouldn't you like to have a nickel for every time a room freshener (a weasel in itself) told you it would make your home "smell fresh as all outdoors"? Well, they can say it, because smell, like taste and flavor, is a subjective thing. And, incidentally, there are no less than three weasels in that phrase. "Smell" is the first. Then, there's "as" (a substitute for the ever-popular "like"), and, finally, "fresh," which, in context, is a subjective comparison, rather than the primary definition of "new."

31   Now we can use an unlimited number of combinations of these weasels for added impact. "Fresher-smelling clothes." "Fresher-tasting tobacco." "Tastes like grandma used to make." Unfortunately, there's no sure way of bringing these weasels down to size, simply because you can't define them accurately. Trying to ascertain the meaning of "taste" in any context is like trying to push a rope up a hill. All you can do is be aware that these words are subjective, and represent only one opinion—usually that of the manufacturer.

Style and *Good Looks*

32   Anyone for buying a new car? Okay, which is the one with the good looks? The smart new styling? What's that you say? All of them? Well, you're right. Because this is another group of subjective opinions. And it is the subjective and collective opinion of both Detroit and Madison Avenue that the following cars have "bold new styling": Buick Riviera, Plymouth Satellite, Dodge Monaco, Mercury Brougham, and you can fill in the spaces for the rest. Subjectively, you have to decide on which bold new styling is, indeed, bold new styling. Then, you might spend a minute or two trying to determine what's going on under that styling. The rest I leave to Ralph Nader.

Different, Special, and *Exclusive*

33   To be different, you have to be not the same as. Here, you must rely on your own good judgment and common sense. Exclusive formulas and special combinations of ingredients are coming at you every day, in every way. You must constantly assure yourself that, basically, all products in any given category are the same. So when you hear "special," "exclusive,"

or "different," you have to establish two things: on what basis are they different, and is that difference an important one? Let me give you a hypothetical example.

34   All so-called "permanent" antifreeze is basically the same. It is made from a liquid known as ethylene glycol, which has two amazing properties: It has a lower freezing point than water, and a higher boiling point than water. It does not break down (lose its properties), nor will it boil away. And every permanent antifreeze starts with it as a base. Also, just about every antifreeze has now got antileak ingredients, as well as antirust and anticorrosion ingredients. Now, let's suppose that, in formulating the product, one of the companies comes up with a solution that is pink in color, as opposed to all the others, which are blue. Presto—an exclusivity claim. "Nothing else looks like it, nothing else performs like it." Or how about, "Look at ours, and look at anyone else's. You can see the difference our exclusive formula makes." Granted, I'm exaggerating. But did I prove a point?

A Few More Goodies

35   At Phillips 66, it's performance that counts.

Wisk puts its strength where the dirt is.

At Bird's Eye, we've got quality in our corner.

Delicious and long-lasting, too.

Very quickly now, let's deflate those four lines. First, what the hell does "performance" mean? It means that this product will do what any other product in its category will do. Kind of a backhanded reassurance that this gasoline will function properly in your car. That's it, and nothing more. To perform means to function at a standard consistent with the rest of the industry. All products in a category are basically the same.

36   Second line: What does "strength" or "strong" mean? Does it mean "not weak"? Or "superior in power"? No, it means consistent with the norms of the business. You can bet your first-born that if Wisk were superior in power to other detergents, they'd be saying it, loud and clear. So strength is merely a description of a property inherent in all similar products in its class. If you really want to poke a pin in a bubble, substitute the word "ingredients" for the word "strength." That'll do it every time.

37   Third line: The old "quality" claim, and you fell for it. "Quality" is not a comparison. In order to do that, we'd have to say, "We've got better quality in our corner than any other frozen food." Quality relates only to the subjective opinion that Bird's Eye has of its own products, and to which it is entitled. The word "quality" is what we call a "parity"

statement; that is, it tells you that it is as good as any other. Want a substitute? Try "equals," meaning "the same as."

38   Fourth line: How delicious is delicious? About the same as good-tasting
is good-tasting, or fresher-smelling is fresher-smelling. A subjective opinion regarding taste, which you can either accept or reject. More fun,
though, is "long-lasting." You might want to consider writing a note to
Mr. Wrigley, inquiring as to the standard length of time which a piece of
gum is supposed to last. Surely there must be a guideline covering it. The
longest lasting piece of gum I ever encountered lasted just over four hours,
which is the amount of time it took me to get it off the sole of my shoe. Try
expressing the line this way: "It has a definite taste, and you may chew it
as long as you wish." Does that place it in perspective?

39   There are two other aspects of weasel words that I should mention here.
The first one represents the pinnacle of the copywriter's craft, and I call it
the "Weasel of Omission." Let me demonstrate:

Of America's best-tasting gums, Trident is sugar-free.

40   Disregard, for a moment, the obvious subjective weasel "best-tasting."
Look again at the line. Something has been left out. Omitted very deliberately. Do you know what that word is? The word that's missing is the word
"only," which should come right before the name of the product. But it
doesn't. It's gone. Left out. And the question is, why? The answer is, the
government wouldn't let them. You see, they start out by making a subjective judgment, that their gum is among the best-tasting. That's fine, as far
as it goes. That's their opinion, but it is also the opinion of every other
maker of sugar-free gum that his product is also among the best-tasting.
And, since both of their opinions must be regarded as having equal value,
neither one is allowed the superiority claim, which is what the word
"only" would do. So Trident left it out. But the sentence is so brilliantly
constructed, the word "only" is so heavily implied, that most people hear
it, even though it hasn't been said. That's the Weasel of Omission. Constructing a set of words that forces you to a conclusion that otherwise could
not have been drawn. Be on the lookout for what isn't said, and try to fill
the gaps realistically.

41   The other aspect of weasels is the use of all those great, groovy, swing-
ing, wonderful, fantastic, exciting and fun-filled words known as adjectives. Your eyes, ears, mind, and soul have been bombarded by adjectives
for so long that you are probably numb to most of them by now. If I were to
give you a list of adjectives to look out for it, it would require the next five
hundred pages, and it wouldn't do any good, anyway. More important is
to bear in mind what adjectives do, and then to be able to sweep them
aside and distinguish only the facts.

42   An adjective modifies a noun, and is generally used to denote the quality or a quality of the thing named. And that's our grammar lesson for today. Realistically, an adjective enhances or makes more of the product being discussed. It's the difference between "Come visit Copenhagen," and "Come visit beautiful Copenhagen." Adjectives are used so freely these days that we feel almost naked, robbed, if we don't get at least a couple. Try speaking without adjectives. Try describing something; you can't do it. The words are too stark, too bare-boned, too factual. And that's the key to judging advertising. There is a direct, inverse proportion between the number of adjectives and the number of facts. To put it succinctly, the more adjectives we use, the less we have to say.

43   You can almost make a scale, based on that simple mathematical premise. At one end you have cosmetics, soft drinks, cigarettes, products that have little or nothing of any value to say. So we get them all dressed up with lavish word and thought images, and present you with thirty or sixty seconds of adjectival puffery. The other end of the scale is much harder to find. Usually, it will be occupied by a new product that is truly new or different. . . . Our craving for adjectives has become so overriding that we simply cannot listen to what is known as "nuts and bolts" advertising. The rest falls somewhere in the middle; a combination of adjectives, weasels, and semitruths. All I can tell you is, try to brush the description aside, and see what's really at the bottom.

Summary

44   A weasel word is a word that's used to imply a meaning that cannot be truthfully stated. Some weasels imply meanings that are not the same as their actual definition, such as "help," "like," or "fortified." They can act as qualifiers and/or comparatives. Other weasels, such as "taste" and "flavor," have no definite meanings, and are simply subjective opinions offered by the manufacturer. A weasel of omission is one that implies a claim so strongly that it forces you to supply the bogus fact. Adjectives are weasels used to convey feelings and emotions to a greater extent than the product itself can.

45   In dealing with weasels, you must strip away the innuendos and try to ascertain the facts, if any. To do this, you need to ask questions such as: How? Why? How many? How much? Stick to basic definitions of words. Look them up if you have to. Then, apply the strict definition to the text of the advertisement or commercial. "Like" means similar to, but not the same as. "Virtually" means the same in essence, but not in fact.

46   Above all, never underestimate the devious qualities of a weasel. Weasels twist and turn and hide in dark shadows. You must come to grips with them, or advertising will rule you forever.

47   My advice to you is: Beware of weasels. They are nasty and untrainable, and they attack pocketbooks.

1. Where does Wrighter define *weasel words?* According to Wrighter, each of the following is a "weasel": *help, like, virtual, acts, can be, up to, as much as.* Why does Wrighter include each in his list?

2. What is a "Weasel of Omission"?

3. In what ways can adjectives function as weasels?

4. Wrighter refers to "romancing the product" (paragraph 13). What does this phrase mean? What can we infer about people who would construct such a term to express what this one does?

5. What are "subjective weasels"?

6. Wrighter states in paragraph 28, "Asking the right questions will prove beneficial." What point is he illustrating?

7. Wrighter obviously relishes the power of language. Mark places where we hear Wrighter taking particular delight in the sound of his own language.

8. Wrighter says in his conclusion, "You must come to grips with them [weasel words], or they will rule you forever." Is the author overstating this case in using a word like *rule?*

9. Wrighter performs several interesting rhetorical feats in his introduction. Look closely at his first two paragraphs, and comment on his use of *and* to begin sentences, his use of parallel structure, and the relationship he creates between the two paragraphs that make up the introduction.

10. How would you describe Wrighter's tone? What relationship does he establish with his audience, and how does he establish it?

11. How does Wrighter use the conclusion to make his essay come full circle?

Assignments

1. During the next few days, write down some of the weasel words that you hear in television commercials. Do the same for weasels that you find in print ads. Do you notice any weasels that Wrighter omits?

2. Wrighter's writing style is distinctive. In a short essay, describe his style, and explain why you believe his style helps or hinders him in arguing his case convincingly.

3. Imagine that you work as an ad writer. Your task is to compose the copy (that is, the printed words) for an ad publicizing the virtues of one of your college courses. Compose the ad copy, using whatever weasels are appropriate.

It's Natural! It's Organic!
Or Is It?

Consumer Reports

Consumer Reports, published by Consumers Union, comments on the quality and performance of consumer products and also discusses consumer issues. Here, *Consumer Reports* investigates the word *natural* and the food industry's discovery of the word as a marketing tool. *Natural* carries weight with buyers today, but for advertisers, *natural* apparently means greater sales and little else.

1   "No artificial flavors or colors!" reads the Nabisco advertisement in *Progressive Grocer*, a grocery trade magazine. "And research shows that's exactly what consumers are eager to buy."

2   The ad, promoting Nabisco's *Sesame Wheats* as "a natural whole wheat cracker," might raise a few eyebrows among thoughtful consumers of Nabisco's *Wheat Thins* and *Cheese Nips*, which contain artificial colors, or of its *Ginger Snaps* and *Oreo Cookies*, which have artificial flavors. But Nabisco has not suddenly become a champion of "natural" foods. Like other giants of the food industry, the company is merely keeping its eye on what will produce a profit.

3   Nabisco's trade ad, which was headlined "A Natural for Profits," is simply a routine effort by a food processor to capitalize on the concerns that consumers have about the safety of the food they buy.

4   Supermarket shelves are being flooded with "natural" products, some of them containing a long list of chemical additives. And some products that never did contain additives have suddenly sprouted "natural" or "no preservative" labels. Along with the new formulations and labels have come higher prices, since the food industry has realized that consumers are willing to pay more for products they think are especially healthful.

5   The mass merchandising of "natural" foods is a spillover onto supermarket shelves of a phenomenon once confined to health-food stores, as major food manufacturers enter what was once the exclusive territory of small entrepreneurs. Health-food stores were the first to foster and capitalize on the growing consumer interest in nutrition and are still thriving. Along with honey-sweetened snacks, "natural" vitamins, and other "natural" food products, the health-food stores frequently feature "organic" produce and other "organic" foods.

6   Like the new merchandise in supermarkets, the products sold at health-food stores carry the implication that they're somehow better for you— safer or more nutritious. In this report, we'll examine that premise, looking

at both "natural" foods, which are widely sold, and "organic" foods, which are sold primarily at health-food stores. While the terms "natural" and "organic" are often used loosely, "organic" generally refers to the way food is grown (without pesticides or chemical fertilizers) and "natural" to the character of the ingredients (no preservatives or artificial additives) and to the fact that the food product has undergone minimal processing.

7   *Langendorf Natural Lemon Flavored Creme Pie* contains no cream. It does contain sodium propionate, certified food colors, sodium benzoate, and vegetable gum.

8   That's natural?

9   Yes indeed, says L. A. Cushman, Jr., chairman of American Bakeries Co., the Chicago firm that owns Langendorf. The word "natural," he explains, modifies "lemon flavored," and the pie contains oil from lemon rinds. "The lemon flavor," Cushman states, "comes from natural lemon flavor as opposed to artificial lemon flavor, assuming there is such a thing as artificial lemon flavor."

10   Welcome to the world of natural foods.

11   You can eat your "natural" way from one end of the supermarket to the other. Make yourself a sandwich of *Kraft Cracker Barrel Natural Cheddar Cheese* on *Better Way Natural Whole Grain Wheat Nugget Bread* spread with *Autumn Natural Margarine*. Wash it down with *Anheuser-Busch Natural Light Beer* or *Rich-Life Natural Orange NutriPop*. Snack on any number of brands of "natural" potato chips and "natural" candy bars. And don't exclude your pet: Feed your dog *Gravy Train Dog Food With Natural Beef Flavor* or, if it's a puppy, try *Blue Mountain Natural Style Puppy Food*.

12   The "natural" bandwagon doesn't end at the kitchen. You can bathe in *Batherapy Natural Mineral Bath* (sodium sesquicarbonate, isopropyl myristate, fragrance, D & C Green No. 5, D & C Yellow No. 10 among its ingredients), using *Queen Helene "All-Natural" Amino Peptide Shampoo* (propylene glycol, hydroxyethyl cellulose, methylparaben, D & C Red No. 3, D & C Brown No. 1) and *Organic Aid Natural Clear Soaps*. Then, if you're so inclined, you can apply *Naturade Conditioning Mascara with Natural Protein* (stearic acid, PVP, butylene glycol, sorbitan sesquioleate, triethanolamine, imidazolidinyl urea, methylparaben, propylparaben).

13   At its ridiculous extreme, the "natural" ploy extends to furniture, cigarettes, denture adhesives, and shoes.

The Selling of a Word

14   The word "natural" does not have to be synonymous with "ripoff." Over the years, the safety of many food additives has been questioned. And a consumer who reads labels carefully can in fact find some foods in supermarkets that have been processed without additives.

15   But the word "natural" does not guarantee that. All too often, as the above examples indicate, the word is used more as a key to higher profits. Often, it implies a health benefit that does not really exist.

16   *Co-op News*, the publication of the Berkeley Co-op, the nation's largest consumer-cooperative store chain, reported on "two 15-ounce cans of tomato sauce, available side-by-side" at one of its stores. One sauce, called *Health Valley*, claimed on its label to have "no citric acid, no sugars, no preservatives, no artificial colors or flavors." There were none of those ingredients in the Co-op's house brand, either, but their absence was hardly worth noting on the label, since canned tomato sauce almost never contains artificial colors or flavors and doesn't need preservatives after being heated in the canning process. The visible difference between the two products was price, not ingredients. The *Health Valley* tomato sauce was selling for 85 cents; the Co-op house brand, for only 29 cents.

17   One supermarket industry consultant estimates that 7 percent of all processed food products now sold are touted as "natural." And that could be just the beginning. A Federal Trade Commission report noted that 63 percent of people polled in a survey agreed with the statement, "Natural foods are more nutritious than other foods." Thirty-nine percent said they regularly buy food because it is "natural," and 47 percent said they are willing to pay 10 percent more for a food that is "natural."

18   According to those who have studied the trend, the consumer's desire for "natural" foods goes beyond the fear of specific chemicals. "There is a mistrust of technology," says Howard Moskowitz, a taste researcher and consultant to the food industry. "There is a movement afoot to return to simplicity in all aspects of life." A spokeswoman for Lever Bros., one of the nation's major food merchandisers, adds: " 'Natural' is a psychological thing of everyone wanting to get out of the industrial world."

19   Because consumers are acting out of such vague, undefined feelings, they aren't sure what they should be getting when they buy a product labeled "natural." William Wittenberg, president of Grandma's Food Inc., comments: "Manufacturers and marketers are making an attempt to appeal to a consumer who feels he should be eating something natural, but doesn't know why. I think the marketers of the country in effect mirror back to the people what they want to hear. People have to look to themselves for their own protection." Grandma's makes a *Whole Grain Date Filled Fruit 'n Oatmeal Bar* labeled "naturally Good Flavor." The ingredients include "artificial flavor."

Is "Natural" Better?

20   "Natural" foods are not necessarily preferable nor, as we have seen, necessarily natural.

21   Consider "natural" potato chips. They are often cut thick from unpeeled potatoes, packaged without preservatives in heavy foil bags with fancy lettering, and sold at a premium price. Sometimes, such chips include "sea salt," a product whose advantage over conventional "land" salt has not been demonstrated. The packaging is intended to give the impression that "natural" potato chips are less of a junk food than regular chips. But nutritionally there is no difference. Both are made from the same food, the potato, and both have been processed so that they are high in salt and in calories.

22   Sometimes the "natural" products may have ingredients you'd prefer to avoid. *Quaker 100% Natural* cereal, for example, contains 24 percent sugars, a high percentage, considering it's not promoted as a sugared cereal. (*Kellogg's Corn Flakes* has 7.8 percent sugar.) Many similar "natural" granola-type cereals have oil added, giving them a much higher fat content than conventional cereals.

23   Taste researcher Moskowitz notes that food processors are "trying to signal to the consumer a sensory impact that can be called natural." Two of the most popular signals, says Moskowitz, are honey and coconut. But honey is just another sugar, with no significant nutrients other than calories, and coconut is especially high in saturated fats.

24   While many processed foods are less nutritious than their fresh counterparts, processing can sometimes help foods: Freezing preserves nutrients that can be lost if fresh foods are not consumed quickly; pasteurization kills potentially dangerous bacteria in milk. Some additives are also both safe and useful. Sorbic acid, for instance, prevents the growth of potentially harmful molds in cheese and other products, and sodium benzoate has been used for more than 70 years to prevent the growth of microorganisms in acidic foods.

25   "Preservative" has become a dirty word, to judge from the number of "no preservative" labels on food products. Calcium propionate might sound terrible on a bread label, but this mildew-retarding substance occurs naturally in both raisins and Swiss cheese. "Bread without preservatives could well cost you more than bread with them," says Vernal S. Packard, Jr., a University of Minnesota nutrition professor. "Without preservatives, the bread gets stale faster; it may go moldy with the production of hazardous aflatoxin. And already we in the United States return [to producers] 100 million pounds of bread each year—this in a world nagged by hunger and malnutrition."

26   Nor are all "natural" substances safe. Sassafras tea was banned by the U.S. Food and Drug Administration several years ago because it contains safrole, which has produced liver cancer in laboratory animals. Kelp, a seaweed that is becoming increasingly fashionable as a dietary supplement, can have a high arsenic content. Aflatoxin, produced by a mold that can grow on improperly stored peanuts, corn, and grains, is a known carcinogen.

27   To complicate matters, our palates have become attuned to many unnatural tastes. "We don't have receptors on our tongues that signal 'natural,' " says taste researcher Moskowitz. He points out, for instance, that a
panel of consumers would almost certainly reject a natural lemonade "in
favor of a lemonade scientifically designed to taste natural. If you put real
lemon, sugar, and water together, people would reject it as harsh. They are
used to flavors developed by flavor houses." Similarly, Moskowitz points
out, many consumers say that for health reasons they prefer less salty
food—but the results of various taste tests have contradicted this, too.

The Tactics of Deception

28   In the midst of all this confusion, it's not surprising that the food industry
is having a promotional field day. Companies are using various tactics to
convince the consumer that a food product is "natural"—and hence preferable. Here are some of the most common:

29   *The indeterminate modifier.* Use a string of adjectives and claim that "natural" modifies only the next adjective in line, not the product itself. Take
Pillsbury Natural Chocolate Flavored Chocolate Chip Cookies. Many a buyer
might be surprised to learn from the fine print that these cookies contain
artificial flavor, as well as the chemical antioxidant BHA. But Pillsbury
doesn't bat an eyelash at this. "We're not trying to mislead anybody," says
a company representative, explaining that the word "natural" modifies
only "chocolate flavored," while the artificial flavoring is vanilla. Then
why not call the product "Chocolate Chip Cookies with Natural Chocolate
Flavoring"? "From a labeling point of view, we're trying to use a limited
amount of space" was the answer.

30   *Innocence by association.* Put nature on your side. *Life Cinnamon Flavor High
Protein Cereal,* a Quaker Oats Co. product, contains BHA and artificial
color, among other things. How could the company imply the cereal was
"natural" and still be truthful? One series of *Life* boxes solves the problem
neatly. The back panel has an instructional lesson for children entitled
"Nature." The box uses the word "Nature" four times and "natural"
once—but never actually to describe the cereal inside. Other products
surround themselves with a "natural" aura by picturing outdoor or farm
scenes on their packages.

31   *The "printer's error."* From time to time, readers send us food wrappers
making a "natural" claim directly contradicted by the ingredients list. We
have, for example, received a batch of individually wrapped *Devonsheer*
crackers with a big red label saying: "A Natural Product, no preservatives."
The ingredients list includes "calcium propionate (to retard spoilage)."

32   How could a manufacturer defend that? "At a given printing, the printer
was instructed to remove 'no preservatives, natural product' when we

changed ingredients, but he didn't do it," says Curtis Marshall, vice president for operations at Devonsheer Melba Corp.

33   *The best defense.* Don't defend yourself; attack the competition. Sometimes the use of the word "natural" is, well, just plain unnatural. Take the battle that has been brewing between the nation's two largest beer makers, Miller Brewing Co. and Anheuser-Busch. The latter's product, *Anheuser-Busch Natural Light Beer*, has been the object of considerable derision by Miller.

34   Miller wants the word "natural" dropped from Anheuser-Busch's advertisements because beers are "highly processed, complex products, made with chemical additives and other components not in their natural form."

35   Anheuser-Busch has responded only with some digs at Miller, charging Miller with using artificial foam stabilizer and adding an industrial enzyme instead of natural malt to reduce the caloric content of its *Miller Lite* beer.

36   No victor has yet emerged from the great beer war, but the industry is obviously getting edgy.

37   "Other brewers say it's time for the two companies to shut up," the *Wall Street Journal* reported. "One thing they [the other brewers] are worried about, says William T. Elliot, president of C. Schmidt & Sons, a Philadelphia brewery, is all the fuss over ingredients. Publicity about that issue is disclosing to beer drinkers that their suds may include sulfuric acid, calcium sulfate, alginic acid, or amyloglucosidase."

38   *The negative pitch.* Point out in big letters on the label that the product doesn't contain something it wouldn't contain anyway. The "no artificial preservatives" label stuck on a jar of jam or jelly is true and always has been—since sugar is all the preservative jams and jellies need. Canned goods, likewise, are preserved in their manufacture—by the heat of the canning process. Then there is the "no cholesterol" claim of vegetable oils, margarines, and even (in a radio commercial) canned pineapple. Those are also true, but beside the point, since cholesterol is found only in animal products.

An Approach to Regulation

39   What can be done about such all-but-deceptive practices? One might suggest that the word "natural" is so vague as to be inherently deceptive, and therefore should not be available for promotional use. Indeed, the FTC staff suggested precisely that a few years ago but later backed away from the idea. The California legislature last year passed a weak bill defining the word "organic," but decided that political realities argued against tackling the word "natural."

40   "If we had included the word 'natural' in the bill, it most likely would not have gotten out of the legislature," says one legislative staff member.

"When you've got large economic interests in certain areas, the tendency is to guard those interests very carefully."

41   Under the revised FTC staff proposal, which had not been acted on by the full commission as we went to press, the word "natural" can be used if the product has undergone only minimal processing and doesn't have artificial ingredients. That would eliminate the outright frauds, as well as the labeling of such products as Lever Bros.' *Autumn Natural Margarine*, which obviously has been highly processed from its original vegetable-oil state. But the FTC proposal might run into difficulty in defining exactly what "minimal processing" means. And it would also allow some deceptive implications. For instance, a product containing honey might be called "natural," while a food with refined sugar might not, thus implying that honey is superior to other sugars, which it is not.

42   A law incorporating similar regulations went into effect in Maine at the beginning of this year [1980]. If a product is to be labeled "natural" and sold in Maine, it must have undergone only minimal processing and have no additives, preservatives, or refined additions such as white flour and sugar.

43   So far, according to John Michael, the state legislator who sponsored the bill, food companies have largely ignored the law, but he expects the state to start issuing warnings this summer.

Questions on Content

1. Is the article concerned only with the word *natural*, or does it have another subject as well?

2. Where does the article most clearly state its opinion of the food industry's use of *natural?*

3. Where does the article limit its discussion of *natural?*

4. Why is Howard Moskowitz (first mentioned in paragraph 18) quoted so often?

5. How is emphasis on "natural" foods part of a larger social trend?

6. Paragraph 19 focuses on Grandma's Food Inc. and quotes its president. What reason might there be for discussing this particular company?

7. Why is *natural* placed in quotation marks throughout the article?

**Questions
on Structure
and Style**

8. What is the function of paragraph 10? Of paragraph 20?

9. Paragraph 12 contains lists of chemical ingredients found in certain products. What effects do these lists create?

10. The article clearly takes a stand against deceptive use of the word *natural*. Which words and expressions in the article contribute to its unmistakable tone? How would you describe that tone?

Assignments

1. This article contains no true conclusion. Write a concluding paragraph, keeping in mind your answer to the first content question above.

2. The article discusses *natural* as it applies to food products, but *natural* can be an important word in many contexts. For example, we often say we want to look natural, or we describe certain types of undesirable behavior as unnatural. Think of a context in which the word *natural* has become important. In an essay, define the word as it is used in the context you've chosen, and give examples illustrating your definition. To help clarify your definition, you might contrast the correct use of *natural* with its incorrect use.

A Consumer's Guide
to Social Offenses

Stuart Berg Flexner

████████████

No one wants to be embarrassed, and—for a price—we needn't
be. Advertisers have devised a long list of distressing ailments
and conditions (usually described in manipulative terms) for
which they, of course, have correctives. In this essay, Stuart Berg
Flexner, co-author of the *Dictionary of American Slang* and chief
lexicographer of *The Oxford American Dictionary*, reviews the history of scare tactics in American advertising, detailing how effective advertisers have been in creating and popularizing language
that makes life's embarrassments profitable for manufacturers.

████████████

1   B.O., athlete's foot, and halitosis are unknown to most of the world outside the United States—not because other people don't suffer from them
but because the terms have been coined or popularized here by advertising
men. Since our 1840s patent medicine men, American advertisers have
used scare tactics to sell their wares. When there hasn't been a well-known
disease their products could cure they have often invented one or made a
merely socially embarrassing condition sound like a dread disease by giving it a name.

2   In 1895, C. W. Post introduced his all-grain brew Postum, claiming not
only that it made "red blood" but that it cured *coffee nerves*, a malady then
unknown both to doctors and to the general public, but which we have
been aware of ever since. Thus the advertisement for the cure gave birth to
the term, if not the ailment.

3   *Dandruff* (1545 in English, akin to Old Norse *hurf*, scab, scurf) and
psoriasis (1684 in English from the Greek *psōriasis*, to have the itch) are old
words and ailments that have been made part of the popular vocabulary by
the advertising of preparations to cure them. *Ringworm* (an English word of
about 1425) of the foot is also a real ailment though it was seldom mentioned until it was widely called *athlete's foot* (1928) when Absorbine Jr. first
advertised itself as a remedy for it. More recently, a manufacturer of a
preparation to relieve itching in the groin area has popularized the term
jock strap itch (mid 1970s, soon shortened by the public to *jock itch*) for this
ailment which, now that it has a pithy, masculine name, is also talked
about more than before.

4   *Halitosis* (an 1874 English word, from Latin *helitus*, breath, plus *-osis*,
condition, especially a pathological condition) was a little-known medical
word referring to specific breath odors that doctors could use to diagnose

The term *athlete's foot* was popularized in 1928 when Absorbine Jr. advertised itself as a cure for it. Before that, the antiseptic preparation had been advertised only as giving relief from muscular aches, bruises, burns, cuts, sprains, and sunburn. This ad appeared in 1930 (W. F. Young, Inc.).

patients' diseases until Listerine mouthwash ads claimed it fought "insidious *halitosis*" and defined it as bad breath in general, beginning in 1921 (for the first ten years Listerine ads followed the word *halitosis* with the explanation "bad breath" or "unpleasant breath" in parentheses, knowing full well that most people had never heard of the word before).

5   The worst social offense, however, was not scratching one's head, elbows, feet, or groin, or even having bad breath, but underarm odor, caused by underarm perspiration—and this was indeed offensive and widespread before the routine daily shower and home washing machine. By clogging the pores, masking the odor, or combining with the perspiration, various preparations could eliminate this offense. Such preparations became available and were widely advertised in the 1920s, the advertisements then mainly being aimed at women, both because sleeveless dresses were the style, making the odor more obvious, and because many men thought their own odor was somehow manly. Thus as early as 1924 liquid Odorono was advertised as a "perspiration corrective"—for both the underarms and the feet—whose protection could last for days. Its ads popularized a blunt new term, saying that when Odorono was used under the arms it would prevent *underarm odor*. Similar liquids and creams joined the war against underarm odor and underarm perspiration stains on clothing so that during the 1930s both women and men were removing the underarm *shields* they had added to their dresses and suits to absorb perspiration and using an *underarm deodorant*, often a cream such as Mum, whose early advertising slogan was the punning *Mum's the word*. Not until the 1960s did manufacturers call the all-too-vivid yet somewhat passive sounding *underarm deodorant* by the more active, scientific sounding name *anti-perspirant*, and now that almost everyone took daily showers, deemphasized underarm odor in favor of emphasizing that the product stopped *wetness*, a new euphemism for underarm clothing stains.

6   The hallmark of scare ads against underarm and other body perspiration odors, however, was Lifebuoy Health Soap's campaign. In 1933, millions of Americans began to laugh at and use the abbreviation *B.O.* to mean *body odor*, as popularized by the advertising of this orange-colored, peculiar-smelling (the ads said it had a "crisp odor"), oddly shaped bathsoap. Soon the two-note foghorn warning ^{B}o was known to everyone through radio ads—and Lifebuoy was the best-selling soap in America. By 1935, *body odor* was such an accepted term that Lux laundry soap was advertising that women should "Lux underthings after each wearing to wash away stale body odors."

7   With the success of *halitosis* and *body odor*, modern advertising continued to coin and popularize terms for both real and imaginary ailments and embarrassing conditions. In the 1930s and 40s there were ads for products which would help prevent everything from *irregularity* (a euphemism for constipation) to *pink toothbrush* (caused by bleeding gums), followed by ads

for products that could prevent that horror of horrors *tattletale gray* (left on laundry from using too mild a laundry soap), *dishpan hands* (in general use by 1944, red hands from using too strong a dishwashing soap), *tired blood* (from not having enough iron in one's diet), and, echoing the earlier "tattletale gray," *ring around the collar* (mid 1970s, from not using a liquid detergent that removed collar grime from shirts in a home washing machine).

8   If there was any doubt after the 1920s, 30s, and 40s that advertising could popularize a term, the history of *chlorophyll* set it to rest. Only scientists had heard of *chlorophyll* (from the Greek *chlor/chloro*, light green, greenish yellow, plus *-phyll/phyllo*, leaf), the green coloring matter in plants essential for photosynthesis, until the late 1940s, when the substance was first claimed to be able to "fight unwanted odors." Soon there were Nullo pills, advertised as a product that "kills body odors and bad breath . . . Safe as a lettuce leaf . . . contains nature's chlorophyll." Next came the 1951 ads for the lozengelike Clorets "makes breath kissing sweet . . . contains chlorophyll," and by 1952 a torrent of products advertising chlorophyll as their special ingredient, including at least 30 tablets and lozenges sold as breath sweeteners, 11 toothpastes and tooth powders, 9 chewing gums, 8 brands of dogfood, 4 mouthwashes (for humans), and one brand of cigarette. The chlorophyll fad began to fade the following year, though some of the products are still with us and the word has become a part of the general vocabulary, now found in all desk dictionaries and known to almost every school child from basic science classes.

Questions on Content

1. What are scare tactics in advertising? Why have American advertisers found them effective?

2. Why did advertisers appeal first to women in selling "underarm odor" preventatives?

3. Why does Flexner devote a complete paragraph to Lifebuoy soap? Why does he do the same for chlorophyll?

4. Does Flexner approve or disapprove of the advertising tactics he describes? How do we know?

5. What is the function of paragraph 3? How does it relate to paragraph 2?

6. As he moves between ideas, Flexner consistently provides smooth transitions. Circle transitional words and expressions in the article.

Assignments

1. Flexner's article has no true conclusion. Write a concluding paragraph, keeping Flexner's thesis in mind as you write.

2. Flexner traces the history of scare tactics used to sell cures for "real and imaginary ailments and embarrassing conditions" (paragraph 7). Think of other products designed for ailments and conditions of the type Flexner discusses ("feminine hygiene" products and carpet deodorants, for example), and write an essay explaining the role language plays in selling these products. Be sure to study actual advertisements before you write, and use the ads as source material in your essay.

Six Advertisements
for Analysis

Reprinted here are three advertisements for consumer goods and three examples of institutional and corporate advertising. The ads are as different in some ways as the products and organizations themselves; in other ways, they follow well-established advertising practice. They all were no doubt designed by professionals skilled at attracting audiences. Ads such as these are expensive to produce, and the manufacturers and organizations paying for them naturally believe that the ads will work. As you examine them, consider what the ads assume about their audiences, and look for both differences and similarities in their use of language as a marketing tool.

Only Sony could turn this simple idea into the most advanced CD changer around.

When Sony set out to create the world's most sophisticated CD changer, we looked no further than the carousel. A classic engineering design that has provided countless hours of entertainment for millions.

The result is the new Sony CDP-C70 DiscJockey® CD changer.

Its unique 5-disc carousel design uses less parts than conventional "magazine" type models. So not only do you get more reliable performance but the fastest disc to disc access time of any CD changer in the industry.

Which means spending a lot less time loading and unloading your discs. And more time listening.

The CDP-C70 also comes with the ultimate in convenience features. Like our exclusive Custom File Display. It remembers the location and title of each disc you've loaded into your CD changer. For up to 226 different discs! What's more, the C70 even lets you play the newest 3 inch discs without the need of an adapter. Add to this, 32 selection programmability and random track "Shuffle Play," and you'll have the maximum enjoyment of your

music. But the real beauty of these features is that they both can be controlled from the comfort of your chair with the supplied Remote Commander.®

Of course, the CDP-C70 is also endowed with some of the most sophisticated technology you've come to expect from The Leader in Digital Audio.™ Such as a 4x oversampling digital filter and dual D/A converters, for superb music reproduction.

Usually, most CD changers try to strike a balance between reliability, convenience and performance. But thanks to its ingenious design, only the Sony CDP-C70 delivers.

SONY®
THE LEADER IN DIGITAL AUDIO™

(Sony Corporation of America)

This ad originally appeared in *Digital Audio Magazine.*

"Then you'd like a Family Physician."

"I sure do like my doctor. You see, Family Physicians care for the *whole person.* Unlike doctors who specialize only in certain medical areas, Family Physicians give each patient personalized, overall health management. In other words, they specialize in *you.*"

No doctor can specialize in everything.

That's not possible. But Family Practice does prepare a doctor to work in all the major medical areas. Every day, Family Physicians care for hundreds of thousands of patients — from newborns to grandparents — dealing with almost every kind of health care need people have.

This *is* possible, because most of the needs you and your family normally have simply do not require more specialized knowledge in any one medical area than your Family Physician is qualified to provide.

In fact, Family Physicians need to refer patients to other specialists in only 10-15% of the cases.

Keeping up-to-date.

Required ongoing education means Family Physicians have to keep up-to-date in new treatments and technology. And Board Certified Family Physicians *must pass* recertification examinations every six years. These Family Practice requirements help to assure continuing quality care for you and your family.

Saving you money by specializing in you.

Since a Family Physician can handle most of the family's health care needs, it is normally more cost-efficient to have this one doctor than to have separate doctors for mom, dad and the children.

Another saving can result from the Family Physicians' emphasis on providing care in their offices. You will be hospitalized only when your Family Physician believes hospital services are essential to proper management of your care.

Obviously, the greatest economy of all comes from staying well, and Family Physicians really focus on preventive health care.

If you would like to have more information about Family Practice, or assistance in finding a Family Physician in your area, write to: *Family Physicians Care For America, P.O. Box 5311, Kansas City, MO 64131-0311.*

FAMILY PHYSICIAN
The one doctor who specializes in you.

This message sponsored by The American Board of Family Practice and The American Academy of Family Physicians.

(Courtesy of The American Board of Family Practice and The American Academy of Family Physicians)

This ad originally appeared in *Family Circle.*

Would you apply?

N ot likely. Not if you're a college graduate who could start in another field at what a teacher earns after 15 years on the job.
That's why America desperately needs teachers. One million teachers between now and 1990. By every measure, we're going to be several hundred thousand short.

Imagine if we were talking about a shortage of physicians and surgeons. A massive teacher shortage has just as serious consequences on our society. Who will be there to prepare future generations to enter all the professions if there aren't enough teachers to do the job?

Shortages already exist all across this country, because for years college students in droves have chosen not to become teachers. In 1967, 22% of all college freshmen planned on teaching. By 1985 only 6% of the students polled said they wanted to teach.

What keeps college students from wanting to be teachers?

First and foremost, pay.

Right now there are four million Americans certified to teach who aren't in the classroom. And one-quarter of all education graduates decided never to seek teaching jobs. Countless more considered education but decided not to make it their major.

America has lost a generation of teachers. To fill in the gaps, schools are using teachers out of the fields of expertise or uncertified teachers to make sure classrooms aren't empty. This severely hurts the education process and masks the severity of the teacher shortage.

In a recent gallup poll, commissioned by the NEA, 80% of the American people favor higher teacher salaries. Almost half of those surveyed—41%—said they are willing to pay higher taxes to see that teachers are paid properly.

Americans want it. America desperately needs it.

Qualified teachers, paid professional wages. So that becoming a teacher is once again a respected and valued choice.

nea
The Subject is Excellence.

This ad originally appeared in the *National Review*.

You know how it was as a kid. You stared at the sand long enough and out of the corner of your eye you spotted something no one else saw. And it was the catch of the day.

We look at the oil business like that. We can drill where everyone else does. Or we can use innovation to drill where no one has drilled before. We can build new refineries. Or we can apply new technology to the ones we have so they work more efficiently.

That's why we were one of the pioneers of the North Sea drilling venture known as Ekofisk. A city at sea, it was the first major oil field ever discovered in Western Europe.

We led the way in low-cost, high efficiency refining technology for the production of quality premium unleaded fuels. And when others saw no potential in bottom-of-the-barrel crude, we developed the process that refines it into high quality gasoline.

And below our offshore rigs, a thriving undersea world complete with mussels, starfish, and scallops tells our environmental story. They regard the structure as a natural reef, and we don't see any reason to tell them otherwise.

Like a child searching for treasure, when you're looking for the undiscovered it doesn't matter as much where you look as how wide you open your eyes.

For more information write to Patricia Marshall, Phillips Petroleum, 16D-4 Phillips Bldg., Bartlesville, OK 74004.

Phillips Petroleum Company
Performing to meet
the challenge of change.

IF YOU LOOK HARD ENOUGH, YOU'LL BE SURPRISED WHAT YOU MIGHT FIND.

(Courtesy Phillips Petroleum)

This ad originally appeared in *Harper's Magazine*.

Questions on Content

1. The following words and expressions may seem common, but examine their meanings within the context of each ad. Be alert for *ad-language*, a language distinct from the one we normally hear from our family, friends, teachers, and others with whom we have day-to-day experience.

   Sony classic, conventional, the industry, the ultimate, convenience features, maximum enjoyment, real beauty, endowed, delivers

   Magnavox a mess, ordinary typewriter, a pain, a lot more than type, features just go on and on, very smart

   Olympus Olympus technology, led the way, decidedly, corporate commitment, history-making, marvel, customary passion, famous, some engineering whim, marketing void, technological response, human needs

   Family Physician specialized, whole person, health management, major medical areas, health care need, qualified, ongoing education, Board Certified Family Physicians, continuing quality care, cost-efficient, proper management of your care, the greatest economy, preventive health care

   NEA interpersonal skills, manage, certification, by every measure, serious consequences, in droves, chosen not to become teachers, pay, out of the fields of expertise, uncertified teachers, the education process, paid properly, qualified teachers, professional wages, a respected and valued choice

   Phillips Petroleum Company the catch of the day, use innovation, new technology, the pioneers, venture, quality premium unleaded fuels, bottom-of-the-barrel crude, high quality gasoline, thriving undersea world, our environmental story, the structure, treasure, performing, the challenge of change

2. In each ad, what words or expressions appear repeatedly? What words or expressions are actually synonymous and represent an effort to say the same thing in different words?

3. In advertising jargon, the *selling idea* of an ad is the single line that sums up the major theme or idea of the ad. What is the selling idea of each ad reprinted here? What words or expressions are used to capture

that idea, perhaps becoming the ad's *slogan*—the phrase repeated or emphasized throughout the ad and meant to plant itself in the audience's mind?

4. Modifiers are often vital in advertising language. A car isn't simply new; it's "brand new" or "refreshingly new." A soap gives more than moisture; it gives "precious moisture." Beef isn't just beef; it's "tender, juicy beef." What modifiers are used in each of the six ads? What purposes do they serve?

5. In "Types of Propaganda" (pages 418–424), the authors list seven devices often used to sway political opinion: name calling, glittering generalities, transfer, testimonial, plain folks, card stacking, and bandwagon. These devices also serve advertisers, who are certainly concerned with influencing the public. Identify any examples of these propaganda devices in the ads.

6. To what audience is each ad appealing? How do we know?

7. What does each ad assume about its audience's tastes, habits, aspirations, weaknesses, and fears?

Questions on Structure and Style

8. Visualize the person speaking to us in each ad. What does this person look like? What is the person wearing? Create a clear mental picture of the speaker, and then describe the speaker's tone. *How* does the person utter the words we hear?

9. Examine the visual elements of each ad—the elements called *art* and *graphics* in advertising jargon. These accompany the *copy*, the words printed on the page. What links are there between the copy and the art and graphics? Generally, how do all these elements relate to each other?

1. In an essay, explain which of the six ads you believe will succeed best. Be sure to substantiate your assertions by citing specific evidence from the ads.

2. The copy in each of the six ads was written by skilled advertising professionals—writers who intend to persuade, not inform. Rewrite one of the ads, translating its copy into simple, honest English. As you do so, note how often "honest" English becomes difficult to decide on, so be prepared to defend your word choices.

Additional Assignments and Research Topics

1. In choosing their language, advertisers carefully consider their audience (that is, the segment of the buying public to whom they're appealing). Age, race, sex, and economic and social status are all important in determining how ads are written. Find examples of ads for the same product or similar products that demonstrate the ways advertisers adjust their appeals to their intended audience, and in an essay or report to your class, analyze how the ads differ and why. (One way to begin your research is to examine magazines aimed at different audiences, such as sports magazines and news magazines.)

2. Advertisers clearly design some ads to appeal mainly to men and others to appeal mainly to women. Review at least five ads for beer and five for detergents. What differences do you see in the advertisers' language? What does the language reveal about the products, the advertisers' assumptions, and the public's tastes and habits?

3. Stuart Berg Flexner discusses scare tactics in advertising ("A Consumer's Guide to Social Offenses," page 399). Such tactics aim at the heart, not the head, for they appeal to our emotions. Find several examples of ads that use a strongly emotional appeal, and analyze how the language in the ads contributes to this appeal. Be sure to gather source material carefully. Do not rely on your memories of ads. Quote with precision. Most importantly, don't allow your emotions to affect your study.

4. "Types of Propaganda" (page 418) examines devices used to affect opinions for political purposes, but advertisers often use these same devices. Find ads that use propaganda devices, and in a report to your class, explain how the advertisers have used each device.

5. Many colleges produce pamphlets highlighting their virtues as educational institutions. These pamphlets review educational philosophy, academic resources, and campus life—all for the purpose of attracting new students or financial contributions. Locate pamphlets from several colleges and universities, and examine them as examples of advertising.

How do they use language as a sales tool? What is each selling? What does their language reveal about their intended audiences? Discuss your findings in an essay.

6. Assume you've been hired to write the copy for an advertisement soliciting subscriptions to a new magazine. The magazine is aimed at college students and includes articles on academic life nationwide, popular culture (particularly music, movies, and books), and fashion. Write the ad, using any advertising techniques (or tricks) you believe might help.

7. Think of an action you once performed primarily because you believed something that appeared in advertising. In an essay, explain why the advertising persuaded you, paying particular attention to language and its role in convincing you that something was true. Remember that advertising does not only urge us to purchase goods and service; at times, it seeks to make us donate to charities, volunteer our time, vote for candidates, and believe that we should do many other things.

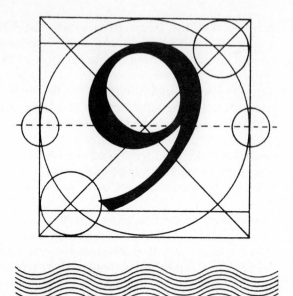

The Political
Voice

C onsider the stereotypical image of politicians, the one so dear to cartoonists. The politician stands before a crowd, sleeves rolled to the elbows, arms in the air, and—always—mouth wide open. This popular image reminds us how automatically we associate politicians with words. We do so because we understand, as politicians do almost instinctively, that language has immense power to inspire, reassure, and deceive. Any study of language must eventually look at the ways that politicians use language for these purposes, and this chapter's reading selections do just that.

Using language for political purposes often means expressing a truth in ways that will generate action. *How* we express a truth can sometimes distort that truth, however. "Types of Propaganda," the first selection, reviews common techniques for bending the truth for political (and other) purposes. George Orwell's famous essay "Politics and the English Language" comments on the sad condition of modern political discourse, in which expressing the truth accurately and gracefully often seems of little importance.

Arthur Schlesinger's "Politics and the American Language" offers a historian's analysis of how politicians today use language and the historical reasons for those uses. E. E. Cummings's poem "next to of course god america i" satirizes the political speechmaker, demonstrating how effectively art can capture the sound and spirit of a voice, and William Safire's "The Case of the President's Case" analyzes one politician's skillful choice of words. Paul Chilton, in "Nukespeak: Nuclear Language, Culture, and Propaganda," explains how language itself has helped create a world in which we accept nuclear weapons as one more element of modern life, and Stephen F. Cohen's argument, "Slanting the News against the USSR," takes aim at distortions in American political reporting. The chapter concludes with two political speeches for analysis: John F. Kennedy's Inaugural Address and Ronald Reagan's First Inaugural Address.

All these readings emphasize how inseparable politics and language are. Politicians use words as tools, the tools of leadership. We who listen should recognize these tools. They're designed to work on *us*.

Types of Propaganda

Institute for Propaganda Analysis

Many terms are tossed about carelessly in political discourse, and *propaganda* is one of them. The word is valuable, however, because it allows us to focus on the many tactics of politicians (and others) who use language to deceive. These tactics are detailed in the following extended definition. The essay, written in 1937, refers to people and places that have faded from newspaper headlines, but its message remains pertinent. Headlines change, but propaganda endures.

1   If American citizens are to have clear understanding of present-day conditions and what to do about them, they must be able to recognize propaganda, to analyze it, and to appraise it.

2   But what is propaganda?

3   As generally understood, *propaganda is expression of opinion or action by individuals or groups deliberately designed to influence opinions or actions of other individuals or groups with reference to predetermined ends.* Thus propaganda differs from scientific analysis. The propagandist is trying to "put something across," good or bad, whereas the scientist is trying to discover truth and fact. Often the propagandist does not want careful scrutiny and criticism; he wants to bring about a specific action. Because the action may be socially beneficial or socially harmful to millions of people, it is necessary to focus upon the propagandist and his activities the searchlight of scientific scrutiny. Socially desirable propaganda will not suffer from such examination, but the opposite type will be detected and revealed for what it is.

4   We are fooled by propaganda chiefly because we don't recognize it when we see it. It may be fun to be fooled but, as the cigarette ads used to say, it is more fun to know. We can more easily recognize propaganda when we see it if we are familiar with the seven common propaganda devices. These are:

1. The Name Calling Device
2. The Glittering Generalities Device
3. The Transfer Device
4. The Testimonial Device
5. The Plain Folks Device
6. The Card Stacking Device
7. The Band Wagon Device

5   Why are we fooled by these devices? Because they appeal to our emotions rather than to our reason. They make us believe and do something

418

we would not believe or do if we thought about it calmly, dispassionately. In examining these devices, note that they work most effectively at those times when we are too lazy to think for ourselves; also, they tie into emotions which sway us to be "for" or "against" nations, races, religions, ideals, economic and political policies and practices, and so on through automobiles, cigarettes, radios, toothpastes, presidents, and wars. With our emotions stirred, it may be fun to be fooled by these propaganda devices, but it is more fun and infinitely more to our own interests to know how they work.

6   Lincoln must have had in mind citizens who could balance their emotions with intelligence when he made his remark: ". . . but you can't fool all of the people all of the time."

Name Calling

7   "Name Calling" is a device to make us form a judgment without examining the evidence on which it should be based. Here the propagandist appeals to our hate and fear. He does this by giving "bad names" to those individuals, groups, nations, races, policies, practices, beliefs, and ideals which he would have us condemn and reject. For centuries the name "heretic" was bad. Thousands were oppressed, tortured, or put to death as heretics. Anybody who dissented from popular or group belief or practice was in danger of being called a heretic. In the light of today's knowledge, some heresies were bad and some were good. Many of the pioneers of modern science were called heretics; witness the cases of Copernicus, Galileo, Bruno. Today's bad names include: Fascist, demagogue, dictator, Red, financial oligarchy, Communist, muckraker, alien, outside agitator, economic royalist, Utopian, rabble-rouser, troublemaker, Tory, Constitution wrecker.

8   "Al" Smith called Roosevelt a Communist by implication when he said in his Liberty League speech, "There can be only one capital, Washington or Moscow." When "Al" Smith was running for the presidency many called him a tool of the Pope, saying in effect, "We must choose between Washington and Rome." That implied that Mr. Smith, if elected President, would take his orders from the Pope. Likewise Mr. Justice Hugo Black has been associated with a bad name, Ku Klux Klan. In these cases some propagandists have tried to make us form judgments without examining essential evidence and implications. "Al Smith is a Catholic. He must never be President." "Roosevelt is a Red. Defeat his program." "Hugo Black is or was a Klansman. Take him out of the Supreme Court."

9   Use of "bad names" without presentation of their essential meaning, without all their pertinent implications, comprises perhaps the most common of all propaganda devices. Those who want to *maintain* the status quo

apply bad names to those who would change it. . . . Those who want to *change* the status quo apply bad names to those who would maintain it. For example, the *Daily Worker* and the *American Guardian* apply bad names to conservative Republicans and Democrats.

Glittering Generalities

10   "Glittering Generalities" is a device by which the propagandist identifies his program with virtue by use of "virtue words." Here he appeals to our emotions of love, generosity, and brotherhood. He uses words like truth, freedom, honor, liberty, social justice, public service, the right to work, loyalty, progress, democracy, the American way, Constitution defender. These words suggest shining ideals. All persons of good will believe in these ideals. Hence the propagandist, by identifying his individual group, nation, race, policy, practice, or belief with such ideals, seeks to win us to his cause. As Name Calling is a device to make us form a judgment to *reject and condemn*, without examining the evidence, Glittering Generalities is a device to make us *accept and approve*, without examining the evidence.

11   For example, use of the phrases "the right to work" and "social justice" may be a device to make us accept programs for meeting labor-capital problems, which, if we examined them critically, we would not accept at all.

12   In the Name Calling and Glittering Generalities devices, words are used to stir up our emotions and to befog our thinking. In one device "bad words" are used to make us mad; in the other "good words" are used to make us glad.

13   The propagandist is most effective in the use of these devices when his works make us create devils to fight or gods to adore. By his use of the "bad words," we personify as a "devil" some nation, race, group, individual, policy, practice, or ideal; we are made fighting mad to destroy it. By use of "good words," we personify as a godlike idol some nation, race, group, etc. Words which are "bad" to some are "good" to others, or may be made so. Thus, to some the New Deal is "a prophecy of social salvation" while to others it is "an omen of social disaster."

14   From consideration of names, "bad" and "good," we pass to institutions and symbols, also "bad" and "good." We see these in the next device.

Transfer

15   "Transfer" is a device by which the propagandist carries over the authority, sanction, and prestige of something we respect and revere to something he would have us accept. For example, most of us respect and revere

our church and our nation. If the propagandist succeeds in getting church or nation to approve a campaign in behalf of some program, he thereby transfers its authority, sanction, and prestige to that program. Thus we may accept something which otherwise we might reject.

16   In the Transfer device, symbols are constantly used. The cross represents the Christian Church. The flag represents the nation. Cartoons like Uncle Sam represent a consensus of public opinion. Those symbols stir emotions. At their very sight, with the speed of light, is aroused the whole complex of feelings we have with respect to church or nation. A cartoonist by having Uncle Sam disapprove a budget for unemployment relief would have us feel that the whole United States disapproves relief costs. By drawing an Uncle Sam who approves the same budget, the cartoonist would have us feel that the American people approve it. Thus the Transfer device is used both for and against causes and ideas.

Testimonial

17   The "Testimonial" is a device to make us accept anything from a patent medicine or a cigarette to a program of national policy. In this device the propagandist makes use of testimonials. "When I feel tired, I smoke a Camel and get the grandest 'lift.' " "We believe the John L. Lewis plan of labor organization is splendid; C.I.O. should be supported." This device works in reverse also; counter-testimonials may be employed. Seldom are these used against commercial products like patent medicines and cigarettes, but they are constantly employed in social, economic, and political issues. "We believe that the John L. Lewis plan of labor organization is bad; C.I.O. should not be supported."

Plain Folks

18   "Plain Folks" is a device used by politicians, labor leaders, businessmen, and even by ministers and educators to win our confidence by appearing to be people like ourselves—"just plain folks among the neighbors." In election years especially do candidates show their devotion to little children and the common, homey things of life. They have front porch campaigns. For the newspapermen they raid the kitchen cupboard, finding there some of the good wife's apple pie. They go to country picnics; they attend service at the old frame church; they pitch hay and go fishing; they show their belief in home and mother. In short, they would win our votes by showing that they're just as common as the rest of us—"just plain folks"—and, therefore, wise and good. Businessmen often are "plain folks" with the

factory hands. Even distillers use the device. "It's our family's whiskey, neighbor; and neighbor, it's your price."

Card Stacking

19   "Card Stacking" is a device in which the propagandist employs all the arts of deception to win our support for himself, his group, nation, race, policy, practice, belief, or ideal. He stacks the cards against the truth. He uses under-emphasis and over-emphasis to dodge issues and evade facts. He resorts to lies, censorship, and distortion. He omits facts. He offers false testimony. He creates a smoke screen of clamor by raising a new issue when he wants an embarrassing matter forgotten. He draws a red herring across the trail to confuse and divert those in quest of facts he does not want revealed. He makes the unreal appear real and the real appear unreal. He lets half-truth masquerade as truth. By the Card Stacking device, a mediocre candidate, through the "build-up," is made to appear an intellectual titan; an ordinary prize fighter, a probable world champion; a worthless patent medicine, a beneficent cure. By means of this device propagandists would convince us that a ruthless war of aggression is a crusade for righteousness. Some member nations of the Non-Intervention Committee send their troops to intervene in Spain. Card Stacking employs sham, hypocrisy, effrontery.

The Band Wagon

20   The "Band Wagon" is a device to make us follow the crowd, to accept the propagandist's program en masse. Here his theme is: "Everybody's doing it." His techniques range from those of medicine show to dramatic spectacle. He hires a hall, fills a great stadium, marches a million men in parade. He employs symbols, colors, music, movement, all the dramatic arts. He appeals to the desire, common to most of us, to "follow the crowd." Because he wants us to "follow the crowd" in masses, he directs his appeal to groups held together by common ties of nationality, religion, race, environment, sex, vocation. Thus propagandists campaigning for or against a program will appeal to us as Catholics, Protestants, or Jews; as members of the Nordic race or as Negroes; as farmers or as school teachers; as housewives or as miners. All the artifices of flattery are used to harness the fears and hatreds, prejudices, and biases, convictions and ideals common to the group; thus emotion is made to push and pull the group onto the Band Wagon. In newspaper articles and in the spoken word this device is also found. "Don't throw your vote away. Vote for our candidate. He's sure to win." Nearly every candidate wins in every election—before the votes are in.

Propaganda and Emotion

21   Observe that in all these devices our emotion is the stuff with which propagandists work. Without it they are helpless; with it, harnessing it to their purposes, they can make us glow with pride or burn with hatred, they can make us zealots in behalf of the program they espouse. As we said at the beginning, propaganda as generally understood is expression of opinion or action by individuals or groups with reference to predetermined ends. Without the appeal to our emotion—to our fears and to our courage, to our selfishness and unselfishness, to our loves and to our hates—propagandists would influence few opinions and few actions.

22   To say this is not to condemn emotion, an essential part of life, or to assert that all predetermined ends of propagandists are "bad." What we mean is that the intelligent citizen does not want propagandists to utilize his emotions, even to the attainment of "good" ends, without knowing what is going on. He does not want to be "used" in the attainment of ends he may later consider "bad." He does not want to be gullible. He does not want to be fooled. He does not want to be duped, even in a "good" cause. He wants to know the facts and among these is included the fact of the utilization of his emotions.

23   Keeping in mind the seven common propaganda devices, turn to today's newspapers and almost immediately you can spot examples of them all. At election time or during any campaign, Plain Folks and Band Wagon are common. Card Stacking is hardest to detect because it is adroitly executed or because we lack the information necessary to nail the lie. A little practice with the daily newspapers in detecting these propaganda devices soon enables us to detect them elsewhere—in radio, news-reel, books, magazines, and in expressions of labor unions, business groups, churches, schools, political parties.

Questions on Content

1.   Briefly explain the "present-day conditions" mentioned in paragraph 1.

2.   Explain the difference between propaganda and scientific analysis.

3.   What is the difference between the devices of name calling and glittering generalities?

4.   Explain the devices of transfer and card stacking.

5.   The essay asserts that "our emotion is the stuff with which propagandists work" (paragraph 21). Explain.

6. What response do the authors of this essay want from their audience?

7. This essay, written in the 1930s, refers to specific people and events. Many of the references may seem dated. What present-day people and events would be appropriate replacements for those named at the end of paragraph 7 ("Today's bad names include . . .")?

**Questions
on Structure
and Style**

8. Where is the thesis? Is it fully developed in the essay?

9. Classification is the rhetorical device used to organize this essay, but definition and comparison and contrast are also important. Find examples of these other rhetorical devices.

10. What is the function of paragraph 4?

11. How effective is the conclusion of this essay?

12. No single author is named for this essay, but does the essay sound impersonal or "bureaucratic"? Why or why not?

Assignments

1. Using dictionaries and encyclopedias, determine the etymology of the word *propaganda*. Then in a paragraph, explain how the etymology is related to today's customary use of the word.

2. *Propaganda* tends to have a negative connotation. In an essay, discuss the positive and useful functions of propaganda. Before starting, reread the definition of propaganda given in paragraph 3. Be sure to provide concrete examples.

3. This essay, though still relevant, was written in 1937, prior to the television era. Do you think the American public, thanks to television, is more— or less—able to recognize propaganda today? Respond in a paragraph or an essay.

Politics
and the English Language

George Orwell

"The English language is in a bad way," and politicians are largely to blame. This belief underlies the following well-known essay by George Orwell (pen name of Eric Blair), an Englishman best remembered as the author of *1984* and *Animal Farm*. Orwell moves carefully through many examples of flawed, often deceptive, political language and leads us to six rules for the effective use of language in any context, not just politics. But political language is central to the essay. For the author, this language "is designed to make lies sound truthful and murder respectable, and to give an appearance of solidity to pure wind."

1 Most people who bother with the matter at all would admit that the English language is in a bad way, but it is generally assumed that we cannot by conscious action do anything about it. Our civilization is decadent and our language—so the argument runs—must inevitably share in the general collapse. It follows that any struggle against the abuse of language is a sentimental archaism, like preferring candles to electric light or hansom cabs to aeroplanes. Underneath this lies the half-conscious belief that language is a natural growth and not an instrument which we shape for our own purposes.

2 Now, it is clear that the decline of a language must ultimately have political and economic causes: it is not due simply to the bad influence of this or that individual writer. But an effect can become a cause, reinforcing the original cause and producing the same effect in an intensified form, and so on indefinitely. A man may take to drink because he feels himself to be a failure, and then fail all the more completely because he drinks. It is rather the same thing that is happening to the English language. It becomes ugly and inaccurate because our thoughts are foolish, but the slovenliness of our language makes it easier for us to have foolish thoughts. The point is that the process is reversible. Modern English, especially written English, is full of bad habits which spread by imitation and which can be avoided if one is willing to take the necessary trouble. If one gets rid of these habits one can think more clearly, and to think clearly is a necessary first step towards political regeneration: so that the fight against bad English is not frivolous and is not the exclusive concern of professional writers. I will come back to this presently, and I hope that by that time the meaning of what I have said here will have become clearer.

Meanwhile, here are five specimens of the English language as it is now habitually written.

3   These five passages have not been picked out because they are especially bad—I could have quoted far worse if I had chosen—but because they illustrate various of the mental vices from which we now suffer. They are a little below the average, but are fairly representative samples. I number them so that I can refer back to them when necessary:

1. I am not, indeed, sure whether it is not true to say that the Milton who once seemed not unlike a seventeenth-century Shelley had not become, out of an experience ever more bitter in each year, more alien [sic] to the founder of that Jesuit sect which nothing could induce him to tolerate.
   Professor Harold Laski (*Essay in* Freedom of Expression)

2. Above all, we cannot play ducks and drakes with a native battery of idioms which prescribes such egregious collocations of vocables as the Basic *put up with* for *tolerate* or *put at a loss* for *bewilder*.
   Professor Lancelot Hogben (Interglossa)

3. On the one side we have the free personality: by definition it is not neurotic, for it has neither conflict nor dream. Its desires, such as they are, are transparent, for they are just what institutional approval keeps in the forefront of consciousness; another institutional pattern would alter their number and intensity; there is little in them that is natural, irreducible, or culturally dangerous. But *on the other side,* the social bond itself is nothing but the mutual reflection of these self-secure integrities. Recall the definition of love. Is not this the very picture of a small academic? Where is there a place in this hall of mirrors for either personality or fraternity?
   Essay on Psychology in Politics (*New York*)

4. All the "best people" from the gentlemen's clubs, and all the frantic fascist captains, united in common hatred of Socialism and bestial horror of the rising tide of the mass revolutionary movement, have turned to acts of provocation, to foul incendiarism, to medieval legends of poisoned wells, to legalize their own destruction of proletarian organizations, and rouse the agitated petty-bourgeoisie to chauvinistic fervor on behalf of the fight against the revolutionary way out of the crisis.
   Communist Pamphlet

5. If a new spirit *is* to be infused into this old country, there is one thorny and contentious reform which must be tackled,

and that is the humanization and galvanization of the B.B.C. Timidity here will bespeak canker and atrophy of the soul. The heart of Britain may be sound and of strong beat, for instance, but the British lion's roar at present is like that of Bottom in Shakespeare's *Midsummer Night's Dream*—as gentle as any sucking dove. A virile new Britain cannot continue indefinitely to be traduced in the eyes or rather ears, of the world by the effete languors of Langham Place, brazenly masquerading as "standard English." When the voice of Britain is heard at nine o'clock, better far and infinitely less ludicrous to hear aitches honestly dropped than the present priggish, inflated, inhibited, school-ma'amish arch braying of blameless bashful mewing maidens!

Letter in Tribune

4   Each of these passages has faults of its own, but, quite apart from avoidable ugliness, two qualities are common to all of them. The first is staleness of imagery; the other is lack of precision. The writer either has a meaning and cannot express it, or he inadvertently says something else, or he is almost indifferent as to whether his words mean anything or not. This mixture of vagueness and sheer incompetence is the most marked characteristic of modern English prose, and especially of any kind of political writing. As soon as certain topics are raised, the concrete melts into the abstract and no one seems able to think of turns of speech that are not hackneyed: prose consists less and less of *words* chosen for the sake of their meaning, and more and more of *phrases* tacked together like the sections of a prefabricated hen-house. I list below, with notes and examples, various of the tricks by means of which the work of prose-construction is habitually dodged.

Dying Metaphors

5   A newly invented metaphor assists thought by evoking a visual image, while on the other hand a metaphor which is technically "dead" (e.g., *iron resolution*) has in effect reverted to being an ordinary word and can generally be used without loss of vividness. But in between these two classes there is a huge dump of worn-out metaphors which have lost all evocative power and are merely used because they save people the trouble of inventing phrases for themselves. Examples are: *Ring the changes on, take up the cudgels for, toe the line, ride roughshod over, stand shoulder to shoulder with, play into the hands of, no axe to grind, grist to the mill, fishing in troubled waters, on the order of the day, Achilles' heel, swan song, hotbed.* Many of these are used without knowledge of their meaning (what is a "rift," for instance?), and incompatible metaphors are frequently mixed, a sure sign that the writer is

not interested in what he is saying. Some metaphors now current have been twisted out of their original meaning without those who use them even being aware of the fact. For example, *toe the line* is sometimes written *tow the line*. Another example is *the hammer and the anvil,* now always used with the implication that the anvil gets the worst of it. In real life it is always the anvil that breaks the hammer, never the other way about: a writer who stopped to think what he was saying would be aware of this, and could avoid perverting the original phrase.

Operators or Verbal False Limbs

6   These save the trouble of picking out appropriate verbs and nouns, and at the same time pad each sentence with extra syllables which give it an appearance of symmetry. Characteristic phrases are *render inoperative, militate against, make contact with, be subjected to, give rise to, give grounds for, have the effect of, play a leading part (role) in, make itself felt, take effect, exhibit a tendency to, serve the purpose of, etc., etc.* The keynote is the elimination of simple verbs. Instead of being a single word, such as *break, stop, spoil, mend, kill,* a verb becomes *a phrase,* made up of a noun or adjective tacked on to some general-purpose verb such as *prove, serve, form, play, render.* In addition, the passive voice is wherever possible used in preference to the active, and noun constructions are used instead of gerunds (*by examination of* instead of *by examining*). The range of verbs is further cut down by means of the *-ize* and *de-* formations, and the banal statements are given an appearance of profundity by means of the *not un-* formation. Simple conjunctions and prepositions are replaced by such phrases as *with respect to, having regard to, the fact that, by dint of, in view of, in the interests of, on the hypothesis that;* and the ends of sentences are saved from anticlimax by such resounding commonplaces as *greatly to be desired, cannot be left out of account, a development to be expected in the near future, deserving of serious consideration, brought to a satisfactory conclusion,* and so on and so forth.

Pretentious Diction

7   Words like *phenomenon, element, individual* (as noun), *objective, categorical, effective, virtual, basic, primary, promote, constitute, exhibit, exploit, utilize, eliminate, liquidate,* are used to dress up simple statements and give an air of scientific impartiality to biased judgments. Adjectives like *epoch-making, epic, historic, unforgettable, triumphant, age-old, inevitable, inexorable, veritable,* are used to dignify the sordid processes of international politics, while writing that aims at glorifying war usually takes on an archaic color, its characteristic words being: *realm, throne, chariot, mailed fist, trident, sword,*

shield, buckler, banner, jackboot, clarion. Foreign words and expressions such as *cul de sac, ancien régime, deus ex machina, mutatis mutandis, status quo, gleichschaltung, weltansschauung,* are used to give an air of culture and elegance. Except for the useful abbreviations *i.e., e.g.,* and *etc.,* there is no real need for any of the hundreds of foreign phrases now current in English. Bad writers, and especially scientific, political and sociological writers, are nearly always haunted by the notion that Latin or Greek words are grander than Saxon ones, and unnecessary words like *expedite, ameliorate, predict, extraneous, deracinated, clandestine, subaqueous* and hundreds of others constantly gain ground from their Anglo-Saxon opposite numbers.* The jargon peculiar to Marxist writing (*hyena, hangman, cannibal, petty bourgeois, these gentry, lacquey, flunkey, mad dog, White Guard,* etc.) consists largely of words and phrases translated from Russian, German, or French; but the normal way of coining a new word is to use a Latin or Greek root with the appropriate affix and, where necessary, the *-ize* formation. It is often easier to make up words of this kind (*deregionalize, impermissible, extramarital, non-fragmentary,* and so forth) than to think up the English words that will cover one's meaning. The result, in general, is an increase in slovenliness and vagueness.

Meaningless Words

8   In certain kinds of writing, particularly in art criticism and literary criticism, it is normal to come across long passages which are almost completely lacking in meaning.† Words like *romantic, plastic, values, human, dead, sentimental, natural, vitality,* as used in art criticism, are strictly meaningless, in the sense that they not only do not point to any discoverable object, but are hardly ever expected to do so by the reader. When one critic writes, "The outstanding feature of Mr. X's work is its living quality," while another writes, "The immediately striking thing about Mr. X's work is its peculiar deadness," the reader accepts this as a simple difference of opinion. If words like *black* and *white* were involved, instead of the jargon words *dead* and *living,* he would see at once that language was being used in an improper way. Many political words are similarly abused. The word

---

* An interesting illustration of this is the way in which the English flower names which were in use till very recently are being ousted by Greek ones, *snapdragon* becoming *antirrhinum, forget-me-not* becoming *myosotis,* etc. It is hard to see any practical reason for this change of fashion: it is probably due to an instinctive turning-away from the more homely word and a vague feeling that the Greek word is scientific.

† Example: "Comfort's catholicity of perception and image, strangely Whitmanesque in range, almost the exact opposite in aesthetic compulsion, continues to evoke that trembling atmospheric accumulative hinting at a cruel, an inexorably serene timelessness. . . . Wrey Gardiner scores by aiming at simple bull's-eyes with precision. Only they are not so simple, and through this contented sadness runs more than the surface bitter-sweet of resignation." (*Poetry Quarterly*)

Fascism has now no meaning except in so far as it signifies "something not desirable." The words *democracy, socialism, freedom, patriotic, realistic, justice,* have each of them several different meanings which cannot be reconciled with one another. In the case of a word like *democracy,* not only is there no agreed definition, but the attempt to make one is resisted from all sides. It is almost universally felt that when we call a country democratic we are praising it: consequently the defenders of every kind of régime claim that it is a democracy, and fear that they might have to stop using the word if it were tied down to any one meaning. Words of this kind are often used in a consciously dishonest way. That is, the person who uses them has his own private definition, but allows his hearer to think he means something quite different. Statements like *Marshal Pétain was a true patriot, The Soviet Press is the freest in the world, The Catholic Church is opposed to persecution,* are almost always made with intent to deceive. Other words used in variable meanings, in most cases more or less dishonestly, are: *class, totalitarian, science, progressive, reactionary, bourgeois, equality.*

9   Now that I have made this catalogue of swindles and perversions, let me give another example of the kind of writing that they lead to. This time it must of its nature be an imaginary one. I am going to translate a passage of good English into modern English of the worst sort. Here is a well-known verse from *Ecclesiastes:*

> I returned and saw under the sun, that the race is not to the swift, nor the battle to the strong, neither yet bread to the wise, nor yet riches to men of understanding, nor yet favour to men of skill; but time and chance happeneth to them all.

10   Here it is in modern English:

> Objective consideration of contemporary phenomena compels the conclusion that success or failure in competitive activities exhibits no tendency to be commensurate with innate capacity, but that a considerable element of the unpredictable must invariably be taken into account.

11   This is a parody, but not a very gross one. Exhibit (3), above, for instance, contains several patches of the same kind of English. It will be seen that I have not made a full translation. The beginning and ending of the sentence follow the original meaning fairly closely, but in the middle the concrete illustrations—race, battle, bread—dissolve into the vague phrase "success or failure in competitive activities." This had to be so, because no modern writer of the kind I am discussing—no one capable of using phrases like "objective consideration of contemporary phenomena"—would ever tabulate his thoughts in that precise and detailed way. The whole tendency of modern prose is away from concreteness. Now analyze

these two sentences a little more closely. The first contains forty-nine words but only sixty syllables, and all its words are those of everyday life. The second contains thirty-eight words of ninety syllables: eighteen of its words are from Latin roots, and one from Greek. The first sentence contains six vivid images, and only one phrase ("time and chance") that could be called vague. The second contains not a single fresh, arresting phrase, and in spite of its ninety syllables it gives only a shortened version of the meaning contained in the first. Yet without a doubt it is the second kind of sentence that is gaining ground in modern English. I do not want to exaggerate. This kind of writing is not yet universal, and outcrops of simplicity will occur here and there in the worst-written page. Still, if you or I were told to write a few lines on the uncertainty of human fortunes, we should probably come much nearer to my imaginary sentence than to the one from *Ecclesiastes.*

12   As I have tried to show, modern writing at its worst does not consist in picking out words for the sake of their meaning and inventing images in order to make the meaning clearer. It consists in gumming together long strips of words which have already been set in order by someone else, and making the results presentable by sheer humbug. The attraction of this way of writing is that it is easy. It is easier—even quicker, once you have the habit—to say *In my opinion it is not an unjustifiable assumption that* than to say *I think.* If you use ready-made phrases, you not only don't have to hunt about for words; you also don't have to bother with the rhythms of your sentences, since these phrases are generally so arranged as to be more or less euphonious. When you are composing in a hurry—when you are dictating to a stenographer, for instance, or making a public speech—it is natural to fall into a pretentious, Latinized style. Tags like *a consideration which we should do well to bear in mind* or *a conclusion to which all of us would readily assent* will save many a sentence from coming down with a bump. By using stale metaphors, similes, and idioms, you save much mental effort, at the cost of leaving your meaning vague, not only for your reader but for yourself. This is the significance of mixed metaphors. The sole aim of a metaphor is to call up a visual image. When these images clash—as in *The Fascist octopus has sung its swan song, the jackboot is thrown into the melting pot*—it can be taken as certain that the writer is not seeing a mental image of the objects he is naming; in other words he is not really thinking. Look again at the examples I gave at the beginning of this essay. Professor Laski (1) uses five negatives in fifty-three words. One of these is superfluous, making nonsense of the whole passage, and in addition there is the slip *alien* for *akin,* making further nonsense, and several avoidable pieces of clumsiness which increase the general vagueness. Professor Hogben (2) plays ducks and drakes with a battery which is able to write prescriptions, and, while disapproving of the everyday phrase *put up with,* is unwilling to look *egregious* up in the dictionary and see what it means; (3), if one takes

an uncharitable attitude towards it, is simply meaningless: probably one could work out its intended meaning by reading the whole of the article in which it occurs. In (4), the writer knows more or less what he wants to say, but an accumulation of stale phrases chokes him like tea leaves blocking a sink. In (5), words and meaning have almost parted company. People who write in this manner usually have a general emotional meaning—they dislike one thing and want to express solidarity with another—but they are not interested in the detail of what they are saying. A scrupulous writer, in every sentence that he writes, will ask himself at least four questions, thus: What am I trying to say? What words will express it? What image or idiom will make it clearer? Is this image fresh enough to have an effect? And he will probably ask himself two more: Could I put it more shortly? Have I said anything that is avoidably ugly? But you are not obliged to go to all this trouble. You can shirk it by simply throwing your mind open and letting the ready-made phrases come crowding in. They will construct your sentences for you—even think your thoughts for you, to a certain extent—and at need they will perform the important service of partially concealing your meaning even from yourself. It is at this point that the special connection between politics and the debasement of language becomes clear.

13   In our time it is broadly true that political writing is bad writing. Where it is not true, it will generally be found that the writer is some kind of rebel, expressing his private opinions and not a "party line." Orthodoxy, of whatever color, seems to demand a lifeless, imitative style. The political dialects to be found in pamphlets, leading articles, manifestos, White Papers and the speeches of undersecretaries do, of course, vary from party to party, but they are all alike in that one almost never finds in them a fresh, vivid, home-made turn of speech. When one watches some tired hack on the platform mechanically repeating the familiar phrases—*bestial atrocities, iron heel, bloodstained tyranny, free peoples of the world, stand shoulder to shoulder*—one often has a curious feeling that one is not watching a live human being but some kind of dummy: a feeling which suddenly becomes stronger at moments when the light catches the speaker's spectacles and turns them into blank discs which seem to have no eyes behind them. And this is not altogether fanciful. A speaker who uses that kind of phraseology has gone some distance towards turning himself into a machine. The appropriate noises are coming out of his larynx, but his brain is not involved as it would be if he were choosing his words for himself. If the speech he is making is one that he is accustomed to make over and over again, he may be almost unconscious of what he is saying, as one is when one utters the responses in church. And this reduced state of consciousness, if not indispensable, is at any rate favorable to political conformity.

14   In our time, political speech and writing are largely the defense of the indefensible. Things like the continuance of British rule in India, the Russian purges and deportations, the dropping of the atom bombs on Japan,

can indeed be defended, but only by arguments which are too brutal for most people to face, and which do not square with the professed aims of political parties. Thus political language has to consist largely of euphemism, question-begging, and sheer cloudy vagueness. Defenseless villages are bombarded from the air, the inhabitants driven out into the countryside, the cattle machine-gunned, the huts set on fire with incendiary bullets: this is called *pacification*. Millions of peasants are robbed of their farms and sent trudging along the roads with no more than they can carry: this is called *transfer of population* or *rectification of frontiers*. People are imprisoned for years without trial or shot in the back of the neck or sent to die of scurvy in Arctic lumber camps: this is called *elimination of unreliable elements*. Such phraseology is needed if one wants to name things without calling up mental pictures of them. Consider for instance some comfortable English professor defending Russian totalitarianism. He cannot say outright, "I believe in killing off your opponents when you can get good results by doing so." Probably, therefore, he will say something like this:

> While freely conceding that the Soviet regime exhibits certain features which the humanitarian may be inclined to deplore, we must, I think, agree that a certain curtailment of the right to political opposition is an unavoidable concomitant of transitional periods, and that the rigors which the Russian people have been called upon to undergo have been amply justified in the sphere of concrete achievement.

15   The inflated style is itself a kind of euphemism. A mass of Latin words falls upon the facts like soft snow, blurring the outlines and covering up all the details. The great enemy of clear language is insincerity. When there is a gap between one's real and one's declared aims, one turns as it were instinctively to long words and exhausted idioms, like a cuttlefish squirting out ink. In our age there is no such thing as "keeping out of politics." All issues are political issues, and politics itself is a mass of lies, evasions, folly, hatred and schizophrenia. When the general atmosphere is bad, language must suffer. I should expect to find—this is a guess which I have not sufficient knowledge to verify—that the German, Russian and Italian languages have all deteriorated in the last ten to fifteen years, as a result of dictatorship.

16   But if thought corrupts language, language can also corrupt thought. A bad usage can spread by tradition and imitation, even among people who should and do know better. The debased language that I have been discussing is in some ways very convenient. Phrases like *a not unjustifiable assumption, leaves much to be desired, would serve no good purpose, a consideration which we should do well to bear in mind*, are a continuous temptation, a packet of aspirins always at one's elbow. Look back through this essay,

and for certain you will find that I have again and again committed the very faults I am protesting against. By this morning's post I have received a pamphlet dealing with conditions in Germany. The author tells me that he "felt impelled" to write it. I open it at random, and here is almost the first sentence that I see: "[The Allies] have an opportunity not only of achieving a radical transformation of Germany's social and political structure in such a way as to avoid a nationalistic reaction in Germany itself, but at the same time of laying the foundations of a cooperative and unified Europe." You see, he "feels impelled" to write—feels, presumably, that he has something new to say—and yet his words, like cavalry horses answering the bugle, group themselves automatically into the familiar dreary pattern. The invasion of one's mind by ready-made phrases (*lay the foundations, achieve a radical transformation*) can only be prevented if one is constantly on guard against them, and every such phrase anaesthetizes a portion of one's brain.

17   I said earlier that the decadence of our language is probably curable. Those who deny this would argue, if they produced an argument at all, that language merely reflects existing social conditions, and that we cannot influence its development by any direct tinkering with words and constructions. So far as the general tone or spirit of a language goes, this may be true, but it is not true in detail. Silly words and expressions have often disappeared, not through any evolutionary process but owing to the conscious action of a minority. Two recent examples were *explore every avenue* and *leave no stone unturned*, which were killed by the jeers of a few journalists. There is a long list of flyblown metaphors which could similarly be got rid of if enough people would interest themselves in the job; and it should also be possible to laugh the *not un-* formation out of existence,* to reduce the amount of Latin and Greek in the average sentence, to drive out foreign phrases and strayed scientific words, and, in general, to make pretentiousness unfashionable. But all these are minor points. The defense of the English language implies more than this, and perhaps it is best to start by saying what it does *not* imply.

18   To begin with it has nothing to do with archaism, with the salvaging of obsolete words and turns of speech, or with the setting up of a "standard English" which must never be departed from. On the contrary, it is especially concerned with the scrapping of every word or idiom which has outworn its usefulness. It has nothing to do with correct grammar and syntax, which are of no importance so long as one makes one's meaning clear, or with the avoidance of Americanisms, or with having what is called a "good prose style." On the other hand it is not concerned with fake simplicity and the attempt to make written English colloquial. Nor does it

---

* One can cure oneself of the *not un-* formation by memorizing this sentence: *A not unblack dog was chasing a not unsmall rabbit across a not ungreen field.*

even imply in every case preferring the Saxon word to the Latin one, though it does imply using the fewest and shortest words that will cover one's meaning. What is above all needed is to let the meaning choose the word, and not the other way about. In prose, the worst thing one can do with words is to surrender to them. When you think of a concrete object, you think wordlessly, and then, if you want to describe the thing you have been visualizing you probably hunt about till you find the exact words that seem to fit it. When you think of something abstract you are more inclined to use words from the start, and unless you make a conscious effort to prevent it, the existing dialect will come rushing in and do the job for you, at the expense of blurring or even changing your meaning. Probably it is better to put off using words as long as possible and get one's meaning as clear as one can through pictures or sensations. Afterwards one can choose—not simply *accept*—the phrases that will best cover the meaning, and then switch round and decide what impression one's words are likely to make on another person. This last effort of the mind cuts out all stale or mixed images, all prefabricated phrases, needless repetitions, and humbug and vagueness generally. But one can often be in doubt about the effect of a word or a phrase, and one needs rules that one can rely on when instinct fails. I think the following rules will cover most cases:

i. Never use a metaphor, simile or other figure of speech which you are used to seeing in print.
ii. Never use a long word where a short one will do.
iii. If it is possible to cut a word out, always cut it out.
iv. Never use the passive where you can use the active.
v. Never use a foreign phrase, a scientific word or a jargon word if you can think of an everyday English equivalent.
vi. Break any of these rules sooner than say anything outright barbarous.

These rules sound elementary, and so they are, but they demand a deep change of attitude in anyone who has grown used to writing in the style now fashionable. One could keep all of them and still write bad English, but one could not write the kind of stuff that I quoted in those five specimens at the beginning of this article.

19   I have not here been considering the literary use of language, but merely language as an instrument for expressing and not for concealing or preventing thought. Stuart Chase and others have come near to claiming that all abstract words are meaningless, and have used this as a pretext for advocating a kind of political quietism. Since you don't know what Fascism is, how can you struggle against Fascism? One need not swallow such absurdities as this, but one ought to recognize that the present political chaos is connected with the decay of language, and that one can probably bring about some improvement by starting at the verbal end. If you

simplify your English, you are freed from the worst follies of orthodoxy. You cannot speak any of the necessary dialects, and when you make a stupid remark its stupidity will be obvious, even to yourself. Political language—and with variations this is true of all political parties, from Conservatives to Anarchists—is designed to make lies sound truthful and murder respectable, and to give an appearance of solidity to pure wind. One cannot change this all in a moment, but one can at least change one's own habits, and from time to time one can even, if one jeers loudly enough, send some worn-out and useless phrase—some *jackboot, Achilles' heel, hotbed, melting pot, acid test, veritable inferno,* or other lump of verbal refuse—into the dustbin where it belongs.

Questions on Content

1. Define the "dying metaphor." How can we determine whether a metaphor is alive or dead?

2. What does Orwell mean by "operators or verbal false limbs" (paragraph 6)?

3. What does Orwell assert about the use of foreign words and expressions in writing?

4. Orwell believes that "the decline of a language must ultimately have political and economic causes" (paragraph 2). Why?

5. Orwell criticizes many features of political language. Does he offer any solutions? If so, where?

6. Orwell's language is decidedly British. Make a list of five words or expressions that demonstrate this.

Questions on Structure and Style

7. Comment on the tone Orwell establishes in the opening paragraph. Does he sustain this tone throughout the essay? If so, how?

8. Orwell establishes his thesis in paragraph 2. Identify this thesis, and comment on how successfully he develops it.

9. Find examples of analogy and figurative language in paragraphs 2, 13, and 16.

10. How does Orwell use the five "representative samples" in paragraph 3?

11. In paragraphs 3, 4, 9, and 12, Orwell makes statements that are important to the essay's organization. Locate these statements, and identify their purposes.

12. Orwell provides a list of rules in paragraph 18. The final rule is, "Break any of these rules sooner than say anything outright barbarous." Is Orwell begging the question? How is this statement (and its language) consistent with the essay's tone? Does this rule weaken the list or strengthen it?

13. In paragraph 18, Orwell refers to "the kind of stuff" he quotes in paragraph 3. What is the effect of such colloquial language? Is it appropriate here?

Assignments

1. Prepare a topical outline of this essay. Is the essay tightly organized? How would you describe the organizational pattern? Answer in a paragraph.

2. Orwell wrote "Politics and the English Language" in 1945. Is it more or less relevant today? Include three specific examples that support your opinion.

3. Choose a sample of prose from a textbook, professional journal, or political speech, and write an essay discussing how Orwell would react to it.

4. Reread Orwell's list of rules in paragraph 18, and examine the essay as a whole with these rules in mind. Does Orwell follow his own advice about using language? Answer in an essay. Be sure to provide specific examples to substantiate your claims.

Politics
and the American Language

Arthur Schlesinger, Jr.

Language and politics are intimately linked. So too are language and history (as Chapter 4 emphasizes), and in the following essay, Arthur Schlesinger, Jr., explains the role of language in American political history. Although he is one of America's foremost contemporary historians, Schlesinger has also worked for liberal political leaders (among them Franklin D. Roosevelt and John F. Kennedy). In his analysis, nineteenth-century changes in our society "began to divert the function of words from expression to gratification"—until today, when political language neither inspires nor reassures but, instead, rejects reason itself and should prompt from all of us a "raid on the inarticulate."

In our time, political speech and writing are largely the defense of the indefensible.

George Orwell

1   It takes a certain fortitude to pretend to amend Orwell on this subject. But "Politics and the English Language"—which I herewith incorporate by reference—was written more than a generation ago. In the years since, the process of semantic collapse has gathered speed, verified all of Orwell's expectations, and added new apprehensions for a new age. Americans in particular have found this a painful period of self-recognition. In 1946 we comfortably supposed that Orwell was talking about other people—Nazis and Stalinists, bureaucrats and sociologists, Professor Lancelot Hogben and Professor Harold Laski. Now recent history has obliged us to extend his dispiriting analysis to ourselves.

2   Vietnam and Watergate: these horrors will trouble the rest of our lives. But they are not, I suppose, unmitigated horrors. "Every act rewards itself," said Emerson. As Vietnam instructed us, at terrible cost, in the limit of our wisdom and power in foreign affairs, so Watergate instructed us, at considerably less cost, in the limits of wisdom and power in the presidency. It reminded us of the urgent need to restore the original balance of the Constitution—the balance between presidential power and presidential accountability. In doing this, it has, among other things, brought back into public consciousness the great documents under which the American government was organized.

3   The Constitution, the debates of the Constitutional Convention, *The Federalist Papers*—how many of us read them with sustained attention in earlier years? A few eccentrics like Justice Black and Senator Ervin pored over them with devotion. The rest of us regarded them, beyond an occasional invocation of the Bill of Rights or the Fourteenth Amendment, as documents of essentially historical interest and left them undisturbed on the shelf. Then, under the goad first of Vietnam and then of Watergate, legislators, editors, columnists, even political scientists and historians—everyone, it would seem, except for presidential lawyers—began turning the dusty pages in order to find out what Madison said in the convention about the war-making power or how Hamilton defined the grounds for impeachment in the sixty-fifth Federalist. Vietnam and Watergate are hardly to be compared. One is high tragedy, the other low, if black, comedy. But between them they have given the American people a spectacular reeducation in the fundamentals of our constitutional order.

4   One cannot doubt that this experience will have abiding political significance. The effect of Vietnam in exorcising our illusions and chastening our ambitions in foreign affairs has long been manifest. Now we begin to see the effect of Watergate in raising the standards of our politics. But I am less concerned initially with the political than with the literary consequences of this return to our constitutional womb. For, in addition to their exceptional qualities of insight and judgment, the historic documents must impress us by the extraordinary distinction of their language.

5   This was the age of the Enlightenment in America. The cooling breeze of reason tempered the hot work of composition and argument. The result was the language of the Founding Fathers—lucid, measured, and felicitous prose, marked by Augustan virtues of harmony, balance, and elegance. People not only wrote this noble language. They also read it. The essays in defense of the Constitution signed Publius appeared week after week in the New York press during the winter of 1787–88; and the demand was so great that the first thirty-six Federalist papers were published in book form while the rest were still coming out in the papers. One can only marvel at the sophistication of an audience that consumed and relished pieces so closely reasoned, so thoughtful and analytical. To compare *The Federalist Papers* with their equivalents in the press of our own day—say, with the contributions to the Op Ed page of the *New York Times*—is to annotate the decay of political discourse in America.

6   No doubt the birth of a nation is a stimulus to lofty utterance. The Founding Fathers had a profound conviction of historical responsibility. "The people of this country, by their conduct and example," Madison wrote in *The Federalist*, "will decide the important question, whether societies of men are really capable or not of establishing good government from reflection and choice, or whether they are forever destined to depend for their political constitutions on accident and force." The substitution of

reflection and choice for accident and force proposed a revolution in the history of government; and the authors of *The Federalist* were passionate exemplars of the politics of reason.

7   The Founding Fathers lived, moreover, in an age when politicians could say in public more or less what they believed in private. If their view of human nature was realistic rather than sentimental, they were not obliged to pretend otherwise. *The Federalist,* for example, is a work notably free of false notes. It must not be supposed, however, that even this great generation was immune to temptation. When the Founding Fathers turned to speak of and to the largest interest in a primarily agricultural nation, they changed their tone and relaxed their standards. Those who lived on the soil, Jefferson could inanely write, were "the chosen people of God . . . whose breasts He has made His peculiar deposit for substantial and genuine virtue." Such lapses from realism defined one of the problems of American political discourse. For, as society grew more diversified, new interests claimed their place in the sun; and each in time had to be courted and flattered as the Jeffersonians had courted and flattered the agriculturists. The desire for success at the polls thus sentimentalized and cheapened the language of politics.

8   And politics was only an aspect of a deeper problem. Society as a whole was taking forms that warred against clarity of thought and integrity of language. "A man's power to connect his thought with its proper symbol, and so to utter it," said Emerson, "depends on the simplicity of his character, that is, upon his love of truth, and his desire to communicate it without loss. The corruption of man is followed by the corruption of language. When simplicity of character and the sovereignty of ideas is broken up by the prevalence of secondary desires, the desire of riches, of pleasure, of power, and of praise . . . words are perverted to stand for things which are not."

9   "The prevalence of secondary desires," the desire of riches, pleasure, power, and praise—this growing social complexity began to divert the function of words from expression to gratification. No one observed the impact of a mobile and egalitarian society on language more acutely than Tocqueville. Democracy, he argued, inculcated a positive preference for ambiguity and a dangerous addiction to the inflated style. "An abstract term," Tocqueville wrote, "is like a box with a false bottom; you may put in what you please, and take them out again without being observed." So words, divorced from objects, became instruments less of communication than of deception. Unscrupulous orators stood abstractions on their head and transmuted them into their opposites, aiming to please one faction by the sound and the contending faction by the meaning. They did not always succeed. "The word *liberty* in the mouth of Webster," Emerson wrote with contempt after the Compromise of 1850, "sounds like the word *love* in the mouth of a courtezan." Watching Henry Kissinger babbling about his honor at his famous Salzburg press conference, one was irresistibly

reminded of another of Emerson's nonchalant observations: "The louder he talked of his honor, the faster we counted our spoons."

10   Other developments hastened the spreading dissociation of words from meaning, of language from reality. The rise of mass communications, the growth of large organizations and novel technologies, the invention of advertising and public relations, the professionalization of education—all contributed to linguistic pollution, upsetting the ecological balance between words and their environment. In our own time the purity of language is under unrelenting attack from every side—from professors as well as from politicians, from newspapermen as well as from advertising men, from men of the cloth as well as from men of the sword, and not least from those indulgent compilers of modern dictionaries who propound the suicidal thesis that all usages are equal and all correct.

11   A living language can never be stabilized, but a serious language can never cut words altogether adrift from meanings. The alchemy that changes words into their opposites has never had more adept practitioners than it has today. We used to object when the Communists described dictatorships as "people's democracies" or North Korean aggression as the act of a "peace-loving" nation. But we are no slouches ourselves in the art of verbal metamorphosis. There was often not much that was "free" about many of the states that made up what we used to call, sometimes with capital letters, the Free World; as there is, alas, very often little that is gay about many of those who seek these days to kidnap that sparkling word for specialized use. Social fluidity, moral pretension, political and literary demagoguery, corporate and academic bureaucratization, and a false conception of democracy are leading us into semantic chaos. We owe to Vietnam and Watergate a belated recognition of the fact that we are in linguistic as well as political crisis and that the two may be organically connected. As Emerson said, "We infer the spirit of the nation in great measure from the language."

12   For words are not neutral instruments, pulled indifferently out of a jumbled tool kit. "Language," wrote Coleridge, "is the armoury of the human mind; and at once contains the trophies of its past, and the weapons of its future conquests." Language colors and penetrates the depths of our consciousness. It is the medium that dominates perceptions, organizes categories of thought, shapes the development of ideas, and incorporates a philosophy of existence. Every political movement generates its own language-field; every language-field legitimizes one set of motives, values, and ideals and banishes the rest. The language-field of the Founding Fathers directed the American consciousness toward one constellation of standards and purposes. The language-field of Vietnam and Watergate has tried to direct the national consciousness toward very different goals. Politics in basic aspects is a symbolic and therefore a linguistic phenomenon.

13   We began to realize this in the days of the Indochina War. In the middle 1960s Americans found themselves systematically staving off reality by

allowing a horrid military-bureaucratic patois to protect our sensibilities from the ghastly things we were doing in Indochina. The official patter about "attrition," "pacification," "defoliation," "body counts," "progressive squeeze-and-talk," sterilized the frightful reality of napalm and My Lai. This was the period when television began to provide a sharper access to reality, and Marshall McLuhan had his day in court.

14   But the military-bureaucratic jargon could be blamed on generals, who, as General Eisenhower reminded us at every press conference, habitually speak in a dialect of their own. What we had not perhaps fully realized before Watergate was the utter debasement of language in the mouths of our recent civilian leaders. How our leaders really talk is not, of course, easy to discover, since their public appearances are often veiled behind speeches written by others. I know that President Kennedy spoke lucidly, wittily and economically in private. President Johnson spoke with force and often in pungent and inventive frontier idiom. President Nixon's fascinating contribution to oral history suggests, however, a recent and marked decline in the quality of presidential table talk. "A man cannot speak," said Emerson, "but he judges himself."

15   Groping to describe that degenerate mélange of military, public relations and locker-room jargon spoken in the Nixon White House, Richard N. Goodwin aptly wrote of "the bureaucratization of the criminal class." It was as if the Godfather spoke in the phrases of the secretary of health, education and welfare. When one read of "stroking sessions," of "running out of the bottom line," of "toughing it out," of going down "the hang-out road," or "how do you handle that PR-wise," one felt that there should be one more impeachable offense; and that is verbicide. But what was worse than the massacre of language, which after all displayed a certain low ingenuity, was the manipulation of meaning. The presidential speech preceding the release of the expurgated transcripts was syntactically correct enough. But it proclaimed in tones of ringing sincerity that the transcripts showed exactly the opposite of what in fact the transcripts did show. "He unveils a swamp," as the *New Yorker* well put it, "and instructs us to see a garden of flowers." In the Nixon White House, language not only fled the reality principle but became the servant of nightmare.

16   "The use of words," wrote Madison in the thirty-seventh *Federalist*, "is to express ideas. Perspicuity, therefore, requires not only that the ideas should be distinctly formed, but that they should be expressed by words distinctly and exclusively appropriate to them." Madison was under no illusion that this condition of semantic beatitude was easy to attain. "No language is so copious," he continued, "as to supply words and phrases for every complex idea, or so correct as not to include many equivocally denoting different ideas. . . . When the Almighty himself condescends to address mankind in their own language, his meaning, luminous as it must be, is rendered dim and doubtful by the cloudy medium through which it

is communicated." Nevertheless, Madison and his generation thought the quest for precision worth the effort. It is an entertaining but morbid speculation to wonder what the Founding Fathers, returning to inspect the Republic on the eve of the two-hundredth anniversary of the independence they fought so hard to achieve, would make of the White House tapes.

17   The degradation of political discourse in America is bound to raise a disturbing question. May it be, as Tocqueville seemed to think, that such deterioration is inherent in democracy? Does the compulsion to win riches, pleasure, power, and praise in a fluid and competitive society make the perversion of meaning and the debasement of language inevitable? One can certainly see specific American and democratic traits that have promoted linguistic decay. But a moment's reflection suggests that the process is by no means confined to the United States nor to democracies. Language degenerates a good deal more rapidly and thoroughly in communist and fascist states. For the control of language is a necessary step toward the control of minds, as Orwell made so brilliantly clear in *1984*. Nowhere is meaning more ruthlessly manipulated, nowhere is language more stereotyped, mechanical, implacably banal, and systematically false, nowhere is it more purged of personal nuance and human inflection, than in Russia and China. In democracies the assault on language is piecemeal, sporadic, and unorganized. And democracy has above all the decisive advantage that the preservation of intellectual freedom creates the opportunity for counterattack. Democracy always has the chance to redeem its language. This may be an essential step toward the redemption of its politics.

18   One must add that it is idle to expect perfection in political discourse. The problem of politics in a democracy is to win broad consent for measures of national policy. The winning of consent often requires the bringing together of disparate groups with diverging interests. This inescapably involves a certain oracularity of expression. One remembers de Gaulle before the crowd in Algeria, when the *pieds-noirs* chanted that Algeria belonged to France, replying solemnly, "Je vous comprends, mes camarades"*—hardly a forthright expression of his determination to set Algeria free. Besides, oracularity may often be justified since no one can be all that sure about the future. The Founding Fathers understood this, which is why the Constitution is in many respects a document of calculated omission and masterful ambiguity whose "real" meaning—that is, what it would mean in practice—only practice could disclose. Moreover, as Lord Keynes, who wrote even economics in English, once put it, "Words ought to be a little wild, for they are an assault of thought upon the unthinking."

19   Keynes immediately added, however: "But when the seats of power and authority have been attained, there should be no more poetic license." Madison described the American experiment as the replacement of

* "I understand you, my friends."

accident and force by reflection and choice in the processes of government. The responsibility of presidents is to define real choices and explain soberly why one course is to be preferred to another—and, in doing so, to make language a means not of deception but of communication, not an enemy but a friend of the reality principle.

20   Yet presidents cannot easily rise above the society they serve and lead. If we are to restore the relationship between words and meaning, we must begin to clean up the whole linguistic environment. This does not mean a crusade for standard English or a campaign to resurrect the stately rhythms of *The Federalist Papers*. Little could be more quixotic than an attempt to hold a rich and flexible language like American English to the forms and definitions of a specific time, class, or race. But some neologisms are better than others, and here one can demand, particularly in influential places, a modicum of discrimination. More important is that words, whether new or old, regain a relationship to reality. Vietnam and Watergate have given a good many Americans, I believe, a real hatred of double-talk and a hunger for bluntness and candor. Why else the success of the posthumous publication of President Truman's gaudy exercise in plain speaking?

21   The time is ripe to sweep the language-field of American politics. In this season of semantic malnutrition, who is not grateful for a public voice that appears to blurt out what the speaker honestly believes? A George Wallace begins to win support even among blacks (though ambition is already making Wallace bland, and blandness will do him in too). Here those who live by the word—I mean by the true word, like writers and teachers; not by the phony word, like public relations men, writers, and teachers—have their peculiar obligation. Every citizen is free under the First Amendment to use and abuse the words that bob around in the swamp of his mind. But writers and teachers have, if anyone has, the custodianship of the language. Their charge is to protect the words by which they live. Their duty is to expel the cant of the age.

22   At the same time, they must not forget that in the recent past they have been among the worst offenders. They must take scrupulous care that indignation does not lead them to the same falsity and hyperbole they righteously condemn in others. A compilation of political pronouncements by eminent writers and learned savants over the last generation would make a dismal volume. One has only to recall the renowned, if addled, scholars who signed the full page advertisement in the *New York Times* of October 15, 1972, which read, as the *New Yorker* would say, in its entirety: "Of the two major candidates for the Presidency of the United States, we believe that Richard Nixon has demonstrated the superior capacity for prudent and responsible leadership. Consequently, we intend to vote for President Nixon on November 7th and we urge our fellow citizens to do the same."

23   The time has come for writers and teachers to meet the standards they would enforce on others and rally to the defense of the word. They must

expose the attack on meaning and discrimination in language as an attack on reason in discourse. It is this rejection of reason itself that underlies the indulgence of imprecision, the apotheosis of usage, and the infatuation with rhetoric. For once words lose a stable connection with things, we can no longer know what we think or communicate what we believe.

24   One does not suggest that the restoration of language is all that easy in an age when new issues, complexities, and ambiguities stretch old forms to the breaking point.

> . . . Words strain
> Crack and sometimes break, under the burden,
> Under the tension, slip, slide, perish,
> Decay with imprecision, will not stay in place,
> Will not stay still.*

Each venture is therefore the new beginning, the raid on the inarticulate with shabby equipment always deteriorating in the general mess of imprecision of feeling. Yet, as Eliot went on to say, "For us, there is only the trying. The rest is not our business." As we struggle to recover what has been lost ("and found and lost again and again"), as we try our own sense of words against the decay of language, writers and teachers make the best contribution they can to the redemption of politics. Let intellectuals never forget that all they that take the word shall perish with the word. "Wise men pierce this rotten diction," said Emerson, "and fasten words again to visible things; so that picturesque language is at once a commanding certificate that he who employs it, is a man in alliance with truth and God."

Questions on Content

1. Schlesinger says that his essay is an amendment to Orwell's (paragraph 1). In what ways does Schlesinger suggest that Orwell was prophetic?

2. What did Vietnam and Watergate reveal about our use and abuse of language?

3. Why does Schlesinger admire the prose of our Founding Fathers? Why is the prose of even the best contemporary politicians so different?

4. What did Tocqueville mean when he said, "An abstract term is like a box with a false bottom; you may put in what you please, and take them out again without being observed" (paragraph 9)?

---

* T. S. Eliot, "Burnt Norton," sec. V, *Four Quartets.*

5. How does Schlesinger characterize President Nixon's language? Should Schlesinger's well-known political liberalism affect our reaction to his opinion?

6. Schlesinger states, "The winning of consent . . . inescapably involves a certain oracularity of expression" (paragraph 18). What does he mean?

7. Why does the author discuss eighteenth-century American history at such length?

Questions on Structure and Style

8. The last sentence of paragraph 10 contains a clear example of parallel construction. Find other examples in the essay.

9. Schlesinger quotes Emerson five times, and he concludes the essay with one of these quotations. Why?

10. The sentence structure in this essay is often quite complex, yet sixteen of the twenty-four paragraphs begin with short sentences. What effect does this achieve?

Assignments

1. Assume the role of George Orwell, and write an essay commenting on Schlesinger's style and language. How would Orwell have reacted to Schlesinger's essay?

2. Schlesinger concentrates on American political language from World War II through the Nixon presidency. Find examples of prose from the Carter and Reagan administrations, and write an essay analyzing political language during these presidencies.

3. Compose a topical outline of this essay (as you may have done with Orwell's), and in a paragraph, describe the essay's organization. If you've outlined both essays, write a paragraph comparing their organization.

next to of course god america i

e. e. cummings

Political voices are often unmistakable. Here, e. e. cummings presents his version of one such voice—or perhaps all of them. In his familiar style, the poet satirizes politicians through their language, achieving a ghastly accurate rendering of political speech at its worst.

"next to of course god america i
love you land of the pilgrims' and so forth oh
say can you see by the dawn's early my
country 'tis of centuries come and go
and are no more what of it we should worry
in every language even deafanddumb
thy sons acclaim your glorious name by gorry
by jingo by gee by gosh by gum
why talk of beauty what could be more beautiful than these heroic happy dead
who rushed like lions to the roaring slaughter
they did not stop to think they died instead
then shall the voices of liberty be mute?"

He spoke. And drank rapidly a glass of water

Questions on Content

1. The poem contains two voices. Where does the second voice enter, and what is its function?

2. What is the poem's theme?

3. Describe Cummings's attitude toward the political voice he captures.

4. Does Cummings want only to make us laugh? What other reaction is he hoping for, if any?

Questions on Structure and Style

5. List five of the many clichés in the poem. What effect does Cummings achieve by running them together?

6. What is the effect of "by gorry/by jingo by gee by gosh by gum" (lines 7–8)?

7. Punctuation and capitalization are more regular in the last line. Why does the poem become more conventional here? Why does Cummings leave out the final period?

Assignments

1. To reveal what any poem means, we need to examine its structure and language. In an essay, discuss the content of Cummings's sonnet in light of its structure and language. In other words, discuss *what* the poem says by examining *how* it says it.

2. Cummings's poem is a good example of satire. In a paragraph, explain the value of a satire like this one. What can satire do that can't be done through some other approach? Use the poem as an example to illustrate your ideas.

3. Try to write your own satire (essay or poem) on language and behavior. Possible subjects might be your friends or family, or perhaps public figures, such as religious leaders or Hollywood celebrities. Remember that satire involves ridicule (usually through exaggeration) and reveals the author's beliefs about the subject of the satire.

The Case of
the President's Case

William Safire

As a speechwriter for Richard Nixon, William Safire helped shape the public statements of a president. In the following analysis of the language of Ronald Reagan's second inaugural address, Safire, now a columnist for the *New York Times*, defends Reagan's apparently deliberate decision to ignore a grammatical rule. As Safire points out, sometimes grammatically *correct* language is simply not the *right* language, given what the speaker wants to achieve with words.

1   "To the ramparts!" writes Ethel Hubbard of Williston Park, L.I. "President Reagan, in his Inaugural Address said, 'If not *us*, who?' For shame. He should have said, 'If not *we*, who?' "

2   From Richard Hall at the Lovett School in Atlanta comes this dismayed reaction: "My colleagues and I spend a good bit of energy attending to details such as pronoun case and agreement in students' writing. It bothers me to see such a crass error coming from the President on such an important occasion and, further, to find no one calling him to task on it."

3   The responsibility devolves upon me, your local grammarian, to do it here, in a column devoted to soft sell of linguistic standards. If not in this space, where? If not me, who?

4   Or should that be—if not I, whom? If not me, whom? If not I, who?

5   The President's rhetorical question, which he has been asking since his California Governor days, involves an error in case. Let's get down to cases on *case*.

6   People hung up on Latin and Greek are case-hardened. You will hear them throwing around words like *ablative, vocative, dative, nominative* and *genitive* as if they still mean something to modern English. They do not. I don't want to be accusative, but the case for *case* in the language we speak today is limited. Useful, but limited, to be defended in a narrow area.

7   When a young person heavily in touch with his own feelings comes up to an English teacher and says, "What's with this *case* jazz?" the best response is: "Do you believe in relationships?" Of course, today "relationships" is all—no commitment, no hurting, just touch lives and run.

8   Same with *case*. Grammatical case is the relationship between classes of words to indicate their functions in a sentence. (Means nothing; try again.) *Case* is a word that describes how certain words relate to the words around them. (Better. I hear you.) The doer of an action is in one category and has

to relate to the receiver of an action. The doers are subjects, in the *subjective* case; the receivers are objects, in the *objective* case. These *subjective* and *objective* cases are frequently married in sentences; just as in real life, the words in each case are tempted to have outside affairs, and those relationships of belonging or possessing are done in the sleazy motel rooms of the *possessive* case. (You're on a roll, man; lay it on me.)

9   What sort of crowd do you find in the *subjective* case? That's the domain of the doers, the assertive big-shot types, *I, we, he, she, they, who,* all looking out for Number One.

10   On the other hand, if you go to a disco for *objective* cases, you get a lot of slow dancing and meek acceptances from the likes of *me, us, him, her, them* and *whom*.

11   When the two cases get together, you have clear relationships: *I* hit *her. We* clobbered *him. They* sued *us*. When the two cases branch out to impose their ownership or lust to be possessed, they relate to the *possessive* case: I got *mine.* He's got *his.* They got *their* or *theirs.* Who got *whose.*

12   Let's play a little game to show how happy we can all be when we stick within our case-assigned relationships: *subjective* gets *possessive* for the *objective*. Here goes: *I* got *mine* for *me. We* got *ours* for *us. He* or *she* got *his* or *hers* for *him* or *her. They* got *theirs* for *them. Who* got *whose* for *whom.*

13   That is the state of relationships in the perfect world, with every word knowing its case the way Victorians knew their places. Now that we have steeped ourselves in the meaning of case and accepted its simple and orderly scheme, I have troubling news: we live in an imperfect world.

14   One of the linguistic problems of the real world stems from our tendency to take verbal shortcuts. We leap from peak to peak and expect the listener to fill in the valleys. When we speak or write and omit words that we expect to be understood, we are engaging in *elliptical construction,* and that's where much of the confusion about case takes place.

15   Take, for example, the President's catchy question: "If not us, who?" Let's assume he meant "If *we* do not make the hard decision, then *who* will?" In that case (using *case* in two meanings), what he meant to say was "If not *we, who?*"

16   But wait. What if his elliptical construction were built this way: "If hard decisions are not made by *us,* then by *whom* will they be made?" In that case, he meant "If not *us, whom?*"

17   The trick is to be consistent within the case: if he goes *subjective,* it should be *we/who;* if he goes *objective* case, it should be *us/whom.*

18   "The President's question represents a clear failure in pronoun-case agreement," charges Mr. Hall. He is correct: Mr. Reagan, to agree with himself, should have said either, "If not we, who?" or "If not us, whom?"

19   Now—who is going to walk up to el Presidente and accuse him of corrupting the grammar of the nation's youth?

20   Not me.

21   Why not? Haven't I fearlessly corrected his pronunciation of *liaison* (he used to say "lay-i-zon," but has now admitted error and changed his ways). Has he not been castigated in this space for going to the "well" too often. (In his most recent press conference, his answers began: "Well, we're going to stay with the treaties. . . ." "Well, the Treasury plan. . . ." "Well, remove it in the sense of its present structure. . . ." "Well, what I'm saying is. . . ." "Well, I was actually speaking to some clergymen . . ." and six more "wells." I may go to a press conference to ask, "How are you feeling, Mr. President?" just to let him use the word in a substantive sense.)

22   The reason for today's timorousness is my own use of the natural-sounding "Not *me*" just above. The correct answer was "Not I," because that is my ellipsis for "I am not the one" or "The one to do it is not I." But I would not say "Not I" because I am a native speaker passionately in love with Norma Loquendi, and she wouldn't be caught dead saying the snooty-sounding, pedantic "Not I."

23   In the same way, if Norma and I were holding hands outside the Oval Office and the President called out "Whozat?" we would reply "It's us." If we were to reply with the formally correct "It is we," the President would think he was being approached by a couple of reactionary linguistic kooks.

24   In the real world, case has been taking a bit of a buffeting in the last couple of generations. Today it is pedantry to insist on the subjective case (*I, he, we*) when the objective case falls more naturally on the ear. The English teacher who hears such permissiveness from a language maven need not be dismayed: "*Us* Tareyton smokers" and "*them* guys" still sound as unschooled as "*Me* Tarzan, you Jane," and "between you and *I*" is still incorrect. Their students should be taught why such constructions make the speakers appear to be straining to be members of the underworld or make writers seem condescending or illiterate. (The use of *their* at the beginning of that sentence, referring back to "the English teacher" in the previous sentence, though not so obvious a blunder, is a misuse of the possessive case, which, had it not been picked up by an astute rewriter, would have been the source of great embarrassment. Next week: pronoun-antecedent agreement.)

25   A good case can be made for the consistent use of case—in most cases. Similarly, a neat and logical argument can be put forward for clarity in personal relationships, with married people, and single people living together, and happy hermits all by themselves—but some mixing of categories is definitely taking place.

26   The great question is: should case-crossing—the breakdown of absolute consistency in grammatical case rules—be furiously resisted, quietly tolerated, openly condoned, or actively encouraged?

27   Put me down for quiet toleration in formal writing, open condonement in speech. When it comes to usage President Reagan is a rhetorical

roundheels, as befits a politician seeking empathy with his audience. He is the McGovern of pronoun-case agreement, an accommodationist of the first order.

28   He was fully aware that, even in an Inaugural Address, the formal "If not we, who?" or "If not us, whom?" would have seemed laughably stilted. He chose the comfortable "If not us, who?" and Norma Loquendi wriggled in enthusiastic agreement, which is why, in this matter, the legion of the rampart-dwellers would do well to get off his case.

Questions on Content

1. Exactly what error in grammatical case did Ronald Reagan make in his Second Inaugural Address? How does Safire react to those who have written to him about this error?

2. What does Safire mean when he says, "People hung up on Latin and Greek are case-hardened" (paragraph 6)? What is the correct term for Safire's humorous *case-hardened*?

3. What is an elliptical construction? How is it relevant to Reagan's error in case?

4. Explain what Safire means by the following: "Today it is pedantry to insist on the subjective case (*I, he, we*) when the objective case falls more naturally on the ear" (paragraph 24). Can you think of other examples that illustrate this belief?

Questions on Structure and Style

5. Discuss the relationship between the first and last paragraphs of Safire's essay. Why is the relationship particularly effective?

6. What audience does Safire have in mind? How can we tell?

7. Paragraph 6 ends with a sentence fragment, one of several that Safire uses in his essay. His use of such fragments is clearly intentional. Find other examples of sentence fragments in the essay, and give possible reasons why Safire, a language authority, chooses to use these fragments rather than complete, grammatically correct sentences.

8. Paragraph 20 consists of one sentence—actually, a reduced elliptical construction. Some may call it a fragment. What is its purpose? That is, what tasks does Safire accomplish with the two words?

Assignments

1. After rereading Safire's essay, become a grammarian, and write a set of rules about the functions of the three cases in English, rules as they may appear in a handbook of English grammar. Be sure that your explanation is both clear and as concise as possible. Then compare your rules with those composed by your classmates.

2. In paragraph 14, Safire states: "One of the linguistic problems of the real world stems from our tendency to take verbal shortcuts." In an essay, explain this phenomenon, providing specific examples from both written material and from language as you have heard it used. (One helpful step may involve defining both the "real world" and the other, unnamed world with which it often conflicts.)

Nukespeak: Nuclear Language, Culture, and Propaganda

Paul Chilton

The way that we talk about nuclear weapons directly affects what
we do with them. This idea guides Paul Chilton, a professor of
linguistics at Warwick University (England), as he examines the
vocabulary that has enabled scientists, politicians, military planners, and others to persuade the public that nuclear weapons are
necessary. According to Chilton, debate about such weapons has
relied on irrational thinking and superstition so that the resulting
"discussion" amounts to propaganda.

1   In totalitarian regimes, official state propaganda fills the hole of silence left
by the censor. It is clearly and recognizably framed off from all other
writing and talk. For that very reason it may not be heeded; people may
even develop a healthy art of skeptical reading between the lines. Of
course, propaganda in totalitarian states does not need to be effective: the
army and the secret police are a more impressive short-term silencer.

2   In Western democracies, though you may be watched, you will probably
not be imprisoned for expressing dissident views or unpalatable facts, and
few people, I imagine, would question that this is a preferable state of
affairs. However, contrary to conventional wisdom, this does not mean
that in Western societies, censorship and propaganda do not operate, and
operate effectively, despite the fact that there is no official censor or propaganda office. Noam Chomsky has pointed out that "state censorship is
not necessary, or even very effective, in comparison to the ideological
controls exercised by systems that are more complex and more decen-
tralized."[1] Indeed ideological control may be more effective for not being
recognizably framed off from the rest of discourse. To quote Chomsky
further:

> A totalitarian state simply enunciates official doctrine—clearly,
> explicitly. Internally, one can think what one likes, but one can
> only express opposition at one's peril. In a democratic system
> of propaganda no one is punished (in theory) for objecting to
> official dogma. In fact dissidence is encouraged. What this sys-
> tem attempts to do is to fix the limits of possible thought: sup-
> porters of official doctrine at one end, and the critics . . . at the
> other. . . . No doubt a propaganda system is more effective

[1] *Language and Responsibility,* Harvester Press, 1979, p. 20. Chomsky is specifically discussing Vietnam, but what he says applies equally to official doctrines on the cold war and nuclear weapons.

> when its doctrines are insinuated rather than asserted, when
> it sets the bounds for possible thought rather than simply im-
> posing a clear and easily identifiable doctrine that one must par-
> rot—or suffer the consequences.[2]

3   Chomsky is referring here to the way the American press excluded certain views on Vietnam in the 1970s, but parallels can be drawn with the
manipulation of the nuclear debate in the British media. . . . Alongside
simple exclusion, of course, there are the equally effective techniques of
ridicule, deemphasis, smear, and so on.

4   In addition to these methods of censorship, there is also a likelihood that
"the bounds for possible thought" about the nuclear issue are influenced
in a more positive way—in the sense that both official and popular utterances about nuclear weapons and war use language in such a way that
nuclear weapons and war are familiarized and made acceptable. This is the
basic idea of "nukespeak."

5   To coin the term "nukespeak" itself is to make three main claims. First,
that there exists a specialized vocabulary for talking about nuclear weapons
and war together with habitual metaphors, and even preferred grammatical constructions. Secondly, that this variety of English is not neutral and
purely descriptive, but ideologically loaded in favor of the nuclear culture;
and thirdly, that this *matters,* insofar as it possibly affects how people think
about the subject, and probably determines to a large extent the sort of
ideas they exchange about it.

6   Granted that nukespeak exists, one is led to ask who is responsible for it.
Clearly not some Orwellian grammarian rewriting the English language in
the Ministry of Truth. One way of answering the question is to see nukespeak as a symptom of the nuclear culture we have forged for ourselves, as
an indication of the depth of its penetration into our mentality. The post-
Hiroshima world has had to create new images and vocabulary to encapsu-
late the inconceivable—literally inconceivable—phenomenon of nuclear
fission/fusion and its moral implications. The development of the atomic
bomb was not a smooth transition from existing weaponry, but a catastrophic jump to a new order of experience in science, politics, and
everyday life. In 1945 it was popular to refer to this jump as a "revolution"
which would itself "revolutionize" human behavior, and to communicate
about such matters on the fringe of experience and imagination places
strain on our symbolic systems. The language used to talk about the new
weapons of mass extermination was partly a reflection of an attempt to slot
the new reality into the old paradigms of our culture. It was also no doubt a
language that served the purpose of those who were concerned to per-
petuate nuclear weapons development and deployment.

[2] As above, pp. 38–9.

7   This is the second way of looking at nukespeak, to see it not just as a kind of mass response to a crisis of comprehension, but as a controlled response directed by the state in conjunction with other interested parties, and to see it as a means of constraining possible thought on the nuclear phenomenon. In the consolidation and dissemination of nukespeak the media are crucial, their function being to pass on nuclear language from producer to consumer along a one-way channel.

8   Once you begin to look closely at nuclear language, you get the strong impression that in spite of the scientific background, in spite of the technical theorizing, most talk about nuclear war and weapons reflects irrational, not to say, superstitious, processes of thought. Myths, metaphors, paradoxes, and contradictions abound. There is no time here to unravel all the complexities: I aim merely to point out some of the features and landmarks in the linguistic control of nuclear ideology.

The Birth of the Bomb

9   The first atomic explosion was at Alamogordo in the New Mexico desert on July 16, 1945. It appears that many of the scientists involved were genuinely overwhelmed by the spectacle and deeply disturbed by the implications. Many more people, scientists and nonscientists alike, were overwhelmed and disturbed when atomic explosions destroyed Hiroshima and Nagasaki later the same year. One soldier who saw the first test is reported to have said: "The long-haired boys have lost control." Others too have been impressed by the fact that the people behind the "atomization" (as it was sometimes popularly called in 1945) of Hiroshima and Nagasaki were civilized and cultured men.[3] Patriotic fervor, political naivety, and the myopia of scientific specialization doubtless played a part.

10   But after the explosion, what sense did they and the general public make of the experience? Nicholas Humphrey has recently stated the question like this: "I do not see how any human being whose intelligence and sensibilities have been shaped by traditional facts and values could possibly understand the nature of these unnatural, otherworldly weapons."[4] One explanation—the one I want to outline here—is that it is precisely certain traditional patterns of thought which make it possible to come to terms with, if not strictly to "understand," nuclear explosions. We have traditional ways of talking, myths, symbols, metaphors, which provide safe pigeonholes for what is "unnatural" or "otherworldly." This is a dangerous tendency in human culture, one which perhaps helps to explain the spellbound ambivalence of our attitudes toward the bomb.

[3] Cf. Thomas Wiseman, referred to in *The Guardian*, Nov. 5, 1981, p. 10.
[4] The Bronowski Memorial Lecture. See *The Listener*, Dec. 29, 1981, p. 494.

11   One of the physicists who left the atom bomb project when it no longer seemed necessary, Joseph Rotblatt, points to a related tendency:

> While everybody agrees that a nuclear war would be an unmitigated catastrophe, the attitude towards it is becoming similar to that of potential natural disaster, earthquakes, tornadoes, and other Acts of God. . . .[5]

12   Robert Oppenheimer, the director of the first tests, seems to have handled his own experience of the explosions in terms of traditional images. He called the first test site "Trinity"—that most mysterious of theological concepts. (Interestingly, the sacred threesome has reappeared in the form of "the Triad," that is the "convention," the nuclear "strategic" and the nuclear "theater" forces of NATO.) It is said that he had been reading John Donne's sonnet "Batter my heart, three personed God. . . ." At the moment of detonation, so the story continues, a passage from sacred Hindu literature "flashed" across his mind:

> If the radiance of a thousand suns
> were to burst into the sky,
> that would be like the
> splendour of the Mighty One . . .

And on beholding the monstrous mushroom cloud he recalled another line: "I am become Death, the shatterer of worlds."

13   This was not an idiosyncratic response. After Trinity an official report was rushed to President Truman, who was then meeting at Potsdam with Churchill and Stalin:

> It [the explosion] lighted every peak, crevasse and ridge of the nearby mountain range with a clarity and beauty that cannot be described. . . . It was the beauty the great poets dream about. . . . Then came the strong, sustained, awesome roar which warned of doomsday and made us feel that we puny things were blasphemous to dare to tamper with the forces heretofore reserved to the Almighty.[6]

The religious vocabulary and phrasing are unmistakable, and are typical of the way the politicians and the press spoke later. In religious cultures the awful and the anomalous are allied with the supernatural, and the supernatural is both dangerous and sacred. Such familiar patterns of thought and talk somehow seem to have made the bomb both conceivable and

---

[5] Cited in *Overkill* by John Cox, Pelican, 1981, p. 10.
[6] Quoted by Nicholas Humphrey. See *The Listener*, Dec. 29, 1981, p. 498.

acceptable. There is also another deep-seated cultural stereotype that has served to mythologize the sorry history of Oppenheimer himself, as well as to alleviate the guilt of the physicists. This is the stereotype of Faust, the overweening genius with dangerous access to the secrets of the universe.

14   Oppenheimer declared, Faust-like, in 1956: "We did the Devil's work." To what extent did he act out the role? He certainly appears, or is portrayed as, a late Renaissance stereotype—like Faust ambitious, individualistic, immersed in science and culture.

15   Some of the scientists may indeed have been mythologizing themselves. Wiseman thinks that "what they really were doing, and they must have been aware of it as they were doing it, was challenging the whole system of God and the whole of the Judeo-Christian morality that up to then said certain things are prohibited by God."[7] Others have cast them in the traditional roles. Lord Zuckerman speaks of the "alchemists of our times, working in secret ways which cannot be divulged, casting spells. . . ." In one recent film about Oppenheimer, his scientist-biographer explicitly describes him as a Faust figure.[8] In traditional cultures such figures are dangerous; they have to be purged. It's therefore not surprising that in the McCarthyite witch hunts Oppenheimer was ritualistically cast out of the body politic. My point is that the recycling of symbolic thought, talk, and actions has helped to bring us to terms with the invention of the bomb. It is a dangerous game to play in the nuclear age.

16   It is important to realize that this recycling was fostered by politicians and the press. In August 1945 there emerged a new consensus language, speaking of the atomic bomb in terms of religious awe and evoking simultaneously the forces of life and death. One useful consequence of such language, if not one of its actual motivations, was to appear to diminish human control, responsibility, and guilt. Its immediate political function was to obscure the fact that, strictly, the bomb project need never have been completed, and the bomb itself never dropped.

17   The problem, for the press, linguistically speaking, was what words to use to refer to the new thing, how to capture a new concept, but also how to conceal from the many the horror that had been glimpsed by the few. There is a kind of gruesome poetry in the resulting style. Rarely is the atomic bomb described in totally negative terms. When the *Times* called it "the new and terrible weapon of annihilation,"[9] this was exceptional. Some letter writers criticized it vigorously, but the contrary was evidently the editorial policy of the established papers.

18   Like the scientists, journalists expressed themselves in terms of incomprehension and ineffable awe. The *Times* called the scale of destruction

[7] Quoted in *The Guardian*, Nov. 5, 1981.
[8] *After Trinity* by John Else.
[9] Aug. 10, 1945, p. 5.

"stupendous," "beyond belief," and declared its "bewilderment."[10] The verbal reactions of eyewitnesses of Hiroshima and Nagasaki were dutifully reported: " 'My God,' burst out every member of the crew as the bomb struck." "The whole thing was tremendous and awe-inspiring," said a Captain Parsons of the U.S. Navy.[11] The *Daily Mail* spoke of the problem for the human mind in confronting what human minds had produced: "The test for our survival . . . is whether the solution of the problems raised by the splitting of the atom lies within the human brain." This was dismissed by the *Daily Worker* as "mumbo jumbo," "medieval superstition," and "mysticism." Actually, both papers were making a valid point. At the end of the week the *Observer* gave a sermon on what it called "a week of wonders," mystified the bomb by referring to it simply as "A" (for "atom," but also for alpha, source of creation), and compounded the mystification by calling it "destruction's masterpiece." Such paradoxical expressions abound in the press rhetoric of that week.

19   There emerged a small set of evocative, positively valued words for describing the bomb and its effects. They are interesting for the notion of nukespeak not only because they stretch existing meanings but also because their use often seems to originate in specific sources—politicians' speeches, and the public utterances of the military. The papers picked them up both in reporting and in comment, and not only repeated them incessantly, but spawned on them a whole network of associations and metaphors.

20   The press did not in fact, in the first instance, report Hiroshima and Nagasaki direct; it reported official utterances *about* them. The speeches of Truman and Churchill on August 6, 1945, were quoted verbatim, but they also provided the core of the subsequent bomb rhetoric developed in the papers. Two key passages in Truman's speech were seized upon:

> It is an atomic bomb. It is the *harnessing of the basic power of the universe*. . . .

and

> The *force* from which *the sun* draws *its power* has been *loosed*. . . .

The key words here seem to have triggered off a whole series of associations which have their basis in the language of religion and myth. Churchill, reported verbatim in the *Times* of August 7, provides an example of this, one that was to yield still more reverberations:

[10] Aug. 8, 1945, p. 5; Aug. 9, p. 4; Aug. 13, p. 4.
[11] *Daily Worker*, Aug. 8, 1945, p. 1, and other papers.

> *By God's mercy* British and American science outpaced all German efforts. . . . This *revelation of the secrets of nature*, long mercifully *withheld from man*, should arouse the most solemn reflections in the mind and conscience of every human being capable of comprehension. We must indeed *pray* that these awful *agencies* will indeed *be made to conduce to peace* among the nations, and instead of wreaking measureless havoc upon the entire globe they may become a *permanent fountain* of world *prosperity*.

So the select few capable of comprehending the problem are let off with "solemn reflections"—that is, pious platitudes well illustrated in the surrounding verbiage, and copiously regurgitated by editorialists. How do the rhetorical tricks work?

21   Churchill does not refer directly to the event that inspired the speech, but instead to the "revelation of the secrets of nature." In the next few days it became commonplace to describe the development and dropping of the bomb in such a way as to make it a natural (or supernatural) process somehow outside human control. That perspective is underscored by a grammatical tactic—using the passive construction with no mention of the causative agent. The "secrets of nature" have been "long withheld." By whom? When agents are omitted readers and hearers normally have to make an inference from context, if possible, and if not possible, make speculative guesses that are plausible in some framework of belief. Or, more conveniently, they can just leave the question unasked. Here readers are strongly encouraged (by words like "pray" and "revelation") to suppose that God was the agent. In fact, what Churchill left implicit was to be amplified for *Times* readers by the Dean of Salisbury in a letter on August 10: "God made the atom and gave the scientists the skill to release its energy. . . ." More "solemn reflections" followed. A letter of August 13 actually amplifies Churchill's phrase "God's mercy": "By the same token it might be claimed that through divine grace English-speaking scientists were able to make their original discoveries of the vast source of energy. . . ."

22   Thus one is left with the supposition that men were not ultimately responsible for the invention and use of the atomic bomb; it was given to them by some outside force. This is not all. In Churchill's phrase "will be made to conduce to peace," there is no clear reference to who will do the making (God again?). Moreover, the atomic bombs ("these awful agencies") themselves, and not humans, are presented as the agents of peace or destruction. It is the bombs that "conduce to peace" (whatever that means) or "wreak havoc." The final image ("perennial fountain") of life-giving water is a potent symbol in traditional culture, and is used to insinuate the belief that the bomb is a "power" for good.

23   The *Times*'s leading article for August 8 gives some idea of how the catch phrases and grammatical tricks could be used to construct a kind of poetic

pseudosolution to the problem. The mushroom cloud becomes a meta-phor—and an excuse:

> An impenetrable *cloud* of dust and smoke . . . still *veils* the un-doubtedly stupendous destruction wrought by the first impact in war of the atomic bomb. . . . A *mist* no less impenetrable is likely for a long time to *conceal* the full significance in human affairs of the *release* of the *vast and mysterious power locked* within the in-finitesimal units of which the material structure of the universe is built up. . . . All that can be said with certainty is that the world stands in the presence of a *revolution in earthly affairs* at least as big with potentialities of good and evil as when the *forces* of steam and electricity were *harnessed* for the first time. . . . Science itself is neutral, like the *blind forces of nature* that it studies and aspires to control. . . . *The fundamental power of the universe*, the power *manifested* in the *sunshine* that has been recognized from the re-motest ages as the sustaining *force* of *earthly life*, is *entrusted* to earthly hands . . . the new *power* [must] be *consecrated* to peace not war. . . .

24   It isn't difficult to spot the verbal and thematic similarities between this passage and the sources cited earlier. The methods are similar—the exploi-tation of familiar traditional images evoking supernatural activity, and the subtle manipulation of grammatical forms; and so is the general presenta-tion of the atomic bomb as something paradoxically good and evil but predominantly good, and as something outside human responsibility.

25   One of the most prominent words in the speeches and press reports is "power," closely followed by "force." Religious associations are never far beneath the surface. Here's a sample: *Basic Power of the Universe, the funda-mental power of the universe, the new power, the irresistible power, vast and mysterious power, mighty power, power manifested in the sunshine, power for healing and industrial application, mighty force, new force, powerful and forceful influence.* . . . All these phrases are elicited by the news of the destruction of Hiroshima and Nagasaki. The advantage of intoning the word "power" lay in the fact that it implied both supernatural forces and at the same time beneficial technological applications. This way of talking, together with the failure to report the full horrific details (reports of Hiroshima and Nagasaki casualties were at first presented as Japanese propaganda), made it pos-sible to conceive that the atomic bomb and its use had been a good thing. A *Sunday Times* book reviewer thought Nagasaki should be remembered as "A-B day," but the ambivalence of current attitudes towards the bomb was such that he did not know whether it should be celebrated "with universal rejoicing as heralding Man's entrance into a Kingdom of Power and Glory, or with a dirge."[12]

---

[12] Aug. 12, 1945.

The Naming of the Bomb

26   Describing the architects of the atomic bomb, Lord Zuckerman has said that "the men in the nuclear laboratories on both sides have succeeded in creating a world with an irrational foundation." This is usually taken to mean that the highly rational activities of scientists have led to the production of weapons with no clear rational purpose—weapons as technical solutions in search of a problem. It can mean too that the strategic doctrine based on, even generated by such weapons, is paradoxical or self-contradictory—MAD. And it can mean, as E. P. Thompson has written, that "mystery envelops the operation of the technological 'alchemists.' 'Deterrence' has become normal . . . and within this normality, hideous cultural abnormalities have been nurtured and are growing to full girth." The naming of weapons systems, seemingly trivial, well illustrates this last point.

27   The accumulation of nuclear weapons beyond the point strictly required in a theory of mutual destruction has been said to serve a symbolic purpose, in the sense of creating political and diplomatic advantage. But there may be more to it than this. I want to suggest that the publicly known nicknames given to weapons systems are a symptom of their progressive assimilation into our culture, and also that such names serve to advertise this fact to the domestic population. The way they do it is something like this. There are deeply ingrained patterns of symbolic thought (some researchers think they are innate tendencies of the human mind) which are used to organize, classify, and "normalize" our experiences of the world. Such patterns are present in mythology, religion, and many other domains. "When a human mind, even a scientist's mind, is overcome by bewilderment, it runs for shelter to the archetypes of pre-scientific thought. . . ."[13] Thus, while nuclear weapons represent the most advanced scientific thinking, their role in human affairs is handled in a subrational, mythological fashion.

28   The Cold War itself is deeply subrational, and the symbols used to express it reflect the fact. In a common image two tribes oppose one another—the Eagle and the Bear. To see how this is ideologically loaded, consider the contrasting attributes of these two totems: one soars to the skies, is wise, and all-seeing; the other is heavy, clumsy, stupid, and half blind. Weapon names are the mythological insignia of the two tribes, and there is a similar relationship between the two sets of names we have given them. Not quite all, but most of the NATO weapons are given two names: LGM-30F/G is also called Minuteman, for example. The nicknames come from Greco-Roman and Scandinavian mythology, and from the more recent "mythology" of national history. They form a meaningful pattern.

[13] *Robert Oppenheimer* by M. Rouze, Souvenir Press, 1962, p. 23.

The nicknames given to Soviet weapons, on the other hand, are generally based on an initial letter and are designed to disparage or to be meaningless: Saddler, Sasin, Scarp, Sego, Savage, Bison, Blinder, Bear . . .

29   As we saw earlier, atomic and nuclear weapons were perceived as awesome and incomprehensible. A slot in our classification of reality had to be found for them, and to christen them was the first step. Rites of naming are rites of incorporation into social life; the officially unnamed in many cultures, including Christian, are in a state of nature (as opposed to society) and sin; they are perceived as dangerous. But even before naming them, weapons are humanized. They have fathers (Edward Teller, "father of the H-bomb"), though no mothers; they grow from infants ("baby nukes") to old age (NATO's allegedly "aging" forces) in a family ("the ICBM family"); they retire ("retiring Polaris force") and make way for the young ("new generation MX ICBMs").

30   The pattern of development of the names is itself revealing. There are four categories: human types and roles (less popular now); artefacts of human culture—tools, hand weapons (increasingly popular); animals (never very much used); and gods and heroes (most prominent). The early atom-test scientists under Oppenheimer referred to the first atomic device as "the gadget"—not strictly a name, but a synonym that made the momentous experiment feel familiar, homely, and useful. And when the "gadget" was accepted into the life of the nation in the form of a usable bomb, it acquired a name. The uranium bomb detonated over Hiroshima was called "Little Boy," the plutonium bomb dropped on Nagasaki, "Fat Man." They were thus familiarized as amiable human stereotypes. But that was *before* the deed was done and the cataclysmic effects brought home. After the event there were new naming tendencies which reflected the sense of supernatural awe. The human designations lingered on, however, though their effect is now not only to familiarize but also to confer a military status and a patriotic role.

31   The 1960s saw "Little Boy" promoted to "Corporal," and later to "Sergeant" (both of these were tactical, short-range missiles). At about the same time "Honest John" also appeared in Europe, equipping BAOR [British Air Force operations] and the French forces. Then there were the "Minutemen," intercontinental ballistic missiles of which we have now had three "generations," the latest having been "MIRVed" with 200-kiloton warheads. The word "Minuteman" may not mean much to a European. To an American patriot it refers to the heroic militiamen of the American Revolutionary War who were trained to turn out at a minute's warning. Thus this inconceivably devastating weapon is given a place in national folklore. And if you didn't know about that, there is also the odd fact that the name of this particular missile also spells "minute [small] man"—odd because that too scales down the weapon's size, and recalls "Little Boy."

32   Animal names are not much used. They seem to be largely reserved to designate Soviet weapon systems. But one is worth mentioning because it illustrates the often bizarre way in which nuclear planners elaborate their semicoded talk. In the 1960s a system was investigated which could dodge ABMs (Anti-Ballistic Missiles). It was nicknamed "Antelope"—a beast that is agile at high altitudes. A further refinement was called "Super-Antelope." This had the notorious successor "Chevaline," a name which ought to mean (in French) "horselike." Its popularity may owe more to its streamlined sound to the English ear, but it had to have a meaning too, and Lawrence Freedman notes that "there is a belief in the Ministry of Defense that Chevaline refers to a species of antelope which is akin to a mountain goat and is supposed to share with the new warhead the ability to move in a variety of directions at high altitudes."[14]

33   The symbolism of height as well as of depth, the symbolism of sky and earth, life and death, is contained in the structure of many traditional myths. But the system is plainer in the imposing *classical* names that accommodate our weapons of mass annihilation in the structures of traditional culture. There are the gods of the sky, thunder, blinding light, who are both creators and destroyers. "Polaris" (submarine launched ballistic missile dating from 1950s) is the "stella polaris," the pole star, traditional top of the celestial sphere. "Skybolt" was a missile project canceled in 1962. "Thor" (an American IRBM kept in Turkey in the 1950s and early 1960s) was the Scandinavian god of thunder. "Jupiter" (another IRBM, accompanying "Thor") was the Latin sky-god of rain, storms, and thunder. "Atlas" (an American missile of the 1950s) was a Titan, condemned to stand in the west to stop the sky falling down—an uncannily apt expression of "deterrence" dogma. The "Titans" themselves (the largest of the American ICBMs, carrying a nine-megaton warhead) were a "monstrous and unconquerable race of giants with fearful countenances and the tails of dragons."[15] Then there are the gods of the depths. The largest of the American submarine-launched ballistic missiles is called "Poseidon," the Greek god of earthquakes and of the sea, who calls forth storms. Poseidon had a brother Pluto, the ruler of the Underworld, and the French have a mobile nuclear missile called "Pluton," and a new "generation" in gestation known as "Super-Pluton."

34   These names enable us to classify the "unnatural, otherworldly" weapons, though the actual mythological classification still keeps them precisely in that category. But the more recent trend is to mythically classify them as a part of human culture rather than as part of nature (or supernature), which is alien, terrifying, and dangerous. This is a return to the era of "the gadget." Nuclear weapons appear again with the names of human

---

[14] *Britain and Nuclear Weapons*, MacMillan, 1980, p. 48.

[15] *Dictionary of Greek and Roman Biography and Mythology*, edited by W. Smith.

artefacts, though this time they are predominantly tools of combat with strong associations in national folklore.

35   "Trident" (the Mark II Tridents are high-precision MIRVed and MARVed systems which will arm Poseidon submarines) is not only the god Poseidon's weapon, but also Britannia's. The symbolism may not be without impact on some British minds. There is also a smaller, "tactical" surface-to-surface "Harpoon." The highly significant technical innovation in the arms race represented by the cruise missile is called a "Tomahawk" —though this one can travel 1,500 miles with a 200-kiloton warhead. From medieval military history we have the "Mace," an early form of cruise missile developed in the 1960s. NATO forces in Europe are armed with "Lances"—artillery missiles that can deliver conventional, nuclear, or neutron shells up to 75 miles. And the neutron shell itself has been variously christened in ways that illustrate the present point. The term "enhanced radiation weapon" is a rather unsubtle euphemism, and when Reagan's decision to deploy the thing in Europe was announced in 1981, the popular British press did its best to justify it. They did so in a way very similar to the naming process that produced lances, maces, and the rest.

36   The *Sun* (August 10, 1981) said: "It [the neutron weapon] will give Europe a *shield*. . . ." Who would object to a purely defensive shield? We would, after all, not need a shield if there were no aggression. The *Daily Express*'s Denis Lehane, in a piece entitled "This Chilling but Vital Evil," shows how spurious arguments can be spun out from logically weak but emotionally powerful analogies. Lehane says he is seeking to rebut the charge that "the neutron bomb is a moral evil . . . because it kills people but leaves buildings largely intact." Here is his response:

> Well, so does the *bow and arrow!* The neutron weapon is for Western Europe today what the English longbow was for Henry V and his army at Agincourt in 1415.
>   It is a weapon of chilling efficiency and destructive power which counter-balances the enemy's superiority in sophisticated armour. . . .

37   There is a crude logic here which goes something like this. The neutron weapon destroys people, not property. The longbow destroys people, not property. Therefore, the neutron weapon "is" a longbow. But the longbow is good (and picturesque). Therefore, the neutron weapon is good.

38   Comparison with accepted primitive weapons is not the only way in which nuclear weapons are classified as part of human culture, and thus as nondangerous. The neutron "gadget" has reportedly been referred to in some quarters as a "cookie cutter." Now to associate it with the kitchen and cooking is significant, because in our myths it is the cooked as opposed to the raw that marks human culture out from the untamed forces of

nature. The natural and supernatural is also mythically associated with noise, culture, and quiet, and "Cruise" and "Pershing," aside from their referential meaning, may well use sound symbolism to convey speed and civilized silence. "Pershing," apart from being historically apt (he was the U.S. commander who established the American Expeditionary Force in Europe against the initial opposition of the French and British in 1917) may well be onomatopoeic ("purr" in the first syllable) for some hearers. With these points in mind note finally that it has been said of the American nuclear superpower: "You must speak *softly* when you carry a *big stick*."[16]

39   There is then a trend in the "naturalization," or rather the *acculturation*, of the nuclear phenomenon. Instead of being symbolically classified as objects of supernatural awe, nuclear weapons now tend to be classified as safe and usable instruments. This shift has clearly accompanied the gradual shift in strategic doctrine toward a more pronounced doctrine of warfighting, of which the nicknames are the public propaganda face.

The Bomb Made Safe

40   Like advertising, propaganda in western democracies has to sell a product. "Deterrents," like detergents, also have to be sold. Taxpayers buy weapons in the sense that they choose the governments who buy them— though in terms of defense policies the choice has not been too broad. Of course, governments can spend your money without telling you (as in the Chevaline development and the Trident decision), but if the arms race is at all "democratized," and facts about cruise, for instance, become known, then specific propaganda becomes necessary. When propaganda is not concealed in "objective" and "balanced" reporting in the media, it may take the guise of respectable advertising. One is reminded of cigarette advertising. Once people come to believe that cigarettes and missiles might be dangerous for them, the producers have to work hard to modify, eliminate, or repress that belief.

41   When the plans to deploy cruise missiles became known during 1980, the population in and near the proposed bases received glossy brochures.[17] On the front is a drawing of a sleek windowless aircraft sailing through azure skies. It has no military markings. Unlike the familiar image of the missile pointed toward the heavens, this one is horizontal and has no tail of fire and smoke. Because of the way it is drawn, it appears to cruise silently past your left ear as you read the text. The first thing the pamphlet does, then, is not to explain the technical facts but to trigger a vague

[16] Denis Healey, reported in *The Guardian*, Nov. 6, 1981.
[17] Available from the Ministry of Defense.

emotional response to the word "cruise." The dominant metaphor of the pamphlet is not, however, that of the travel agent, but rather the insurance broker. Beneath the drawing, in bold type, is the following statement: "A vital part of the West's Life Insurance." This odd metaphor is actually quite common in the parlance of nuclear strategists and those who advocate deterrence theory. Indeed, metaphors and analogies of all kinds are disturbingly prevalent in what is often claimed to be highly rational discourse.

42   It is not just that the association of "Life" with weapons of death and destruction is bizarre. The expression "life insurance" is odd to start with. You insure against theft or fire and you can insure against death too but you then have to call it not "death insurance," but life insurance. The advantage of doing so is first that you suppress the taboo word, and second that you read the phrase (unconsciously no doubt) as "that which insures, ensures, or assures life." Perhaps it is some such irrationality that makes the phrase effective in relation to missiles, since it scarcely makes sense as a literal analogy. If you buy an insurance policy, someone will benefit when you die; but it won't deter death from striking you, though you may have a superstitious feeling that it will. The supposedly rational argument that the cruise deterrent will ward off the death of the West is thus sustained by a doubly irrational metaphor.

43   The rest of the pamphlet follows the pattern of a commercial brochure. There is a series of questions and answers, or rather pseudoquestions and pseudoanswers, of which more below, and a wallet flap containing a separate leaflet, which does little more than repeat the material written on its glossy container. On the flap itself, however, is a color photograph of a Transporter Erector Launcher (TEL) ("about the same weight and size as large commercial vehicles" according to the legend). Its raised pod forms one side of a triangle; a line of fir trees forms the other. The foreshortening reduces the impression of the length of the vehicle. A man in green and dark glasses leans against the cab, and the line projected by his arms as well as the direction of his gaze intersects very low with the missile pod, to reduce the impression of height.

44   The back page is devoted to other aspects of making the weapon seem civilized and convenient. "What will the Cruise Missiles do in peacetime?" We are assured that "the exercises will be arranged to cause the least inconvenience to the public" and that "busy road traffic periods will be avoided." But "Are Nuclear Weapons Safe? What happens if there is an accident?" You will be reassured to know that "Nuclear Weapons are designed to the highest safety standards and [that] the greatest care is taken in their handling and storage." The same might be claimed of television sets and electric light bulbs. However, in case any reader had some other notion of "safe" in mind, he has the appropriate question asked for him: "Will Basing of Cruise Missiles in this Country make us a Special

Target if there is a War?" This and the preceding question are the only ones that expect a yes/no answer. The answer is "No," and the reason is the "sad truth . . . that no part of this country . . . will be safe from danger whether we have Cruise Missiles or not." There is a good deal of fudging and hedging here, if not actual self-contradiction, and the fuzziness starts with the formulation of the question. Who is supposed to be asking the questions? Any British inhabitant, or specifically those near the bases at Molesworth and Greenham Common? Who is the "Special Target"? "Us" in Molesworth or "us . . . in this Country"? What the pamphlet seems to be doing is to deny that the bases are "special" or "priority" targets, and offering the cold comfort of a sort of randomized danger in time of war.

45   It is interesting that this, the most crucial question of the cruise controversy, is handled in this way. It is not just ignored, but raised at the end of the pamphlet, sandwiched between a "question" on "safety" and one on cost (in general, questions relating to wartime and peacetime matters are alternated and thus associated throughout the pamphlet). Moreover, the contradictions are scarcely veiled. But what carries weight in the act of reading is that emphatic "No," which establishes an intention to deny and reassure: the reader will use that perceived intention to interpret the rest of the confusing text. This is a species of doublespeak and its significance is clear in the light of the 1980 civil defense exercises, which included the cruise bases on their list of nuclear strikes.

46   The technique in the pamphlet as a whole is reminiscent of the distortions of "balanced" reporting and discussion. Opposition as such is not silenced, but what constitutes opposition is predefined—the "limits of possible thought" are fixed in advance, and the permitted degree of opposition is handled in such a way by those who control the medium that it is neutralized or marginalized. The cruise pamphlet sets up dissident questions on its own terms and knocks them down without possibility of reply. Most of the questions are phrased in such a way that they presuppose an assertion of the official view. The supposed questioner is made to say not "Are nuclear weapons necessary?" which is the fundamental question, but "Why are nuclear weapons necessary?" This presupposes the statement "nuclear weapons are necessary," and places the "questioner" in the role of tentative enquirer approaching someone with superior knowledge and authority. Similarly, (s)he does not say "Does NATO need more nuclear weapons?" but has the question "Why does NATO need more nuclear weapons?" put in their mouth.

47   No one will buy an insurance policy unless they are convinced that they are at risk. Hence the front page of the brochure is devoted to insinuating the Russian threat. This does not mean that there is no threat or risk— clearly there is—but the situation cannot be rationally appraised by dealing in half-truths and innuendo; the verbal techniques draw on the inherent (and necessary) vagueness of human language. When a hearer or reader

interprets an utterance he assumes that the speaker has a specific intention and that he is speaking in relation to some shared context. This means that speakers can make indirect assertions, leaving readers to draw relevant inferences, while speakers can disclaim responsibility. There is the added bonus that insinuated propaganda is probably more effective than bald declarations.

48   Consider the principal actors in the front page text. On the one hand "We." In English this word is ambiguous: "we" including "you," and "we" excluding "you." The actual situation is that "we" (Ministry of Defense propaganda writers) are addressing "you," but the reader is clearly intended to assume the "we" includes her or him. Otherwise (s)he is committed to assuming that (s)he does not "want to live at peace." "We" who "want to live in peace" are then indirectly and directly identified with "The United Kingdom," with "We in the West," and with "NATO." Interestingly, there is no reference to the United States. The pronouns "we" and "us" are also defined in relation to "they" and "them," those outside the "we" group. In "we want to live at peace," the reader may be prompted by a number of contextual cues to stress the "we," thus simultaneously inferring that *"they"* do *not* want peace. And the phrase "But it takes two to make agreements and progress has been slow" infers that "they" have been recalcitrant but "we" have not.

49   Consider now the actions and mental states attributed to the principal actors in the various verb phrases. The vocabulary is not peculiar to the pamphlet, but is typical of the current rhetoric of the arms race. It is characterized by evocative vagueness, though a perusing reader may be left with the general impression of detailed definiteness.

50   Modal verbs expressing possibility, necessity, desire are most frequently attributed to "us." So "we" *"want* to live," *seek* to disarm, *"must* be stronger," *"need* to strengthen" (implying that "we" are not currently "strong"). Cruise missiles *"can* go a long way to achieving this aim"—"this aim" being a tortuous back reference to the equally vague "need to strengthen." All this strongly suggests passivity, lack, and inaction. "We" also "persuade"—a verbal activity; our military activities are limited to "basing," and "we" "have been falling behind," in a modally ambiguous sentence, the Russians "see we are weak."

51   "They," on the other hand, are not characterized by needs, wants, and lacks, but by definite actions and possessions. "They" "have been rapidly building up their military strength"; the Soviet Union "spends 12% of its national wealth each year on its armed forces," and "This is over twice the proportion spent by the NATO allies." This sounds both authoritative and precise (all the more so because of the "about"), but it is a misleading piece of noninformation. Accurate information on Soviet military spending and valid methods of comparison are notoriously difficult to come by. The figures given are in any case relative—they take no account of the absolute

difference in "national wealth."[18] The main aim is not to inform but to induce the reader to infer aggressive Soviet intentions.

52   Note also the prevalence of the present and perfect tenses, which imply definiteness, reinforced by repetition: "the Russians . . . have been rapidly building up . . . The Soviet Union spends . . . The Warsaw Pact countries have massive forces . . . They have large conventional forces . . . They also have . . . Finally they have . . ." "Their" weapons are described as "massive," "large," "very large," "modern," whereas existing NATO weapons are not mentioned at all. If "they" is read with contrastive stress, as it might well be, the reader might infer from the statement "*They* also have short and medium range nuclear weapons" that "*we*" do not have such weapons. However, the cunning pamphleteer has included an ambiguous "also"; so that if challenged, he could always claim that he meant it to mean "they as well as us." Finally, notice the phrases "to start a war" and to "risk a war against us"; it is "they," the Russians again, who are the logical subjects of these actions.

53   The distribution of vocabulary and grammatical devices is systematic, but will probably go unnoticed. Most readers seem to store *meanings* in memory rather than words and phrases, and may not question the details. They will be left with the impression of a powerful alien threat to "us," to their group. On these irrational premises is laid a spuriously rational logic. We are peaceful and weak. The Russians are warlike and strong. Conclusion: "NATO *therefore* needs to strengthen its defenses." How? "By basing Cruise Missiles, etc."

54   This is the first statement about these mysterious objects, or indeed the first mention of any NATO armaments. But we are not yet told what cruise missiles are or how they operate. We are told merely (for the second time) that "the Cruise Missile is a vital part of the West's life insurance," whatever that can mean. More succinctly, we are then told that "Cruise Missiles are (not 'would be' or 'might be,' but *are*) a deterrent."

55   The fact that they are classified as "a deterrent," before their characteristics are divulged, is a significant ploy. It predisposes the reader to think of them in a certain fashion. In the first place "deterrent" seems to have become for many people in certain contexts a synonym—and a dangerous

---

[18] See *SIPRI Yearbook 1981*, pp. 147–169 ("World military expenditure and the current situation") for further comments on this kind of distortion, e.g.: "One constantly finds, in Western discussions of Soviet military expenditure, that military spokesmen and others use the *dollar* estimate for the level of military expenditure, since that gives you a very high figure, and the *rouble* estimate for the rate of growth in that expenditure, since that method gives the higher figure for the rate of growth. This is, of course, not the only problem in producing sensible, and comparable, figures for rates of growth; one of the other main problems [is] the measurement of quality change.

    Using constant price figures (rather than the misleading proportion of national wealth), SIPRI notes "that there is a rough parity of resources devoted to military purposes. . . ." It also points out that "the one country in NATO Europe which had a military spending boom is the UK, with an average annual volume increase each year over the three years from 1977 to 1980 of 4.5%. This is an extraordinarily high figure. . . ."

one—for "nuclear missile." So Cruise is classified first of all as just another nuclear missile—without the word "nuclear" ever having to be used about "our" weapons. (Equally the nuclear warhead and its explosive yield are never mentioned in the semitechnical details provided inside the brochure: the missiles just "hit their targets.") In the second place, in the single word "deterrent" an important claim is made—namely, that the things do, as a matter of actual fact, "deter." That is to say, they prevent or hold back (depending on your individual use of the term) some enemy (the Russians, clearly) from doing something they are claimed, as a matter of fact, to be about to do—attack us. All that appears to be implied, in context, in the semantic structure of the term. Indeed, as this potent single word is habitually used, it encapsulates the whole cold war ideology.

56   The cruise missiles pamphlet is not an isolated example. Its rhetorical ploys are typical of current official discourse concerning defense matters and relations with the Soviet Union. Such discourse is scarcely conducive to a rational evaluation either of Soviet policy or of our own defense needs. Rather it is the typical stuff of which western propaganda is made. And it is all-pervasive. That is why much of this article has had to be written in inverted commas.

Questions on Content

1. In the quotation from Noam Chomsky in paragraph 2, the following statement appears: "No doubt a propaganda system is more effective when its doctrines are insinuated rather than asserted." What does Chomsky mean? How is this point relevant to Chilton's argument?

2. According to Chilton, what is the purpose of *nukespeak*?

3. Explain the following statement: "The language used to talk about the new weapons of mass extermination was partly a reflection of an attempt to slot the new reality into the old paradigms of our culture" (paragraph 6).

4. Chilton states in paragraph 7 that nukespeak is a "controlled response." Why is this statement vital to his argument?

5. Who is Robert Oppenheimer, and why does Chilton choose to discuss Oppenheimer's reaction to the first atomic explosion?

6. What does the acronym MAD stand for? Why is this concept crucial to our understanding of nuclear weapons today? What can we say about the connotations of the acronym itself?

7. According to Chilton, what are the four major categories of names for nuclear weapons?

Questions on Structure and Style

8. For what audience is Chilton writing? How can we tell?

9. The introduction of this essay consists of the first eight paragraphs. How does Chilton use transitions among these eight paragraphs? Where does he state his thesis?

10. What does the last sentence of the essay mean? Does it create an effective closing?

Assignments

1. A. Read George Orwell's "Politics and the English Language" (beginning on page 425). In an essay, respond to Chilton's argument as you believe Orwell would.
   B. Read Stephen F. Cohen's "Slanting the News against the USSR" (beginning on page 473). In an essay, respond to Chilton's argument as you believe Cohen would.

2. Are you frightened by, or at least concerned about, the naming process that Chilton describes in his essay? Respond in a paragraph.

3. Study the names of a commodity such as cars, detergents, or cigarettes. In an essay, analyze the naming process that seems evident in the names chosen by the manufacturers. To whom are the manufacturers appealing, and what tactics are they employing in naming their products? (Remember that the tactics Chilton describes are commonly used by most advertisers.)

Slanting the News against the USSR

Stephen F. Cohen

This essay bluntly states an opinion that some may consider controversial: When discussing the Soviet Union, American political reporting regularly distorts the truth. Stephen F. Cohen is a professor of Soviet politics at Princeton University. He here builds an argument against the misrepresentation, biased language, and prejudice that he believes are hallmarks of American coverage of Soviet affairs.

1   America's renewed crusade against the "Soviet threat," from Central America, Western Europe and the Middle East to outer space, has reopened an old question: Do American newspapers, magazines and television networks, with their collective power to shape public opinion and influence government policy, give concerned citizens a balanced view of the Soviet Union?

2   Whether purposely or inadvertently, they fail to do so in at least three fundamental ways. The first is through a pattern of media coverage that systematically highlights the negative aspects of the Soviet domestic system while obscuring the positive. Soviet crop failures and abuses of political liberties have been the regular focus of American news stories since the early 1970s, but expanded welfare programs and rising standards of living have gone largely unreported.

Lack of Balance

3   Nor is the disparity corrected by what passes for informed analysis, even in widely respected publications. Efforts to show both Soviet achievements and failures are exceedingly rare, whereas wholesale vilifications of the Soviet Union appear frequently. A 1982 article in the *Wall Street Journal* by the influential academic Irving Kristol, for example, informed readers that the entire Soviet system is simply a "regime of mafioso types" with "pathological" beliefs and "with no popular roots." The problem is not that the opposite is true but that, as a *Washington Post* correspondent returning from Moscow concluded several years ago, "If Americans know anything about the Soviet Union, we probably know what is bad about it."

4   The second media offense is more subtle. Objective political analysis requires language that is value-free. But much American commentary on

Soviet affairs employs special political terms that are inherently biased and laden with double standards. Consider a few of them. The United States has a government, security organization and allies. The Soviet Union, however, has a regime, secret police and satellites. Our leaders are consummate politicians; theirs are wily, cunning or worse.

Prejudicial Language

5   Obviously, the two systems are not alike, but such prejudicial language is incompatible with fair-minded analysis. In 1982, for example, the CIA reported the existence of 4 million Soviet "forced laborers." The report, based largely on the fact that all Soviet penal inmates must work, was widely and uncritically publicized in the media, sometimes with references to "slave labor." But convicted prisoners in most American penitentiaries must also work. Does that mean we, too, have "forced laborers"?

6   Finally, there is the media's habit of creating a popular perception that the Soviet Union is guilty of every charge made against it. In recent years, initial newspaper and television reports virtually convicted the Soviet leadership of the following offenses: increasing military spending by an ominous 4 to 5 percent a year; invading Afghanistan in order to seize Persian Gulf oil; attempting to assassinate the Pope; waging chemical warfare ("yellow rain") in Southeast Asia; and destroying what it knew to be a Korean commercial airliner carrying 269 passengers. Subsequent less-publicized evidence disproved some of those charges and raised serious doubts about the others. Nonetheless, it seems that in the minds of most Americans, the Soviet Union remains guilty of all of them. The result is increased acceptance of Cold War policies.

7   Can anything be done to correct this wicked-witch image of the Soviet Union? People who acknowledge the problem say we need more information to overcome widespread ignorance about complex Soviet realities.

8   But knowledge alone will not solve the problem. A growing body of more balanced information about Soviet life has been available since the 1960s. It has had little positive impact on the media or on public opinion. We know far more about the Soviet Union than we do, for example, about China, which receives far more favorable press attention. And no amount of information would prevent William Schneider, a high-level science and technology official in the Reagan Administration from writing or publishing this judgment: "The Soviet state has contributed practically nothing at all to science, culture, art, industry, agriculture, or to any other field of human endeavor."

9   Clearly, the problem is also American indifference or resistance to balanced information about the Soviet Union. Other countries frequently

receive favorable coverage in the US media because of America's traditional sympathy for them or because of domestic lobbying in their behalf. No such pro-Soviet factors are at work in the United States, and anti-Soviet lobbies stand ever ready to explain away facts that might suggest some improvement in the Soviet system. Thus, in the February 1983 *Commentary,* the eminent contributing editor Walter Laqueur writes: "There are at present in the Soviet Union relatively few political prisoners. . . . This is not because the Soviet Union is a less repressive regime, but on the contrary, because it is repressive *and* effective."

10   The solution, if there is one, requires not simply new information but old-fashioned American common sense and fairness. Common sense would tell us that the Soviet leadership had no motives for some of its alleged crimes. Fairness would not allow us to defame a nation that has suffered and achieved so much. Both have been lacking in our thinking about Soviet realities. The reason must be embedded in our history and needs. As an American historian of US attitudes toward the Soviet Union concluded, "When talking about the USSR, Americans were really talking about their own nation and themselves."

Questions on Content

1. Identify the three ways in which, Cohen believes, American reporting fails to give a balanced view of the Soviet Union.

2. Is Cohen responding to propaganda in this essay? Does he intend something else?

3. What does Cohen object to in a 1982 CIA report about "forced laborers" (paragraph 5)?

4. Cohen concludes his essay with this quotation from an American historian: "When talking about the USSR, Americans were really talking about their own nation and themselves." What does this mean?

Questions on Structure and Style

5. Examine Cohen's opening paragraph. Is his purpose apparent? Is his thesis clearly stated?

6. What is the purpose of the first sentence of paragraph 2? Should this sentence appear in the first paragraph?

7. What audience is Cohen addressing? How can you tell?

8. Is Cohen's argument convincing? Why or why not?

Assignments

1. Make a topic outline of this essay, and write a paragraph discussing its organization.

2. Locate articles about the Soviet Union in various newspapers and news magazines. Choose sources that reflect a range of political ideologies. Then write an essay responding to Cohen's assertion that "much American commentary on Soviet affairs employs special political terms that are inherently biased and laden with double standards" (paragraph 4).

3. If you agree with Cohen's thesis, do you believe that American media should be more objective in their portrayal of the USSR? Soviet news agencies are often accused of lacking any objectivity about the United States. Does (or should) this affect your reaction to American reporting? Write a paragraph responding to these questions.

Two Presidential Speeches

Presidents compose their inaugural addresses with great deliberation (and with help from advisers and professional speechwriters). These addresses are intended to inspire, reassure, and establish a tone as well as to articulate political philosophy and priorities. The following two speeches are examples of the language two presidents chose as befitting a historic occasion.

John F. Kennedy's Inaugural Address (1961)

Vice President Johnson, Mr. Speaker, Mr. Chief Justice, President Eisenhower, Vice President Nixon, President Truman, Reverend Clergy, fellow citizens:

1   We observe today not a victory of party but a celebration of freedom—symbolizing an end as well as a beginning—signifying renewal as well as change. For I have sworn before you and Almighty God the same solemn oath our forebears prescribed nearly a century and three quarters ago.

2   The world is very different now. For man holds in his mortal hands the power to abolish all forms of human poverty and all forms of human life. And yet the same revolutionary beliefs for which our forebears fought are still at issue around the globe—the belief that the rights of man come not from the generosity of the state but from the hand of God.

3   We dare not forget today that we are the heirs of that first revolution. Let the word go forth from this time and place, to friend and foe alike, that the torch has been passed to a new generation of Americans—born in this century, tempered by war, disciplined by a hard and bitter peace, proud of our ancient heritage—and unwilling to witness or permit the slow undoing of those human rights to which this nation has always been committed, and to which we are committed today at home and around the world.

4   Let every nation know, whether it wishes us well or ill, that we shall pay any price, bear any burden, meet any hardship, support any friend, oppose any foe to assure the survival and the success of liberty.

5   This much we pledge—and more.

6   To those old allies whose cultural and spiritual origins we share, we pledge the loyalty of faithful friends. United, there is little we cannot do in a host of cooperative ventures. Divided, there is little we can do—for we dare not meet a powerful challenge at odds and split asunder.

7   To those new states whom we welcome to the ranks of the free, we pledge our word that one form of colonial control shall not have passed away merely to be replaced by a far more iron tyranny. We shall not always expect to find them supporting our view. But we shall always hope to find

them strongly supporting their own freedom—and to remember that, in the past, those who foolishly sought power by riding the back of the tiger ended up inside.

8   To those people in the huts and villages of half the globe struggling to break the bonds of mass misery, we pledge our best efforts to help them help themselves, for whatever period is required—not because the communists may be doing it, not because we seek their votes, but because it is right. If a free society cannot help the many who are poor, it cannot save the few who are rich.

9   To our sister republics south of our border, we offer a special pledge—to convert our good words into good deeds—in a new alliance for progress— to assist free men and free governments in casting off the chains of poverty. But this peaceful revolution of hope cannot become the prey of hostile powers. Let all our neighbors know that we shall join with them to oppose aggression or subversion anywhere in the Americas. And let every other power know that this Hemisphere intends to remain the master of its own house.

10   To that world assembly of sovereign states, the United Nations, our last best hope in an age where the instruments of war have far outpaced the instruments of peace, we renew our pledge of support—to prevent it from becoming merely a forum for invective—to strengthen its shield of the new and the weak—and to enlarge the area in which its writ may run.

11   Finally, to those nations who would make themselves our adversary, we offer not a pledge but a request: that both sides begin anew the quest for peace, before the dark powers of destruction unleashed by science engulf all humanity in planned or accidental self-destruction.

12   We dare not tempt them with weakness. For only when our arms are sufficient beyond doubt can we be certain beyond doubt that they will never be employed.

13   But neither can two great and powerful groups of nations take comfort from our present course—both sides overburdened by the cost of modern weapons, both rightly alarmed by the steady spread of the deadly atom, yet both racing to alter that uncertain balance of terror that stays the hand of mankind's final war.

14   So let us begin anew—remembering on both sides that civility is not a sign of weakness, and sincerity is always subject to proof. Let us never negotiate out of fear. But let us never fear to negotiate.

15   Let both sides explore what problems unite us instead of belaboring those problems which divide us.

16   Let both sides, for the first time, formulate serious and precise proposals for the inspection and control of arms—and bring the absolute power to destroy other nations under the absolute control of all nations.

17   Let both sides seek to invoke the wonders of science instead of its terrors. Together let us explore the stars, conquer the deserts, eradicate disease, tap the ocean depths and encourage the arts and commerce.

18   Let both sides unite to heed in all corners of the earth the command of Isaiah—to "undo the heavy burdens . . . (and) let the oppressed go free."

19   And if a beach-head of cooperation may push back the jungle of suspicion, let both sides join in creating a new endeavor, not a new balance of power, but a new world of law, where the strong are just and the weak secure and the peace preserved.

20   All this will not be finished in the first one hundred days. Nor will it be finished in the first one thousand days, nor in the life of this Administration, nor even perhaps in our lifetime on this planet. But let us begin.

21   In your hands, my fellow citizens, more than mine, will rest the final success or failure of our course. Since this country was founded, each generation of Americans has been summoned to give testimony to its national loyalty. The graves of young Americans who answered the call to service surround the globe.

22   Now the trumpet summons us again—not as a call to bear arms, though arms we need—not as a call to battle, though embattled we are—but a call to bear the burden of a long twilight struggle, year in and year out, "rejoicing in hope, patient in tribulation"—a struggle against the common enemies of man: tyranny, poverty, disease and war itself.

23   Can we forge against these enemies a grand and global alliance, North and South, East and West, that can assure a more fruitful life for all mankind? Will you join in that historic effort?

24   In the long history of the world, only a few generations have been granted the role of defending freedom in its hour of maximum danger. I do not shrink from this responsibility—I welcome it. I do not believe that any of us would exchange places with any other people or any other generation. The energy, the faith, the devotion which we bring to this endeavor will light our country and all who serve it—and the glow from that fire can truly light the world.

25   And so, my fellow Americans: ask not what your country can do for you—ask what you can do for your country.

26   My fellow citizens of the world: ask not what America will do for you, but what together we can do for the freedom of man.

27   Finally, whether you are citizens of America or citizens of the world, ask of us here the same high standards of strength and sacrifice which we ask of you. With a good conscience our only sure reward, with history the final judge of our deeds, let us go forth to lead the land we love, asking His blessing and His help, but knowing that here on earth God's work must truly be our own.

1. In paragraph 2, Kennedy asserts that his world is different from and, at the same time, similar to the world of "our forebears" (paragraph 1). What does he mean?

2. Describe Kennedy's attitude toward the United Nations.

3. What is Kennedy's attitude toward our adversaries?

4. What does Kennedy imply is a major goal for his administration?

5. Most paragraphs in this address are brief—one is as short as six words. Why does Kennedy favor this form? How does it contribute to his speaking style?

6. Paragraph 23 consists of two questions. What rhetorical strategy is Kennedy using here?

7. Kennedy often uses figurative language, such as "beach-head of cooperation" and "jungle of suspicion" (paragraph 19). Find three other examples of figurative language, and explain how they contribute to the address.

8. This speech is filled with the rhetorical devices of balance, parallel structure, and repetition. Find three examples of each device. What effect does each device create?

9. Kennedy's address contains many phrases that are carefully designed to be memorable. List three that seem particularly well crafted. Why do they stand out?

10. Overall, what effect does Kennedy hope to create with the ideas and language of this speech? Moreover, how does he himself wish to appear to his audience?

Assignments

1. Looking back, we can now see how this speech was an integral part of the 1960s, when John F. Kennedy's youth and enthusiasm inspired a generation of Americans. Write an essay discussing how an audience of the 1980s would respond to the tone, style, and content of this speech.

2. In an essay, describe and evaluate Kennedy's expression in this address. Pay attention to the rhetorical devices of balance, parallel structure, repetition, and figurative language, and consider the effects these devices create.

3. Write your own address, focusing on three key issues that affect college-age students of your generation.

Ronald Reagan's First Inaugural Address (1981)

1   To a few of us here today this is a solemn and most momentous occasion. And, yet, in the history of our Nation it is a commonplace occurrence. The orderly transfer of authority as called for in the Constitution routinely takes place, as it has for almost two centuries, and few of us stop to think how unique we really are. In the eyes of many in the world, this every-4-year ceremony we accept as normal is nothing less than a miracle.

2   Mr. President, I want our fellow citizens to know how much you did to carry on this tradition. By your gracious cooperation in the transition process you have shown a watching world that we are a united people pledged to maintaining a political system which guarantees individual liberty to a greater degree than any other, and I thank you and your people for all your help in maintaining the continuity which is the bulwark of our Republic.

3   The business of our Nation goes forward. These United States are confronted with an economic affliction of great proportions. We suffer from the longest and one of the worst sustained inflations in our national history. It distorts our economic decisions, penalizes thrift, and crushes the struggling young and the fixed-income elderly alike. It threatens to shatter the lives of millions of our people.

4   Idle industries have cast workers into unemployment, human misery, and personal indignity. Those who do work are denied a fair return for their labor by a tax system which penalizes successful achievement and keeps us from maintaining full productivity.

5   But great as our tax burden is, it has not kept pace with public spending. For decades we have piled deficit upon deficit, mortgaging our future and our children's future for the temporary convenience of the present. To continue this long trend is to guarantee tremendous social, cultural, political, and economic upheavals.

6   You and I, as individuals, can, by borrowing, live beyond our means, but for only a limited period of time. Why, then, should we think that collectively, as a nation, we're not bound by that same limitation? We must act today in order to preserve tomorrow. And let there be no misunderstanding—we are going to begin to act, beginning today.

7   The economic ills we suffer have come upon us over several decades. They will not go away in days, weeks, or months, but they will go away. They will go away because we as Americans have the capacity now, as we've had in the past, to do whatever needs to be done to preserve this last and greatest bastion of freedom.

8   In this present crisis, government is not the solution to our problem; government is the problem. From time to time we've been tempted to believe that society has become too complex to be managed by self-rule, that government by an elite group is superior to government for, by, and of

the people. Well, if no one among us is capable of governing himself, then who among us has the capacity to govern someone else? All of us together —in and out of government—must bear the burden. The solutions we seek must be equitable with no one group singled out to pay a higher price.

9   We hear much of special interest groups. Well, our concern must be for a special interest group that has been too long neglected. It knows no sectional boundaries or ethnic and racial divisions, and it crosses political party lines. It is made up of men and women who raise our food, patrol our streets, man our mines and factories, teach our children, keep our homes, and heal us when we're sick—professionals, industrialists, shopkeepers, clerks, cabbies, and truckdrivers. They are, in short, "We the people," this breed called Americans.

10   Well, this administration's objective will be a healthy, vigorous, growing economy that provides equal opportunities for all Americans with no barriers born of bigotry or discrimination. Putting America back to work means putting all Americans back to work. Ending inflation means freeing all Americans from the terror of runaway living costs. All must share in the productive work of this "new beginning," and all must share in the bounty of a revived economy. With the idealism and fair play which are the core of our system and our strength, we can have a strong and prosperous America, at peace with itself and the world.

11   So, as we begin, let us take inventory. We are a nation that has a government—not the other way around. And this makes us special among the nations of the Earth. Our government has no power except that granted it by the people. It is time to check and reverse the growth of government which shows signs of having grown beyond the consent of the governed.

12   It is my intention to curb the size and influence of the Federal establishment and to demand recognition of the distinction between the powers granted to the Federal Government and those reserved to the States or to the people. All of us need to be reminded that the Federal Government did not create the States; the States created the Federal Government.

13   Now, so there will be no misunderstanding, it's not my intention to do away with government. It is rather to make it work—work with us, not over us; to stand by our side, not ride on our back. Government can and must provide opportunity, not smother it; foster productivity, not stifle it.

14   If we look to the answer as to why for so many years we achieved so much, prospered as no other people on Earth, it was because here in this land we unleashed the energy and individual genius of man to a greater extent than has ever been done before. Freedom and the dignity of the individual have been more available and assured here than in any other place on Earth. The price for this freedom at times has been high. But we have never been unwilling to pay that price.

15   It is no coincidence that our present troubles parallel and are proportionate to the intervention and intrusion in our lives that result from

unnecessary and excessive growth of government. It is time for us to realize that we're too great a nation to limit ourselves to small dreams. We're not, as some would have us believe, doomed to an inevitable decline. I do not believe in a fate that will fall on us no matter what we do. I do believe in a fate that will fall on us if we do nothing. So, with all the creative energy at our command, let us begin an era of national renewal. Let us renew our determination, our courage, and our strength. And let us renew our faith and our hope.

16   We have every right to dream heroic dreams. Those who say that we're in a time when there are no heroes, they just don't know where to look. You can see heroes every day going in and out of factory gates. Others, a handful in number, produce enough food to feed all of us and then the world beyond. You meet heroes across a counter. And they're on both sides of that counter. There are entrepreneurs with faith in themselves and faith in an idea who create new jobs, new wealth and opportunity. They're individuals and families whose taxes support the government and whose voluntary gifts support church, charity, culture, art, and education. Their patriotism is quiet but deep. Their values sustain our national life.

17   Now, I have used the words "they" and "their" in speaking of these heroes. I could say "you" and "your," because I'm addressing the heroes of whom I speak—you, the citizens of this blessed land. Your dreams, your hopes, your goals are going to be the dreams, the hopes, and the goals of this administration, so help me God.

18   We shall reflect the compassion that is so much a part of your makeup. How can we love our country and not love our countrymen; and loving them, reach out a hand when they fall, heal them when they're sick, and provide opportunity to make them self-sufficient so they will be equal in fact and not just in theory?

19   Can we solve the problems confronting us? Well, the answer is an unequivocal and emphatic "yes." To paraphrase Winston Churchill, I did not take the oath I've just taken with the intention of presiding over the dissolution of the world's strongest economy.

20   In the days ahead I will propose removing the roadblocks that have slowed our economy and reduced productivity. Steps will be taken aimed at restoring the balance between the various levels of government. Progress may be slow, measured in inches and feet, not miles, but we will progress. It is time to reawaken this industrial giant, to get government back within its means, and to lighten our punitive tax burden. And these will be our first priorities, and on these principles there will be no compromise.

21   On the eve of our struggle for independence a man who might have been one of the greatest among the Founding Fathers, Dr. Joseph Warren, president of the Massachusetts Congress, said to his fellow Americans, "Our country is in danger, but not to be despaired of. . . . On you depend

the fortunes of America. You are to decide the important question upon which rests the happiness and the liberty of millions yet unborn. Act worthy of yourselves."

22   Well, I believe we, the Americans of today, are ready to act worthy of ourselves, ready to do what must be done to ensure happiness and liberty for ourselves, our children, and our children's children. And as we renew ourselves here in our own land, we will be seen as having greater strength throughout the world. We will again be the exemplar of freedom and a beacon of hope for those who do not now have freedom.

23   To those neighbors and allies who share our freedom, we will strengthen our historic ties and assure them of our support and firm commitment. We will match loyalty with loyalty. We will strive for mutually beneficial relations. We will not use our friendship to impose on their sovereignty, for our own sovereignty is not for sale.

24   As for the enemies of freedom, those who are potential adversaries, they will be reminded that peace is the highest aspiration of the American people. We will negotiate for it, sacrifice for it; we will not surrender for it now or ever.

25   Our forbearance should never be misunderstood. Our reluctance for conflict should not be misjudged as a failure of will. When action is required to preserve our national security, we will act. We will maintain sufficient strength to prevail if need be, knowing that if we do so we have the best chance of never having to use that strength.

26   Above all we must realize that no arsenal or no weapon in the arsenals of the world is so formidable as the will and moral courage of free men and women. It is a weapon our adversaries in today's world do not have. It is a weapon that we as Americans do have. Let that be understood by those who practice terrorism and prey upon their neighbors.

27   I'm told that tens of thousands of prayer meetings are being held on this day, and for that I'm deeply grateful. We are a nation under God, and I believe God intended for us to be free. It would be fitting and good, I think, if on each Inaugural Day in future years it should be declared a day of prayer.

28   This is the first time in our history that this ceremony has been held, as you've been told, on this West Front of the Capitol. Standing here, one faces a magnificent vista, opening up on this city's special beauty and history. At the end of this open mall are those shrines to the giants on whose shoulders we stand.

29   Directly in front of me, the monument to a monumental man, George Washington, father of our country. A man of humility who came to greatness reluctantly. He led America out of revolutionary victory into infant nationhood. Off to one side, the stately memorial to Thomas Jefferson. The Declaration of Independence flames with his eloquence. And then, beyond the Reflecting Pool, the dignified columns of the Lincoln

Memorial. Whoever would understand in his heart the meaning of America will find it in the life of Abraham Lincoln.

30   Beyond those monuments to heroism is the Potomac River, and on the far shore the sloping hills of Arlington National Cemetery, with its row upon row of simple white markers bearing crosses or Stars of David. They add up to only a tiny fraction of the price that has been paid for our freedom.

31   Each one of those markers is a monument to the kind of hero I spoke of earlier. Their lives ended in places called Belleau Wood, The Argonne, Omaha Beach, Salerno, and halfway around the world on Guadalcanal, Tarawa, Pork Chop Hill, the Chosin Reservoir, and in a hundred rice paddies and jungles of a place called Vietnam.

32   Under one such marker lies a young man, Martin Treptow, who left his job in a small town barbershop in 1917 to go to France with the famed Rainbow Division. There, on the western front, he was killed trying to carry a message between battalions under heavy artillery fire.

33   We're told that on his body was found a diary. On the flyleaf under the heading, "My Pledge," he had written these words: "America must win this war. Therefore I will work, I will save, I will sacrifice, I will endure, I will fight cheerfully and do my utmost, as if the issue of the whole struggle depended on me alone."

34   The crisis we are facing today does not require of us the kind of sacrifice that Martin Treptow and so many thousands of others were called upon to make. It does require, however, our best effort and our willingness to believe in ourselves and to believe in our capacity to perform great deeds, to believe that together with God's help we can and will resolve the problems which now confront us.

35   And after all, why shouldn't we believe that? We are Americans.

36   God bless you, and thank you.

Questions on Content

1.   What "special interest group" is Reagan most interested in serving?

2.   What does Reagan believe is the most important issue facing his administration?

3.   Explain the following: "The Federal Government did not create the States; the States created the Federal Government" (paragraph 12).

4.   Why does Reagan paraphrase Winston Churchill in paragraph 19? What parallel is he attempting to draw?

5. Why is Martin Treptow (paragraphs 32–34) important to Reagan's address?

Questions on Structure and Style

6. Reagan refers to Dr. Joseph Warren (paragraph 21) and Martin Treptow (paragraphs 32–34), yet most of his audience has probably never heard these names before. Why does he mention them? How do these references contribute to Reagan's style in this address?

7. What is the tone of this speech?

8. Overall, what effect does Reagan hope to create with the ideas and language of this speech? Moreover, how does he himself wish to appear to his audience?

Assignments

1. In this speech, Reagan makes certain assumptions about the American people, assumptions that we can infer from his ideas and language. Are these assumptions different from those Kennedy makes in his inaugural address? Respond in an essay.

2. Write an essay comparing the language of Reagan's First Inaugural Address with that of Kennedy's 1961 Inaugural Address. Examine the level of diction, tone, and rhetorical devices each president used.

Benderly discusses recent discoveries about the startling ways in which the human brain handles language.

Computers aren't the first invention to affect language; television and the telephone have left their influence, too. But the computer is one of the most recent and thus most visible technological forces stretching and molding language. Regardless of its shape, however, language will survive as long as we do. Technology may change it, but language comes with a better guarantee than any machine: It won't become obsolete.

Four Hang-ups

William Zinsser

Anyone who has felt intimidated by machines will appreciate William Zinsser's candid and witty discussion in *Writing with a Word Processor*, from which this chapter is taken. Zinsser identifies four "blocks" that often prevent us from accepting word processing. Zinsser is a writer, editor, and teacher (and author of a selection in Chapter 1 of this book), but his reflections on word processing incorporate the feelings of people in many fields—the humanities, science and technology, and commerce and industry.

1   I found myself thinking about some of the psychological blocks that people would bring to their first encounters with a word processor. Different blocks would be brought by different people, but all of them would be injurious and would have to be confronted and cleared away.

2   The hardest thing for me to think about was the idea of getting along without paper. The idea is alien to everything we know in our bones. People have been writing on paper, or papyrus, for four or five thousand years—long enough, anyway, to get into the habit. Paper is where we transact most of the routine business of life: letters, postcards, notes, lists, memos, bills, checks, receipts, notices, reminders to ourselves. Writing something on paper is one of the basic comforts. Even those of us who keep messy desks know that if we just burrow long enough in the piles of stuff we'll find the scrap of paper we're looking for—the one we didn't throw away because we knew that someday we might need it. The nightmare is to lose the crucial nugget of information: the recipe torn from a magazine, the name of the perfect little country inn, the phone number of a plumber who will come on Saturday.

3   Writers are unusually afraid of loss. The act of writing is so hard that just to get anything on paper is a small victory. A few terrible sentences are better than no sentences at all; they may at least contain a thought worth saving, a phrase that can be reshaped. The important thing is that these fragments exist somewhere in the physical world. The paper that they're written on can be held, stared at, marked up, put aside and reexamined later. Ten or twenty pages can be spread out on the floor and rearranged with scissors and paste. Scissors and paste are honorable writers' tools. So is the floor.

4   I could hardly imagine throwing all this away—not only the paper itself, but the security blanket. With my new word processor I would type my words and see them materialize on a screen. At that moment the words

would, I suppose, exist. But would they *really* exist? Not in any sense that I had ever thought of words before. They would be mere shadows of light. If I pressed the wrong key, couldn't they just vanish into thin air? (No air is thinner than the air into which a writer starting out on a word processor thinks his words will vanish.) Or even if I pressed the right key and stored my words correctly overnight on a disk, would I be able to call them back in the morning? Would I ever see them again? The chances of my never seeing them again struck me as high. I didn't trust what I couldn't hold. Paper was the one reality in writing.

5   That was my first block. I wondered how I would get past it—and if I would.

6   The second block was what I'll call the humanist hang-up. This is the snobbery of liberal-arts types who don't understand science or technology and don't want to. It's a group that I belong to myself, so I know its biases and phobias. Our unifying belief is that science has somehow been the cause of everything that has messed up the world and made it so complex and impersonal. If it would just go away. If we could just be left to our exquisitely sensitive appreciation of art and music and literature, of history and philosophy and the classics—the really civilized fields.

7   Perhaps we aren't snobs so much as we are cowards. We're afraid of how stupid we feel in the presence of science, and so we take refuge in feeling superior. We have never had an aptitude for math or chemistry or engineering, and we are fearful that we won't understand what we read and hear every day about quantum physics, or solid state electronics, or gene splicing, or quasars and quarks. These are mysteries too arcane for us dummies to fathom. Better not to try.

8   But what really makes us dummies is that we give up so easily. I often think of the pleasure I've lost by shying away from fields that I thought would be too hard to grasp. Only in recent years have I started to glimpse the elegance of the physical and mathematical world by reading the work of scientists who also were writers—men and women like Rachel Carson, Lewis Thomas, Margaret Mead, René Dubos, Jeremy Bernstein and Loren Eiseley. They seem to me to be the true humanists. I envy them their gift for seeing the world whole and not in isolated parts.

9   Most of us who are afraid of science are also uncomfortable with machines. As a boy I was never taught to tinker and to fix things, and as a man I have lived in a society of servicemen who will repair what has gone wrong. When a piece of machinery breaks, my instinct has always been to hit it, or to yank at it—to force it, somehow, to lurch back into action. It's the blind instinct of a man who regards machines as his enemy. Only later does it occur to me that the broken gadget was built to operate by a series of logical steps and that I might locate the problem by tracing those steps. Even then the idea that I might be able to fix it is almost inconceivable, and when I occasionally succeed I tend to think it was mostly luck.

10   It's not that I disapprove of technology. On the contrary, I'm grateful for its blessings. I love to drive a car, though I have only a vague notion of what is under the hood or how the combustion engine works. I love to fly in a plane, though I'm fuzzy about the law of aerodynamics that holds such an immense object up in the sky. Surely it defies that other law (which I also hope nobody asks me to explain)—the law of gravity. I'm a fan of the electric light, but my knowledge of the ohm is limited to crossword puzzles—and that goes for the erg and the ampere and the watt.

11   The point is that it's not necessary to understand the wonders of technology in order to enjoy them, and this should be as true of computers as it is of cars. Yet there is no end of grumbling about them. "I don't want to have anything to do with computers," I keep hearing people say. I used to say it myself, and part of me still continued to think it.

12   That was obviously a hang-up.

13   The third block is the exact opposite of the one I have just described. It belongs to all the people who are not liberal-arts types—people whose bent is for science and technology and commerce and industry. Their block is that they don't think they have to bother to learn how to write clear English. At the IBM showroom I had seen enough of the word processor to suspect that it could greatly help people to clean up their sentences by focusing their mind on the act of writing and revising. But over the years I had also seen enough writing by America's technical and business people to feel that they are almost beyond salvation.

14   Here is a typical example of how corporate America conducts its daily business in memos:

> Product usability objective setting should be a direct outgrowth of the initial opportunity definition of your program, plus the specific usability oriented information gathered during priority setting and the requirements definition activity.

15   It's little short of criminal to inflict such a memo on a group of employees or colleagues. How much energy do Americans expend every day trying to figure out what people in authority are trying to say? How many good ideas are lost in the murk of Memoville? How many official explanations totally fail to explain? Consider how the airlines tell their passengers—in a notice stapled to every ticket—what to expect if a flight is overbooked:

> OVERBOOKING OF FLIGHTS
>
> If there are not enough volunteers the airline will deny boarding to other persons in accordance with its particular boarding priority.

16   This kind of writing is endemic to American life. Much of what is disseminated by businesses, banks, insurance companies, manufacturers, technical firms, government agencies, educational systems and health institutions—both internally and to the public—is as hard to decipher as an ancient rune, and a great deal of it makes no sense at all. This is because the people who are doing the writing don't stop to think that this is in fact what they are doing. Writing is something that "writers" do.

17   But writers are only a fraction of the population. The rest of the citizens are in some other line of work, and vast numbers of them write something during the day that gets foisted on other people. Yet very few people realize how badly they write and how badly this hurts them and their career and their company. People are judged on the basis of who they appear to be in their writing, and if what they write is pompous or fuzzy or disorganized they will be perceived as all those things. Bad writing makes bright people look dumb.

18   How did we get into this fix? It's the humanist hang-up in reverse. People who never had a knack for words usually hated English when they were in school and stopped taking it as soon as they could. Now, out in the world where they need to write, they are as afraid of writing as I am afraid of science. They have writing anxiety. They don't know how to start.

19   One way to start is to realize that writing is a craft, like carpentry or cabinetmaking, with its own set of tools, which are words. Writing is not some sort of divine act that can only be performed by people of artistic bent, though obviously a gift for words is helpful. Writing is the logical arrangement of thought. Anybody who thinks clearly should be able to write clearly—if he learns how to use the tools. Anybody whose thinking is muddy will never write clearly.

20   To clarify what we write, it is important to see what we are writing and to constantly ask, "Have I said what I wanted to say?" Usually we haven't. Even for a professional writer very few sentences come out right the first time, or even the second or third time. Almost every sentence has some flaw: it's not clear; it could mean several different things; it's not logical; it's cluttered with unnecessary words or phrases; it has too many words that are long and lifeless; it's pretentious; it lacks rhythm.

21   These are problems that a writer systematically attacks. Like a watchmaker or any other artisan, he wants to build something that works as simply and as smoothly as possible—with no extra parts to get in the way—and he fiddles with his materials until they are right. Nonwriters don't do this. Nobody has told them that rewriting is the essence of writing—that their first draft is probably poor and that they have a second and a third chance to make it better. The worst offenders tend to be bosses who dictate to a secretary. Most people's spoken sentences are full of repetition and disarray. Therefore the man who dictates should see what he has said after it has been typed. One of the things he will see is that he could have said it in half the number of words.

22   Seeing is a key to writing. What the word processor could do is to revolutionize the way we think about words by displaying them for our consideration and giving us an instant chance to reconsider them. It will also draw far more people into the act of writing. In a few years, professional men and women in every field and at every level will be writing on word processors to conduct their daily business. I hope that as their words appear on the terminal screen they will begin to see them as tools that they can use like any other tools—without fear, and maybe even with pleasure.

23   The fourth block is the typing block.

24   A word processor has the same basic keyboard as a typewriter; therefore, anyone who uses it must know how to type. But a surprising number of otherwise competent professional people—especially men—have never learned this fundamental skill. For many men it's a sexist hang-up: typing is something women do. It's all right for men to type if they are writers; their image has been validated by macho authors like Hemingway and by movies about tough reporters in snap-brim hats. But for a man with executive ambitions to sit down at a typewriter and bang out a memo or a letter is an indignity. Better to have Miss Smithers ("a really wonderful gal") do it, even if she can't get to it until tomorrow.

25   What is lost, among other things, is independence. A person who can type is a person in control of an important area of his life: how he communicates with other people. Most writers, for instance, type their own letters—it's quick, and the writing is warm and direct. I would hate to filter what I say through Miss Smithers, wonderful though she is. What I type is who I am. When a secretary is brought into the act, writing stiffens and loses its spontaneity.

26   These, of course, are subjective reasons, related to my feelings about the writing process and about the role of women in America's offices. But there is a practical reason that is far more compelling. With the advent of computers it will be crucial for managers and other people who work in offices to have "keyboard skills."

27   "Suppose a manager must get in touch with the London or San Francisco office," said a recent piece in *The New York Times* analyzing the office of the future. "To operate at maximum efficiency he or she will not interrupt a secretary for a quick memo but will sit down at the keyboard and type. During a typical day a business manager might use terminals several times to write memos to out-of-town offices. Productivity is the key."

28   Nor will there be as many secretaries to interrupt. "The number of young, semi-skilled people for clerical jobs continues to decline," the *Times* noted. "This means that there will be more direct-support computers for managers who do not have enough people support. Middle management officers will certainly be typing."

29   Ironically, many bright and educated young women have avoided learning how to type—or admitting that they already know how—because they

have seen how often this skill gets them deflected from a possible good job into one that is clerical and demeaning. The word processor could be the answer to everybody's problem because it isn't stereotyped by sex. Although it's just a glorified typewriter, it doesn't look like a typewriter. It's modern and sleek. You'd almost expect to see it on the command deck of the starship *Enterprise*. A woman can sit at its keyboard and not be taken for a secretary. So can a man.

30   Anybody can learn to type. It's one of those skills that becomes habitual with practice, like driving a car. If typing is your block, invest in a typing course. Don't get stuck with the hang-ups of today when everyone else is flourishing in the office of tomorrow.

Questions on Content

1. For Zinsser, what was most difficult about adjusting to a word processor?

2. What four "blocks" does Zinsser identify? Which of them might apply to your own reaction to word processing?

3. What does Zinsser mean by "the humanist hang-up" (paragraph 6)? Do you believe it actually exists, or is he merely generalizing from his own feelings?

4. According to Zinsser, how can a word processor help people with writing anxiety?

5. Zinsser objects to the prose he quotes from "corporate America" in paragraph 14 and from an airline in paragraph 15. What do his objections tell us about Zinsser himself?

6. The author cites two important reasons why business people should do their own typing rather than rely on someone else. What are these reasons? Do you find them convincing?

Questions on Structure and Style

7. What organizational strategy does Zinsser employ in "Four Hang-ups"? Why is it particularly appropriate?

8. For what audience is Zinsser writing? How can we tell?

9. What is the purpose of the sentence that ends paragraph 29? Why are its shortness and simplicity vital to its purpose?

Assignments

1. One central point Zinsser makes is that writers acquire habits that are difficult to break. Try making changes in your own writing habits. If you write your first drafts with pencil and paper, try composing on a typewriter (or better yet, on a word processor). If you usually compose on a typewriter, try writing in longhand. Then write an essay assessing your writing habits and the problems you faced when you tried to change them.

2. Zinsser pays particular attention to two groups: "liberal-arts types" and "people whose bent is for science and technology and commerce and industry." Determine which of the two groups you belong to (if you believe you belong to either), and write an essay responding to the attitudes toward technology that Zinsser attributes to your group. Be sure to address the issue of technology and its effect on writing.

Machinespeak

Hugh Kenner

━━━━━━━━━

The language we venerate reveals our values and attitudes, and because computer languages constitute our contemporary "reserved knowledge," we face serious trouble. This bleak conclusion underlies Hugh Kenner's definition of computer languages, which, as he explains, are unlike human language but represent what people *think* language is—and also epitomize how people treat each other today. Kenner is a professor of humanities at Johns Hopkins University.

━━━━━━━━━

> *Ah the creatures, the creatures,*
> *everything has to be explained to them.*
> Samuel Beckett

1   That which a time truly venerates, its reserved knowledge, the lore not for the laity (who are defined, precisely, by their nonpossession of it); the formulae which will conjure the god to speak and enable their human possessors to think as largely as gods: such arcane stuff goes into a language apart, to have learned which (since no one grows up speaking it) is by definition to have become learned; and it was at one time Hieroglyphic, and at another time Scholastic Latin, but in our time is fragmented into dialects called FORTRAN and LISP and COBOL and even BASIC, variants of the authentic speech of the thunder which is called Machine Language, and is very elegant but barely comprehended save by veritable machines, and looks like this:

00000000	00111010
00000001	00001000
00000010	00000000

. . . This austerity is in 0's and 1's because—come on, you know that much—and its words are eight characters long because 8 is $2 \times 2 \times 2$ and we are in a domain where all goes by twos, and as to what it means, that depends on the reader: INTEL 8080? Motorola 6800? Unlike you and me, partially shaped by our reading, that reader was fully defined before the language was. To write Machine Language your primary need is to know *all* about your reader (as you can; there is a little booklet).

2   Like Cuneiform, Machine Language is made of many identical elements, tedious to write and easily miswritten. There was a time when

programmers wrote zeroes and ones all day long, and a few neoclassicists still do, but in these late days the Higher Level Languages are ubiquitous. They allow you to write something another human being can follow, and with less likelihood of error, in part because you can reread it yourself, in part because you need bestow less attention—ideally, none—on what is going on inside the machine. Since machines can't understand Higher Level Languages, another program called Interpreter or Compiler stands between. (Interpreter and Compiler are not quite the same, but equivalent for our purposes.) The Compiler-writers are the true High Priests, since it is they who must encode the conventions and skirt the ambiguities of the language in which the programmer is going to write. The programmer in turn is at the service of someone who wants a job done, and the whole arcane art is both necessary and possible because we have blundered into a culture abristle with jobs that entail much exact repetition. A Higher Level Language is a system of abbreviations that works by defining repeated portions exactly.

3   Suppose you run an office whose sole business is to produce typed copies of messages like the following:

> The farmer in the dell
> The farmer in the dell
> Heigh ho the merry o
> The farmer in the dell.
>
> The farmer takes a wife
> The farmer takes a wife
> Heigh ho the merry o
> The farmer takes a wife.
>
> The wife takes a child
> The wife takes a child
> Heigh ho the merry o
> The wife takes a child.

—and so on, as the dog takes a cat, the cat a rat, the rat a cheese; whereupon

> The cheese stands alone
> The cheese stands alone
> Heigh ho the merry o
> The cheese stands alone.

This will be recognized as a reasonable model of secretarial output; form letters are not otherwise structured.

4   In the early years you gave the typist written copies to copy, but all that changed with Miss Quickwit, whose flying fingers could generate anything in the office repertoire once you'd prompted her with a few hints on "how it goes." The nature of these hints is obvious from the way we abbreviated three stanzas in the example above. "The Farmer in the Dell" is characterized by a tune, a little sequence of variables, and some rules of combination, and out of her sense of these Miss Quickwit could generate it afresh whenever it was wanted.

5   But Miss Quickwit one day put trivial occupations behind her, having met a typewriter salesman whose socks she aspired to wash; whereupon Personnel sent up Dora, who could neither carry a tune nor remember whether the cheese came after the rat or before the dog. Dora needed explicit written instructions, which soon got longer than the ditty itself and to no avail because she kept misreading them; indeed a complete prose specification for producing "The Farmer in the Dell" is apt to sound like an excerpt from *The Golden Bowl,* a book Dora couldn't follow either.

6   Dora was accordingly replaced by a computer, even dumber than she but unflappable. Its neurons never flag, its iron fingers never tangle, but it can neither carry a tune nor begin a new line without being told. So it needs totally unambiguous instructions, for which the Higher Level Language called MACROGENERATOR seems suitable. They look like this:*

```
§DEF, VERSE, <_1_1
Hey ho the merry o _1
>;
§DEF, LINE, <
The _1 wants a _2>;
§DEF, FORM, <§VERSE,§LINE,_1,_2;;>;
§VERSE,
The farmer in the dell;
§FORM, farmer, wife;
§FORM, wife, child;
§FORM, child, dog;
§FORM, dog, cat;
§FORM, cat, rat;
§FORM, rat, cheese;
§VERSE,
The cheese stands alone;
```

The swing, the beat, the bucolic lilt are gone; but if what you want is a typed copy, that will get it typed, and no customer need ever know that transistors have disposed the words he reads.

---

* Based on an example in Bryan Higman, *A Comparative Study of Programming Languages,* 2nd ed. (London, 1977), p. 81. MACROGENERATOR was invented by C. Strachey in 1965.

7   One can puzzle out how it works. A little study suggests that the symbol § marks the beginning of a new unit of attention, something analogous to a sentence, terminated by a semicolon. It also seems that "DEF," (= "definition") heads something the machine is to stash away for future reference. There are three of these, and they may be regarded as lexical definitions, for use in a convention like the following: "When you come upon the defined term, e.g. VERSE, substitute its definition." Within a definition, _1 marks a place where a further substitution will be made; such instances are serially numbered, _1, _2, etc.

8   When the machine encounters a statement unpreceded by "DEF," it takes its cue to be up and doing. So it deals with

> §VERSE,
> The farmer in the dell;

by substituting the supplied words for each _1 in the definition of VERSE, and types out stanza one. The next task,

> §FORM, farmer, wife;

is a little more complicated. "FORM" has been defined as a VERSE in which the place of the variable is taken by something called LINE, and LINE has the pattern, "The _1 takes a _2." So it concocts a provisional "FORM,"

> The _1 takes a _2
> The _1 takes a _2
> Heigh ho the merry o
> The _1 takes a _2

Into this, at a second stage, "farmer" and "wife" are inserted to fill out the pattern "LINE"; and with no more to be done stanza two is typed.

9   In the same way, working down the list, the machine compiles and executes each stanza in turn; and if it makes no mistakes that is not thanks to luck or miracle, but because *the program and the output are exactly equivalent*. The program, with its list of variables and its unambiguous instructions about their treatment—unambiguous because specified by the conventions of the programming language—is simply *a compact way of writing the output*.

10   Whereupon much mystery vanishes, for this is generally true. Think of the computer as a machine to print what for some reason we want printed: "The Farmer in the Dell," or thirty-five thousand utility bills, or all the words W. B. Yeats used in his poems, arranged in alphabetical order. It differs from the typewriter at which I sit in only one respect, that instead of typing in what you want to get out, you type in instructions for generating what you want to get out.

11   The discipline of devising these instructions is justified only by the time it saves in the long run. The arithmetic of utility bills is trivial, but there are so many of them; it is easier to state the rules, supply the meter readings, and leave the rest to busy hardware. Or we may want a result, 3.141592653589793, which takes seconds to type but took even Leonhard Euler an hour to arrive at, involving as it does the formation of many terms in a series and the addition of these; better state a rule and let the machine obey it, over and over and over.*

12   Over and over and over is the most general principle; it is quicker to write a program than to arrive at and write out the result only when the problem is such that the instructions can specify simple operations that get done many times. Why, at this phase of human history, we confront so many such problems is a question for another occasion, though no study of Higher Level Languages will permit us to stray from it very far.

13   These languages have a number of interesting peculiarities, beginning with the fact that nobody speaks them. Walter Ong has reminded us repeatedly that Medieval Latin was peculiar in being first learned at a writing desk and then spoken, a fact which encouraged certain geometric criteria of style: a sentence was elegant when its diagram was. Still, once learned, Latin *was* spoken. Programming languages are never spoken at all. Even in context, a fragment of FORTRAN conveys nothing to the most expert ear:

READ (5, 100) N, MAXIT, EPSILON, BIGGST
NPLUS 1 = N + 1

while this PL/I horror, where every mark is significant, is utterly unpronounceable:[†]

$$\text{ANGLES(I)} = 2\text{*ATAND(SQRT((S-A(IND(I,1)))\text{*}(S-A(IND(I,2))))/}$$
$$(S\text{*}(S-A(IND(I,3)))));$$

Both are intelligible to the practiced *eye*, but being eye language they stay obdurately "out there," in the eye's external domain, remote from tongue and ear, guarding their inviolate distance from the human psyche (Ψῡχή, breath, spirit) and pedantic about minute differentiations.

14   Eye languages? *Lingua* means "tongue." Why it is plausible to call such things languages at all is an interesting story. Late in the seventeenth century, and for complex reasons deriving partly from the emergence of printing, partly from missionaries' reports of the Chinese ideograph, it had

---

* The number, of course, is *pi* to fifteen places. Euler in fact got twenty places in that eventful hour, but since he was one of the three greatest mathematicians in history, a 25 percent handicap seems fair.

† The PL/I example is from Gerald M. Weinberg, *The Psychology of Computer Programming* (New York, 1971), p. 29.

become plausible to accord the written primacy over the spoken. In written syntax, it seemed, lay the logic of the language. A "word" was an entity existing in space like a chair, and its spatial existence was identical with the way it was spelled. (Spelling grew standardized.) Linguistic skill got called "literacy"; the literate were cautioned against writing the kind of thing they spoke. Mere speakers were improvisers, mispronouncers, corrupters. So language was removed from the tongue, and came to connote some orderly system of signs and of rules for combining them, impossible to master without pencil and paper. There ensued a craze for devising "philosophical" languages, purged of ambiguity, rational in mapping the taxonomies of creation, capable of effecting their syntactic transactions in accordance with the movement of reason and in no other lawful way. (Mathematicize "reason," and you are close to the computer.) These were written languages, equipped with systems of phonemes as if by afterthought. It is among the "philosophical" languages of the seventeenth century that we must seek precursors for the programming languages of the twentieth, in which "words" are quite explicitly mnemonics (the flesh is weak), and programmers are enjoined to make them pronounceable: POINT and POUND, not PQRST and PQSRT on which a machine won't stumble but a human will.* Speakability seems a regrettable afterthought.

15   If saying PQSRT is hard, remembering it is hard too, because it is a list and not a story, space-bound, not time-bound. Lists, it seems, forced the development of writing itself. If we are to trust its current decipherment, Linear B was devised to record inventories, not to preserve speech. An inventory is a string of nouns, so chirographically controlled systems tend to be noun-oriented and have trouble with the verb, the part of speech that affirms. Thus the "philosophical" languages were better at taxonomizing than at affirming anything save the logical relationships inherent in the taxonomy.

16   For a taxonomy is a diagram like an inverted tree, down which we travel, alert at the branching-points, to arrive at the place of some entity in the scheme of things. To devise a philosophical language you have only to arrange that the phoneme structure of each term shall indicate its location on the tree. When you do this you are, true, assigning names; but with this important difference from Adam's activity that you are not *calling* the thing by its name, but *using* the name as a mnemonic for the thing's location. "Rainbow" for John Wilkins (1668) was "Det*a*," *De* signifying the Genus *Element*; *t* its Fifth Difference, Meteor, a brightness in the air; *a* the first Species of the Difference and pronounced like the *o* in *cot*.† To name an

---

* This kind of point gets made routinely in books on programming style, the emergence of which in the 1970s suggests that the art is regarded by its practitioners as emerging from barbarism. It is no longer enough that programs merely *work*.

† John Wilkins, *Essay Towards a Real Character and a Philosophical Language* (London, 1668), p. 415.

arch of colors "Det*a*" is to guide someone's finger down a diagram, designating branches left and right. To name it "Rainbow" is to affirm its selfhood in something like a trumpet's tongue. This matters, and not only because "rainbow" records the centuries-old consensus of the English-speaking peoples, but because when we hear "rainbow" we hear affirmed an arching colored shining ("that is its name": our naïveté is profound) whereas when we read "Det*a*" we think of the system wherein "Det*a*" marks a place. The system alone is real.

17   In the programming languages likewise names are arbitrary, bestowed ad hoc by the programmer to the end that the Central Processing Unit (CPU) shall allocate memory spaces consistently. The only real referent of a name is a location. Thus in our program for "The Farmer in the Dell" the entry "DEF, VERSE" in seeming to define "verse" in effect instructs the CPU to allocate a sequence of locations to which any further call of "VERSE" will refer it. Instead of "VERSE" we might have used "RATS" or "SQZX," anything at all so long as we kept the usage consistent. The machine cares only for consistency, and "VERSE" does prompt fallible humans.

18   Similarly with the sentence: the salient event is not a predication but a branch: not an impingement on affirmed substantiality but a choice of *this* course, hence a rejection of *that.* Branches correspond to natural-language words like *if* and *then* and *as* and *for,* even *a* and *the* (any member of an array? or a specified member?). Such structures have been probed by numerous twentieth-century writers. William Carlos Williams fifty years ago wrote a poem (called "Poem") with the structure:

> As the . . . over the . . . of the . . .
>   first the . . .
>   then the . . .
>   . . . . .

It pertains to a cat. And, "not consequent on the cat but precedent to the cat," I wrote of this poem some years ago; "a pattern proffered and conceivable as pure syntax, but a pattern which the cat renders substantial."[*] The poem's tension is that of a cat against a verbal cat's cradle. Likewise Sam Beckett in 1944:

> Mrs. Gorman called every Thursday, except when she was indisposed. Then she did not call, but stayed at home, in bed, or in a comfortable chair, before the fire if the weather was cold, and by the open window if the weather was warm, and, if the weather was neither cold nor warm, by the closed window or before the empty hearth.[†]

* Hugh Kenner, *The Pound Era* (Berkeley and Los Angeles, 1971), p. 400. For the poem, see Williams's *Collected Earlier Poems* (Norfolk, 1951), p. 340.
† Samuel Beckett, *Watt* (Paris, 1953), p. 139.

Computer folk will intuit how this can be flowcharted (see the accompany-ing chart). This mirrors the structure of most nontrivial programs. All happenings are choices among options, in a field defined without ambi-guity, and closed.

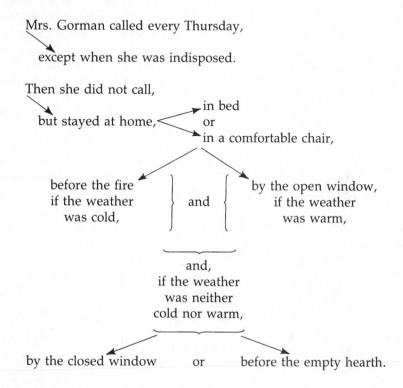

Mrs. Gorman called every Thursday,

except when she was indisposed.

Then she did not call,

but stayed at home, in bed
or
in a comfortable chair,

before the fire
if the weather
was cold,   and   by the open window,
if the weather
was warm,

and,
if the weather
was neither
cold nor warm,

by the closed window   or   before the empty hearth.

19   With nouns reduced to taxonomic arbitrariness, with sentences arranged as branching systems, the classic declarative gesture, affirmation, grew problematic as long ago as the seventeenth century. To affirm, what might that mean? It soon grew dubious. Affirmation was apt to connote opinion, something not scientific. (*Scientific* means "trust nobody.") What might one still say? One might narrate one's procedure and one's observations, implying that they could be repeated; one was then not asking to have one's judgment trusted but one's result verified. Or one might assert, in the Boolean algebra of classes, that sets were, or were not, or were only partially, subsets of other sets, as anyone might verify by retracing the reasoning. But these seem debilitated literary forms, despite Wordsworth's success with the former and Beckett's with the latter. The programming languages supply a new incentive for composition. In them, having just conceived something to be done, one can devise instructions for an execu-tant who will promptly do it. Beckett's fans will empathize with this fulfillment of the fantasies of the blind immobile Hamm; and will note how

ever more tightly his playscripts bind the actors, *Waiting for Godot* recognizably a play, but *Play* a program.

20   The programming languages are thus unique in having only one mood, the imperative. Despite appearances, they permit no affirmations. What looks like an algebraic statement, $a = b$, is in fact an instruction ("*b* belongs in box *a*; put it there"). Into an affirmation the psyche flows. Having affirmed that—affirmed anything—I am committed; there is a meaning to "I," and to commitment, and to the terms of the affirmation, which I underwrite. I say it is so, having seen that it is so. But to move things in and out of boxes is mere filing, mere efficiency, proper to a domain where you do nothing but give trivial orders.

> HAMM: I feel a little too far to the left.
> (*Clov moves chair slightly.*)
>
> Now I feel a little too far to the right.
> (*Clov moves chair slightly.*)
>
> I feel a little too far forward.
> (*Clov moves chair slightly.*)
>
> Now I feel a little too far back.
> (*Clov moves chair slightly.*)
>
> Don't stay there,
> (*i.e. behind the chair*)
>
> You give me the shivers.
> (*Clov returns to his place beside the chair.*)
>
> CLOV: If I could kill him I'd die happy.
> (*Pause.*)*

Happy! The voice of INTEL 8080, the Central Processing Unit. The orders that we now give to computers are the same we once gave to meek men in shirtsleeves. "Farrington?" cried a voice in James Joyce's story "Counterparts," a voice out of a head "like a large egg,"

> —Farrington? What is the meaning of this? Why have I always to complain of you? May I ask you why you haven't made a copy of that contract between Bodley and Kirwan? I told you it must be ready by four o'clock.

Farrington, c. 1904, was a human Xerox machine; nowadays the voice from the egg screams for a Xerox repairman. And in advanced societies microcircuitry has supplanted Clov, with feedback loops to obviate Hamm's finickiness and center his chair. All rolls on wheels toward certain

---

* Samuel Beckett, *Endgame* (New York, 1958), p. 27.

liberations. Still, mapped by Higher Level Languages, certain habits remain, purged of *Endgame*'s melodrama but not of dubiousness.

> A precise definition of language is an elusive thing, but we come fairly close to one if we say that a language consists of a set of objects called its vocabulary, which can be combined into linear strings in accordance with certain rules known as its grammar, for communication to a recipient with the intention of inducing activity in the recipient relative to certain specific features abstracted from a general situation.*

Such a statement, it seems fair to say, could only have been formulated late in the twentieth century. A vocabulary is "a set of objects"; sentences are "linear strings"; and the purpose of "inducing activity" specifies the imperative as the normal mood. (A later sentence permits the indicative as a special case, when the activity to be induced is "a mere 'awareness.' ") It describes the Machine Languages with studied exactness. If it seems an acceptable statement about language in general, that is because the machine and its languages epitomize what men have come to think of language during humanity's three most recent centuries. Men's technology images what they really believe, embodying deep decisions made long prior to "the state of the art." Scrutinized like our poems, our machines have similar things to disclose to us: in this instance, that during the years between Descartes and Chomsky we have fallen imperceptibly into the habit of regarding one another, much of the time, as machines.

Questions on Content

1. What distinction does Kenner make between "Compiler-writers" and programmers?

2. What point does Kenner illustrate with "The Farmer in the Dell" (paragraphs 3–10)?

3. What does Kenner identify as the major difference between typewriters and computers?

4. How do written and spoken language differ?

5. Explain the meaning of this sentence: "An inventory is a string of nouns, so chirographically controlled systems tend to be noun-oriented and have trouble with the verb, the part of speech that

---

* Higman, *A Comparative Study*, p. 7.

affirms" (paragraph 15). How is this idea relevant to Kenner's thesis?

6. How is a name (such as *rainbow*) different from a list (such as *Deta*)?

Questions on Structure and Style

7. Where does Kenner state his thesis? Why does he position it as he does?

8. The opening sentence of this essay is long and complicated. Paraphrase the first sentence. Is it an effective opening?

9. Kenner is a humanist writing on a technical subject. How does this affect the essay's tone? Does it, or should it, affect tone at all?

10. What effect does the author achieve with examples from literature—Beckett, Joyce, and even "The Farmer in the Dell"?

11. How would you describe Kenner's use of examples in paragraphs 4 through 6? What do such examples—and their purpose—tell us about the author?

Assignments

1. The organization of "Machinespeak" might seem confusing, but the essay is carefully structured. Outline the essay, showing its major parts and their relationships.

2. The following definition of language is by the noted linguist Archibald Hill:

Language is the primary and most highly elaborated form of human symbolic activity. Its symbols are made up of sounds produced by the vocal apparatus, and they are arranged in classes and patterns which make up a complex and symmetrical structure. The entities of language are symbols, that is, they have meaning, but the connection between symbol and thing is arbitrary and socially controlled. The symbols of language are simultaneously substitute responses and can call forth further stimuli and responses, so that discourse becomes independent of an immediate physical stimulus. The entities and structure of language are always so elaborated as to give the speaker the possibility of making a linguistic response to any experience.

In a paragraph or essay, explain how you believe Kenner would react to this definition. Be concise but specific.

3. Kenner ends by saying, ". . . we have fallen imperceptibly into the habit of regarding one another, much of the time, as machines." In an essay, explain why you agree or disagree with this opinion. (You may use Kenner's essay as a starting point if you wish, but you needn't rely on it.)

Hacking the English
Language to Bits and Bytes

Erik Sandberg-Diment

Computers seem to be everywhere, and so does "computerese,"
the language this new technology has spawned. But according to
Erik Sandberg-Diment, "techno-babble" is a divisive force in the
linguistic habits of Americans, and in this essay (which first appeared in the *New York Times Magazine*), he responds to many
examples of the "computer Esperanto that defies comprehension
by the uninitiated."

1 Not even the estimable George Orwell foresaw that by the year before 1984
men would modify their language to accommodate machines. Perhaps, as
some critics have said, Orwell foresaw nothing, but just reversed the last
two digits of 1948 to label his polemic against the world as it then was.
Whatever the case, there is nothing in "1984" that anticipates the dialect of
Newspeak known as computerese.

2 At its most basic, this dialect is a techno-babble of bits, bytes and bauds,
mixed with such scrambled numerics as "RS-232" and "64K." With this
cant, amazingly enough, the neophyte computer enthusiast quickly becomes conversant, at least enough to assume the role of verbal threat or
bore at cocktail parties.

3 Just beyond the basic vocabulary needed to enter a computer store lies
the manufacturers' marketing jargon. Here's where one comes across code
words like "upgradable," as in "upgradable double density." This is apt to
mean that the manufacturer has not quite figured out how to introduce a
computer with the particular feature in question. Meanwhile, however, he
will be glad to sell you whatever machine he does have, and if and when
he figures out how to incorporate the new feature, he will be glad to add it
to your machine for a small extra charge.

4 The word "feature" itself often describes a design mistake which, since it
couldn't economically be changed, comes to be touted as the greatest advance since the development of microelectronics itself. Features are usually
stressed in the initial product announcement, along with the assurance
that the product is available now or soon. "Now" means within three to 12
months. "Soon" means never.

5 The next step in the subtle dominance of computerese over normal
English occurs after the actual acquisition of a personal computer. In the
broadest sense, this vernacular development comprises "game English,"
which derives not so much from the shoot-'em-down arcade games as

from the verbal adventure games so beloved by the proponents of information technology, who consider them the new open sesame of intellectual development.

6   In these pictureless games, the participant reads his way through an adventure or mystery on the screen, much as he would read one of those popular "choose-your-own-adventure" books in which one skips around from section to section, the direction of the story being determined by the way the questions are answered. Each of his moves is quickly matched by a computer riposte. Unfortunately, the vital visual, phonic, contextual and etymological complexities of human language, not to mention its ambiguities, are far beyond the sustained scope of even the very best computers and programs available today. Thus a simplistic electronic patois reduces communication to the abrupt verb/noun staccato of "go west," "take knife," "go exit" and so on, with the verb always preceding the object and all intervening modifiers or other linguistic luggage that add depth and emotion to our verbal intercourse being disallowed.

7   If the vocabulary of game English is limited to a very structured set of verbs and nouns, neither remains what it was for long in computerization. Nouns are as likely as not to become verbs—to format, to interface, to just about anything. Perfectly ordinary adjectives absorb the function of nouns; "open," for instance, is what one computer fan says to another when he means "open parenthesis."

8   On the other hand, predicates are often reduced to a similar uniform letter affixed to the end of a word in what is called the P convention. A typical construction would be "eat-P," meaning "do you want to eat?"— not necessarily peas.

9   At this stage, the budding computerist is still accessible to mere mortals. However, after a certain period of increasing computer involvement, a fine line—over which lies total incomprehensibility to all but fellow hackers— is crossed.

10   The term "hack" has many meanings in English, from the basketball foul of striking an opponent's arm to a worn-out horse to a person who abandons professional integrity for the sake of personal gain. What most of these definitions have in common is a negative connotation. So leave it to computerese to invert the emotions and raise the term "hacker" to a pedestal of the highest acclaim. Among computer enthusiasts, a real hacker is a demigod, for he is an expert capable of intense bursts of program writing, often called "hack attacks," one who has a true and exclusive love of all things computerish, and usually one who has more than a little skill at electronically breaking into other people's computer systems across the land.

11   People who have reached the hacking stage are often fun-loving pranksters. A few are the embodiment of the antisocial, malevolent techno-freak that some people who are not computer enthusiasts imagine the advanced

hacker to be. Still fewer appear perfectly "normal" outside of their silicon-saturated work environments. What they all have in common is a multi-layered computer Esperanto that defies comprehension by the uninitiated.

12   Interestingly enough, the assemblage of monosyllables such as "glork," "foo," "bar" and "gronk" bear a certain resemblance to the verbal exercises of a baby as it learns to speak. Other terms, like "snail mail," for messages delivered by the United States Postal Service, as opposed to those transported electronically, are more widely comprehensible.

13   All this techno-babble has been codified by an electronic-minded Dr. Samuel Johnson (although as yet no Boswell has appeared) and can be accessed through various computer data bases. For those who intransigently refuse to deal with printouts, "The Hacker's Dictionary," compiled by Guy L. Steele et al., is to be released by Harper & Row before Christmas [1983]. As they say in the book world these days, it's a good read.

Questions on Content

1. What is "game English" (paragraphs 5 to 8)? Why does Sandberg-Diment consider it important to his discussion?

2. Why does the author devote an entire paragraph (paragraph 10) to the word *hack?*

3. In what ways does computerese resemble "the verbal exercises of a baby as it learns to speak" (paragraph 12)? What effect does Sandberg-Diment intend when he makes this comparison?

4. Identify the stages that the student of computerese passes through before becoming an expert in techno-babble.

5. In criticizing computerese, is the author criticizing computers themselves?

Questions on Structure and Style

6. Describe the author's tone. How does it relate to his purpose in writing the essay?

7. What audience is Sandberg-Diment addressing? Cite specific evidence from the essay to support your answer.

1. Carefully consider Sandberg-Diment's opinion of computerese.
   A. If you have worked with computers, point out how your own experience confirms or contradicts the author's assertions about language and computer use.
   B. If you have never worked with computers, explain why, as a fellow "computer outsider," you agree or disagree with the author's opinions.

2. In paragraphs 3 and 4, Sandberg-Diment discusses manufacturers' jargon. In an essay, analyze the marketing jargon of another product. (The automobile and travel industries are likely targets, but there are many other possibilities.) Cite specific examples from advertisements to substantiate your claims.

French Resistance

Hannah Benoit

French may still be the language of love and haute cuisine; in science and technology, however, there is little justification for the feeling of linguistic supremacy that the French have cultivated and, in fact, institutionalized. In the following essay, Hannah Benoit highlights the relatively tolerant linguistic attitudes of the United States through an examination of French linguistic chauvinism. As Benoit suggests, the worst enemy of the French language may well be the French.

1   An American tourist in France, armed with only a high school knowledge of French, may well tremble at the thought of asking a native for directions. The question may evoke only a sneer if the visitor inadvertently requests the quickest way to *la guerre* (war) rather than *la gare* (the railroad station). In France, the French language commands divine status. And one does not mess with the linguistic gods.

2   In international spheres, however, French is ailing. Although it probably retains its rank as the language of love, it has long been surpassed by English in science, medicine, and high technology. Not only is English the lingua franca of the sciences, it is also the tongue that gives rise to most technical neologisms, since new words are coined by those who first have need for them. The French created quiche, but the Americans invented the microchip.

3   The French have traditionally sought linguistic purity, resisting the "loan words" that are casually accepted into most other languages. For more than 20 years the French government has officially opposed the infiltration of anglicisms into the mother tongue. To President Charles de Gaulle, the exorcism of such demon *Franglais* words as *le businessman* and *le jumbo jet* was a matter of state. His successor, Georges Pompidou, created the High Commission for the French Language, which in turn spawned more than a dozen committees charged with coining French substitutes for the wicked English words.

4   Science and technology have been prime targets of the commission. The *Journal Officiel* (the French equivalent of our *Federal Register*) regularly publishes lists of forbidden Anglo-Saxon words, along with the preferred French counterparts. The official lexicon for the nuclear industry appeared in 1973. Henceforth, French bombs would create not fallout but *retombees radioactives*. An emergency shutdown of a *surregenerateur* (breeder reactor) would not be called a scram, as in English, but *un arret d'urgence*. Meltdowns would apparently remain unspeakable; no French word was given.

Preserving the Language

5   In 1975 the French legislature passed a law mandating the use of French in government documents and school textbooks. The media were also encouraged to comply. In 1982 the Minister of Research and Industry wrote to top French scientists to implore them to publish only in French. He also declared that he would boycott French conferences conducted in any foreign language. He must be staying home a lot; by one estimate some 75 percent of French scientists speak English at such gatherings.

6   Recent lists of forbidden words have covered the communications and computer industries. Although Sony's personal, portable stereo is known the world over as a Walkman, the French are supposed to call it *un baladeur* (a stroller). And computer users must discard their software and hardware in favor of *le logiciel* and *le materiel*.

7   "The government has been pretty good at modifying people's behavior," claims Jean-Louis Poirier, a French-born energy engineer who has worked in the United States for the last eight years. Although people may resist such cumbersome terms as *suramplificateur* when the punchier *booster* is available, a word like *informatique*, which has been accepted into common usage, rolls off the tongue perhaps more easily than does *data processing*. "The new words will be used on TV and by journalists," says Poirier, "and people follow that pattern."

8   Although French scientists often speak English at their own conferences, they bring a stubborn *chauvinisme* with them to scientific gatherings in other countries. At a recent Chicago meeting of the International Standards Organization, everyone spoke English except the French; they insisted upon an interpreter. "The French will come to an American conference with a videotape in French," says Poirier, "and expect people to understand. It's a typical problem."

Japanese Hospitality

9   By contrast, Japan, America's number one competitor in high technology, has extended a characteristic hospitality toward the English language. Beginning in junior high school, all Japanese children study English, and those who go on to college rack up a decade's study of it. "Japanese engineers may not necessarily be able to *speak* English," says Dr. Eleanor Westney of the MIT-Japan Science and Technology Program, "but they can read it and therefore keep up with the literature of their fields."

10   Technical Japanese, says Westney, is liberally sprinkled with English words that have been made to conform to Japanese phonetics. They use the term *computer*, for example, but pronounce it *komputah*, with a

prolonged "ah" sound. And because in Japanese a consonant sound is almost always followed by a vowel sound, *diode* is said as *diodo*, and *chip* is *chippu*.

11   This language-splicing sometimes results in hybrid phrases. The Japanese term for *optical fiber* is *hikari fibah*, which combines the Japanese word for light with the English word *fiber*.

12   "English has a certain cachet in Japan," notes Westney, "and the Japanese feel very comfortable using it." And since Japan regards itself as a technological newcomer, she adds, it makes an effort to stay informed about international developments. "Part of this effort," says Westney, "is a foreign-language competence."

13   Despite the benefits of knowing and using a foreign language, however, it may take a *coup d'etat*, or at least a *tour de force*, to get France to adopt a *laissez faire* attitude toward foreign words—no matter how *au courant* they may become.

Questions on Content

1. How do the French and Japanese attitudes toward anglicisms differ?

2. Can you think of historical reasons for France's resistance to "loan words" from English?

3. Why is English the "lingua franca" of the sciences? What problem does this present for the High Commission for the French Language?

4. What differences might you expect to find between technical French and technical Japanese?

5. What is Benoit's attitude toward French linguistic chauvinism? Cite specific evidence from her essay.

Questions on Structure and Style

6. Discuss the author's strategy in the opening paragraph and the transition between the first two paragraphs.

7. What important point does Benoit make in her concluding paragraph? Is the way she makes this point consistent with her tone in the rest of the essay?

Assignments

1. Do you believe that the linguistic attitude in the United States is closer to the chauvinism of France or the more open attitude of Japan? Using this question as a base, consider the broader issue of language tolerance in the 1980s. Present your thoughts in an essay.

2. Linguistic chauvinism often manifests itself in other ways. For example, how should American public schools treat non-native speakers of English and speakers of minority dialects? Many educators believe that our schools should encourage linguistic unity; others believe that we should be more tolerant and develop bilingual and bidialectical programs. Argue one of these positions in an essay.

The Multilingual Mind

Beryl Lieff Benderly

Even though it often serves as a point of reference in a discussion
of computers, the human brain is not a computer. Recent discoveries about how the brain handles language reaffirm the brain's
unique status—and its mystery. Beryl Lieff Benderly, an anthropologist and author, here reviews some of what we have learned
about the powerful and subtle entity that is responsible for both
language and our understanding of it.

1   For the first four or five days after a stroke, a Swiss-German woman we'll
call Hilda spoke only Italian. Gradually, however, she shifted to French,
and the Italian faded away. Ten days later her usual home language, German, began to emerge and the French to disappear.

2   Before developing his brain tumor, Mr. Wang, who came to the United
States from China as an adult, had handled both Chinese and English
fluently. As the disease progressed, however, he lost the ability to read and
write his native language but kept it in his acquired one.

3   What's going on here? Ordinarily we wouldn't expect a head injury to
affect different languages differently. In a great majority of strokes and
other brain lesions, in fact, losses are similar in all the victim's languages.
But once in a while someone like Mr. Wang or Hilda comes along—
someone whose case tests the rule and raises a question that has increasingly interested scientists of the brain. Does the bilingual brain handle
language differently from the brain that manipulates only one language?
Is it possible that the same brain may even handle different languages
differently?

4   For decades scientists thought they knew how the brain deals with language: in the right-handed monolingual male who is the typical experimental subject, the left cerebral hemisphere, which controls the body's
right side, also controls linguistic processing; the right hemisphere, on the
other hand (and literally so—it controls the left side), accounts for other,
nonverbal abilities—spatial reasoning, music, grasping the whole of an
idea or impression rather than analyzing its parts. But, says Loraine Obler
of Boston's Veterans Administration Medical Center, it now appears that
"particularly in the early stages of language learning, there's more right-
hemisphere involvement than you'd expect." And the right hemisphere
remains surprisingly important even after a second language is completely
mastered. To her this is a "stunning" finding.

5   Your Latin teacher, of course, knew long ago about the ineffable benefits of foreign conjugations and declensions. But precisely because they were so ineffable—a presumed increase in grammatical awareness, for example, or a supposedly enhanced sensitivity to semantic meaning—they were largely ignored by scientists. An accumulating body of evidence now suggests that bilingualism does indeed mean deeper differences than the ability to converse with foreigners. Obler and her colleague Martin Albert write in the 1978 book *The Bilingual Brain*: "Knowledge of multiple languages has anatomical consequences." And some researchers believe those anatomical consequences may find expression in specifically bilingual strategies for language processing, perhaps even in differing perceptions of the universe.

6   As is well known by now, studies of brain lateralization have become one of the hottest fields in science since psychologist Roger Sperry's dramatic finding that the two hemispheres of patients whose brains had been surgically split not only appeared to handle different functions but also to approach processing—even cognition—in strikingly different ways. Because scientists can only rarely experiment directly with living human brains, they use techniques like tachistoscopy and dichotic listening to get at what they want to know. By presenting different stimuli to each ear or visual field respectively, these methods allow scientists to measure differential reactions. Assuming that the left hemisphere processes signals to the right ear or right visual field, and vice versa, researchers take differences in reaction time or level of performance to indicate divergence between the abilities or involvement of the two hemispheres.

7   Neurosurgeon George Ojemann and psychologist Harry Whitaker had a rare opportunity to test two bilingual brains directly. Combining word tests with electrical stimulation of two surgical patients—English-Spanish and English-Dutch bilinguals respectively—they mapped the actual areas of the dominant hemisphere where each language was represented. "Within the center of the language area of each patient, there appeared to be sites common to both languages," they write. "Peripheral to this . . . are sites with differential organization of the two languages. There is a tendency for those sites concerned with a given language to cluster together." In other words, the two languages share some brain space, but each also has areas of its own. Surprisingly, the second language appears to occupy more cortex area than the first. Ojemann and Whitaker speculate that perhaps learning a second language takes "a large number of neurons located over a wide area," and that with growing familiarity, this number may shrink.

8   Speaking two or more languages obviously imposes extra burdens: keeping the two systems separate, retrieving the right word from duplicate sets for each meaning, placing incoming messages in the proper pigeonhole.

For the bilingual, every linguistic situation is a choice, every possibility has a twin in the background. Could the right hemisphere help with the extra work? Could it make the bilingual, in the words of psychologists Jyotsna Vaid and Wallace Lambert of McGill University, "more sensitive to a variety of input cues"? Bilinguals appear to be abler to distinguish among auditory and visual stimuli. One example is their greater ability to distinguish figure from ground, that is, to pick an object in a picture out of its background. And Vaid and Lambert believe bilinguals are "more field-independent." That is, they do better on the well-known psychological test requiring them to set a rod to true horizontal, regardless of the position of a lighted frame surrounding it. Some researchers believe this test measures general independence—although this interpretation is coming under increasing attack. Could it be significant that those who learned their second language early appear to be most field-independent of all?

9   Indeed, Vaid and Lambert go on, "age of onset of bilingualism has provided the least equivocal results in behavioral studies." Comparisons of people who spoke two languages from infancy or early childhood with others who acquired a second language in their teens or later have shown significant differences, not so much in superficial aspects like fluency or speed, but in deeper methods of processing. It appears, for example, that the very early bilinguals take a more semantic—a more left-hemisphere—approach to understanding. Those who became bilingual later seem to use strategies more related to the right hemisphere. Asked to tell whether words were French or English, for example, persons fluent in both from early childhood seemed to analyze them semantically—at the level of meaning—even though that was not appropriate to the task. The later bilinguals seemed to judge more on the basis of physical features of the words, like melody or combinations of sounds; thus, suggests the McGill University research group, it may be that "the phonetic, syntactic, and semantic components of the [later] bilinguals [are] more differentiated neurophysiologically than those of the [early] bilinguals."

10   These differences persist over many years, Obler believes. Decades after losing any trace of a foreign accent, generations after building a huge vocabulary and mastering a vast store of slang, a person who learned a second language in late childhood will still process it somewhat differently from one who learned it in the cradle. Indeed, bilingualism in infancy or early childhood might well alter a person's whole general approach to language. Such persons have "been confronted early in life with a verbal environment of unusual complexity, in which underlying order is difficult to discover because the rules belong to two structures, not one. As a result, they seem to have developed special facility for seeking out rules and for determining which are required by the circumstances," writes psychologist S. Ben-Zeev. Her research found that elementary school pupils fluent in

both Hebrew and English were quicker and subtler when analyzing verbal material and more adept at seeking out "the underlying dimensions of the patterns they confront." Just as your Latin teacher always said, they had a special sensitivity to language. And perhaps more to the point, studies are suggesting that multilingual children stabilize their lateralization for language earlier than other children.

11   But is their extra work load the only reason that bilingual brains divide the job of processing differently from monolinguals? Does something inherent in bilingualism cause them to prefer or require special strategies? Or do different languages actually imprint themselves differently on the two hemispheres? Again, the evidence is spotty and inconclusive, but suggestive.

12   Clearly we can't consider "language" a single, unitary phenomenon. It involves both receptive processes—those concerned with receiving and understanding messages—and expressive ones—those concerned with sending them. Just as clearly, two different languages might present quite different sorts of stimuli. The world's thousands of tongues are astonishingly diverse in every conceivable dimension. Their spoken versions include a vast range of sounds, arranged in innumerable ways. Some emphasize consonants, others, vowels. A few African languages even include clicks of the tongue and lips. In many, a word's meaning depends on its pitch. The written forms march across the page from left to right, as in English; from right to left, as in Hebrew; or from top to bottom, as in Chinese. They construct the written word out of units representing single sounds, complete syllables, or entire ideas. They use scores of different notations.

13   Not surprisingly, the brain seems to handle linguistic material, in part, according to its physical form. Tadanobu Tsunoda of Tokyo Medical and Dental University has found that right-handed Westerners and Chinese process vowels on the left if they occur along with consonants and on the right if they occur alone. Right-handed Japanese and Polynesians, however, process all vowels on the left. Is that because lone vowels in Western languages tend to be inarticulate expressions of emotion (a right-hemisphere task), while Japanese and Polynesian permit all-vowel sentences?

14   This type of difference can occur even within a single language. Japanese has two distinct writing systems, the phonetic *kana* and the ideographic *kanji*, which appear to be processed in opposite hemispheres. In a few recorded cases, brain lesions have damaged one type of reading without touching the other. Yiddish and Hebrew, which run from right to left, also seem to favor more right-brain involvement. Yiddish-English bilinguals, according to Albert and Obler, appear "more balanced between the hemispheres"; even so, they show an advantage in the right visual field when

reading English. Could this in part account for greater left-brain involvement in that language?

15   Indeed, a research group led by Linda Rogers at the University of British Columbia suggests far more radical and profound differences among languages. The anthropological linguist Benjamin Lee Whorf first proposed the idea that language is not only a medium for discussing reality but also a means of structuring it. In his theory, the grammatical and semantic features of a given tongue shape the world view of its speakers.

16   Whorf compared the structure of Hopi to that of English and concluded that Hopi tends to involve the individual in his surroundings, while English tends to isolate him from them. English divides experience into objects (nouns) that perform or undergo actions (verbs). Hopi views reality as a flow of eventuations of varying lengths, which are specified by suffixes. Eventuations may be as fleeting as a thunderclap or as durable as a mountain. If Whorf is right, Rogers and associates speculate, then the more holistic or "appositional" Hopi language ought to involve the right hemisphere more than "propositional" English, which emphasizes "abstraction from the perceptual field." And indeed, when they tested bilingual Hopi-English children in their two languages, the electroencephalograms showed more activity on the right side while using Hopi. But the experimental design is not perfect, the authors warn, because no native English speakers also fluent in Hopi could be found for the study. Nevertheless, they assert, "it seems most unlikely . . . that the results obtained would have derived from the order in which languages are learned." As we have seen, however, other researchers believe that the order of learning may have an important differentiating effect. And further confounding the result is another study by Warren Ten Houten, a sociologist at UCLA, and associates, suggesting that socially subordinate individuals generally show greater right-hemisphere involvement. Could the low social position of the Hopi language rather than its grammatical structure be responsible for the observed effect?

17   For now, these speculations must remain precisely that. Other researchers report that bilinguals generally, including Native Americans, appear to process both their languages on the same side. Despite—or, perhaps, because of—these uncertainties, however, this entire field of research is vast and fertile, although as yet lacking in fixed landmarks. Indeed, couldn't the whole traditional notion of how the brain handles language be a historical accident? Simply because of where they lived, researchers have generally studied right-handed, monolingual speakers of Indo-European languages. The effects of a particular linguistic situation were generalized into universal rules of neurology. How much and what kind of revision the picture needs will not be clear for years. All that researchers can definitely say for now is that the brain handles language in a manner far more flexible, adaptable, and mysterious than anyone had imagined.

**Questions
on Content**

1. What are some of the differences between the right and left cerebral hemispheres?

2. Because scientists can only rarely experiment with living human brains, what must they often do instead?

3. Why do scientists find it surprising that in bilingual people, the second language occupies more cortex area than the first?

4. Every language has phonetic, syntactic, and semantic components. What do these terms mean?

5. What is the difference between receptive cerebral processes and expressive processes?

6. Who is Benjamin Lee Whorf? What idea did he first propose, and why does Benderly refer to him in her essay?

7. Benderly explains that Hopi is more "appositional" than English, which is more "propositional" (paragraph 16). Why is this difference important to researchers?

**Questions
on Structure
and Style**

8. How effective are paragraphs 1 and 2 as an opening? What relationship is there between the two paragraphs?

9. Where does the author state her thesis? What form does it take? What does Benderly achieve by choosing this form? How does her thesis relate to the essay's closing sentence?

10. Benderly twice refers to "your Latin teacher" (paragraphs 5 and 10). Why does she do so, and what effect does she create by using *your*, the second-person possessive pronoun?

Assignments

1. Interview someone who has been bilingual for many years. Ask questions about dreaming, thinking, and

communicating with other people, including those who are bilingual in the same languages. Prepare an informal presentation of your findings.

2. Among educated societies, the United States is, sadly, one of the most monolingual. What problems does this create for our nation? In an essay, explore this question, and propose ways to increase bilingualism.

Additional Assignments and Research Topics

1. Today it's common to hear leaders in education and industry insist that it is just as important for college and perhaps even high school graduates to be computer literate as to be literate in English and math. Write an essay responding to this position by examining the importance of computer literacy for your generation.

2. Assume the roles of William Zinsser and Erik Sandberg-Diment, and write a five-minute dialogue in which the two compare their ideas on the value of computers in our society.

3. The introduction to this chapter quotes Max Frisch's definition of technology: "The knack of so arranging the world that we don't have to experience it." In an essay, discuss this definition, paying particular attention to technology's effects on our use of language.

4. The following poem was written by a computer programmed to produce syntactically correct sentences and parallel stanzas. Write an essay analyzing the poem. Why was a computer able to produce it?

   A lustful twig can twiddle up to the tenderness of a spoon
   And can kill the motion of wisdom.
   But the brain beside gay power heals the action of earth
   While the tenderness of a spoon heals the lustful twig.

   A happy muffin shall bask under earth of night
   And can ensnare the pond up charity of earth.
   But the activity of charity strengthens sorrowful faith
   While the earth of night beseeches the happy muffin.

   A wanton gate may gurgle under the gate of the age of a star
   And should worship a gay shovel.
   But frail wisdom ensnares the endurance of night
   While the gate of the age of a star pursues the wanton gate.

   A moody cloud shall ponder over the motion of a shovel
   And should beseech the goodness of beauty.
   But war over nature worships a wanton goat
   While the motion of a shovel strengthens the moody cloud.

5. In her essay "French Resistance," Hannah Benoit asserts that English is "the tongue that gives rise to most technical

neologisms, since new words are coined by those who first have need for them" (paragraph 2). In other words, language constantly changes to meet the changing needs of its speakers. Write an essay examining an area other than computers that has added new words to our lexicon. Consider, for example, video games, CB radios, videocassette recorders (VCRs), music systems, sports, music, politics, or national defense.

6. Imagine that Hugh Kenner, Hannah Benoit, and Beryl Lieff Benderly are on a panel to discuss the issues of language and technology and monolingualism in the United States. What major points will each assert? What fundamental differences or agreements can you foresee?

Acknowledgments

(continued from page iv)

Robert Burchfield. "Dictionaries and Ethnic Sensibilities" from *The State of the Language*, Leonard Michaels and Christopher Ricks, eds., reprinted by permission of the author and the University of California Press.

Paul Chilton. "Nukespeak: Nuclear Language, Culture, and Propaganda" from *Nukespeak: The Media and the Bomb*, Crispin Aubrey, ed. Reprinted by permission of Comedia Publishing Group.

Stephen F. Cohen. "Slanting the News against the USSR" reprinted from *The Nation*, May 12, 1984. Copyright © 1984 The Nation Company, Inc.

Consumer Reports. "It's Natural! It's Organic! Or Is It?" Copyright 1980 by Consumers Union of United States, Mt. Vernon, NY 10553. Reprinted by permission of *Consumer Reports*, July 1980.

e. e. cummings. "next to of course god america i" is reprinted from IS 5 poems by e. e. cummings, edited by George James Firmage, by permission of Liveright Publishing Corporation. Copyright © 1985 by e. e. cummings Trust. Copyright © 1926 by Horace Liveright. Copyright © 1954 by e. e. cummings. Copyright © 1985 by George James Firmage.

Ossie Davis. "The English Language Is My Enemy" reprinted from the *Negro History Bulletin*, April 1967, by permission of the Association for the Study of Afro-American Life and History, Inc.

Paul Dickson. "Smile, Dr. Fuchs, Your Fuchsia Is Bright" is reprinted from *Smithsonian Magazine*, September 1986.

Peter Elbow. Excerpt from *Writing without Teachers* by Peter Elbow. Copyright © 1973 by Oxford University Press, Inc. Reprinted by permission.

Stuart Berg Flexner. Excerpts from *Listening to America*. Copyright © 1982 by Stuart Berg Flexner. Reprinted by permission of Simon & Schuster, Inc.

Francine Frank and Frank Anshen. Excerpt reprinted from *Language and the Sexes* by Francine Frank and Frank Anshen by permission of the State University of New York Press. Copyright © 1983 by State University of New York. All rights reserved.

Otto Friedrich. "Of Words That Ravage, Pillage, Spoil" reprinted by permission from *Time*, January 9, 1984. Copyright 1984 Time Inc. All rights reserved.

Donald Hall. Excerpt from the Introduction, "An Ethic of Clarity," in *The Modern Stylists*, reprinted with permission of The Free Press, a Division of Macmillan, Inc. Copyright © 1968 by Donald Hall.

Rich Hall. Ten Sniglets reprinted with permission of Macmillan Publishing Company from *More Sniglets* by Rich Hall and Friends. Copyright © 1985 by Not the Network Company.

J. N. Hook. Extract reprinted with permission of Macmillan Publishing from *Family Names: How Our Surnames Came to America* by J. N. Hook. Copyright © 1982 by J. N. Hook.

Philip Howard. Abridged from *The State of the Language: English Observed* by Philip Howard. Copyright © 1984 by Philip Howard. Reprinted by permission of Oxford University Press, Inc.

Pico Iyer. "In Praise of the Humble Comma" reprinted by permission from *Time*, June 13, 1988. Copyright 1988 Time Inc. All rights reserved.

Lane Jennings. "Brave New Words" reprinted from *The Futurist*, June, 1981, by permission.

Diane Johnson. "Doctor Talk" from *The New Republic*, August 18, 1979, reprinted by permission of *The New Republic*, © 1979, The New Republic, Inc.

Hugh Kenner. "Machinespeak" by Hugh Kenner reprinted from *The State of the Language*, Leonard Michaels and Christopher Ricks, eds. Used by permission of The University of California Press, © 1980 The Regents of the University of California.

Alfie Kohn. "Sex and Status and a Manner of Speaking," *The Boston Globe*, May 4, 1987. Reprinted by permission of the author.

Jeff Kunerth. "Sometimes the Liveliest Words," originally published as "Slang—Linguistic Follow-the-Leader" by Jeff Kunerth, January 22, 1985. Used by permission of *The Orlando Sentinel*.

John Leo. "Journalese: A Ground-breaking Study" reprinted by permission from *Time*, September 1, 1986. Copyright 1986 Time Inc. All rights reserved.

John Leo. "What's in a Nickname?" reprinted by permission from *Time*, January 19, 1987. Copyright 1987 Time Inc. All rights reserved.

Malcolm X. Excerpts from *The Autobiography of Malcolm X*, by Malcolm X with Alex Haley. Copyright © 1964 by Alex Haley and Malcolm X. Copyright © 1965 by Alex Haley and Betty Shabazz. Reprinted by permission of Random House, Inc.

H. L. Mencken. "American English," originally published as "A New Nation in the Making," from *The American Language, One Volume Abridged*, by H. L. Mencken. Copyright © 1963 by Alfred A. Knopf, Inc. Reprinted by permission of Alfred A. Knopf, Inc.

Casey Miller and Kate Swift. Excerpt from *Words and Women* by Casey Miller and Kate Swift. Copyright © 1976 by Casey Miller and Kate Swift. Reprinted by permission of Doubleday, a division of Bantam, Doubleday, Dell Publishing Group, Inc.

Florence Miller. "Why EdSpeak Endures," *The New York Times*, January 4, 1987. Copyright © 1987 by The New York Times Company. Reprinted by permission.

Donald M. Murray. "Internal Revision: A Process of Discovery," from *Research on Composing: Points of Departure*, edited by Charles R. Cooper and Lee Odell. Copyright © 1978 by the National Council of Teachers of English. Reprinted with permission.

Frances Norris. "Legal Trees" as originally published in the June 1988 issue of *The Atlantic Monthly*. Reprinted by permission of the author.

Michael Olmert. "Points of Origin" reprinted from *Smithsonian Magazine*, August 1982, by permission of the author.

George Orwell. "Politics and the English Language," copyright 1946 by Sonia Brownell Orwell; renewed 1974 by Sonia Orwell. Reprinted from *Shooting an Elephant and Other Essays* by George Orwell by permission of Harcourt Brace Jovanovich, Inc., the estate of the late Sonia Brownell Orwell, and Martin Secker & Warburg Ltd.

Thomas Palmer. "Spanglish: Hispanics and the Bilingual Dilemma," *The Boston Globe*, April 27, 1987. Reprinted courtesy of *The Boston Globe*.

Jack Rawlins. Excerpt from *The Writer's Way* by Jack P. Rawlins. Copyright © 1987 by Houghton Mifflin Company. Used with permission.

Hugh Rawson. Excerpt from the Introduction, "Euphemisms," reprinted from *Dictionary of Euphemisms and Other Doubletalk*. Copyright © 1981 by Hugh Rawson. Used by permission of Crown Publishers, Inc.

Paul Roberts. Chapter 3, "Something About English" (printed here as "A Brief History of English"), and Chapter 27, "How to Say Nothing in Five Hundred Words," from *Understanding English* by Paul Roberts. Copyright © 1958 by Paul Roberts. Reprinted by permission of Harper & Row, Publishers, Inc.

Richard Rodriguez. Excerpt from *Hunger of Memory* by Richard Rodriguez.

Copyright © 1981 by Richard Rodriguez. Reprinted by permission of David R. Godine, Publisher.

William Safire. "The Case of the President's Case," *The New York Times*, March 10, 1985. Copyright © 1985 by The New York Times Company. Reprinted by permission.

William Safire. "Hypersexism and the Feds," *The New York Times*, May 26, 1985. Copyright © 1985 by The New York Times Company. Reprinted by permission.

Erik Sandberg-Diment. "Hacking the English Language to Bits and Bytes," *The New York Times*, September 13, 1983. Copyright © 1983 by The New York Times Company. Reprinted by permission.

Arthur Schlesinger, Jr. "Politics and the American Language" reprinted from *American Scholar*, Autumn 1974, by permission of the National Education Association and the author.

Muriel R. Schulz. "Is the English Language Anybody's Enemy?" reprinted from *ETC*, Vol. 32, No. 2, 1975, by permission.

Dorothy Z. Seymour. "Black Children, Black Speech," originally published as "Black English," reprinted from *Commonweal*, February 1972, by permission of Commonweal Foundation.

Anne H. Soukhanov. Definitions from the "Word Watch" column as originally published in *The Atlantic Monthly*. Reprinted by permission of the author.

Anne H. Soukhanov. "Welcome to the Web of Words." Copyright © 1987 by Houghton Mifflin Company. Adapted and reprinted by permission from *Welcome to the Web of Words: Marking Terms for the American Heritage Dictionary Citation Files.*

Wallace Stegner. "Good-bye to All T__t!" by Wallace Stegner. Copyright © 1965 by Wallace Stegner. Reprinted by permission of Brandt & Brandt Literary Agents, Inc.

Marvin H. Swift. Reprinted by permission of the *Harvard Business Review*. "Clear Writing Means Clear Thinking Means . . ." by Marvin H. Swift (January/February 1973). Copyright © 1973 by the President and Fellows of Harvard College; all rights reserved.

Lewis Thomas. "Just That One Thing," originally published as "Social Talk" from *The Lives of a Cell* by Lewis Thomas. Copyright © 1972 by the Massachusetts Medical Society. Originally published in the *New England Journal of Medicine*. Reprinted by permission of Viking Penguin, Inc.

Susan Trausch. "English Spoken Here . . . Sort Of," *The Boston Globe*, April 17, 1988. Reprinted courtesy of *The Boston Globe*.

John Updike. "A&P," copyright © 1962 by John Updike. Reprinted from *Pigeon Feathers and Other Stories*, by John Updike. By permission of Alfred A. Knopf, Inc. Originally appeared in *The New Yorker*.

Geoffrey Wagner and Sanford R. Radner. "Taboo: The Sacred and the Obscene" from pp. 223–232 of *Language and Reality* by Geoffrey Wagner and Sanford R. Radner. Copyright © 1974 by Harper & Row, Publishers, Inc. Reprinted by permission.

George Will. "In Defense of the Mother Tongue," from *Newsweek*, July 8, 1985, © 1985 Newsweek, Inc. All rights reserved. Reprinted by permission.

Carl P. Wrighter. "Weasel Words: God's Little Helpers" from *I Can Sell You Anything*, by Carl P. Wrighter. Copyright © 1972 by Ballantine Books, Inc. Reprinted by permission of Ballantine Books, a Division of Random House, Inc.

William Zinsser. "Four Hang-ups" from *Writing with a Word Processor*. Copyright © 1983 by William K. Zinsser. Reprinted by permission of the author.

William Zinsser. "Simplicity" from *On Writing Well*. Copyright © 1980 by William K. Zinsser. Reprinted by permission of the author.

Index

To the Student:

We hope that you will take a few minutes to fill out this questionnaire. Your response will help us to plan future editions of *About Language*. Please answer those questions you care to, detach this sheet, and mail it to English Editor, College Division, Houghton Mifflin Company, One Beacon Street, Boston, MA 02108. Thank you.

Name of college or university _____

Name and number of course _____

Name of instructor _____

Other books assigned in course _____

	Excel-lent	Good	Fair	Poor	Didn't Read
THE PROCESS OF WRITING					
Elbow Freewriting	___	___	___	___	___
Rawlins Five Principles for Getting Good Ideas	___	___	___	___	___
Roberts How to Say Nothing in Five Hundred Words	___	___	___	___	___
Murray Internal Revision: A Process of Discovery	___	___	___	___	___
Swift Clear Writing Means Clear Thinking Means . . .	___	___	___	___	___
Zinsser Simplicity	___	___	___	___	___
Iyer In Praise of the Humble Comma	___	___	___	___	___
Hall An Ethic of Clarity	___	___	___	___	___
NAMES AND NAMING					
Hook From a World without Surnames	___	___	___	___	___
Miller/Swift Women and Names	___	___	___	___	___
Bolton Putting American English on the Map	___	___	___	___	___
Leo What's in a Nickname?	___	___	___	___	___
Dickson Smile, Dr. Fuchs, Your Fuchsia Is Bright	___	___	___	___	___
DICTIONARIES					
Malcolm X Get Hold of a Dictionary	___	___	___	___	___
Soukhanov Welcome to the Web of Words	___	___	___	___	___
Olmert Points of Origin	___	___	___	___	___
Burchfield Dictionaries and Ethnic Sensibilities	___	___	___	___	___
LANGUAGE DEVELOPMENT					
Thomas Just That One Thing	___	___	___	___	___
Barber The Origin of Language	___	___	___	___	___
Trausch English Spoken Here . . . Sort Of	___	___	___	___	___
Roberts A Brief History of English	___	___	___	___	___
Mencken American English: The Period of Growth	___	___	___	___	___
Jennings Brave New Words	___	___	___	___	___
SLANG, TABOO, AND EUPHEMISM					
Kunerth Sometimes the Liveliest Words	___	___	___	___	___
Updike A&P	___	___	___	___	___
Wagner/Radner Taboo: The Sacred and the Obscene	___	___	___	___	___
Rawson Euphemisms	___	___	___	___	___
Friedrich Of Words That Ravage, Pillage, Spoil	___	___	___	___	___
Stegner Good-bye to All T__t!	___	___	___	___	___

LANGUAGE, IDENTITY, AND DISCRIMINATION

Davis The English Language Is My Enemy! ___ ___ ___ ___ ___
Seymour Black Children, Black Speech ___ ___ ___ ___ ___
Rodriguez Aria: A Memoir of a Bilingual Childhood ___ ___ ___ ___ ___
Palmer Spanglish: Hispanics and the Bilingual Dilemma ___ ___ ___ ___ ___
Will In Defense of the Mother Tongue ___ ___ ___ ___ ___
Kohn Sex and Status and a Manner of Speaking ___ ___ ___ ___ ___
Frank/Anshen Of Girls and Chicks ___ ___ ___ ___ ___
Safire Hypersexism and the Feds ___ ___ ___ ___ ___
Schulz Is the English Language Anybody's Enemy? ___ ___ ___ ___ ___

JARGON

Howard The Two Sides of Jargon ___ ___ ___ ___ ___
Johnson Doctor Talk ___ ___ ___ ___ ___
Leo Journalese: A Ground-breaking Study ___ ___ ___ ___ ___
Miller Why EdSpeak Endures ___ ___ ___ ___ ___
Norris Legal Trees ___ ___ ___ ___ ___

LANGUAGE AND ADVERTISING

Boorstin The Rhetoric of Democracy ___ ___ ___ ___ ___
Wrighter Weasel Words: God's Little Helpers ___ ___ ___ ___ ___
Consumer Reports It's Natural! It's Organic! Or Is It? ___ ___ ___ ___ ___
Flexner A Consumer's Guide to Social Offenses ___ ___ ___ ___ ___
Six Advertisements for Analysis ___ ___ ___ ___ ___

THE POLITICAL VOICE

Institute for Propaganda Analysis Types of Propaganda ___ ___ ___ ___ ___
Orwell Politics and the English Language ___ ___ ___ ___ ___
Schlesinger Politics and the American Language ___ ___ ___ ___ ___
cummings next to of course god america i ___ ___ ___ ___ ___
Safire The Case of the President's Case ___ ___ ___ ___ ___
Chilton Nukespeak: Nuclear Language, Culture, and Propaganda ___ ___ ___ ___ ___
Cohen Slanting the News against the USSR ___ ___ ___ ___ ___
Kennedy Inaugural Address (1961) ___ ___ ___ ___ ___
Reagan First Inaugural Address (1981) ___ ___ ___ ___ ___

LANGUAGE AND TECHNOLOGY

Zinsser Four Hang-ups ___ ___ ___ ___ ___
Kenner Machinespeak ___ ___ ___ ___ ___
Sandberg-Diment Hacking the English Language to Bits and Bytes ___ ___ ___ ___ ___
Benoit French Resistance ___ ___ ___ ___ ___
Benderly The Multilingual Mind ___ ___ ___ ___ ___

1. What language issues not included in this edition would you recommend be included in future editions? _____
_____

2. Did you use the questions and assignments following each selection? _____ Were they helpful in understanding the selections? _____ What other type of material not included in this book do you think would help you to better understand the selections?
_____

3. Please make any additional comments or suggestions on the text that you would care to.
_____
_____
_____
_____